SECRET STATE

The Pursuit of Former Premier Brian Burke and ex-Minister Julian Grill

Julian Grill

Connor Court Publishing

Published in 2022 by Connor Court Publishing Pty Ltd.

Copyright © Julian Grill

All Rights Reserved.

Not to be reproduced without the permission of the Copyright holders.

Connor Court Publishing Pty Ltd.
PO Box 7257
Redland Bay QLD 4165
sales@connorcourt.com
www.connorcourt.com

ISBN: 9781922449870

Cover Design by Elle Deslandes

Printed in Australia.

I dedicate this book to my dear wife Lesley, our late daughter Siobhan and my son Shannon, who were severely traumatised by the events described in this book, but who staunchly remained loyal throughout.

Julian Grill

Contents

Author's note	vii
Significant dates	ix
Introduction	xiv
1. CCC hype produced only hurt	1
2. CCC 'court' revives Star Chamber procedures	15
3. CCC inquiries a process of vilification	29
CCC inquiries fail to find crime or corruption 33	
Norm Marlborough becomes a target 40	
Media vilification continues unabated 52	
CCC attack renewed in 'Lobbyist Inquiry' 61	
4. Smiths Beach approval frustrated, undermined	73
CCC punishes McKenzie family 92	
5. Where it all began: Smiths Beach and Busselton council election	107
SBAG website raises queries 116	
The CCC's Smiths Beach report 123	
6. 'Lobbyists Inquiry' – CCC v Burke & Grill, Round 2	131
Burke, Grill homes raided 136	
The Tony McRae inquiry 158	
7. CCC resorts to Parliament – and fails again	179
Privilege committee findings 196	
CCC triggers its decline 201	
8. Burke, Grill ban feeds 'corruption' myth	227
Players in the Ian Campbell debacle 241	
Lobbying strategy misunderstood 249	
9. Why innocent people need protection from the CCC	253
10. McGinty defends CCC's miserable track record	263
Improper, corrupt conduct claimed 269	

11. The CCC's weaknesses and mistakes start to emerge — 278
    Parliamentary Inspector slams CCC's police oversight 294
    Police culture abused judicial system 300
    Parliamentary committee rejects CCC methods 305
    Case studies illustrate police-CCC tensions 311

12. Corruption, dysfunction, conflict exposed in CCC — 327
    P I Murray's dramatic annual report 338
    Roberts-Smith – McCusker conflict 355
    Brigadier Silverstone – A man with a past 366

13. CCC leadership marked by turmoil, controversy — 383
    The bureaucrats take over 392
    Chasing the prize 'scalps' 398
    Smiths Beach 'findings' fall flat 411
    The persecution of Dr Wally Cox 414
    The McKechnie reappointment 424

14. 2008 Election: A CCC casualty — 427
    Carpenter-McGinty media rift 434
    McGinty takes on *The West* 441
    CCC 'casualties' cost Labor government 454

15. Helping Andrew Forrest crack the iron ore duopoly — 462
    'Binding contracts' causes problems 480

16. Brian Burke – the 'godfather' — 493
    'Old money' turns hostile 498
    Cabinet confidentiality emerges as an issue 508
    Public servants, councillors cleared 519

17. Burke and Bryce – WA's best Labor government — 527

18. 'Corruption' – No case to answer — 538
    Crown's case faced problems 550

19. CCC prosecutions 'unlawful' – Senior Counsel — 558

Index — 567

Author's Note

For an inexperienced writer like me, this book was not easy. The story has myriad aspects that need to be captured without incurring the risk of defamation.

In writing this note, I have to confess to episodic emotions of guilt.

There were manifold people hurt and damaged by the CCC hearings, inquiries and actions. I am not equipped to describe their individual plights, but I do know that they were underserving of their fates. Ultimately, they would not have been injured if not for me.

Thus, to help me present my narrative, I have sought the help of others.

Firstly, my wife Lesley, who grieves every day from the death of our daughter Siobhan, who was most grievously affected by the CCC process. Lesley typed the manuscript and acted as a gentle critic.

Secondly, Mark Irving, well-known journalist, was my first and essential editor. His wise cuts and rewording of some critical passages were very important.

Thirdly, Carmel Galati, Mark's wife and defamation law specialist. Without her, the book could not have gone ahead.

Fourthly, I thank my proof-reader, Doug Durack. Another journalist, whose work has been invaluable.

Lastly, my second editor, experienced journalist Jerry Maher, who took a personal interest in the narrative. Apart from shortening what was still an overlong manuscript and further knocking it into shape, Jerry reassured me that the narrative was worthwhile and needed telling.

It is a lonely business writing a book on your own and I am forever grateful for Jerry's moral support.

Julian Grill
August 2021

Significant Dates

Date	Event
25 February 1988	Brian Burke retires from WA Parliament after 15 years, the last five as Premier.
10 February 2001	Julian Grill retires from WA Parliament after 24 years, seven of them as a Minister in ALP governments.
March 2001	Julian Grill establishes lobbying business as sole trader, mostly in mining matters. Later, Julian Grill Consulting is set up with wife Lesley, specialising in lobbying, issues management and government, stakeholder and community relations.
May 2002	Burke joins Grill's lobbying business.
May 2002	Grill and Burke engaged by Canal Rocks Pty Ltd to assist progress of the proposed Smiths Beach resort development near Yallingup, for which planning approval had been delayed for about 18 years.
3 July 2003	*Corruption and Crime Commission Act 2003* creates WA's Corruption and Crime Commission (CCC).
1 January 2004	District Court Judge Kevin Hammond is the inaugural Commissioner of the CCC.
March 2005	Canal Rocks decides to support pro-development candidates – not sitting councillors – in the forthcoming Busselton Shire Council elections through anonymous donations to campaign funds.
7 May 2005	Busselton Shire Council elections.
Late 2005	A complaint is made to the CCC that Canal Rocks made improper payments to Busselton Shire councillors.

2005-2006	CCC obtains warrants to bug Grill and Burke residences, phones and electronic communications. The CCC breaks into Grill's West Perth residence to plant electronic communications bugs and places camera in lamppost outside.
March 2006	The CCC starts secret hearings as part of its inquiry into the Smiths Beach development project. The inquiry is centred on the Busselton election and associated matters.
23 October 2006	The CCC starts public hearings into the Smiths Beach development project.
8 November 2006	The CCC raids the homes of Burke and Grill, removing boxes of hard copy and digital files, as well as computers. Media are present for the raid on Burke's home.
8 November 2006	The CCC starts releasing telephone intercepts in public hearings, revealing that it had obtained warrants to "tap" the phones of Burke and Grill. The taped phone conversations revealed no crime or corruption.
8 November 2006	The CCC announces it is extending the Smiths Beach Inquiry into the actions of senior public servants in relation to the business affairs of Burke and Grill – the Lobbyists inquiry.
9 November 2006	Norm Marlborough resigns from Parliament after being humiliated as a witness in the CCC's Smiths Beach inquiry and being sacked from the Ministry by Premier Carpenter.
12 February 2007	Public hearings start in the Lobbyists Inquiry.
20 March 2007	CCC Commissioner Kevin Hammond announces his resignation from the post, two years ahead of time. The resignation is effective from 31 March 2007. His draft report on the Smiths Beach inquiry had been completed. The Lobbyists Inquiry report has not been completed.

5 June 2007	Len Roberts-Smith appointed CCC Commissioner.
5 October 2007	The Smiths Beach report is tabled in WA Parliament under the name of Acting Commissioner Neil McKerracher – five months later than expected. CCC Executive Director Brigadier Michael Silverstone announces its completion.
6 September 2008	WA Labor loses the "unloseable" State election. Publicity generated by CCC inquiries is seen as a crucial factor.
6 November 2008	CCC accuses Burke and Grill of corruption as a result of the Lobbyists Inquiry. The charges relate to a draft pearl oyster hatchery policy.
15 June 2009	Solicitors for Burke and Grill advised that DPP has taken over the corruption case against them.
20 April 2010	Supreme Court trial on corruption charges commences.
10 May 2010	Burke and Grill acquitted of the corruption charge.
31 January 2011	CCC Commissioner Len Roberts-Smith resigns as CCC Commissioner before his term is completed.
14 September 2011	Supreme Court Appeals Court upholds DPP appeal and orders a retrial of Burke and Grill on corruption charges.
21 November 2011	Former District Court judge Roger Macknay appointed CCC Commissioner.
2 February 2012	Burke and Grill acquitted of corruption after DPP decides not to proceed with the prosecutions. Five years and three months had passed since the start of the Lobbyists Inquiry.
2 November 2013	Information starts to emerge that officers in the CCC's covert Operations Support Unit have been disciplined for misconduct.

18 July 2013	The CCC informs the Parliamentary Inspector Michael Murray of suspected misconduct by CCC officers in the OSU. Conflict develops between the CCC and PI Murray when the PI decides to refer the misconduct matters to the police for investigation, rather than to the DPP as recommended by the CCC.
5 November 2013	CCC Commissioner Roger Macknay resigns. He delays his departure at the request of the Attorney-General.
24 March 2014	Mr Macknay leaves his post as CCC Commissioner. He is the third Commissioner to retire without completing his term and without any apparent preparation for a successor.
15 October 2014	P I Murray's 2013-2014 Annual Report is tabled in WA Parliament. It contains criticism of the CCC's handling of misconduct by CCC officers, and of impeding the police investigation. There is wide media coverage.
October 2014	CCC long-serving Executive Director Brigadier Michael Silverstone resigns.
6 November 2014	CCC makes a special report to Parliament disputing assertions made by PI Murray in his Annual Report.
28 April 2015	Former Supreme Court Judge John McKechnie is appointed CCC Commissioner.
17 June 2015	A special report by P I Murray providing additional information about misconduct by CCC officers is tabled in WA Parliament.
20 March 2020	P I Michael Murray resigns.
April 2020	The parliamentary Joint Standing Committee on the CCC blocks Commissioner McKechnie's reappointment as Commissioner.
21 October 2020	Matthew Zilko SC is appointed PI.

25 June 2021	Commissioner McKechnie is reappointed CCC Commissioner by a special Act of Parliament initiated by the McGowan Labor Government.

Introduction

This is a story about justice. Or, more correctly, injustice. Rampant, blatant, ruthless injustice conducted by the apparatus of the State of Western Australia in a nation that prides itself on embracing all the protections of an enlightened western society.

It is the story of a remorseless and unjustified pursuit of two individuals and their most unfortunate friends and associates, carried out with all the covert investigative and penal powers of an autocratic regime. It is also the narrative of the shameful carnage visited upon a collection of civilians, innocent public officers and their shocked families.

Alongside this, it illustrates the failure of the mainstream media to perform one of its core roles – that is, to present the facts in a fair and unbiased manner. Instead, the media enthusiastically played the role of a Star Chamber-style prosecutor.

I am acutely aware that this book will have no significance if it is seen to comprise merely sectional pleas on behalf of myself and my onetime business partner, Brian Burke, the former Premier of WA.

That is not to suggest for a moment that I do not want to clear my name and regain my reputation. I do. Desperately.

And it does not mean that I do not wish to demonstrate how badly and unfairly Brian Burke was defamed. Of course I do. However, even more I want some recognition for those innocents who were incidentally caught up in the maelstrom and had their careers, reputations and lives destroyed.

Details will come later but first some brief facts.

In December 2002, Justice Geoffrey Kennedy of the Supreme Court of WA completed a Royal Commission into the WA Police Service. It uncovered significant and ongoing corruption – not unsurprisingly, perhaps, considering the police force had historically policed itself.

A principal recommendation of Justice Kennedy's report was the establishment of a permanent police oversight body. Hence, Geoff Gallop's Labor Government created the WA Corruption and Crime Commission (CCC) in January 2004. The CCC Act was steered through Parliament by Attorney-General Jim McGinty.

For several years previously, WA had an Anti-Corruption Commission (ACC), which enjoyed jurisdiction over public servants. However, the ACC's powers were thought to be inadequate. In particular, it did not hold public hearings and did not prosecute. It left prosecutions to the police.

Consequently, the new CCC was conferred massive powers, including the imposing powers of a royal commission with all of the coercive capability that went with that. It also had the faculty to suspend all aspects of procedural fairness.

Additionally, it was given capacious eavesdropping powers and multi-million-dollar equipment and resources to back it up. To top it off, the legislation specifically sanctioned public hearings, where witnesses could be humiliated and fatally demeaned before the asserted evidence of wrongdoing could be properly tested. In all, it constituted an awesome package, manifestly open to misuse.

It was recognised at the outset by State Parliament that such imposing capabilities required a set of very strong oversight safeguards to prevent abuse. In this book, I will present data that demonstrate those safeguards were manifestly inadequate.

For its first big test case, the CCC chose a resort development proposal at Smiths Beach in WA's south-west.

In 2004, Brian Burke and I had been hired to advise and lobby for the long-delayed project, south of Yallingup. The proposal was to develop a 21-hectare site at Smiths Beach to provide 272 accommodation units, 104 homes and 1700 square metres of commercial space.

This dazzling development was opposed by an "environmental" group calling itself the Smiths Beach Action Group (SBAG). At its core were a couple of local real estate developers. Out of this process, a complaint was made to the CCC alleging that some Busselton Shire councillors had been bribed to support the development.

It was at about this time, in late 2004 or early 2005, that the CCC commenced a highly secret investigation, Operation Tiberius. That was the internal code name for a relentless pursuit of Brian Burke and Julian Grill, beginning with covert eavesdropping and concluding in Australia's High Court.

In early 2005, a number of people, including Brian and me, were called to give evidence in secret to the CCC. It was quickly established that no such bribery had taken place. Or, at least, it should have been so established, as no evidence of bribery was presented.

Nonetheless, the CCC process continued for another decade. It included ancillary punitive parliamentary committee hearings and a long procession of initially dubious, and ultimately failed, prosecutions.

The Smiths Beach Inquiry was extended and widened into sensational public hearings in October 2006 and in early 2007 into the so-called Lobbyists Inquiry. This later investigation was just a rambling and ultimately unproductive fishing trip into the lobbying activities of Burke and Grill.

How did it continue for so long, hurt so many innocent people and bring down the Carpenter Labor State Government? These are central questions explored in this book. But without going into specifics, some things are clear:

1. The new CCC had invested a huge amount of resources and prestige in proving itself in its first big inquiry.

2. The CCC Act was the progeny of Jim McGinty, who was not prepared to concede its defects or accept it had fallen at the first hurdle.

Some readers will remember that the media coverage was sensational, incessant, unprecedented and ultimately misleading.

In the final analysis, the CCC's multiple investigations amounted to nothing more than a 10-year fizzer, but a fizzer that nonetheless mowed down the lives and careers of scores of innocent victims.

Records show that of the 40-odd prosecutions launched or initiated by the CCC in connection with the Smiths Beach and

Lobbyists inquiries, only one very minor charge had a recorded conviction – and even that finding has been seriously questioned.

This book will also assert that the CCC illegally assumed prosecution powers, which it unscrupulously used to persecute a range of bewildered witnesses.

Ultimately, it emerged that most of this unproductive and highly injurious conduct was undertaken by several officers at the heart of the powerful investigative and administrative wings of the CCC, who themselves acted either corruptly in some cases or incompetently in others.

This story has not previously been told because of its complexity, scope and duration, and also because of the effects the devastating and misleading coverage had on its victims.

But it is now time the story was told, and time that the authorities acknowledge that what transpired was an injustice that caused lasting damage.

If a meaningful section of the public, or a proportion of our community's opinion leaders, don't recognise the elements of a seriously compromised justice system in the following pages, then I have wasted my time. If no one says, "There but for the grace of God go I and my family", then I have failed. You, the reader, will be the judge.

But as strongly as I feel about these egregious past injustices, it is for the future that I fear the most. The CCC Act is still in place with its woefully inadequate safeguard and redress mechanisms.

In its current form, it can be used as a vehicle for judicial and political repression. If a totalitarian regime were to be set up in WA, the CCC Act would be an archetype vehicle and the Smiths Beach, Lobbyists and associated interrogations would be a working blueprint for its implementation.

There is no place in a democratic society for such a badly designed and dangerous piece of legislation as the CCC Act.

1

CCC HYPE PRODUCED ONLY HURT

At the end of March 2007, news coverage of what was being described as the Corruption and Crime Commission's "success" was overwhelming. Its high-profile investigations in the Smiths Beach, Lobbyists and D'Orazio[1] terms of reference had exploded like a bomb in the Australian media.

Additionally, the associated CCC-initiated Parliamentary Committee inquiries were contemporaneously contributing to the media sensation. Prematurely, in my view, prior to any of the Commission's reports being released, four unfortunate ministers in the WA Carpenter Government – John Bowler, Norm Marlborough, John D'Orazio and Tony McRae – had been crushed and forced to resign. A fifth, Ljiljanna Ravlich, was demoted.

After the Smiths Beach and Lobbyists inquiry reports were presented, several of the State's most talented public servants were suspended with disciplinary proceedings commenced; Norm Marlborough was on criminal charges; multiple proceedings were recommended against Busselton Shire councillors; some eminent lawyers were referred for prosecution; one of our clients was in the same position and another was prosecuted; and Brian Burke and I were to be subject to multiple penal proceedings.

There had never been anything approaching this level of exposure of perceived illegality and impropriety in Australian political history. If the CCC and the awestruck media were to be believed, this was the most sensational scandal ever to engulf WA.

Additionally, businesses were ruined, reputations destroyed, promising political careers and prospects for others were snuffed out, and families traumatised with fear, shame and helplessness.

---

[1] John D'Orazio was a minister in the Carpenter Labor Government until May 2006. He was investigated over allegations of misconduct in 2003 with two public officers. The CCC found in 2006 he did not engage in misconduct.

Our innocent clients, such as Smiths Beach's proponent David McKenzie and mining identity Nathan McMahon, were demeaned and criminal charges recommended against them.

Following completion of the CCC-initiated Parliamentary Committees of Inquiry and their reports presented, Legislative Council MPs Shelley Archer (ALP) and Anthony Fels (Liberal), and ex-Senator Noel Crichton-Browne, all of whom were only incidentally involved, were publicly pursued with prosecutions recommended.

If you craved a life of drama, this was the place to be. The human toll from these ruinous proceedings was immense.

While not immediately apparent, all of those mentioned above (except John D'Orazio, whose tragic story I shall deal with separately) were people associated with Brian Burke and Julian Grill. It was as if Perth was the corruption and crime centre for the developed world, and all of that implied corruption was focused on Brian and me.

I should explain now, because it is essential to a basic understanding of the CCC process, that the CCC Act strictly limits its jurisdiction to crime, corruption and impropriety by "public officers" and organised crime and *not* private citizens. Page 14 of the CCC's Smiths Beach Report notes:

> The Commission's function is to deal with allegations of misconduct concerning public officers.

That is because in all free and democratic countries the concept of unleashing the CCC's extraordinary powers on ordinary citizens is beyond contemplation. The populace would not knowingly countenance a full-on police state.

It is a central theme of this book that the CCC was acting beyond or at the very margin of its jurisdiction in both the Smiths Beach and Lobbyists inquiries, and that the parliamentary inquiries engendered by the CCC were an adjunct to that process.

My rationale is that, although the inquiries should have been impartial investigations into "public officers", they were in fact a ruthless pursuit of two individuals – Brian Burke and Julian Grill. But the bottom line is that we could only be pursued under the CCC Act by maintaining allegations against unsuspecting and blameless public officers.

In fact, in nearly all cases the allegations were later found to be unfounded. It was akin to carpet-bombing a civilian population in the hope of killing a couple of combatants.

In all, some 40 criminal prosecutions were initiated by the CCC and numerous public service disciplinary proceeding were recommended. Some pundits, including former Senator and Hawke Government Minister Robert Ray (in a report of a specially commissioned inquiry into the ALP's 2008 WA election defeat) and the then WA State Secretary of the ALP, Simon Mead, maintained that the CCC inquiries brought down the Carpenter Government at the 2008 election.

For "CCC inquiries", read "the activities of Burke and Grill".

Stephen Smith, the former Federal Minister for Defence, made a similar claim in a speech in the House of Representatives on 12 May 2011.[2]

The CCC public hearings commencing on 23 October 2006 were contrived and sensational. They created "shock, horror" headlines in the media, and continued to do so for many months and years throughout Australia. Vicious cartoons ridiculed Burke, Grill and Marlborough.

Numerous innocent parties were forever damaged by the stream of highly prejudicial and carefully selected evidence. The resulting tangle of pathology ensured that Burke and Grill were perceived as scoundrels of the first order.

It was like an avalanche that engulfed, overwhelmed and mercilessly battered. There was no way of arresting it, defending oneself, or responding meaningfully. We were unable to shield our families, who suffered terribly.

The hapless public servants were in the same wretched position. It badly hurt loving wives and children to hear that their husband/

---

[2] *The West Australian*, 13 May 2011.

father was supposedly corrupt. Apparently, we became so toxic that the least association was lethal for a person's moral wellbeing.

The process continued remorselessly, day after day, for months and ultimately years. No one wanted to hear any explanation, much less the media.

Outrageously, when I was sensationally arraigned before the Legislative Assembly of Parliament in "Court Session", a most unusual event, I was not permitted to speak one word in my own defence. I would have received a fairer hearing at a Stalinist show trial.

Highly derogatory and injurious accusation continued one on top of the other as the public hearings extended into 2007. All had to be endured in silence. The CCC process did not allow response within the CCC tribunal. With the never-ending flow of adverse accusation, and the CCC's media department confidentially feeding the media beast, there was no avenue to mount any meaningfully counter argument and no point in trying.

The CCC hearings systematically poisoned public opinion and prepared the ground well before we were examined. As early as the end of 2006, prior to the publication of any of the CCC's highly damaging reports, the media had firmly and collectively made up their mind. The verdict was clear and seemingly unimpeachable: The hapless public officers, as well as Brian Burke and me, were all convicted in the court of public opinion.

Of what, no one was quite clear. But whatever it was, it was "appalling". In any event, what was happening to us suited the media pack's "gotcha" predisposition. In Brian Burke they had a nationally known figure who was vulnerable to an aggressive media campaign. They did not want to spoil a good story by questioning the accuracy of the underlying facts. The niceties of natural justice did not trouble them in the least and pack hunting was their speciality.

However, while the media were the crucial conduit for the inflammatory storyline, it was the largely faceless CCC operatives who painstakingly fashioned the narrative and reaped the abundant glory. One of my lawyers suggested, "The people who most fear the CCC are the innocent".

In the *Australian Financial Review* on 30 December 2006 (substantially in advance of any report), the victors and the vanquished had already been declared by a frenzied media. In *The West Australian*, journalist Sean Cowan bizarrely compared the Smiths Beach investigation to a one-sided Native American scalping party. Cowan wrote:

> Corruption-fighting bodies are all about scalps. And for the Corruption and Crime Commission, 2006 has been like the Battle of Little Big Horn.[3]

Cowan then identified some of those high-profile scalps, while continuing a torrent of highly prejudicial invective against Brian Burke.

The odds against Custer were long, but he at least had his cavalry to fight alongside him. The odds against the CCC targets were infinitely worse. In late 2006 and early 2007, there were precious few journalists who were brave enough, or foolish enough, to question the methods of the CCC or look behind the superficial outpouring of highly detrimental (but untested) calumny.

Our situation in WA and Federal ALP ranks was dire. Some in the "radical" Left instinctively went in for the kill. Long-term animosity between Brian Burke and WA Attorney-General Jim McGinty had made sure of that. Most of our remaining parliamentary friends and colleagues deserted us and either joined the ranks of those calling for our exclusion and penalisation, or exited the arena.

While the legal profession, almost unanimously, was privately aghast and critical of the CCC processes, their formal written protests to the Government were seemingly ignored.

The great majority of the high-profile political commentators and social justice advocates would not speak a word in our defence. I now identify that failure as moral cowardice as they must have been aware that the CCC process denied natural justice.

It was a bitter lesson that, if a person is deeply unpopular or hated, it is very difficult to find a defender no matter how just their cause may be. We had our families, our few closest friends, and our lawyers

---

[3] *The West Australian*, 30 December 2006, p. 2.

only. The CCC had the deep pockets of the State, plentiful human resources, a piece of diabolical legislation of which the 1970s Cambodian dictator Pol Pot would have been envious, an oversight body that fell asleep at the wheel and, most importantly, massive media support.

It was an abuse of power, but no one of consequence was publicly prepared to assert that at the time.

Worse, our enforced silence in the face of this onslaught was taken by the public as an indication, if not an admission, of our culpability. There was no other choice for us but to patiently wait, in the hope that there would be a lull; for an occasion when we could present another side to the story.

Reluctantly, I have to concede that the CCC understood the psychology of its public operations and was deftly able to depict its targets in the most unflattering of terms. Constant repetition of derogatory innuendo was a much-used tool. The public was informed in a variety of ways that we were crooks. There is an old, but true, saying about political campaigning: "When the proponents of a particular political message become heartily sick of hearing the same refrain, you know that it is just starting to get through to the public."

Months of repellent media coverage had its effect, whether the abhorrent allegations were true or not. It was like acid rain that never ceased.

The spectre of our supposed greed was one continually played up by the CCC.

To give you some idea, on each occasion that I was examined I would be laboriously questioned on our business charging structure and the success fees that we earned.

I regret to report that this line of attack, although extraneous to the issues being investigated, was highly effective. So effective was it, in terms of negative perceptions, that the Colin Barnett-led WA Coalition Government was later persuaded to legislatively ban "success fees".

There was never any evidence that such fees were the slightest of problems, but this was not the impression that the CCC generated.

For anyone who might disagree with me, I challenge you to find a case. And not withstanding its irrelevance, it was a theme that the journalist pack was all too eager to take up and use to great effect.

If I concede that there was a tiny number of journalists who queried the CCC methods, and some who felt sympathy for the hapless public servants, there was none among the media ranks who would explicitly defend Brian and me. That would have been akin to committing professional suicide.

This dark motivation was epitomised by Tim Treadgold in the *WA Business News* under the heading: "Greed can appear in many guises".[4] In this article, Treadgold unfairly described the Smiths Beach project as "a get rich (quick) scheme", and unjustly implied that all those associated with it were avaricious.

The potency of the image of greed, as a highly undesirable human trait, was unmercifully exploited by the CCC. We were stereotyped as manipulative and greedy.

The public abhors rapacious individuals. However, when I think back over my many failings, which I reluctantly admit to myself and strive to remedy, I do not discern that greed is one of them.

Unfortunately, the next thing I say will sound just as self-serving, but it has to be said and I don't know any other way to put it. On entering Parliament, I took a major pay cut. I have always donated substantial time and money to charity. My life has been built around helping others and as a lawyer and parliamentarian I am well equipped for that. Brian Burke never stops helping people.

Nonetheless, what I might think of myself was really of no importance in this battle. The critical consideration was the pernicious image the CCC presented of us, our unfortunate clients and the public officers, and the initial triumph it had in fostering that image. It was devastating. They demolished us all. It was a mismatch.

As I shall detail later, by this yardstick the CCC was frighteningly successful. Although ultimately unable to prove the vast majority of its allegations of criminality and impropriety, it triumphed in turning Burke and Grill into reviled figures of public hatred.

---

[4] *WA Business News*, 2 November 2006, p. 26.

The close link between the CCC and the media, and the CCC's command of the critical public psychology, was demonstrated by the proceedings on 8 November 2006 when the CCC officers executed search warrants on Brian Burke's home. Surprise, surprise, the media also attended to film the raiding squad and the procession of officers leaving with boxes of files, computers and other possible exhibits.

My view is that it was highly unethical for the CCC to tip the media off about the raid. Such graphic and vividly descriptive images in the media count immensely in degrading the reputation and standing of the distressed quarry. Journalists salivate over such opportunities. These are priceless visuals.

Additionally, in modern politics and contemporary presentation of a case, the creation of appearances is salient for the generation of outcomes. It is trite but true: "Power corrupts and absolute power corrupts absolutely." The CCC was able to act in a way that the police could only fantasise about. We live in the day of the 20-second grab, continuous media feed and the polemics of the moment.

On the other hand, I concede that we made the CCC's task easier in some critical ways. Initially, I resolutely kept to a no-comment position when aggressively accosted by the assembled media pack.

As a group (but not normally as individuals), the media can be rude, provocative and belligerent. As I pushed through the throng, entering or exiting, on the many occasions that I was called to give evidence, I was assailed by anonymous, but calculated, insults. These barbs are thrown in the hope that you will react badly for the cameras.

You would have seen it on TV. The uninitiated witnesses flinch, duck their heads, try somehow to hide and sometimes run. A few hurl back invective at the media group. It never looks good, but having been there I can't help but feel sorry for them all.

Nonetheless, although I was always polite, my tight-lipped "no comment" position won me no friends.

Brian Burke took to wearing a distinctive fedora hat to the hearings. For reasons unexplained, it became his CCC hat and the focus of a myriad of pictures and belittling cartoons. To my knowledge, he had never worn that hat before or since.

It became his conspicuous media hallmark and autographed copies were a big money spinner at charity auctions for months. My heart goes out to him on this matter.

If things were bad for us by December 2006, then after the Smiths Beach hearings our public image inevitably became worse, with the public hearing of the multiple issues within the Lobbyists term of reference beginning in early 2007.

With its highly restrictive rules on our ability to respond, these hearings became a picnic for the CCC and a feeding frenzy for the media.

To release the Smiths Beach report on 5 October 2007, the Executive Director of the CCC, Michael Silverstone (in the unexplained absence of a serving Commissioner at the time), held a highly publicised media conference on the steps of Parliament House in Perth.

The reality was that, despite the massive resources applied, the CCC Report was conspicuously empty in respect to evidence of either corrupt activity or criminality by "public officers". The initial central thesis of the CCC case – the suggestion that our client had made improper payments to Busselton Shire councillors – had collapsed. That left the CCC like the emperor with no clothes.

To compensate for this failure, the CCC contrived to dress up its Smiths Beach report with melodramatic and specious "findings". I shall explain later how these 'findings' were of zero legal consequence, but they made dramatic copy. These sensationalised "findings" were made against senior State Government public servants and local government councillors, and included an outrageous attack on the innocent David McKenzie, the leader of the Smiths Beach development team.

But Burke and Grill were singled out for special treatment and the most deleterious comment. That is, we were front and centre in the second paragraph of the media release that was issued at Mr Silverstone's press conference.

In featuring Burke and Grill, the CCC had shown its hand. It had somehow escaped the attention of Mr Silverstone and the CCC that the CCC had no jurisdiction over us. In the final analysis, these quite specious findings had no legal standing.

But power was once defined as "having control of the microphone". It was certainly Silverstone who had control. On that day, on the steps of Parliament House, he had the nation's media at his attendance and in his thrall.

Later, as the Lobbyists terms of reference reports dribbled out through 2007 and 2008, the intensity of adverse public opinion and media censure became even more severe and agonising for our families. We were treated with odium and revulsion. It mattered little that the CCC ultimately failed miserably to prove their high-octane assertions.

My loyal wife, Lesley, and I were frequently abused in the street and other public places. Fair weather friends simply vanished. Clients cancelled our engagements.

Our daughter, Siobhan, who worked in State Parliament, was effectively ostracised and lastingly traumatised. The parliamentarians, with one or two exceptions, with whom she had been on friendly terms, turned their backs on her and figuratively "sent her to Coventry". This was a cruel strike to a vulnerable and innocent young woman. They were, in effect, visiting the perceived sins of the father on the daughter.

Lesley and I became social outcasts. Many of our good and enduring friends could not run the risk of being seen publicly with us. This sort of treatment can be emotionally injurious, even to a seasoned lawyer and politician like me. I had to will myself to venture out publicly and I feared turning up to a function where most knew me, but where I would be studiously ignored.

I have always maintained that bravery is a very rare commodity. Certainly, that is my long experience of politics. Consequently, when some heroic soul at one of these functions took pity on me and spoke to me, I was highly relieved and secretly very grateful.

However, as grim as I found it, I know that Lesley and Siobhan had it many times worse. Lesley tried not to go outside. She was intimidated by the media gauntlet that assembled at the front gate every time the CCC focused on an issue. The telephone was a cause of apprehension as some of the media were forceful and abrupt. On top of that, we were aware by then that all our telephone conversations were eavesdropped. The serene Sue Burke was always composed, but she must have silently suffered.

Siobhan came from work at Parliament in early 2007 to our home nearby. She was crying, highly distressed and trembling uncontrollably. She was almost incoherent. It took some time, but Siobhan finally conveyed to me that she had overheard in Parliament House that the CCC was going to charge John Bowler and me with corruption.

My attempts to pacify her were only partially successful. In fact, her information turned out to be correct; but the image of her distress will never leave me.

My son, Shannon, was shocked and angry that his family could be so shabbily and unjustly treated and developed the habit of revealing his surname only when obliged to. But otherwise, his reserves of inner strength left him largely untouched.

I was also mortified to hear reports that the targeted public officers and their families were in some cases doing it even harder.

As mentioned, the CCC was not just dominant in its own tribunal and in the media, but also with Parliament, where the parliamentarians were stunned and intimidated. Once the Smiths Beach and Lobbyists terms of reference hearings were completed, the CCC turned its attention to State Parliament where it was determined to pursue my friend John Bowler, then the Member for Kalgoorlie, Brian Burke's long-time family friend Shelley Archer MLC, and Noel Crichton-Browne's friend Anthony Fels MLC.

In this arena, the CCC met some early resistance in the form of the Legislative Council President Nick Griffiths. He was not going to be bullied by the CCC, but ultimately the Carpenter Government exerted sufficient pressure on the President and the Speaker to see two Special Committees of Inquiry set up, ostensibly targeting the MPs referred to above.

However, those in the know were aware that the real objectives were the isolation and further humiliation of Burke and Grill, and an attempt to convict us and our parliamentary friends for "abuse" of the parliamentary processes. These parliamentarians were all intimates of ours.

The evidentiary basis for these hearings were mainly tapes of CCC eavesdropped conversations on Brian and my phones that the CCC "generously" made available to the parliamentary committees.

However, once again, the CCC was entirely frustrated in its attempts to gain convictions. It was too impetuous and simply out of its depth in the parliamentary arena. Nonetheless, the destructive process, not the outcome, was ruinous to careers and lives.

The time taken for these events I am describing to unfold was significant. For Brian Burke and his large, close Catholic family, and for me and my family, this CCC process and the tribulation that has accompanied it began when we were first called before the CCC secret hearings in early March 2006.

These unpublicised tribunal hearings were so secret that we were prohibited under the CCC Act from disclosing their existence to even our wives.

I invite you to envisage that situation, where on pain of possible imprisonment one had to be either disingenuous or downright dishonest with one's closest companion as to one's whereabouts for large portions of the day. I did finally manage to gain a retrospective exemption from CCC Acting Commissioner Gail Archer so that I could tell my wife where I had been, on one occasion only. The situation at home was becoming ridiculous.

From early 2006, this CCC matter was with us unabated, challenging our levels of resolve and draining our financial resources. The last court case was not completed until 2014. The surveillance bugs in our home, by which Lesley felt so violated, have not been removed, as far as we know. We are still shunned by sections of the ALP and others.

The great majority of the victimised public servants never recovered.

In its early years, the CCC was the toast of the town. It was perceived as the most successful corruption-fighting organisation in

Australia. Infamously, almost immediately the hearings commenced, the parliamentary oversight committee, whose task was meant to be as watchdog over the CCC, became a fawning cheer squad for the CCC's worst excesses.

Parliamentarians were afraid and cowed into obeisance and Parliament was bending over backwards to do CCC bidding. From the outset, the parliamentary Liberals and Nationals were delighted, as it created turmoil in Government ranks.

Some radical elements of the ALP supported and acclaimed each denial of natural justice committed by the CCC. The Government supported these proceedings, for reasons I shall explain later.

The CCC stood omnipotent and seemingly impervious to correction or restraint.

It is consequently of considerable irony to observe that (with the exception of one minor charge of misleading evidence) the CCC was not successful in any of its many recommended criminal prosecutions stemming out of the two CCC inquiries or Parliamentary Committee inquiries; has not seen a favourable outcome from any of its recommended public service disciplinary proceedings; has not had removed or disciplined any local government councillors; nor witnessed the implementation of the substantial part of its advocated policy from its reports.

I shall return to this irony later.

Were there any exemplars from this pernicious tragedy? Without doubt there were. Ultimately, we were saved by the integrity of our contemporary legal system. As you will see in this book, it has not always been the case that WA was so well served.

The State's legal profession bodies were alarmed at the CCC's appropriation of legal rights and protections forged by our historic common law and statutes over the centuries. They made those concern known.

Our personal lawyers were magnificent and so were the courts. But our redemption was led by Malcolm McCusker QC. He alone publicly challenged the CCC straight out with full frontal engagement on questions of evidence, morals and fair procedure.

The CCC responded by seeking to muzzle him with a Supreme Court injunction. They failed and his witheringly accurate opinions prevailed.

He is a prince among lawyers.

Second was ex-Judge Michael Murray who persisted against considerable odds to expose the rogue unit within the CCC and who negotiated an acceptable level of oversight of CCC operations. He is one of the heroes.

2

CCC 'COURT' REVIVES STAR CHAMBER PROCEDURES

I appreciate that readers when contemplating the CCC's initial so-called "success" will express surprise that I would question whether the CCC was actually investigating matters of significant criminality. Put colloquially, this scepticism can be expressed as: "Where there is smoke, there must be fire."

My firm response is that there was neither smoke nor fire, but the CCC was able to give the contrary impression by employing profoundly unfair methods.

I contend that the unprecedented initial (apparent) triumph of the CCC depended upon the abrogation of the venerated common law principles of justice and procedural fairness, painstakingly built up and fought for over the centuries by our forefathers. That is, the core tenets of our inherited law, based on our fundamental moral beliefs.

Archbishop Desmond Tutu held:

> Freedom and liberty lose out by default when good people are not vigilant. If you are neutral on injustice, you have chosen the side of oppression.

In respect to the "triumph" of the CCC, I suggest that we revisit Rudyard Kipling's celebrated poem "If", wherein he penned the unforgettable lines:

> *If you can meet with Triumph and Disaster*
> *And treat those two imposters just the same;*
> *If you can bear to hear the truth you've spoken*
> *Twisted by knaves to make a trap for fools.*

The so-called CCC "triumph" was ultimately proven to be ephemeral, as we shall see.

Our inherited British system of legal justice rests upon certain basic precepts. They include:

(a) The right to be informed of the nature of the charge and accusation. (This right was never extended to us and in fact was actively blocked.)

(b) The freedom to question and cross-examine your accuser's evidence. (This was never allowed.)

(c) The liberty to give evidence in your own defence. (We were never given this opportunity. We were restricted to answering a narrow set of CCC questions.)

(d) The ability to call witnesses in defence. (We could not call any witnesses.)

(e) The opportunity to argue your own case and comment on evidence. (This was never allowed at the hearings. We could reply in writing on the draft CCC reports, but that was after the hearings were concluded and our comments could be, and were, easily ignored by the CCC. That part was done in secret. The public and the media had no way of making any judgement on either the draft report or our responses, as our lawyers' written objections never saw the light of day. If we had publicised them, we would have been in contempt of the CCC and could have gone to jail. What it all meant was that in the face of this tsunami of CCC-inspired hostile commentary, we never once had the opportunity or the forum to present any coherent, argued and public rebuttal. Remember, at this crucial stage it was all about public perceptions. Witnesses lived or died on these perceptions. Please make no mistake: this is where careers were destroyed and reputations lost. Forever.)

(f) The ability to appeal against the "findings". (There was no avenue of appeal to a court or person who could quash or amend a CCC finding.)

(g) Proof of criminally related matters "beyond reasonable doubt" is the normal standard. (The CCC openly admits that it does not use this standard of proof for its "opinions". It maintains [unfortunately correctly] that its statute allows it to use the civil standard of "proof on the balance of probabilities".

(h) The right to remain silent. (That was denied.)

(i) The right of an accused to speak confidentially with his/her lawyer and counsel, commonly known as "legal professional privilege". (Under intense cross-examination [in a separate case before the Magistrates court], a senior CCC officer was forced to concede that the CCC eavesdropped on telephone conversations between Brian Burke and his lawyer, Grant Donaldson. The CCC was not only trashing one of the law's most sacrosanct principles, it was covertly using the information against witnesses.)

(j) An embargo on hearsay evidence. (Hearsay evidence is allowed under the CCC Act and was often employed.)

(k) The prerogative to produce exculpatory or explanatory evidence. (On page 3 of his opening address in the Smiths Beach hearing, Commissioner Hammond ordered: "Documents and statements can only be produced by counsel assisting. Other legal representatives have no right to tender documents or statements and no right to call for the production of documents."

Right to be informed of the allegation

I mention this again separately as it is such a fundamental part of justice. Many years ago, when a youth at the University of WA, I read Franz Kafka's book "The Trial" and saw Orson Welles' film of the novel.

Its moving description of injustice left an indelible impression on me. It tested credibility to believe that such legal oppression could exist. It was therefore astonishing to witness it actually happening in Australia in 2006/7.

As a State Cabinet minister, I travelled to Prague and visited the Kafka memorials. He died in 1924, but his three sisters were murdered in Nazi concentration camps during World War II because they were of the Jewish faith. Kafka is said to be one of the most influential writers of the 20th century, but the bulk of his writing was not published during his lifetime.

"The Trial" is one of his best-known works. It tells the story of a man arrested and prosecuted by a remote, inaccessible authority, with the nature of his crime revealed neither to him nor the reader. On the last day of the protagonist's thirtieth year, two men arrive to execute him. He offers little resistance. They lead him to a quarry where he is expected to kill himself, but he cannot. The two men then execute him. His last words describe his own death as "like a dog".

Please forgive my presumption, but I believe that there are parallels between "The Trial" and the experiences of witnesses before the CCC. I try to highlight them through this book.

The CCC's first major investigation was into the proposed Smiths Beach resort development on a site near Yallingup in WA's southwest. Public hearings commenced in October 2006.

When I was first summoned to give evidence in secret session in March 2006, I was given no indication of specific matters of interrogation. I had been involved in the Smiths Beach development application process for some years and knew that it was a complex, difficult and many-faceted saga. It had "lots of moving parts", as they say.

Although I readily appreciated that I was to be questioned on Smiths Beach, I could only speculate as to the nature of the CCC investigation and the matters upon which I would be examined. Nor was I aware that I was under threat. I did not see the need for legal representation. Consequently, I did not embark upon any preparation. When on 6 November that year I gave evidence for the first time in the glare of the media, I was no more enlightened as to the subject of my forthcoming inquisition.

At around that time, well-known veteran lawyer Malcolm Hall had a letter published in *The West Australian*. He ominously predicted that if the CCC continued its practice of keeping witnesses in the dark as to the nature of their examination, it was likely that there would be a resulting spate of unfair charges for giving false testimony.

History distressingly demonstrates how perspicacious Malcolm Hall was. After the CCC failed to prove criminality, it began to allege that our testimony was dishonest and then brought futile charges alleging false testimony.

Mistakenly, before I was subject to open interrogation by the CCC in November 2006, I assumed that I would be questioned on roughly the same material on which I had given evidence in secret session in March 2006. I was anxious not to contradict my previous testimony.

My counsel, Jeremy Allanson SC, consequently requested a copy of my earlier secret evidence. The CCC responded that by virtue of its statute I was not entitled to a copy. However, I had permission to attend at the CCC offices and peruse my earlier answers. With Mr Allanson, I presented myself at the CCC office in St Georges Terrace and, under supervision, read my part of the 6 March transcript.

By reason of threat of penal sanction, I can never disclose the content of that evidence, but I can inform you that refreshing myself was a barren exercise. I can only legally disclose that the various subjects of my public examination bore little resemblance to my previous secret interrogation. It was never explained why we had to endure both public and private hearings.

It might seem irrelevant, but I explain this to readers to indicate that there appeared to be very little continuity in respect to the investigative process, or the implied nature of our supposed wrongdoing. As a consequence, it was extremely difficult to obtain any sense of how we were alleged to have transgressed or whether we were supposed to have transgressed at all.

Because of the public interrogations of other witnesses in October 2006, it was becoming apparent that the CCC was pursuing suggestions of wide-scale bribery and/or improper influence of Busselton Shire councillors. Specifically, that meant payments to councillors in return for support of the Smiths Beach development through the shire planning processes.

These were serious assertions. I hasten to add that they were never proved. In fact, they were unsoundly based because the CCC failed to appreciate the distinction between payments to councillors for favours and completely legal payments to council *candidates* for campaign expenses *prior* to their election. These sensational imputations simply unravelled and were ultimately never fully pursued by the CCC.-

In the meantime, however, the CCC was able to gain appreciable traction in the minds of the public and create considerable excitement in the media by airing these spectacular, but erroneous, claims. These damning assertions had the effect of thoroughly prejudicing public opinion from the outset.

By the time I gave my first public evidence on 6 November 2006, the media and the public had been turned savagely against us. Talkback media was primed and full of venom.

Our lawyers were concerned. My wife, Lesley, was alarmed. I could almost feel the malice as I pressed through the media scrum to face interrogation. Some of the journalists were disrespectful.

Surprisingly, once in the witness box I was barely questioned on this seemingly critical subject of alleged improper payments. The CCC seemed much more interested in the structure of my business and the fee-charging model. Moreover, no one subsequently queried why I was not seriously examined on this bribery imputation. I can only conclude that by the time I came to give evidence the CCC had realised that the bribery imputations had no legal basis.

Moreover, for all of the fanfare over this aspect of the matter in October 2006, it never rated a mention in the final report. It was jettisoned by the CCC. However, the CCC never corrected the initial highly prejudicial impressions. At no time did it make any attempt to amend the record or explain why the sensational insinuations had not been pursued.

Just as disappointingly, State Parliament's oversight committee (the Joint Standing Committee on the Corruption and Crime Commission, or JSCCCC) never questioned the CCC's propriety in raising such false and prejudicial evidence and then furtively dropping it, without explanation. I will explain later that a differently composed JSCCCC under Nick Goiran MLC was ultimately extremely critical of the CCC's general approach to public hearings.

Lamentably, the media, having headlined the scandalous primary allegations in October 2006, failed to inquire how or why they had disappeared. The media (largely) behaved like intellectual lemmings.

No one seems to have raised the question: "What has happened to those sensational allegations we built our lead stories around?"

It has been said that people think in herds. It shall be shown later in this book that people go mad in herds. Put bluntly, the media (with a couple of very rare exceptions) did not do its duty. It got nowhere near its oft professed, lofty ideals of fearlessly presenting the facts.

This became a hallmark of the CCC process as the public hearings continued and later when the charges were laid. But as I shall detail, the parade of allegations and inferences of so-called "impropriety" just kept failing to match the actual evidence. Then they were abandoned without further mention.

My highly reputed lawyers (Jeremy Allanson, now a Supreme Court judge, Tom Percy QC, Steven Penglis SC, Ante Golem, Sharad Nigam and Ben Gauntlett), although puzzled at what the CCC was driving at, could see through the verbal fog where the media could not, and kept on assuring me that no impropriety had been revealed. Brian Burke and David McKenzie (our client) had similar reassurance from their counsel.

That was all reassuring, but it was a different world out there in media land where most of the commentators could see only sensational copy and a few worthy malefactors. In the absence of some public correction by the CCC, these failed contentions produced an environment of perceived felonious activity.

It was a case of shifting sands. We never knew what impropriety we were supposed to have committed. I shall enlarge on that as we go along. Our counsel feared that the CCC, so as to catch witnesses out and lure them into making mistakes in their evidence, was not giving them the opportunity to prepare for their testimony.

It was not until 28 October 2008, before Magistrate Wheeler's Court on two charges against me of knowingly giving false evidence (on which I was resoundingly exonerated), that we had the first hard evidence that our lawyers' suspicions were correct. Under cross-examination by Tom Percy, CCC senior investigator RM Ingham was drawn into making a revealing admission. On page 45 of the official transcript, the following exchange is documented:

> **Percy:** The element of surprise is usually a valid operational method in that case?
>
> **Ingham:** It is.
>
> **Percy:** That is a method that is employed, isn't it?
>
> **Ingham:** It is one that is used, yes.

On 3 March 2010, in the trial of similar charges against Brian Burke, there came further confirmation of the "methods" of the CCC. From page 34 to page 48 of that transcript, there follows the revealing cross-examination of Mr Ingham by Grant Donaldson QC. Quoted below are elements of that testimony.

Page 36:

> **Donaldson:** In this matter, that is the Smiths Beach inquiry and the public officers' inquiry, no witness who was summoned was given any indication prior to them being summoned to give evidence as to specific matters that they were going to be asked questions about?
>
> **Ingham:** I'd accept that.

Page 38:

> **Donaldson:** Would you accept…that it is difficult for people to prepare to give accurate evidence…if they have no inkling of what matters they're going to be asked about?
>
> **Ingham:** I would if they didn't know.

Page 40:

> **Donaldson:** So you know that the CCC was listening in to conversations that Mr Burke was having with me? …
>
> **Ingham:** Yes.
>
> **Donaldson:** Were they handed to counsel assisting?
>
> **Ingham:** Yes.
>
> **Donaldson:** …you knew that I was his counsel.
>
> **Ingham:** Yes.
>
> **Donaldson:** …you would understand them in the

ordinary course to be confidential? To be the subject of legal professional privilege?

Ingham: Yes

A number of disturbing matters emerge from this evidence of Mr Ingham. They include:

(a) Despite a legislative recommendation that a CCC witness was to be given the general scope and purpose of the inquiry, such information was kept to an absolute minimum.

(b) Brian Burke was not given any indication of the specific matters upon which he was to be interrogated in public session on 6 November 2006. Worse, the CCC operatively contrived to keep him unenlightened.

(c) The CCC failed to honour an undertaking given to Brian's lawyers to provide advice on witnesses who may give evidence adverse to him.

(d) Those specific matters were used to ground later charges of false testimony against Brian.

(e) A clear acknowledgement by Mr Ingham that this situation would have made it "difficult for people to prepare to give accurate evidence".

(f) That the CCC secretly listened to tapes of telephone conversations that Brian had with his counsel, Mr Donaldson. It was conceded by a senior CCC officer that such tapes should normally attract "legal professional privilege".

(g) The CCC secretly used that information to prepare for its examination of Brian.

It could never be said that Brian Burke actually misled the CCC because the CCC had surveillance tapes of telephone conversations and copies of emails, detailing exactly what he had previously said.

The hearings were not an information-gathering exercise. As I maintain later in this chapter, the public hearings of October and November 2006 was when the inquiry turned from investigation to entrapment. And that was the submission put to the Magistrates Court by Grant Donaldson SC (page 42 of transcript).

I submit, therefore, that the common law and statutory "right to be informed of the nature of charge and accusations" against Brian and others was actively attenuated.

Interestingly, Mr Ingham brazenly defended the questionable ethical posture adopted by the CCC. In evidence, he seems to be saying that the CCC had made a considered decision to keep us in the dark. See page 37 of the transcript:

> **Ingham**: The commission hearings aren't a court. They're part of the investigation and I would suggest in the same way that a police officer doesn't tell a murder suspect, 'This is all the evidence we've got'... What do you say?

Technically, Mr Ingham is correct. The CCC is not legislated to act as a court of law and its role is akin to that of a police force. However, there are other factors to consider. In truth, the CCC in public session masquerades as a court and gives every outward impression of being a court, with all of the gravitas, impartiality and protection a court normally bestows.

When one steps into the CCC hearings, it proffers the appearance of being a court. The CCC actually built a chamber, as part of its offices, for public hearings. It is physically set up exactly like a courtroom, not like a police interrogation room. Its outward, but superficial, formalities are designed to make the process appear identical to detached courtroom procedures. The public and the media find it difficult to make any distinction.

It is not appreciated that the Commissioner presiding is not an impartial judge, but is in fact in close consultation, every step of the way, with the Counsel Assisting, who for much of the time acts as a prosecutor. These two, together with the senior investigators, plan the interrogation of the witnesses at the beginning of each day.

In other words, the Commissioner's role is the antithesis of that of a wise and neutral judge overseeing an impartial trial. Its benign outward appearance is a façade, but it works for the CCC. The public is never conscious of how partisan the whole procedure can be.

This is not a place where the truth, the whole truth and nothing but the truth is presented. If the truth is ever displayed at these hearings, it is a one-dimensional truth that reflects one jaundiced perspective only.

If Mr Ingham is technically correct when he likens the role of the Commission to that of the police, he hides some very ugly truths.

The first such disturbing truth is that the CCC has immensely more powers than a police officer. It has amplified spying and surveillance powers, and it can compel witnesses to give evidence against their will and to incriminate themselves. Police officers certainly can't do that.

The CCC can operate in public hearings and make preposterous and highly damaging accusations about witnesses with near total impunity. Police officers have no such rights and fewer protections.

Police interrogations are highly confidential. The CCC can bring down decidedly injurious public reports on the basis of very subjective assessments of the evidence. Police officers have to present their cases in court where rules of evidence and natural justice apply.

The CCC does not have to prove its cases beyond reasonable doubt in an impartial court of law as police do.

But, most importantly, being examined by the police doesn't put one at risk of losing your job, your spouse and your reputation.

Infamous Star Chamber recalled

In bestowing on the CCC the most extensive powers of any such body in Australia, the WA Parliament recognised the need to prevent an abuse of those powers and correctly endeavoured to make the exercise of the powers subject to certain safeguards. Shortly, I will examine how those safeguards have been exposed as inadequate.

The legislature also granted the Commission a free rein on the type and ambit of the procedures it could adopt when it acted as a public tribunal. In its questionable wisdom, the CCC embraced the decidedly prejudicial and unfair procedures that had been applied in the Cole Royal Commission into the Australian building industry.

Past royal commissions in WA have broadly adopted "liberal" sets of procedures where witnesses were generally given notice of accusations, could contribute evidence on their own behalf to correct misconceptions, and their counsel could cross-examine witnesses and re-examine their own clients.

There has also historically been some statutory oversight by the WA Supreme Court, control over hearsay evidence, and counsel for witnesses could make submissions in open sessions on the facts and on the law.

In adopting the Cole procedures, these normal safeguards were confiscated. Bear in mind that royal commissions are relatively rare and are set up in response to exceptional circumstances. They may have considerable powers, like the CCC (without its eavesdropping capability), but they have defined terms of reference and a specific, limited life. On the other hand, the CCC can range far and wide and is with us every day of the week.

I would also remind readers that British based common law countries have not for hundreds of years given permanent tribunals power equivalent to those conferred on the CCC. You have to go back to the infamous Star Chamber for an equivalent. That body became a byword for injustice.

At the CCC, I was represented initially by Jeremy Allanson and later by Tom Percy and senior Herbert Smith Freehills partner Steven Penglis, who was brilliantly assisted by Ante Golem. Those of you who might be cynical about lawyers need to stand in our shoes for a while. When you are under serious and ceaseless legal, political and media attack, they are about the only thing you can hold on to. They are your bastions and reassuring friends. Against all the odds, they take your side. I am so grateful to them, as was Brian Burke for his lawyers.

The procedural CCC rules were so restrictive and so limiting that none of my lawyers said more than a few words during the whole of my numerous CCC appearances. In fact, Mr Allanson made the point that he was permitted to do so little in the hearings that he felt embarrassed to take my money. In simple terms, our lawyers were never allowed to represent our interests properly.

A dangerous mix of extreme powers, almost non-existent procedural safeguards, an ability to act in secret, an expropriation of normal natural justice protections was always problematic. Add to that inadequate oversight capacity and you have all the makings of a potential rogue agency.

In due course, that is exactly what came about.

Finally, I would observe that there was a certain inflection point where the CCC exercise turned from one of gathering evidence to the start of a witch-hunt. I believe that point was reached at about the time of our first public examination on 6 November 2006. For reasons that I shall explain in Chapter 5, "Where it all began: Smiths Beach and Busselton council elections". I believe that it was only then that it dawned on the CCC that the allegations of improper payments to councillors would just not fly.

In that regard, Counsel Assisting Stephen Hall SC, in his opening on day one of the Smith's Beach hearing (page 7 of the transcript) referred to the principal areas of inquiry.

One was, "whether <u>elected representatives</u> (my emphasis) had received funding from the developer and whether that funding had been adequately disclosed". The other was, "whether decisions made in the approvals process have been subject to undisclosed or improper influence".

By the time Smiths Beach hearings were completed on 6 December 2006, and although Mr Hall was still referring to the same two central issues in his final summation, his tune had changed in a significant aspect. On page 1377, he states:

> The evidence has indicated that the regulations dealing with electoral funding are inadequate.

This is an oblique way of conceding that no laws have been broken. And, although it was never made explicit, that is what the final report confessed to by its very silence on the issue.

This situation should have been conceded by the CCC much earlier. In respect to Smiths Beach, all the significant evidence had actually been given prior to the commencement of public hearings in October 2006. There had been extensive secret testimony in

March 2006. Additionally, the "targets" had been subject to one of the most far-reaching electronic surveillance operations ever seen in Australia.

When the CCC publicly interrogated us, it was armed with a mountain of transcribed documents of the relevant conversations. The CCC investigators knew the answers to their own questions better than we did. They were testing our memories, ever vigilant for the slightest mistake.

As you shall see during the reading of this book, no impropriety of substance was ever found against us. It was a search and destroy mission, with roughly the first year devoted to "search" and the public hearings and beyond to "destroy".

There should be no surprise that two sets of hearings (that is, Smiths Beach and Lobbyist) and the Parliamentary Committee inquiries were loaded, in a procedural sense, against essentially innocent witnesses and produced a series of needless injustices.

The real surprise was that Commissioner Kevin Hammond allowed such an oppressive system to dominate proceedings.

Was he pressed too far by an over ambitious investigative wing of the CCC? Was he strained by political or media considerations? Why did he resign in such bizarre circumstances without completing either inquiry and without a replacement?

We shall examine these crucial questions in Chapter 13, "CCC leadership marked by turmoil, controversy".

3

CCC INQUIRIES A PROCESS OF VILIFICATION

Some years had to elapse before the legal scoreboard decisively demonstrated the woeful win/loss ratio achieved by the CCC in the Smiths Beach and Lobbyists inquiries.

In contrast, when it came to calumny and character assassination, the CCC was top scorer and leading wicket-taker with its swift and entirely ruthless performance. The partisan and procedurally unfair public hearing process despatched to oblivion the precious reputations of parliamentarians, public servants and innocent individuals alike.

In terms of targeting, there appears to have been only one criterion: Did the quarry have any association or affinity with Brian Burke or Julian Grill? However, there is no doubt it was Burke and Grill who were the primary targets. We were in the cross hairs. In *The Weekend Australian* Magazine of 6-7 June 2015, Andrew Burrell asserted that Burke had the status of "Australia's most vilified man".

An interesting epithet for a person who, during most of his time as Premier, was the most popular public office bearer in the country. It was a decisive and ruinous fall from grace. I would argue that, in large part, it was due to the machinations of the CCC.

In this chapter I shall detail how trenchant, demeaning and personal this traducement became. I shall also try to demonstrate how good reputations can be expropriated by a rampant state-owned organisation such as the CCC, even when it fails in all of its primary objectives.

In the interest of veracity, I should clearly indicate that Brian Burke's collapse in public esteem did not commence with the CCC. In the first instance, it stemmed from the Royal Commission into the Government's Business Dealings (commonly known as the WA Inc. Royal Commission) in the early 1990s and his indirectly related conviction for over-claiming on a travel account.

It is correct that, in the minds of the public, WA Inc. was about Brian Burke. However, in informed circles there remained considerable sympathy for Burke over both the royal commission findings and his expenses conviction.

As I explain elsewhere in this book, the WA Inc. inquiry exposed very little of substance outside of the losses on the Petrochemical Industries Company Ltd (PICL) project, which was not even on the horizon when Brian retired from Parliament.

In respect to the travel account matters, some compassion extends to Brian because the defective claim forms were completed by a public servant and not by Brian himself. Furthermore, many other parliamentarians in analogous circumstances (including high-profile MPs such as Tony Abbott and Carmen Lawrence) were simply allowed to repay the over-claimed amounts without prosecution.

For Brian to be sent to jail in this similar fact situation seems disproportionately harsh.

Notwithstanding some significant elements of sympathy for Brian in the ALP (and elsewhere), Premier Geoff Gallop "banned" Burke and me as lobbyists in 2004. This action by Dr Gallop was not explained at the time and has never been justified in any legally clarifying way. Depressingly, Premier Gallop received considerable media acclaim when the CCC appeared to justify his judgement in the initial media onslaught coming out of the CCC hearings.

I am critical of Gallop on this score because he was intelligent and experienced enough to know the CCC processes were conspicuously unfair. He should not have needed the likes of Malcolm McCusker QC, the WA Law Society and the Criminal Lawyers Association to explain why the CCC procedures were a blatant denial of natural justice.

Thus, the initial denigration of Brian Burke and me as lobbyists began with Gallop. But there were others who took the Gallop line by unfairly and brutally attacking Brian on the basis of his influence within the ALP – that is, before the CCC hearings got started.

Liam Bartlett in *The Sunday Times* of 29 January 2006 had these remarkably harsh comments to make in the context of the ALP leadership election:

> The biggest problem facing the Carpenter Government is memory loss. The unabashed acknowledgement this week that convicted thief and liar Brian Burke is a fully functioning powerbroker within ministerial ranks is not only an affront to every voter in the state, it is proof that the ALP has forgotten the mistakes of the past ....
>
> It's also a condemnation of the valiant efforts of past premier Geoff Gallop to separate the Government from the scandalous WA Inc. years.
>
> Police Minister Michelle Roberts confirmed the worst during the jostling for votes that led to caucus installing Alan Carpenter as Premier. Ms Roberts was asked if she had talked to the disgraced former premier and she replied: "I have spoken to Brian. He contacted me and I asked for his support and for the support of the Old Right ...".
>
> Brian Burke's five self-indulgent years as premier were investigated by a royal commission that cost the taxpayers $30 million (in 1990 dollars). Burke's legal fees from the public purse represented $1.7 million of that figure and, in the end, a seven-volume report delivered by three eminent jurists painted a clear picture of a man quite prepared to break the rules and place our system of government at risk.
>
> Burke's then Deputy David Parker admitted to the commission in the witness box that Burke's government sought to "live by concealment".
>
> He was a premier prepared to put in place a secret commission so that his brother, Terry, could make $600,000 out of the millions that Burke demanded in campaign donation from business mates.

The Bartlett piece continued for several more ferocious paragraphs, but I am sure the reader has already got the picture. It was one of the most vituperative media excoriations of a political figure that has ever been put on paper.

But was it factually accurate and was its major premise correct? The answer to both questions is a decisive "no". The job of collecting funds for the ALP was awarded by the State ALP Secretary, Michael Beahan, whose integrity has never been questioned, and not by the Premier. I know as a fact other people were also offered the job that Terry Burke took up on retirement. There was no secret commission. The 25 per cent commission was well canvassed within the party and was 8 per cent below the rate charged by the previous incumbent.

David Parker was never Burke's deputy premier. That position was always occupied by Malcolm Bryce. Parker never said the Burke Government "lived by concealment". He unguardedly said "all" governments lived by concealment. It was a philosophic statement that historically was not too far off the mark.

It is correct, however, that Gallop said publicly on a number of occasions that former leaders like Burke should have no part in policies or the business of the party. Well, I respect Gallop's right to have such an opinion, but there is no rule or custom of the party that suggests that. And Gallop has no right to claim he alone can decide who can and who cannot exercise his or her democratic right within the party forums. History presents no precedent for such a proposition.

Former Prime Minister Billy Hughes carried on in Federal Parliament and continued to be a power broker well after he was deposed as Prime Minister. Gough Whitlam was always a formidable figure within the ALP. Peter Dowding continued to play a political role, as did other former ministers. Former Liberal Prime Minister Tony Abbott has also exercised that right.

Numerous deposed leaders have carried on their careers and exercised political influence. It is well known that senior ALP leaders such as Neville Wran, Paul Keating and Bob Hawke kept up their connections within the ALP – and have used those contacts to build up very lucrative national and international businesses. Their activity has attracted very little adverse public comment.

It was no secret that Jim McGinty was assessing his prospects of returning to the leadership of the party when Gallop resigned. Ministers Michelle Roberts and Alan Carpenter were also in the field. Brian Burke maintains that when Michelle Roberts approached him to support her candidacy it had the potential to change the voting dynamic within the Caucus, as it would reunite the old and the new Right (of which Roberts was the leader) factions. That alliance, together with the help of the Centre faction, would exceed McGinty's numbers within his support base in the Left faction.

As it transpired, after the possibility of the Right reuniting became public, McGinty did not persist with his candidature and the Left threw its support behind Alan Carpenter.

Once McGinty was eliminated, both sections of the Right also supported Carpenter, who was elected unopposed. It was the last throw of the leadership dice for McGinty, who was somewhat embittered and resigned at the next election.

This was the second time McGinty had been within grasp of the premiership and we should not underestimate how desperately he wanted the job. It was well known McGinty and Burke were fierce antagonists. This episode over the premiership did not improve matters.

However, whatever perspective you take on this ALP leadership battle, the Bartlett article ensured Burke's public reputation (unfairly) took a considerable hit in early 2006. It is a mystery what motivated Bartlett to write such a partisan piece, or how he came upon such a collection of incorrect facts. He clearly must have had a source within the ALP. However, even worse was in store for Brian Burke and those close to him later in 2006.

CCC inquiries fail to find crime or corruption

After the biggest and most sophisticated covert surveillance operation carried on in WA (and possibly Australia), and after a full round of secret interrogations in early 2006, the CCC commenced public hearings on Smiths Beach on 23 October 2006. These proceedings, with a three-month hiatus, ran into public hearings on the Lobbyists term of reference for three weeks from 12 February 2007.

I have to confess that it is a distressing experience to open my files on the adverse and degrading publicity that emanated from these two public inquiries. Clearly, the most direct target of the hearings' constant vitriol was Brian Burke, but I was effectively his business partner and each venomous phrase applied to him was also visited on me.

The poisonous implications brought great shame on my family. My wife and my daughter were particularly traumatised. I know Burke's close-knit family was similarly affected. But beyond that, scores of people were dragged in, tainted, wounded and left damaged by the process. I felt responsible for the damaged public servants and their families.

Before I expound on some of the more pernicious consequences of the hearings, I want to explain that once the dust had settled and the reputational lethal allegations and innuendo were put to rest, the score card on actual proof of wrong-doing was decisive.

After eight years of CCC surveillance and hearings, parliamentary committee inquiries and court cases, the CCC was not able to make out one sustainable instance of serious criminality or corruption.

It launched or recommended more than 40 criminal cases on essentially technical matters arising out of the hearings, mainly for alleged misleading evidence. It failed to record a conviction on all but one case, where a fine was imposed.

The CCC did make some highly subjective "findings" of impropriety. However, the logic and integrity of most of these "findings" were severely challenged and found to be unsound by the Parliamentary Inspector (PI) and independent review tribunals. In any event, the PI, Malcolm McCusker, put the status of these CCC "findings" in perspective in a letter to Busselton Shire Councillor Anne Ryan dated 31 December 2008, where he stated:

> It is, obviously, little consolation for you to be reminded that the CCC 'opinions' are no more than that. They are not 'findings' and certainly are not conclusive.

I would comment that the CCC does *not* have the jurisdiction under its Act of Parliament to make findings against private citizens. However, its opinions in its reports about private citizens and those opinions as reported in the media gave the incorrect impression that they were "findings".

Nonetheless, the CCC was devastatingly destructive of peoples' reputations. In many cases, the defamed persons never recover and the CCC's untested "opinion" is used against the injured parties for the rest of their lives. That is, in the ways they are affected in their employment, in their public standing, in their social status and family life.

There are many examples I could easily quote. Several fine and innocent public servants were never reinstated, even after the CCC allegations against them were found to be baseless. But just to give one specific instance, I refer again to Ms Ryan the former Busselton Shire Councillor.

Some years ago, after some excellent years in local government, Ms Ryan retired and moved interstate. The CCC's Smiths Beach Inquiry had "found" she *may* have breached a Public Service code of practice in the way she declared campaign funding. However, as a question of law, the Public Service code of practice did not apply to her or any other local government councillor. Consequently, she was not charged with any offence or breach.

Nonetheless, she was left with this so-called CCC "finding", because she had no venue to challenge such a "finding".

When Ms Ryan returned to Busselton in 2015 and again stood for local government election, she was uncharitably attacked in a local newspaper on the basis of the CCC "finding" as being "tainted". It was very distressing for her and on top of that she lost the election.

The Smiths Beach CCC hearings commenced on 23 October 2006. Florid reports of the testimony were on the front page of *The West Australian* and carried by all substantial media outlets across Australia almost immediately. The headlines on the next day and 25 October were targeted and highly prejudicial.

The West headlines shrieked: "Councillors paid $50,000 by lobbyists"; "Burke the broker in payment to councillors"; "Fishy smell lingers over Canal Rocks"; "Agent had fears of 'sham deal'"; "Secret deal Burke's idea, probe told"; and, "Burke named in corruption probe" in the coverage of the first few days of the hearings."

An atmosphere of implied bribery and palpable corruption was instantly created. The impression was lamentably indelible and, although quite untrue, remains to this day. The media sensationalised the drama. *The West*, for instance, on the first day of coverage, ran the story of the $50,000 payouts to councillors on page one, with a second article that took up most of page 13.

The truth was that no councillor was paid a cent. Six or seven new candidates for possible election to the Busselton Shire Council were given a share of $45,000 to help with their campaigns. The assistance was completely legal and ultimately the CCC impliedly conceded this fact by dropping the allegations without explanation and making no adverse finding on this previously incendiary issue.

The hearing rules did not allow for any correction or even explanation of the issues contemporaneously with the hearings.

We were almost instantly outcasts who were viewed as "untouchable". Anything we said in our own defence outside of the hearings was viewed as self-serving and not worthy of serious contemplation. With the exception of one or two loyal souls, our clients deserted us out of a sense of self-preservation.

Premier Alan Carpenter openly said that we were "toxic", as though any contact with us defiled others. Regrettably, it was true, but not in the way he meant. Jim McGinty was not so generous. On the ABC he said that Burke was "evil". Tragically, the public officers we had dealt with, and who thereby had been unwittingly enmeshed in the events, were necessary sacrifices because, by virtue of the CCC legislation, Burke and I could only be attacked through them.

Despite everything, I can't throw off an overwhelming sense of guilt, especially when my path crosses theirs and we meet face to face. I feel most badly with their partners. I am impelled to try to explain to them what truly happened, but I never have the time required and I can't find the words. I sense they blame me for the misfortunes of their husbands and wives and I know that I can never put the situation right. I hope that maybe this book will help. I extend my best wishes to them.

The "Fishy smells lingers over Canal Rocks" headline featured a big picture of David McKenzie, the chairman of Canal Rocks, and former Busselton Councillor Fraser Smith. It was apparent that McKenzie was also being made a special quarry by the media, who appeared to be working in tandem with the CCC.

Almost unbelievably, the CCC was producing special press kits for the media to guide the nature of the coverage. These kits included recordings of telephone conversations that, although tendered in proceedings, ran the risk when presented in kit form of being taken out of context.

Councillor Fraser Smith was presented by the CCC as a leading witness.

My impression has always been that Cr Smith and Mr McKenzie were friends.

Smith had helped select the candidates who were assisted at the council election by our client, Canal Rocks. He was a successful candidate himself in the 2006 election, but did not require help with campaign funding. Smith's evidence at the Smiths Beach hearings did not ultimately damage McKenzie.

However, I believe that the conflict of allegiance devastated Smith. He was one of the first victims of the hearings. He resigned prematurely from council, had what appeared to be a nervous breakdown and when I last heard had moved away from the area. He was a thoroughly decent human being, but a certain casualty.

For Mr McKenzie, it was his first of many traumatic encounters with the CCC, but he was wretchedly tainted from the first day. He was a secondary target, but was also an innocent victim. In the final analysis there were no "findings" of criminality or corruption against him. In due course, the CCC laid charges alleging he had misled the inquiry (on inconsequential matters). They were eventually thrown out of court. However, he lost the Smiths Beach project, much of his real estate business and, as I explain elsewhere, it wounded his family.

The CCC and the media wasted no time in scapegoating Norm Marlborough. The second day of the hearings produced another sensational story with *The West* running a headline "Minister enmeshed in CCC hearing", with the almost breathless sub-headline "Former shire president puts Burke, Marlborough, Canal Rocks chief at meeting".

The former Shire President was Beryl Morgan and the story ran with a picture of her, head bent down, seemingly crying. She had just completed her public CCC evidence, mainly concerning a luncheon in Fremantle where the CCC was trying to make the case that Ms Morgan was being offered a South West Development Commission job as a payoff for unspecified services she performed for Canal Rocks.

The West photographer caught Ms Morgan in a pose that exhibited her as a picture of contrition. But contrition for what? It was a non-story dressed up as an embryonic scandal. In truth, it was totally innocent. That is, a luncheon meeting of Brian Burke, David McKenzie, Beryl Morgan, Norm Marlborough and myself when Ms Morgan was seeking a position with the South West Development Commission (SWDC).

But it was amazing what a fuss was made of it by the CCC. Marlborough, who was the responsible Minister at the time, made no commitment, but in due course opted for his own reasons not to recommend her.

To this day, I don't see how the story of the luncheon added to the CCC narrative. It was not alleged that she acted with other than propriety and no "findings" of any sort were made against her.

However, she became part of the CCC trail of carnage. After the hearing, this Order of Australia recipient became unemployable. Up until that time she was endowed with a Freeman of the City of Busselton award, mainly for her long and outstanding social work in aid of the sick, the aged and the poor. After the hearing, the stigma was such that some councillors unsuccessfully moved to rescind the honour.

When the CCC reconvened its hearings on 31 October 2006, the knives were vindictively unsheathed for Marlborough. The next day (1 November 2006) *The West* ran the headline "Minister 'lobbied' for project". The import of the story by Daniel Emerson and Sean Cowan was that it was improper and/or corrupt for Minister Marlborough to advocate support for Canal Rocks' Smiths Beach development.

This banner was quite misleading because the event referred to in the article took place in June 2005, well before Marlborough was a minister. But even if the headline had been true, supporting an employment-generating project was not in any way improper and in no way corrupt.

A similar theme of implied impropriety and a corruption taint was pursued on the 2 November 2006 by Sean Cowan and Daniel Emerson of *The West* in a front-page story under the headline: "Secret deal Burke's idea, probe told".

The first paragraph stated:

> Former premier Brian Burke was named in a *corruption probe* (my emphasis) yesterday as the man who hatched a complex plot for thousands of dollars to be channelled secretly from a *controversial property developer* (my emphasis) to Busselton council candidates via a dormant lobby group.

This choice of wording gave an extremely sinister representation to Burke's actions. However, correctly expressed and stripped of its inflammatory rhetoric the paragraph should have benignly read: "Anonymous donors contribute thousands of dollars to new candidates in Busselton Shire elections." Such contributions were completely legal under the *Local Government Act* (see Chapter 4).

In specific terms, the Smiths Beach inquiry was not a "corruption probe". No evidence of corruption was ever produced. No such findings were ever made. The property developer (Canal Rocks) comprised a group of inoffensive mostly "mum and dad" investors headed up by a respected suburban real estate agent, David McKenzie.

The development itself did become controversial, largely because the Gallop Opposition (and later Government) announced, prior to the 2001 election, that in Government it would retrospectively strip the project of approvals lawfully obtained under the Court Government.

That stripping of lawful approvals was a political action done largely at the behest of local vested interests (see Chapter 4).

Retrospective regulation, to confiscate property rights already passed and gazetted, as was the case in this instance, is exceptional, especially where no compensation is offered.

Obviously, the proponent, Canal Rocks, had committed very substantial resources and money on planning for the development on the basis of the Government approvals. That was lost without any offer of recompense. Further, the Gallop Government refused to recognise that loss and arrogantly rejected any contact or dialogue with Canal Rocks. I have never witnessed anything more unfair in all of my 24 years in Parliament.

Usually, the media would have been expected to be outraged by such treatment of a group of citizens. On principle, newspapers like *The West Australian*, *The Australian* and *Australian Financial Review* would have been highly critical of such high-handed government. In the situation of Smiths Beach and Canal Rocks, however, there was not the slightest expression of concern.

Much of the misleading campaign of denigration was directed toward creating the impression of the "greed" of the Canal Rocks group and, unfortunately, myself and Brian Burke. Not one shred of hard evidence was produced to back this smear campaign.

Nonetheless, sections of the media dutifully picked up and amplified the CCC's "greed" theme. Tim Treadgold wrote an article on financial greed in the *WA Business News* of 2 November 2006. He labelled the project a "get rich (quick) scheme" by investors motivated by "rampant greed".

Norm Marlborough becomes a target

The West of 3 November 2006 again targeted Marlborough with two front-page articles (one an opinion piece) by Robert Taylor, Sean Cowan, Amanda Banks and Daniel Emerson under the headlines "Yet another Cabinet crisis for Carpenter" and "When will the Premier ever learn?"

The background to the stories was that Premier Carpenter had lifted the Gallop ministerial contact ban on Burke and me and that

Burke's friend Norm Marlborough had finally been appointed to Cabinet. The clear objective of *The West* story was to induce the Premier to dismiss Marlborough. The rest of the media were also baying for blood. The first paragraph of the larger of the front-page articles was as follows:

> Alan Carpenter refused to say whether he retained confidence in beleaguered Small Business Minister Norm Marlborough yesterday after it was revealed at the *corruption* (my emphasis) probe that the Peel MPs election campaign had received $5000 from property developer Canal Rocks.

The clear implication was that the $5000 was a payment to Marlborough for services rendered. The word was not actually used, but the newspaper was referring to a payment akin to a "bribe". I postulate that such a conclusion would have been legitimately found only if the facts put forward by the CCC were correct.

But here was the problem: the CCC facts were demonstrably erroneous. No such money was paid to Marlborough's election campaign. The funds were for tickets to an ALP fundraiser hosted by Kim Beazley and every cent went into the ALP central account.

The Sunday Times, not to be outdone, quickly escalated the matter into a full-blown $100,000 scandal, in a story by Joe Spagnolo in its edition of 5 November 2006. It began:

> Electoral Commission officials have intensified an investigation into the ALP donations scandal, which now involves more than $100,000. The scandal could go much deeper than a $5000 cheque given by developer Canal Rocks to Labor MP Norm Marlborough.

This was a disgraceful and unjustifiable beat-up by the paper. It did transpire that $116,000 was raised at the Beazley function and the ALP had to file a corrected form in respect to the $5000 donation. However, there was never the slightest evidence that Marlborough had behaved other than properly. There was never a scandal.

The West later carried a correction on 16 November 2006 by Amanda Banks. However, the rectifying story had little of the prominence of the original articles and only a tiny fraction of the impact. Incredible damage was done. The CCC never redressed the position. Nor did *The Sunday Times*.

This situation underscores the manifest unfairness of the Smiths Beach and Lobbyists inquiry processes. Taking witnesses by surprise, as they did in this case, prevents a considered reply being made or a credible explanation being presented. Further, by not allowing an opportunity for a witness to present rebuttal evidence, partial and faulty evidence can be paraded as fact, with horrendous consequences for reputations – as happened in these sets of hearings.

After this episode of patently erroneous evidence and mistaken conclusions, *The West* (but not the CCC) started to become slightly more wary of making unfounded inferences. On 8 November 2006, the newspaper's Gary Adshead had this to say in an analysis piece buried at the bottom of page 13:

> Unless the CCC has an ace up its sleeve, then the past three weeks spent examining the links between a resort development near Yallingup and the Busselton council's elections will have been more about name dropping and whether the hat Brian Burke wore to his hearing was a Panama or a fedora.

It went on to talk about the use of "well connected and skilled lobbyists like Mr Burke and Julian Grill", but concluded, "thus far the knockout punch proving bribery hasn't been delivered".

After the CCC hearing on 8 November 2006, Premier Carpenter sacked Marlborough from his Ministry. To make the event ever more dramatic, Marlborough – devastated and humiliated – resigned from Parliament entirely. The CCC had the "scalp" that it had telegraphed to the media it would get.

Marlborough was a desolate man. The one job he had aspired to all his working life, and which made his politically orientated wife Ros and family so proud of him, that of an MP and Government minister, was gone.

So was his will to live. Marlborough saw himself as being in disgrace and having betrayed his beloved Labor Party. He was in such a shattered state that he was committed to a psychiatric hospital within days. Burke and Grill were once again placed on the banned list by a frantic Carpenter.

The West banner front-page headlines of 9 November 2006 screamed: "I got it wrong, admits besieged Carpenter".

There was one central issue that triggered the sacking and two ancillary matters. The first concerned a private phone used exclusively for calls between best friends Norm Marlborough and Brian Burke. The two ancillary matters concerned a possible job on the SWDC (mentioned above) and an answer to a Parliamentary question. *The West* story by Robert Taylor and Sean Cowan summed it up this way:

> In his evidence Mr Marlborough admitted buying a new mobile telephone *registered to his wife* (my emphasis), days after he was sworn in as Minister for Small Business and the South West in February this year, purely so he could speak to Mr Burke.
>
> The pair spoke about keeping Mr Marlborough's *new* (my emphasis) phone line secret to avoid having his links with Mr Burke all over the papers. In a later conversation, Mr Burke provided his friend with an answer to a question put to him in Parliament about the level of contact between the men.
>
> And in another phone call, recorded in August, Mr Burke urged Mr Marlborough to appoint former Busselton Shire president Beryl Morgan to a plum position on the South West Development Commission. Mr Marlborough told Mr Burke that it was a "done deal".

The phone was not new, but Robert Taylor got the story mostly right. Norm Marlborough did use the term "done deal", but his actions contradicted his words. The inference was that Marlborough was prepared to appoint Ms Morgan without going through the normal government appointments process.

I refer to the luncheon in Fremantle, mentioned earlier, where Brian Burke introduced Ms Morgan to Marlborough. Marlborough and I left together. When we were in my car, he told me immediately that he would not recommend Ms Morgan for the job at the SWDC as she had been a recent National Party candidate for Parliament. He was too much of an ALP tribal warrior to appoint political opponents to plum jobs.

Additionally, later documentary evidence from the SWDC disclosed that Marlborough was going to recommend to Cabinet completely different individuals for approval. Also, that all appointments were going through the proper processes in any event.

The tragedy of the CCC hearings was that Marlborough was never permitted to adduce this exculpatory evidence. It could have and should have been produced, but it only came to light publicly when the CCC unsuccessfully later tried to prosecute Marlborough for giving false testimony to the Smiths Beach hearing.

I have checked with Ros Marlborough and she advises that the phone was not new, as indicated by the CCC. She maintains the phone was an old one that had been in the family for some time. But it is conceded it was re-activated for exclusive use between Norm and Brian.

However, it is not a crime or improper for Marlborough to have a non-government, personal phone for his own private use. I submit the critical issue relates to the use to which the phone was put. Was it used properly or improperly? I argue that it was not improperly used.

Further, in regard to the SWDC job, a whole host of people, including me, lobbied Marlborough on behalf of third parties interested in these positions. We were all told by Marlborough that our respective candidates would be sympathetically considered. It was not printed in *The West*, but in the highlighted telephone conversation between Marlborough and Burke, Marlborough could not initially recollect Ms Morgan from the Fremantle luncheon. That's an indication of how much importance he gave to the issue.

As mentioned, hard evidence later emerged that he was never going to recommend her for appointment. The Supreme Court, when called upon in due course, expressly exonerated Marlborough on this issue.

The real case for possible allegations of impropriety or criminality by Marlborough was that the private phone may possibly have been used to pass on confidential Cabinet information to Brian Burke. This was always the innuendo and it was an accusation of a serious nature. It was covered in a separate analysis by Robert Taylor in *The West* on 9 November 2006. The headline ran: "Premier risked Cabinet integrity".

I respect Taylor as a journalist, and he later adopted a somewhat different attitude to the Smiths Beach and Lobbyists inquires, but in this story he really laid on the invective with a trowel, predicting that when the CCC reconvened on 4 December it would concentrate on whether Marlborough had passed on details of confidential Cabinet deliberations to his friend, Brian Burke.

He said the CCC had signalled this by taking Marlborough through the Ministerial Code of Conduct in relation to cabinet confidentiality. If Marlborough had breached the Code of Conduct in his many telephone conversations with Brian, his inclusion in the Cabinet would have serious implications for the State.

Premier Carpenter would have to take responsibility for Cabinet's deliberations being compromised and would have difficulty maintaining the confidence of other Ministers – and the public.

I believe it was entirely improper for Taylor to remark on these important issues without the benefit of seeing any evidence. You, the reader, be the arbiter, but in my assessment he was pronouncing Burke and Marlborough guilty of breaching cabinet confidentiality, especially when he concluded: "The whole State has been let down."

This was an extraordinary piece. Taylor was the chief political reporter at *The West* and he was implying for the politically astute that, if the facts were as he had been led to believe they might be by the CCC, *The West* may be forced to campaign for the removal of the Premier. This was serious stuff by any assessment.

The "Cabinet leaks" line was not taken up by Taylor alone. It was adopted by the media generally.

This was a remarkable turn of events. This inquiry was no longer just a witch-hunt for Burke and Grill. Like a cancer it had metastasised into something even more dangerous. It had the real potential to knock out Premier Carpenter and destroy the Government.

McGinty must at least have had the stirrings of panic. Here was the CCC, an agency that he had created and fostered, setting up to demolish the Carpenter Government.

Very much on the defensive and in survival mode, Carpenter insisted, "that no decision taken by his Cabinet had been compromised by the relationship between his Minister and the former Premier" (Burke). But the matter was out of his hands now. The CCC and its senior counsel were clearly in control and the masters of destinies.

But then a strange thing happened, or more correctly, didn't happen.

Contrary to the bold assertion made by Taylor, Marlborough was not recalled on 4 December. Indeed, he was never resummoned on the Smiths Beach matter at all. Although Brian Burke was recalled and extensively cross-examined for nearly all of the sitting day on 4 December, he was not questioned on a possible breach of cabinet confidentiality.

In fact, the subject was never again raised seriously by the CCC in the context of Smiths Beach. Nor was it the subject of a "finding" in the Smiths Beach report.

As we shall see, although the CCC did raise the broad issue of cabinet confidentiality in the Lobbyists public hearings, the accusation went nowhere.

The question consequentially arises: What happened at the CCC between 8 November 2006 and when the CCC next sat on the 4 December 2006? The likelihood of a major and serious violation of the law in respect to Cabinet discussion was a real issue robustly conjectured by CCC counsel Stephen Hall on the former date. It was the most critical concern raised to that point and took up the larger part of Marlborough's interrogation.

The divulging of Cabinet secrets is a serious offence under the Criminal Code. It could carry a long term of imprisonment. The matter of the so-called "secret phone" and its possible use to infringe cabinet secrecy was the most devastating blow to Marlborough and

Burke's standing in the community of all of the issues canvassed in the long-running set of inquiries.

Put more simply, if there was no breach of Cabinet secrets, the innocent use of the "secret phone" by very close friends lost all of its sinister overtones.

Most people never quite understood, among the plethora of imputations raised at the CCC public hearings, just what it was that Brian Burke and I were supposed to have done wrong or how it was imagined we might have transgressed.

But two items stood out. Recently, at an informal morning coffee meeting with a group of my old ministerial colleagues, the only two matters that were recollected clearly in our discussion of the CCC inquiries was the intrusive nature of covert surveillance used on Lesley and my home, and the "secret phone" with the inference of breach of cabinet confidentiality.

The inferences of breaches of cabinet confidentiality were made at a time when the media were beginning to doubt the efficacy of the Smiths Beach Inquiry. After the inferences were made, the scalp of Marlborough was secured and the position of Premier Carpenter was placed under threat, the CCC media stocks took an explosive turn for the better.

But why was this deadly issue seriously canvassed in the Smiths Beach hearing and not substantially touched on again? Possible alternative explanations are:

(a) The CCC received a gentle hint from the Government that it had gone too far.

(b) There was in fact no evidence of any breach of cabinet confidentiality by Marlborough in the possession of the CCC. The CCC had knowledge of every phone call made between the two friends, as all those phone calls were monitored. In other words, the CCC would have had information of any such breach and would have been able to pinpoint and act upon it. The fact that the CCC produced no evidence of an infraction and took no action seems to speaks for itself.

(c) The CCC, in its own right, came to the conclusion these were matters outside of its terms of reference and desisted in that line of inquiry.

We can speculate, but we shall never know. This unresolved situation is troubling because of the flamboyant coverage given to the issue in the media.

The cartoons that ridiculed Marlborough were particularly cruel and must have added to his significant distress. He was likened successively to a counterfeiter, a little grossly fat man who had a telephone explode in his face while supposedly talking to Brian Burke, was depicted as an easily manipulated chimpanzee, and Burke, Marlborough and I were drawn to look like flying pigs.

A picture of Marlborough in *The Sunday Times* of 3 December 2006 had been altered to distort his face and give him the most outrageous black eye. Put simply, the media treated him as fair game and seemed not to care how cruel it was.

The media wasted no time in visiting all of Carpenter's problems on Burke, Marlborough and myself (by inference). *The West*, as an example, ran a front-page article on 11 November 2006 under the headline: "Labor hits new low after Burke fiasco".

The story went on to quote from a specially conducted poll that indicated the ALP vote in WA had fallen 19 points since the election eight months earlier. The innuendo was that Burke and I had been primarily responsible.

In the same paper, on page 4, was an article by Jessica Strutt concerning Ljiljanna Ravlich, the Minister for Education. The headline stated: "Ravlich admits to calls and meeting with Burke".

The tacit message in the headline and story was that any contact by anyone in government with Burke was sinister.

Ravlich was removed from the significant Education portfolio and her position in Cabinet within weeks of this article in *The West*. Although she was reappointed to Cabinet in 2007, it was for the lesser responsibilities of Local Government and Racing and Gaming.

Media vilification continues unabated

By this time there were some very harsh judgements being made about us by members of the media. Typical of those denunciations was that of Andrew Burrell in *The Australian Financial Review* on 11 November 2006.

Burrell wrote in broad-brush terms of "overwhelming evidence presented to the WA Inc. Royal Commission that Burke ran a corrupt government". I have dealt with this issue elsewhere, but I have to say again: No such corruption was even alleged, let alone proved. When all the dust had settled, the official findings of the Royal Commission into Government Business Dealings (WA Inc.) were quite to the contrary.

The Royal Commissioners, in fact, said that they found "little evidence of illegality and no evidence of corruption". Burrell could have discovered these facts himself if he had gone to the proper source – the royal commission report.

However, for the sake of completeness and accuracy, I should concede that it is correct that after the conclusion of the royal commission David Parker (Peter Dowding's deputy, not Burke's) was charged and convicted for perjury related to evidence given at the commission. I emphasise, that did not in any way reflect on Brian Burke or the rest of Cabinet.

In the same article, Burrell stated:

> That evidence also shows that Burke's character hasn't changed: He clearly lied to the Corruption and Crime Commission when he gave evidence on the amount of phone contact he had with Marlborough as a minister. Burke said it was a couple of times a week; the phone records showed it was as often as 10 times a day.

We need to be explicit here as to exactly what Burrell was alleging in a newspaper read in every corner of Australia. He was asserting not only that Burke was a corrupt Premier presiding over a corrupt government, but that the corruption had continued on in my lobbying business.

Further, that Burke had deliberately lied to the CCC under oath on the issue of the much-hyped question of the phone calls made to and from Marlborough. I say "much-hyped" because of the depth and scope of the coverage. *The West* actually established a free telephone line where people could listen to recordings of the eavesdropped Burke/Marlborough conversations.

On top of that, *The West* devoted a double-page feature story in the same edition to written transcripts of the same four phone conversations. Several other articles referred to the same issue.

It was extraordinary coverage and was bound to cause extensive damage to reputation. In the wash-up, the CCC, unable to link the telephone calls to any impropriety, was forced to treat it as a non-issue. But *The West* (I think, essentially out of ignorance) persisted with the damaging untruths. Even after the CCC's Smiths Beach Report had been tabled, in an article relating to John Halden on the very subject of leaking of Cabinet confidential information, Robert Taylor wrote:

> One of the defining moments of the CCC's lobbyists' inquiry was when ministers Norm Marlborough and John Bowler were shown to have leaked Cabinet considerations to Mr Burke and Mr Grill. [5]

It was clear testimony as to how persistent untrue innuendo can be.

I have already commented on the false allegation of corruption. Burrell's accusation that Brian lied is on similar shaky terrain. On 6 November 2006, when examining Burke, Stephen Hall, Counsel Assisting, laid a trap (see page 954 of transcript). The dialogue went this way:

> **Hall:** How often would you speak?
>
> **Burke:** To Mr Marlborough?
>
> **Hall:** Yes?
>
> **Burke:** A couple of times a week, I guess.
>
> **Hall:** Has that changed at all in the – since he was appointed a minister?

---

[5] *The West Australian*, 31 May 2008.

Burke: Yes.

Hall: In what way?

Burke: It's decreased in frequency.

Hall: How often would you speak to him before then?

Burke: Three or four times, five times."

I would interpose here that Mr Hall was not asking these questions to elicit information. CCC staff had already searched the records. Marlborough was assailed with the results of the research when he was brutally interrogated by Mr Hall just two days later. As we now know, it was a ferocious grilling that Marlborough was not emotionally equipped to deal with.

Mr Hall returned to the same subject on 4 December 2006 when the CCC cross-examined Burke for the third time. The trap set on 6 November 2006 was sprung by Mr Hall. On page 1177 of the transcript, he said to Burke (in part): "Now, you may recall that when Mr Marlborough was giving evidence, I said to him that in the days following the connection of this (secret) phone there were 10 calls on 5 February ...?"

So that's where Burrell got his 10 calls a day from. But that is also where the misleading numbers are derived. The 5 February 2006 date is a high-water mark that came about in the euphoria of Marlborough's elevation to Cabinet. For the CCC to imply through Mr Hall that 5 February was a representative day was a major exaggeration of the frequency of calls.

However, in a very rare episode in the Smiths Beach inquiry, a witness was allowed some very small latitude to actually take on the CCC. Brian Burke challenged Mr Hall's figures and won the debate. It was revealed that the CCC had calculated that there were 542 calls between Burke and Marlborough over the relevant 11-month period.

But, as Brian was able to point out, many of the phone calls he made to Marlborough went unanswered; almost half by Burke's calculation. And that calculation was not contradicted by the CCC (which was in a position to know). Far from being 10 calls a day, as implied by the CCC, the number that resulted in dialogue was probably more likely to be in the order of five a *week* as Brian has suggested.

To put this into some perspective, Brian made 8272 outward calls during this same period. He was a prolific phone user.

The comments made by Burrell were in truth a terrible libel of Burke. They have never been retracted. These, and other defamations like them, were all too numerous during this traumatic period. They seemingly had such momentum as to appear at the time to be irresistible. Their impact was like a sledgehammer to the reputations of those targeted.

Much later, in 2015, Burrell wrote a more considered feature article on Brian for *The Weekend Australian's* Magazine. It was balanced and fair; however, there was no redress of the November 2007 falsehoods.

I cannot finish this matter without making one more thing clear. That is, that the CCC should have known at all relevant times that the 10 phone calls a day was a vastly exaggerated number. But it was the number put out there for media and public consumption. Burrell and the *Australian Financial Review* certainly bought it.

Beazley is drawn into media morass

There was another aspect of the CCC-inspired media avalanche that was tasteless and destructive of the human spirit. I am referring to the manner in which the federal Leader of the Opposition, Kim Beazley, was forced to denounce his lifelong friend, Brian Burke.

It was a gradual and demeaning process that effectively began when Premier Carpenter told the media on 9 November 2006 that henceforth Burke and Grill were *persona non grata* again. This was confirmed in a front-page story by Taylor in *The West Australian* of 14 November, under the headline: "Premier enforces lobby gag on Burke".

The first paragraph of the story summed it up:

> Alan Carpenter effectively cut off the livelihood of Labor power broker Brian Burke and his partner Julian Grill

yesterday, saying his Government would establish a register for lobbyists but the pair would not be allowed on it.

This triggered a media debate that went on for weeks.

There was a phrase, first used by Geoff Gallop and Jim McGinty that "Burke and Grill were toxic" and any contact with us could be contaminating. It was this notion that was quickly employed in respect to Kim Beazley. That is, any contact by Beazley with Burke would infect and corrupt the federal Opposition Leader.

Kim Beazley Sen. and Brian Burke's fathers had much in common. Tom Burke was Beazley's best man. They were elected to Federal Parliament in the war years (Burke 1943 and Beazley 1945); they were both articulate anti-communists; and at separate times they were each touted as possible leaders of the federal party.

Kim Beazley (junior) and Brian Burke were comrades in arms in the ALP and fought many torrid policy and internal election battles within the WA ALP on behalf of the Right wing of the party. These battles were made more poignant because the Right was rarely in the majority in an ALP still pursuing the "socialist objective" and under the domination of rampant old-style left-winger Joe Chamberlain.

Immense pressure went on to Beazley in late November 2006 from within the Labor Party and from all sections of the media, which could smell blood, for him to denounce and abandon his oldest, and I believe closest, political friend. We need to bear in mind that at this very time Beazley was about to come under very serious attack for leadership of Federal Labor by Kevin Rudd.

Initially, Beazley resisted the calls to desert Burke and responded that he wanted to wait and see what came out of the completed CCC inquiry. However, the media and elements within the ALP were insistent. Beazley's position was unethically put on the line.

The incessant pressure worked. On 16 November 2006, *The West* triumphantly ran a front-page banner headline proclaiming: "I'll banish Burke too, says Beazley".

However, even that was not enough for the media. They insisted that Beazley disavow the friendship and completely forsake his old childhood pal. *The West's* front-page story of 16 November by Andrew Probyn and Robert Taylor reported as follows:

> Kim Beazley is set to follow Alan Carpenter's lead with a register of political lobbyists that will exclude his good friend Brian Burke, revealing yesterday that future Federal Labor ministers would be banned from talking to the former premier.
>
> But, in almost the same breath, Mr Beazley refused to sever personal ties with Mr Burke.

Probyn ran a page 11 comment piece in the same paper under the headline: "Big Kim must say bye-bye to B-B".

In the article, Probyn goes on to deal with the essence of the Beazley/Burke relationship: "He was sort of one of those friends you inherit automatically," Probyn quotes Beazley as saying in Peter FitzSimons' biography, *Beazley*.

> When your parents know each other, and the family are friends, they are almost like cousins. But then we became friends, real friends. In the Labor Party you can have a lot of mates, but he was a friend.

Not all of the media pressed for Beazley to terminate his friendship with Burke. There was even one lonely objection to this course of action within *The West*, where Paul Murray had this to say in his column of 18 November 2006:

> There's a poisonous smell of McCarthyism hanging in the air around Perth. This time the thought police aren't looking for Reds under the bed: they're looking to see if Brian Burke has been in it.
>
> For example, the attempt this week by a national newspaper to tar Opposition Leader Kim Beazley for being one of hundreds attending a Burke organised Labor Party fund raiser – at which the former premier was not even present – has a whiff of McCarthyism about it.
>
> The national broadcaster reported that Mr Beazley was

forced to 'defend' his 50-year friendship with Brian Burke as a result.

What sort of society do we have when the media tells people who they can and can't have as friends? Surely politicians should be judged on their actions.

That did not prevent *The West* from running highly demeaning cartoons of Beazley and Burke on their editorial pages in the paper's editions of the 16 and 20 November 2006. The ongoing cartoon storm was a degrading and crippling process. It was an inundation of derision that included all of the major papers across Australia, and most of Perth suburban and WA regional papers. It was impossible to escape. It often included me, but it always featured Brian.

When Beazley was appointed WA's next Governor in April 2018, he declared Burke was a "lifelong friend" and would remain a friend, but he would keep the personal and professional separate.

I do not allege that Beazley's friendship with Brian was the cause of his removal as Federal Opposition Leader. However, it can credibly be argued that Beazley's internal detractors could have used Beazley's vulnerability as a catalyst when the successful challenge was mounted against him.

There are many who believe that Beazley would have made a fine Prime Minister. I am one of them. Perhaps the best we never had. Even more agree that the history of the ALP would have been a happier and more successful one with Beazley at the helm.

Even the comedian Sacha Baron Cohen (alias Borat) got into the act by featuring in a rather demeaning set of cartoons in *The West* of 18 November 2006 lampooning lobbying in WA. Burke, in the great majority of these depictions, was drawn as a sinister, raincoat-garbed, Panama hat-wearing fat man in dark glasses. I can assure you that it is demoralising to be reviled and ridiculed day after day without end in this fashion.

I featured enough in this lampooning to really hurt my family, but the quarry they really loved to hate was Burke. Many people would be emotionally shattered after a few days of such treatment. Try eight years.

For Marlborough, the ridicule of the cartoons multiplied his disgrace. His humiliation was almost total. I wasn't present when he publicly announced that he would resign, but Jessica Strutt gives the flavour of his desperation in a story in *The West* of 10 November 2006. In part, it went like this:

> A visibly shattered Norm Marlborough faced the media early yesterday to announce he would quit State Parliament.
>
> Dressed in a dark pinstriped suit, the Peel MLA emerged just after 10am to concede he could not stay in Parliament.
>
> Slightly stooped and red in the face, Norm Marlborough admitted he had betrayed the Labor Party and was 'paying the price' for his friendship with Brian Burke.
>
> Marlborough described Burke as a mentor, confidante and friend, saying:
>
> "I simply haven't had the capacity or the will to control that friendship and the evidence of the last 48 hours has highlighted that. I feel I've let my family down (and) I feel I've let the Labor Party down."
>
> Marlborough told the media throng that in retrospect there were things that occurred that should not have, but he would leave it to the CCC to decide if he had committed a crime.

His wife was asked how her husband was coping was quoted as saying: "He's very sad. At the moment he's just very exhausted."

Norm and Ros Marlborough were Labor "true believers". Norm knew nothing else but the ALP and the unions. Ros' family worked intimately with Prime Minister John Curtin. Together she and Norm organised the ALP branches in their area, raised the money for the electoral campaigns and ensured that the polling booths were properly manned.

As I explain elsewhere, Marlborough was never charged with any substantive matters under CCC investigation. In fact, there was not even any "finding" of impropriety against him, for what that is worth. There just wasn't any evidence of wrongdoing.

So why did he confess to some possible crime and why did he resign from Parliament? The reality was that Marlborough was in a profound state of shock. He was not in a condition to make any judgment. I had tried to contact him after he gave evidence at the CCC to offer him support. I felt very concerned about his welfare. He did receive my messages, as I later discovered, but I never got through personally.

I believe that, apart from Ros and his immediate family, he was alone, cut off from independent guidance. His initial legal counsel was not able to help him and he had no media advice. His former colleagues in Parliament had deserted their friend. They were cowed by the brutality of the CCC onslaught.

Clearly, it was immoral for the CCC to take such a vulnerable individual by surprise. It was the perfect example of trial by ambush and decision by media. Marlborough's family blamed Brian Burke and to a lesser extent me for his predicament. On one occasion, at one of the CCC hearings, his brother-in-law, Syd Shea, whom I always counted as a friend, followed me into the toilet and offered to knock my head off "for what you have done to Norm".

It was clear to me that the family was deeply immersed in a broiling sea of emotional wreckage. I was relieved to escape from the toilet unharmed. I bear Syd Shea absolutely no ill will and we later resumed a very good relationship.

However, this concept that I had harmed Norm confounded me. I saw him as a victim of an unethical CCC. On the other hand, at that time his family perceived Norm as a manipulated casualty of Burke and my commercial interests. It was not until then that I fully appreciated just how thoroughly the unjust CCC narrative had been accepted by the public.

Brian Burke saw the truth of public sentiment more quickly than me. He identified that he was lethally noxious to the ALP and he resigned on 9 November 2006. It was the front-page story of *The West* and it was news across the country. Robert Taylor, Amanda Banks and Graham Mason wrote the story (in part) as follows:

> WA Labor tore itself apart yesterday after powerbroker Brian Burke quit the party, Alan Carpenter threatened to resign and backbenchers said they would defy the Premier's edict not to have contact with Brian Burke.

Later in the article Carpenter was quoted as follows:

> I gave them (the ALP) the choice between Brian Burke and myself and the Labor Party has chosen me and I'm glad that they have because, if you want to have people like me in public life, then you can't have people like Brian Burke destroying everything that we try to do.

It would be obvious to readers that Carpenter and the media were over-dramatising the situation. There was no real contest between Brian Burke and Alan Carpenter. Burke openly conceded that he was yesterday's man. Nearly 20 years out of Parliament, an unfortunate stint in prison in the meantime, followed by just about the worst media beating up that we have ever witnessed. In truth, it was a walkover.

It was only later that the pretext, that is, the perception of the leaking of secret cabinet business, was found to be unsupportable.

It was curious that someone like Carpenter, who had been in the ALP for such a short time and who was only going to be around in the party for another 20 months before he embarrassingly lost office, could pass such a derogatory judgment on the former Premier who had led the party out of the political wilderness in 1983, who was considered by most pundits to be easily the highest-achieving WA Labor Premier, and whose family was steeped in the party history.

It was also indicative of the prevailing atmosphere that Carpenter could not publicly identify exactly what Burke had done wrong and didn't think that was even necessary. This latter mentioned point was actually taken up in *The West* article:

Political analyst and Curtin University Professor Greg Craven questioned what Mr Burke had done to warrant being thrown out of the ALP. 'No matter how undesirable contact with Brian Burke may be politically, there's not yet a law saying you can't talk with Brian Burke. We may be moving in that direction but we're not there yet,' Professor Craven said.

Speaking before Mr Burke's resignation was known, senior Labor Senator Mark Bishop said: "Mr Carpenter should consult widely and exhaustively before expelling Mr Burke from the ALP. I've never heard of anyone being expelled for lobbying a minister."

Treasurer and ALP Deputy Leader Eric Ripper conceded, "the Government could not guarantee that cabinet confidentiality had not been breached". This did, of course, contradict his leader, Alan Carpenter, who strongly maintained otherwise.

Jim McGinty actually went so far as to allege unacceptable conduct on the part of Burke. He is quoted in the same *West* article as follows: "Alan Carpenter has drawn a line in the sand and made it abundantly clear that he is about getting rid of people who are sapping our political system of integrity."

Here again, McGinty, like Carpenter, was not able to specify any improper conduct or a breach of the law by Burke.

Labor State MP Fran Logan was less sophisticated. He was quoted in the same article as saying: "As far as Brian Burke goes, I say good riddance to bad rubbish."

These comments were all made shortly after the question of the breach of cabinet confidentiality was raised by Stephen Hall in his interrogation of Marlborough on 8 November 2006. They were not to know that these imputations were to be dropped like a red-hot brick when the CCC resumed public hearings on the 4 December.

Deeply wounded and upset, Brian resigned. He did not consult me, as his close business partner, on his resignation. If he had, I would have advised him against it on two grounds. First, as far as I knew, he had committed no impropriety. Secondly, on the basis of the rules of the party and the law, there was no legitimate way that he could be expelled.

Sadly, Kim Beazley agreed with Brian's actions. The first two paragraphs of a story on 10 November 2006 by Rhianna King of the Canberra office of *The West* were as follows: "Brian Burke did the right thing by himself and the party in resigning from the ALP, Federal Labor leader Kim Beazley said yesterday. Mr Beazley said that while Mr Burke was an old friend of his, he had no choice but to stand down as an ALP member."

The West of 10 November 2006 also ran an article by their then Chief Crime Reporter Gary Adshead evidencing the fact that the business community and most of our clients had deserted us.

In writing the article Adshead made the allegation that Brian was a power junky. It begs the question of why, if Burke was power hungry, he quit politics after exactly five years and never make any attempt to return. Strange behaviour for a so-called power junkie.

As for the lobbying, it was not a job of choice. Even for me it was a trial. It was well paid, but in most part harrowing. In truth, it was the most demanding work I have ever done and it severely affected the state of my health. For Burke, it was no different. He told me on a number of occasions that the intensity of the tasks was placing him under such extreme pressure that he did not think he could carry on for much longer.

But for Burke there was no realistic alternative. He had used up all of his savings on lawyers. After he was released from jail he was almost unemployable in Australia and the only job he could obtain was provided by the late Lang Hancock, away from his family in a grimy industrial town in the vicinity of Vladivostok, Siberia. He still had to feed his family, and his two youngest children were students who lived at home.

One of the ironies was that all of our clients swore by the integrity of our operational methods and appreciated the effort we injected into our work. But I don't want to be too melodramatic about our gravely diminished public standing. I have never seen myself as a victim. A target yes, but not a victim. We were big boys and should be able to look after ourselves.

Inevitably, however, the public took its cue from the media on the issues raised in the CCC hearings. Letters to the editor and Perth talkback radio were uniformly hostile to Brian and me. Even though it was not clear what misdemeanour we had committed, significant elements of the citizenry were howling for blood.

The State Opposition took up this same theme. It slavishly followed the media line. Proof of an offence by Burke or Grill was irrelevant. Hysteria was the order of the day.

When former National Party MP Max Trenorden went further and made a media statement indicating that he would introduce legislation to strip MPs found guilty of committing an offence of their superannuation I became concerned for my wife as that would have left her without an income in her later years. I initially sustained a very substantial pay cut to enter Parliament and I had contributed heavily to that superannuation over a 24-year period. It would have been a major financial blow.

Trenorden made it clear the legislation would be aimed at Burke and me.

Attorney-General McGinty (as I detail elsewhere in this book) actually made a high-profile promise to legislate to confiscate the superannuation of any MP found guilty of a serious offence. In fear, on his resignation Marlborough cashed in his superannuation so that it was out of harm's way.

Ultimately, no such bill was introduced. I suspect that that was because wiser heads realised just how dangerous such legislation could be and what a huge disincentive it would be for any young person contemplating public service through a parliamentary career.

CCC attack renewed in 'Lobbyists Inquiry'

On 8 November 2006, the day the CCC secured Norm Marlborough's "scalp", Counsel Assisting Stephen Hall announced a "turning point" and "major extension" in the inquiry.

I have called this extension the "Lobbyists Inquiry" to distinguish it from the Smiths Beach Inquiry.

This "turning point" – or as Mr Hall put it, "change in the nature of the investigation" – was an announcement that certain witnesses would be recalled for further examination on 4 December 2006. He explained it this way:

> ... on evidence available to the Commission there is reason to believe that some witnesses who appeared to date have been less than completely frank and honest in their evidence. The Commission intends to recall a number of witnesses when the hearings resume. They will be advised shortly of the requirement to return.
>
> If witnesses persist in deliberate untruthfulness they run the risk of committing further offences under the CCC Act. Witnesses should also appreciate that it is very much in their own interest not to aggravate their position by continuing to maintain a false story.

No one would deny the right of the CCC to test the evidence of witnesses with further examination. However, brazenly broadcasting the recall of witnesses, using the words employed, was to prejudge the issue and stigmatise everyone recalled as a potential criminal liar.

I mention here a letter of 9 February 2011 by Acting Parliamentary Inspector Chris Zelestis QC to the CCC Commissioner commenting on this passage, in which he states that Mr Hall was in fact contravening Section 23 of the CCC Act by raising the matter of potential criminal offences. I quote below from Report No 25 of the Joint Standing Committee on the CCC (JSCCCC), page 22:

> No power at all is given to the Commission in that regard. It would be inconsistent with a person's right to a fair trial upon an allegation of commission of an offence to allow the Commission to make public statements about the commission of offences. Thus, the prohibition in s. 23 is of fundamental importance in preserving the basic elements of the system of justice that prevails in Western Australia.

Consequently, there is a clear duty on the part of those conducting the inquiry to be extremely careful of witnesses' reputations.

Especially where, as in this case, those giving testimony were being deprived of all of the normal protections of the law. This announcement of recall of witnesses was recklessly playing fast and loose with the good name of innocent people.

As well as Brian Burke, David McKenzie and myself, six public officers, mostly senior public servants, were recalled. None of the public officers was a friend or close associate of Brian or me and all had impeccable public records. They did not deserve this humiliation.

Although I am jumping ahead of myself slightly, I think that it is appropriate to mention that Commissioner Hammond made matters much worse when on 20 March 2007 in an address he gave to the Institute of Public Administration Australia (IPAA) he said, ". . . inevitably charges will be laid as a result of these investigations".

These words demonstrated a contempt for the witnesses. Additionally, he was plain wrong. No charges were laid on any substantive issue in the Smiths Beach Inquiry.

Some might have said that by that time the reputations of Burke and Grill had been so badly impeached that they were already beyond redemption. I would have to agree. By the end of 2006, there was not much that went wrong in WA that was not laid at our feet. I cringe when I write it, but the fact was we were hated and shunned. But the blameless public servants were in a different category and did not deserve to be condemned in this way.

The frenzy created by the CCC hearings was highlighted in a motion for an urgent debate in the Legislative Assembly, introduced by Opposition Leader Paul Omodei on 21 November 2006. It read:

> That this House censures the Premier and members of his Government for undermining public trust and confidence in WA politics by allowing disgraced former Labor Members of Parliament Brian Burke and Julian Grill to influence the decisions of Government.

The acrimonious and unedifying debate that ensued added no clarity to Norm Marlborough's supposed misdemeanours. It generated much more heat than light when the Opposition Leader irresponsibly asserted: "We now have corruption at the heart of Government in WA." Such irresponsible comments are, unfortunately, broadcast and have consequences. Two years later a London-based lifestyle ratings agency marked Perth down because of reported high levels of corruption.

On the question of wrongdoing, there was nothing more specific than this nebulous statement by Omodei: "After the disgraceful revelations of the CCC last week." However, it was apparently sufficient to label me as "disgraced", a term the media picked and continued to apply to me.

It was simply trial by denunciation. Omodei appeared to believe that it was a scandal because: "Brian Burke and Julian Grill had influence over ministers and over the bureaucracy right through the system of government." Readers would appreciate that this is not yet a crime in Australia. He seemed oblivious to the uncontentious fact that all lobbyists aspired to have influence with ministers and bureaucrats.

Also, he seemed to take the view that all such officers were supine wimps who went weak at the knees in our presence. To be fair, Gallop and Carpenter adopted the same false logic. No one attempted to produce evidence that we had made improper representations or offered inducements.

On the one occasion when the CCC rather belatedly made such an allegation in the Broome pearling matter (over which the CCC unsuccessfully tried to convict Brian Burke, Nathan Hondros and me for corruption), it was thrown out by the Supreme Court without the need for us to even answer it. I deal with this in Chapter 18.

If there had been any credible evidence adduced that Marlborough had breached cabinet confidentiality, then Omodei may have had a possible case. But just like the CCC, he failed on this point. However, lack of facts did not slow or stop Omodei from asserting, "...having Norm Marlborough in his ministry was a direct conduit straight to the Cabinet (for Brian Burke)".

The motion was defeated along party lines, as you might have expected.

The debasing of Brian and my characters through the media continued without relief through to the end of 2006 and beyond.

On 23 November 2006, Barry House, the shadow science minister and later President of the Legislative Council, put out a media release in which he claimed Brian and I had put Australia's bid for the giant (international) Square Kilometre Array (a massive radio telescope) in jeopardy because of lobbying we did for a haul road (that is, a road dedicated to the carriage of mined ore) on behalf of a mining client.

There was little truth in the allegation and it ultimately went nowhere, but it made us appear as though we were prepared to endanger the national interest for monetary gain. It was a hurtful and damaging accusation.

Six days later, on 29 November 2006, *The West* ran a story implying that Resources Minister John Bowler had improperly given environmental approval to Griffin Coal's new $400 million power station at my behest. There was no evidence whatsoever to support this untrue claim and again it collapsed.

The story almost certainly had its genesis in the CCC. It was later revealed that the CCC was investigating this issue at the time. The publicity surrounding this accusation did not improve our communal status. It was never withdrawn and consequently the public were left with the impression of impropriety.

On 7 December 2006, a senior representative of one of our few remaining clients rang from Sydney reporting that his company had been excluded by the Department of Housing and Works from a 3,000-lot housing development because its joint venture partner had engaged my company to help with the approvals processes.

It was not contended we had done anything improper; it was just another entirely unfair example of guilt by association. It was a severe body blow for me and more particularly to our blameless client. There was nothing I could do to remedy the situation.

Tony Barrass, in a full-page feature article in *The Australian* on 8 December 2006, likened our work to the Godfather Part II. The headline adopted that name with a very unflattering picture of Brian Burke. It was a vitriolic piece that seized every opportunity to demean Brian, whom he compared to Svengali, the fictional character of Jewish origin who manipulates others with evil intent. It sought to rip to shreds what was left of Brian's national reputation.

Typically, the story was not able to identify any actual evidence of wrongdoing, but that appeared to be unimportant.

When Joe Spagnolo of *The Sunday Times* referred to us on 10 December 2006, he used this language:

> The fallout from the Smiths Beach investigations, which so far has claimed the scalp of a Labor minister and lifted the lid on the shadowy world of lobbyists Brian Burke and Julian Grill – who have wrapped their tentacles around ministers, heads of departments and public servants – will not be enough for Liberals to win government.

Descriptions like this don't enhance your social standing.

Our treatment in the mortgage brokers' scandal is worth mentioning in this context. Put briefly, my lobbying company was engaged by litigation funding company IMF after Jim McGinty, as Attorney-General, disputed aspects of an understanding that the Gallop Government would pay adequate compensation to the victims.

On behalf of the victims, IMF commenced legal proceedings against the Government. When that suit bogged down because of certain tactical manoeuvres by the Government, my company (i.e. Burke and I) was engaged to break the deadlock. Our modest fees were set out in an open contract. It needs to be understood that the lawsuit and other proceedings were being taken without any risk to the victims. IMF shouldered all the risk and picked up all of the costs, which they could only recoup from the proceeds if there was success.

Put very briefly, we did our job and a $30 million settlement offer was arranged. But that was where McGinty personally stepped in. A large part of our campaign on behalf of the victims was directed at McGinty because the victims believed he had previously promised the compensation in the 2001 election campaign.

Pursuant to the proposed settlement, IMF would receive $3.4 million to compensate it for $1.4 million in costs incurred to that date and another $2 million to administer the deal – that was $3 million (22.5%) short of the fee that IMF had originally negotiated with the victims. That entailed five years' work by IMF.

Amanda Banks in *The West* on 13 December 2006 reported it this way:

> At least 360 elderly victims of the finance broker's scandal have died waiting for yesterday's $30 million State Government compensation offer.
>
> (but) …the families and estates of those who did not survive will be among an estimated 3,000 victims who will benefit from the offer, which comes almost six years after Labor gave an election promise to support their increasingly bitter bid for compensation.
>
> The Government deal comes with a caveat restricting how much can be paid to litigation funder IMF and includes a proviso that none of the cash will get paid to former premier Brian Burke for his lobbying on behalf of the group.
>
> Mrs Michelle Roberts (the Minister for Consumer Protection announcing the offer) said while Attorney-General Jim McGinty had overseen the negotiation of the offer, he stood aside from taking the deal to Cabinet after concerns about his relationship with (IMF's) Mr McLernon, who was his cousin.

IMF managing director Hugh McLernon reluctantly indicated that he would recommend the acceptance of the conditional offer and would try to recoup the $3 million it was owed under its contractual entitlement with his clients from the (second) action against certain professionals who he claimed had wrongly advised the victims.

However, on 23 December 2006 (refer to email from me to Burke), Mr McLernon rang me to advise he had received a letter from Tim Sharp of the State Solicitor's office confirming the terms of the offer as presented in Amanda Banks' story, and additionally making clear the conditions that no part of the settlement sum could go to Burke and Grill, and that IMF cannot take advice from Burke.

However, Mr Sharp had rung Mr McLernon a couple of days after the letter was received to advise further that McGinty had personally intervened in the matter and required two more conditions:

The additional $3 million could not be collected from the proceeds of the second action between the victims and the professional advisers.

Burke and Grill cannot be involved in acting in relation to the second action against the professional advisers.

These two conditions related to the non-government side of the action. How the Government could legally or morally exclude us was a mystery.

On 19 January 2007, Banks ran a further front-page story about jeopardy to the settlement because of McGinty's insistence in nearly halving the IMF fee owing. She quoted McGinty as follows: "I think that they (IMF) are seeking to claim excessive fees and I think to propose to hit the victims with a double-whammy on future actions is unconscionable."

It was apparent that McGinty was using the old political trick of claiming the moral high ground. It did not fool the victims. One of them was referred to in Banks' article as follows:

> Investor Ann Hemsley, who is represented by IMF, called on Mr McGinty to stop interfering with investors' individual contractual arrangements. "As a Christian, when I make an agreement, I stick by my agreement and I don't want to be forced to change it," Ms Hemsley said. "We are not a democratic country anymore."

I do not know the exact terms of the settlement of the Government's part of the action. However, I do know the victims were paid. I believe that it might have been the subject of a confidentiality agreement to which I was not privy.

As for Brian and myself, we did not want to endanger any settlement to a group of victims who had been treated despicably on two occasions. We did not fight any of McGinty's conditions and we did not share in the proceeds of settlement. Privately, we thought we had been treated vindictively, but we did not take those concerns to the media. In any event, I doubt we would have been listened to. By that time, our status had fallen to such a low ebb that we were below contempt in the eyes of many people.

Before I finish on the IMF issue, I want to indicate clearly to the reader that at no time was it ever hinted that we behaved other than with complete propriety in relation to the mortgage broker's issue.

One last thing on this matter – the legal façade created when McGinty arranged for Minster Roberts to take the proposed settlement to Cabinet. In my view, if there was a perceived conflict of interest, then McGinty should not have been involved in the settlement at all. We can only assume from the phone call by Mr Sharp to Mr McLernon that within a few days of the supposed handover of the matter to Roberts, McGinty seemed to be back setting new conditions.

It would be interesting to know whether Cabinet gave its approval to those new conditions. There was nothing on the public record in relation to them. It would have been quite improper if no such Cabinet approval was given. Even if it was given, it was still an egregious abuse of power.

But it was more than McGinty. Brian and I were fair game for all sides of politics. Liberal MP Dr Steve Thomas, the state shadow spokesperson for the environment, alleged in Parliament, according to an article in *The West* on 14 December 2006, that the Labor Government had set an unrealistically cheap price for the land and seabed at a new development at Port Coogee. Further, he stated that Burke and Grill had been involved.

It was correct that Brian and I had been involved in this highly successful development, but the price of the land had been set by the previous Liberal Government. Alannah MacTiernan, as Planning Minister, responded in her own robust style. According to Luke Morfesse, *The West's Inside Cover* columnist, it went as follows:

> After question time, Ms MacTiernan was seething, saying Dr Thomas was "pathetic" and "completely off the mark".
>
> "To run off at the mouth and make allegations of corruption, which was the subtext of the questions, when the

whole deal was done by their government, shows the Opposition doesn't do its homework," she told IC.

"It's all right to say you're going fishing, but you've got to have bloody bait on your line first."

It wasn't much for Burke and Grill, but it was the closest in a long time that we had come to a win in public. Otherwise, the remainder of 2006 was just as painful. There was no let-up in the media onslaught.

This assumption of exposed corruption was generally accepted in all the media. The CCC had successfully implied massive corruption without actually making any specific allegations.

In a commercial sense, 2006 ended on a disastrous note for our business as we lost the great bulk of our clientele. One or two stuck with us, despite the odium of doing so. However, on 21 November 2006 an employee of Griffin (our remaining client) who I shall not name rang to advise me that he had been contacted by telephone by someone from Alan Carpenter's office, advising that if Griffin wanted access to the Premier, then it should come direct.

The implication was that Griffin should not use us. It was clearly an attempt to put the finishing touches to our financial ruin. Until that time, both Premiers Gallop and Carpenter had kept their distance from Griffin. What came next, however, was quite breathtaking. According to the Griffin employee, the Government employee dropped the name Roger Cook from lobbyist company CPR and advised that, "...it was OK to use that avenue to the Premier and his staff".

In my experience, the advocacy of a lobby firm by a Premier was quite unprecedented. Roger Cook, of course, has been Deputy Premier of the McGowan Labor Government. He had previously worked in McGinty's ministerial office. To my surprise and gratitude, Griffin Chairman Ric Stowe continued to retain my company.

The period between the end of 2006 and the beginning of the Lobbyists Inquiry in early 2007 was something of a lull between two storms, but already we were hated outcasts. While our lawyers kept on reassuring us the Smiths Beach Inquiry had failed to elicit any illegal activity, and while the rest of the legal profession appeared to support that view, it was a different matter altogether with the media and the public.

There was a disturbingly ugly polarity in the public mind. On the one hand, there was the seeming "white knight" in the form of the CCC valiantly exposing corruption. Counterpoised, in the dark role of the accused, were Burke and Grill. It was a founding myth of this scenario that the CCC was dispassionately dispensing justice while extending the rule of law to Burke and Grill. It would take many gruelling years before this obscene distortion was unmasked.

Perhaps to round out this chapter I should also mention Bill Shorten, because *The West Australian* did so, on 6 January 2007, just to spice up its coverage. It was a vicious article by Kim MacDonald under the headline: "Labor's rising star is rattled by Burke links". It began:

> It's no secret that anyone in the Labor Party these days is determined to be seen running a million miles from disgraced former Premier Brian Burke.

The story referred to a dinner that Burke and I had arranged for Shorten at West Perth restaurant Perugino so he could meet 20 or so members of the WA media. Shorten was then running for Federal Parliament in the Victorian seat of Maribyrnong.

The theme of the article was to demonstrate just how much "on the nose" Burke and I were. It referred to the fact Shorten had returned to Burke a $20,000 campaign donation and how Shorten had been forced to deny access to his former friend for the sake of his political future. It was apparent, however, and to his credit, that Shorten, under a fusillade of aggressive media demands, had refused to personally denounce Burke.

MacDonald was aware of the former friendship between the two, but was not conscious of how deep it went.

The true story was that Burke had played a critical role in Shorten's career. It is well known Shorten's parliamentary vocation was built upon his Australia-wide leadership of the giant Australian Workers Union. In 2004/5, national control of that union was evenly balanced with the WA Branch, headed by Tim Daly, holding a critical block of votes.

Daly was onside with Shorten, but he looked like being deposed in an election by a renegade candidate from the alumina industry. Shorten sent a raw Paul Howes (who went on to succeed Shorten as National Secretary of the AWU) to WA to run Daly's campaign. However, he also convinced Burke to throw his weight behind the effort. In turn, Burke asked my wife, Lesley (an experienced campaigner) and me, to help organise. We agreed.

It was a close-run thing, with the final vote being quite tight. Daly won narrowly and changed history. Shorten could send back the $20,000, but he was not going to condemn Burke and thereby demonstrate ungratefulness for the help that he was given.

Regretfully, although I can provide facts and argument that show Burke and I were not involved in any corrupting conduct, the years of constant public denigration create myths and finally long-lasting prejudice. In *The West* of 19 May 2017 (a page 5 article by Daniel Emerson), former Premier Colin Barnett still talked about, "…the Gallop-Carpenter government, which lost five ministers to scandal".

In *The West* of 14 June 2017 (page 5), a story by Dylan Caporn ran with the headline: "Premier (McGowan) warns Cabinet off Burke".

In *The West* of 19 June 2017 (page 4), an article by Daniel Emerson and Gary Adshead reported on Premier McGowan's office blocking the appointment by Minister Michelle Roberts of Emiliano Barzotto as chief of staff. The only reason advanced for the blocking was that Mr Barzotto had "historical connections with Mr Burke".

But is that fair? Is that due process?

In Australia and other developed countries, we are smug when we moralise about lack of fair process in other countries. But, in reality, we sometimes embrace the same debased ethic and perpetrate the same injustices, but by other means.

Who stood up and exposed the CCC when it ruined so many lives without producing any specific evidence of wrongdoing? The answer is, a tiny handful. Most of those who should have, didn't.

4

SMITHS BEACH APPROVAL
FRUSTRATED, UNDERMINED

The Smiths Beach Inquiry was an extensive and dramatic CCC probe into a proposal by Canal Rocks Pty Ltd to develop a luxury tourist and residential precinct at Smiths Beach near Yallingup in WA's South West.

The inquiry began in March 2006 with secret hearings, followed by public hearings starting in October. It was unmatched in WA in terms of scale and the extensive use of state-of-the-art surveillance equipment. This was an encounter where the might and wealth of the State apparatus was deployed against puny unsuspecting individuals.

Contrary to public expectations, it would find no corruption or criminality, but was distinguished by unwarranted character assassination, destroyed careers and broken lives.

The CCC should have recognised soon after the inquiry started that its expected crime and corruption did not exist; the evidence simply was not there. But the CCC proceeded – and at great cost.

"Why?" is one of the questions explored in this book.

Before detailing the inquiry, its conclusions and aftermath, let me outline its genesis.

The planning approval history of Smiths Beach Development (Guide) Plan (SBDGP) was a shameful bureaucratic exercise that displayed all the worst elements of delay, procrastination, manipulation, reversal and cowardice by government.

It illustrates how difficult it was for a group of modest "mum and dad" investors in WA to successfully negotiate the gauntlet of WA's labyrinthine approvals process while being obstructed by a determined group of agitators.

That group of agitators was the Smiths Beach Action Group

(SBAG), which portrayed itself as a community association of environmentally concerned, but otherwise disinterested, citizens. But I evince evidence that it was something more than that.

Moreover, the CCC embraced the SBAG's doubtful narrative and exhibited it as its own, without allowing Canal Rocks to present the real, alternative picture.

Also, I shall point to data in this and succeeding chapters that demonstrates how this important project was ultimately a victim of brutal politics, and how those politics spectacularly blew up in the face of the Carpenter Labor Government.

The proposal for Smiths Beach, on nearly 41 hectares of land with a near beach front location, was in the opinion of many experts a potential world-class adornment to the general area. It was about 10 kilometres by road south of picturesque Yallingup township on the dramatic coastline between Cape Naturaliste and Cape Leeuwin.

The development would not only have complemented a majestic sweep of sandy beach and rocky headland, but would have created something very special by way of tourist and visitor amenity. Few sites in WA offer such inherent capacity for a tourist resort of interstate and international potential.

The development was desperately needed to capture the undeniable potential on that stretch of coast; that is, a dazzling architectural and landscaped design to elevate it above the ordinariness of many WA coastal settlements.

Additionally, it would have produced abundant new jobs in the extensive construction phase, and much-needed long-term hospitality and tourism employment thereafter.

The original proposed development encompassed two upmarket resort hotels several cafes, wonderful beach amenities and a surf club; facilities not available elsewhere in the area at that time. Estimated capital expenditure was $330 million, a considerable investment in the 1990s.

No one associated with the proposal undervalued the beauty and uniqueness of this rare, north-facing and, consequently, sheltered site. The property sloped from its southern heights down to the protected beach, thus giving splendid views of the vivid blue-green waters of the bay and the dramatic shoreline as it stretched north.

It is a very special place, just beyond the northern end of an extensive national park.

Brian Burke and I were engaged on the Smiths Beach project in May 2002 by David McKenzie, director of Canal Rocks Pty Ltd. The development proposal had been badly bogged down and it proved to be our most difficult consulting engagement.

Our client's Development Plan had evolved through years of protracted consultation with local communities and was an offspring of the geographically much larger Leeuwin Naturaliste Regional Plan (LNRP).

The catalyst for the LNRP was a proposal in 1985 for a safe boat harbour to be constructed in Geographe Bay at Point Picquet, about halfway between Dunsborough and Eagle Bay. There was no such safe haven facility on this treacherous coast for hundreds of kilometres between Bunbury in the north and Augusta in the south. Local boat owners craved such a protected amenity.

The South West Development Authority was the proponent for this haven and, as its minister in 1985, I took the proposition to Cabinet. However, the wealthy denizens of Eagle Bay (essentially Perth-based millionaires with luxury holiday homes on this part of the coast) did not all desire such a facility on their doorstep. They lobbied government to oppose it.

Although a majority of ministers favoured the proposal, at least two resisted it. The compromise motion that succeeded at Cabinet ordered a planning study on the question of whether and where settlements and facilities such as boat harbours could be placed on this coast. Thus, the LNRP was born.

I was present with Planning Minister Bob Pearce when he launched the study at Caves House in Yallingup in 1985. It was expected then that the study would take a year. We were naïve and enthusiastic young ministers. As it turned out, the LNRP was not completed until some 13 years later when it was gazetted in September 1998. It recommended no new development sites on this very long coast and limited development to four existing sites. One was Smiths Beach.

Highly respected planning firm Chappell and Lambert put forward the first Tourist and Residential plan for Sussex Location 413 (Smiths Beach), owned by Canal Rocks, in October 1986.[6] Final approval for a development did not come through until 2012 – 26 years after the LNRP was launched. It was a clear failure of the planning system.

Sadly, at the end of that massively expensive and draining process, Canal Rocks, totally depleted of its finances, had to be wound up. The site was sold by the National Australia Bank (NAB) as mortgagees in possession to a private developer. However, to this day, no development has taken place on this magnificent site. The potential for a much-desired international class facility has been lost.

These are the sad but true facts, verifiable on the public record.

That the planning system can be conducted to result in such delays should be a matter of grave concern for those in the community who are interested in good public policy and efficient government decision-making. The community is the loser.

No government can be proud of what happened at Smiths Beach, but you would not have picked this up from the CCC hearing or its final report because David McKenzie was never allowed to tell his story. It was strictly one-way traffic against his company's project.

When the outline DNRP was finally approved in 1998, it was apparent that the affluent NIMBY (Not-In-My-Back-Yard) homeowners at Eagle Bay had got their way. There was not going to be any boat harbour within the plan area. However, the actual scope of those new facilities allowed on Location 413 was very much in contention, with both state and local government having a shared jurisdiction.

It was in this situation, at a local and more intimate level, where the necessary more detailed Development Guide Plan (DGP) had to be approved, that pressure could be exerted on local councillors by

---

[6] Chappell and Lambert's submission of 15 October 1997 to the Busselton Shire's Director of Planning and Development, Nigel Bancroft, p. 2.

antagonistic power brokers and concerned citizens alike, to prevent or minimise development. That did not mean that raw politics, at a State Government level, failed to play a decisively negative role. It did, as I shall explain.

Nevertheless, the Busselton council, despite a ferocious campaign by the Smiths Beach Action Group (SBAG), initially gave approval in principle for Canal Rocks' Development Guide Plan when it first came up in early 2001. However, the planning approval process was not quite completed prior to the February 2001 State election.

The election of the Gallop Government was a game changer. Geoff Gallop had promised at a public meeting organised by the SBAG as part of the 2001 election campaign, to substantially cut back the size of the development. Consequently, after nearly a decade and a half, it was almost back to square one for Mr McKenzie.

To understand the basic economics of the project, the reader has to appreciate two important things. First, that the state planners' demand that deep sewerage and water had to be brought in from distant Dunsborough was very, very expensive. Secondly, the only way of financing the development was to have a healthy element of residential housing. To diminish that was to kill the project.

The Gallop Government was initially, essentially ignorant of these two basic parameters and that is where the trouble started.

The Court Government-approved Leeuwin–Naturaliste Ridge Policy (Statement of Planning Policy 1998), attached to the LNRP, allowed for up to one-third of the accommodation development on Sussex Location 413 to be applied to permanent residential use and the balance of the developable land was to be applied to tourist accommodation.

Early on it was proposed by Canal Rocks that more than one fifth (8.5ha), at the higher more rugged western end, be gifted to the state for Principal Ridge Protection purposes. That was in addition to a sizeable portion within the developable area being reserved for public open space, foreshore reserve and other communal purposes.

However, in all, by a variety of autocratic planning edicts and demands, as I shall explain, the owners were instructed that they would ultimately lose more than half the land to the State, as a condition of development.

In contrast, the adjacent existing (and future) developments at Smiths Beach, although admittedly smaller, did not have to surrender any part of their properties to the State. For instance, take the renovated and extended neighbouring development to Canal Rocks at Smiths Beach. This was coincidentally named Canal Rocks Beach Resort, and it comprised 50 new strata-titled apartments. At no stage did it give up any land. Moreover, it had a plot ratio (density of development) that Mr McKenzie's company could only dream of.

Lee-Anne Petchell, writing in *The West* on 30 December 2004, correctly commented:

> The Canal Rocks Beach Resort near Yallingup will be redeveloped into a $40 million resort. But unlike its controversial neighbour at Smiths Beach it has raised hardly a ripple in the local community.

She was dead right, but there was not a shred of equity or fairness in this process. It was hard to understand why the Government was demanding to take so much of the freehold land from Mr McKenzie's Canal Rocks as a condition of granting permission for development on the remainder. It was not as though the State required it for any specific purpose. It would only compromise the development by adding to the adjacent national park, which was thousands of square kilometres in extent.

The land in question was an obsolete, grown-over and ecologically degraded grazing property. This can be verified by pictures in the Shire's archives.

As I shall elucidate, public opinion against the Smiths Beach development was whipped up in local circles by the SBAG on a number of dubious premises. Prominent among those pretexts was the allegation that the people funding the Canal Rocks proposal were rich and greedy.

The truth was that the proponents making up the syndicate that put the initial development proposal funds together were not rich at all. In the main, they were ordinary middle-class people who were looking for a real estate development project investment that might help fund their retirement in their old age.

The project funding was to be borrowed. These modest investors were not looking for a killing.

Another allegation was that the development was too big for the area. But that was dictated by the Government's demand for scheme water to be brought in from distant parts.

Because of its isolated position it was acknowledged at the outset that the infrastructure costs would be immense. Water, power and sewerage had to be brought in a very long way.

This costly infrastructure was demanded by the planning and environmental authorities. If the size of the development was too small, the project could not cover the cost of the required infrastructure. It was a simple equation, but one publicly ignored by the opponents, who in fact knew better.

When finally approved in 2012, development was permitted on only 12 of the site's nearly 41 hectares. It was just not commercially feasible. This was not only grand larceny by the State, but it robbed the people of the South West of critical employment opportunities. It inevitably ended in tears. The project was just overloaded with costly and unnecessary conditions. No one benefited—except present and future rival local developers.

The headline of a report by Neale Prior and Usman Azad in *The West Australian* of 4 October 2014 (page 117) advised: "NAB dumps $10m on Smiths Beach sale wipeout".

That headline neatly summed up the situation, but it did not mention that all the investors lost their money, too. There was no resort, no jobs, no important infrastructure to be shared by others and no land handed back to the Government.

This headline followed the sale of the land by receivers Korda Mentha for $10 million to a private owner at the behest of the NAB. There are no current serious plans to develop Smiths Beach. The Government's cumulative land grab and demand for expensive infrastructure, simply made any project unviable.

Nor was it publicly mentioned by the proposal's detractors that the development, if it proceeded, was to bring significant environmental benefits to the Smiths Beach locality in general. As mentioned above, the Smiths Beach domain was already partly developed for tourism purposes by other owners before Canal Rocks started its planning process. Such existing facilities were 40 years old, of standard design and aesthetically were of no outstanding architectural merit. In a word, they were basic.

However, the significant potential problem was that they were sewered with septic tanks and extracted their drinking and domestic water from local bores. Unfortunately, this remains the situation today, even though these sites have since been very substantially expanded and modernised in term of accommodation.

The ecological benefits were clear. Septic tank sewerage may be acceptable for a few years, but inevitably, because of the steep slopes and extremely sandy soils over granite rock, the contaminated waste fluids ultimately find their way down to the water table and dunes near the beach.

Serious questions of public health then arise, as the authorities are acutely aware.

Unbelievably, existing developments at Smiths Beach were permitted by the Busselton Shire to substantially expand their residential capacity and construct other facilities such as cafés without making provision for deep sewerage or permanent reticulated water service *after* the deep sewerage and permanent reticulated water obligation was imposed on Canal Rocks.

The only condition pressed upon the other developers was a duty to hook into the Canal Rocks sewerage and water facilities, if and when they were established.

Stunningly, there was no complaint from the (seemingly environmentally zealous) SBAG or the State Government and shire council about the reliance on septic tanks or bore water on these adjacent sites.

The Canal Rocks concept was to produce a Smiths Beach tourism resort and residential development plan that would lift the area above the great mass of undistinguished and aesthetically inferior

WA coastal settlements and provide stunning amenities that would attract tourist and visitors from all over the world.

Anyone who had a rudimentary knowledge of such matters in WA could attest that the residential part of the development would have to generously subsidise the initially loss making the tourism element.

The extremely fragile nature of the economics of regional tourism developments was emphasised in a report by expert Alan Boys, a director of Hotel and Leisure Advisory Pty Ltd, for Canal Rocks on 29 May 2002.

Thus, if one had the motivation, the obvious way to destroy the proposed Canal Rocks development was to reduce the residential component and increase the tourism elements. As we shall see in ensuing pages, that is exactly the path the opposition to the Smiths Beach development took.

Much opposition came almost entirely from the SBAG, which, astonishingly, had at its core two of the area's most prominent land developers in Kevin Merrifield and Bill Mitchell. Each had made fortunes in land development, both locally and further afield.

Other active members of SBAG appear to be a small group of friends and associates of these two promoters. To say the least, they were unusual figures to be heading up what was presented to the public as an "environmental group". The SBAG president for some years, Bob McKay, was also engaged in a development.

To make matters even more bizarre, Kevin Merrifield actually had a land sub-division development underway (and later a resort development) in the same general area at the same time Smiths Beach was being considered. Likewise, Bill Mitchell was finalising a tourism/residential development at Regency Beach Club at Dunsborough.

Mr Merrifield, through his company, according to a report by Elicia Kennedy in the *Busselton-Margaret River Times* of 20 September 2001, was proposing a 49-lot residential subdivision on his Millbrook Road property, close to Smiths Beach. It included plans for chalets, a restaurant and guesthouse.

The Merrifield project was to be developed on 100ha of land surrounding historic Millbrook Farm. At the time of writing and for some time now, Merrifield has been lobbying for the town planning scheme to be amended to allow for uses such as hotel, tavern, reception centre, holiday resort, tourist accommodation, winery, exhibition centre and more on his land.

The planning staff at the Busselton Shire recommended amendments to the initial Merrifield development plan because of heritage and environmental concerns (mainly frog habitat and vegetation removal).

Despite those environmental and heritage considerations, I understand that this proposal ultimately received approval in a modified form. However, I bring it to the attention of readers because, although it was contemporaneous with the Smiths Beach proposal and had more obvious heritage and environmental implications, it seems to have escaped the public attention of the SBAG altogether.

Mr Mitchell's development at Regency Beach Club was also substantial and put forward in the same general time frame as Smiths Beach. According to the shire minutes of 17 January 2001, it amounted theoretically to 70 accommodation units, parking facilities, heated outdoor pool, tennis court, café reception/office etc. Additionally, six permanent residential occupation units were later included.

All of this was to be contained on 4ha only of prime beach front land in Dunsborough on Geographe Bay. This proposal got up, but it stretched the planning guidelines.

What I have been able to pick up from the public papers concerning Mr Mitchell's environmental record regarding his properties during this period suggests that there was much that was marginal.

Mr Mitchell had significant problems at a property he owned on Juniper Road, south of Smiths Beach. The situation is well covered in a story by Janet Wainwright, in *The Sunday Times* of 21 May 1999, where she began:

> Developers who encroached into the Leeuwin Naturaliste National Park and damaged vegetation have been given the go-ahead to build four houses.
>
> The Augusta-Margaret River Shire Council agreed that

developer Bill Mitchell and his partner John Jakovich could build the houses on the Leeuwin Naturaliste Ridge, north of Gracetown. This is despite CALM condemning the siting of the houses as "most unsuitable".

There were two initial problems with the development. The first is that Mr Mitchell encroached on the national park and damaged vegetation.

The second initial problem was that he commenced construction without the necessary shire permit. He is quoted in the article as saying, "I did not realise that building permission was needed".

Mr Mitchell ultimately received approval for the four houses on the ridge because he maintained he had been promised that right when he purchased the property in 1994.

However, few in the community were happy with his actions. It transpired that Mr Mitchell and his partner had actually constructed massive 10m-high sand pads for these large houses on the top of the ridge. Final shire approval made the partners reduce these sand pads by five metres. It is testimony to Mr Mitchell's pugnacious style that he ultimately got his proposal through the shire.

According to Wainwright, the council's planning committee recommended the sand pads be removed altogether and plans rejected.

Wainwright reported:

> CALM's regional manager at Bunbury, Bob Chandler, said CALM stood by its original advice that the building sites were the worst possible on the (104ha) block for the protection of landscape values on the ridge, but the council had planning powers.
>
> The spokesman for both the Cape to Cape Alliance and the Leeuwin Conservation Group Bill Meiklejohn said that council's own planning policy was that "no development should be permitted that would affect the landscape". The acting president of the Gracetown Progress Association Wayne Baddock said the council had not paid enough attention to the area. There should never be

approval for buildings adjoining CALM land on a sensitive area of ridge.

When the developers cleared CALM land and earthworks without approval, the council had the opportunity to revoke approval.

The houses are bulky and visually assertive. A photograph in the press of part of the interiors indicates that they are luxurious. However, the first and last impression is of a Normandy Beach, Second World War-type bunker, with sweeping and strategic views of the terrain. Great for maximising rental return, but totally incongruous in an area designated by the State as having outstanding national environmental significance.

Nevertheless, if we are handing out plaudits for chutzpah it must be awarded to Mr Mitchell over Smiths Beach. One of the major tools to diminish the Canal Rocks development used by the SBAG was the assertion of loss of visual amenity if the Canal Rocks approval went ahead.

Essentially, the contention was that some of the Canal Rocks development could be seen from the beach over the sand dunes.

However, Mr Mitchell had built a mansion, his own personal residence, on the very top of the ridge overlooking Smiths Beach with extensive views of the coast. It was clearly visible for miles around.

The disposition of Bob McKay towards Smiths Beach was of the most puzzling. One of the persistent and incorrect assertions used by SBAG supporters was that the Busselton Shire Council was duped into approval of the original Canal Rocks plan in 2001 because it was not fully informed of the scope and nature of the proposal.

That was the line initially led to ALP hopeful Adele Farina and Alannah MacTiernan of the Gallop Labor Opposition after it was approved by the Richard Court Government, but before the ALP ultimately decided to oppose the size of the Smiths Beach development.

However, as a Busselton Shire Council appointee, Mr McKay was a member of Court Government Minister Graham Kierath's Leeuwin-Naturaliste Ridge Planning Policy Review Steering Committee from 24 July 1997 to 3 August 1998.[7] This was the same committee that recommended a one-third/two-thirds residential/tourism split on the Smiths Beach development that SBAG and the Gallop Government retrospectively opposed.

Further, Mr McKay was a serving councillor on the Busselton Shire when these parameters were fully discussed and advocated for acceptance in 1998. There is no indication that Councillor McKay had any real problems with the Canal Rocks development proposal at that critical time. In fact, at the Council meeting of 24 September 1997 Mr McKay moved a detailed amendment that endorsed the one-third/two-third residential tourism split at Smiths Beach and would have had the effect of increasing the land available for development.

His public posture changed some years later after he had left the Council and subsequently joined SBAG and became an opponent of the development. But whatever his reasons for a change of heart, any suggestion that the Busselton Shire was not fully aware of the intrinsic nature of the Canal Rocks project just doesn't equate with the facts. Beryl Morgan, the other Busselton Shire councillor on the committee, swears that the shire was fully and completely informed.

As mentioned earlier, I believe that crude political forces were to play a pivotal and grave role in what should have been an impartial planning process.

Court Government Planning Minister Graham Kierath approved the plan in 1998 provided that up to one-third of the accommodation development on Location 413 may be for permanent residential use.

On 14 November 2000, after further extensive public consultation, the shire approved Canal Rocks Development Guide Plan for Location 413 for advertising. That would have ended the planning process. However, the period for advertising ran up against the date for the State Election in February 2001 when ALP leader Geoff Gallop was pitted against the incumbent, Premier Richard Court.

---

[7] See letter from Graham Kierath to Mike Swift, CEO Shire of Busselton, of 24 July 1997, and letter from Gail Priest, Manager/Council Services, Shire of Busselton, to Ministry of Planning of 4 August 1998.

Consequently, the proposed advertising was delayed.

In the interim, before the State Election, the SBAG was set up by Mr Merrifield, Mr Mitchell and associates. The SBAG opposed the development as approved by the Court Government and (subject to advertising) the shire.

The initial part of the SBAG strategy was to influence government to change the planning guidelines for the project. That entailed reducing the vital residential component of the proposal.

The Court Government, having seen the proposal through the extensive and arduous planning and community consultation process and having gazetted the LNR-SPP, was unlikely to amend it.

But then along comes the February 2001 election and Adele Farina as a new ALP Upper House candidate. This opened up a new opportunity for the development's opponents.

Informed political pundits were aware that Labor could win. Additionally, that the Gallop Opposition, with its aspiration to green credentials (and preference votes), may be induced to critically limit the development.

Ms Farina, in the year 2000, was an ambitious young lawyer with a long history as an ALP political staffer and operative. She was part of the Centre faction and had coveted a parliamentary career for many years. She had her heart set on the Legislative Assembly seat of Perth, which was being vacated by Diana Warnock, another member of the Centre faction.

Ordinarily, Adele Farina would have been endorsed by the ALP for the Perth seat. But because of inter-factional machinations, John Hyde was duly selected and subsequently elected. Adele was very disappointed in me as the Center Faction negotiator and did not hide the fact.

She found a saviour in Brian Burke, who, on behalf of the Right faction, offered her endorsement for the Right's effective position in the South West Province seat. Adele accepted this offer and became the second candidate on the ALP election ticket. This was a winnable position, but this was an area where Labor traditionally did not do well. For Adele Farina to succeed, the ALP vote had to be maximised during the campaign. The ALP campaigned in favour of limiting the size of Smiths Beach.

It was a strange situation as, although Adele Farina was in fact a nominee of the Right and held a position on the ticket the Right commanded, she remained nominally in the Centre. Her ambiguous factional position was later at the core of her startling denunciation of Brian Burke at the close of the CCC public hearings into Smiths Beach.

Ms. Farina always had strong mentors. For most of her political life in the Labor Party, firstly as a staffer and later as a parliamentary aspirant, it was Bob Pearce – the former Minister for Planning. After she left Pearce's office, she obtained a law degree and worked for Qantas as an in-house lawyer.

However, her real interest was always politics and she consistently craved a parliamentary position. She achieved this, with Brian's considerable support, when she was elected as an Upper House member for the South West Region in the February election.

I am not privy to the exact details, but it seems that Merrifield and Mitchell approached Ms Farina in the lead-up to that election for support in opposing the Smiths Beach development. Moreover, I have reason to believe she was expecting Merrifield and Mitchell's support at the election.

Subsequently the ALP gave a commitment that the ALP, if elected, would downsize the Canal Rocks project – and it kept its side of the deal. There is a newspaper picture of fit-looking Geoff Gallop emerging from the water at Smiths Beach accompanied by a story indicating that if an ALP Government was elected it would cut back the size of the Canal Rocks proposed development.

Gallop would later proclaim to anyone who would listen that his was a "process-driven" government. Well, the process was dramatically diminished in the case of Smiths Beach. Gallop never went near the developer and rejected any consultative path. As a consequence, he could not be fully aware of the sensitive economics of the project.

There had been no government or independent expert study casting doubt on the previous government's planning or environmental decisions, before Gallop promised to amend them.

The SBAG's ferocious public attacks on the project and the usual soft and sympathetic reception the media gave to environmental protests had seemingly put the development proposal out of favour prior to the 2001 election.

Ignoring any possible benefits of this prestigious (and, in truth, economically delicate) development, Gallop appears to have adopted the new fashionable bandwagon.

It was not on the horizon prior to the 2001 election, but in embracing Bill Mitchell's (and Kevin Merrifield's) opposition to the Smiths Beach development, Adele Farina was adopting a new mentor, who in due course would be locked in a deadly struggle with her political mentor, Brian Burke.

This was later evidenced when Mr Mitchell was extensively quoted in terms quite hostile to the Burke-supported Smiths Beach development in late 2006. One instance was a response to questions from Liz Jackson on a one-sided ABC TV *Four Corners* program, shown on national TV at the height of the subsequent CCC hearings.

It was clear that the *Four Corners* team had spent considerable time with Mr Mitchell, Mr Merrifield and SBAG in producing the program. It did not reveal that SBAG's executive was dominated by developers and that at least two of their developments in the same general area had the potential to compete with Canal Rocks for sales and patronage.

Liz Jackson rang me when the *Four Corners* team was making preparations for the program in an effort to procure my participation. I met with her twice at the Mount Street Café in Perth. I discussed it with other experienced figures in the media and on the second meeting told Jackson that I could not partake because I could not trust that the program was not just a set up.

About the same time, on 13 December 2006, Mr Mitchell issued a media statement on Smiths Beach that demonstrated just how close he had become to Adele Farina. It referred to her extraordinary denunciation of Burke at the closing of the CCC's public hearings into

Smiths Beach. Among other highly depreciatory averments, she accused Brian of blackmailing her.

I refer to this curious testimony elsewhere in this book and explain how its relevance was so tenuous that even the CCC deleted all reference to it in its final report.

The CCC has never explained why the clearly defamatory and ultimately irrelevant evidence of Farina was called. A further unexplored question was why Mr Mitchell seemed to have coordinated his media release with Farina's strange evidence.

I know of no evidence, apart from Adele Farina's belated assertion at the hearing, which supports any conclusion that Burke placed undue pressure on her.

It was SBAG that asked Ms Farina to make representations to her parliamentary colleagues on the subject of Smiths Beach. And it was a person close to the SBAG and its executive members who made the complaint of alleged corruption or criminality to the CCC that set the whole sad CCC process in motion.

Adele Farina was always a close Centre faction colleague of the shadow Planning Minister Alannah MacTiernan. In due course it was MacTiernan and Gallop who substantially amend the Court Government's decision on the Smiths Beach plan.

Because of the secrecy provisions of the CCC Act, the public (and the accused persons) will never know exactly which allegations the CCC relied on to obtain its search warrants for Brian and my homes. But we can be absolutely certain, because of the trigger point for any CCC investigation, that the initial complaint must have entailed accusations of possible felonious or seriously improper activity.

The only possible illegality was the false allegation, entertained and publicised by the CCC, that we paid Busselton shire councillors in a bid to win their support for the Smiths Beach project. As I explain in Chapter 5, this never happened.

The "payments to councillors" matter died immediately when the law was belatedly understood by the CCC. It was another embarrassing back-down by the CCC, but the damage had been done – to our reputations and the project.

It was not until around the beginning of May 2002 that Brian and I began working for Canal Rocks and that is when Adele's divided loyalty dilemma began to crystallise.

This came after the Gallop Government announced in November 2001, through the Planning Commission, that the Minister would move to amend the already legislated SPP to reduce the Smiths Beach residential area from 33.3 per cent to 25 per cent and increase the tourism area from 66.6 per cent to 75 per cent.

This amendment would have made the project unviable. As indicated, it was a decision taken without reference to the proposed developer. In fact, the Gallop Government obdurately and unfairly refused to consult with Canal Rocks prior to our engagement.

It is a severe indictment of the professed even-handedness of government. Whenever did a serious proponent of a $333 million development (in money of that day) not have the ability to meet one-on-one directly with the responsible minister? This situation was dreadfully disheartening, as Canal Rocks simply wished to present their case to the decision makers.

Canal Rocks members were particularly baffled and depressed when they were acquainted with the fact that Minister MacTiernan had had at least two meetings with the SBAG group. One such meeting was in Mr Mitchell's palatial home (that I have mentioned previously) on the high ridge overlooking the Smiths Beach site. It was never explained why the Planning Commission, after being perfectly happy with the Leeuwin-Naturaliste Regional Plan and associated Statement of Planning Policy (which approved the 2/3 to 1/3 split) right up until the 2001 election, changed its position.

Canal Rocks was treated wretchedly.

There were two conspicuous matters, however, that had changed since the gazettal of the SPP in September 1998 – that is, after two decades of the most intensive community consultation. The first was that Messrs. Merrifield and Mitchell, by assiduous lobbying, had turned a vocal section of the public and parts of the media against the project. Their public campaign of denigration and stigmatisation of Canal Rocks was devastating.

Whatever else one might say about Messrs. Merrifield and Mitchell, they were astute operators and persistent lobbyists. That is not surprising as they had spent many years on the other side of the fence as determined developers.

The second matter was that there had been a change of government. Just to be clear, I would never argue that an incoming regime does not have the right to change or amend planning decisions of its predecessor. Nonetheless, continuity and certainty from one government to the next is important and a necessary aspect of good governance. I would contend that the incoming government should exercise that power to change past democratically made decisions very judiciously.

However, despite Canal Rocks being an innocent injured party that had patiently and dutifully followed the laborious planning and consultative processes, it was now unfairly cast as the greedy villain who was supposed to be despoiling the coast.

You will not find one word of this in the subsequent CCC Smiths Beach report, but when the planning rules were changed, the Gallop Government's media machine swung into action and, with the enthusiastic support of the SBAG, it stigmatised decent and honest people, including David McKenzie and the "mum and dad" investors, as acquisitive plunderers.

No one would accuse me of being overly emotional, but I considered the attacks on the personnel and families associated with Canal Rocks to be so discriminatory as to almost bring tears to my eyes and to make me quiver at the appalling indignity and unjustness of the situation.

The SBAG railed publicly at the "loss of coastline", failing to mention that the planning process had not condoned one new settlement on the long study area coast and that, at Smiths Beach itself, 95 per cent of the foreshore was to be placed in secure public reserve. Or that the larger part of the freehold land was ultimately to be vested in the State by way of a gift from Canal Rocks.

Nor did it allude to the fact that all of the beaches and most of the development area would remain totally accessible to the public.

No mention was made that the much maligned (by SBAG) density in Canal Rocks proposal was considerably less than that for already existing development or the new development on an adjacent site to Canal Rocks.

Mr McKenzie's family suffered terribly as a result of the undeserved public condemnation by SBAG and later by the highly prejudicial public hearings of the CCC.

Ultimately, Mr McKenzie was cleared by the WA Magistrates Court and Supreme Court of all imputations of an improper or criminal nature, but the process took years, and in the meantime his previously immaculate reputation was shredded by the CCC process.

His business was once the most successful real estate agency in Claremont. It had been built on years of scrupulously honest practice. After the Smiths Beach matter hit the headlines and he was drowning in adverse media comment, the clientele fell away dramatically. He was snubbed in the street and actively discriminated against. There are numerous beautiful and brave people in the Western Suburbs, but when they decide to close ranks, as a mass, they can be quite ruthless and cold.

I watched David McKenzie and his wife, Fiona, at a Nedlands Golf Club event at about the time of the CCC hearings. In the words of that English idiom, they were "sent to Coventry". Few in attendance were brave enough to be seen to be speaking to them. Observing, I can only say that the scene was pitiable and I felt deeply distressed for them.

CCC punishes McKenzie family

David McKenzie was not the only target. Fiona, his vivacious wife, was also a quarry of the CCC. Because of the covert nature of the CCC operation I don't have the full details, but some appalling facts are clear. In mid- to late-2006, the CCC's eavesdropping apparatus focused on my home picked up telephone conversations between my wife, Lesley, David's wife, Fiona, and Fiona's assistant (whom I won't name for privacy reasons). Fiona was a professor and head of department at a Perth university.

The conversation centred on the probable employment of a candidate for a vacant research position in Fiona's department. The candidate was well known to Lesley and Fiona's assistant and they both supported his appointment. It is not known publicly exactly what the CCC investigators thought was unsound with the appointment process, but it is acknowledged that the CCC launched a full investigation into the engagement.

Such investigations by the CCC are meant to be confidential, but it soon became the talk of the university campus. Bad news travels and, given the nature of academia, it was accompanied by the usual element of negative speculation. A number of academics were questioned and Fiona and her assistant were aggressively interrogated. Witnesses who saw them afterwards attested to the fact that both had been weeping. I have no doubt that the intrusive probe was both humiliating and demeaning. They both had to take time off work.

Like so much of what was done by the CCC during this period, nothing came of their pointless and highly destructive foray. However, it left an eminent scholar who had always enjoyed an unblemished record, Fiona, profoundly shaken and forever fearful.

The quite apparent insensitivity of the CCC makes me wonder whether its investigators have any appreciation of the potential damage they can do with their clumsy fishing trips. In the case of the McKenzies, they have come through the long CCC ordeals with their precious reputations intact, but with significant financial loss and huge emotional damage.

We can never accurately plumb the depth of others' feelings, but their actions are often a good and more evident proxy. David McKenzie sharply reduced his operations in Claremont and moved his business to another suburb. He told me that he had lost much of his confidence, lacked enthusiasm, and his faith in the goodwill of other people was diminished.

Fiona judiciously amended her professional name. Their three children moved to another state to make their futures.

For an important aspect of the long-running saga, I go back to 2002. Not long after Brian Burke and I agreed in May 2002 to act for Canal Rocks, Brian contacted MPs Graham Giffard and Adele Farina. Our assignment was to strategise and lobby the Gallop Government in an endeavour to bring about a viable Smith's Beach development.

The first element of that task was to set up some liaison between Canal Rocks and the Government. Giffard and Farina were ALP Upper House members and parliamentary secretaries. That is, assistants to a minister or junior ministers. Farina was particularly relevant as she represented the South West and was directly helping Alannah MacTiernan in the Smiths Beach area.

At the time, Brian and I were not aware of Farina's relationship with Mitchell and Merrifield.

Brian arranged for Giffard and Farina to be briefed by Canal Rocks on their planning problem at Smiths Beach. Giffard met with Canal Rocks on 2 May 2002 and it was agreed that Farina should be briefed by Mr McKenzie and the Chappell and Lambert planning team on 30 May 2002 at the firm's Subiaco office.

Giffard was also to attend. Bob Mercer from respected engineers Wood and Grieve was present, as was environmental scientist and highly regarded consultant Alan Tingay and well-known planner Ian Everett. I also attended. Old habits die hard and as an old-fashioned lawyer I took notes.

Brian, who had made the arrangements, could not attend.

Although I had some doubts about Farina's comportment at the meeting, she told me afterwards that she was impressed by the presentation and was inclined to assist. Giffard informed me that he was similarly persuaded.

Despite these words, when I spoke to Brian by phone later in the day, I expressed my hesitancy about Farina's commitment to ensuring Canal Rocks received a fair hearing by the Government. At times, she had displayed irritability and doubt. I recounted my disquiet about her manner. I shall never forget Brian's reaction. Brian strongly disagreed, believing Adele was firmly on side.

For quite some time his view proved to be correct. As far as I am aware, and certainly as Brian asserted, Farina appeared to co-operate in taking steps to acquaint Minister MacTiernan with the true situation on the crucial question of the adequacy of residential lots.

In fact, a few months later Farina attended a meeting in my home where tactics and strategy for Smiths Beach were discussed and she appeared to support the Canal Rocks project strongly. At that meeting, and at afternoon tea with Lesley and myself afterwards, she seemed to be quite relaxed and comfortable. There was no hint of her later condemnation of Brian.

I have a hypothesis on the reason for her change of attitude, which I shall explain shortly.

The second task for Brian and I was to demonstrate to the Government that the proposed amendment to the SPP did not compute financially and would render this showpiece development, with delivery of its quality features and superior amenities, financially impossible.

It was almost certain that no senior government member had actually looked at the practical economics or done the maths. For instance, it was well known in tourist development circles that there could be a 15-year lag from commencement before the tourism component would start paying back money. In the meantime, the residential element would have to carry the whole project.

The politicians making the decisions were naïve and distressingly green on these basic realities. Unfortunately, so were most of the public servants, who had little expertise in this arena. Messrs. Merrifield and Mitchell, on the other hand, as seasoned project developers, would have been alert to the risk that any significant reduction of the residential area, or "yield", could destroy the viability of the project. Thus, the pivotal exercise was for Burke and Grill to put the real numbers together in an easily accessed and understood format.

The next exercise was to establish that highly credible experts stood behind those numbers. As well as the respected professionals mentioned above, Canal Rocks engaged venerated planners and landscape consultants in the form of Brian Haratsis and Chris Dance.

Mr Haratsis is an author and strategic economic adviser operating in the property sector, both locally and internationally. Mr Dance was an eminent Melbourne-based landscape architect who had been recommended by the WA Department of Planning.

The third exercise was to encourage the formation of a group close to MacTiernan that she would listen to on the subject of the Canal Rocks proposal. That was where Giffard and Farina (and also Norm Marlborough) came in. Later, Karl White, from the Department of Planning joined. I believe that it was he who introduced MacTiernan to the elusive, but essential, financial facts of life.

That group did in fact convince the Minister to at least meet with Burke and me and later to finally give Canal Rocks members a hearing. This all sounds very logical and straightforward, but in truth it is always difficult to persuade people to change their minds when they have already nailed their colours to the mast. To put it brutally, even where the facts are overwhelming, as I think they were in this case, there has to be a face-saver.

MacTiernan is a very interesting character to say the least. I do not for a moment pretend to understand her. It has, however, become clear to me that I sometimes aggravate her. As a consequence, I must warn you that I am not unbiased on this subject. She has developed something of a national profile (ex- Federal MHR), which, because of her outgoing personality, she carries off well.

She perplexed some people close to her. To me, there is a definite personality contradiction displayed in her nature and actions. As a Minister she went through a lot of senior staff. I have spoken to some of them. They admire her work ethic, but find her difficult.

Also, she has an endearing feature: she is brave. Unfortunately, an all too uncommon character trait in politics. My experience is that, if you can sit down and quietly go through the facts with Alannah, logic prevails. And so ultimately it largely happened with Smiths Beach. But it was far from plain sailing and not as definitive as we would have preferred.

Brian Burke and I have been through many of these project approval processes. It is not a difficult task to whip up unreasonable, but forceful, opposition to any significant development in WA, especially if it is on the coast. One famous instance was the Hillarys boat harbour and tourist development on Perth's northern beaches. I discuss this issue in Chapter 17.

A further example was the Anchorage marina and coastal village south of Fremantle on which we acted as consultants after it ran into planning approval difficulties due to an anti-development group that was able to give the public impression that the project was highly unpopular.

At a rally planned by opponents of the project, we ensured that more locals turned out to support the project than the opponents could bus and drive in. It broke the back of the hostile campaign. The development has since largely been built and by all criteria is a major success.

There are other examples that I could recite, but these two sufficiently demonstrate how public "support" and "opposition" can be misrepresented and misconceived. Both of these model projects came within a whisker of rejection because the objectors were able to give the impression that, first, there would be an environmental catastrophe if it proceeded, and secondly, by deftly manipulating the media to present the view that the public was decisively opposed.

It is my view that this happened with Smiths Beach.

In the case of Smiths Beach, there was bound to be some element of local opposition. The main industry in the area is tourism and tourism accommodation is a large part of that. Understandably, existing accommodation providers don't want more competition.

But Smiths Beach was not about the existing casual holiday industry. It was about creating a handsome new destination, a different, more professional industry, offering luxury and appealing to a much wider clientele.

SBAG's reluctance to nominate an acceptable size to the development, continued pushing for reductions in numbers of residential blocks and webpage suggested a different story.

There is a point, in all of these conflicts, where the interests of the wider community have to be balanced against the more commercial interest of existing hospitality providers.

Usually, the greater interest is sustained by government support for the development. Sadly, this was not the case in this instance.

Our approach to Minister MacTiernan, on the other hand, was backed by hard figures and credible argument. It did not immediately create a turnaround, but ultimately some progress was made.

Highly regarded legal counsel Les Stein QC, then WA's pre-eminent planning barrister and university lecturer on planning laws, and well-known planning lawyer Paul McQueen were engaged by Canal Rocks to protest the lack of fair process to the Minister, but it seemingly fell on deaf ears.

It became clear to us in July 2002, as a result of a report of meetings between Mr Haratsis, MacTiernan, her adviser Vince McMullen and Paul Frewer from the Planning Department, that the Minister had early on acquired a very adverse impression of Canal Rocks. It was said at one of these meetings that the developer "wanted to squeeze every last dollar out of the development".

Ominously, Mr Haratsis also reported that Ms Farina, who accompanied him to his meeting with the Minister, "was not of much help". It was also reported that government had an unrealistically low estimate on the cost of bringing services to Smiths Beach.

In a meeting on 22 July 2002 with Department of Planning officers and MacTiernan's staff, it was alleged that Canal Rocks was exaggerating the cost of infrastructure.

It is hard to understand how anybody came to this conclusion as the main part of that infrastructure was the reticulated sewerage and water that had to come from distant Dunsborough. The Water Corporation's (first) estimate on cost was readily available to the Minister's office. It was $16 million for water and sewerage alone, as part of total infrastructure costs of $27 million. That is approximately $42 million in today's (2021) dollars.

As a consequence, the independent company Egan National Valuers, appointed by the bank (NAB), recommended that the development not proceed in 2002 unless the Government was prepared to relent on its proposed 75 per cent tourism, 25 per cent residential split.

As the Government had done no detailed assessment of costs, and the Minister had had no separate meeting with Canal Rocks (apart from at a public meeting in Bunbury, chaired by the Minister to which both the developer and the SBAG were invited) and therefore had no independent basis to doubt Canal Rocks' *bona fides*, I can only conclude that the Minister's impressions were informed by her contacts with SBAG. But however it happened, there was no doubt that the Minister's mind had been largely poisoned at an early stage.

Nonetheless, there was something of a breakthrough in late July 2002 when MacTiernan appointed a young planner from her department, Karl White, to take further submissions on the development and make recommendation to her. She did not tell us directly, but Mr White informed us later that his Minister had ultimately come to the view that her initial proposed amendment would in fact make the project unviable. (See email from Brian Burke dated 15 August 2002.)

Also, there was an implied, but belated, acknowledgement that the Department of Planning had not had sufficient expertise to accurately model revenue from the tourism component.

Liaison by Canal Rocks with Mr White continued during August, September, October and November of 2002. On the evening of 13 November 2002, Brian and I met with Minister MacTiernan at Parliament House to discuss the project. This was a critical meeting. Parliament House is never a good venue for a serious meeting as one is often confronted with the continual ringing of the division bells calling ministers away to vote.

I remember the meeting well for another reason: MacTiernan looked dead beat and overworked. She could barely keep her eyes open.

One matter she raised was the need for budget accommodation during the peak of the season. The Minister was keen that people on modest incomes, like her typical Armadale constituents, had the same opportunity to enjoy the benefits of Smiths Beach as more wealthy visitors.

You couldn't fault her motives, but the inclusion of an eco-tourism lodge and campsite, which was then added to the plan by Canal Rocks on our advice (we had some considerable doubts, but could see no alternative) did not in any way contribute to viability. It certainly did not make the banker happy. But it was the critical "face-saver" that allowed for a more reasonable residential/tourism split.

However, to give MacTiernan her due, she did show some real interest in the project and also put pressure on Water Corp to get serious about providing the sewerage and water infrastructure and reviewing its initial costings.

After taking her proposal to Cabinet, MacTiernan announced her long-awaited decision on the amendment to the Statement of Planning Policy (SPP) on 2 January 2003. This process had added a delay of almost two years to the project. In broad terms, the amendment allowed 30 per cent (the pre-2001 election figure was 33.33 per cent) for residential accommodation and 70 per cent for tourism purposes. It was a case of "palm tree justice".

All that can be said is that it was an improvement on the Gallop Government's initially announced 25/75 split.

Minister MacTiernan had come a long way in understanding the critical economic factors of the project and, in a roundabout way, had become a supporter. In fact, she went so far as to recommend a change in planners to give the project a more acceptable profile to Government. It was a proposal readily taken up by Canal Rocks and her recommendation, Perth-based Roberts Day, became the new planners.

Shortly afterwards, Canal Rocks brought on board one of Australia's leading consultant project managers, Clifton Coney Stevens, to administer and control the enterprise. I believe this action was partly motivated by Kevin Merrifield's public and private assertions (to me on 1 March 2002) that Canal Rocks' executives had no development experience.

Regrettably, MacTiernan's decision was completely opaque. There was no reasoning or explanation attached to it. There was no disclosure of Karl White's actual recommendation and the advice the Department of Planning gave her was never revealed.

Even worse, no one could explain what could actually be done on the "tourist" component of the land. The 30 per cent residential component was an improvement on the initially announced 25 per cent, but none of the expensive planning experts retained by Canal Rocks could be sure whether it was enough to make the project economic. Nevertheless, they were hopeful enough for Canal Rocks to make a hesitant decision to press ahead to the next phase.

My view, with the help of hindsight, is that at this juncture it would have been better for the Canal Rocks investors to sell the land and walk away.

This important icon project was slowly throttled by protracted legal argument over the next nine years on what constituted an "acceptable level of development". For those up close, it was like watching a slow-motion train wreck.

One of the tragedies was that this area needed the tourists and the long-term employment that this project would have generated. This was a beautiful but job-poor region.

Prime tourism destinations at Smiths Beach and Mauds Landing (adjacent to famous Ningaloo Reef, south of Exmouth) were crying out for quality resort developments to attract tourism, investment and jobs. In fact, they were two of just a handful of prime sites in regional WA where you could have some expectation that interstate and international visitors could be attracted in numbers.

Not only did Smiths Beach and that coast generally offer magnificent coastal scenery, it was backed by the renowned Margaret River wine and vineyard domain.

I was also aware from my days as WA Tourism Minister that the Government had expended considerable time, resources and money in unsuccessful attempts to draw an international resort company to regional WA.

It is my belief that although MacTiernan eventually got the message, Gallop was never interested. Neither Mauds Landing nor Smiths Beach proceeded.

Nor did any other similar project on this immense and largely untouched Western Australian coast during the eight-year period of the Gallop/Carpenter Governments. This was at a time when preparations should have been in hand for the end of the "once in a century" resources boom and the State's economy diversified.

The dismal results speak eloquently for the regime's lack of resolve and purpose. Compare the record of the Burke Government. I make no apology for the comparison. During the five-year tenure of the Burke administration, WA's two largest tourist attractions were planned and built against trenchant opposition. They were the Burswood Casino and Resort Complex on a garbage dump on the edge of the Swan River and the Hillary's Marina. Both were controversial and entailed punishing "anti" campaigns.

Additionally, a number of boat harbours and safe beaches were constructed in the extended Perth/Fremantle area during the Burke period. None of this was easy.

Interestingly, Brian Burke commented to me a few years ago that no new coastal development projects, either in the metropolitan area of Perth/Fremantle or in the regions, had progressed without our involvement, either as parliamentarians or lobbyists.

The distinguishing feature with Brian and me was that once we judged that the proposal was ecological sustainable and otherwise meritorious, we actually went out and fought hard for it.

After Minister MacTiernan's decision to allow a 30/70 residential/tourism split, there was a faint, but real, hope by Mr McKenzie that once the State Government had made its decision on implementing its amendment to the SPP that Canal Rocks would, after some 17 years, be allowed to get on with the job.

That glimmer of hope began to fade almost immediately. What followed was that the SBAG signalled it would continue to frustrate Canal Rocks. As I have mentioned previously, SBAG seemed never to be satisfied. It commenced a new campaign to further limit the project. It made it abundantly apparent that it would take MacTiernan's SPP amendment and turn it into a straightjacket that would further restrict development.

The SBAG opposition campaign was many-pronged and apparently well-funded, with its own permanent website. It entailed a high-profile hostile media campaign and a constant, behind-the-scenes process of lobbying state and local government officers and elected members.

However, the arena for the conflict would migrate from the state ministerial jurisdiction to the domain of the Busselton Town Council (previously known as the Busselton Shire), which also had to amend its own planning policy for the area before the development could proceed.

I became afraid in February 2003 that if the Shire of Busselton process became a protracted conflict, similar to the SPP amendment vicissitudes, the project would just die.

As planning negotiation proceeded with the shire, Mr Merrifield's public demeanour hardened, through the CCC hearings and the long-drawn-out aftermath. He was a star CCC witness at the Smiths Beach public hearings and I believe it was his line that the CCC adopted. If you read the media and the transcripts, you shall see that it was unremittingly inimical.

To enhance its community consultation expertise, in early 2003 Canal Rocks engaged social planner and former public servant Allan Tranter and his highly regarded company Creating Communities to liaise with local residents and interest groups. Mr Tranter was previously the acting head of the Department of Sport and Recreation. His company has consulted to most of WA's foremost corporations.

With Mr Tranter, new prestigious planners (Roberts Day) and new project development managers (Clifton Coney Stevens) and NAB providing the development funds, Canal Rocks should have been free of any allegation of lack of expertise. However, as one perceived problem was cleared away another arose.

Against all precedent, the Busselton Shire Council (BSC) gave as much status to the SBAG in the planning process as it did to Canal Rocks. Unbelievably, SBAG was formally consulted by BSC on a similar basis as Canal Rocks.[8]

---

[8] See minutes of the Shire of Busselton, Director Planning and Building Services Report of 26 February 2003.

This in effect meant that Messrs. Merrifield, McKay and Mitchell – who all had their own competing projects in progress at or around that time – were privy to and consulted on all of the aspects of the Canal Rocks development. From the perspective of fairness and public policy, this was not a healthy situation.

When Mr Merrifield gave evidence to the CCC on 26 October 2006, he referred to himself as a retired property developer who had not been involved in commercial property development for 16 years. When challenged on this point by Busselton Shire Councilor Anne Ryan shortly thereafter, he claimed that the (substantial) commercial development of his Millbrook Property did not count because he owned the land. I am not sure how many town planners would agree with that definition.

I won't take the reader through the chaos of the Busselton Shire planning process for the rest of 2003 and beyond. It was a depressing quagmire that continued on during the whole of that year and another nine, until 2012 when it was still not fully resolved – and when Canal Rocks finally gave up and went into liquidation.

There are many town planning professionals who advocate that major planning powers should be removed from local government. After witnessing the performance by the Shire of Busselton on this important project, I have joined those ranks. The State Government has recently started down that road.

It is too time consuming to cover the expensive Supreme Court and State Administrative Tribunal proceedings that ensued. Considerable amounts were spent on media promotion. Full-page newspaper pictures of star footballer Ben Cousins (against Smiths Beach) and test cricketer Justin Langer (for) accompanied the media debate.

It was bitter and furious.

How a development on an old degraded grazing property, already approved once, with a smaller footprint than was initially under consideration and one that had already been through 15 years of state government planning approval process could take another 11 years before a Development Guide Plan is finalised is hard to understand, to put it mildly.

The new burden placed on the developer, Canal Rocks, in 2003 by the BSC was very substantial. Apart from the usual bevy of onerous bureaucratic planning requirements, the shire now demanded a whole batch of new studies. They included a landscaping and rehabilitation plan, an archaeological survey, a landscaping and amenities assessment report, a fire management plan, a report on all the elements of tourist development, a report on the mixture of residential development (maximum density R25), and a full report on how reticulated water, sewerage and power was to be implemented. The shire made visual amenity and environmental values its overarching concerns.

These extensive demands were reluctantly accepted by Canal Rocks, as long as they were allowed to get on with the job.

However, the reader needs to appreciate two things. First, such studies and reports required extensive interaction with, and approval from, some 20 State and Federal Government departments and offices. Second, demands of this breadth had never previously been made on other developers at Smiths Beach or any other development in the Busselton Shire.

More gravely, however, the shire took the highly unusual step of deciding to amend its Town Planning Scheme (TPS No. 20) to limit the scope of development before it had serious communication with Canal Rocks. That is, ahead of Canal Rocks' proposed consultation program with the community on the type of development plan that would be acceptable for the site, and prior to an opportunity for a new draft Development Guide Plan (DGP) to be developed by the fresh Canal Rocks team.

Actually, it was the reverse of accustomed procedures.

The fact that SBAG had been able to produce 3000-plus signatures in opposition to the first DGP weighed heavily with government and continued to do so.

I don't want readers to conclude that there was little local support for the Smiths Beach project. There was clear, but restrained, support from a majority of local, high-end wine producers who could see that Smiths Beach would translate into enhanced sales.

It is my own private opinion that in bending over backwards to appease the 3000 SBAG signatures, the Government was exposing itself to the accusation of naïvety.

The council's hasty decision to restrictively amend the relevant Town Planning Scheme 20 (TPS No. 20) (No. 56) before a DGP was submitted by Canal Rocks, apart from being very unorthodox, was not well thought through and had some unintended and undesirable consequences for the shire.

What was a shock for the council was that in prematurely limiting and circumscribing the TPS without a developer-sponsored development guide plan, the council was placing itself in the extraordinary position of the landowner and thereby took upon itself some of the normal responsibilities of the developer, including the onus of producing the necessary environmental assessment and report at a probable cost of $1 million.

This was an impossible and ridiculous position for the shire that would not have come about if it had adhered to the normal sequence of timing. As it eventuated, the shire was forced into the position of having to abandon amendment No. 56 and its officers commenced work on a replacement amendment No. 92. It took nearly another two years for amendment No. 92 to be produced. This amendment was less prescriptive, but still highly demanding and oppressive.

I concede that I do not have formal expertise in town planning. However, I was Minister for Regional Development and Minister for the South West. In fact, I set up the South West Development Authority, and I have been closely involved in numerous regional projects.

As a consequence, I claim some small standing for my view that no substantial quality development will in future be built on the magnificent Smiths Beach site while the current provisions of the Town Planning Scheme remain in place.

A few people may be happy and benefit from that situation. However, the general population in the Busselton Shire, in terms of jobs and amenity, will be the big losers. This was an opportunity to do something brilliant in terms of a multi-purpose tourist mecca. It was blighted by partisan opposition, government faint heartedness and incessant bureaucracy.

5

WHERE IT ALL BEGAN: SMITHS BEACH AND BUSSELTON COUNCIL ELECTION

The CCC's inquiry into the Smiths Beach resort development had immense unintended repercussions, including, I would argue, a change of State Government in 2008.

Although on the first day of public hearings, 23 October 2006, Counsel Assisting Stephen Hall quite properly declared, "It was not the CCC's role to reach any conclusions on the merits of the proposed development",[9] the hearing then went on to present the nature of the Smiths Beach development in very adverse terms.

Mr Hall did not appear to be armed with financial modelling when he implied that the development was highly profitable. He said:

> The development of land for residential and tourist purposes can be highly lucrative; profits in the hundreds of millions of dollars are not unusual.[10]

The implication to most people was that there was so much money to be made the proponents were being avaricious. This was to be a recurring theme of Smiths Beach and all associated inquiries. The targeted parties were portrayed as rapacious.

Throughout the hearing, it was mischievously conjectured that the developers had not paid sufficient attention to proper planning or to environmental and aesthetic considerations. I hope that in Chapter 4 I have painted a different and more faithful picture of just how concerned our client, Canal Rocks, was in respect to all these important considerations.

The core of the complaint that initiated the Smiths Beach inquiry related to the 2005 Busselton Shire election. The actual complaint

---

[9] See page 7 of the hearing transcript.
[10] Ibid., p. 8.

will forever remain secret because of the CCC legislation. However, much of the CCC's investigation centred on the election and associated matters.

This, in turn, gave birth to the false assertion that Canal Rocks made improper payments to Busselton Shire councillors. The innuendo, if not an outright allegation, was that the councillors were thereby suborned. An appreciation of this matter is pivotal to an understanding of the inquiry.

This is a brief history.

In mid-2003, Canal Rocks employed former Senator Noel Crichton-Browne to liaise with local identities in the Busselton and Yallingup area. His long experience in regional affairs and his friendship with people such as Shire President Troy Buswell (later the WA Treasurer and Leader of the Opposition) and former Shire President Beryl Morgan was an advantage.

On the 24 October 2003, Mr Crichton-Browne reported to Canal Rocks director David McKenzie, Brian Burke and me by email that he thought a majority of the council was "opposed to the development in its present form as I understand matters".

Of concern to Canal Rocks was the position of Cr Buswell, who had taken over as Shire President from Ms Morgan in 2003. Buswell had privately told social planner and former public servant Allan Tranter, Mr Crichton-Browne and Mr McKenzie that he conditionally supported the Canal Rocks project (refer to email of 4 November 2003 from Burke to Mr McKenzie).

Once again, the situation was complicated and debased by politics. At the same time, Buswell was embarking upon a parliamentary career by seeking Liberal endorsement for the WA Legislative Assembly seat of Vasse. It was a highly public affair and hotly contested.

In late 2003, Buswell was not inclined to publicly take on issues that could adversely reflect on his electability because endorsement for Vasse by the local Liberal Party selection panel was in the balance.

As a repercussion of the Council's unenthusiastic attitude to the project, the concept evolved of supporting new candidates at the next election who would strongly endorse appropriate tourism development and job-creation in the Busselton Shire.

From my perspective, the backdrops to the 7 May 2005 Busselton Shire Council election, and the role played by Canal Rocks in the election, was as follows.

On the 30 March 2005, I attended at a meeting at Mr McKenzie's office in Claremont. I was present for only a short time, but it is my understanding that at this meeting a decision was taken to provide support for pro-development candidates in the Busselton election in May.

According to the evidence given to the CCC on 24 October 2006 by Fraser Smith (a former Busselton Shire councillor), and in conformity with the notes I made at the March meeting, the following people attended: Brian Burke, Mr Crichton-Browne, Mike Swift (ex-Busselton Shire CEO), Mr Fraser Smith (a possible candidate), Paul Downie (from public relations firm Porter Novelli), Ms Beryl Morgan (although I think that she arrived after I departed) and Joe White (a Dunsborough real estate agent) who joined the meeting by phone.

All of this was much pawed over by the CCC and subject to numerous media articles. Fortunately, I am an inveterate note keeper and paper hoarder. Consequently, on most occasions I have a contemporaneous note.

Brian Burke informally chaired the meeting while I was present. Even though the meeting was held at Mr McKenzie's office, my notes suggest he was not present while I was there. My notes indicate there was discussion about incumbent councillors and some possible candidates for the May 2005 election, the scope and cost of a possible campaign, and who might contribute funds to a war chest. Brian estimated expenditure of $45,000.

I have no specific file note on the subject, but a few weeks later it became my understanding that the financial help would be channelled through a third-party agency, similar to the time-honoured way the WA Liberal Party is partially funded – that is, through the 500 Club, whereby individual donors are not named.

The legitimacy of the process was made clear in expert evidence called by the CCC in its public hearings on the 23 October 2006. Testimony from Phillip Richards (see transcript page 110), the acting manager Local Government Elections for the WA Electoral Commission, made it clear in response to Counsel Assisting:

> There is no prohibition on receiving anonymous gifts. And there's no requirement for donors of gifts to complete any forms.

At the meeting in Mr McKenzie's office on 30 March 2005, I indicated support for the concept of assisting pro-development candidates in the May election. Certainly, it was bold and audacious plan. However, the process was perfectly proper and acceptable in a democratic society.

In due course, I arranged for one of my clients, WR Carpenter (a property arm of Griffin Coal) and a friend, Glyn Crimp, to donate. Both WR Carpenter and Mr Crimp were engaged in developments in the Busselton Shire and both were very disappointed at the glacial pace of planning approval.

They were never aware of the names of the candidates and had no contact with them. Nor did they know who else contributed to the election fund.

The May council election did not come within my compass and I played no role, except as mentioned above. Nor was I included on the normal email stream that accompanies such electoral activity. As a consequence, my email and hard copy files are largely silent in this subject. What I now relate is mostly derived from the sworn statements of witnesses at the CCC hearings.

However, I hasten to assure you that I am not ducking for cover. Despite my limited knowledge of the processes of funding the candidates, I always approved and endorsed the concept and the goal.

In general terms that evidence disclosed:

1. The Independent Action Group (IAG), organised by Brian Burke and its President Greg Dean, assumed the role of the third-party agency to collect and pay out donations in aid of

the campaigns of selected pro-development candidates. This entity had previously been used by us to pursue successful campaigns on behalf of grocers in the shopping hours referendum and associated matters.

2. Around $47,600 was contributed to the IAG account; $10,000 from WR Carpenter, $6000 from Glyn Crimp and $31,700 from Canal Rocks.
3. Six candidates were assisted: Anne Ryan, Adrian Gutteridge, Wayne Lupton, Hamish Burton, John Triplett and Alan McGregor.
4. Some funding was also offered to Fraser Smith. He declined help, but played an important part in recruiting other candidates. He was a close friend of Mr Joe White, who helped in the campaign. They attracted local business and tradesmen Adrian Gutteridge, Hamish Burton and Wayne Lupton as nominees.
5. Mr Crichton-Browne was employed by IAG to liaise with existing councillors and assist candidates in their campaigns.
6. Ms Morgan, Mr White and Mr Smith primarily selected the candidates who were supported. Ms Morgan had a friendship with Ms Ryan and knew Mr Triplett and Mr McGregor. Ms Morgan arranged a telephone hook-up for Ms Ryan and Mr McGregor with Brian Burke to discuss election campaigning.
7. Mr McKenzie interviewed some of the candidates prior to them being extended assistance. He maintained in evidence that he did not brief any of the prospective candidates on the Canal Rocks proposal or seek their support for the project. There is no evidence to contradict this statement.

As far as the evidence indicates, none of the candidates (with the possible exception of Ms Ryan) knew who the donors were or the amount of the donations to the IAG account. For instance, the candidates were never apprised of the WR Carpenter and Glyn Crimp contributions. Some candidates may have conjectured that Canal Rocks was involved because of the interest shown in their nomination by Mr McKenzie. In fact, the CCC found that only one aspirant

– Ms Ryan – did have constructive notice of Canal Rocks support at the time of the election.

The motive for Brian and Mr McKenzie using the third-party agency of IAG to help fund the election campaigns was to retain the anonymity of Canal Rocks. *This was made perfectly clear by Mr McKenzie in evidence* on more than one occasion in 2006.

Mr McKenzie and the CCC knew as a matter of law that if the elected candidates were aware that Canal Rocks had contributed to their election expenses, they would be precluded from voting on any Canal Rocks associated matters that came before the council. Put simply, it was very much in Canal Rocks' interest to be incognito as a donor. And it was perfectly legal.

Mr McKenzie was always cautious and proper. He told Brian he was not prepared to commit Canal Rocks to anonymously supporting candidates unless he had clear legal opinion that it was legitimate. As a result, Brian organised advice from well-known Perth legal firm Fiocco Lawyers and Malcolm McCusker QC.

His daughter, Sarah Burke, was a practitioner at Fiocco at the time, but that did not reflect adversely on the calibre of the advice. John Fiocco, the principal, has an impeccable reputation and is additionally a professor at the University of Western Australia. Malcolm McCusker's massive legal reputation needs no elucidation.

As to the actual legal advice given, I can't assist. Mr McKenzie's lawyer claimed legal professional privilege on that advice and it has never been made public. Consequently, neither has the CCC seen it. However, I know that Canal Rocks did proceed to fund the candidates after receiving the advice.

Also, revealingly, once the CCC was informed of the provenance of the legal opinion, all inferences that assistance to the candidates may have been illegitimate was discontinued. No adverse finding was made by the CCC on this issue. Nor was any negative or unfavourable comment on this matter made in Counsel Assisting's summing up at the end of the public hearings.

Unfortunately, the media never really understood this important point and, in the absence of any proper public clarification by the CCC, the media continued to imply that this anonymous aid to selected candidates was somehow irregular. In response to that, I simply say that such donations were quite legal and, in fact, had been a consistent part of WA's political system for a very long time.

The CCC was clearly flying a kite initially and in my view was harmfully mischievous in first raising this as a serious issue on day one. Counsel Assisting, Mr Hall, in his opening said the second of two areas of focus "was whether elected representatives have received funding from the developer" (page 7 of CCC transcript, 23/10/2006).

However, while making anonymous donations was legitimate, the candidates had a clear regulatory duty to disclose such donations. Candidates had a responsibility to file a Form 9A making declaration of any assistance received within the period commencing six months prior to the election and three days after the election for unsuccessful candidates, and "start date" for successful candidates. I shall not go into the technicalities, but it is incumbent for candidates to identify "the true source of the gift, *if known* (my emphasis)".

Of the five candidates who received donations, Messrs Lupton, Gutteridge and Burton were unsuccessful and Ms Ryan and Mr Triplett were successful. All of these candidates indicated IAG was the source of the funding. In the cases of Messrs Lupton, Gutteridge and Burton, the CCC concluded in due course that they had insufficient information to identify Canal Rocks as a contributor.

In the case of Ms Ryan, the CCC was to opine she should have made more inquiry as to the "true source" of the electoral funding and, if she had done so, she would have had sufficient information to conclude that Canal Rocks was a donor when she nominated and later when she voted in council on a motion that concerned Canal Rocks.

In respect to Mr Triplett, the CCC decided that although Mr Triplett did not have enough facts to identify Canal Rocks as a donor when he nominated for election, there was later sufficient information to that effect and, as a result, he concealed a conflict-of-interest situation. These were opinions only of impropriety against Ms Ryan and Mr Triplett. However, the CCC was not confident enough in these opinions to recommend any prosecutions.

In the next chapter, I quote from a letter from Parliamentary Inspector Malcolm McCusker that casts real doubt on the CCC's logic in giving these types of vague opinions.

The Smiths Beach Action Group (SBAG) was highly agitated over the election of Ryan and Triplet.

There is an interesting set of exchanges between the candidates who received funding from IAG and the Smiths Beach Action Group (SBAG). It shed light on just how determined and desperate a group the SBAG was.

The exchange commenced with a three-page letter sent to each of the five candidates mentioned above, by one Bayfield Ian Collison on 20 May 2005; that is, after the 7 May election and after the candidates had filed their form 9As that identified IAG as the source of their election funding.

The letter warned each of the candidates they could be charged under the Local Government (Election) Regulations 1997 and fined up to $5000. Mr Collison alleged in the letter that IAG was "not a legal entity" and for the form 9A to be legitimately completed, "the name of individual(s) with who you have dealt in receiving the gift" would have to be stated.

The missive from Mr Collison was clearly highly intimidating to relatively unsophisticated people not versed in the law. He not so modestly identified himself as an "eminently experienced, recently retired barrister and solicitor of 40 years standing". Also, he disingenuously indicated that he was merely a "voter". In truth, as later became quite apparent, he was someone who was very close indeed to the SBAG decision-making group.

Despite the coercive tone in Mr Collison's letter, the legal argument presented was clearly wrong. The facts were that IAG was a legal entity, properly registered as a "not for profit" organisation. This was impliedly acknowledged by the CCC (see page 46 of CCC, Smiths Beach report).

Not content with pressurising candidates by mail, Mr Collison and prominent SBAG member Kevin Merrifield took to challenging them in person. On 16 May 2005, Mr Merrifield rang Mr Lupton and made a time for himself and Mr Collison to meet him at a Dunsborough coffee shop that day.

At that meeting and in a subsequent letter dated 20 May 2005, the pair questioned the provenance of Mr Lupton's election funding in his official statutory form 9A and suggested that Mr Lupton had knowingly taken election funding directly from Mr McKenzie and thus, by implication, of making a false form 9A return.

Mr Lupton had never met or had any contact with Mr McKenzie and was clearly of the impression the funding for his campaign had exclusively come from IAG. Ultimately, even the CCC accepted his position. But Mr Lupton had to endure two face-to-face meetings with Messrs Collison and Merrifield and several blustering letters from Collison on behalf of SBAG.

It is of relevance to note that Mr Collison was also a real estate developer operating in the area. That meant all of the prominent SBAG activists were developers; something that most people were not aware of, partly because their developments were done in private company names.

The meetings were acrimonious in the extreme. Threats of legal proceedings were exchanged. Much of the acrimony stemmed from the initial assertion from Mr Merrifield and Mr Collison at the first meeting on 16 May 2005 that Mr Lupton had agreed with them that Mr McKenzie had financed his campaign.

Mr Lupton's evidence to the CCC showed he believed the pair was trying to "verbal" him, and he remained highly aggrieved over a year later when he appeared before the CCC in October 2006. That was despite the fact Messrs Merrifield and Collison tried to retrieve the situation by giving a form of apology in a letter on 7 June 2005, in which Mr Collison wrote:

> If, as you now state, we have misunderstood what you maintained you told us, and have misrepresented you, then both Kevin and I apologise for that.

In the same letter, Mr Collison gave up the impression he was acting as an interested "voter", stating clearly:

Kevin and I called the meeting representing the Smiths Beach Action Group.

It is beyond doubt that Mr Lupton was an innocent party in all of this process. Nonetheless, he came out of it in a highly stressed condition with a feeling he had been bullied and threatened.

The SBAG also sought out other candidates over campaign funding, which left them feeling angry and intimidated. About a week after the shire election, the SBAG arranged a meeting with Ms Ryan and Mr Triplett at Smiths Beach. According to Ms Ryan's CCC evidence of 26 October 2006, the SBAG members at the meeting were Bill Mitchell, Bob McKay and Mr Merrifield.

The evidence of both Mr Triplett and Ms Ryan was that the SBAG trio accused them of being aware that their campaign funding came from Mr McKenzie. Both newly elected councillors denied any such knowledge. Ms Ryan said the confrontation became "quite heated".

I relate some of this material concerning the encounters between members of the SBAG and the council candidates to highlight how differently the SBAG group operated in contrast to most environmental action groups. With SBAG, there was no recognised ecologist or environmentalist among its hierarchy. Also, whether it was by legal letter or face-to-face meeting with the SBAG, there was a feeling of threat and penalty.

SBAG website raises queries

It is worthwhile looking at some of the operational methods used by SBAG in pushing the case against Canal Rocks, starting with the SBAG website.[11]

There are two matters that stand out in this slick presentation. It looked like a strictly environmental group. The webpage goes almost immediately to a picture of Smiths Beach Bay. There is then a film clip with the picture of the beach and the bay as a backdrop.

Professor Jessica Meeuwig, a marine scientist at the University of WA, makes a presentation about the number and unique nature of

---

[11] www.savesmithsbeach.com

fish life off this coast. She then proceeds to make an emotional appeal for more marine parks to be established, where fishing is not allowed. The clear imputation is that this coast should be a marine reserve and that the proposed Smiths Beach development represents a threat to that. The presentation is authorised by Piers Verstegen from the WA Conservation Council.

Nice image, I suppose, but is this the real purpose of the SBAG campaign? During the whole long process of Smiths Beach there had never been expressed any previous proposal for a marine park. Also, under the "maps" section of the website, there is the line:

> Note that site lies directly between two areas of *Coastal National Park* (my emphasis). The vegetation on the site currently provides a link between the areas of National Park.

The logical implication is that the Smiths Beach should be incorporated into an extended national park. This impression was certainly not conveyed to the CCC in any of Mr Merrifield's public testimony. At all times, he insisted the SBAG supported the Smiths Beach resort development, albeit one with a smaller footprint.

And that broaches the second issue I want to raise; that is, the SBAG's website to a casual viewer has the impact of conveying the feeling that *no development at all* should take place at Smiths Beach. The script in the body of the webpage is artfully worded to confound the uninformed. The text talks about "protecting the area from inappropriate development". Inappropriate development is nowhere defined, or in any other way elucidated. The impression conveyed is that *any* development would be "inappropriate".

Prominent, at the top of the website, is an invitation to donate to a "voluntary community campaign". There is no advice concerning the type of goals to which such a campaign might be directed. Nor is there a name of any person one might want to contact to clarify the matter.

The contact section of the webpage mentions the Shire of Busselton and the Minister for Planning's respective websites. No name of any SBAG official, member or contact is provided. Right down the bottom of this Contacts section there is a reference to the Save Smiths Beach Facebook page, which appears to be inactive.

I have obtained a copy of the original SBAG constitution dated 12 February 2001. It is available from the Department of Commerce. Publicly, the SBAG gives the impression that it had 2,000 members; that it is a mass organisation with many highly motivated voting members. My subsequent search of documents from the department discloses the names of only eight members, who also make up the eight-person executive committee, three of whom are Kevin Merrifield, Robert McKay and William Mitchell.

It appears the SBAG was controlled by the developer group.

The SBAG is an incorporated body under the State Associations Incorporations Act. There are responsibilities and duties under this Act to keep a members' register, hold annual general meetings, elect office bearers, appoint executive committees, keep accounts and prepare an annual financial statement for members.

It may be possible that these actions have taken place as there is no requirement to account publicly in this way. My searches have not been able to determine how many members the SBAG had in 2006 or before.

There is a question mark over the SBAG's fund-raising activity. It has long been the law in WA that an association, like SBAG, before it can solicit or raise funds from the public has to abide by the Charitable Collections Act. Quite specifically, an association by law is required to have a government-issued licence pursuant to the Act. A search of the official register on 20 June 2015 failed to disclose the name of members of the Smiths Beach Action Group or the entity itself as a licence holder.

One wonders whether the SBAG, as a "community" organisation, actually has elections. Mr Merrifield has been "acting chairman" for many years now. By statute and pursuant to its constitution, the SBAG has to have a secretary who normally deals with the formal and informal business of the association. I may have missed it, but nowhere in all the data that I have waded through have I found the name of anyone who performs the central secretarial function.

'Concerned Citizens Group' a precedent

Being the head of such an organisation was not a unique experience for Mr Merrifield. In May 2000, when he was running into difficulties with Busselton Shire officers in respect to environmental and heritage issues on the development of his Millbrook property, he used the "Concerned Citizens Group".

This "group" led by Mr Merrifield was highly critical of the shire's executive officers and publicly browbeat the council for some weeks. *The Busselton and Margaret River Times* (now the *Busselton Dunsborough Times*) in its 4-11 May 2000 edition quoted shire CEO Mike Swift as saying:

> What they (the Concerned Citizens Group) are asking for is against the principles of natural justice. They're demanding transparency but saying they want the meetings to be held behind closed doors – I consider that to be hypocritical. I am uncomfortable with the examples being used by Mr Merrifield... He has four interests in the matters being discussed, specifically related to the examples he personally brought up six times. He is an adjoining landowner, he is involved in a joint venture to develop the property, he has entered into at least one contract to buy that land and his son is running the tourism business on the site. I was concerned about that conflict of interest. I was worried he was pushing his personal agenda without making his own interests clear. When we checked them out (the group's complaints) we haven't been able to find anything wrong.

In a related story in the same edition, journalist Beth Jinks reported Mr Merrifield's response as follows:

> Mr Merrifield denied he had any hidden agenda and said that the group was only interested in ensuring the concerns that existed in the community about the Busselton Shire were brought forward and dealt with appropriately.

And so it went for several weeks. Ultimately, Mr Merrifield had to amend his plan, as I have already related. However, the tactics of Mr Merrifield in using the Concerned Citizens Group was to give force and impetus to his accusations against council staff. Some in the council felt quite intimidated. And, of course, he had a definite private interest; that is, his Millbrook development.

There are parallels with the CCC's ill-fated Smith Beach inquiries. Bear in mind that someone very close to the SBAG made the initial complaint that commenced the CCC's inquiries.

In about late 1986, I was the Minister for the South West, superintending the Bunbury 2000 project. This was a program of intense regional development to substantially transform the City of Bunbury – economically, socially and aesthetically.

It was a resounding success. Part of the aesthetic transfiguration was to take the railway shunting yards, marshalling facilities, workshops and other railway amenities out of their strategic site between CBD and beautiful Koombana Bay and relocate them out of town.

This opened up three huge blocks of land for redevelopment for public and community purposes as the city's new civic heart. There was a public competition among teams of developers and architects on how one of these blocks should be redeveloped for a shopping centre and other related facilities.

A syndicate of which Mr Merrifield was a member put in a proposal for consideration. The South West Development Authority set up an expert panel to make a recommendation on which of the four or five finalists should be selected to do the development. The public was also invited to participate by voting for their preferred development. The panel was to take the popular vote into account, but the popular vote was not necessarily to be decisive. At the end of the process, a recommendation was made to me and I announced it.

Although at the time I was on very good personal terms with Mr Merrifield, it was not his consortium that I announced as the winner.

Some weeks later I received a visit from a senior police detective at my ministerial office. The officer told me the syndicate that included Mr Merrifield had made an official complaint that I had accepted an inducement from the winning tenderer and the officer was required to question me about the allegation.

I advised the police officer the charge was preposterous, but I agreed to answer any questions he had there and then, without resorting to a lawyer. I then submitted myself to an interrogation. At the completion of the questioning, the officer told me my answers confirmed his prior investigation and he had concluded that the accusation of bribery against me was baseless.

In both the Bunbury issue and later in the Smiths Beach issue, serious allegations on the basis of speculation were made against me and my associates.

Because of the secrecy provisions of the CCC Act, we shall never know the official source or the exact wording of the Smiths Beach complaint. However, we can reasonably deduce that the allegations must have been of a serious nature because the CCC officers would not have established and met the high threshold to obtain eavesdropping warrants.

I am not saying Mr Merrifield made the complaint to the CCC, but I have strong reason to believe that it was a person closely related to the SBAG. And the unchallenged ABC *Four Corners* program mentioned in Chapter 4 above gives substantial weight to that proposition.

I also relate this story is to contrast the two different approaches taken by the police, on one hand, and the CCC on the other. Neither the police nor (ultimately) the CCC found any serious criminal activity. However, in the case of the police, they resolved the issue quickly and effectively by checking out the evidence and interviewing the relevant parties with dispatch.

The CCC on the other hand set up an elaborate and expensive surveillance system, held private hearings and took two sets of highly publicised evidence (for some witnesses). In all, it took three years to bring down a report. Worse, in the process the CCC caused very considerable trauma, ruined reputations and snuffed out promising careers. You could well ask, what for?

Consideration of the SBAG website also hints that SBAG's motivation was to destroy the Smiths Beach project and make any future proposal unviable. It is not only the website, but the Facebook page referred to on the website I mentioned above. As far as I can see, there is only one posting on the site and it comes from the SBAG itself. That states:

> 2013 Update: After a decade long community campaign, Smiths Beach can be enjoyed as a rugged rural, scenic coastal place. See the website for details. The developer that sought to inappropriately build a tourism town on the hill has gone into liquidation. The campaign seeks a generous supporter/s to purchase the site.

This can easily be interpreted as a request for a "green" investor – the type of investor who bought the controversial Gunns' woodchip mill site in Tasmania and all the infrastructure and closed it down permanently.

While I am on the subject of the SBAG's webpage, it is also worth mentioning some ongoing anomalies. As indicated above, the website has links to media releases and other comments that are highly detrimental to Canal Rocks and its proponents.

For instance, there is a story relating to the charging of David McKenzie with giving misleading evidence to the CCC. Although there has been plenty of time since that event, there is no correction to the website in either withdrawing the original story or mentioning the fact that Mr McKenzie was resoundingly acquitted.

There are other references in the links to the website that are clearly designed to give the fallacious impression the CCC found corruption in its hearings and/or the Canal Rocks proponents were guilty of corruption.

When you look at all of this in perspective, it is easy to see that the SBAG was successful in bringing about a situation where, with the Gallop Government's help, it destroyed a highly desirable policy and planning outcome that had been embraced by government over a long period of years.

In other words, it opposed the outcome of a process set up and endorsed by the Burke, Dowding and Lawrence Labor Governments, adopted by the Court Government and is still (in theory) government policy today. As indicated above, although I believe that Alannah MacTiernan finally woke up to what was actually happening, the Gallop Government lacked the courage and the will to take the issue on and promote and defend it, as it should have done.

The CCC's Smiths Beach report

The Smiths Beach inquiry report[12], dated 5 October 2007, was tabled in State Parliament under the written hand of Acting Commissioner Neil McKerracher QC.

There were some perplexing questions about its tabling that I deal in detail elsewhere, but briefly the main questions include:

1. As this report was effectively complete before Commissioner Hammond retired on 31 March 2007, why did he not table it then?
2. Why was there a seven-month delay?
3. Why was the Commissioner's report amended before final release and on whose authority? After all, Mr Hammond heard the evidence and was therefore able to form opinions about the witnesses and the evidence.
4. What was the full extent of the report's alteration after Commissioner Hammond departed?
5. Why did Mike Silverstone, the Executive Director of the CCC, preside at the press conference on the steps of Parliament House, and issue the accompanying media release when the report was tabled? He had no role in hearing evidence or writing the report. Why did not one of the acting commissioners, whose job it was, preside?

I leave further consideration of these questions to later chapters, but I mention these unexplained issues because they form a confounding backdrop for analysis of the report itself. Also, by raising these questions I want to signal my scepticism generally concerning the legitimacy of the report.

---

[12] *Report on the Investigation of Alleged Public Sector Misconduct Linked to the Smiths Beach Development at Yallingup*, CCC of WA, 5 October 2007.

Nonetheless, it is essential for readers to be informed on the nature of the findings of this report to understand the dynamics of this, a most convulsive period in WA political history. The section below sets out the report's major findings (actually "opinions"), with some essential explanatory comment from me.

Mike Allen

Mike Allen was a senior officer at the Department of Planning. The CCC made a finding that he agreed to a request from Brian Burke to appoint a particular officer (Ms Pedersen) to write one of the planning reports on Smiths Beach and that that constituted misconduct. The CCC recommended that disciplinary action be taken against Mr Allen under the *Public Service Act*.

Most unjustly, such a referral, whether successful or not, would mean the loss of Mr Allen's job.

Punitive proceedings were duly commenced. Petrice Judge, a senior public officer from the Department of Premier and Cabinet, conducted the inquiry and she determined there had been no misconduct.

We know quite a bit about this episode as Parliamentary Inspector Malcolm McCusker investigated and wrote a long report on it dated the 10 March 2008. This report was quite an eye-opener. It found:

1. Crucial available exculpatory evidence, later gleaned by Ms Pedersen, was ignored by the CCC and there was no explanation of why it was not referred to in the CCC report.
2. There was no instruction by Mr Allen to Ms Pedersen to write the alleged planning report.
3. There was no such planning report and one was not contemplated at that time.
4. Crucial witnesses were not called (Ms Clegg, Ms Cherrie and Mr Singleton). Their evidence would not have supported the CCC's conclusions.
5. Mr Allen was not given his statutory right under Section 86 to rebut the draft report.

6. The CCC was not able to identify hard facts that supported its opinion.

The chief CCC investigator, Mark Ingham, stated to Mr McCusker when interviewed that he did not recommend the finding against Mr Allen. That leaves open the question of who did.

Later, the CCC brought what are known in the law as "process charges" against Mr Allen for false testimony. They were dismissed in court. Outrageously, Mr Allen was never reinstated.

Paul Frewer

Paul Frewer was Deputy Director of the Department of Planning and the Acting Director of the Department of Water. In the report, the CCC gave an opinion that he did not make the required declaration to the effect that he had been approached by Brian Burke over the deferral of a motion relating to a planning decision affecting Canal Rocks (our client) at a meeting of the South West Regional Planning Committee.

The CCC asserted that this failure was misconduct and recommended disciplinary proceedings against Mr Frewer pursuant to the public service Act. Once again, the misconduct proceedings were set up and extensive evidence taken. The misconduct charge was dismissed because the CCC investigation was again found to be woefully inadequate.

Evidence to establish the CCC opinion wasn't there and it was demonstrated that, if the CCC had investigated adequately, it would have found that Mr Frewer had in fact made a declaration about being lobbied.

In this matter, too, the PI made a comprehensive report [13] in which he was scathing of the CCC's investigation and opinion. You can read the detailed reasons online, but I quote the first paragraph of the PI's report:

> There was no justification for the Commission's finding that Mr Paul Frewer was guilty of 'misconduct', nor for

---

[13] *Report on the Corruption and Crime Commission's Findings of "Misconduct" by Mr Paul Frewer, Parliamentary Inspector of the CCC of WA*, 8 February 2008.

recommending that a 'relevant authority' consider taking disciplinary action against him.

But Mr Frewer had already been relieved of his job and was never re-employed by government.

Mark Brabazon

Mark Brabazon was a senior officer in the Department of Conservation and Land Management.

The CCC report included the following opinion or finding (p. 74):

> That consideration should be given to the taking of disciplinary action against Mark Brabazon by the Director General of the Department of Environment and Conservation. This is in regard to his integrity in relation to his dealing with the allegations of bias made by Mr Burke against a CALM employee and in providing Mr Burke with advice on how ministerial approval could best be achieved. This includes the withholding of concessions to the department he worked for.

This was not a finding of actionable "misconduct", as are the two other above-mentioned findings. It was a CCC opinion that Mr Brabazon acted with a lack of integrity.

Though readers might not appreciate fully the fine distinction, space prevents me from going into a detailed explanation. But I assure readers that, if pursued and upheld, this was a career-ending finding.

Mr Brabazon chose to fight the opinion with the help of PI Chris Steytler. It was time consuming, but on 27 August 2009, nearly two years after the delivery of the opinion, the CCC was obliged to table an amendment to its Smiths Beach report that cleared Mr Brabazon of all adverse opinion.

Wally Cox

Dr Wally Cox was the Chairman of the Environmental Protection Authority.

The CCC made a finding of misconduct against him and recommended he face disciplinary proceedings. The basis of that finding was:

> On the 17 May 2006, Dr Cox accepted an invitation from Mr Grill to attend a lunch hosted by Messrs Burke and Grill, specifically knowing from Mr Grill that Smiths Beach was to be discussed at the lunch. This lunch and the discussion occurred at a time when Dr Cox had before him and his agency a Strategic Environmental Assessment (SEA) lodged by Canal Rocks Pty Ltd and affecting Smiths Beach. In accepting the invitation and attending the lunch, Dr Cox deliberately sought to avoid a perception of a conflict of interest by asking Mr Grill to shift the proposed location for the lunch to a more discreet place. The acceptance of the invitation and attendance by Dr Cox to this private lunch when he knew the agenda for discussion and knew (or should have known) that the Canal Rocks SEA was before him and his agency, constituted the performance of functions as a public officer in a manner that was not impartial.

The finding or opinion by the CCC was in my view a nonsense and when the matter came before the Public Service disciplinary process, the accusation was roundly dismissed.

It was sheer invention for the CCC to allege that for Dr Cox to discuss Smiths Beach with Brian and me while a SEA was in place amounted to impropriety. In fact, a SEA contemplates an ongoing dialogue between the EPA and our client. There was no embargo on our involvement. In suggesting otherwise, the CCC was simply placing its ignorance on display. One can thus appreciate why the CCC lost so many court cases in relation to these issues.

Additionally, and although it does not matter either way, the CCC admitted in its report that it could not prove that Smith Beach was discussed at the luncheon. It wasn't, and Dr Cox and I told them so, on oath, in the strongest of terms.

Mr Cox lost his job, never to be re-employed, even after he was cleared.

There was an obvious element of vindictiveness in the treatment of these innocent public servants.

Norm Marlborough

The CCC report made the finding that:

> Mr Marlborough, by agreeing with Mr Burke that he would appoint Ms Morgan to the South West Development Commission in circumstances where the relevant merit of Ms Morgan holding such a position was unknown, failed to act with integrity in the performance of his duties.

This again was just an opinion of the CCC and was not a finding of misconduct. Unfortunately, there was no legal avenue for such an opinion to be tested in a court and in any event Marlborough had resigned from Parliament altogether before the report came down.

However, it later became crystal clear that Marlborough never at any time appointed or intended to appoint Ms Morgan.

Considering that during the hearings the CCC was irresponsibly implying that Marlborough was the recipient of bribes, the final accusation in the report was trivial. By this stage, however, the CCC had driven Marlborough out of Parliament and into a mental hospital.

It was really shoddy stuff and Marlborough deserves an apology from the CCC.

The CCC did take action against Marlborough on two charges of allegedly giving false testimony. They were dismissed in the Magistrates Court.

Ms Philippa Reid, Ms Anne Ryan and Mr John Triplett

The CCC expressed opinions that each of these Busselton Shire councillors conducted themselves in ways that (theoretically) could constitute misconduct under the CCC Act. However, these findings carried no weight, no laws were broken and no prosecutions were instituted.

I will not go into the boring detail of whether forms were properly completed and expressions of interest fully recorded. It was trivial stuff, desperately grabbed on to by the CCC to save face. In truth, as the CCC would have quickly become aware in the course of the inquiry, these councillors had never broken the law.

CCC's Counsel Assisting made it clear in his opening address that the inquiry was about whether improper payments were made to councillors. That is just another way of talking about bribes. That word was never used, but it was constantly implied, and the media kept on using the word "corruption".

There was no mention of any of this in the report, because the penny finally dropped with the CCC that there was no evidence.

Brian Burke and Julian Grill

At the start, Counsel Assisting the CCC described the Smiths Beach inquiry as an investigation into corruption, criminality and serious impropriety. No findings in respect to any of these heads of activity were made against either Brian Burke or me in the report.

Nonetheless, despite the absence of this allegation in the actual report, CCC Executive Director Mike Silverstone's media release asserted that Burke and Grill "influenced or attempted to influence public officers to engage in misconduct".

This was complete fantasy – to spice up the press release, I suspect. I ask: Which public officers, when and how? The only possible candidate is Mark Brabazon. Surely, we were entitled to have some detail of this if it was being seriously alleged?

The CCC has amended its report to exclude Mr Brabazon, who I never met.

Further, I ask: What was Mr Silverstone doing in making arguably the CCC's most important media release? It was not his role as an administrator. His was not a legal or judicial role. He was an ex-soldier. Why didn't the Acting Commissioner put out the press release and attend the media conference? It was his responsibility.

I deal more specifically with Mr Silverstone in Chapter 12, but I mention now that he later received a stingingly adverse mention from PI Michael Murray. The PI held that Mr Silverstone was "ultimately responsible for the organisational environment in which the OSU culture existed".[14] That is, the Operational Support Unit of the CCC in which extensive illegality and rogue activity by some of its officers was eventually exposed.

Later, a number of charges for giving false testimony were brought against Brian Burke, me and others. That was all superficial window dressing to mask the failure of the inquiry. In any event, all except one minor false evidence charge were unsuccessful.

I suspect that when readers see this meagre and ultimately fragile set of findings, they will be surprised. Wasn't this all supposed to be about corruption, I can imagine people asking. What about the media pyrotechnics? All those ministers had to resign, observers may exclaim.

The response is that in the longer term, as I shall detail, it was proved that no ministers were guilty of any offences or actionable impropriety. The situation was CCC hype and the vast bulk of the media jumped the gun.

Criminal charges

I deal with this more fully in Chapter 18, but it has long been my view and the strong opinion of my lawyers that, if left to the independent Director of Public Prosecutions (DPP), the failed false evidence charges that the CCC prosecuted against me would not have seen the light of day. At the very best, they were marginal, but in reality, they were misconceived.

Similar charges proffered against the likes of Brian Burke, Mike Allan, David McKenzie, Norm Marlborough and others failed (except one).

Extraordinarily, it has recently been made clear by a decision of the Supreme Court of WA that the CCC had no legal authority to initiate the charges.[15] That simply means the prosecutions were illegally commenced. What a shameful embarrassment for the CCC.

---

[14] *Parliamentary Inspector's report on misconduct and related issues in the Corruption and Crime Commission, Report No. 19*, June 2015 JSCCC, p. 38.
[15] Supreme Court of Western Australia, A -v- MAUGHAN (2016) WASCA 128, July 2016.

6

'Lobbyists inquiry': CCC v Burke & Grill, Round 2

With the accompaniment of huge media fanfare, a so-called "extension of inquiry" was announced by CCC Counsel Assisting Stephen Hall on 8 November 2006 in the following way:

> ... the Commission's investigations extend beyond the conduct of public officers and the policies and procedures relating to elections and planning decisions with regard to the proposed Smiths Beach Development. The Commission is investigating whether senior public officers have engaged in serious abuse of power in a range of other matters, not restricted to Smiths Beach ..."[16]

It sounded imposing. But how much credence should to be given to this perplexing statement? The media certainly regarded it as momentous, with journalists falling over themselves to file dubious CCC-inspired copy.

But later, viewed with hindsight in the cold light of day, the results should evoke no pride. After the CCC fell well short of legal and media expectations in the Smiths Beach matter, it arrogantly proceeded to put together further hearings targeting the same people.

The ensuing series of public hearings in February and March 2007 had a single thread of interest. In contradiction to the assertions of Mr Hall, the new hearings were only peripherally about public officers. In reality, they became a succession of inquisitions into the business affairs of Brian Burke and Julian Grill and a list of their clients.

I have therefore called the hearings the "Lobbyists inquiry".

The words "extension of inquiry" implies some continuity with the Smiths Beach inquiry. As it ultimately transpired, the only link

---

[16] Transcript of Proceedings, Public Examination, on 8 November 2006, p. 1085.

between the Smiths Beach Inquiry and the new set of inquiries was Burke and Grill.

Furthermore, when these "extended" hearings commenced, it is unlikely that the CCC could have had any actual evidence of criminal activity or corruption by public officers that would have justified such an inquiry. If such evidence existed, it has never been made public.

Ultimately (except in one minor exception, where the court made a finding against public officer Gary Stokes, but refused to record a conviction), the CCC was unable to find any wrongdoing by public officers.

It is my contention that, if the CCC possessed information of wrongdoing by Burke and Grill at that time, then, because we were not public officers, there was an explicit obligation for the CCC to report the matters to the police. No such report was made.

It was clear enough then, but since the High Court's highly publicised decision on *Cuneen v the NSW Independent Commission Against Corruption*, it is beyond doubt the CCC has no jurisdiction to investigate private individuals in respect to their own private business affairs.

Brian Burke and I were obviously not public officers over whom the CCC had jurisdiction.

Put another way, if the Lobbyists hearings were really only about Burke and Grill, they were of dubious legal validity.

However, in his opening address on 12 February 2007, Mr Hall did not specifically mention any public officers, but singled out Brian and me for unfair comment, as follows:

> This is not an inquiry into the consultancy business of Messrs. Burke and Grill, however, there is reason to be concerned that in respect of some other clients, *methods* (my emphasis) have been used that have led to or may have led to misconduct by public officers.[17]

Mr Hall was directly fingering us and no one else – and before

---

[17] Opening Address by Commissioner Hammond on 12 February 2007, p. 11.

one word of evidence was given. It was never made clear what these "methods" were supposed to be, or how these methods transgressed acceptable conduct.

Notwithstanding the omission of this little detail, the Lobbyists public hearings commenced by pre-judging Brian and me in extremely adverse terms. It was like a bizarre scene out of Alice in Wonderland, with the Queen of Hearts proclaiming: "sentence before verdict, off with their heads".

This set of hearings was to have national significance and permanently damage a lot of blameless people.

I argue that if the CCC was really concerned about public officer delinquency, it should have impartially addressed itself to the question of whether public officers had transgressed laws, regulations and/or government policies; that is, a genuine inquiry into some suspected or alleged misconduct for which there is some hard evidence, rather than an obscure fishing excursion into the affairs of Burke and Grill in the hope or expectation, or even suspicion, that the expedition would throw up evidence of misconduct.

Overall, and in retrospect, it can be seen that despite the massive publicity generated and the chaos engendered, the CCC failed almost totally in the Lobbyists inquiry. No infringements of any consequence by public officers – and certainly no evidence of corruption – were uncovered. But reaching that conclusion took eight long years, and the valuable reputations of many innocent witnesses were sacrificed in the process.

Also, in the final analysis, the CCC was not able to point to any material instances where Burke and Grill's "methods" in respect to the matter the CCC was investigating were other than proper. I contend that there were never adequate grounds to embark on this set of public hearings.

The anonymous letter

But before I venture into the actual events of the Lobbyists inquiry, I shall deal briefly with the "anonymous letter" mystery that evolved at the same time and which characterised this tumultuous period.

On the 27 December 2007, my wife Lesley collected the following letter from our letterbox. I have removed the names of the CCC officers.

> Dear Julian,
>
> I write to you because I think you, Mr Burke, Mr D'Orazio and others investigated by the CCC have been done an injustice.
>
> I have recently heard an investigator of the CCC, officer X, whilst in the company of work colleague, officer Y, say that the CCC manipulates its powers to get telephone intercept warrants. This is how X said it works (and Y nodded).
>
> The legislation that gives interception warrants (I don't know its name, sorry) does so only for serious offences. X said for offences of 7 years imprisonment. But for most of the offences the CCC investigates against public servants, the actual offence that is suspected is not that serious. X said that if they put on their warrant application the offence that they actually had evidence for, they would never get the warrant.
>
> So, what they do is put on the warrant application that they suspect the offence of corruption so that they can get their warrant. Then, when they get their evidence from the telephone intercepts the charge of 'corruption' is either dropped by the DPP, at the last minute, or they run with the corruption charge (along with the more minor charges) at trial, but don't mind losing the 'corruption' charge because the other ones usually win.
>
> X said that lawyers or the courts have not worked this out yet. X said that if they lost the power to get telephone intercepts, they couldn't do much at all.
>
> He also said that there is a section that defines what a 'reasonable suspicion' is in order to get telephone intercept warrants. It is in the CCC Act itself. X said that this section wouldn't ever be "satisfied" for their warrant appli-

cations because they knew that they could not prove the offence of 'corruption' on the evidence they have at the time of making their warrant applications.

X finally said that this is how the CCC has had so much success. Y then said that if this was ever tested at court the warrant would be "knocked out".

Mr Grill, I think that this is so wrong. In fact, I am disgusted. I hope by writing to you that I help you and others who have been affected by the shameful practises of the CCC.

We referred this missive to Mr McCusker, the Parliamentary Inspector (PI), with a request that he investigate the serious allegations and obtain a copy of the CCC affidavit that grounded the application for the warrants that had sustained Operation Tiberius – the code name given to its overall operation, presumably after the famous Roman general and emperor.

In short, the CCC strongly opposed our access to the document and the PI was not able to obtain the warrant affidavit for my lawyers. We were extremely disappointed, but accepted the situation.

However, my lawyers raised the issue some years later in the Supreme Court after Brian Burke, Nathan Hondros and I were charged with corruption, as related in Chapter 18.

My counsel, Tom Percy, argued before Justice Murray that the content of the affidavit be made available. My legal team relied on the above letter to fight the CCC's attempts to block our access to the documents. This is a changing area of law, but generally speaking, at that time, courts only allowed the disclosure of the affidavits supporting the warrant applications in exceptional circumstances.

The DPP opposed the disclosure of the affidavit. But the interesting thing was that the CCC took matters a step further by obtaining leave to intervene in the proceedings and directly argue against disclosure. Both argued that there were no exceptional circumstances. They also contended that the anonymous letter could be bogus. My lawyers and I did not agree with these arguments.

The logic was simple. The corruption case against us relied in part on evidence obtained pursuant to the secret surveillance warrant or warrants. If the warrants were obtained by a possibly fallacious affidavit, as suggested in the anonymous letter, then the warrant may be invalid and the evidence inadmissible.

When Mr Justice Murray handed down his decision on 12 April 2010, he denied our access to the material and we still do not know what was contained in that affidavit. The basis for denial of access to the affidavit was that, "the identity of the (letter's) author has not been established ... The genuineness of the author has not been established ... There is really nothing to show that this letter was not concocted".

Although not stated, it could easily be concluded that Lesley, or I, or some unidentified party had composed the letter and hand delivered it to our mailbox. Although I consider it outrageous, one might also presume that Lesley or I had a motive for such action, but what would motivate a third party?

But the really interesting issue was that in the letter we received on 27 January 2007, the author named actual individuals at the CCC. And the interesting question was which third party would have been able to identify X and Y by name?

Lesley and I had no knowledge of such people at that time. My inclination is to believe that the anonymous letter writer was the same person who later blew the whistle on colleagues in the "rogue officers" scandal referred to in Chapter 12.

Following the logic, it all fits together.

Burke, Grill homes raided

But returning to the public hearings. Despite the media enthusiasm for another headline-creating inquisition, there were one or two journalists who were a bit puzzled by the "extension of inquiry". To begin with, the media did not initially know what to make of the CCC's remarks about the "escalation" of the inquiry.

Writing in *The West Australian* on 11 November 2006, State Political Editor Robert Taylor was perplexed. He wrote:

> When CCC lawyer Stephen Hall adjourned the hearing on Wednesday, he said the CCC's inquiry had now widened from an investigation into Smiths Beach to whether "senior public officers had engaged in serious abuses of power in a range of areas".
>
> That's got a lot of people around town wondering whether the CCC is rapidly becoming the arbiter of what is and is not politically appropriate.[18]

As time would ultimately tell, this assessment would prove to be particularly prescient.

The raids on Brian's and my home/offices, was coordinated on 8 November 2006 with the extension of the inquiry. My wife, Lesley, was at home alone at the time and had to bear the full brunt of the CCC's four-hour raid, before being joined by our son, Shannon. Her description of events indicates that it was highly traumatic and very intimidating.

As Lesley identified the various files and documents and showed the raiding team around, the CCC filmed her on video. She was guarded by a female officer and prevented from going to the toilet on her own. Life has not prepared guileless and sensitive people like Lesley for such a confronting situation. And nor should it.

I have viewed the film and although she was trembling and reduced to tears, Lesley behaved in a dignified and cooperative manner throughout. I had the impression that a couple of the CCC officers actually admired her.

The CCC seized more than 20 boxes of paper material relating to more than 50 clients. They also took Lesley's and my personal computers and various computer storage disks.

This so-called "extended inquiry" was said to relate to senior public officers. As far as I can ascertain from the available information, no public servant was ever the subject of a CCC-initiated search warrant or phone taps. The public officers, in my view were like props in a movie. They were necessary, but it was never about them.

---

[18] *The West Australian*, 11 November 2006, p. 4.

I have retained a copy of the search warrant used on 8 November 2006. The name of the Supreme Court judge who was convinced by the CCC to issue the warrant has been blacked out. However, the warrant clearly mentions "suspected serious misconduct".

It was similar in wording to the warrants issued to allow the CCC's electronic surveillance (phone tapping) on us. Under the *Telecommunications Act*, the alleged conduct had to amount to a crime punishable by at least seven years jail before such a warrant could be issued. The Parliament treats these matters very seriously because such warrants can easily be abused.

What was supposed to constitute this particular alleged "misconduct" was never disclosed. The CCC affidavit supporting the application for the warrant is secret under the law and therefore not normally meant to be divulged publicly.

If it was similar to affidavits used by the Independent Commission Against Corruption (ICAC), the NSW equivalent of the CCC, where there was a study into abuse of warrants, the odds are that it has a less than 50 per cent prospect of being veracious.

What we do know with certainty, however, is that in the set of Lobbyists public hearings the CCC was never able to produce evidence that amounted to such a crime.

Having lived through this protracted nightmare and reflected on it every day since, I have come to the conclusion that the CCC never had hard evidence of criminal activity by me or Brian Burke or any public servant for that matter, but may have believed that if it could gain access to all of our business and personal records and examined them minutely enough, its officers might find such evidence. The fact that the "extension of inquiry" and the home raids took place on the same day is of some significance.

In the case of the CCC's raid on Brian's home, the media were in full attendance.

It seemed as though, before the public hearings commenced, the CCC used its PR machine and friendly elements in the media to build up anticipation and momentum in the public consciousness of imminent exposure of serious public corruption.

I concluded that the extension of inquiry could not proceed in December, as indicated by Mr Hall, because it would not leave sufficient time for the CCC investigators to trawl through the mountain of data seized from our homes.

My conjecture proved to be correct. The public hearing was put back until February. Notwithstanding the delay, the CCC was exceedingly active. Clearly, it had selected its targets and, through the media, its PR machine (as I shall explain) was unethically poisoning community opinion ahead of any public hearings.

Minister John Bowler, my long-time friend and my successor in the Goldfields seat of Eyre in the Legislative Assembly, was made first cab off the rank for this iniquitous media treatment. On 29 November 2006, *The West Australian* ran a story by Graham Mason under the headline: "Doubts raised over coal plant approval".

The thrust of the story was that Bowler had conspired with me, while he was acting Minister for the Environment, to nefariously grant approval for my client, Griffin Coal, to proceed with a second new power plant in Collie. As I explain elsewhere in this book, there was never any validity in this imputation, but it was the first shot in a public offensive to impugn Bowler and me.

Also, as I again explain elsewhere, CCC officers had already boasted at Parliament House that they would be charging us for corruption. Tragically for Bowler, the story (although incorrect) was crudely effective.

The Carpenter Government was by then super sensitive to any hint of scandal. One unverified media story of putative impropriety was enough to engender panic in the Government. In this case, the untrue imputation was sufficient to see Bowler immediately lose the prized Resources portfolio in Cabinet.

A second assault was launched against Bowler in an article by Robert Taylor and Sean Cowan in *The West Australian* on 16 December 2006 under the headline: "Bowler faces corruption probe over link to Burke in land deal".

The story stated:

> The CCC is investigating a decision by Local Government Minister John Bowler which cleared the way for a client of Brian Burke, the financial powerhouse Macquarie Bank, to develop a big tract of land at Whitby in the Perth Hills.
>
> The *West Australian* understands that CCC officers have conducted extensive interviews in recent weeks with staff at Macquarie Bank's wholly owned land development subsidiary, Urban Pacific, which employed Mr Burke and Mr Grill as lobbyists in the Whitby deal.
>
> As Resources Minister, Mr Bowler ordered the Department of Industry and Resources to remove its objection to mining land at Whitby Falls being rezoned to residential.[19]

And on it went. Such information should never have been leaked to the media prior to any public hearing.

Taylor ran a follow-up story seven days later under the headline: "Questions over Bowler's decision to clear mining land for housing".[20]

The article basically argued the case that the actions of Bowler were highly improper and suggested that he had been motivated by his relationship with Brian and me. In due course this became the CCC "Whitby Inquiry", which I deal with below.

How could this information have got to the media? The word "Exclusive", prominently displayed under Taylor and Cowan's bylines, suggests that the two journalists were briefed by elements within the CCC.

Political analysts talk about passing the "pub test", but with media leaks like those presented in the three articles mentioned above, Bowler was adjudged guilty by the public well before the Whitby and other hearings commenced. The media's arrogance in virtually declaring Bowler corrupt was only possible because of underpinning by a power-intoxicated CCC.

---

[19] *The West Australian*, 16 December 2006, p. 1.
[20] Op. Cit., 23 December 2006, p. 11.

As it turned out, the media stories were wrong. No evidence of corruption or criminal conduct against Bowler was ever produced. However, the public was left with a contrary opinion. The leaking was as unconscionable as it was damaging.

Conveniently for the CCC in the Whitby matter, it was not disclosed that Iluka, Australia's biggest and most profitable heavy minerals miner, had sold the subject land to our client for residential development only after it came to the conclusion that local community opposition to mining was so intense that it could not be overcome – and it was not economically viable.

As I detail below, there were several other vital matters concerning Whitby that the CCC did not reveal. By omitting this pertinent information, the CCC prejudicially distorted the factual landscape.

The CCC, well before any evidence was heard, prematurely telegraphed its intention and contemptuously endeavoured to affect public opinion prior to the hearings on Whitby and another planned CCC inquiry.

A further such episode was evidenced before the CCC's Wanneroo Council inquiry. In another "Exclusive" on 19 December 2006 by Taylor, beginning on the front page of *The West Australian* and continuing with a larger story on page 5, the substance of the Wanneroo Council inquiry was unveiled more than two months before it commenced.

It was not an isolated case. As early as 14 January 2006 (nine months before the Smiths Beach public hearing commenced), *The Weekend Australian* ran a story about the impending Smiths Beach inquiry. The article by Amanda Banks was replete with confidential details concerning the case and names of witnesses. It specifically linked Burke and me.

No matter how you looked at it, this leak was a very serious error of judgment.

The continued and loose use of the words "corrupt" and "corruption" in media reports in association with the names Brian Burke and Julian Grill had an inevitable effect, so that even where corruption was not proved (as it was not in any of these cases) the public was left with the indelible impression of profound turpitude stamped on their mind.

Add a multi-dimensional character like Brian Burke, and an ALP that had decided to eat its own, and the truth becomes unidentifiable.

When Commissioner Hammond opened the Lobbyists hearings on 12 February 2007, he embarked upon a 10-page discourse in justification of the probe. Much of that was taken up with three matters.

First, a rationalisation of why the CCC would, in its discretion, withhold from witnesses the normal basic provision for procedural fairness and natural justice as applied in courts of law and similar tribunals.

Second, an argument why the inquiry had to be held in public, rather than *in camera*. It took some time, but ultimately the parliamentary oversight committee, the Joint Standing Committee on the Corruption and Crime Commission (JSCCCC), had a special inquiry into the question of the CCC's public hearings and produced Report No. 25 of March 2012. I deal with this issue more fully in Chapter 12.

But briefly, the report was highly critical of the CCC's failure to protect the reputations of witnesses. Chairman Nick Goiran stated in his foreword (among other things):

> …the Committee's strong belief that there is much that could be done by the CCC to improve the public examination process; …the CCC has not done enough to preserve procedural fairness, and this has been to the great detriment of many CCC witnesses; the CCC's discretion to open examinations to the public 'has miscarried in the past' and regards this as a significant issue.[21]

Third, Commissioner Hammond outlined the special arrangements that the CCC was making for the media. That included an exclusive media room, unique access to exhibits, special press kits, arrangements for filming of the Commission and Counsel Assisting's addresses, and so on.

These arrangements went further than those usually counte-

---

[21] Foreword to JSCCCC Report No. 25, March 2012.

nanced in a court of law. Bernard Keane from *Crikey* got it right in his online article of 23 February 2007, when he wrote:

> The CCC's media unit works hard to ensure that details of each day's carefully selected and salacious evidence and one sided assertions by counsel are widely reported. Transcripts are made available to the media well before they are publicly available. MP3 recordings of phone taps are provided promptly to media but are not available at all to the public on the CCC website, which means that the media may report those extracts they consider most "compelling", and members of the public have no way of knowing whether the context is accurate.[22]

It was an unholy alliance. This obsequious fawning on the media, background briefing of selected journalists, and granting of "exclusives" to a favoured few by the CCC PR machine was an extremely unhealthy degeneration of what was proffered to the public as an impartial inquiry.

I believe that this dubious process predisposed the media against witnesses and encouraged the Fourth Estate to turn a blind eye to the fundamentally inequitable denial of natural justice.

This throws up the embarrassing question of just what was the end game of this prolonged set of inquisitions, reports and abortive trials that finally resulted. This has never been clearly spelt out, so that there may be some specific criteria to measure "success", as this was to become a touchy issue.

The CCC, on the defensive, has since said that success should not necessarily be gauged in terms of numbers of crime or corruption convictions. So, what was the actual goal? It has never been revealed.

And why, if the CCC was not especially interested in convictions, did it recommend prosecutions on so many inconsequential procedural matters, as it did with Brian Burke, me and others close to us? There has never been an answer.

One thing is apparent, however: The CCC never made any overall

---

[22] crikey.com.au, 23 February 2007.

public assessment of the Smiths Beach and Lobbyists inquiries and measured it up against the tens of millions of dollars expended on the lengthy operation.

I suspect that the CCC did not want a catalogue of the foreshortened careers, broken lives and destroyed and diminished reputations that it had engendered. Or the trial by media debacle it ultimately descended into.

In fact, there is a credible argument that these CCC hearings cost the taxpayers many additional millions of dollars over and above the direct cost because of the fear engendered, loss of motivation and reduced productivity in the public service.

After trawling through the 50 or so sets of files taken from my home and others from Brian Burke's home office, the CCC selected several for full intensive public examination. These were the issues that mesmerised the media for months and gave rise to seven more years of failed prosecutions and human misery.

They can be summarised as follows.

The Whitby matter

Extraordinarily, this ultimate calamity was the CCC's finest hour. This was its dubious pinnacle. The miserable best that it could do. After the passage of eight years, in July 2013 the CCC finally proved a case on a substantive issue coming out of the twin Smiths Beach and Lobbyists inquiries.

However, as history now records, following an immense and almost entirely futile procession of judicial and semi-judicial efforts that I shall explain, the courts refused the CCC demands that a conviction be recorded. The CCC's single success, if you can really call it that, on a matter of any substance against a public officer was hollow and pointless. It was a pyrrhic victory. Viewed objectively, with the benefit of hindsight, it can be fairly described as ignoble.

I should explain, for clarity, that the CCC did also obtain one solitary conviction on a procedural matter against a third party, who was not a public officer. I outline this matter in Chapter 16. However, no matter how the CCC might like to dress it up, this too was only a very minor win.

The success on a single substantive issue, in the Whitby matter, did not give rise to any celebration in the CCC. In fact, quite the contrary.

There was no popping of champagne corks at the CCC. It would aggressively try to defend its record to the public, but the procession of prematurely resigning CCC commissioners (indeed, the absence of a commissioner at all for long periods) plus abject failure in the courts, relates a story at variance with this desired image.

This Whitby matter is a chronicle of rhetorical over-reach, unfulfilled suspicion and an almost demented refusal to confront reality on the part of the CCC.

Forget the initial allegations of corruption by John Bowler. That went nowhere. The ultimate issue in Whitby revolved around the minor issue of a letter sent by the Department of Resources to the Department of Planning on 28 February 2006.

It was said by the CCC that this letter contained confidential information. First, concerning the economics of mining a mineral sands deposit at Whitby Falls, 38km south east of Perth near Mundijong. And, second, the Department of Resource's attitude towards the rezoning of the land in which the deposit was found.

Our client, Urban Pacific, acquired 504ha of land at Whitby Falls in November 2005. Our client subsequently refused an offer by Bemax to be allowed to mine the land. The CCC alleged that it contained $1 billion worth of extractable mineral sands; a gross embellishment of value. Bemax Resources Ltd who had cause to know (mentioned below) put a value of $134 million on it.

The CCC neglected to advise that 75 per cent of the deposit had been confiscated by previous planning decisions.

This is how it happened.

1. The land was purchased by our client for housing from Iluka Resources Ltd, Australia's most successful mineral sands miner. On 16 August 2005, Iluka advised the Government the

deposit was not viable. A further review of the mining proposal's economics, by respected mining services consultants AMC Consultants Pty Ltd, in January 2006, concluded that "indicative analysis is overwhelmingly negative".

2. Subsequent to the sale, Bemax approached DOIR with a case that it should be allowed to mine the tenements before the housing development took place. Bemax was a Saudi Arabian-owned company, which had no track record of mining in WA. It withdrew from the State in July 2011.

3. The CCC failed to disclose relevant matters. There was almost unanimous opposition to mining on this land from within the Gallop Labor Government. There was forceful and sustained community antagonism to mining this deposit. Further, and importantly, Planning Minister Alannah MacTiernan had carriage of the rezoning application. For years as the local MP, she had vehemently opposed mining and fiercely spearheaded the drive for the rezoning.

4. This was a landscape where a beautiful fresh water brook came out of the Darling Scarp over a scenic waterfall. The CCC maintained (see page X of report) that in June 2005, "DOIR advised DPI (the Department of Planning) that it considered that the DOIR had questions about any subdivision prior to mining". I have no reason to doubt that advice was given. However, as I have explained above, what the CCC did not make apparent was that when Iluka subsequently made the presentation of its negative feasibility study to DOIR in September 2005, the department expressed no opposition to the dropping of the mining tenements and the on-sale of the freehold title to the land. Urban Pacific bought the land from Iluka for fair market value for residential housing, on the basis that the question of mining had been well and truly settled in the negative. Any mineral at Whitby had no strategic importance. Dr Jim Limerick, the then Director General of DOIR, referred to it in evidence as a "minnow".[23]

---

[23] Dr Jim Limerick's evidence on p 662 of Lobbyists Transcript Hearing.

Additionally, the WA Environmental Protection Authority (EPA) had not given approval for mining and in my view was never likely to because of the probable despoliation of this scenic area and the emphatic nature of the local opposition.

Thus, the case put forward by the CCC was also fundamentally in error in two respects.

First, the CCC gave the erroneous impression that Burke and Grill unethically suborned the acting director of the Department of Resources, Gary Stokes, into supporting the rezoning against government policy and contrary to the public interest. As I have explained, there was no element of validity in this CCC proposition. It ultimately dropped this allegation, but not before it did a lot of damage.

Secondly, the CCC massively overstated the gravity of the situation. This is the language used at the commencement of the hearing and in the final report:

> The Commission conducted these hearings publicly in order to expose and make the public aware of matters that could represent *serious abuse of power by senior public officers* (my emphasis).[24]

This was grandiloquent hyperbole to describe what turned out to be a line-ball lapse of judgment on the question of the release of a not very important letter by Gary Stokes to Brian Burke. Both the Public Service Board and the courts later adjudged the lapse by Mr Stokes as trivial.

So, what on earth was the CCC doing in tying up massive amounts of money, time and human resources on a matter where, ultimately, no corruption was alleged and the court was not even prepared to record a conviction?

On 27 February 2007, *The West Australian* ran a prominent story by Daniel Emerson under the headline: "Senior officer leaked rezoning letter to Burke".

The story said in part:

> The career of senior bureaucrat Gary Stokes is under a

---

[24] CCC Whitby Report, p. xi.

cloud after an intense grilling in the CCC yesterday revealed he had leaked information to Brian Burke which his boss considers confidential.[25]

Mr Stokes in evidence conceded that he had provided the requested letter to Brian Burke; had requested that Burke keep it confidential; and that "possibly" he shouldn't have disclosed it.

The CCC found that Mr Stokes engaged in serious misconduct by reason of his releasing to Burke a copy of the letter dated 28 February 2006, already referred to, from Dr Limerick (head of DOIR) to the Director General of Department of Planning (DPI), Gregory Martin. That letter assessed the mining potential of the land based on figures from Bemax.

Mr Stokes gave it to Brian Burke on 23 March 2006. It was alleged by the CCC that this information was financially confidential and that it revealed the posture of DOI over the issue of rezoning.

Brian liked to have tangible evidence, comparable to a letter, which confirmed the advice we gave to our clients. He would be the first to concede that he made a mistake in requesting a copy of the letter from Mr Stokes because it opened Mr Stokes up to attack. However, it was hardly a hanging offence.

And there were substantial mitigating factors. Chief among them were that the information on Bemax's economics for mining the deposit was already in the public domain and that DOIR's position on rezoning the land was previously known within the industry.

In respect to Bemax's business (or economic) model, this was never a secret. In fact, it was a conspicuous part of Bemax's strategy to disclose and promote its financial case. If Bemax was to have any standing at all, it depended upon convincing government and the public that the community would be better off under its financial model of development.

I would add that well before the letter was even contemplated, Bemax had requested a meeting with Brian Burke and me. As that meeting, Bemax gave us the financial details of its proposed pro-

---

[25] *The West Australian*, 27 February 2007, p. 6.

ject with the request that we convince our client to accept their offer.

Consequently, the public nature of Bemax's estimated financials disposes of the CCC's claim that they were confidential. The second proposition put forward by the CCC was that the 28 February 2006 letter was confidential because it revealed the DOIR's attitude towards rezoning. This was a nonsense, as I shall explain.

With Whitby, we always knew that DOIR supported the sale. We knew because we spoke to the public servants directly and they gave us frank and honest answers.

There was some conflict between some officers within DOIR, but this was never kept a secret. Government is not normally a secret society, nor should it be.

The CCC knew (but played down) the fact that our client owned the land outright; not government nor anyone else. That meant that our client had a complete veto over mining, just as someone cannot come along and mine the ground under your house.

Additionally, it needs to be born in mind that the letter of 28 February 2006 was not sent by Mr Stokes to Brian Burke until 23 March 2006. By that time its content was old news. No wonder the courts were not prepared to record a conviction.

It may have impressed our client that Brian could provide them with a copy, but it did not add to the sum total of their knowledge on the subject. For instance, I have never seen the letter and never needed to.

After the CCC public hearings on Whitby were complete, in March 2007, the CCC urged the Director General of the Department of Premier and Cabinet to bring disciplinary proceedings against Mr Stokes for passing the letter to Burke. The Director General complied and commenced formal proceedings under Section 81 of the *Public Sector Management Act*, which among other penalties could strip Mr Stokes of his position.

Mr Stokes was a highly respected public servant who did not have a blemish against his name. He had recently held the high post of WA's Agent General in London.

To the chagrin of the CCC, the s.81 proceedings concluded that Mr Stokes had been guilty of only a minor breach of discipline and no substantial penalty was applied.

The displeasure of the CCC at this result was graphically evident when Commissioner Len Roberts-Smith finally tabled the CCC report on the Whitby matter on 3 October 2008. Not for the first time, the CCC churlishly rejected the umpire's decision. In fact, the CCC in its displeasure took the most immoderate step of attacking the Public Service disciplinary process outright.

It called for the "Director General of the Department of Premier and Cabinet (to) review the operation, process and appropriateness of outcomes of the disciplinary provisions of the *Public Sector Management Act 1994*".[26] In other words, a giant dummy spit by the CCC, which was quite happy to accept the Section 81 process until the time it came down with decisions that did not suit it.

But the CCC was not prepared to leave the matter there. It then commenced criminal proceedings against Mr Stokes for making an unauthorised disclosure to Brian Burke. It also inadvisedly commenced complementary criminal proceedings against Brian.

The media, without the opportunity of hearing anything of the other side of the story, placed the worst construction on the events. As an example, *The West Australian* printed a prominent story by Amanda Banks under the headline: "Official caught in Burke's web".

It stated:

> Former high-ranking public servant Gary Stokes may be charged with *corruption* (my emphasis) for leaking confidential information to lobbyists Brian Burke and Julian Grill *in a bid for promotion* (my emphasis).[27]

Ascribing this unworthy motivation to Mr Stokes, on the basis of suspicion alone, is terribly unfair. It destroyed his career.

There was another aspect of CCC's actions that smacked of injustice. That was the risk of double jeopardy.

---

[26] Summary CCC Report on Whitby, 3 October 2008, p. 11.
[27] *The West Australian*, 4 October 2008, p. 5.

Put briefly, it is my submission that it is questionable for the CCC to encourage s.81 proceedings (where Stokes job was in jeopardy), put the accused through the trauma and cost of that action and then commence criminal prosecutions, making much the same allegations, when the CCC hierarchy is not happy with the s.81 result.

It is not just my view. The Parliamentary Inspector to the NSW Independent Commission against Corruption (ICAC), David Levine QC, has also warned of the potential for iniquitous double jeopardy situations in the similar ICAC process.

Mr Levine also said, "... the anti-corruption body had abused its power in pursuing relatively trivial matters".[28] That is exactly the course I am suggesting that the CCC embarked upon in respect to Messrs. Stokes and Burke over Whitby.

Morality aside, the CCC, through the DPP, ensured criminal charges were laid against Mr Stokes (for providing the letter) and against Burke (for procuring the letter). These charges ran the course of a long and highly publicised judicial process, which I won't take the reader through. A decision was handed down on 3 December 2013 by Magistrate Robert Young.

Brian was acquitted with cost being awarded in his favour. Rania Spooner from *WA News* in an online story that same day stated:

> Mr Burke has now been acquitted of the final of eight charges brought against him by the CCC, which have spanned more than seven years.

The story continued:

> With his wife by his side outside court Mr Burke described the lengthy prosecutions against him as 'intolerable' and suggested he had been unduly targeted by the corruption watchdog.

It was a different outcome for Mr Stokes. He was convicted. Senior Counsel for the DPP, Bruno Fiannaca, pressed for a weighty penalty, but the CCC was to be bitterly disappointed. Like every other independent person who looked at this matter, Magistrate Young formed

---

[28] *The West Australian*, 15 March 2016.

the opinion that Mr Stokes' transgression was little more than trivial. He imposed a modest fine, but ignored the CCC's demands on penalty and refused to record a conviction.

I am told by people who know that there were elements within the CCC who were apoplectic. They had insisted on bringing criminal charges against both Mr Stokes and Brian Burke, but were no further advanced than they were four years earlier after the result of the s.81 proceedings were announced.

Not to be deterred, the CCC dipped again into the public purse. Unabashed, it launched the expensive Supreme Court process of appealing Magistrate Young's decision not to record a conviction. It should be noted the CCC continued to use taxpayers' money seemingly without fear. It was a remorseless process that placed Mr Stokes' freedom in jeopardy once again.

According to an online article,[29] the DPP argued on behalf of the CCC "a spent conviction was not appropriate because the magistrate had erred in regarding the offence to be a minor example of its type".

It was not a proposition that WA's highest court was prepared to entertain. The appeal was rejected. Mr Stokes was free, with no stain on his record, but at another huge cost in human capital. This formerly highly respected career public servant had been emotionally pulverised over the six-year ordeal. His reputation and public service job had been lost, as had his marriage.

The Fortescue Metals Group (FMG) inquiry

At no time was it any secret that Julian Grill Consulting was engaged by Andrew Forrest on behalf of FMG. Our task was to help facilitate government approvals for this huge new iron ore project in the Pilbara. It was a wild ride, to say the least, but one full of challenge and exhilaration. I deal with it in Chapter 15, "Helping Andrew Forrest crack iron ore duopoly".

The CCC's public inquiry into this matter began in February 2007, but the report was not tabled until 14 September 2009. This inordinate delay has never been explained.

---

[29] *Perth Now*, 31 July 2013.

The public hearings revolved around whether Resources Minister John Bowler and his chief of staff, Simon Corrigan, had disclosed Cabinet confidential information to Brian Burke and me. However, it (like Whitby) deteriorated into a dry technical argument about what was confidential.

Ironically and ultimately, it was determined that none of it was confidential. In the final analysis, no impropriety was found.

Nonetheless, the CCC investigations unfairly led to the sacking of Bowler from the Ministry and expulsion from the ALP. And because any affinity with Burke and Grill, no matter how innocent, was treated like a strict liability offence, the public service careers of two fine young officers, Simon Corrigan and Timothy Walster, also were snuffed out.

The final report exonerated them all, but the unfair publicity, which resulted in a trial by media, destroyed the careers of all three. It is hard to imagine how this long-winded inquiry could ever have been justified.

Extraordinarily, it also directly led to the loss of Government, as I elucidate in Chapter 15.

The Bowler bookkeeping inquiry

John Bowler was a particular quarry of the CCC. He was also my close friend. Initially, I understand from a highly placed source within Parliament House that some CCC officers were proclaiming on one of their visits that they would "get Bowler and Grill for corruption". That dated back to before the Lobbyists hearings commenced.

That proclamation was a disturbingly indiscreet assertion, but it had no evidentiary basis. But just imagine how damaging this must have been to Bowler. Parliament House is a well-known hotbed of rumour and gossip. I knew of this reckless allegation within 30 minutes of it being made. People started avoiding Bowler like the plague.

Ultimately, the CCC's grand claims of official corruption degenerated into trivia. However, in the meantime, the CCC's actions did immense damage, not just to John Bowler, but to the fabric of government.

The CCC admits in its report No 7 of 2008 (page 5) that the inquiry also considered whether Bowler, Burke and Grill entered into a criminal conspiracy. There was not a shred of credible evidence for that assertion.

It beggars belief, but as part of the Lobbyists hearings on 26 and 27 February 2007, the CCC actually conducted an inquiry into record keeping in Bowler's ministerial office. Moreover, 21 months later, in November 2008, it produced a 72-page report on the subject and breathlessly announced:

> Mr Bowler had made arrangements to avoid any documentary or electronic record being kept of contacts and communications with Mr Julian Fletcher Grill and Mr Brian Thomas Burke.[30]

It was a finding of no consequence, as there was no requirement to keep such records. But that was the pathetic best the CCC could do. The CCC went on to find that it was a "breach of discipline". But no-one is sure what that means. There was no evidence that either Brian or I was aware that our communications with Minister Bowler's office were not recorded and I can assure you that we weren't.

But who would keep such records, if the penalty for innocent contact with Burke and Grill was dismissal, as it was with the Federal Minister for the Environment, Ian Campbell?

Although the CCC hearings initially gave the impression that Bowler did favours for Burke and Grill, and this was reflected in the media coverage, the CCC was not able to evince such evidence and it was ultimately reflected in the CCC report where no such findings were made.

Sadly, this exoneration came far too late to save Bowler. By the time the CCC report was brought down in November 2008 he had successively been sacked as Resources Minister, thrown out of the Ministry and expelled from the ALP. His problem stemmed from his preparedness to meet with Brian and me.

---

[30] Summary, *Report on Behalf of Procedure Privileges Committee of Legislative Assembly Report on Issues Relating to Record Keeping in Ministerial Office of Hon John James Mansell Bowler MLA*, 6 November 2008, p. 1.

That reflects on the original Gallop ban. It placed ministers like Bowler and public servants like EPA Chairman Dr Wally Cox in a very difficult position.

However, in the case of Bowler, Premier Alan Carpenter had publicly lifted the ban before Bowler was involved. But not in truth. Evidence emerged at the CCC hearings that he still privately told his ministers not to deal with us.

Dr Gallop chose not to put the original prohibition order in writing and failed to give an answer to a letter from my wife asking for an explanation. It took two months from 22 November 2006 to 24 January 2007 for Mal Wauchope, the Director General of the Department of Premier and Cabinet, to answer my own letter inquiring about the extent of the ban.

Mr Wauchope advised that it extended to ministers and ministerial officers, but it still left open the question of whether it applied to departmental officers. In the absence of any clear direction from the Premier, most heads of departments acted as though there was no ban.

Ministers were naturally confused.

I maintain that this autocratic dictate perplexed and distressed at least some of Gallop's Cabinet colleagues, who quietly continued to meet with us.

It is my belief that the CCC's abortive attempt to prosecute Nathan Hondros, the former chief of staff to Fisheries Minister Jon Ford, Burke and me for conspiracy to corrupt stemmed from Ford's maladroit attempt to camouflage the fact he was dealing with us. I explore this further failure by the CCC in Chapter 18, "'Corruption' – No case to answer".

John Bowler and Yeelirrie

The next part of the CCC campaign against John Bowler was the Yeelirrie Tenement matter. This component of the Lobbyists hearings was the subject of a separate report, dated 16 November 2009.

The scenario was as follows: In February 2006, Bowler, the Minister for Resources, asked a favour of me – not the other way around, as the public was led to believe.

Our client, Precious Metals of Australia (PMA), had applied for tenements on a location known as the Yeelirrie State Agreement area, southwest of Wiluna. It contained a substantial uranium deposit. The background was that while Liberal governments favoured uranium mining, as did successive Federal Labor Governments, WA Labor governments did not.

For this and other economic reasons, the Yeelirrie ore body and other uranium deposits in WA had remained undeveloped. Neither had the wider Yeelirrie Agreement area been worked for more than 35 years.

This is a highly unusual situation. The *WA Mining Act* was written on the strict basis of "use it or lose it" – that is, roughly speaking, either a tenement is actively explored or mined, or it becomes liable for forfeiture.

Notwithstanding that the area was subject of a State Agreement, PMA's lawyers advised that there was a legal possibility to apply for exploration licences in its favour in the Yeelirrie area because owner BHP had not complied with the *Mining Act* regulations. Other companies had come to the same conclusion and made similar applications, all of which were listed for hearing in the Warden's Court.

BHP, faced with the possible loss of the tenements, approached the Mines Department and the Minister for special assistance. I remind readers that BHP was a long-standing and ferocious lobbyer of government.

It was contemplated by the Mines Department, the Minister and BHP that, rather than leave the matters to the impartial judgment of the court, the Minister would use an extraordinary provision in the *Mining Act* (Section 111A) to snuff out PMA's legal rights (and the other applicants' rights) and restore BHP to its former position as unchallenged holder of the subject tenements.

When Minister Bowler contacted me, he said he was reluctant to use s.111A because it was a provision that was only applied in the most extreme circumstances and where it was clearly in the state or national interest. As a consequence, he said, he had rung me to request that I approach our client (PMA) to suggest that it voluntarily withdraw its claims.

We did contact PMA and received the reply that it most reluctantly agreed, in principle, to withdraw its action. However, its directors imposed conditions.

It proposed that it be allowed to peg some tenements in the agreement area that were surplus to BHP's requirements. To further that proposal, I organised a set of negotiations with BHP.

In discussion with Bowler, it was agreed that I should have some additional time to hammer out a settlement between BHP and PMA. I told the Minister that if he made it apparent to BHP that he was about to invoke the extraordinary s.111A power, I would lose any leverage that I might have to bring about an agreed outcome. He consented to an extension.

However, as it transpired, he mistakenly allowed the Section 111A letters to be sent to our client and other affected companies. It was Bowler's agreement to give me time to bring about an arrangement between PMA and BHP that the CCC tried to allege was corrupt.

This was an absurd proposition. Arriving at a satisfactory arrangement to bring about the voluntary withdrawal of the PMA applications was just a normal commercial negotiation. Such negotiations occur every day and should never be characterised as improper.

In its zeal to find some basis to somehow incriminate Bowler, the CCC disregarded two very important factors. First, BHP was asking Minister Bowler to employ a powerful, seldom-used, statutory power. Secondly, it involved the confiscation of PMA's normal legal right to have its case heard in court.

Additionally, this extreme option was conferring a major benefit on a huge transnational company in circumstances that went against the history and spirit of the *Mining Act*.

So, what was the outcome of the CCC public hearing and report? The end point was really a damp squib. In its report published on 16 November 2009 (20 months after the hearing) the CCC offered the "opinion" that Bowler's actions in agreeing to give me more time to fashion a commercial settlement constituted serious misconduct.

Many independent lawyers would strongly disagree. But the CCC was not going to chance the rejection of its "opinion" in a court of law. In the final analysis the CCC found:

> The Commission considers that the evidence which would be legally admissible in a criminal trial is not likely to be sufficient to properly found a charge of corruption under Section 83 of *The Criminal Code* against Mr Bowler, and accordingly does not recommend further consideration of that.[31]

Nor did the CCC make any recommendation of disciplinary action. So much for the CCC officers' assertion to parliamentary officers in Parliament House that they would "do John Bowler and Julian Grill for corruption". In fact, Julian Grill wasn't mentioned in the findings at all.

The City of Wanneroo (several issues)

This was an elaborate fishing trip.

As usual, there was only one shared element. That was the presence of Burke and Grill in contact with the council.

No findings of substance were made.

The Tony McRae Inquiry

Tony McRae must be the unluckiest MP of this period. I doubt that he was initially a target of the CCC when the Smiths Beach inquiry began, or that he had the slightest idea that he might become one. But he soon did, and he lost his career.

When the CCC's McRae Inquiry report was released on 21 November 2008, Minister McRae was the lone recipient of a "serious

---

[31] Executive Summary of the *Report on the Investigation of Alleged Public Sector Misconduct in Connection with the Activities of Lobbyists and Other Persons – A Ministerial Decision in Relation to Applications for a Mining Tenement at Yeelirrie*, p. xv.

misconduct" "opinion" from the CCC. I suspect that I was initially the real quarry for a charge akin to "bribery" of McRae.

In October 2006, he was Assistant Minister for Planning. My belief is that when the documentary evidence taken from my house in the CCC raid of 8 November 2006 was shown to be quite inadequate to implicate me in wrongdoing, the focus was switched.

Thereafter, McRae was said to have deceived me about the timing of an announcement of a planning decision relating to land at Gingin north of Perth. That land was owned by our client, David Lombardo and his family.

The planning decision was made by Minister McRae in our client's favour on 9 October 2006. McRae overturned a previous decision requiring Lombardo's application for rezoning to go through the costly and time-consuming business of re-advertising.

Everyone, including the CCC, ultimately agreed that McRae's determination in our client's favour had been made in an entirely open and above-board manner. Both the Town Planning Commission and the relevant Department of Planning officers recommended and supported the decision.

That did not prevent Phillip Urquhart, Counsel Assisting for the CCC, from persistently suggesting in cross-examination of McRae that he had made his finding in our client's favour because of past donations we had made to McRae's earlier election campaigns, and some support that Burke and I lent to his efforts to become a Cabinet Minister.[32]

These suggestions by Mr Urquhart went nowhere. However, it should have been clear to the CCC that such suggestions were bound to do irreparable damage to McRae's reputations in the interim. It was a quite wrong for Mr Urquhart to raise these imputations of bribery in such an aggressive and public way. It was akin to throwing red meat to the lions.

Minister McRae's planning decision in the Lombardo family's favour was conveyed to me, in general terms, when his Chief of Staff, Rewi Lyall, rang me on 10 October 2006. Mr Lyall advised that our

---

[32] Transcript, 22 February 2007, p. 593.

client's application had been granted and that I would be relatively satisfied "but could not go into further detail as the Minister hadn't actually signed the letter yet".

The next matter in the sequence of events was the most crucial and had profoundly deleterious effects on the careers of both Minister McRae and Mr Lyall.

What transpired was that McRae rang me the following day (11 October 2006). The phone conversation was quite long and was somewhat complicated (for details, see transcript at page xvi of CCC report), but in brief terms can be summarised as follows:

1. In answer to a question from McRae, I told him that Mr Lyall had informed me that there was a written brief coming up for him to sign off and that would make our client reasonably happy.
2. McRae said, "Okay".
3. Additionally, McRae told me that the decision on the Gingin land may not be signed off for a week or two and hadn't yet come to him. He would follow it up.
4. I said that Lesley and I would be attending his fund-raising dinner in several days' time.
5. McRae intimated that numbers for the function were a bit thin and he was thinking about postponing it. He sought my opinion.
6. I responded by indicating that if he did postpone I would talk to Brian Burke about helping him with a well-patronised fund-raiser at a later date.
7. McRae advised that he would postpone as he just did not have the attendance numbers.

At the CCC public hearing, and in its later report, the CCC interpreted this conversation this way: McRae had committed serious misconduct "by deliberately (albeit subtly) linking the exercise of his Ministerial power to approve the Lombardo development, to gaining assistance from Mr Grill for this political fund-raising, Mr McRae took advantage of his public office."

It is important to understand that this CCC interpretation of the conversation was on the lesser standard of "on the balance of probabilities" and not on the higher standard of "proof beyond reasonable doubt" – that is, the civil standard, not the criminal standard.

In reality, the CCC "finding" relied upon on interpretation of what was going on in McRae's mind at the time of the conversation with me. That is, the CCC was taking on the role of mind-reader.

Former WA Premier Peter Dowding is a long-standing friend of Tony McRae and he was outraged by the opinion expressed by CCC Commissioner Len Roberts-Smith in the November 2008 report. At a public meeting a few months later at the Constitutional Centre in West Perth, attended by many of Perth's legal elite, Dowding took Mr Roberts-Smith to task over the decision and received a resounding round of applause.

One of Dowding's central points was that to use the lesser standard of proof, in circumstances where the evidence was thin and where McRae's whole political future was in the balance, was unfair and inappropriate.

Mr Roberts-Smith fell back on the defence that he was entitled to use that standard, and it was sanctioned by the CCC Act, where he was expressing an "opinion" only. While Mr Roberts-Smith may have been technically correct, every bone in my body impels me to embrace Dowding's reasoning. I believe that in a matter as subjective and uncertain as this one, and where you are assessing a person's possible innermost thoughts and motivations, it was wrong and unfair to deprive McRae of the benefit of reasonable doubt.

But I go further. I assert that Mr Roberts-Smith was wrong in his reasoning, even on the lesser standard. Dead wrong. His facts and his logic only stand up superficially. When examined forensically, the reasoning falls to pieces.

The essential argument presented by the Commissioner was that McRae temporarily withheld from me the fact that our client's development plan would not have to be re-advertised, as we had originally requested, so that I would have an incentive to help with his fundraiser. The problem with Mr Roberts-Smith's case was that I already knew when McRae rang on 11 October 2006 that our client's appeal had been granted and I told him so.

Furthermore, the Department of Planning had written to our client the day before advising that their appeal had been upheld.

Brian Burke and I did not need any incentive to help McRae. We had a long and quite public history of helping him and a long inventory of helping other ALP candidates and members with fundraising functions over many years.

Look at it this way: I was the person who was supposed to have been misled. I was not called to give evidence on this matter. How could the CCC assume that I was deceived without asking me? I can assure the reader, I was not.

Another problem with this set of CCC procedures, as I have previously explained, is that the CCC accusations and opinions were never contestable or appealable. This was a point that was expounded upon by Dowding at the Constitutional Centre meeting mentioned above.

Like many other CCC witnesses, McRae was taken by surprise and confronted by covert telephone recordings that he was in no way prepared for. At no time was he able to call witnesses or other evidence in his own defence. He couldn't even give evidence in his own right. McRae was strictly limited to answering a narrow set of CCC questions.

The media was brutal. It accepted in the Tony McRae matter the superficial assessments made by Counsel Assisting at the original hearing. The media were not interested in any questioning of the CCC's fragile assumptions or the way the CCC had deprived McRae of any procedurally fair hearing.

The media wasted no time. It rushed to judgment immediately after the CCC hearing and pronounced guilt, nearly two years before the CCC report was brought down.

There was a huge unflattering picture of Tony McRae and smaller, but prominent, mug shots of lugubrious ex-ministers John D'Orazio, Norm Marlborough, John Bowler and Ljiljanna Ravlich.

The accompanying stories, by Robert Taylor and Sean Cowan,

dwelt as much on the recent demise of the other four ministers featured as it did with McRae. It neatly bundled up all five matters and laid it at the feet of Premier Carpenter for the sin of giving his imprimatur for Burke and Grill to have access to his ministers. The newspaper's editorial of the same day thundered:

> The moral cancer in the factions of the Labor Party has spread to Cabinet – and Mr Carpenter must accept that he is partly responsible for allowing that to happen.

The Taylor/Cowan article, either negligently or deliberately, muddied the waters in a pivotal way. Whatever the reason, it set the scene. It stated:

> … Environment Minister Tony McRae had asked lobbyist Julian Grill for fundraising help *while* (my emphasis) dealing with a planning proposal put forward by one of Mr Grill's clients.

This statement was simply untrue, as it gives the impression that McRae had not made his decision before he rang me. However, even Commissioner Roberts-Smith was quite explicit on this point in his report. He said (page xxix of the Executive Summary):

> … his solicitation of fund-raising assistance. In fact, he had already discharged that particular function of his office – and it had been done entirely properly, based, as it was, on Departmental advice.

The West quoted McRae in response:

> Outside the CCC, Mr McRae said he would not resign from Cabinet. "I think it's clear from the commission's hearings that I've done absolutely nothing wrong and acted with absolute propriety", he said.

Essentially, my view is that on the critical question of whether McRae actually requested my help for an alternate fund-raiser, the hard evidence was non-existent.

This view was shared by the Parliamentary Inspector, Malcolm McCusker. Having seen the rancorous media coverage, he preemptively wrote an 11-page epistle to the CCC on 11 April 2008 warning that any adverse finding or opinion against McRae would be unsafe. The letter is attached to the CCC report as an appendix.[33] It is worth reading and is quite compelling.

At paragraph 28, Mr McCusker has this to say:

> At no time in the discussion did Mr McRae suggest that Mr Grill should organise for him an alternative fund-raising event, instead of the event which Mr McRae had already scheduled for the 19th October 2006. The suggestion by Mr Grill, that he and Mr Burke *could* (my emphasis) do that was neither solicited by Mr McRae nor adopted.

As readers now know, Mr Roberts-Smith rejected the central thrust of Mr McCusker's letter and made the adverse "finding", or opinion, which was part of the devastating process of confiscating McRae's career. In making that non-reviewable, non-appealable finding, Mr Roberts-Smith must have appreciated that the evidence was extremely thin.

This almost tragic situation is reflected in the words of High Court Chief Justice Murray Gleeson AC QC in a 1998 speech:

> ... the ever-widening gap between what is required to be done in a court of law to prove that a person is guilty of misconduct, and what is sufficient outside a court of law, to create about a person such an atmosphere of suspicion, distrust and hostility, that for all practical purposes it does not matter whether anything can be proved against him.[34]

This quotation is entirely appropriate to McRae's situation and is made even more pertinent when it is appreciated that Mr Roberts-Smith was present for not one word of the public examination of McRae. This was surely a case where McRae's credibility was in issue and it was essential for the decision maker to be there in person.

---

[33] Appendix 1, to CCC Report into activities of AD McRae and RE Lyall dated 21 November 2008, page 157. Letter from Parliamentary Inspector Malcolm McCusker to acting CCC Commissioner CP Shanahan SC, dated 11 April 2008.
[34] *The Australian*, online edition, 14 March 2016.

But in February 2007 (the time of the CCC hearings), the media was in high dudgeon and demanding heads. McRae's fate was not going to be decided by cool legal deliberations. His future would be left to a sanctimonious media and brutal political contrivance.

The Fourth Estate simply went into overdrive. They wanted to be in on the kill. One of the seven stories in *The West* of 24 February 2007 was by high-profile analyst by Sky News TV commentator Professor Peter van Onselen.

Normally a levelheaded correspondent, van Onselen appeared to lose all sense of rational perspective. He maintained, in the light of the McRae matter, that Carpenter should either resign or mount a massive campaign to reform a scandal-plagued WA Labor Party. The van Onselen article shrieked:

> The scandals revealed by the CCC have now given him the impetus to make the changes needed.
>
> It's high time the good people in the Labor Party stood up to be counted. They should get behind Mr Carpenter and launch an all-out assault on reform, no matter how messy the process gets. WA will be better for it. We are not talking about one or two bad eggs here, we are talking about corruption and deal making that permeates through all levels of the party.
>
> ... This week the CCC exposed just how rotten the Labor Party in this State truly is ... The fact that Brian Burke and Julian Grill have had their tentacles totally immersed in the Labor Party organisation in WA for more than 30 years is not an easy thing to transform. But the time is now and Labor at least has the right Premier in play, to make the changes.[35]

This was some pretty pompous journalism. It sounded good and was just the stuff to sell newspapers. And it largely accorded with the general perceptions being purveyed by the CCC and the national media at that time. But where was the "corruption"? After many years and tens of millions of public money, the CCC could not prove one case.

---

[35] *The West Australian*, 24 February 2007, p. 7.

And what "deal making" was Professor van Onselen referring to? We were never told. Even the CCC did not allege that there was any deal done between McRae and myself. This was just unsupportable, broad-brush libel.

Obviously, Professor van Onselen comes from a different era to me. In most of my history in the party, rank and file voluntary service was the order of the day. My wife, and both of our children, Shannon and Siobhan, dedicated thousands of hours of unpaid work to the ALP.

If the professor had done his homework, he would have appreciated how seldom I accessed the so-called "parliamentary perks". He would also have known that during 24 years in Parliament, I never took one cent of party or union money and always contributed from my own funds to other ALP candidates' election campaigns.

Brian Burke probably had an even more illustrious record of contribution towards others in the party. Certainly, the list of achievement of his government is without peer in Western Australian ALP history.

So why did Professor van Onselen use such a malicious epithet in respect to Burke and me? He simply did not have the historical knowledge.

Remarkably, however, Peter van Onselen's "rational perspective" marvellously returned to him in an article that he published in *The Australian* of 22 March 2014. The article was headed: "Modern Star Chamber must be bought to account".

It was a devastating critique of the procedures adopted by the CCC's sister body, ICAC, in NSW. It was written in the context of proceedings in NSW, but the professor made it clear that it applied to the CCC.

He stated:

> The ICAC in NSW, as well as similar star chambers in other states and federally, are very good at one thing in particular, besmirching reputations.
>
> Yes, sometimes they are exposing corruption, but at what price to our rule of law? At what price to the reputations

of the innocent who get dragged through the proverbial mud?"³⁶

I won't go through the whole article. But the last paragraph is worth repeating:

> The problem is not necessarily the notion of a body such as ICAC designed to root out corruption. Rather it is when the body itself is put above the very rule of law it is designed to uphold.

About this time, or slightly earlier, the professor rang me and we had a coffee in a cafe in my street. It was then that he told me that he had worked for the precursor of the NSW ICAC, the NSW Crime Commission, and was concerned about some of their procedures, and I informed him of the CCC's confiscation of our procedural fairness rights. I like to think, but do not know, that I had some influence on him.

While the public may have been led to believe that there had been a transgression of the law by both McRae and Burke in their respective roles, the legal profession had a much clearer view of the absence of any incriminating evidence and of the methods being employed by the CCC.

In the *Sunday Times* of 25 February 2007, there was a small, but highlighted, piece by its regular legal commentator, Tom Percy QC.

In his direct, no-nonsense style, Mr Percy stated:

> … innocent people who were called to CCC hearings to give evidence were crucified by the media. Members of Perth's legal profession intend to lobby Attorney-General Jim McGinty to re-examine CCC procedures.

The article continued:

> But Mr McGinty seems unmoved. "We always knew there was going to be pain with the CCC," he said. "It's a bit more than we anticipated, but this is about maintaining ethical standards of government and that is what the public is demanding."

---

³⁶ *The Australian*, 22 March 2014, p. 20.

I suggest that this response by McGinty was glib and uncaring. Legal experts of the highest repute later demonstrated that the safeguards against abuse of the CCC's immense powers were simply inadequate. It has not been proved, but it is my strong suspicion that McGinty's refusal, as Attorney-General, to act upon fair criticism of the CCC led to a situation where some CCC officers came to regard themselves as untouchable and above the law (see 12, "Corruption, dysfunction, conflict exposed in CCC").

The West editorial of 9 December 2015 (page 26), when referring to this expose, quoted the contemporaneous comments of current CCC Commissioner John McKechnie:

> Yesterday, Mr McKechnie acknowledged that the CCC's reputation was blighted and it would take more than a little publicity to reassure the public and regain its trust.

With all of the adverse media coverage and pressure from the usual suspects within the ALP to dismiss McRae, it became evident that primitive political consideration would decide the impasse. It was not pretty.

Carpenter's decision to sack McRae was made on Sunday 25 February 2007 and was the sensationalised lead story that evening and the next day. Various articles (including all of the front page), an editorial and an Alston cartoon took up a large part of *The West Australian*. That paper unequivocally supported Carpenter's actions.

It adopted the easy self-righteous position. It was a set of articles reeking of moral vanity. McRae maintained that the decision was based on "extraordinary unfounded suppositions, propositions and innuendo". As I have already mentioned, his position was very strongly supported in writing by Malcolm McCusker.

It was buried away at the end of an article on page 4, but Daniel Emerson and *The West* did give one paragraph of coverage to a neutral commentator's view of the decision:

> Constitutional law expert Professor Greg Craven said Mr McRae had done nothing wrong, but Mr Carpenter had to ask him to resign to protect the Government's credibility.

There was to be a strange twist on this when exactly the opposite occurred at the 2008 State election. This is explained in Chapter 14, "2008 Election: A CCC casualty".

Even in February 2007 it was a lot more politically complicated than that. The seeds of discontent, which would later have serious repercussions, were sown in the ALP, as witnessed by Emerson's story, where furious assertions by Kevin Reynolds were aired (to quote the headline), "Premier captive of Left, McGinty: union boss". The story continued:

> Union heavyweight and Labor Party Faction powerbroker Kevin Reynolds lashed out yesterday at Alan Carpenter for ending the Cabinet career of Tony McRae and labelled the Premier a 'captive' to dominant forces within the party. The Construction, Forestry, Mining and Energy Union boss, a powerful figure in the Centre faction which supported Mr McRae's rise thorough Labor ranks, said Mr McRae had done nothing wrong and claimed his ignominious exit had been orchestrated by Attorney-General Jim McGinty and his Left faction.

In the final analysis, McRae lost his position in Cabinet, never to return. He stayed in Parliament, but was really a lost, disenchanted, but brave political warrior. It's reported that he has made many unsuccessful attempts to have the CCC "opinion" withdrawn. He still believes that he was the victim of political intrigue.

As befits his character, he courageously fought for his seat at the next election the following year. With his weakened standing and the CCC adverse opinion linked to his name, he lost and so did the Carpenter Government. It was one of the closest election results WA had ever seen. I analyse it in Chapter 14.

The sad irony was that if Carpenter had retained McRae's seat of Riverton, he would most likely have held on to the Treasury benches. Riverton was won by Mike Nahan, who later became Opposition Leader.

As for McRae's innocent chief of staff, Rewi Lyall, he was but one more CCC fatality. His sin was being overheard by the CCC talking on the phone to me, where I agreed to make a modest contribution to a charitable cause he was supporting.

But the Carpenter Government was sanctimoniously ruthless. No finding was made against Mr Lyall by the CCC, but he nonetheless lost his job. It was made clear that he was not welcome in the WA public service. He had to move interstate to find employment.

Concluding thoughts

My essential point about the Lobbyists inquiry is that there was a monumental estrangement between the CCC/media-generated propaganda and the provable facts.

I have not related much of the media coverage on these Lobbyist issues, because of reasons of space. But let me assure you, the media was unwaveringly condemnatory. Some was malicious. Nearly all implied corruption. The giant chasm between this coverage and the ultimate outcomes surely must have been an embarrassment to some journalists and editors.

Julian and Lesley Grill and Brian and Sue Burke are confronted by the media as they leave a CCC hearing. Lesley and Sue attended every CCC and court hearing.

A photographer created what some people thought was a pertinent image when Julian Grill was at the front gate of his West Perth apartment. The CCC used the media to foster a community belief that Grill and Brian Burke had committed serious crimes. Just one serious charge was laid and it was not successful.

Mike Allen, pictured with his wife Beth, was a senior officer in the Department of Planning. The CCC wrongly accused him of agreeing to a request by Brian Burke to appoint a particular officer to write a report on the Smiths Beach development. There was no such request and no report was ever written. Despite being cleared of any misconduct, Mr Allen was never reinstated to the public service.

Dr Wally Cox, Chairman of the Environmental Protection Authority, was accused by the CCC of misconduct because he had lunch with Brian Burke and Julian Grill while the Department of Environment – not Dr Cox's department – was assessing the Smiths Beach proposal. He was stood down and although the Public Service Commission later dismissed the misconduct allegation he was not reinstated to his position.

The CCC conducted several investigations into John Bowler's performance as Resources Minister in an effort to uncover corruption or illegality is his relationship with Brian Burke and Julian Grill; particularly with Grill whose Goldfields seat of Eyre he won in 2001 after Grill retired. Nothing was found. The CCC interest in Bowler cost him his place in Cabinet and he was pressured into resigning from the ALP in March 2007. He contested the 2008 election as an independent and easily won the seat of Kalgoorlie.

Julian Grill and Brian Burke show the strain of facing a corruption charge related to a pearl industry draft policy, the most serious of all the unsuccessful charges they faced. They walked free from the WA Supreme Court.

Brian Burke's Panama hat became a signature piece of clothing at his many CCC hearings and subsequent court appearances. In later years, similar hats signed by Burke were auctioned at charity fund-raising events.

Alston's cartoon in *The West* on 14 November 2006 highlights the futility of Premier Alan Carpenter's attempt to end Burke and Grill's influence on the Labor government by banning his members from having contact with the lobbyists.

John Quigley (left) was among a group of Perth solicitors who were critical of the CCC's performance in a number of areas and were prepared to challenge what they saw us unfair or unjust outcomes.

Kevin Hammond (right), the inaugural Commissioner of the CCC, was appointed on 1 January 2004. In the three years until his early resignation on 31 March 2007, he presided over the CCC's two high-profile investigations, the Smiths Beach and Lobbyists inquiries – both focussed on Brian Burke and Julian Grill. Neither inquiry secured convictions for corruption or illegal conduct in respect to the matters enquired into.

Lesley and Julian Grill leave court after Julian's acquittal on false evidence charges. The CCC's intensive attack on Julian included tapping the Grills' phones, bugging their home and installing a hidden camera in a lamp post near the front entrance.

Businessman David McKenzie (left) was the promoter of the Smiths Beach resort development. The project's seed capital came from small investors. However, after almost two decades of frustration in the approval process, the project went into receivership and was abandoned. Malcolm McCusker QC (right), before he was appointed Governor of WA, was highly critical of the CCC's procedures and many of its inquiry findings, particularly in relations to senior public servants.

A parody on the Burke and Wills expedition, Alston's cartoon in *Kalgoorlie Miner* on 1 March 2007 was in line with the community perception, created in the media, that Burke and Grill were responsible for the demise of ministers Marlborough, Bowler and McRae, who had been targeted by the CCC. In fact, all three had been dropped from Cabinet because of publicity created by the CCC in its failed attempts to find them guilty of corruption or illegality in their dealings with Burke and Grill.

Premier Alan Carpenter maintained an unenforceable ban on Labor MPs having contact with Brian Burke and Julian Grill; a ban introduced by his predecessor, Geoff Gallop. The sacking of cabinet ministers because of inflammatory media publicity generated by the CCC cost Carpenter the "unlosable" 2008 election, when Labor failed in four seats previously held by the dumped ministers.

A series of CCC inquiries into decisions by Resources Minister John Bowler created an impression that Julian Grill was "pulling his strings". None of the CCC investigations found any illegality or corruption in the Bowler-Grill relationship. This cartoon was published in *Kalgoorlie Miner* on 3 March 2007.

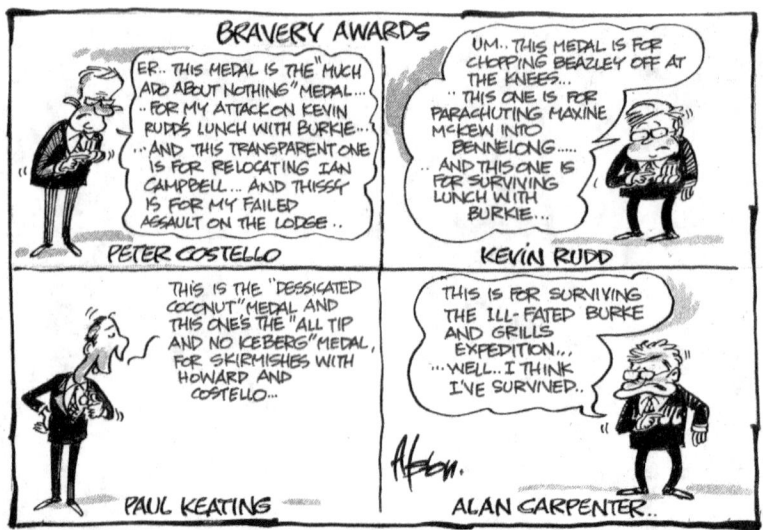

Alston's Bravery Awards cartoon in *The West* on 12 March 2007 was an indication of how the CCC pursuit of Burke and Grill was dominating politics and media across the country.

When Geoff Gallop (left) became Premier in 2001, his government undid a planning approval of the Smiths Beach resort development that allowed sufficient residential development of the site to make the project financially viable. A chain of events that followed included the CCC's Smiths Beach and Lobbyists inquiries. The promising political career of Tony McRae (right) was cut short by a CCC investigation of a silly allegation – based on an intercepted telephone call – that he made a planning decision in exchange for Julian Grill offering to assist a campaign fund-raising event. McRae was cleared of any misconduct but was dumped from Cabinet and lost his seat at the looming 2008 election; a loss that cost Labor government.

7

CCC RESORTS TO PARLIAMENT
– AND FAILS AGAIN

Not content with its own vast powers, in an attempt to skewer its target, the CCC recruited additional muscle – namely, members of the Legislative Assembly (Lower House) and the Legislative Council (Upper House) of the Western Australian Parliament.

This abortive exercise was a flagrant instance of abuse of power. The interventions were both unsuccessful and disastrous.

Unsuccessful, because the attempts to expel from Parliament two MPs, Shelley Archer and Anthony Fels, failed. So too did a threat to force me to apologise or be sent to jail. Moreover, the Director of Public Prosecutions (DPP) point blank refused to bring criminal charges against anyone targeted by the inquiry.

Disastrous because they damaged innocent parties, visited disrespect on Parliament and weakened the Government.

The CCC vehicles were two parliamentary inquiries (one in each house) that stemmed from the CCC Smiths Beach hearings.

I think of these two sets of parliamentary disciplinary committee hearings this way: They were one arm of a CCC-inspired pincer movement aimed at Brian Burke and me. The other arm was the Smiths Beach and Lobbyists inquiries. One arm supported the other.

The uncertain honour of initiating the Upper House committee hearings, the central subject matter of this chapter, resided with two CCC officers who made contact with Giz Watson MLC, Chair of the Upper House Select Committee on Estimates and Financial Operations (SCEFO), on 8 February 2007 and met with her on 12 February. The officers alleged that SCEFO's confidential deliberations may have been improperly disclosed to "third parties" by members of the SCEFO.

They also presented a letter from Kevin Hammond, the Commissioner of the CCC, irregularly demanding the SCEFO agenda and minutes of the 31 January 2007 meeting.

It was apparent that the officers were seeking evidence for a CCC inquiry. That situation was breathtakingly audacious as it sought to reverse centuries of constitutional law. The matters the CCC wanted to inquire into, and demand documents for, were the exclusive jurisdiction of Parliament.

Quite correctly, the CCC request was refused by Nick Griffiths, the President of the Council.

In what amounted to a supercharging of the issue, Commissioner Hammond issued an extraordinary media release attacking the President for frustrating the CCC's inquiries. The CCC's assault was clearly misconceived and the Commissioner was forced to apologise to the committee overseeing the CCC, the Joint Standing Committee on the CCC (JSCCCC).

There is a strong suspicion, however, that the CCC in making the written demand and issuing the defying media statement had rashly decided to take on Parliament and confront its historic privileges. That suspicion received some support from Robert Taylor's article in *The West Australian* of 22 March 2007, where he observed:

> It is, however, hard to understand how the CCC managed to get the press release concerning Mr Griffiths wrong this week when it was well aware of the attitude of the Parliament's presiding officers as early as March 12 when an exchange of letters laid the groundwork for the current standoff.

The impression remained that the CCC, at this giddy time, was sufficiently arrogant to actually challenge Parliament. What's more, the CCC nearly pulled it off. That was because there was a "third column" within the legislature that, possibly out of populism or misplaced zeal, would have supported the CCC.

Contemporaneously, the CCC was also making demands on the Speaker of Parliament's Legislative Assembly, Fred Riebeling, for documents and information from a Parliamentary Committee looking at the sale of mining company Vanadium Resources (our client).

Both sets of demands made by the CCC related to Burke, Grill and Minister John Bowler. They were resisted by the Speaker with cooperation from the President of the Legislative Council. The media love a confrontation and were intensely interested in the history and politics of the issue. Also, it was all rather unique. The public had never seen a powerful institution like the CCC pitted against Parliament.

In articles in *The West* of 22 March 2007, at pages 9 and 15 (parts of which I have already quoted), Robert Taylor set out the background and circumstances of a major standoff. On page 9, under the headline, "MPs use privilege rule to block CCC inquiry", Taylor wrote:

> The LA Speaker Fred Riebeling rejected a request from CCC boss Kevin Hammond to hand over the records of a Parliamentary Committee looking into the controversial sale of Vanadium Resources, stymying the CCC's investigation into former resources minister John Bowler and his relationship with Julian Grill.

In the page 15 article under the heading, "Tussle over a matter of privilege in wonderland", Taylor wrote:

> There has been growing disquiet among politicians when they touch on the hard-won and historic right of parliament in the Westminster system to govern their own affairs.
>
> In pursuit of lobbyists and their influence on government, the CCC chased Labor MPs John Bowler and Shelley Archer and Liberal Anthony Fels back to their parliamentary lair, only to find themselves in a politicians' wonderland ...

The egregiously unfair CCC public hearings into Smiths Beach had wrongly convinced the electorate that rampant corruption had been uncovered. It was emblematic of the CCC's popularity that it was actually in the balance whether Parliament would surrender its historic privileges and hand over the requested documentation.

Parliament's exclusive right to manage its own affairs without outside interference by autocratic forces had been achieved by the mother of all parliaments, the UK's Westminster. It is an essential part of democracy won by the English parliament in a titanic battle with the English kings when the 1689 Bill of Rights was passed.

Presiding officers Griffiths and Riebeling were determined to uphold the common law and resist the CCC's intervention.

The encounter was played out in the media and was carried on with intense vigour. It was not the case, however, that all members of the WA Parliament supported their President and Speaker. For instance, National Party Leader Brendon Grylls opposed Mr Riebeling in the Assembly.

> The moment it is reported that the WA Parliament is using parliamentary privilege to block further investigations by the CCC is the moment the public loses more faith in this institution, Mr Grylls said.

Premier Carpenter was also reported in *The West* as having said on 22 March 2007 that he "did not want anything to stand in the way of CCC investigations".

Additionally, the populist Legislative Assembly member for Avon, Max Trenorden, took the side of the CCC by moving to debate the privileges question in relation to CCC demands. That proposal was tantamount to removing the handling of the dispute from the presiding officers.

It was clear then that the two presiding officers were under extreme pressure from both within parliamentary ranks and from outside to roll over and accede to the CCC demands.

It is interesting to note that the CCC was publicly and highly questionably canvassing the prospect of criminal charges at that early stage and upon what appeared to be very slender evidence.

This is how it works. The CCC is empowered by its legislation to make findings of "impropriety" by public officers, and it is empowered to furnish evidence to other agencies, the police or the Attorney General that may be used in a prosecution (s. 18 (h)). But the CCC is *expressly forbidden* by Section 23 of its Act to publish or report on the committal of a criminal offence by any individual under investigation.

In a story by Adam Gartrell in *Perth Now* (Murdoch Press) of 20 May 2007, it was reported that, "The retiring head of the Corruption and Crime Commission, Kevin Hammond, said today charges were inevitable from the recent high-profile public hearings".

The next day, in the same publication, Amanda O'Brien repeated the Hammond assertion about inevitable charges and went on to quote Mr Hammond on an assertion that phone tap investigations were only used "to investigate crimes that were punishable by imprisonment of at least seven years".

The West Australian was also quoting the Hammond letter of demand on Parliament "so the CCC could advance its investigation, with a view to further hearings and disciplinary action or criminal charges". (See Robert Taylor article, page 9 of 22 March 2007.)

But, because of the public nature of the CCC hearings and the explicit media coverage, the populace was aware of exactly which individuals were under investigation and therefor candidates for charges. Consequently, in my opinion, the CCC was effectively in breach of s. 23.

By March 2007 (see Taylor article page 2 of 31 March 2007) *The West* was referring to the CCC inquiries as investigations into the activities of lobbyists Brian Burke and Julian Grill.

My contention about Section 23 transgressions was later generally supported in a written opinion by highly respected Christopher Zelestis QC. This opinion was referred to with approval in JSCCCC Report No 17 of 2011.

After Commissioner Hammond's public opinions of criminality, what was left of our client base was bolting for the door.

A possible explanation for Hammond's outburst about the possibility of "criminal" activity is that he wanted to turn up the pressure on Parliament in the raging media war.

However, Griffiths and Riebeling held their nerve. They were on well-tested constitutional ground. They prevailed. The documents were withheld from the CCC.

At the time, the "win" by the presiding officers was not universally popular and/or well understood, even by some Members of Parliament. By way of explanation, I provide the following comment: Parliament is a body elected and unelected by the people, and it is a bulwark against the possible tyranny of kings initially, and now of government and government institutions such as the police and, in many countries, the secret police. Free speech by MPs in Parliament is among the essential freedoms exercised under the heading of "parliamentary privilege".

Freedom for Parliament to regulate its own affairs is another aspect of parliamentary privilege. The pragmatic reason behind this is that the executive of government (read cabinet, police, CCC, departmental heads, political parties, etc.) should not be able to dictate to the people's elected representatives in Parliament.

These are freedoms and rights that are essential in a democracy. They are protections for citizens more than safeguards for parliamentarians. Readers would have noted that in countries like Russia and China, where they don't have these rules, their parliaments are routinely ignored and overridden by their leaders.

These rights are not some empty perks of office, as unfairly implied by some of the media. They do not exist in totalitarian states and, unfortunately, are now taken for granted in places like Australia, where the history of the long fight for their establishment has largely been forgotten.

In defending these "freedoms" or "rights", the presiding officers did a considerable service to free government. They prevailed against a generally hostile media and an apathetic public, and in spite of some undermining from within their own political party.

Parliament, however, while maintaining the principles of parliamentary privilege, was forced, because of the pressures that I have mentioned, to compromise with the CCC. The main element of that compromise was that Parliament would itself investigate the CCC accusations. In respect to the Council, that meant the accusation that confidential material about a possible inquiry into Western Australia's "iron ore policy" was improperly leaked to third parties by members of the SCEFO committee. In the Assembly it meant allegations akin to corruption by John Bowler and myself.

The remainder of this chapter confines itself to comments on these remarkable proceedings in the Council and to similar (and no less sensational) proceedings in the Assembly.

With regard to the committee hearing in the Council, we had to contend with a secret "trial" with secret witnesses, secret evidence and unsuspecting accused.

Pursuant to the compromise mentioned above, on 21 March 2007 the Upper House appointed a Select Committee of Privilege (SCP). Its terms of reference were:

> Whether there has been any disclosure of deliberations of the Standing Committee on Estimates and Financial Operations (SCEFO) relating to a proposed inquiry into the State's Iron Ore Industry.

The three-person committee comprised Chairman Murray Criddle (National Party), Barry House (Liberal Party) and Adele Farina (ALP). The reporting date was to be no later than 30 May 2007, but it dragged on until 15 November 2007.

This seemingly inauspicious committee made numerous debatable findings and recommendations and was to prematurely and unfairly truncate the parliamentary careers of Upper House members Anthony Fels (Liberal) and Shelley Archer (Labor). Foremost among other outcomes were recommendation of criminal charges against the two MPs, together with Noel Crichton-Browne, Brian Burke and company director Nathan McMahon for supposedly giving misleading evidence to the committee.

Additionally, the committee alleged that I had also given misleading evidence to its inquiry and that I should apologise to the Council. Further it found that Pippa Read (electorate officer to Nigel Hallett MLC) and respected Perth lawyers Robert Edel and Alexander Jones had all made unauthorised disclosures of the SCEFO, but that no penalty be applied.

The final SCP report gives the misleading impression that the inquiry was inspired by Parliament and conducted by the Upper House, in the normal manner of all such committees. The truth was that the inquiry was a direct product of CCC machinations, as explained above.

Most unusually, the CCC provided the bulk of the relevant interrogation material for the SCP. Even more unusually, outside barrister Phillip Urquhart was made a committee member. Mr Urquhart had a close association with the CCC. It was, in reality, a complementary set of inquiries to the CCC's investigations into Smiths Beach and Lobbyists.

Like those two previous inquiries, it was never the investigation of a crime. It was an investigation in search of a crime.

As it transpired, it was every bit as misconceived and damaging to innocent parties as the two wider CCC inquiries. It was just part of the same old witch-hunt. When the background history is considered, one comes to the conclusion that the true motive of the CCC in engendering the SCP process was an endeavour to prove that Burke, Grill and their associates had behaved improperly (and perhaps illegally) in their attempt to have a parliamentary inquiry held into the State's so-called "iron ore policy".

This "criminal" aspect of the matter was confirmed by Commissioner Hammond, who was quoted by Robert Taylor in *The West Australian* in these terms:

> Mr Hammond had asked for the information so the CCC could advance its investigation, with a view to further hearings and possible disciplinary or criminal charges.[37]

Stated simply, the CCC was not interested in a mere breach of parliamentary rules for which there was normally no serious penalty. It was interested in establishing "criminality".

Be in no doubt that there were very big stakes involved here, both

---

[37] *The West Australian*, 22 March, 2007, p. 5

at a legal and commercial level. The history behind the setting up of the SCP had its genesis with the substantial iron ore deposit at Shovelanna, 25km from Mt Newman in WA's mineral-rich Pilbara, and a dispute between the giant Hamersley Iron Pty Ltd (Rio) on the one hand and two junior companies, Cazaly Resources Limited and its partner Echelon Resources Limited (our client), on the other.

When Rio Tinto failed to apply correctly for the renewal of the mining lease for Shovelanna on 26 August 2005, Cazaly made claim for the tenement, as it was entitled to under the Mining Act. In normal circumstances, Cazaly would have succeeded and been registered as the lessee. However, on 21 September 2005 Rio Tinto lodged a submission with the Government requesting it to use its discretionary power to refuse Cazaly's application under rarely applied Section 111A of the *Mining Act*.

On 21 April 2006, John Bowler, as Resource Minister, peremptorily terminated Cazaly's application, thus allowing the highly valuable tenement to be retained by Rio.

This most unusual, but legal, action was taken on advice to the Minister from his department. That advice was "that special treatment" be accorded to iron ore tenement holders (at that time it effectively meant just Rio Tinto and BHP) and a much broader discretion exercised than would normally be allowed under the Mining Act. This advice was given pursuant to the Mines Department's "iron ore policy".

I emphasise that there was no mention of this policy in legislation and it had been put in place informally as an administrative tool by departmental officers.

The trigger for the initial demand by the CCC for documentation from the Council and the subsequent setting up of the SCP was evidence given by witnesses at the Smiths Beach hearing. That was testimony to the effect that Cazaly and Echelon were requesting, through its lawyers and my consulting company, to have an inquiry of the "iron ore policy" established in a committee of the Council.

We always openly admitted that fact, but strongly assert that such action is completely proper. The CCC, on the other hand, built its case against us on the erroneous assumption that such a pursuit was illicit. As history shows, the SCP miscarried in all of its principal objectives.

It is apparent the SCP treated the so-called "iron ore policy" as a form of holy writ. From the perspective of much of the mining industry, there are at least three serious problems with this view:

(a) The policy appears not to be in writing and consequently can be arbitrarily interpreted.
(b) The policy was not accessible to the mining industry or to the public and couldn't be scrutinised.
(c) The policy is not mentioned in the *Mining Act*, and consequently had an uncertain legal standing.

It is believed in mining circles that the policy had been used for 40 years, right up to 2007, to lock new and/or smaller aspiring companies out of the Pilbara – the world's most productive iron ore province and Australia's most valuable export product. Multinationals Rio Tinto and BHP had dominated the region, almost exclusively, for many years on the back of this vague policy. As a result, it has long been the subject of suspicion and hostility by many of Australia's smaller mining companies.

After the Minister terminated Cazaly's application, Cazaly's board sought legal opinion from senior counsel. On 1 August 2006, Cazaly released an opinion by Wayne Martin QC (later Chief Justice) which concluded, "there was no ground or basis on which the Minister could lawfully exercise his powers under Section 111A of the Mining Act".

Cazaly briefed Gadens Lawyers and barrister Malcolm McCusker QC to challenge Minister Bowler's decision. (Mr McCusker subsequently became WA's Governor, but was then the State's best-known, and one of its most respected, barristers.)

On 4 August 2006, Cazaly sought a judicial review of the Minister's decision by the Supreme Court of WA. This was seriously big money litigation. Every element of the encounter was fully reported in the media.

On 28 August 2006, the court rejected Cazaly's application and a subsequent appeal to the High Court of Australia met a similar fate. That put an end to all judicial proceedings, but going back to the time before Minister Bowler had used Section 111A – that is, in February 2006 – Cazaly and Echelon had opened another battle front, and that was to seek a Legislative Council (SCEFO) inquiry into WA's so-called "iron ore policy".

Generally, it was proposed that an open inquiry would determine whether such a policy, as best it was publicly known at the time, was in the State's best interest. On 21 February 2006, Echelon engaged Burke and Grill to help bring about such an inquiry.

Cazaly had already taken on lobbyist Peter Clough for a similar mission. Brian and I brought in former Liberal Senator Noel Crichton-Browne to help with the task as the Liberals and their partners, the National Party, had a majority in the Upper House, where it was proposed such an inquiry be held.

I believe that our client's primary concept was designed to put Rio Tinto under considerable pressure so that it was more amenable to a negotiated settlement of the dispute. However, I also believe that it genuinely believed that the undisclosed "iron ore policy" was an affront to open government.

When Brian and I first met Echelon directors Matthew Rimes and Ian Middlemass on 21 February 2006, they requested that we co-operate with Cazaly directors Clive James and Nathan McMahon, Cazaly's lawyers Robert Edel and Alexander Jones from Gadens, and Cazaly's counsel, Malcolm McCusker, in initiating the inquiry.

We were also requested to work with Peter Clough, who apart from acting for Cazaly was also at times a lobbyist for BHP. Cazaly had, in anticipation of success with the Shovelanna tenement, arranged an offtake (sales) agreement with BHP.

Cazaly was the applicant for the Shovelanna tenement, but Echelon had negotiated a 14 per cent interest. It was explained that the tenement had been in existence in one form or another since 1972, had not been mined, and had only been lightly explored. The implication was that, apart from the fact that Rio Tinto had not properly renewed the tenement, it had possibly failed to work the deposit in accordance with the *Mining Act* and, but for the vague terms of the "iron ore policy", the tenement was liable for forfeiture.

Despite the lightness of the exploration program on the tenement, it was known that it contained millions of tonnes of high-grade ore and consequently was worth billions of dollars.

The SCEFO at the relevant times (between 30 October 2006 and 1 February 2007) comprised Chair Giz Watson (Greens), Ken Travers and Shelley Archer (both ALP), Anthony Fels and Nigel Hallett (both Liberal).

For those readers who are interested in background details, Chapter 4 of the SCP report dated November 2007, under the heading, "Background to the Establishment of The Committee", reasonably correctly sets out the critical matters that led to the setting up of the SCP.

I mention at this point that Mr Clough, our counterpart lobbyist employed by Cazaly, was never called as a witness and did not feature at all in the SCP inquiry. That is curious to say the least, as he was party to the whole plan, cooperated in its delivery and was privy to most of the same meetings and information as Brian Burke and me. This situation further confirmed that Burke, Grill and their close associates were the intended targets of the inquiry.

Thus, at the urging of the CCC, the SCP was set up. This potentially punitive inquiry should never have taken place. My primary ground for that view is that the decision by the SCEFO committee to inquire into the "iron ore policy" had not yet been taken. The SCP investigation was entirely premature. There was no decision to proceed with an inquiry into the iron ore industry and, in fact, it never went ahead.

Normally and inevitably, at the early stage of any serious inquiry before a parliamentary committee, a broad range of consultations with affected parties and stakeholders takes place. Many people, both inside and outside of Parliament, by necessity, become aware of a likely term of reference. Sometime it is even canvassed in the media. There is nothing confidential about these processes and nor should there be.

The CCC was not deterred by this line of logic, however. And when the matter of the so-called leaks was referred to the SCP, the CCC had a very significant, and in my view improper, influence on these proceedings. It was only much later, after many months of hearings, reports and legal consideration, that the folly of the exercise was revealed.

Although the SCP recommended criminal charges against a number of hapless individuals, as I explain below, those proposals were rejected by the Director for Public Prosecutions. Ultimately, it was all a giant waste of time. Unfortunately, that was only after much human damage was inflicted on blameless witnesses.

The committee members took themselves very seriously. On page iii of the Summary of the Final Report, it makes the pretentious boast:

> Shortly after embarking upon this inquiry, it became readily apparent that this was potentially one of the most important challenging inquiries in the history of the Legislative Council.

Such grandiloquence was not justified in the text of the report and wasn't shared by Upper House President Griffiths, who later said to me: "The whole matter was much ado about nothing."

Many in our community are unaware that the WA Parliament can, due to its ancient leftover powers, imprison citizens directly or refer persons for criminal charges. As happened in this case. I should mention that it is the contention of many legal authorities and other enlightened parliaments, including our own Federal Parliament, that while the essential democratic parliamentary privileges are just as important as they were when first implemented, the punitive powers of imprisonment are outdated, oppressive and unnecessary.

The SCP committee, if it was looking for illegality and criminal charges, as the CCC proclaimed, was beset with the problem that in those circumstances, where individuals' liberty and reputations were ultimately in jeopardy, the investigating body (that is, the SCP) should at least have been obliged to extend procedural fairness to the witnesses.

Unfortunately, the SCP was just not intended for such a task. While it may have been fit to decide on questions of its own procedures and privileges, it was never furnished to make recommendations on issues of forensic criminal guilt or innocence.

The whole process was dangerous from the start, as the following list of reasons highlight:

Firstly, witnesses were never advised at any time that they were exposed to any peril. Most, like me, attended the SCP unrepresented by legal counsel. I had not, at any relevant time, spoken to any member of the SCEFO or its officers and consequently could not have been a conduit for leaks. I was not aware that there was any suggestion that I might have transgressed in any way.

Second, to magnify dramatically the injustice of the procedural unfairness, all of the evidence was taken and heard *in camera*. It was a secret trial. In other words, those in jeopardy were never aware of the evidence being given against them and therefore had no way of responding to it.

Third, a witness against whom a finding is made has to be very careful as to how he or she expresses continued belief in his or her innocence. Any statement that contradicts the finding or reflects badly on the SCP can be punished as an archaic contempt of Parliament and imprisonment can follow.

Fourth, none of the members of the SCP was an experienced jurist trained to impartially sit in judgement on their peers.

Fifth, there was the make-up of the SCP. Murray Criddle as chairman and Barry House as one of its three members were unexceptional and unobjectionable. However, the appointment of Adele Farina was quite extraordinary. At the time of her appointment to the SCP in March 2007, she had only recently given highly damaging evidence to the CCC in public hearings against Brian Burke.

Among other things, she had accused him of blackmail. Her CCC evidence was adduced, without prior notice or warning, just before the Smiths Beach term of reference was closed. That meant that Brian had no possible way of responding to it or defending himself.

The manner in which Farina's evidence was presented by the CCC in the Smith Beach hearings (as I explain in Chapter 16, "Brian Burke – the 'godfather'") was outrageous and his lawyers were shocked at the scandalous denial of justice. Nor was the highly prejudicial evidence directly relevant to the term of reference, even if true.

Brian objected and ultimately his lawyers were able to press the CCC to disregard Farina's evidence altogether in the final Smiths Beach report.

Given this history, it was an enormous shock when Farina was appointed to the SCP where she would sit in judgement of Burke. It gave the appearance that the CCC was stage-managing the process. As might be expected, on two occasions during the SCP hearing Brian objected to the presence of Farina as part of the bench on the grounds of perceived "bias". On 10 September 2007, he raised the question of bias for the second time in these terms (in part):

> Adele has said at the hearing of the CCC that she believed that I was blackmailing her, that she was angry, that she was affronted, that she was upset and in a number of different ways she expressed views that I do not believe can be accommodated by her persistence on this committee … I fail to see how Adele can say these things about me and then sit in judgement on me. I will leave that for the committee to consider. It is an unfairness.

Farina did not step down. Nor, it would appear, was there any pressure on her from the other two members of the SCP or her party to withdraw. They seemed to be blind to the blatant danger of bias.

It is revealing to note the ultimate response on this question of "perceived bias" in the SCP's report in November 2007. Curiously, the Committee does not deny the bias. In fact, it almost glorified in it. The report stated:

> All Members of Parliament have a party, factional or friendship bias of some description and, if the no bias rule was applied strictly, it would be impossible to appoint Members to select committees of privilege.

This self-serving justification by the SCP ignores that what they perpetrated by including Farina was a flagrant denial of fair process.

Sixth, there was no settled avenue or process for review of findings, or appeal from them, as you would find in a court of law.

Seventh, was the role of the CCC. Its transcripts of bugged conversations formed a large part of the evidence. However, CCC officers gave additional secret evidence to the SCP on four occasions. Not even the identities of those CCC officers were disclosed. One was left with a secret trial with secret witnesses.

What an unbelievable farce. That evidence is secret to this day.

Unprecedentedly, the SCP was weaponised when barrister Phillip Urquhart, who had also worked extensively with the CCC as Counsel Assisting on its associated hearings on Smiths Beach, was present with the SCP during the second half of its hearings and appeared to do most of the interrogation. We can only presume that the CCC was not happy with progress to that date.

Eighth, the legal procedures developed over the years by the courts of justice to ensure fair hearings were not employed by the SCP. These principles and precepts were arrogantly swept aside by a committee that seemed to be proud of the fact that it was not obliged to conform to internationally recognised standards of fairness and equity. On page 400 of the SCP report, the Committee makes the following pompous and disdainful remark:

> Indeed, the Committee received many submissions from witnesses' legal counsel that objected in great length to the Committee's procedures and erroneously sought to compare the processes of a parliamentary committee to those commonly found in adversarial court proceedings.

This haughty statement must surely be entirely unacceptable in any modern society. The concept that a person could be tried and potentially sent to prison in the circumstances where they are not informed of the charge against them and, deprived of hearing and testing the evidence presented to condemn them, was eliminated in most British Parliamentary countries when the notorious Star Chamber was abolished in 1641.

The Star Chamber became, and continues to be, a prime symbol of the use and abuse of power by the establishment in England. The members of the SCP were unable to recognise that its methods were the same as the long-abolished tribunal.

As soon as Commissioner Hammond indicated that the CCC wanted to investigate possible "criminality", the Parliament should have indicated that that was a job for the police and the courts, not for Parliament. We now know that Parliament was encouraged by the CCC to embark upon a dangerous wild goose chase.

The standard adopted by the Legislative Council for interrogations are well below the minimums set out in the United Nations. For instance, Article 10 of the UN Universal Declaration of Human Rights clearly states:

> Everyone is entitled in full equity to a fair and public hearing by an independent and *impartial* tribunal (my emphasis) in the determination of their rights and obligations and of any criminal charges against them.

Somehow the SCP did not consider that this universal safeguard, to which Australia has subscribed for 65 years, applied to it.

Ninthly, the SCP seemed to focus almost exclusively on Brian Burke, Noel Crichton-Browne, me and those associated with us. That focus appeared to go well beyond the terms of reference. Just to remind you, the term of reference dealt exclusively with the question of whether there was an unauthorised disclosure from the SCEFO.

On my second appearance before the SCP, Mr Urquhart focused his interrogation on our lobbying fees, both by way of retainer and success fees. There appeared to be a preoccupation with whether we were likely to receive or did receive fees from Cazaly. At one stage in the hearing, on 8 October 2007, I was coerced at the demand of the SCP and against my strong protests, to ring my wife from the committee hearing room. Lesley did our business accounts and the SCP wanted to ascertain whether we received any payment from Cazaly.

My wife's answer was in the negative, but I couldn't understand why this line of questioning was being used. It had no direct relevance to the terms of reference. Quite naturally, I then became suspicious that Mr Urquhart was using the question of fees to discredit us. That is, in the same way that had been employed so odiously, but successfully, by the CCC in the Smiths Beach and Lobbyists terms of reference.

As explained earlier, the CCC in these two inquires made an exaggerated extravaganza of fees and deliberately amplified the success payments. In one case, involving Precious Metals of Australia, the CCC gave the media the idea that Brian and I had received a success fee of $1.7 million. Headlines across Australia trumpeted the allegation. The true figure was $70,000.

I wrote asking that the information be corrected. The CCC ignored my request. *The Australian* ran a small retraction. I believe that the CCC had a strategy to make us look greedy and excessively self-interested. Having established that concept, it was possible to make people believe almost anything about us.

In the instance of the SCP, the committee – especially after Mr Urquhart took the role of the inquisitor – became obsessed in trying to establish that Burke and Grill were employed by Cazaly and either received fees from that company or may have become entitled to such fees. As explained earlier, we were engaged by Cazaly's junior partner (14 per cent) Echelon, *not* by Cazaly.

Our success fee with our client (Echelon) was quite modest and should not have been of any interest to the SCP. In fact, during my first interrogation by the SCP the question of fees was not a subject of discussion. It was only later, when the CCC effectively took over the proceeding of the SCP and Mr Urquhart assumed the questioning, did the subject of fees apparently become a critical matter of interest.

Privilege committee findings

I have mentioned above that the SCP held its inquiry *in camera* and that witnesses were not privy to other witnesses' evidence. Also, I advised that most of this evidence remains secret to this day. The exception to that is the limited transcript evidence selected by the Committee to publicly justify its report's conclusions.

However, the CCC contended that it was being fair just because it wrote to each relevant witness once the report was drafted, but before its public tabling in Parliament, informing of any adverse findings against the witness and inviting comment.

Letters were sent out to affected witnesses on 16 October 2007 and the deadline for comment was 23 October 2007 at 5.00pm. Just six working days to review and comment on a 496-page report! But we were never given access to the secret SCP inquiry transcript. This was never a serious exercise in fairness by the SCP and CCC.

On the innocent impression that I was simply being called to give background information, I did not seek to be legally represented at the hearings. The draft findings came as a bolt out of the blue and caused me to immediately engage highly reputed Herbert Smith Freehills lawyers Steven Penglis and Ante Golem.

The draft findings in the SCP report, as they applied specifically to me, were as follows:

The Committee's Preliminary Findings

Finding 1

The Committee finds that Mr Brian Burke, Mr Julian Grill, Mr Noel Crichton-Browne, Mr Nathan McMahon, Managing Director, Cazaly Resources Limited, Mr Clive Jones, Joint Managing Director Cazaly Resources Limited, Mr Robert Edel, Partner, DLA Phillips Fox, and Mr Alexander Jones, Senior Associate, DLA Phillips Fox, together devised and implemented a strategy to attempt to influence the proceedings of the Standing Committee on Estimate and Financial Operations for an improper purpose, being the opportunity for commercial gain by way of the subsequent possibility of influencing and manipulating legal proceedings then on foot before the Court of Appeal of the Supreme Court of Western Australia.

Specifically, the strategy involved using a parliamentary committee inquiry to:

Discredit the Government's iron ore policy; and

> Encourage Rio Tinto Limited to settle legal proceedings on terms favourable to Cazaly Resources Limited.

The Committee further finds that a central element of the strategy was to obtain information by way of disclosures of the deliberations of the Standing Committee on Estimates and Financial Operations.

This attempt to influence the proceedings of the Standing Committee on Estimates and Financial Operations for an improper purpose is a contempt of Parliament.

> **Finding 2**
>
> The Committee finds that, on a date unknown, Mr Julian Grill provided Mr Brian Burke with copies of documents that had been requested of Mr Grill by the Committee in a private hearing, and that Mr Grill had further advised Mr Burke of the fact that those documents had been requested by the Committee.
>
> The provision of the documents and the accompanying disclosure of the private proceedings of the Committee is a breach of privilege and a contempt of the Parliament.

My lawyers (Herbert Smith Freehills) were aghast at the intellectual and legal flaws of logic and denial of justice in the findings and responded swiftly and definitively by letter, dated 23 October 2007.

In brief, Mr Penglis made the following points:

1. The Report's findings were beyond and outside the terms of reference and the Committee had no jurisdiction.
2. The evidence and basis of the findings were not identified. The Committee was requested to furnish same.
3. The Committee actively misled me as to the nature of the hearings.

Readers may not be surprised to learn that none of Mr Penglis' questions was responded to.

On 30 October 2007, Malcolm McCusker, the Parliamentary Inspector of the Corruption and Crime Commission, alarmed at what appeared to be a SCP running off the rails, wrote to the President of the Council, Nick Griffiths. The letter referred to a joint legal opinion by Mr McCusker and senior NSW barrister Richard Price, which had already been sent to the SCP. The sending of such a letter is extremely unusual. Indeed, I know of no other instance.

Writing on behalf of DLA Phillips Fox lawyers Robert Edel and Alexander Jones, Mr McCusker said he and Mr Price believed there were serious issues with the conduct of, and procedure adopted by, the Select Committee of Privilege. They had grave concerns.

While not being permitted to provide details, because of Council confidentiality rules they said:

- The Committee had no authority to deal with issues outside the terms of reference.
- It appeared the Committee had pre-judged a number of issues and was not approaching those issues in an impartial, unbiased way.
- The Committee had acted contrary to standing orders and in breach of the principles of natural justice and fairness.
- As a result, their clients had been unfairly treated and the Committee's fact-finding processes and its conclusions had been, and would be, seriously flawed.

The letter suggested President Griffiths could see details of their concerns by obtaining from the Committee the joint McCusker/ Price legal opinion. If the Committee did not comply with that request, Mr Griffiths is advised to refer the matter to the House for possible investigation of the issues raised.

President Griffiths replied on 6 November 2007, agreeing that the matters raised by Mr McCusker and Mr Price were serious.

He said the SCP was due to report to the House on 15 November. If there was any question of the Committee having acted outside of its terms of reference, or contrary to correct procedure, the House had the opportunity to refer the matter to the Standing Committee on Procedure and Privileges for consideration.

Mr Griffiths asked for permission to table Mr McCusker's letter in the House.

There are two interesting elements of the President's sympathetic reply. Firstly, he makes it clear that although the matters raised in the joint opinion are "serious" his hands are tied and he would (reluctantly) have to leave a decision to "the House". That is, where political, rather than legal, considerations would be paramount.

Secondly, he asked permission to table Mr McCusker's letter in the House. It was so tabled on the 15 November, at the same time that the SCP final report was tabled. The tabling of McCusker's letter had no effect on the Legislative Council, which had already set its political course, as dictated by ALP and Coalition party leadership.

With the media, however, it was a slightly different matter.

At this time, it was blindingly apparent that President Nick Griffiths was becoming very concerned and uncomfortable, if not alarmed, at the CCC's incursion into parliamentary matters and also by the secret activities of the SCP.

There is no doubt that, as President of the Council, Mr Griffiths had his own sources of information concerning the CCC's highly questionable influence over the proceedings of the SCP. No doubt his concern was likely to have been inflamed by the fact that the first draft finding, as notified to me and as mentioned above, was straight out of the CCC playbook.

An assertion of "improper purpose" in an alleged attempt to influence the proceedings of the SCP over the "iron ore policy" was the central matter in a separately proposed CCC inquiry, as brought up in CCC open session of 28 February 2007. In the final analysis, this separate CCC inquiry did not go anywhere because it was a breach of parliamentary privilege as explained earlier in this chapter. But the almost identical wording was just too much of a coincidence.

Also, as had been eloquently explained in the letters from Steven Penglis and Malcolm McCusker, the question of "improper purpose" was clearly outside of the terms of reference for the SCP. I can also disclose, although technically I am probably breaking the law of Parliament because of the secret nature of the SCP inquiry, that "improper purpose" was not even raised with me as an issue when I gave evidence on two occasions. Nor was it included in the terms of reference for the SCP inquiry.

It is quite alarming, but it appears "improper purpose" had not been mentioned in any of the SCP proceedings before evidence had been completed and the report drafted.

Notwithstanding, "improper purpose" suddenly and inexplicably turns up as the main finding of the SCP. It is fair to surmise that the CCC had got up its own term of reference through the back door. Unlike Adele Farina, Nick Griffiths was an experienced court lawyer who appreciated immediately that something had gone badly wrong in the SCP.

CCC triggers its decline

Until the exposure of the draft report to some of the witnesses, the activities of the SCP had gone on under the radar and free of any scrutiny.

Much more alarmingly, politicians were intimidated by the CCC's extensive powers and its imposing media-created standing. Several had already seen their careers snuffed out, or severely jeopardised.

Perhaps Mr Griffiths appreciated that it was a very unhealthy situation. I believe that was the motivation for his public tabling of the McCusker letter. Mr McCusker was the most publicly respected lawyer in WA, while Mr Price was one of the most sought-after barristers in the country.

I maintain that in tabling Mr McCusker's letter simultaneously with the SCP report, Mr Griffiths knew that it would be a significant counter point to the report and its findings.

He would also have appreciated that it could raise considerable doubts about the shrouded interplay between the SCP and the CCC. As subsequent events demonstrated, he was correct. Unsuspected then, the tabling of the McCusker letter was a turning point. That was the day when, imperceptibly at first, the CCC's star began to wane.

Surprisingly, it was also the time when the critical seeds of destruction were sown for the Carpenter Government. The CCC and the SCP had just gone too far. Too many people concluded that this SCP report was not credible.

The SCP quoted the *sub judice* rule as the second basis for its implausible finding of "improper purpose".[38] The SCP dealt with the evidence for such a finding in one paragraph in an extremely superficial way, which was fatuously ridiculous and convinced no one.

The third justification for the finding of "improper purpose" was a faulty allegation that "Cazaly disguised the fact that it was promoting the inquiry".

It was never a secret that Cazaly and Echelon were promoting such an inquiry. In fact, when I approached the Association of Mining Exploration Companies (AMEC) to support the proposed SCEFO inquiry into the "iron ore policy", I made it abundantly clear that it was being promoted by Cazaly and Echelon. I went so far as to suggest that AMEC contact Cazaly and Echelon to discuss the proposed inquiry.

AMEC took this advice, before writing to the SCEFO supporting an inquiry.

There is a clear paper trail documenting those facts and it is very hard to understand how these and other similar facts could escape the attention of the SCP in drafting its final report.

Lastly, on this subject of "improper purpose", I ask why this issue was not raised with me on either occasion when I was examined; and why, when my lawyer Steven Penglis requested in his letter to the SCP of 23 October 2007 some grounds for such a finding, they were not provided. One can only assume that the issues were not raised with me and the grounds were not provided to Mr Penglis because the committee was aware of just how fragile and susceptible to scrutiny the committee's reasons were.

The SCP insensitively damaged quite a number of innocent individuals, as will be shown.

Cazaly company director Nathan McMahon was one against whom the SCP recommended the investigation of a criminal charge. It related to answers he gave to Mr Urquhart about Cazaly's relation-

---

[38] Report, pp. 81-2. See p. 82, para 7.14.

ship with Brian Burke and me. The SCP performed intellectual contortions to try to prove that Brian and I had entered into a contract of employment with Cazaly. It seems evident that that was because the CCC and the SCP wanted to tie us into a hypothetical $600,000 success payment from Cazaly.

It is my belief that the CCC then wanted to somehow take the next step of discrediting us as "venal" and then to allege some sort of specific corruption against us. How else can the CCC's fetish with the success payment be explained? How else could an inquiry into an alleged leak from a parliamentary committee turn into a witch hunt over a possible success fee?

There was evidence of a payment of an *ex-gratia* success fee:

> At 1.22pm on the 25th May 2006, Mr Burke emailed Mr Grill to advise that on that day Mr McMahon had offered them 100,000 fully paid Cazaly shares if they succeeded with the Shovelanna matter by Christmas, in addition to the success fee from Echelon. Mr Burke advised Mr Grill that he had accepted Mr McMahon's offer.[39]

Apart from that email, which all of the relevant parties could not recall in any detail, there was no clear evidence of the success fee, although no witness denied it may have been offered. Nor was there any motive or reason to deny it.

From our point of view, it was a non-issue, but for its own reasons the CCC made an immense fuss over it. When Mr McMahon gave evidence, he was (according to the report) examined at length over the success fee. And then threatened with criminal prosecution because he could not remember the detail of the offer he made to Brian.

As far as I was concerned, it amounted to no more than a possible future *ex-gratia* offer. All very nice, but certainly not legally enforceable and certainly it did not amount to an "engagement". We strictly took our instructions from Echelon's directors.

Given these facts, it is very hard to understand how any responsible body could make a finding of false evidence. Ultimately, my

---

[39] Report. p. 92.

judgement proved correct. The Director of Public Prosecutions refused outright to prefer charges against Mr McMahon.

I canvas the issue of Nathan McMahon because of the threat that a covert and largely unaccountable body like the CCC, linked to a secret inquiry like the SCP, poses to ordinary citizens.

Forget the politicians and lobbyists like myself for the moment. Mr McMahon was the managing director of a small WA mining company. He was trying to earn an honest living. He had an impeccable record. His company was operating lawfully pursuant to the State's *Mining Act*.

Unlike Rio, he was not petitioning the Government for special favours. Cazaly was a junior Australian company acting on the best legal advice it could buy and with an experienced lobbyist, Peter Clough, to guide it through the political minefield.

Instead of being treated fairly and respectfully, Mr McMahon was tried in a secret court before being paraded as a delinquent and ultimately made the subject of a seriously threatened criminal charges.

He had no idea that he would be accused of criminal conduct. It would have come as a bombshell. Images of a lamb to the slaughter come to mind.

There were five referrals by the SCP to the DPP for investigation of criminal prosecution for alleged false evidence under s. 47 of the Criminal Code. Those were in relation to Noel Crichton-Browne, Brian Burke, Anthony Fels, Shelley Archer and Nathan McMahon.

Quite properly, the DPP subsequently refused to proceed with them.

There were nine other non-criminal findings of either alleged unauthorised disclosing proceedings of the committee, or asserted false evidence. They attracted minor parliamentary penalties, such as making an apology, but none can really be taken with any degree of confidence or gravitas because of the dangerous degree to which natural justice, due legal process and transparency were denied to the witnesses.

Everyone appreciates that parliamentary rules may make proceedings at a SCP inquiry confidential, but some critical threshold questions arise: Are conversations preparatory to settling the terms of reference and the arrangements prior to commencement of taking evidence, subject to confidentiality? Distinguished lawyers would argue in the negative.

Almost invariably, suggestions for terms of reference for an inquiry come from a third party, as happened in this case. It is natural that there will be discussion between third parties and at least one member of a committee as to how the terms of reference might be framed and who might support those terms of reference.

Simultaneously, members of a proposed inquiry panel shall, and do, seek advice from other interested persons and experts as to whether an inquiry is wise and whether the terms of reference are adequate.

In fact, most, if not all members of the SCEFO, took the position that conversations and proceedings leading up to an inquiry were *not* confidential.

Shelley Archer was one of the obvious CCC targets of the wider Smiths Beach/Lobbyists inquiries and of the SCP inquiry. I hold the view this was solely because of her long friendship with Brian Burke. It was "guilt by association".

Ms Archer was born on 15 October 1958 as one of 16 children in a working-class family. Her father was a battler who had become an official of the Australian Workers Union in Derby. For many years she was a single supporting mother who obtained work in the union movement and married well-known unionist Kevin Reynolds. Becoming a member of parliament was the fulfilment of a dream for her.

Archer had been in Parliament for less than a year when she was appointed to the SCEFO, so she was still very inexperienced. Archer indicated to the SCP:

> The matter that was before the committee, in my view, was not an inquiry and could be discussed.

That is a similar position to that embraced by Watson, the Chair.

Finally on this subject, I would venture the opinion that committee confidentiality procedures were developed over the decades to protect only highly confidential testimony and the premature release of reports. They do not apply to discussion that may take place prior to the inquiry being commenced.

I happily concede that Archer passed on some limited information to Brian Burke concerning progress towards setting up the inquiry. Fels imparted even less such information to Mr Crichton-Browne. No argument from me there. But were these transgressions? Did they warrant investigation for criminal proceedings? The relevant facts and a history of what next transpired comes up resoundingly in the negative.

Anthony Fels, analogous to Shelley Archer, was a comparatively new and inexperienced Member of Parliament (he took office on 25 May 2005). While Archer was approached by Brian to move for the setting up of an inquiry into the State's "iron ore policy", Fels was similarly approached by Mr Crichton-Browne. He advised Mr Crichton-Browne on the progress made on establishing this important investigation into Australia's most significant export industry.

All of this was done before any terms of reference were settled and before there was any final decision to proceed with the inquiry. His friendship with Mr Crichton-Browne appears to be the major motivating factor for the CCC attention.

Fels always strongly asserted that he "did not disclose any deliberations" of the SCEFO.[40]

The SCP also made findings against Brian Burke. Firstly, for passing on to our client and their lawyers two separate sets of information provided by Archer concerning the disposition of SCEFO members towards the holding of an inquiry into the "iron ore policy". The SCP deemed these to be "secondary disclosures".

They were very rare findings indeed, as nowhere is "secondary disclosure" defined or proscribed. The SCP could not point to any precedent for a similar finding. It is a dubious concept and it would certainly not stand up in a court of law. No penalty against Brian was recommended by the SCP on the first of these two findings of sec-

---

[40] Report, p. 272.

ondary disclosures. On the second, however, it demanded an apology.

More serious, though, was the finding by the SCP that Brian gave false evidence to the SCP committee. It took on a more acute aspect because potentially that could have triggered criminal prosecution and jail. So far as can be made out from the limited actual evidence made available in the report, his testimony was reasonably accurate, given that there were (understandably) some matters that he could not recall.

Essentially, it all boiled down to the question of whether discussions prior to the establishment of the inquiry were committee deliberations, as discussed above. It is not conclusive, as the DPP did not publish detailed reasons, but it would not be an unfair inference to suggest that when the DPP declined to take the matter further, it was agreeing that Burke (and Watson, Fels and Archer) were correct in that their disclosures made prior to the setting-up of the inquiry were not part of the deliberations.

Mr Crichton-Browne was dealt a similar hand by the SCP to that of Burke. The so-called "facts" were slightly different, but he was ordered to apologise and to be investigated for criminal proceedings. Once again the DPP declined to proceed with the SCP recommendation of criminal proceedings.

Additionally, the SCP made the following finding against me:

> Between 13th June 2007 and 10th September 2007, Mr Julian Grill provided Mr Brian Burke with copies of documents that had been requested of Mr Grill by the Committee in a private hearing and that Mr Grill had further advised Mr Burke of the fact that these documents had been requested by the Committee. The provision of those documents and the accompanying disclosure of the private proceedings of the Committee is a breach of privilege and a contempt of Parliament.[41]

I was ordered to apologise.

---

[41] Report, p. 398.

A lawyer or a trained observer could see what was happening here. The SCP, having failed to produce any adverse matter of substance against me and others, was trying to score on a technical procedural matter.

Moreover, there are two major flaws with this finding. Apart from the fact that the SCP on its own admission[42] was incapable of identifying the documents, there was absolutely *no* evidence that I had told Brian that the "documents had been requested by the Committee".

This was an unacceptable distortion of the evidence by the SCP.

Secondly, I was confident, as were my lawyers,[43] later supported by an eminent Queens Counsel, that the provision of my own private papers to Brian was not a disclosure to him of SCP proceedings. Later events justified that confidence.

In summary on this issue, there is no role for the CCC in matters of this type. The unfortunate incursion of bodies such as the CCC into the SCP is entirely aberrant and without precedent in the British Westminster system. It should never happen again.

The tabling of the SCP report

After nearly nine months of secrecy, the SCP finally broke cover on 13 November 2007 when Chairman Murray Criddle tabled the final report in the Legislative Council. It was virtually an unamended copy of the Draft Report. However, those who thought that was the end of the matter were badly mistaken.

The report exploded on to the media and its consequences were to dominate political events for weeks. It was not readily apparent then, but ultimately it would become a major factor in the defeat of the Carpenter Government in the 6 September 2008 State Election. The report was the catalyst for a political tectonic plate shift on the West Coast.

The West Australian sensationalised the SCP report, with the whole of its front page consumed and follow-up stories taking up all

---

[42] Report, pp. 395-6.
[43] See Herbert Smith Freehills letter of 23 October 2007 (appendix number has to be added in due course, see reference to it on page 63 above).

of page 10.⁴⁴ The front-page headline screamed: "Secret MPs probe finds 10 guilty of contempt" – and included unflattering photographs of Mr McMahon, Mr Crichton-Browne, Archer, Burke and Fels.

Page 10 featured large pictures of Adele Farina, Barry House and Murray Criddle. A sub-headline shrieked: "Five face criminal charges".

The media, generally, really gave it the treatment.

However, it was not quite the "tour de force" that the CCC had been hoping for. In a sub-headline, and prominently in the front-page story, was the news that, "QC Malcolm McCusker had 'grave concerns' about the way the committee was run". *The West* had picked up on Mr McCusker's letter, tabled by Legislative Council President Nick Griffiths.

As I have written previously, Mr McCusker was WA's pre-eminent barrister and had championed and won the release of a number of innocent, wrongly convicted individuals – notably the exoneration of Andrew Mallard who had wrongly spent 12 years in jail for the murder of Pamela Lawrence; and the exculpation of the Mickleberg brothers, who spent years in prison on the basis of phoney evidence manufactured by the police.

Additionally, he had a rare quality: he was brave. Consequently, when Mr McCusker repeated his misgiving in the media about the proceedings and findings of the SCP inquiry, people took notice.

Intriguingly, Committee Chair and Leader of the Greens Giz Watson was also vocally critical of the report. She stated:

> I think that they have applied a very high test ... I've looked into this closely and I can find no similar finding in any Westminster Parliament, that simply discussing the possibility of an inquiry should lead to the finding of contempt.⁴⁵

Brian Burke, on the phone from Ireland to *The West Australian*, summed it up neatly:

---

⁴⁴ *The West Australian*, 14 November 2007.
⁴⁵ *The West Australian*, 14 November 2007, p. 1.

The findings were head scratchingly bizarre. How can it be contempt to repeat gossip that was not confidential about an inquiry that was never held? The decision to hold secret meetings meant the committee was fatally flawed from the start.[46]

The key to future events was that the tabling of the report was in fact an unintended watershed for the CCC in respect to its critical relations with *The West Australian*. More importantly, it was to lead to a public falling-out between the Carpenter Government and the editorial staff of *The West*. At that time, *The West*, as the only local daily newspaper, dominated the media.

However, in respect to the SCP, while sensationally covering the report, the paper effectively backed Parliamentary Inspector of the CCC Malcolm McCusker against the CCC. From then on, the CCC did not have the same traction with the media.

By way of example of how decisively *The West* turned on the SCP I refer to the story by the newspaper's State Political Editor, Robert Taylor, of 14 November 2007. After Taylor referred to the shockwaves in the legal and parliamentary circles that had accompanied the release of the SCP report and Mr McCusker's doubts about that report, Taylor said:

> The opinion of Mr McCusker, appointed by Attorney-General Jim McGinty as the watchdog of the CCC, cannot be ignored just because usual suspects Brian Burke, Julian Grill and Noel Crichton-Browne are involved …

Taylor went on to ask whether the CCC and not Parliament was setting parliamentary processes and definitions, commenting that the CCC appeared to have taken control of the SCP inquiry, used secretive methods and evidence, and had its own lawyer seconded into the SCP. He observed that such actions would have an impact in the way democracy would work in the State.

He then wrote:

> The bottom line is that this inquiry came about because

---

[46] *The West Australian*, 21 December, 1994.

people were discussing what a committee may or may not inquire into.

That's what parliamentary committees do.

It's hard to see how they will operate in the future if they can't discuss the prospects of an inquiry with people outside their own walls.

And how does Mr McGinty decide on the committee's recommendation to assess a finding of false evidence against his political enemy, Mr Burke, when his appointee, Mr McCusker, has such serious misgivings about the process?[47]

The Carpenter Government, however, after the report's release and under the influence of Attorney-General McGinty made a number of strategic errors. It misread the shift in sentiment at *The West*.

The first error was continued behind-the-scenes support of the CCC's involvement in the parliamentary committee process. The second was to abandon the basic principles of natural justice and persist with endorsement of the secret SCP inquiry report, despite Mr McCusker's severe misgivings.

The Government unsoundly calculated that the ascendant popularity of the CCC was such that principle and precedent could be put at risk. At that time, the fact that broad public opinion was still running hotly and strongly against Burke and Grill and anyone close to them was masking the fact that in small, but growing, sections of the media – and in large components of the legal profession, in some elements of the business community and even portions of the ALP and union movement – there was the beginnings of disquiet over the spectre of "secret police" style CCC oppressing the populace.

Carpenter and McGinty appear to have been blind to this developing shift in the public mood.

A third error flowed from that blindness, but still came out of left field. Rewinding to 7 November 2007, a week before the tabling of the report, Taylor wrote a front-page story in *The West* under the headline: "Furore looms over secret MPs probe".

---

[47] *The West Australian*, 14 November 2007, p. 10.

The first paragraph of Taylor's story set the scene:

> A political firestorm is brewing over the use of CCC tapes at a parliamentary inquiry which threatens the careers of top Perth lawyers and business people.

Taylor clearly had prior access to information touched upon by Malcolm McCusker's letter of "grave concern" to Nick Griffiths.

Taylor followed up his story in the next day's newspaper with a further article on the covert hearings, the questionable and alarming use of the CCC tapes and the Carpenter Government's resort to secrecy on a number of other contentious fronts. This second story was headed: "Old-style secrecy makes a comeback".

Both of these high-profile stories contained information about the extraordinary use of CCC covertly taped material in the SCP inquiry. As mentioned, these stories preceded the public tabling of the SCP report. It was supposedly confidential information, up until the publication of the report on 13 November 2007.

This compounding third mistake came about when, on 13 November 2007, the Legislative Council resolved to investigate the "leaks" of confidential SCP report material that was the basis of Taylor's two articles.

Taylor was the obvious target of the inquiry. Murray Criddle moved the motion to set up the new inquiry, and it was strongly supported by the Carpenter Government, which controlled the numbers.

The West did not miss the point that the new Privileges Committee inquiry was aimed at its State Political Editor, and the fact that this committee would not bother to investigate who actually made the leak, only who received it. As the new inquiry had the potential to exact punitive measures up to a jail term for Taylor, it was privately viewed by *The West* as a declaration of war.

In the final analysis, the new Taylor Privileges Committee inquiry, without even calling Taylor as a witness, or seemingly anyone else, decided that Taylor's "conduct offends the dignity of the House", but on this occasion (recommends) "no further action" [48] (my emphasis).

---

[48] Findings and Recommendations, L.C. Standing Committee on Procedure and Privileges Report 14 of 37th Parliament, December 2007, p. 6.

It appeared then that a much more judicious approach had prevailed in the Legislative Council. However, this is where the Carpenter Government made its fourth mistake.

The Government Leader in the Council, Kim Chance, would not accept the report of the Taylor Privileges Committee and successfully moved to have the matter held over to 2008. This was a grave miscalculation. No self-respecting metropolitan newspaper was going to allow its chief state political reporter to be seen to be swinging in the breeze for weeks or months without some retaliation. Paul Murray in an opinion piece in *The West* commented this way:

> The effect of that (non-acceptance of the report) is to keep an axe hanging over Taylor's head – and to intimidate other journalists. Now, Mr Chance is not a complete fool – although a casual observer might be excused for arguing about that on this occasion. But the likelihood is that he has been encouraged to take the stance by others in the Left faction, more intimately associated with the nitty gritty of these issues than he.[49]

By refusing to accept the committee report, the ALP was seemingly keeping open other limited options – one of which was a jail term for Robert Taylor. One wonders what advice Attorney-General McGinty was giving to the ALP parliamentarians at this critical juncture.

Thus, the battle lines between *The West* and the Carpenter Government were set.

It was a battle that was taken on by the Government in the full flight of its arrogance. It was always destined to lose it and that was the way the battle ultimately went. The Government lost the Treasury benches at the next election in less than a year on 23 September 2008. I deal with this in more detail in Chapter 14, "2008 Election: A CCC casualty".

More immediately, what followed during November 2007 was a torrent of stories in *The West* questioning the reasonableness of the CCC methods in a democratic and open society. Murray, writing an

---

[49] *The West Australian*, 11 December 2007, p. 20.

opinion piece on 11 December 2007, concisely summed up the situation as follows:

> Parliamentary Committees rarely have clean hands and in WA they have a long history of acting from crass political motive. That a body with the covert powers of the CCC would hand over phone bug evidence to a group of politicians with axes to grind was always going to be explosive.

The fifth substantial misjudgement was perpetrated when Premier Carpenter self-righteously announced on 14 November 2007 that he would move to have Shelley Archer expelled from the ALP after she resisted his strident demands for her immediate resignation.

Paul Omodei, the Leader of the Liberal Party, followed suit by announcing that he would move for the expulsion of Anthony Fels. It was big news. Nothing like it had happened in WA political history. It provided a front-page story in *The West* the next morning. Carpenter's demand and motion were perceived by many people as being petty, politically divisive, distracting and ultimately bound to fail.

They were thought to be petty because even if the so-called contempt by Archer and Fels were properly found (which most experts severely questioned), they were certainly at the very lower end of the scale. It led in due course to the CFMEU's Kevin Reynolds (the partner of Archer) leaving the ALP and depriving the party of the CFMEU's important financial support.

Contrary to popular belief, an ALP leader cannot on his own account expel a member. There are constitutional forms to be followed. Those proper forms and processes were simply ignored. Archer was given no opportunity to be heard or defend herself on the question of her expulsion. Unhappily, it appears that Carpenter was motivated by pure politics.

Postscript: The aftermath

No one was going to spell it out publicly, but it was readily apparent that Mr McCusker's well-publicised condemnation of the highly questionable SCP process had shaken the Council members and officials.

It was discernible to all but the most recalcitrant MPs that in modern times in a free country it is not acceptable to strip selective "targets" of basic civil rights and legal protection by means of a secret trial. Further, it was appreciated by most that it was not acceptable that the "targets" were unaware that they were in jeopardy. Nor was it fair that the evidence brought against these unsuspecting witnesses was intentionally hidden, even in large part after the findings were brought down.

It was even more apparent (as I shall detail below) to the more fair-minded MPs that it was anathema to any concept of justice to bludgeon acceptance of doubtful committee decisions and demand a confession of guilt in the form of an apology by threat of a jail term. Not even courts of law have the power to coerce compliance with its verdicts in this egregious way. These powers in the hands of the WA Parliament are positively medieval and repugnant.

Remember, these dubious findings by Parliament on the subject of contempt of parliament are not reviewable or appealable. Not even the Australian High Court, the country's otherwise supreme legal authority, had the power to overturn them. For this reason, most Westminster-style parliaments around the world have dispensed with this archaic power to imprison for contempt.

Unfortunately, as I shall explain below, the WA Parliament has an ugly historical record of employing this brutal penal power.

Interestingly, although no MP openly criticised the SCP findings, by its subsequent public actions the Council began the process of distancing itself from the report and establishing the process of reform.

The first step, as referred to above, was for the Standing Committee on Procedures and Privileges to recommend that no action be taken against Robert Taylor.[50] This Standing Committee was quite differently constituted to the Special Parliamentary Committee of Privilege (SCP) that has been extensively referred to above and

---

[50] Report No. 14, Standing Committee on Procedures and Privileges, December 2007.

which had considered matters relating to the "iron ore policy". The Standing Committee was chaired by the President of the Legislative Council, Mr Griffiths (ALP), and it took a very different approach to that adopted by the SCP.

Unlike the SCP, the Standing Committee dealt with the Taylor issue within a few days. It looked at the *prima facie* evidence, concluded quickly that no harm had been done, decided not to call witnesses and proposed that no action be taken.

Kim Chance (ALP), Leader of the Government in the Upper House and a Left faction member, unadvisedly delayed the acceptance of this Standing Committee's report until the first session of Parliament in 2008. In doing so he foolishly alienated *The West*, as mentioned above. I have some sympathy for Chance, however, as it would appear that he was simply carrying out orders "from above", as surmised by Paul Murray.

Secondly, there was a markedly different attitude by the Griffiths-chaired Standing Committee to that adopted by Premier Carpenter on the question of expulsion from Parliament of Shelley Archer. Carpenter badly over-played his hand when he demanded that Archer and Fels be expelled from Parliament.

Academic political analyst professors David Black and Peter van Onselen both expressed doubts about the legitimacy of the process.[51] Consequently, however, when it became apparent the banishment of Archer from the ALP had both left her as a free agent to vote how she pleased and destroyed the Carpenter Government's wafer-thin 18-17 majority in the Legislative Council, the move lost much of its political lustre.

One of Archer's first steps was to help defer the Carpenter Government legislation on prostitution regulation.

When it came to the proposed expulsion of Archer and Fels from Parliament, outside of the hard-line members of the ALP there was virtually no support in the Legislative Council. The expulsion moves failed.

It was evident that many of the Upper House members were dis-

---

[51] *The West Australian*, 17 November 2007, p. 4.

turbed at what had gone on in secret in the SCP, nominally in their names. Additionally, the majority of members were highly surprised at the extent to which the SCP had seemingly been taken over by the CCC.

The third distinction between this more circumspect Council on the one hand and the Carpenter Government on the other was the Council's attitude to the penalties recommended in the SCP report. The SCP had recommended, and the Council initially endorsed, an order that Brian Burke provide an unreserved written apology to the Upper House for the so-called secondary unauthorised disclosure mentioned above.

The Council had a potent, but none the less outrageous, weapon by which to enforce such an order, as it had the capacity to send Brian to jail if he refused to apologise (see SCP Report No 16 of the 37th Parliament) and therefore admit his culpability.

As a consequence of this implied threat of imprisonment, Brian sent two letters to the members of the Legislative Council. Neither was an admission of guilt or an unreserved apology, but both illustrated the absurdity of the SCP process.

It was conspicuous evidence of the Council's changed attitude that it accepted the first letter and mildly requested that Burke desist from sending out any further material that may be deemed confidential.

It was a similar case with Mr Crichton-Browne's ordered "unreserved apology" (see Report No 17 of 37th Parliament). The three-page so-called apology letter of 12 December 2007 was a terse but devastating excoriation of the SCP's performance and conclusions. It had the word "unreserved apology" perfunctorily tacked on to the last sentence, but there was no way that it could properly be characterised as an apology.

Nevertheless, it was ultimately accepted by the Legislative Council.

The SCP had also demanded that I make an apology. On 11 December 2007, my lawyer, Steven Penglis, wrote to the President of the Council. Without going into detail on the highly persuasive three-page epistle, I can disclose that it argued convincingly that the SCP finding against me was "entirely without foundation" and he would not advise me to apologise. As a consequence, I would not be apologising. That is, not even a Clayton's apology.

This rebuff of the Upper House set up a situation analogous to the infamous "Easton affair" where the Council unadvisedly jailed Brian Easton for seven days when he refused to succumb to similar intimidation to apologise for a misdemeanour that he denied. I shall deal with this scandal shortly.

Before my lawyer's letter could be considered, Mr Penglis wrote again to the Council on my behalf on 15 February 2008 enclosing a preliminary opinion from Stephen Gageler SC, one of Australia's foremost jurists and later a highly respected member of Australia's ultimate court, the High Court.

In brief, Mr Gageler's opinion was that the SCP's finding was fatally flawed and that I had done no wrong. The irony of this situation was that on one side there were some of Australia's most esteemed legal minds in Stephen Gageler SC, Richard Price, Malcolm McCusker QC, Grant Donaldson (later Solicitor-General) and Tom Percy QC tendering legal advice that was at odds with the SCP finding. On the other hand, there were essentially faceless, little-known legal advisers for the SCP and the CCC.

Easton was charged with contempt of the Parliament by motion of the Legislative Council in 1995 and, upon conviction, was ordered to appear before the Council and apologise. He refused and was sentenced by the Council to seven days imprisonment.

The conviction resulted from the tabling of a petition in the Council in November 1992. In part, the petition alleged that Opposition Leader Richard Court had improperly provided Easton's former wife, Penny Easton, with confidential information about Easton's severance payment when he left his position as General Manager of the government-owned Exim Corporation.

The petition attracted significant media interest. On 9 November 1992, Penny Easton committed suicide.

Subsequently, Premier Carmen Lawrence denied in Parliament that she had detailed prior knowledge of the petition. A royal commission established by Richard Court in May 1995 after he became Premier found that Lawrence had misled the WA Parliament.

In February 1997, when Lawrence was the Shadow Environment Minister in Federal Parliament, she was charged with three counts of perjury resulting from the findings of the royal commission. She was acquitted of the charges on 23 July 1999. However, her career never recovered from the events.

It was later conceded by independent analysts and commentators that every aspect of the Easton Affair, as it was called, was driven by politics. It is similarly conceded that the Council was almost the last place one would look for impartiality.

It should have been a lesson to all concerned that politics and the need for impartial deliberation do not mix and, if they are forced into the same space, events can spiral unexpectedly and disastrously out of control. It was manifest that the SCP, driven by the CCC, was ignorant of the dire lessons of Easton. But there were wiser and more experienced heads in the Council.

President Nick Griffiths (Labor) was one of them. He had been a busy practising lawyer before entering Parliament, had a very healthy respect for the rule of law and had a deep admiration for Mr McCusker.

A second person was Norman Moore (Liberal), at one time the longest-serving Member of Parliament. He was an experienced and competent minister and long-term Leader of the House. A third was George Cash (Liberal), a parliamentary long-termer, a Master of Laws and a former President of the Upper House.

Under their influence, and with the help of other members, such as Graham Giffard, Ray Halligan, Sheila Mills, Simon O'Brien and Giz Watson, a saner and more reasonable (although I would say still not correct) middle course was adopted. The option of my imprisonment was rejected, after some struggle with a more punitively minded few within the committee.

The demand that I apologise was abandoned. Instead, I was admonished and my right to enjoy the privileges of Parliament House, as a former member, were revoked. As I rarely used Parliament House it was not a serious penalty.

Revealingly, however, the Carpenter Government, which had control over the order of business in the Upper House, was not pleased by what was perceived as a major back-down. It displayed its displeasure by delaying consideration of the committee report, which had been tabled in the Council on 8 April 2008, until 25 June 2008. And that was only after I went public on the long delay on 17 June 2008.[52]

Almost immediately, the outstanding committee reports on Archer, journalist Taylor and Mr Crichton-Browne were all dealt with in the Council. The report on Taylor had been hanging over his head since 6 December 2007. The delay of more than six months smacked of both pettiness and vindictiveness.

Nonetheless, the delay did evoke a considered and balanced comment from one of the original members of the SCP, Barry House, in the short debate on 25 June 2008 when the report was accepted. House, who later went on to be the President of the Council, said:

> The result, I concede, is that some breaches or "contempts" that were reported in the original report could be considered of a minor nature and in other circumstances might not have been reported at all.

I emphasise that this was a very considerable retreat from the original SCP report and must have embarrassed the CCC. House's comments reflect the same judgement as President Griffiths, who used the Shakespearian vernacular to sum the whole long, confused and damaging episode as "much ado about nothing".

However, getting to this point was not as easy as I have made it sound. In the middle of February 2008, a betting person was likely to have wagered that I would be going to jail. Surprisingly, we (Burke, Crichton-Browne and I) acquired an ally out of the blue – *The West Australian* and its editorial staff.

On 20 February 2008, *The West* ran a full front-page story by Kate

---

[52] *The West Australian*, 17 June 2008, p. 11.

Campbell under the headline: "I will go to jail before I apologise: defiant Grill".

The body of the article was sympathetic to reform. *The West* also ran a cartoon by Dean Alston in the same edition that clearly demonstrated that support. A number of letters to the editor in subsequent editions took up the cause.

On 21 February 2008, *The West* editorialised in favour of abolition of the penal powers under the heading: "Upper House's punitive powers have no present justification".

However, please don't think that *The West* was brave enough to support Burke, Crichton-Browne or me personally. Matters had not proceeded quite that far. Despite its explicit support for reform, *The West* clearly felt constrained to dissociate itself from support for us three.

Its editorial also commented that, if the Council sent me to jail, I might be perceived as an unlikely martyr to the cause of democracy.

But *The West* was gradually softening its hard line against us. The lead article on its front page for the same day had the headline: "End Parliament's power to jail Grill". It followed up on 22 February with a third story in three days under the headline: "Grill urges court contempt trials".

Even *The Australian* chimed in with a sympathetic story by Amanda O'Brien under the headline: "Grill to risk jail for reform".[53]

On 23 February 2008, *The West* kept up with what had now become a campaign by publishing a story under the headline: "Lawyers back Grill in parliamentary fight". The article referred to the supportive position taken by the Law Society of Western Australia as articulated by its President Hilton Quail. He said:

> In a modern democracy, it (the Parliament) should refrain from exercising that power (penal power) and enact legislation that ensures that no person is exposed to the risk of jail without fair trial before an independent judiciary.

Additionally, the Bar Association also came out against parlia-

---

[53] *The Australian*, 22 February, 2008, p. 5.

mentary use of the penal powers. Ben Wyatt (former lawyer, Labor MP, and recently retired State Treasurer) was quoted in the story as favouring urgent reform.

Mr Crichton-Browne and I were summoned before the Legislative Council Privileges Committee on 27 March 2008 in an attempt by hard-line elements (sadly, almost all were members of my party, the ALP) of the Upper House to force us to apologise. *The West* carried an article that day under the headline: "Quash contempt finding says unrepentant Grill".

The next day, *The Australian* published a story by Amanda O'Brien under the headline: "Crichton-Browne faces prison". The story featured pictures of Mr Crichton-Browne and myself coming out of the committee hearing room with our respective lawyers, Tom Percy QC and Ante Golem.

On 28 March 2008, *The West* ran a two-page feature under the respective headlines: "Questions of bias hang over politicians" and "Defiant Grill, Crichton-Browne are still refusing to say sorry".

The second article, in part, stated:

> The former Labor Minister (Grill) stood by his claim that he did nothing wrong, there was no evidence to suggest wrongdoing, the committee had no power to order him to apologise and the threat of gaol without fair trial was a denial of natural justice.

My battle with the SCP is detailed in the committee's Report 18, 8 April 2008.

The West continued to carry stories and letters to the editor, up to and including 9 April 2008, when it ran its last article, by Kate Campbell, on the issue under the headline: "Defiant Grill stares down jail threat over apology refusal".

Campbell's story dealt with the retreat by the Council from the brink of using its penal power. *The West* mentioned the "significant victory for the controversial lobbyist" (me), but it modestly did not draw attention to its own important role in that victory.

However, *The West* had not quite finished with McGinty's part in the saga. On the same day, the newspaper carried a separate, but linked, story under the headline: "McGinty shows narrow focus on choice of rules to discipline MPs".

Robert Taylor wrote:

> The decision by an Upper House privileges committee to accept the apology of Noel Crichton-Browne and admonish Julian Grill for a grave contempt of Parliament for refusing to apologise highlights the urgent need for an overhaul of the contempt laws. But even though it is long-held Labor Party policy to reform the laws so that Parliament is not stuck with a choice between a slap on the wrist and a prison sentence, Premier Alan Carpenter and Attorney-General Jim McGinty say such reform is not a priority.

Later in the story Taylor went on to say:

> Yesterday's recommendation from the privileges committee was also, in its own way, another blow to the Corruption and Crime Commission and the select committee that investigated the leaks-to-lobbyists affair with the aid of the CCC telephone intercepts and CCC lawyer Phil Urquhart.
>
> In the end, once again a lot of time and energy was expended on something that never got off the ground.

At a personal level, the lifting of the penal threat was certainly a relief. I did not want to go to jail. I had some fear. I did not publicise it, but I suffer claustrophobia.

Pleasingly, the re-found sanity and rationality of the Council did not end there. There were members who had become convinced that the antiquated powers and penalties for breach of parliamentary privileges and contempt needed to be amended and modernised.

Put succinctly, the Council needed to be dragged into the 21st century. On 12 November 2008, a Select Committee was set up for just that. It comprised Nick Griffiths, George Cash, Kim Chance, Kate Doust, Norman Moore and Giz Watson.

Its Report was No 1 of the 38th Parliament on 7 May 2009, and, according to clause 2.2 of that report, two mentioned catalysts for the Select Committee were the Brian Easton matter and the SCP inquiry and findings, as extensively canvassed above.

The report was the result of scholarly research and, in large part, its conclusions reflected the path taken by other enlightened parliaments around the Western world.

The November 2008 Select Committee was of the common-sense view that it was "for electors to determine who should be Members of Parliament, rather than the House themselves". It recommended that the power of Parliament to expel a member be abolished.

In all, the Select Committee made six recommendations. Despite the fact that there appears to be no opposition to the implementation of these recommendations, this has not yet taken place.

To ascertain the reason for a large part of the delay in taking such action, one needs to look no further than the publicly expressed views of the then Premier Alan Carpenter and the then Attorney-General Jim McGinty, who, while indicating that they had no philosophical problems with the proposed changes, "did not see such reform as legislative priorities".

This casual and unhurried attitude by the two had an air of arrogance about it, perhaps reflecting their disappointment and irritation at the Council's apparent back-down on the so-called "unreserved apologies" by Burke, Crichton-Browne, Grill, and refusal to expel Archer and Fels.

However, this attitude by Carpenter and McGinty flew in the face of the ALP's long-held view that these archaic penalties and procedures should be reformed.

It is worthwhile noting that Herbert Smith Freehills, at its own expense and initiative, gave a powerful detailed submission advocating change. The DPP did likewise.

Penultimately on this sorry saga, I shall briefly consider the fate of the recommendations by the SCP to prosecute Archer, Fels, Nathan McMahon, Noel Crichton-Browne and Burke for allegedly giving false evidence. The Director of Public Prosecution decided not to proceed with charges.

Interestingly, by far the weightiest arguments presented by the DPP's office for not proceeding were its concerns that the *factual* cases against the five potential accused just wouldn't stand up to scrutiny in a court of law. Of course, this is what some of Australia's and WA's best legal minds had told the SCP and the Council in written submissions at the outset.

Depressingly, the DPP's report and notification of its decision not to proceed with prosecutions attracted no publicity. That was more than surprising, it was astounding.

This was the completion of a SCP inquiry that was melodramatically billed as "the most important committee hearing in the history of the Legislative Council". It was never publicly reported that no prosecutions proceeded.

If you search the back copies of the mainstream press today, you will find no reference to the report from the DPP's office wherein the DPP refused to prosecute. The Parliamentary Library staff recently took five days to track down the DPP's report, after initially telling me they couldn't find any reference to it.

There was no debate in Parliament. It appears that it was quietly tabled in the Upper House on 8 August 2011, slipped in among other sundry documents. It certainly was not picked up by the media. Members appeared to be unaware of its existence.

Further, I suspect that it was buried to save embarrassment. After all of the sensational pyrotechnics of the SCP hearings, it ended with a whimper. I believe that those who had spectacularly promoted the hearings just wanted it interred.

But that left the public in the dark on the vexed question of culpability. The impression that certain "targets" had behaved criminally had been made all too well in the media at the time of the hearings. The fact that the accusations had been dropped or discarded was not nearly so well publicised and, in many cases, including this one, was not publicised at all.

So ended one of the Legislative Council's most sensational and extensively hyped episodes.

How could this have happened? How could the CCC have inserted itself into a parliamentary committee and turn that committee into something it was not meant to be. That is, a criminal investigatory tribunal. Perhaps we will never know.

8

BURKE, GRILL BAN FEEDS 'CORRUPTION' MYTH

As ripples from the CCC hearings spread across the nation, unexpected responses included a Coalition prime minister and senior federal minsters performing shamefully, Labor premiers acting like political rookies as they tried to save their skins, and the media still behaving badly.

The Smiths Beach and Lobbyists issues were covered regularly in the national media, but now and again they were actually and sensationally played out on the national stage. Allegations against Ian Campbell and Kevin Rudd as they related to Brian Burke are prominent instances. In both cases, the concept of "guilt by association" was taken to ridiculous levels.

I shall deal with the Rudd matter first, as it gave rise to the Campbell catastrophe.

It is now established that in 2005 Rudd met Brian Burke on three occasions in WA: at a breakfast in May; at a dinner on 1 August; and at a lunch in November.

The backdrop was that in mid-2005, Rudd visited WA to familiarise himself with the State. The John Howard-led Coalition Government, and most of the media, asserted that Rudd was feeling out support around Australia, mainly within the ALP, to topple Kim Beazley as Federal Opposition Leader.

There is no hard proof for that claim and Rudd did not express or present it that way. But the next year, on 4 December 2006, he supplanted Beazley in a caucus election.

Apart from meeting Brian Burke while in WA, Rudd attended functions organised by Brian where he was introduced to influential elements of the WA business world (chiefly clients of Julian Grill

Consulting) and people from the Right and Centre factions of the ALP.

I was present on two of those occasions, both held on 1 August 2005 and both held at Brian's favourite restaurants. The first was a lunch at Kailis Brothers seafood restaurant in Leederville, attended mainly by senior ALP faction members. Burke was not present, but Graham Edwards, his close friend and then a Federal MHR, was master of ceremonies. The lunch was arranged in a discreet function area.

The second reception was a dinner in the stand-alone function centre at Giuseppe Pagliaricci's Perugino Restaurant in West Perth.

Rudd later maintained that he was simply in WA on a familiarisation trip and that he attended these social occasions by coincidence; in other words, they had little or nothing to do with Burke specifically. Well, the two functions I attended were clearly organised for Rudd as the focus and reason for the gathering.

Brian consulted me on the guest list for the dinner at Perugino and he presided at the event. Additionally, I have seen emails that demonstrate Burke was requested by Edwards on behalf of Rudd to do the organisation.

The initial Rudd denials of association with Brian Burke and lame explanations just would not wash with the media. Rudd made a strategic error in initially obfuscating on the obvious Burke connection. This silly prevarication by "Saint Kevin" gave unnecessary oxygen to an outrageous campaign by a desperate PM, John Howard.

The Rudd meetings were not a story in 2005, but they became white-hot issues in March 2007 – firstly, because in August 2005, despite the Premier Gallop's un-elucidated and largely ignored ban, it was still acceptable to associate with Burke or myself. By early 2007 we were an anathema and lethally toxic.

Secondly, by March 2007 Rudd had become the leader of the Opposition.

Thirdly, in 2007 Rudd was beginning to head Howard in the opinion polls.

What next transpired in March 2007 was one of the most shameful episodes in the history of Australian politics. More innocent people were to be irreversibly damaged.

My research indicates that the Rudd/Burke story was broken by Andrew Probyn, the then Federal Political Editor of *The West Australian* on 1 March 2007. Probyn's article was prominently marked as an "exclusive" and had detail that would manifestly prove its accuracy.

Probyn did not disclose who briefed him, but *The West's* editorial staff considered that it was connected to the CCC because that is how they promoted the story. The article began: "CCC Investigation" under the headline, "Rudd feted at Burke's soiree".

The story went on to allege that Rudd, in company with Edwards, had been anointed as Labor's next prime minister at a dinner of 15 to 20 local business leaders at Perugino's restaurant organised by Burke on August 1 2005, some 16 months before Rudd replaced Beazley as ALP Leader. It was also said that Rudd's office had confirmed that he had met with Burke on two other occasions in 2005. That is, at a time when Gallop had a ban on contact with Burke.

Further on Probyn wrote:

> Mr Rudd, when asked if he would ban Federal Labor MPs from having any contact with Mr Burke, said: "As of now, there is from my point of view and the point of view of all the members of my parliamentary team, that is the case."

Once broken, this confected, guilt-by-association story went viral. Every major media outlet in the country wanted a piece of it. There was a truly ugly set of motivations driving the agenda.

Howard required a weapon to batter Rudd. The task for the Prime Minister was substantial. Even after the public revelation of the Rudd-Burke meetings of 2005, Rudd led Howard 45 per cent to 38 per cent as preferred PM and 62 per cent to 42 per cent in satisfaction ratings.[54] In turn, Rudd was determined to disavow Burke, in a sad act of self-survival.

Contemporaneously, there was a legion of dubiously principled

---

[54] Newspoll, as cited in the editorial in *The Australian* 6 March 2007.

journalists who were quite happy to build a major national story on the basis of the equivocal premise that any contact with Brian Burke was immoral.

Additionally, there were Brian's factional competitors who were all too eager to use any fragile pretext to heap revilement on him. It was sick. But it was explosive too. The theme was simple: any person who met with Burke was unfit to be Australia's Prime Minister; or a cabinet minister, if it came to that.

The story consumed most of the front page of *The Australian* the next day, 2 March 2007, under the headline: "Burke scandal engulfs Rudd".

The article featured pictures of Burke, plus Edwards and WA Senator Mark Bishop, who were said to be friends of Brian. These two were thus fingered, tainted and, according to a statement made by Rudd in Federal Parliament, "counselled" for keeping in contact with their long-term friend and political ally.

Just to add drama to the main story, *The Australian* carried a side story by Andrew Trounson and Kevin Andrusiak intimating that Burke, me and our client PMA, were likely to be sued. It began as follows:

> Mining giant Xstrata is considering legal action against its former business partner after the Corruption and Crime Commission this week revealed that a crooked parliamentary report helped extract a $17.5 million settlement from the Swiss-based company.
>
> Xstrata's threat of legal action is the first to flow from the hearings, which have unveiled Brian Burke and Julian Grill's extraordinary influence over government and bureaucracy.
>
> State Attorney-General Jim McGinty yesterday put politicians, public servants and everyone else exposed as having behaved corruptly on notice, saying their assets could be seized under proceeds of crime laws if they were convicted.[55]

---

[55] *The Australian*, 1 March 2007.

Our lawyers thought the threat ridiculous. It was always a beat-up. But the story was clearly designed to demonstrate what undesirable people Brian and I were, and thereby add spice to *The Australian's* feature story by Steve Lewis and Patricia Karvelas, which began as follows:

> Kevin Rudd's bid for government has suffered its first serious blow after the Labor leader admitted to bad judgement in meeting disgraced former West Australian premier Brian Burke on three occasions.

Further on it reported Rudd as saying:

> So therefore, with the benefit of 20-20 hindsight, of course I would not have met with Mr Burke.

Also, it remarked:

> In the most savage attack, Peter Costello said Mr Rudd had been 'morally and politically compromised' through his dealings with the convicted felon.

And:

> Labor's surging popularity has unnerved Coalition MPs – but senior Opposition figures were worried last night that Mr Rudd could come crashing back to earth because of the Burke revelations.[56]

The Australian also ran several page 2 articles that heaped odium on Brian Burke and me and its Letters to the Editor page focused on our presumed "corruption".

As usual, no specifics, of course. Invariably the stories and letters picked up on inferences of corruption from the CCC hearings. These inferences were never proved and in my view were never provable. In fact, in the final analysis, the majority of these assumptions were abandoned without explanation by the CCC.

The Australian Financial Review, not to be left out, ran the story on the same day as its front-page lead by Andrew Burrell and David Crowe. The headline was: "Rudd dragged into Burke scandal".

---

[56] *The Australian*, 17 March 2009.

However, Costello, over eagerly went too far and was quoted in the front-page article as saying: "Anyone who deals with Mr Brian Burke is morally and politically compromised." Costello may have been one of the great parliamentary performers, but ethical considerations aside, this was a particularly reckless utterance that always had immense potential to injure blameless individuals.

In view of the immediate and all-consuming national interest, *The West* upgraded its follow-up story on the issue on 2 March 2007 to a front-page lead. Probyn, who broke the story the day before in what was probably his biggest scoop to that date, must have been disappointed that the original story had only managed to make page 7.

However, it is apparent that the paper's senior editorial team did not initially appreciate what it had. And Probyn's focus on possible political fund-raising may have been somewhat off target.

Chris Johnson, not Probyn, wrote *The West's* lead story on 2 March 2007, under the headline: "Burke liaisons ends Rudd's glorious honeymoon". This appeared to signal that the Howard, Costello, Tony Abbott led attack on Rudd's standing had met its goal. Rudd's poll-driven assent had been arrested. But there was to be a cost and unexpected casualty.

During debate in Federal Parliament on 1 March 2007, the Coalition did in fact line up, as reported in the media, to assail Rudd over his association with Burke. However, all sides in Parliament aligned to condemn Burke. From what I have read, Beazley eloquently defended Rudd, but I can't see where one single parliamentarian spoke a word in Burke's cause.

This was a unique situation. In my experience of parliamentary debate, there is normally at least one contrarian. Not in this case. The view was unanimous: Burke was toxic and contagious. I know that he still had friends and supporters in Federal Parliament, but they had been intimidated into silence. Not one was brave enough to lift their head above the parapet.

Brian Burke was deemed poisonous and too dangerous to be associated with. I have never heard these epithets applied so vehemently to another living soul. These were words usually reserved for mass exterminators.

The question thus arises: What was it about Rudd's contact with Burke that gave rise to such pious wrath? I can't answer that question, but I do have a perspective that I can offer. That is, when Brian was asked to help Rudd acquaint himself with a range of people in WA, it was the most natural thing in the world for him to accept. He has a long family history in the ALP and an extensive list of Labor people, both in WA and interstate, who he has helped personally or financially. In a way, his family, like my family, was married to the ALP.

I am not privately uncritical of some aspects of the Labor Party, but my family and I have never stopped helping the organisation and contributing in terms of time and money to the campaigns of worthwhile individuals within it.

Even now, despite the fact that Brian may have been forced to resign from the ALP, and the ALP may have unmistakably turned its back on him, it does not mean that he does not feel compelled to contribute. It is in his DNA.

The West, in its second effort, shifted into overdrive. On 2 March 2007, in addition to the front page by Johnson, the paper was consumed with the Rudd, Burke and Grill narrative with no fewer than 15 articles and an Alston cartoon dealing with different aspects of the media-perceived "infamy". I shall deal with some of the more distressing aspects.

Of particular concern to my wife, Lesley, was a page 5 story by Amanda Banks and Sean Cowan under the headline: "Burke and Grill face the loss of millions". The first few paragraphs of the story went as follows:

> Brian Burke and Julian Grill could lose millions of dollars in cash and property after Attorney-General Jim McGinty vowed yesterday to enforce tough property confiscation laws if criminal activity is proved as a result of the Corruption and Crime Commission inquiry.
>
> Mr McGinty's warning raises the prospect that MPs, former politicians and public servants caught up in the scan-

dal could lose property under the broad provisions of the *Criminal Property Confiscation Act*, whether or not they are convicted of an offence.

Lesley, through our lawyers, had been made aware that our family home was in particular jeopardy of confiscation because it also doubled as a home office and had been used as the meeting place with a number of our clients. The legal profession generally regarded this Act as a particularly obnoxious and arbitrary piece of legislation that could bring about the most unjust results. Lesley was extremely alarmed because she now saw that McGinty, who was a singular enemy of Brian, was implying that Burke and Grill were particular targets for use of this punitive law.

Do not worry, Mr McGinty, Lesley got your message loud and clear, even though she couldn't quite understand what her husband had done wrong. I expect that Sue Burke, who is an angel of a person, was in the same state of anxiety as Lesley.

To try to alleviate Lesley's anxiety, I heavily mortgaged my share in our home so that my equity was nearly all squeezed out. Also, we started taking up our weekends searching for a really cheap house that we could live in if the worst came to worst.

We found an old timber worker's dwelling in Yarloop, 100km south of Perth, for $60,000, when prices had been depressed due to a public health scare in the town. We were a bit desperate as there was now the possibility that our possessions would be confiscated. Our means of earning income had already come to an end, because our clients had been scared by the CCC hearings.

Additionally, as I have informed readers earlier, there were powerful elements in the Legislative Assembly who were advocating new laws to strip us of our superannuation. We were frantically fighting on multiple fronts.

It is unusual for a reputable paper to comment on a person's looks, but page 2 of *The West* featured a distorted picture of a sinister and misshapen freak next to a photograph the paper had taken of me. The headline stated, "Chameleon Grill is dead ringer",

The story by Luke Morfesse intimated:

> Julian Grill seems to be updating his look. Yesterday in Inside Cover he was doing his best impression of offbeat Hollywood gritter Peter Lorre, who featured in classics such as Casablanca and the Maltese Falcon.
>
> Meanwhile, his photo on page seven of yesterday's paper (that's him on the right) saw him take on the appearance of a more modern star of the big screen, Gollum from Lord of the Rings.

Another prejudicial story in the same addition of *The West* by Mark Drummond was headed: "Builder hired then fired Burke, Grill". [57] It was obviously provoked by the Rudd issue and sourced from the CCC.

The article related to the late construction magnate Len Buckeridge, whose company BGC had a number of problems with the Gallop Government, including the non-performance by the Government on an agreement for Mr Buckeridge to build a private port at James Point in Cockburn Sound.

This was in late 2003. Mr Buckeridge engaged us on a monthly basis because he said he could not get a fair go from the ALP Government. He maintained that this was due to his well-known conservative political and industrial relations views.

His goals seemed reasonable to us. He had in fact been granted a commitment from the previous Richard Court Government to build a new port in Cockburn Sound, south of Fremantle. In the normal course, this agreement would have been respected by an incoming Government, but it was not easily enforceable and the new Gallop Labor Government was playing hardball.

We made some immediate progress on one of BGC's problems, but we only lasted a couple of weeks before we were sacked.

This came about because Brian had the view that if Mr Buckeridge and Kevin Reynolds, as head of the CFMEU, could settle their historic enmity it would bring about a better industrial scene and a better environment for dealing with the Government. Burke then

---

[57] *The West Australian*, 2 March 2007, p. 7.

brokered a meeting between the two and he later reported to me that there had been a breakthrough.

Soon after it was reported in the media that "the BGC chief had agreed to sign a union accord". I had known Mr Buckeridge for many years and admired his dedication to work and his ability to get things done. When the "union accord" story hit the media, he rang me and somewhat apologetically advised that he could not live with publicity that suggested that he was in bed with the unions. Consequently, our consultancy was immediately terminated.

Why *The West* ran this story on 2 March 2007 I do not know. The matter, like many others related to the CCC inquiries, was unsourced, but there was no suggestion that anyone had behaved improperly. It had nothing to do with the prevailing Kevin Rudd issue. I can only guess that *The West* ran it to publicise the fact that we had been sacked and that we were *persona non grata* across the spectrum. If that was the case, it worked, as we were universally reviled and scorned.

Part of the denigration of Brian Burke and me took up the old line pressed by the CCC at its hearings and which I have elaborated elsewhere in this book. The false line developed by the CCC was that we were greedy. Whenever I went into the witness box (which was quite often) I would almost invariably be interrogated on our consultancy fees. It was irrelevant to the matters being investigated, but I have heard from a source close to the CCC that the CCC legal team mistakenly believed that they could link our lump sum success fees to corruption.

Shockingly, during the Rudd controversy in early March 2007 when Brian and I were under the most severe attack, *The West Australian* took the same approach. It focused more on our financial assets, and consultant fees were once again paraded. *The West* conducted a highly intrusive probe into our financial affairs and published the lot, for the entire world to pore over, in a full-page article by Gareth Parker on 5 March 2007. The story was replete with pictures of our respective residences.

It was apparent that the story was designed to show us up as bloated capitalist types. The promo on the front page referred to us as "Filthy Rich". I won't take you through all of the details, but it was obviously linked to McGinty's comment in Parliament the previous week concerning the possible confiscation of our property.

The article ended:

> It all goes to show just how high the stakes are after Attorney-General Jim McGinty invoked the spectre of WA's ultra-tough criminal property confiscation laws last week.

Clearly, *The West* had undertaken an extensive forensic investigation into our finances. What this information had to do with supposed impropriety of public officers is hard to discern. In my experience, this category of high-level financial investigation is reserved for serious crooks. Whether that was the intention or not, that was the unfortunate impression conveyed.

In fact, our fees were set at the industry standard. And our assets acquired in a completely legal manner by a lifetime's saving were certainly not colossal. The work we did without charge was never mentioned.

They say that all is fair in love and politics. I contend that the CCC had no business in this arena. Also, that McGinty behaved prematurely in raising the spectre of confiscation of our property.

The same edition of *The West* also examined the entrails of the Rudd dinner. Under the headline, "Guess who went to dinner", it named and identified in individual photographs the industry heads, union leaders, senior public servants and politicians who attended. Was the story designed to shame those who attended?

However, the two articles mentioned above were only window dressing. The real news was that Ian Campbell, the former Federal Minister for the Environment and Heritage and at the time the Minister for Human Services, had been sacked by John Howard for attending a meeting at which Brian Burke was accidentally present.

A further prominent item was that polling was commencing to indicate that the CCC hearings and their aftermath were beginning to have a substantial impact on WA polling.

The Campbell sacking was entirely unprecedented in Australian political history and, in an election year, created a shock wave throughout the electoral system. It also demonstrated how ruthless and unprincipled Australian politics could become. It was the inevitable result of arguably the most unscrupulous pre-emptive attack launched by a political leader on his opposition number in Australian politics.

It was written up in *The West* by Andrew Probyn on 5 March 2007 with the headline: "Campbell a necessary loss in war on Rudd".

Then followed:

> One of the golden rules of politics is don't have an inquiry unless you know what you'll find.
>
> The other is that you don't launch a double-barrelled attack on a political foe unless you know your own house is in order.
>
> The Howard Government erred on the latter. That's why Ian Campbell got the knife.
>
> To sustain Peter Costello's assertion that anyone who deals with Mr Burke is 'morally and politically compromised', Senator Campbell had to be dealt with swiftly.
>
> The dispatching of Senator Campbell, a senior member of Cabinet, was brutal.

This affair devoured most of the space and time in the country's mainstream media for several days. It was a watershed issue that strangely would be decisive in the 2007 election. *The Australian*, knowing how important it could be, gave it maximum coverage. I can't refer to all the articles, but I include parts of the front-page analysis piece by the late Matt Price on 5 March 2007:

> I don't think people in other States quite understand or understood the influence that Brian Burke and Julian Gill were wielding, embattled West Australian Premier Alan Carpenter said yesterday.
>
> He's dead right. In theory, as Peter Costello and Tony Abbot insist, it seems utterly inexplicable that any self-re-

specting politician or businessman would ever deal with Brian Burke. Forget theory, here's how it works.

Andrew Forrest is one of the Prime Minister's favourite entrepreneurs."

Forrest was at another table in 2005, the now infamous Perugino's dinner featuring Kevin Rudd and Burke. When Burke issued an invitation for prominent West Australians to meet an up-and-coming federal Labor figure, Twiggy answered the call.

Anyone who deals with Mr Brian Burke is morally and politically compromised, was how the Treasurer lambasted Rudd and nailed Ian Campbell last week.

Yet the PM's favourite entrepreneur doesn't merely dine with Burke; for years, Forrest has paid Burke and his business partner Grill for consulting and lobbying services.

According to Fortescue spokesman Julian Tapp, Burke and Grill were deftly able to cut through endless red tape and set up meetings with key bureaucrats and MPs.

That's what lobbyists do, all around Australia. We can assume Howard's favourite entrepreneur paid Burke and Grill handsomely for their efforts.

Forrest and Fortescue employed Burke and Grill through the period when former West Australian Premier Geoff Gallop had slapped a ban on ministers dealing with the pair. Many reputable companies and organisations did the same. If the Costello dictum held true, half the people in Perth's wealthy western suburbs would be "morally compromised".

Except it's not true. For all their dodginess, it's clear Burke and Grill also performed legitimate work for reputable companies, such as helping Fortescue in its battle to run trains down BHP Billiton's Pilbara line.

Grill has never been convicted of a crime, but he served in Burke's government and copped a whack in the WA Inc. royal commission report.

> Grill's partnership with Burke is widely known in Western Australia -like Torvill and Dean, you rarely hear one mentioned without the other.
>
> So, is dealing with Grill a political and/or moral transgression?
>
> During the early 1980s Liberal senator David Johnston was a partner with Grill in a Goldfields law firm and Grill knows numerous Coalition MPs from his period in and around politics."
>
> Campbell, conducting legitimate ministerial business, has been blown apart by friendly fire. The PM is confident nobody else in his Government has had dealings unsavoury or otherwise with Burke.
>
> Burke's lobbying days may be numbered and his perverted political influence is surely on the wane. Having inflicted untold damage on the state and federal Labor Party, the shadowy man in the Panama hat may be in the mood to even the score."

The background to the matter was that, acting on behalf of the WA Turf Club, I had set up a meeting for my client with Senator Ian Campbell, the Minister for Heritage.

The Turf Club was undertaking a major redevelopment to Belmont Park, its second racecourse, on the Burswood Peninsula of the Swan River. The project included a significant residential development plan that had been superintended by my friend, internationally renowned environmental and public transport expert, Professor Peter Newman.

Part of the proposal was for the inclusion of a world class Aboriginal Cultural Centre on part of the land fronting the river. We had held discussions on the project with a representative group of Noongar (South West WA Indigenous Clan) Elders, as organised by Ken Colbung (deceased) an old friend and ally. Mr Colbung held a preeminent position in the WA Aboriginal pantheon and was highly respected by both sides of politics.

The Elders became enthusiastic supporters of the project. That was partly because the Turf Club was prepared to donate the land and sponsor the development of the Aboriginal Cultural Centre. I learned from the Elders that the proposed land had serious significance to the Noongar people.

The meeting with Senator Campbell was designed to introduce the Federal Government to the concept of the heritage and cultural centre and, in due course, to seek Federal support. Ben Wyatt, the State MP for the area and, until his recent retirement, State Treasurer in the WA Labor Government, was a well-known Aboriginal lawyer and a board member of the National Aboriginal Enterprise Corporation. He too was invited to the meeting.

The Turf Club believed that the project could be nationally significant. It was highly appropriate to consult with Heritage Minister Campbell.

One of the ironies of this Turf Club/Burke/Campbell meeting was that it was not originally intended that Burke should attend. Senator Campbell was a long-term friend of my brother-in-law and my sister, Bruce and Grania Keys. Consequently, because I had an amiable relationship with the Senator, I made the arrangement and it was planned that I attend.

As events transpired, I had to be out of town and Brian Burke took my place at short notice. The law of unintended consequences calamitously came into play. It cost Campbell his Cabinet ministry immediately and shortly thereafter his Senate seat.

Players in the Ian Campbell debacle

My comment on the players is as follows.

Peter Costello. As chief attack dog for John Howard, Costello was grossly intemperate, verbally irresponsible and extremely unfair. From his parliamentary coward's castle, he comprehensively traduced Burke's character. None of the calumny was provable. In spearheading the attack with such extravagant and profligate language, he laid the ground for the destruction of the career of his Cabinet colleague Ian Campbell.

Ian Campbell. He was innocent, totally innocent and decent, all the way through the episode. He accepted that he was going to be the sacrifice and fell on his sword without a murmur of rancour.

Tony Abbott. He was the second-ranked attack dog in the co-ordinated assault on Kevin Rudd. History demonstrates that he is particularly adept in this role, but his invective did not have the vicious edge that Costello commanded.

John Howard. The Prime Minister was also true to form. He hid his critical role behind Abbott and Costello and the rest of the team. He did not want to be seen with dirty hands.

However, this pose did not really deceive anyone. It was easily discernible that Howard had engineered the foray and that it was done to save his skin.

For anyone who cared to look beneath the surface and saw the ugly truth, it was evident that the onslaught was profoundly unethical. I assert this for the following reasons: The object of the meeting with Senator Campbell was entirely proper. I maintain that it was virtuous. The Noongar people would have received belated recognition and for the first time since colonisation, would have owned a very valuable piece of riverfront land in Perth. The people of Australia would have gained a brilliant cultural attraction.

Even if one accepts that Brian Burke was somehow tainted (which I don't), it is ridiculous to maintain that an intelligent, highly competent and reputable senior Cabinet Minister like Campbell could be suborned in one isolated 20-minute meeting, where there were several other noteworthy citizens in attendance.

The meeting happened more than a year before any CCC hearings.

While conceding that the attack on Rudd may have been blunted to some extent by the forced resignation of Campbell, it was impossible to hide the callousness and moral void that accompanied Campbell's sacking. It was a ruthless and self-interested knifing by the Prime Minister.

As former ALP Federal Minister and Senator, Graham Richardson is fond of saying, "the mob ultimately work it out". In the 2007 election, the Howard Government not only lost the election, but astoundingly, the PM lost his seat.

The media. In respect to the media, I have tended in the past to mentally absolve them from moral responsibility on the basis that the journalists, editors and owners were just doing their job in a challenging commercial world. However, the older I get and the more of the media copy I review in writing this book, the more naïve I believe I must have been.

In the case of the attack on Rudd it is clear that the bulk of the media aided and abetted a significant attempted political assassination. Whatever one might think of Rudd's later stewardship of the country's affairs, he was most unfairly assailed in an attempt to knock him out of the 2007 election race before he really got started.

With the clear exception of *The Australian's* editorial of 5 March 2007, which pointed out in detail the appalling hypocrisy of Howard's actions (*The West's* editorial of the next day, much to its eternal shame, took the opposite line), the majority of the media ardently went along with Howard's unprincipled attack.

In general, however, the media conspired with Howard and lent legitimacy to this unethical assault.

To do this, the media overwhelmingly supported and propagated the improbable notion that any contact with Burke and Grill, no matter how blameless, was pernicious.

It was a line that Premier Carpenter vigorously promoted. For instance, he is quoted in *The Australian* of 5 March 2007 by Amanda O'Brien (Jim McGinty's former press secretary) in these terms:

> Premier Alan Carpenter has warned up-and-coming young Aboriginal MP Ben Wyatt to have "absolutely nothing to do with Burke and Grill" after revelations Mr Wyatt attended a meeting with Brian Burke at Senator Ian Campbell's office last year.
>
> And the Premier said any Labor MP who continued to have contact with the pair even as a friend do so at their political peril.

It was a clear threat by Carpenter that Wyatt's career prospects would be extinguished if he again associated with us. Unhappily for the precept of freedom of association, it had the desired effect. Wyatt was quoted as saying he would have nothing to do with us.

What Carpenter didn't know and what was never disclosed in the media (but was well known in certain ALP circles) was that this so-called "poisonous influence" of Burke and Grill as described in O'Brien's article was initially responsible for Wyatt's election to State Parliament, in Geoff Gallop's prized seat of Victoria Park.

It is a long and detailed story so I shall keep it short for reasons of space. Put simply, Burke and I had organised critical support and helped put together the numbers to allow Wyatt to win ALP pre-selection for this safe Labor electorate.

Some ungenerous minded people might think that we may have fostered Wyatt on the basis that we could influence him later. That was certainly not the case and no evidence was ever produced that even hinted that we had at any time attempted to induce him to take any particular position on any matter at all.

In fact, Wyatt sought us out for help. Initially, he approached Lesley and me for assistance in his pre-selection because we had been long-time friends of his father, Cedric Wyatt, a former head of the Department of Aboriginal Affairs. We got to know Ben and his vivacious wife Vivian well and attended their wedding. Later we helped with the by-election campaign.

That friendship was acknowledged by Wyatt in his maiden speech on 29 March 2006, where he said:

> … to Julian and Lesley Grill, who have known the Wyatt family since I was a small boy in Kalgoorlie and who have provided me with long hours of political debate and advice, thank you.

Another of the tragic casualties of the CCC hearings was the enforced cessation of that relationship. It hurt Lesley a lot because she had genuine affection for Ben. The truth is that you get close to young people like Ben and Vivian and you come to share their hopes and aspirations.

It is true that our friendship with Cedric never suffered. He still kept calling around and updating us on how the family was prospering. Sadly, we attended his funeral where we met Ben again, but it was not the same.

The Gallop ban was not only repetitiously used by sections of the media, it was also employed extensively in the Parliamentary debates, both State and Federal as we have seen. It was the bedrock rationale for the Howard-inspired assault on Rudd.

But justifying the attack on Rudd, and what was actually the retrospective sacking of Campbell, by reference to the Gallop ban is logically and ethically fraught. That was the case for an extensive list of reasons, including:

- There was no legislative underpinning for the ban.
- It was a devise used by tin-pot dictators.
- It was never put in writing and its scope was nebulous.
- Gallop never advised us of the ban.

Appropriately, with Howard's confected attack on Rudd and the peremptory sacking of Campbell, Steve Pennells of *The West* broached this subject in the 5 March 2007 edition. As far as I can ascertain, it is the only serious examination of the Gallop ban that played such a pivotal role in justifying the attempted poleaxing of Kevin Rudd.

The story was headlined: "The West's exposure of Cabinet power wielded by lobbyist sparked Gallop ban".

There is no doubt that the headline was substantially correct. The rest of the article, although I would strongly take issue with some of its language, laid the essential story bare. It said in part:

> Four years ago this month, former premier Geoff Gallop's denial of Brian Burke's influence within government was rapidly crumbling under a series of explosive revelations in *The West Australian*.
>
> The paper had exposed Mr Burke's lucrative lobbying business and *influences* (my emphasis) over a series of Cabinet decisions and Dr Gallop was left with little choice

but to implement his now famous ban on Mr Burke in a heated interview with *The West Australian*.

With State and Federal ministers falling in the wake of the Corruption-and Crime Commission hearings, it has been easy to forget the climate of a few years ago. But it was this newspaper, along with the *Australian Financial Review's* Mark Drummond (who has since moved to *The West*), which lifted the lid on Mr Burke and Julian Grill's lobbying business in the face of denials and scorn from within Parliament, the State Government and naïve media organisations.

It was *The West Australian* which first revealed that even before Mr Burke's mate Norm Marlborough was elevated to Cabinet, Mr Burke and Mr Grill had privileged access to at least four ministerial offices and their fingerprints over a range of controversial Government decisions.

Changes over payroll tax concessions, the make-up of WA's new racing and gaming body and the Government's approval of Portman Mining's Koolyanobbing expansion plans against Environmental Protection Authority advice had all gone, in full or in part, the way of Mr Grill and Mr Burke's clients."

This paper continued to expose Mr Burke's reach into the Government, including the fact that he still enjoyed high-level access to the office of Deputy Premier Eric Ripper through one of the Government's most senior officials, chief of staff Mike Megaw, long after Dr Gallop's ban. The ALP had also called on Mr Burke to help in an 11th-hour bid to push its controversial plan to break up Western Power through State Parliament.

As the paper continued its investigation, it was subjected to constant attacks – including anonymous emails, intimidation and bizarre incidents like the visit from a small group of country MPs, who were sent to *The West's* parliamentary office one evening by Dr Gallop's fix-it man,

Kieran Murphy, to angrily deny that their decision to successfully lobby Cabinet to reverse a decision on racing legislation had anything to do with conversations they had had with Mr Grill. One of those MPs was John Bowler.

"You've made a big mistake and upset some very powerful people," one lobbyist told *The West* after a story which widened the paper's lobbying probe.

WA business already viewed Mr Burke and Mr Grill as the go-to men. WA Trotting Association president Garry Scott told *The West* he approached Mr Grill for one reason. "You obviously want to be with people you believe are going to be successful," he said.

When the paper revealed Mr, Grill was claiming credit for a Cabinet decision, Dr Gallop admitted that he had no idea Mr Burke and Mr Grill were being paid to influence the outcome.

"I was disturbed to read in *The West Australian* this morning that Mr Grill was claiming responsibility," he told Parliament.

"I was disturbed about that comment because I know how the decision was made and how my Government operates, and that the claim was not true… I was disturbed to read that article in the paper, it is not true. Our Government acts properly and according to due process."

This Pennells article was given an interesting format by the editor. It included pictures of the headlines and large parts of Pennells' previous stories of four years earlier, on 4 October 2002 and 21 April 2003. *The West* was parading its evidence of the verity of its earlier articles.

It is not denied by me for a moment that Brian and I were involved in the decisions that Pennells referred to in his article. In truth, we were party to many more such outcomes. They were our assignments and we performed them as best we could. I can assure readers that

I carried out those tasks as ethically as possible. The Pennells article does not actually assert otherwise.

Pennells essentially asserts that he and *The West* had been correct when they had previously claimed that Burke and Grill had been effective in representing our clients' interest to Government. But that was nothing to be ashamed of. Lobbying *per se* is not dishonourable. Political scientists maintain that it is an essential element of a healthy democracy.

However, the Pennells story also clearly demonstrated that Gallop was desperate to rebut any suggestion that we had any involvement in final decisions made by the Gallop Cabinet.

Lobbying strategy misunderstood

And there was another myth: there was a presumption in the media that our lobbying method mainly entailed the simple contacting of one of our friends in Cabinet. But, contrary to orthodox presumptions, that was rare. It was generally our last option. It was not good business for us to expose Cabinet ministers to charges of cronyism. No lobbyist would last long that way.

We always tried to go through proper channels. Take for instance the very three matters raised initially by Steve Pennells. First, there were "changes over payroll tax concession". The relevant Minister was the Treasurer and Deputy Premier, Eric Ripper. He was a friend of mine, but I do not believe I spoke to him at all over the issue. He certainly denies that I did.

On the other hand, we engaged with the Commissioner for Taxation on three occasions and drafted lengthy written submissions for consideration by his departmental officers. In those submissions we suggest a mechanism that would allow our 12 engineering company clients to survive, and for the State to collect more revenue in the longer term. It was logic and reason that won the day, not contacts.

On the second matter raised by Pennells, namely "the makeup of WA's new racing and gaming body", the applicable minister was another friend, Nick Griffiths. I never spoke to him on the subject.

Burke had the carriage of the matter for us and, as far as I am aware, he never spoke to Griffiths either.

The lobbying of Griffiths was done by Members of Parliament, who in turn had been lobbied by delegations of constituents from the electorates that had substantial numbers of electors with an interest in horse racing. These MPs were deliberately not informed that Burke had made arrangements for them to be lobbied by their constituents.

I was not aware, until I read the Pennells article of 5 March 2007, that Gallop had arranged a delegation of country MPs to attend on *The West* "to angrily deny that their decision to successfully lobby Cabinet to reverse a decision on racing legislation had anything to do with conversations they had had with Mr Grill".

The paradox is that the MPs were telling the truth. There was no need for Burke or me to speak to the MPs. Their own constituents were far more eloquent on the subject than we could ever be.

A similar process was applied when local members convinced the Government to proceed with the multi-million-dollar Marmion Avenue extension to the north metropolitan beach suburbs. The local MPs, who badly wanted the road, lobbied Government ministers, not Burke and Grill. We did co-ordinate the approaches, but at no time did we make advances to ministers. As in the other matters, the arguments, when properly presented, were compelling enough.

In respect to the third issue raised by Pennells, Portman Mining's Koolyanobbing (iron ore) expansion plan, we convinced our client to engage our friend Syd Shea, a former head of the Department of Conservation and Land Management (CALM). Mr Shea carried much of the argument to the Environmental Planning Authority (EPA) and CALM. He spoke their language.

In these three matters nominated by Pennells, when the pertinent ministers may later have been interrogated by Gallop, as I am sure they were, each could say with hand on heart, that they were not lobbied by Burke or Grill.

Thus, when Gallop vehemently maintained in Parliament that Burke and I were not directly involved, he had been truthfully informed by the relevant ministers that they had not been personally approached by either Burke or me and that consideration of the pertinent matter had gone through the normal prudential processes.

However, as I mentioned above, this mistaken belief that we used cronyism to promote our clients' causes was largely brought about because of Gallop's one-dimensional view of the lobbying process.

A curious aspect of this and other elements of our lobbying activity was that the final outcomes were never questioned as being other than fine solutions to difficult problems. The Government was invariably proud of the outcomes that the ministers and Cabinet ultimately arrived at; and the Opposition could not find fault, either.

Any problems only seemed to arise when it was perceived that Burke and Grill may have been involved. By and large we tried to minimise our public exposure. We never advertised, had no webpage and never disclosed the names of our clients.

So how could the Gallop ban possibly lay the foundation for an unprincipled attack on Rudd? How could it render Burke so toxic that one short innocent meeting with Senator Campbell could spell the end to this poor man's career?

Also, there was some irony emanating from Senator Campbell's dismissal. The person who took his place in the Howard Cabinet was WA Senator David Johnson. He had been my partner in my Kalgoorlie legal practice. According to an article by Chris Johnson in *The Australian* of 16 March 2007, Senator Johnson had to assure Howard that he had had no past meetings with Burke before he could take up his cabinet post. "None at all."

Just contemplate that for a moment. It was now supposedly a new criterion for Cabinet appointment that the prospective appointee had never met Brian Burke. Are we then to assume that the thousands of ordinary people and scores of parliamentarians who have met Burke had rendered themselves ineligible for high office?

Just to demonstrate how absurd the confected political situation became, I quote from a further story in *The Australian* of 8 March 2007 by Samantha Maiden:

> Newly anointed Justice Minister David Johnson also

confirmed yesterday he would divest his share portfolio, which contained holdings in two mining companies that he was unaware had also employed Mr Burke's lobbying services.

If that bizarre standard were applied across the board, then most ministers would have been forced to dispose of their stocks or resign. That was true for the simple reason that Burke and Grill had consulted to a large number of Australia's "blue chip" companies.

I am also critical of the media for going after my known political friends in the same way they went after Kim Beazley because of his lifelong friendship with Brian Burke.

The Australian, in an article by Amanda O'Brien of 8 March 2007, forced the former Federal Resources Minister and Special Minister of State Gary Gray to defend his friendship with Lesley and me. Gray and his wife, Deb, had been our close friends for many years through various triumphs and travails of the Labor Party. That friendship was the direct outcome of an even longer association with Deb's father, Peter Walsh (the former Federal Finance Minister), and her mother Rose Walsh.

If they were expecting Gray to desert us, the paper was badly mistaken. He told *The Australian* "he saw no reason to change the friendship between his family and the Grills". Later in the article he is quoted as saying, "friendships were not something he considered disposable".

One of the more extraordinary actions taken as a result of the Rudd/Campbell/Burke/CCC affair was the prohibition that Premier Carpenter placed on his MPs in respect to their speaking about the issue at all. This was an astonishing turn of events, which set another remarkable "first" for WA politics.

In fact, it is arguable that in suppressing his parliamentary colleagues from publicly discussing issues relating to the CCC hearings, Carpenter was in risk of breaching the law.

Presumably the penalty for ignoring the ban was dismissal from the Cabinet, exclusion from promotion or expulsion from the ALP.

As a footnote to the Rudd/Campbell affairs, I reference the paradox of the fact that it spurred sundry other lobbyists in WA to form an association. The *WA Business News'* Mark Beyer broke the story on 22 March 2007. His article featured a smiling picture of Megan Anwyl, the State MP for Kalgoorlie before she lost the ALP bastion to Liberal Matt Birney. Ms Anwyl was quoted as saying, "…the association would represent the industry and seek to educate the public about the legitimate role of lobbyists".

So, at long last, was there going to exist a body of like-minded people that would point out that Julian Grill Consulting's lobbying methods were no different to the industry standard? That there was no accessible evidence that Burke and Grill were in receipt of Cabinet secrets? A brave new organisation, perhaps, to resist trial by media?

Lamentably not. Ms Anwyl proudly announced that Burke and Grill would be "disqualified" from membership from the outset. No correspondence entered into. There was no benefit of any doubt here. Nor was there one scrap of hard evidence presented to justify the brush-off.

9

WHY INNOCENT PEOPLE NEED PROTECTION FROM THE CCC

A reasonable observer would quite properly have expected that the CCC, as a guardian of public sector propriety, would be careful to at least observe the legalities of its own legislation. Sadly, that has not always been the case.

The provisions of Section 23 (now Section 217A) of the CCC Act are quite clear:

> Section 23(1): The Commission must not publish or report a finding or opinion that a particular person has committed is committing or is about to commit a criminal offence or a disciplinary offence.

This provision was obviously enacted to prevent character assassination before a witness could stand a fair trial in a properly constituted court of law.

In its Smiths Beach and Lobbyist inquiries, the CCC ignored that clear injunction. It often made and published findings and comments implying or concluding criminality.

And bear in mind that some of the evidence base used by the CCC in coming to its findings was not admissible in a court of law.

Early on, it became apparent that there were many ways a witness could be discredited without waiting for formal "findings" by the CCC.

They included statements to the media that some witnesses would be charged; lines of questioning that incorrectly implied criminality (as in the alleged Marlborough bribery payments); a focus on and exaggeration of Burke and Grill's legitimate fees; inferences of breaches of Cabinet confidentiality and the charges that could stem from that; leaking prejudicial stories to the media; failure to correct unfounded media impressions of misconduct; highly damaging statements about Burke and Grill in CCC media releases that did not reflect the CCC's official reports; and damming evidence being given against witnesses without any opportunity for the witnesses to offer evidence in rebuttal.

The statements, including inaccuracies, were spun to the media and the public in highly derogatory and damaging language that depreciated the standing of witnesses.

The media effectively branded witnesses GUILTY of specific criminal offences on the basis of CCC evidence and reports that, although not directly asserting specific criminality, simply implied criminal guilt, as I explain below.

Unfortunately, the body that oversees the CCC, the WA Parliament's Joint Standing Committee on the Corruption and Crime Commission (JSCCCC), initially ignored this behaviour.

Eventually, after the demise of the Carpenter Government, and after the receipt of an opinion by Acting CCC Commissioner Christopher Zelestis QC, the JSCCCC adopted a more conscientious approach to its obligations. In 2011 and 2012, it looked afresh at the derogatory and deprecatory observations and throwaway lines used by the CCC Counsel Assisting during public hearings.

That is, the same verbal delicacies that had been eagerly snapped up by a hungry media.

Such damning and flamboyant utterances by Counsel Assisting in hearings of the New South Wales Independent Commission Against Corruption (ICAC) – the equivalent of the CCC – have been the subject of intense nationwide media comment because of the potential to ruin a witness's reputation, and to pre-judge crucial issues.

The WA JSCCCC expressed its consternation at this CCC practice, firstly, in its Report No 17 September of 2011 and, secondly, because of its importance, in its report entitled *The Use of Public Examinations by the Corruption and Crime Commission* (Report No 25, 29 March 2012, pages 20-24).

Remember, the CCC has almost no limit, apart from Section 217A (formerly Section 23) on what it alleges or implies in public hearings (no matter how untrue or slanderous). That is due to a statutory exemption (Section 219 of CCC Act) from the laws of libel and all actions in tort as long as they act in "good faith".

Experience has demonstrated that it is almost impossible to prove "bad faith" or its equivalent, "malice", in a court of law. Given these statutory privileges and the great scope for harm in public hearings, it would have been expected that the CCC should take care to be punctilious in the language it employed in public hearings and report findings.

This is not what the JSCCCC found. Quite the contrary, as can be seen in the committee's statement quoted below.

Some CCC comments amounted to legalised slander.

Calamitously, this persisted for an extended period while the media and public were spellbound and swooning. When challenged on the issue by its parliamentary supervising body, the JSCCCC, the CCC had four justifications.

The first was to blame the media. The second was to define Section 23 so narrowly as to destroy the section's intent; that is, to limit the scope of the section to formal findings only. The third was to try to artificially maintain a distinction between the CCC and the CCC's own Counsel Assisting.[58]

And the fourth, as a fall back, was to acknowledge that there had been isolated breaches in the Smiths Beach hearings five years earlier, but that the CCC had changed its ways since then.[59] However, the CCC's subsequent actions cast grave doubt on that asserted change of ways.

The CCC's argument was that it was not required to take responsibility for statements made by its Counsel Assisting. This reasoning was almost fraudulent. The JSCCCC properly found that the CCC arguments were not justifiable or legitimate.

In coming to conclusions on the CCC and Section 23, the JSC-

---

[58] *The Use of Public Examinations by the Corruption and Crime Commission* (Report No 25, March 2012, p. 22).
[59] See letter from Mark Herron, Acting Commissioner of the CCC, to the JSCCC, Appendix 1 to JSCCC Report No 17, 2011.

CCC drew heavily on one of the State's most highly regarded barristers, Chris Zelestis QC, who then ranked with Malcolm McCusker at the pinnacle of the WA Bar. He was a "lawyers' lawyer" of the highest repute – the "go to" man for significant commercial litigation in WA. He was used by the CCC itself in other important matters.

The JSCCCC report No 25 had this to say on the issue:

> It is, of course, easy to apportion blame for unintended or unfair reputational damage to the media; of greater concern to the Committee is that the CCC has – at best – consistently demonstrated a general disregard for the manner in which the media functions.
>
> Nowhere is this better demonstrated than in the fact that past CCC Commissioners have at times allowed inappropriate questions to be put to witnesses by various counsels assisting the CCC.
>
> Furthermore, that various counsels assisting the CCC have seen it fit – in the context of a public examination wherein the rights of witnesses are severely constrained – to use (to cite but one example) derogatory 'throwaway' lines during questioning also reflects poorly upon some within the Western Australian legal fraternity.
>
> CCC examinations aim to arrive at the truth of some matter, and in aid of this goal witnesses are compelled to answer any question deemed appropriate by the Commissioner. This is a significant departure from a regular court of law, and as such the Committee has long failed to understand why CCC witnesses – and particularly those who appear before public examinations – are so often treated with open hostility.

The JSCCCC report then referred to comments by Mr Zelestis in a 2010-2011 inquiry requested by the Parliamentary Inspector on several statements made by counsel assisting at the close of a series of public examinations, including the Smiths Beach inquiry.

One of these statements included the counsel assisting's opinion that, on evidence available to the Commission, there was reason to believe some witnesses had been less than completely frank and honest in their evidence. And, also that if witnesses persisted in deliberate untruthfulness they ran the risk of committing further offences under the CCC Act.

The JSCCCC report said Mr Zelestis had considered the statements in the context of Sections 22 and 23 of the CCC Act and, according to Mr Zelestis, the statements suggested that some witnesses had, in effect, lied to the CCC (which was a criminal offence under section 168 of the CCC Act). This amounted to the publication by the CCC of an offence and, as such, was in contravention of Section 23 of the Act.

However, the CCC had disagreed with Mr Zelestis' construction of the CCC Act, asserting that, in its opinion, the word "finding" or "opinion" in the context of the Act (read as a whole) must mean the CCC's formal expression of a considered conclusion at the end of a deliberative process.

It was the Commission's opinion that the legislative intent of Section 23(1) was to prevent publication within the Commission's statutory reporting regime of any concluded opinion or finding that an individual was guilty of a criminal or disciplinary offence.

The JSCCCC report goes on to say that Mr Zelestis disagreed with these CCC opinions, stating:

> The express terms of s.23 do not confine the prohibition to a formal expression of opinion at the end of a deliberative process. The nature and purpose of the prohibition are much more fundamental than that.
>
> The purpose of s.23 is clear. Allegations that a person has committed an offence, etc. (including an offence under s.168 of the Act of giving false evidence to the Commission) are to be made and determined in courts and tribunals of competent jurisdiction. No power at all is given to the Commission in that regard.
>
> It would be inconsistent with a person's right to a fair trial upon an allegation of commission of an offence to allow

> the Commission to make public statements about the commission of offences.
>
> Thus, the prohibition in s.23 is of fundamental importance in preserving the basic elements of the system of justice that prevails in Western Australia.

The JSCCCC report comprehensively concurred with Zelestis, and added *inter alia*:

> The role of the CCC is to improve the integrity of the Western Australian public sector; it is not the role of the CCC to determine whether or not a person has committed a criminal offence.

Given the clear conclusions by the JSCCCC, it is disconcerting that the CCC, on 16 and 20 August 2018 respectively, published, firstly, a report into "bribery" and "corruption" in maintenance and service contracts within the North Metropolitan Health Service, and, secondly, a report on "corruption" in Information Technology at the State-owned Horizon Power.

In each case, these reports named public officers and presented a narrative of bribery, corruption and fraud, using those actual words. And in the case of the Horizon Power employees, it specifically recommended corruption and fraud charges be considered against named officers.

Strangely, the CCC report then offered the disclaimer that its recommendation did not amount to a finding!

It all looks rather confusing to me, as I don't believe that a decision on this situation has been made by the courts. To be clear, the CCC did not specifically allege those crimes by the named officers. Instead, it used the term "serious misconduct", which it is permitted to do under its Act.

But the CCC narrative of criminality was obvious and the media was not confused. In a succession of banner headline, front page and otherwise high profile stories extending over weeks, *The West* and to a lesser extent *The Australian* and other media detailed the alleged criminal offences in highly colourful terms.

Surely this is the situation that Section 23 was designed to combat? However, in spite of the strong opinions of Mr Zelestis, I suppose the CCC could argue that the matter had not been decided finally by a court and it was open to the CCC to argue that it had not transgressed. It is not an argument that I would embrace.

Television, newspapers (state and national) and radio went viral on the Health Services and Horizon Power matters. Sensational and incendiary articles were prominent in the media for weeks. Guilty or not, the named officers' careers were finished and their futures destroyed.

Some of these officers were ultimately found guilty, but did that excuse the damning comment prior to trial? At least one of the named targeted officers, however, denies his guilt and conceivably could be acquitted. Should he be publicly branded guilty before he is tried?

The media did not have to be concerned about a defamation suit as they were drawing their material from a privileged CCC report.

Brian Burke and I publicly questioned such dubious coverage.

In a letter to the editor of *The West* published on 22 August 2018, Brian maintained (*inter alia*):

> It's almost impossible to avoid judging someone guilty when the Corruption and Crime Commission publishes its opinion supported by comprehensive detail that is widely reported . . . But declaring their guilt without charging them and giving them their day in court undermines the system of justice in WA.

In a letter to the same paper on 24 August 2018, I had this to say (*inter alia*):

> Section 23 of the *Corruption and Crime Commission Act* states that the CCC 'must not publish or report a finding or opinion that a particular person has committed, is committing or is about to commit a criminal offence or a disciplinary offence'.
>
> This provision is designed to prevent character assassination of a suspect before they have a fair trial.

I was technically wrong about the section number of the Act, as I shall shortly explain.

Brian and I were not entirely alone. On 27 August 2018, *The West* published a letter by Greg Fitzgerald of South Lake (who we did not know) that supported Burke's view. Also, on 28 August 2018 Greg Fitzgerald sent an email to me that copied in an email he had sent to the CCC on 25 August 2018. In that email he asked the CCC:

> (a) Is this (Grill's) reading of the Act correct?
>
> (b) If it is, why has the reports of both of these incidents been released?
>
> (c) Did the CCC release these reports or was it by person/s unknown?
>
> (d) If the CCC has acted in violation of the Act why?"

Mr Fitzgerald also sent me the CCC's emailed reply of 27 August 2018. It was as follows:

> Section 23 of the *Corruption and Crime Commission Act 2003* (now the *Corruption, Crime and Misconduct Act 2003*) was repealed in 2014, and therefore no longer applies.

That was all.

The response from the CCC was technically correct, but what it did not disclose was that Section 23 had been re-enacted in Section 217A of the amended Act.

A follow-up letter by Mr Fitzgerald to the CCC on 31 August 2018 sought advice on how the reports were released to the public when it implied criminal conduct by named officers. The letter was met with a response the same day, advising Mr Fitzgerald to "refer to the Commission's website". But vague and general reference to the CCC website did not answer Mr Fitzgerald's direct question. After that brush off, that is where the situation remains.

Not very satisfactory from the public's point of view.

As a consequence, Mr Fitzgerald made a complaint to the CCC Parliamentary Inspector (PI), Michael Murray. That complaint did not bear any early fruit, but it must have been a part-motivator for a piece in the PI's Annual Report for 2018/19, which was picked up by Nick Butterly in *The West* of 23 September 2019 under the headline: "Watchdog questions CCC name and shame powers".

The Butterly article read:

> The independent inspector of the CCC has questioned whether the powerful body should be able to name and shame people as part of public hearings and investigations.
>
> The question comes as debate grows over the model of a possible Federal corruption body to police bureaucrats and politicians in Canberra.
>
> The CCC has come under fire ever since its creation over its use of public hearings and its selective naming of individuals in reports.

Journalist Paul Murray highlighted a similar case in his column in *The West* on 18 September 2019. It related to a CCC public inquiry into the Exmouth Shire that culminated in a report that made scathing comments relating to serious misconduct over an aquarium contract by CEO Bill Price and Strategic Planning Officer Andrew Forte. These comments and other highly adverse remarks made during the CCC hearing were widely reported and both men lost their jobs and reputations long before the allegations were tested in an impartial court.

In a very short period of consideration, a District Court jury dismissed charges against both men in August 2019. Murray commented:

> Most of the media which had reported the lurid assertions from the public hearings, the CCC report and Commissioner John McKechnie's subsequent media appearances, did not report the results of the case.

Murray went on to ask the critical question:

> Does anyone concede the investigative process would not

have been hampered had the hearings been held in private? Where is the protection of people whose innocence can take years to prove, whilst the unsubstantiated assertion of fact from investigations, publicly made under legal privilege, have already done their damage?

I conclude this chapter by commenting that the assessments of the JSCCCC and Christopher Zelestis could not be clearer. In the Smiths Beach and Lobbyists public hearings, the CCC was chastised by the JSCCCC for contorting the interpretation of its own Act in a manner that then permitted it to smear and malign witnesses.

In the Exmouth Shire, Horizon Power and WA Health Department matters, the CCC appears to have followed a similar path.

These types of reports have the twin propensities of jeopardising a fair trial if and when charges are laid, and can severely impugn, without appeal, the reputation of a witness not put on trial.

As I have stated elsewhere in this book, one of my lawyers always maintained that "those who had the most to fear from the CCC were the innocent".

As it ultimately transpired, the CCC was spectacularly unsuccessful in proving criminality in the interminable Exmouth Shire, Smiths Beach and Lobbyists related prosecutions. Time will tell in respect to the advocated high profile Horizon Power indictments.

10

McGinty defends CCC's miserable track record

I have long conjectured that former Attorney General Jim McGinty was largely responsible for the particularly high level of antipathy and downright hostility emanating from the State Parliamentary Labor Party (SPLP) towards Brian Burke and me over the CCC inquiries.

Brian, for reasons I cannot fathom, has tended to downplay my hypothesis. Perhaps his entrenched loyalty to the ALP won't allow such thoughts; or perhaps it is true, as he has said to me more than once when I have raised the subject, "What does it matter anyhow?"

Well, I am human and to me it does matter. Very much. I think about the treatment handed out to us almost every day of our lives as a consequence of the CCC's activities. How could it not matter that the organisation to whom my wife, Lesley, and I had given most of our working and social life, the ALP, held me in contempt and actively discouraged and shunned contact with me by its members?

McGinty's public comment about Brian Burke and me were continuously jaundiced.

For instance, on 30 December 2008, McGinty is reported to have said:

> The insidious influence of lobbyists on government processes would never have been exposed without the watchdog.[60]

Elsewhere in this book, I refer to the occasion where I was forced to threaten legal action against McGinty before he withdrew an allegation of corruption against me.

Confirmation of the very worst of my suspicions about McGinty's

---

[60] *The West Australian*, 30 December 2008, p. 4.

continued denigration of Brian and me came when I was invited by my barrister, Steven Penglis, to a panel discussion sponsored by Transparency International Australia at leading law firm Herbert Smith Freehills on 7 November 2013. The seminar's purpose was to discuss the question of whether the CCC, established in 2004, had been successful in its goals and performance.

The panellists were McGinty and John Quigley (then Labor's shadow Attorney-General). It was chaired by Elizabeth Macknay (a partner of Herbert Smith Freehills). She is a relative of the then CCC Commissioner, Roger Macknay.

The attendees appeared mostly to be lawyers, but I was informed that there were also several officers from the CCC and a sprinkling of academics and other professionals. My impression was that I would be called on to speak and that my perspective might offer some counterpoint to that of the two panellists.

When I arrived, the mainly young, group of about 50 or 60 practitioners were enjoying pre-seminar drinks. Ms Macknay greeted me warmly but did not mention anything about any speaking role for me.

I was a little perplexed but didn't say anything lest I embarrassed her. Quigley arrived, approached me and we exchanged pleasantries. He seemed to be unaware that I may speak. McGinty came in at the death knock, but didn't meet me and was quickly whisked away to open the substance of the seminar.

McGinty's role in the CCC's Smiths Beach and Lobbyists inquiries is reported in relevant sections of this book, but the confrontation I am about to relate was so unique as to be almost surreal. It was the only time I directly spoke to him about the CCC, but the intensity of the exchange more than made up for the singular nature of the event.

Well-informed readers would appreciate that the CCC and its enabling legislation constituted McGinty's baby. He was inordinately defensive of it. The CCC was born out of the Kennedy Royal Commission into the WA police force.

When McGinty, as Attorney-General, introduced the CCC Bill on 15 May 2003, he painted a glowing picture of a state-of-the-art, crime-fighting body that would "restore the public confidence in the Western Australian Police Service that their corrupt colleagues have eroded" (from Second Reading speech).

However, as events unfolded it became clear that the CCC fell well short of that mark and barely pursued corrupt police at all (which I explain later in this chapter and Chapter 11, "The CCC's weaknesses and mistakes start to emerge").

Additionally, it was demonstrated in various forums that the CCC's accountability mechanisms were distinctly inadequate. However, at the panel discussion to which I was invited, McGinty was in denial of any defects of his offspring, the CCC. He was to jealously evangelise his own creation.

Before I come to that, however, I want to highlight McGinty's formal position as (former) Attorney-General – a position that historically holds very special status within Cabinet and Parliament.

He or she is the principal legal officer of the Crown. They are the guardians of a long, but evolving, tradition of rule by law and fairness before the courts and other tribunals. Attorneys General are '… responsible for maintenance and improvement of WA's system of law and justice.' Traditionally, they exercise important discretions, including, historically, those touching upon life and death.

Consequently, in matters relating to the law, it has been expected that the Attorney General would normally be above issues of politics and remain steadfastly impartial. McGinty appeared to ignore those traditions when it suited him. When it came to Brian Burke and me, his pronouncements were clearly partisan.

I give reference to some of the McGinty's prejudiced remarks at appropriate places in this book and the encounter that I am now relating underlines that predisposition.

The assertive nature of his discourse and the unequivocal character of his conclusions on this highly contentious subject was breathtaking. He assured the audience that the CCC had been highly effective, had beneficially altered the environment within the public service and, although success with prosecutions was not his criteria, that the CCC had a (implausible) 99 per cent success rate.

I am not sure where these fantasy figures came from, but I can assure readers that in respect to the Smiths Beach and Lobbyists terms of reference the numbers were almost the reverse.

This glowing assessment of the CCC failed to mention any of the scathing criticisms previously made by distinguished Queens Counsel Malcolm McCusker, a former Parliamentary Inspector (PI) of the CCC (and later WA Governor), highly respected QCs Chris Steytler and Michael Murray (also both former Supreme Court judges and Parliamentary Inspectors of CCC at material times), and strong implied criticism by the parliamentary Joint Standing Committee on the Corruption and Crime Commission (JSCCCC) in its March 2012 report.

In that report, when dealing with the Smiths Beach and Lobbyists matters, the JSCCCC stated:

> The Committee concurs with the Parliamentary Inspector's opinion that the CCC's discretion to open examinations to the public 'has miscarried in the past' and regards this as a significant issue.[61]

McGinty also failed to mention that the CCC under Commissioner Len Roberts-Smith took the extraordinary and unprecedented step of commencing proceedings in the Supreme Court in an attempt to prevent Parliamentary Inspector McCusker from inquiring into, and commenting on, some of the CCC's actions and activities in the Smiths Beach and Lobbyists terms of reference.

The Department of Premier and Cabinet in the Barnett Government had to publicly intervene to try to sort the dispute out.

This highly embarrassing deadlock was the result of deficiencies in McGinty's legislation. It arose again later between Commissioner Roger Macknay QC and PI Michael Murray QC. In all, it took years to (only partly) resolve. It is both incredible and telling that McGinty failed to mention these events.

It is well understood that the CCC's essential task was to keep po-

---

[61] Chairman's Foreword to the Joint Standing Committee on the CCC Report No. 25, March 2012: *"The use of Public Examinations by the Corruption and Crime Commission."*

lice honest. However, PI Chris Steytler QC had produced a startling report [62] indicating that the CCC had failed to investigate all but one of 381 complaints alleging excessive use of force by the police in a two-year window, and that the CCC had been forced to investigate in that single case by outside pressure.

There was no reference by McGinty to the massive decline of morale within the WA Public Service brought about by the unjust, clumsy and ultimately disastrous persecution of numerous innocent officers in the Smiths Beach term of reference. The highly concerned comments of the Public Service Commissioner on this subject are included in Chapter 5.

Another substantial omission by McGinty was the prison scandal reported on the front page of *The West* on 29 June 2013. According to the headlines, that scandal involved "Guards linked to organised crime figures" and a "Toxic culture of misconduct".

The problem for the CCC was that it had a clear responsibility to help prevent police corruption and crime in WA prisons, and yet some of the CCC's own officers were reported to be involved in prison wrongdoing.[63]

In another front-page story in *The West*, on 28 August 2014, journalist Gary Adshead wrote that the police had established a "taskforce to crack down on crime in WA jails". In other words, the police were taking over part of the CCC's responsibilities. That action highlighted the failure of the CCC in this arena and largely sidelined it, for a considerable time, in relation to prison matters.

By the time of this seminar, there was, in spite of McGinty's exaggerated claims to the contrary when he initially introduced the legislation, overwhelming evidence that too little consideration had been given to the oversight provisions when framing the legislation. This also contributed to the "Rogue Officers" affair covered in Chapter 12.

It has since sensationally emerged by decision of the Supreme

---

[62] Report No 18, *Procedures Adopted by the Corruption and Crime Commission When Dealing with Complaints of Excessive Use of Force by Police*, tabled in WA Parliament on 8 September 2011.

[63] *The West Australian*, 2 July 2013, p. 2.

Court that the CCC, since its inception, has been criminally prosecuting individuals without any such authority.[64] I deal with the issue more fully in Chapter 19, but official figures show that the CCC launched 121 prosecutions illegally.

It would appear that the bulk of these charges were actually instituted after Attorney-General McGinty took no effective action on a recommendation in a report by Gail Archer QC advising that the CCC Act required amending to clarify the highly questionable prosecution power.

If that was not sufficient, McGinty also failed to mention that the CCC's initially much-vaunted powers to investigate organised crime were so badly devised as to be largely inoperable. In truth, McGinty introduced and presided over, in the critical early years, a chaotic piece of defective legislation.

Having made these glaring omissions, McGinty got straight on to the attack and told the seminar that there were four groups of people who had impugned the standing of the CCC. He gave the impression that all four groups were misguided and acted unfairly.

He asserted the first group was motivated by self-interest and comprised those who felt aggrieved by being targeted by the CCC. The second group, he said, was simply conducting an organised attempt to destroy the CCC. It was at this point that McGinty named Brian Burke and Julian Grill as being prime examples of both groups.

I was so shocked at this blatantly slanderous accusation made at a professional gathering that I did not take proper note of what the other two categories were.

Shortly thereafter I was further astounded when the former Attorney-General pulled out a copy of Andrew Burrell's best-selling book "Twiggy" from his papers and waved it in front of seminar members. The book had a chapter that dealt with the role Brian and I had played in the success of the iron ore project of Andrew "Twiggy" Forrest's Fortescue Metals Group (FMG).

Mr Forrest had downplayed our role in the project in the wake

---

[64] *A v Maughan* [2016] WA Supreme Court of Appeal 128.

of the Smiths Beach and Lobbyists inquiries, but Burrell had unearthed substantial documentary evidence of our critical work with FMG.

Improper, corrupt conduct claimed

Having raised this issue, McGinty then embarked upon a harangue on how the CCC had exposed Burke and Grill as parties to improper and corrupt conduct in association with WA public officers, and that this conduct had caused highly deleterious headlines and gravely disturbing comment in media for weeks throughout Australia.

He further went on to say (correctly) that Burrell's book was proof that Brian and I had lobbied Ministers and Members of Parliament despite having been expressly banned at that time (2005/06) from doing so by then Premier Geoff Gallop.

McGinty appeared to be personally affronted by our activity, which he clearly considered to be nefarious. Unambiguously, the bulk of and thrust of his address was a strike at Burke and Grill. We were the real focus of his address and all those who questioned the operations or effectiveness of the CCC were no better and no more credible than we were.

It was apparent that the former Attorney-General considered he had affected a minor coup in exposing us in the way that he described. He sat down at the conclusion of this harangue, looking highly satisfied.

Quigley spoke next. He said that the CCC had done a barely passable job, but also put the view that the CCC had gone too far and had intimidated the public service to the extent that it was no longer properly cooperating with the public.

He also mentioned the destructive Supreme Court confrontation between Mr Roberts-Smith and Mr McCusker. Otherwise, he dealt with narrative material about findings the CCC had made against him personally, but which were later withdrawn. Quigley was at least entertaining, as he always is.

That was followed by two questions, immaterial to this account, from the floor.

The seminar was about to finish and I was anxious to at least make some effort to try to set the record straight after the McGinty onslaught. Despite the fact that I had still not been asked to speak, I decided to make a statement. I was in shock and emotional and my hands were shaking as I commenced. I said:

> Because most of Jim McGinty's discourse has been offensively denigrating of Brian and me, at the outset I want to make it clear that I have always publicly and privately supported the establishment and continued operation of the CCC, but I have grave concerns about its practices and processes and the adequacy of the oversight provisions of the CCC Act.

I then went on to say that CCC activity in respect to me had been accompanied by an unprecedented level of surveillance, including a CCC break-in to our apartment.

Also, that "the planting of bugs in our house and mobile cameras at the front lamppost, together with the full suite of electronic eavesdropping" had severely traumatised my wife Lesley and daughter Siobhan. It had driven us from our home.

Additionally, I added that once the CCC hearings commenced we had sure knowledge that we were in deep trouble, but that we never ever knew of what we were being accused throughout the CCC process. The right to call witnesses, cross-examine witnesses, give evidence on our own behalf or make submissions during the CCC public hearings had been denied.

As quickly as I could, I tried to explain that the screaming headlines that had electrifyingly dominated the state and national media, on which McGinty had just commented, proved to be without substance after more calmly considered examination. So much so that they were quietly dropped by the CCC, never to be raised again.

I mentioned just a few of those headlines, mainly in *The West Australian*:

> "Smelly fingers linger over Canal Rocks" (implied corruption of councillors) 25 October 2006.

"Minister enmeshed in CCC inquiry" (suggested improper appointment to Government job) 26 October 2006.

"Minister lobbied project – Resigned out of shame" (alleged illicit influence by Minister Norm Marlborough) 27 October 2006.

"Greed appears in many guises" (greed drove players in Smiths Beach development) 2 November 2006.

"Premier risks Cabinet integrity" (Cabinet compromised) 2 November 2006.

"Yet another Cabinet crisis" (implied bribery) 3 November 2006.

I mentioned that these hair-raising allegations and many others had destroyed the careers and reputations of innocent parliamentarians and upright public servants – mostly in circumstances where they were not permitted even the basic right to explain or defend themselves before "findings" were made against them.

I asserted the public had been so poisoned by the sustained media barrage that the toxicity remained, even when the allegations were dropped or when they were proved false. I explained that, generally, the CCC rarely issued any corrections and in its privileged statutory position was immune from legal action, except in exceptional circumstances.

I added at the end that my lobbying activity had always been carried on with scrupulous legality, ethics and morality. Then I said directly to McGinty:

> Jim, you appear to be particularly upset by the fact that we continued lobbying for FMG and others after we were banned by Premier Geoff Gallop. Well, apart from the fact that the ban lacked any statutory or regulatory basis, Dr Gallop was never prepared to publicly explain it or put it in writing. Many ministers and most public servants thought, in the circumstances, that it was not justified and simply ignored it. For Brian and my part, we simply got on with our job.

There was much more that I wanted to include about the CCC's damaging practices, but I appreciated that I wasn't a designated speaker and that I had taken some liberties. Consequently, I resumed my seat.

Elizabeth Macknay appeared a little confused about what to do next. Ultimately, she asked McGinty (to whom most of my statement had been directed) whether he wanted to respond. When he got to his feet, it suddenly dawned on me that the former Attorney-General may not have been aware that I had been in the audience when he initially spoke. His face was red and his body language was of a person who had been compromised.

He had arrived at the death knock, had immediately been requested to deliver the opening address, had not spoken to me and may easily have missed me in the crowd. His response was almost meek. Interestingly, he did not dispute anything that I had said. He commented: "I never meant to imply that the CCC was perfect. I did not say that they never made mistakes. I concede that some innocent parties may have been damaged. Amendment has been made to CCC procedures."

I nearly got back to my feet to say: "Yes, that is fine, but the CCC is arguing against any changes to its legislation that would entrench fair procedure, as is, at least in part, extended by its New South Wales counterpart."

However, I didn't further respond and that panel discussion ended there with participants adjourning for further drinks.

Almost immediately, journalist Amanda O'Brien came up to me and said: "You won't be too happy with me. I have taken up a permanent position as a media officer with the CCC."

I responded: "I have no problems with that, and I wish you well. As you have heard, I support the CCC as an institution. I hate corruption and I have observed its debilitating effects overseas."

O'Brien had previously been a press secretary for McGinty and had been a journalist with *The Australian* at the time of the CCC public hearing in the Smiths Beach and Lobbyists terms of reference. She had filed some of the most alarming stories of perceived corruption, but now she volunteered: "I want to say how much I regret some of those stories that I wrote. We were all carried away with the media frenzy. I want you to believe me."

Elizabeth Macknay later emailed me:

> Thank you for joining us at our presentation about the CCC last night. Your contribution was invaluable. I spoke with many clients after the formal part of the evening who commented that your observations gave them a real and practical sense of some of the difficulties (at least historically) with the operation of the CCC.

And now to return to my theory about Jim McGinty's role. At the time of the public hearing on the Smiths Beach and Lobbyists matters, there were persistent rumours that the then Attorney-General was privately and heavily denigrating Burke and Grill to Ministers and Members of Parliament.

However, I had not personally experienced such aspersions until that panel discussions of November 2013. Hearing it directly from McGinty was like receiving a fist in the face. However, the express mention of Geoff Gallop's lobbying ban on Brian and me endorsed my view that it was somehow especially pertinent to him. It added to my suspicion that he may have had a bigger hand in the proscription of Brian and me by Gallop than shows on the public record.

As I have explained elsewhere, when Premier Gallop announced the prohibition in March 2003 he failed to justify it with any facts or assertions of specific improper conduct. It had all the hallmarks of arbitrariness and disappointing arrogance. Lesley was particularly hurt by Dr Gallop's actions, pointing out by letter the sacrifices our family had made for the ALP over decades and asked for some justification of his ban. The Premier disdained any personal reply.

As far as the ban applied to Brian Burke, it was an extraordinary process. No other Premier had boycotted a former Premier of the same party or any other political party. The circumstances were that Gallop surely must have known that he was effectively attempting to confiscate Burke's only substantial source of income.

Brian and I did, of course, extensively discuss the ban. We were unaware of any impropriety on our part.

It remains a mystery what triggered the ban, as Gallop has never explained his reasons, but he has maintained that the CCC public hearings legitimised his actions. I strongly dispute that conclusion.

On the other hand, McGinty's position has always been conspicuously apparent. On 31 March 2007, well before the reports on Smiths Beach and Lobbyists terms of reference were finalised and presented, he was reported by Perth journalist Joseph Poprzeczny in *News Weekly* as follows:

> "Brian Burke's reputation, his own government's reputation he has destroyed: the governments of Peter Dowding and Carmen Lawrence, Brian Burke single-handedly destroyed; he did his best to destroy Geoff Gallop, and now he is doing his best to destroy Alan Carpenter as the premier of this state," said McGinty.
>
> It's even spread nationally and [is] now having a detrimental effect on Kevin Rudd's leadership of the national party.
>
> These people, Brian Burke in particular, are like cannibals: they kill and devour their own friends and supporters, I cannot begin to understand why they do that to their own.[65]

It is hard to imagine a more intemperate statement by an Attorney-General.

McGinty's assertion about the Burke, Dowding and Lawrence governments only had a small element of truth, and then only if Burke had been responsible for the commitment to the failed Petrochemical Industries Company Limited (PICL) project. This potential development related to a major petrochemical and caustic soda plant at Kwinana south of Fremantle, in association with Bond Corporation.

It resulted in a loss of $1 billion to the government and its agen-

---

[65] *News Weekly*, 31 March 2007.

cies, but a large proportion of it was recovered when the (Bell) litigation was finally settled in December 2019. It was by far the biggest issue examined by the Royal Commission into Commercial Activities of Government and Other Activities, set up by Premier Carmen Lawrence.

As I have clarified elsewhere, this project was not even on the horizon when Burke retired. Certainly, he went to jail in 1994 after it was discovered coincidentally to the royal commission that he had wrongly claimed on his travel expense account. That "sin" of erroneous travel expense claims was also committed by many other MPs, including Carmen Lawrence and Tony Abbott, but with no penalty imposed.

Brian's conviction was never central, or even relevant, to the operation of government. He did nothing that reflected adversely on the Gallop Government. The CCC had conspicuously failed to prove that he committed any impropriety.

As I maintain, Alan Carpenter's Government suffered badly as a result of the CCC hearings, but when all of the facts are taken into account, our lobbying activities were not to blame.

Further, the Carpenter Government's standing had recovered entirely soon after the CCC's Smiths Beach and Lobbyists hearings were completed. Carpenter was well ahead in the polls by the end of 2007. As I demonstrate in Chapter 14, Carpenter made a major mistake in calling an early election after McGinty went to war with *The West Australian* and upset other substantial elements of the WA media.

In an *AAP* online article dated 3 March 2009 (the day after he announced his retirement), McGinty is reported this way:

> He did not believe that his three year feud with *The West Australian* newspaper had been responsible for Labor's election defeat, but conceded that it might have been a factor.

Read Chapter 14 and make your own judgment.

In the same article, McGinty was presumptuous enough to speak for several premiers including Peter Dowding, Carmen Lawrence, Geoff Gallop and Alan Carpenter, when he stated:

> If you look at the premiers I served under they all made it quite clear Brian Burke was a figure from the past that didn't represent contemporary behaviour.

This was a jaundiced statement about a man who, in 1983, on behalf of the ALP had finally broken a very long period of conservative hegemony, and set the party up for three consecutive wins. McGinty's allegation (above) concerning the Rudd leadership was just preposterous and doesn't merit response.

Brian Burke's record of achievement as Premier is unsurpassed by any other WA Labor leader. I refer to it in Chapter 16, "Brian Burke – the 'godfather'". Take a look and you will be impressed.

Respected veteran journalist Peter Kennedy makes a more favourable assessment. In his book *Tales from Boomtown*, Kennedy presents the following question and answer:

> So who are the stand-out premiers? Without doubt they are Sir Charles Court and Brian Burke, but for widely divergent reasons.[66]

The assertions by McGinty, in the main, were grievously defamatory. Equally, Gallop considered that he could proscribe us without giving just cause.

How could this occur in a representative democracy with a free press? It was, I believe, to a large degree the result of the way the CCC ran its hearings and influenced the media so that the concomitant media coverage created a toxic environment.

The damage done by the succession of false CCC accusations appeared to be cumulative and enduring, even when, after the passing of time, they failed for want of evidence. It seemed to work for the CCC because neither the public, nor the media, had the ability to review and contrast the CCC's initial extravagant depositions against the exculpatory outcome.

---

[66] *Tales from Boomtown: Western Australian Premiers from Brand to Barnett*, by Peter Kennedy, p. 6.

No one seemed to keep score. The media just neglected (except on a couple of rare occasions) to produce a retrospective assessment. It seemed as though they were just too preoccupied with the prospect of the next so-called "scandal".

It is all made vague by an overwhelming miasma of swirling, but un-evidenced, allegations of impropriety; making it possible for our detractors to allude to "scandal" without referencing one fact.

Few journalists are heroic enough to risk their status on defending contaminated goods.

But in a just society and pursuant to better legislation, the CCC would not have been allowed to attack citizens, damage them significantly and leave them without redress.

11

THE CCC'S WEAKNESSES AND MISTAKES START TO EMERGE

The intention of the *Corruption and Crime Commission Act 2003* was virtuous, but its execution has been shameful. The CCC's inability to address its most crucial role can be traced back to the poor drafting.

No political scientist who has ventured far from Australia's shores could remain ignorant of how seriously rampant corruption has blighted the lives and aspirations of so many citizens of so many countries.

Although Australia has a relatively low incidence of criminal corruption, few in legal spheres do not welcome a strong corruption-fighting body.

However, it is very rare for a new institution such as Western Australia's CCC to enjoy the initial "perceived" success or acclaim that it did. Regrettably, this early promise led to an unhealthy environment where the CCC believed it could do no wrong; and the community seemingly agreed.

An example of the unrealistic euphoria and over-the-top hyperbole employed by legislators in respect to the CCC was reflected on by John Hyde, MLA for Perth and an early chair of the parliamentary Joint Standing Committee on the Corruption and Crime Commission (JSCCCC), which oversees the CCC. In a paper he presented at an international conference during the early years of the CCC he included the comment:

> A few weeks back, some colleagues mused that this had to be the best corruption commission in the world.[67]

Hyde did not say if he agreed. But this and similar statements

---
[67] *The Australian Parliamentary Review*, Autumn 2006, pp. 102-110.

made by a variety of people were doubly disappointing because the JSCCCC was established for the specific purpose of casting a sceptical eye over the CCC's activities.

Within a few years, a more experienced Hyde was to adopt a substantially different perspective on the CCC. However, his comment above indicates how thoroughly the CCC had captured public approval, dominated the media in its own interest, and commanded the legislature and its own watchdog, the JSCCCC, in late 2006, through 2007 and in early 2008.

It was therefore of great interest to observe the CCC, in the period leading up to the writing of this book, slowly becoming a symbol of misuse and abuse of power.

The changed fortune of the CCC had its unfortunate genesis in its initial legislation of May 2003. The seeds of its foremost problem lay in the fact that the Act was far too ambitious and raised unrealistic expectations. It was contemplated that the legislation would embrace a very broad jurisdiction, ranging from minor public service impropriety, through to police corruption and to investigating and prosecuting organised crime.

An additional significant defect was that the CCC was granted immense powers and open-ended discretions, but its overseeing bodies, the JSCCCC and Parliamentary Inspector (PI), were not assigned complementary supervisory powers, suffered insufficient inquiry capability and had no direct ability to critique the CCC's procedures.

Additionally, the injudicious use of "public hearings" had huge capacity to injure innocent parties unfairly. The CCC was, at its core, a secret police force with all of the potential problems such bodies have had traditionally.

There was undeniably an urgent and critical need for a well-resourced body in WA to independently and fearlessly handle complaints against the police. Essentially, until this time, a section of the police force itself had adjudicated alleged malpractice by individual police officers. History repeatedly demonstrated that this "Caesar judging Caesar" model was defective. Few complaints against police were ever upheld and most were not investigated.

As a result, it is difficult to quantify just how much police corruption there was. Some well-informed observers maintain it existed on a mammoth scale.

However, there is considerable anecdotal evidence that when corruption was found by the police internal investigating unit, the perpetrators were requested to resign, with full entitlements, rather than being made to face prosecution.

Unhappily, as we shall see in Chapter 12, "Corruption, dysfunction, conflict exposed in CCC", there was an almost exactly similar situation in that body.

Ultimately, the 2002 Kennedy Royal Commission into the WA police force found substantial criminality. The State Ombudsman and the previous Anti-Corruption Commission had been assigned a role of shining a light on, and prosecuting, police corruption, but they were simply inadequately equipped to do the job.

An arena where it was difficult to obscure police malpractice was when criminal convictions were taken to review in higher jurisdictions by aggrieved appellants. Complaints then came under judicial scrutiny.

There is an embarrassingly long line of cases in WA where this has occurred and where serious police misconduct has been exposed. Deplorably, in many of these cases it has taken much time and effort by crusading lawyers such as Malcolm McCusker and Tom Percy, and determined campaigning journalists such as Estelle Blackburn, for ultimate justice to be done.

Distressingly, the road to justice has been made much harder historically by an arrogant senior judiciary that has often been too uncritical of the provenance of pivotal police evidence.

When lawyers discuss this depressing line of cases, they often start with the conviction for murder of Darryl Beamish. Beamish was the first person to be wrongly convicted for a murder actually committed by WA's most notorious killer, Eric Edgar Cooke. Beamish at the time of the murder was an 18-year-old deaf mute. He was unjustly sentenced to death for the brutal and senseless slaying of young socialite Jillian Brewer in the up-market Perth suburb of Cottesloe on 20 December 1959.

Beamish was ultimately saved from the hangman, but his arrest, trial and aftermath were a media sensation in WA. He served 15 years jail before his death sentence was commuted to life imprisonment. In all, it took 45 years to April 2005 for his conviction to be overturned on appeal at the sixth attempt. That Appeal Court comprised Justices Christopher Steytler, Christine Wheeler and Carmel McLure.

The miscarriage of justice in the Beamish case was the subject of the immaculately researched 2013 book *Presumed Guilty* by well-known journalist and editor Bret Christian. Tom Percy QC described the work as a "masterly, incisive and compelling work that belongs on the curriculum at every law school and every secondary school in this State".

After acquittal, an ever-humble Beamish made it clear that he was not interested in financial compensation for his ordeal. He stated:

> All I ever wanted was truth and justice. I have just wanted everyone to know for sure that I did not kill anyone.[68]

Eric Edgar Cooke conducted a bloody reign of terror and slaughter in inner Perth suburbs from February 1959 to August 1963. No Australian serial killer has ever had an impact on the population of an Australian city in the way that Cooke did on the residents of Perth before his capture in August 1963.[69]

Blackburn, in an article written in *The West Australian* on 21 January 2013, maintained that Cooke admitted to eight murders, 14 attacks on people who survived, five deliberate hit-and-runs and five attacks on sleeping women. He shot, stabbed, mutilated, ran down and strangled his victims. Necrophilia and abuse of Constance Lucy Madrill with a bottle were part of the gruesome picture.

Additionally, he confessed to more than 250 breaking and entering offences. No one was immune to the hysteria and distress that gripped Perth. Many came under suspicion.

---

[68] Statement attributed to Mr Beamish on 1 April 2005, as reported in *The Sydney Morning Herald*, 13 October 2014.
[69] *Australian Serial Killers*, by Paul B. Kidd, Macmillan Australia 2000.

Sometime in 1963, on a date that I cannot now remember, I was apprehended while jogging from my parents' house in Subiaco back to my accommodation at Kingswood College at the University of WA. I had done nothing more suspicious than run through streets late at night. The police questioned me for some considerable time about my movements and my habits before I was released.

Many Perth citizens had the same experience. It all related to the Eric Edgar Cooke crime wave.

Later that year, on 10 August, Shirley McLeod, a UWA science student, was shot dead by Cooke while baby-sitting in Dalkeith. Ms McLeod was intelligent and attractive. I had been taking her out and I was fond of her. Her parents, whom I visited shortly after Shirley's death, were devastated. Her brother, Denis, who was a friend and in my year in law school, was gutted.

Shirley McLeod was unknown to Cooke. There was no motive and no rationale. Just a promising life ended and deep pain for those left behind.

Cooke gave a detailed confession to the police and the Appeal Court of the killing and butchering of Jillian Brewer with a tomahawk and scissors. It contained some material not previously known by the police. Unfortunately, this confession, which was repeated on several occasions, including by Cooke with his hand on a bible just before he was executed on 24 October 1964, came too late to prevent Darryl Beamish being convicted in 1961.

The critical evidence employed against Mr Beamish by the police and prosecution was a highly dubious confession. This material was adduced from Beamish by Detective Owen Leitch, who gained considerable professional status from the conviction and later went on to become Commissioner of Police.

In his book, Christian writes of Leitch:

> Leitch's years as Commissioner of Police were controversial, his term marked by arguments over civil liberties, street demonstrations and trenchant accusations of political bias.[70]

---

[70] *Presumed Guilty*, by Bret Christian, Hardie Grant Books 2013. p. 26.

The presiding judge at the Darryl Beamish trial in 1961 was the Chief Justice, Sir Albert Wolff, and he was to play a pivotal role, not just in the trial, but also in the subsequent appeals.

Beamish always maintained that the signed "confession" was not true and that he was unaware of what he was signing.

Christian commented on the Beamish "confession" on page 28 of his book in the following terms:

> Leitch had extracted a confession to die for. But there were a couple of problems with it. Problems not evident from a casual reading. First, not one word of it was true. Second, because Darryl Beamish had for all his twenty years been totally deaf and could not speak a word. No information from his ears reached his quite normal brain, preventing it from processing sound. No instructions could be sent to his healthy voice box, so Beamish, in common with other profoundly deaf people, unknowingly emitted grunts and squeaks when he was excited or stressed, such as when he was playing football or being accused of murder. Much grimacing, hand and arm gestures accompanied these grunts as he tried to make himself understood to those unable to sign (sign language).
>
> Darryl Beamish pleaded not guilty, but the confessional evidence as advanced by Detective Leitch dominated jury consideration. The case was taken to court by Sir Ronald Wilson, WA's top prosecutor." He later went on to the High Court and subsequently headed up the Commonwealth Royal Commission into "The Stolen Generation".
>
> However, there were many people who could see, almost from the beginning, that there was considerable potential for a gross injustice in the Darryl Beamish case. I believe that that was why the execution did not go ahead and the sentence was commuted by the Brand Government.
>
> After it became public that Eric Edgar Cooke had confessed in graphic detail to Jillian Brewer's murder, the

public disquiet about Darryl Beamish's adjudged culpability only increased.

Many other ordinary citizens were convinced of Darryl Beamish's innocence. For instance, Jim Irwin, Lesley's uncle, gave generously to see that Beamish was represented by competent legal counsel. Later, he also contributed to Lindy Chamberlain's defence fund. Like many of those who subscribed to their innocence, Jim Irwin never lived to see either of them exonerated. However, he epitomised an innate sense of justice that was felt by a working-class man for other ordinary people unjustly accused.

Beamish's lawyers were successful in arranging a second appeal, where Cooke gave direct evidence to a three-judge Appeal Court. Once again, Cooke confessed in detail. Incredibly, Chief Justice Albert Wolff led the bench. That is, in an appeal against his own judgment! Talk about a loaded system.

Justice Wolff was originally a prosecutor from the Crown Law Department and he had a prosecutor's mentality. In the appeal, Ronald Wilson was again leading the attack. Cooke was simply branded a liar.

The prejudicial language used by Wolff and the biased position that he adopted is reflected by Bret Christian in chapters 6, 7 and 8 of his book. In short, Wolff simply, and almost immediately, wrote Cooke off as a "self-confessed liar and utterly worthless scoundrel" whose testimony was not worth considering. Appeal dismissed.

Christian continued:

> Darryl Beamish was a young man of no means and he came from a working-class family. They did not have the means to finance a defence, at trial, or at the appeals that followed. Nonetheless, there were lawyers who were shocked and outraged at what was being meted out to this gentle, disabled young man who had never shown any tendency to violence. One of these was Sir Frances Burt, later Chief Justice and Governor of Western Australia. He was one of the greatest jurists the State has produced. He was drawn to act for Darryl Beamish, although not at the

original trial. Francis Burt acted at a very much reduced fee as he took the case right through to the Privy Council, without success."

The Beamish case disillusioned Burt and brought about a change in his attitude to the criminal justice system.

On page 164, Christian lays out Francis Burt's theory on what happened:

> Sir Francis Burt . . . had a theory about why the truth of the Beamish case remained comprehensively covered up. He says it was influenced by fear that the Jillian Brewer murder had so high a profile, and the violence had been so extreme, that in such a highly charged atmosphere a jittery public would lose confidence in the police and courts were Cooke found to have murdered her – this notion infecting judges as well as police.
>
> A layman's interpretation is that Beamish stayed convicted to protect the System.
>
> Sir Francis added: "Before Beamish, I thought the administration of the criminal law was fair. That case changed my mind."

Christian continued:

> In the Darryl Beamish case, there was no direct objective evidence of his guilt. For instance, it was not established that Darryl Beamish knew Jillian Brewer, had ever been to the scene of the murder, had ever handled the murder weapon, etc. The only evidence that this essentially unaggressive, naïve, profoundly handicapped youth had suddenly, somehow been turned into a homicidal maniac, was the confession obtained by Owen Leitch.
>
> The Appeal Court, if it were going to overthrow the guilty verdict, had to invalidate the confession. That would have entailed a process that would at least have implied that Leitch had manufactured the confession and had committed perjury. In the 1960s, in parochial Perth, that would

have been an earth moving event and just too much for the system.

Ultimately, it took a new generation of Appeal Court judges in 2005 for the egregious wrong to Darryl Beamish to be rectified. In the meantime, a series of innocent people were convicted of extremely serious crimes, but later acquitted after appeal. The consistent thread running through these cases was the substantial suspicion, and in some cases proof, that the police manufactured confessions and other evidence to obtain convictions. The other consistent fact was that there was no effective police oversight body.

I want to give you a flavour of how disastrously distorted the administration of justice became in WA and underline the crucial need for a powerful police integrity body. Perhaps I can do that by quoting a few paragraphs from Tom Percy's speech when he launched *Presumed Guilty*:

> It's nearly 15 years since Estelle Blackburn wrote her epic book *Broken Lives*. It won every award in its category. It captivated the State and won her the Order of Australia. It set two men free. (They were Darryl Beamish over the Jillian Brewer murder and John Button over Rosemary Anderson's murder – author). Most of us liked to think that it would be the end of the line for books like this. This sort of thing was a debacle of the past, wasn't it? Sadly, it wasn't.
>
> In his book, Bret deals comprehensively with the disgraceful litany of cases that have occurred in WA since then.
>
> Colleen Egan's book *Murder No More* documented how Andrew Mallard's case was a huge blot on the copybook of WA justice; a jury and two Courts of Appeal getting the entire case horribly wrong.
>
> And then there is the appalling saga of the Mickelbergs. I hardly need to elaborate on that disaster.
>
> Not to mention cases like Rory Christie, Clark Easterday, Lloyd Rayney. The list is extensive and embarrassing.

Then there are the unresolved miscarriages, like the case of Arthur Greer (still languishing in prison 12 years after his parole date for a murder he almost certainly didn't commit) and who knows how many others?[71]

I would only add that in the case of John Button, the confession material was coerced from a naïve and vulnerable young man who had a bad stutter. It was similar to the confession extracted from Darryl Beamish.

Button always disputed the so-called confession, and irrefutable evidence later emerged by which he was totally exonerated of a murder committed by Eric Cooke. It is an unavoidable conclusion that Button's "confession" was fabricated. It was to the great credit of the late David Malcolm, the Chief Justice, when he overturned Button's wrongful conviction in 2002 – after nearly 40 years.

Chief Justice Malcolm also played the ultimate role in the Mickelberg case, when he wrote the appeal judgement that exonerated the two surviving brothers, Ray and Peter Mickelberg. That was after seven tries at appeal. Justice Malcolm was an exceptional jurist. In both the Button and Mickelberg cases, the police and "the system" fought a fair outcome every inch of the way.

Andrew Mallard was also fragile. He had a significant mental health condition for which he was undergoing psychiatric treatment when he was wrongly convicted of the murder of Pamela Lawrence in her jewellery shop in the Perth suburb of Mosman Park. The case followed the distressing pattern of Beamish and Button.

Mallard spent 12 years of a 30-year jail sentence in prison for a murder that most now know was committed by convicted killer Simon Rockford, who left his prints at the scene of the crime. Mallard refused to sign a confession, but this did not stop the police from alleging a verbal confession, which, despite any direct evidence against him, was enough to obtain a conviction.

That "confession" was much later proved to be a fabrication. Exculpatory evidence had been deliberately suppressed. The scandal went high into the police force. Adverse findings were made against

---

[71] thestarfish.com.au/tom-percy-justice-wa-style/

Assistant Police Commissioners Mal Shervill and David Caporn. The Deputy Director of Public Prosecutions, Ken Bates, had similar adverse findings against him and was likewise forced to resign.

As with Beamish and Button, the painstaking work of bringing about justice was done by another courageous journalist, Colleen Egan, and brilliantly followed up by lawyers John Quigley and Malcolm McCusker.

In the case of the Mickelberg brothers, who spent significant periods in jail before their convictions were quashed, there was clear evidence that senior police actually went out and manufactured evidence. Avon Lovell's books, *The Mickelberg Stitch* and *Litany of Lies*, give the very disturbing particulars on this appalling instance of police dishonesty.

Almost as disturbing was the part played by the senior judiciary within the State. In all cases, the wrongly convicted young men spent significant periods in jail. In all cases, the judges of the day appeared to credulously accept the dubious evidence of the police witnesses. In the Mallard and Mickelberg matters, the cases had to be taken out of WA (to the High Court) before the convictions were overturned.

The Perth Mint Swindle involved three brothers, Ray, Peter and Brian Mickelberg, who respectively received jail sentences of 20, 16 and 12 years after going on trial in 1983. In 2002, midway through the WA (Inc) Royal Commission into police corruption, Detective Tony Lewandowski confessed that he and Detective Don Hancock had fabricated evidence that was used to help frame the brothers.

Disturbingly, such spurious convictions seemed to be the way to promotion. Hancock became head of the Criminal Investigation Bureau shortly after.

After seven attempts at appeal, the brothers were exonerated in 2004, more than 20 years after the convictions.

In a sequel to these events, Hancock was blown up and killed by Gypsy Joker bikie Sid Reid, who maintained it was a payback because Hancock had murdered gang member Billy Grierson by shooting him near Hancock's Ora Banda Hotel in the Eastern Goldfields.

In comparison with the Mickelberg proceedings, the departures from accepted norms of justice in the cases of Rory Christie and Clark Easterday and his co-accused were not so extreme.

Christie was convicted of the murder of his wife on scant circumstantial evidence in 2003 and sent to jail for life. However, after appeal and a second trial, he was entirely acquitted. The appeal and second trial produced new exculpatory evidence that had previously been "lost" by the prosecution.

In the Clark Easterday (and two others) matter, infamously known as the Karpa Gold Swindle, the three men were convicted in 1993 of fraud for supposedly "salting" the Karpa Gold Mine and thereby cheating investors. They went to jail, but an engineer by the name of Michael McGowan, working *pro bono* and spending more than $60,000 of his own money, proved that it was impossible for the mine to have been salted in the way that the prosecution had alleged. The accused were acquitted on appeal.

In each case it was ultimately adjudged that there just wasn't credible evidence to justify the initial prosecutions.

Readers would appreciate that the police power to prosecute is a very potent weapon. Few accused, even where they are thoroughly exonerated, recover – mentally, materially or reputationally – from such an ordeal. Exactly the same comments apply to a situation where the CCC uses its powers to target witnesses in public hearings.

Mr Percy also mentioned Lloyd Rayney and his prosecution for the murder of his wife. It is a matter of record that Mr Rayney was acquitted at trial, and his acquittal upheld on appeal. Some of the police were severely criticised by the trial judge for the procedures and activities they engaged in prior to the trial. Subsequently, Mr Rayney sued the police for comments made prior to trial that "he was the prime and only suspect for the murder". He was eventually awarded $2.62 million in damages, a record.

The suit proved not only that the police got it badly wrong, but also that they have to be very careful concerning negligent comments made publicly during an investigation. Also, it contrasted with the licence given to CCC officers under the CCC Act, where officers can make reckless findings with impunity. I comment on that irony below.

The call for a probe into these grave allegations appears to have elicited little publicly known action. The CCC has a clear jurisdiction to undertake an inquiry. It seems that it has not done so.

Ultimately, because of public concern about police malfeasance, something was in fact done about this situation in WA. A royal commission into police corruption was finally called.

The legacy police culture, handed down over the decades, was made the subject of Mr Justice Geoffrey Kennedy's comments as part of his 2004 report on WA Police Corruption:

> The blue wall of silence, the code, brotherhood, secrecy, loyalty, solidarity and protecting your mates; these are the constructs upon which traditional assumptions about police culture have been built. They shape the behaviour of police officers and are exemplified in the stereotypical 'tough copper', who looks out for his mates and never 'dobs them in', is by nature suspicious, is tough on criminals and does what he has to do to get the job done.[72]

The highest and most primal task of any ruling body is to keep its citizens safe. In modern civilised states, that is principally done by the police force. In other nation states, it can be done by the army or a warlord. In summary, the police are our guardians. But what happens when the guardians abuse their authority or harbour elements of corruption? That is where WA found itself in 2002.

Partly because of the criminal cases like the ones mentioned above, and partially due to what Justice Kennedy referred to as "persistent public concern and foment over several controversial outcomes of investigations by WAPS (WA Police Service) and an abiding public doubt over the integrity of the Police Service",[73] the Kennedy Royal Commission into police corruption was set up on 12 December 2001. The terms of reference allowed Kennedy to go back only to 1985.

There were many people disappointed by that limitation, but there

---

[72] *Royal Commission Into Whether There Has Been Corrupt or Criminal Conduct by Any Western Australian Police Officer, Final Report*, January 2004, p. 31
[73] Ibid., p. 2.

was plenty of material to keep Justice Kennedy and his team busy for more than three years. He took evidence on a number of specific cases of police corruption and illegal conduct. For reasons of space, I shall not review these cases, but I can assure you that some of the disclosures were hair-raising and went to the core of administration of justice.

Justice Kennedy also looked at similar inquiries in other states and places, including the Fitzgerald Commission in Queensland in 1987, the Mollen Commission in New York in 1994, the Wood Commission in NSW in 1997, and the Los Angeles Board of Inquiry of 2000. All of these inquiries uncovered extensive corrupt or criminal conduct ranging from stealing to assaults, perjury, drug dealing and improper disclosure of confidential information.

Justice Kennedy found evidence of the "full range" of those activities by police in WA. He also determined that existing internal and external police oversight bodies were inadequate. He reported:

> What is of more significance is the extent to which WAPS had been ineffective in monitoring those (improper) events and modifying its procedures in order to deal with that conduct and to prevent its repetition.[74]

That comment also embraced the current Anti-Corruption Commission (ACC), which he concluded, "lacked the necessary powers".

Justice Kennedy decided that the oversight inadequacies were so critical that he brought down an interim report in December 2002 recommending the replacement of the ACC by a new more powerful Corruption and Crime Commission.

New legislation to set up that body was assented to on 3 July 2003. The appointments of District Court Chief Judge Kevin Hammond as Commissioner and Malcolm McCusker QC as independent Parliamentary Inspector of the new body were made on 24 December 2003.

As its genesis clearly indicates, the driving necessity for a new CCC body stemmed from the Kennedy Commission into police cor-

---

[74] Ibid.

ruption and from the requirement for an effective police integrity overseer.

It must be said that the State Attorney-General, Jim McGinty, acted on the Kennedy interim report with considerable dispatch. Fighting organised crime was a dubious add-on. The Attorney-General was acutely aware that the CCC was about overseeing police integrity and probity. In the second reading debate on the new CCC Bill, McGinty he had this to say:

> At the last state election, Labor made an important commitment to the people of Western Australia to establish a royal commission into police corruption. In this way we would fight police corruption and restore public confidence in the Western Australia's Police Service.[75]

But if appears not much has changed during the life of the CCC.

The highly distressing case of Scott Austic, which surfaced frequently in WA media over many years, epitomises the problematic nature of the Police/CCC interface and underlines the difficulty the CCC has had in its major responsibility. That is, keeping the police honest.

Mr Austic spent over 12 years in prison after he was convicted in 2009 of the wilful murder of his pregnant lover, Stacey Thorn, at Boddington, 120 kilometres south east of Perth, in 2007. The murder was particularly horrendous, with 21 stab wounds inflicted.

Mr Austic always maintained his innocence and, importantly, his mother fervently believed that he was not guilty. She campaigned and, after considerable legal setbacks, with lawyer Dr Clint Hampson, help from Malcolm McCusker QC and intervention by Attorney General John Quigley, the case was referred back to the WA Court of Criminal Appeal, which quashed the conviction.

In a retrial in the Supreme Court, in November 2020, Scott Austic was finally acquitted.

The media played a very positive role in highlighting the glaring evidentiary anomalies in the case.

---

[75] Extract from Hansard, Legislative Assembly, 15 May 2003, p7861b-7865a Jim McGinty.

The anomalies included the mysterious discovery of critical evidentiary items in areas that had previously been searched and/or searched and photographed by police. The items included the alleged murder weapon, a knife, that later expert evidence concluded could not have inflicted the wounds; as well as unexplained bloodied footprints that did no belong to the accused.

At the trial and subsequently, the defence team inferred that critical evidence had been planted by the police.

On 20 November 2020, *The West* ran a story by Tim Clarke indicating that Mr Austic's lawyers had called for a probe into police conduct during the initial investigation and referral for trial. On 24 November 2020, a story in *The West* by Shannon Hearne raised claims of police corruption.

On 23 November 2020, the ABC's Joanna Menagh reported on the Appeal Court finding of "credible evidence knife, cigarette packet planted at scene".

The call for a probe into these grave allegations appears to have elicited little publicly known action. The CCC has a clear jurisdiction to undertake an inquiry. It seems that it has not done so.

The CCC, when set up, enjoyed a comprehensive set of coercive powers and a clearly expressed priority from Parliament, namely to fight police impropriety and corruption. It was therefore more than strange that the CCC went off on an expensive and extraordinary frolic of its own.

That is, on a seven-year pursuit of private citizens Brian Burke and Julian Grill. In the process of this fundamentally barren chase, it ignored its paramount duty. That was to ensure that the police service operated ethically.

The Burke-Grill escapade consumed tens of millions of taxpayers' dollars. How much of the investigative and legal budget of the CCC that represented I cannot say; but it must have been a substantial part. Some further portion of the resources that were left over must have been deployed fighting the legitimate actions of Parliamentary Inspector Malcolm McCusker.

And what that meant was something that the ALP is still very loath to accept: that is, that this exercise, in real terms, was an indirect assault on the Government.

Although it was not understood at the time, especially by McGinty, who always showed excessive zeal in promoting the CCC, this costly pursuit saw the successive loss of five ministers (depending on how you count), one other Member of Parliament, effective control of the Legislative Council, a host of senior public servants, public service morale and ultimately, government.

As I have explained in other chapters, the CCC could not, under its Act, attack Brian Burke and me directly. The CCC was obliged to carry on that quest by taking down public officers. The whole process turned into an enfeebling assault on government. I discuss this strategic blunder by the government in the Chapter 14, "2008 Election: A CCC casualty".

Parliamentary Inspector slams CCC's police oversight

But back to the police. It took two-and-a-half years of assiduous work by Parliamentary Inspector Christopher Steytler to expose what had actually happened with complaints against the police.

Justice Steytler was appointed Parliamentary Inspector on 1 February 2009. On 8 September 2011, he brought down a report entitled: "Parliamentary Inspector's Report Concerning the Procedures Adopted by the CCC When Dealing with Complaints of Excessive Use of Force by Police."

PI Steytler was previously a skilled and highly regarded Supreme Court and Appeals Bench judge. Distressingly, his report concluded that for at least the period 1 July 2009 to 31 March 2011, the CCC had failed to investigate independently complaints of excessive force by the police.

Of 381 complaints during that period, only one had been investigated by the CCC. All other complaints were simply referred to the police service to handle in its own discretion. That is, just as it did in the bad old days before the Kennedy Royal Commission.

This lack of action by the CCC blatantly contradicted the proper discharge of the CCC's first priority. In a foreword to PI Steytler's report, the chairman of the parliamentary oversight committee, Nick Goiran MLC, confirmed the CCC's principal responsibility:

> The CCC's most important function is to ensure that the work and role of the WA Police is not hampered by misconduct or corruption.[76]

PI Steytler was clearly shocked and outraged by the CCC's indisputable neglect. To underline his point, he detailed two examples of the CCC's dereliction and referred to two other cases where the CCC ignored credible complaints against police officers. Both were instances where it was claimed that extreme violence had been unlawfully used by police officers.

Daniel Emerson wrote a front-page story on the two detailed cases for *The West* on 9 September 2011 under the headline: "Police bashing footage stolen".

It stated:

> CCTV footage of police kicking and Tasering a law professor during an unlawful arrest was burgled from his university office before officers presented edited footage of the incident in court.
>
> Corruption and Crime Commission parliamentary inspector Christopher Steytler revealed the case in a report tabled in State Parliament yesterday that criticised the CCC for investigating just one of 381 allegations of serious policed misconduct in two years.
>
> Mr Steytler recounted the version of events given by the associate professor of law from a Perth university who clashed with police near Fremantle's Esplanade Hotel early on November 2, 2008.
>
> The professor (Robert Cunningham) and a female com-

---

[76] *Parliamentary Inspector's Report Concerning the Procedures Adopted by the Corruption and Crime Commission When Dealing with Complaints of Excessive Use of Force by Police*, Report No 18 of the Joint Standing Committee on the Corruption and Crime Commission, tabled in the WA Parliament on 8 September 2011. p. x.

panion (Catherine Atoms, later his wife) were walking with a friend after celebrating the birthday of the professor, who had not been drinking, when he stopped to help a man who had fallen in a garden bed.

The professor saw two police officers speaking to his female companion when one office grabbed her arm, causing her to scream in pain.

When the professor asked why the officers were giving the woman a move-on notice, they pulled his arms behind his back, pushed him to the street and handcuffed him before one officer tried to trip him by kicking his legs.

He heard someone yell at the police from an Esplanade balcony that that person was recording the incident, before the professor and the woman were Tasered and taken to Fremantle Police Station, where they were charged with resisting arrest.

The footage was erased after police told the witness that night it was too dark to be used as evidence.

Separate CCTV footage from Marine House on Essex Street was released to the professor by police under disclosure provisions on March 2, 2009, after he and the woman pleaded not guilty.

"(But) on or about March 9, 2009, (the professor's) office at the university at which he lectures was broken into and his external hard drive was stolen, along with the CCTV footage of the incident," Mr Steytler said.

The CCTV footage presented in court by police on April 29, 2010, had gaps at the points the Tasering and kicks occurred, he said. The magistrate ruled the arrest unjustified and unlawful, dismissed the charges and accused police witnesses of colluding.

The professor complained to the CCC but it referred the matter to WA Police who, last December, found the officers had acted appropriately.

Mr Steytler noted the internal investigation was by officers from the Fremantle Police Station, who cleared their colleagues.

He said the case "raised some suggestion of tampering with evidence by (WA Police) officers" and the CCC's failure to investigate independently had "serious consequences for the administration of justice".

Mr Steytler also criticised the CCC for failing to investigate middle-aged Lynette Annandale's complaint of police heavy handedness while arresting her for unwittingly driving without a licence in Wembley in 2009.

Acting CCC commissioner Mark Herron said in the report that it only had the resources to investigate 10 per cent of complaints received.

But Attorney-General Christian Porter said the CCC's $120 million yearly budget was not fully spent each year.

Greg Barnes from *Crikey* gave a slightly different emphasis to the story when he wrote online on 12 September 2011: "Judge slams Crime and Corruption Commission over police abuse".

The story read:

> The home page of the Western Australian Corruption and Crime Commission describes the organisation as "a leading Australian anti-corruption body" whose task is to investigate "misconduct in the public sector".
>
> How then did the CCC fail to investigate two cases of gross misconduct on the part of the state's police force? In the first, police assaulted a university professor who subsequently found his office had been broken into and evidence about his case removed; the second case involved a middle aged woman who was on her way to assist some asylum seeker but who, after being stopped by traffic police, ended up being physically and verbally assaulted and placed in police cells and charged with criminal offences.
>
> The woman complained to the CCC, which did nothing about her complaint. Steytler took up the case and wrote

to the CCC chair Len Roberts-Smith, who dismissed the idea that the CCC should investigate the matter. In his view "the woman's complaint, if true, amounted to the use of minor force and intimidation and her behaviour contributed to the way events unfolded".

The second case involves a man, ironically a professor of Law at the University of Western Australia who was, with his girlfriend, assisting a man who had fallen over in Fremantle late at night. Police arrived on the scene and the professor and his girlfriend were assaulted by police and Tasered. They were taken to the local police station. The professor was charged and he obtained CCTV footage of the events.

His office at the university was subsequently broken into and his external hard drive, which contained the footage, was stolen. The professor was acquitted in the Magistrates Court after the magistrate who heard the case made adverse findings against the police involved. The professor complained to the CCC. The CCC undertook an examination of the matter but refused a full investigation.

Steytler was scathing of the CCC's inaction in these cases. "Abuses of power by police officers, especially those involving the use of excessive force, undermine the integrity of, and respect for, the justice system. The system is further undermined when the body relevantly tasked with the external oversight of (police) fails, almost entirely, to conduct independent investigations into serious and credible allegations concerning the use of excessive force. There can be no public confidence in the justice system in the absence of a vigorous, independent investigation of complaints of this kind," Steytler wrote.

One of the CCC's reasons for failing to investigate these matters was cost. But is this the real reason the CCC's priorities? This was the organisation that spent millions of dollars going after former premier Brian Burke and politician Julian Grill over their lobbying activities.

The Chairman Nick Goiran of the JSCCCC had this to say in *The West* on 10 September 2011:

> The CCC's failure to investigate nearly all allegations of serious police misconduct over the past two years gives the public the impression it is protecting the force.

The West editorialised on the issue on 12 September 2011. It made it clear the CCC was well on the way to losing its credibility.

At the conclusion of his report, Mr Steytler recommended:

> The CCC should change its procedures so as to implement the emphasis placed by the CCC Act on police misconduct by independently investigating instances at the upper end of the category of serious and credible complaints concerning the use of excessive force by police, especially complaints concerning the unnecessary discharge of a firearm or Taser.[77]

The firearms element comes from the case of Ian Quartermaine, which I address shortly.

In its submission to the JSCCCC, the CCC opposed the very reasonable proposition put forward by PI Steytler. It was a very informative insight into how the CCC viewed its most important duty. The CCC defensively insisted:

> Its procedures to deal with allegations of excessive use of force against police are appropriate and effective.[78]

The CCC went on to state:

> There is no need for it to independently investigate all credible and serious allegations concerning excessive use of force by WA police.[79]

Some people would find this statement astonishing.

Well, if the CCC was assertively content with its performance, then no-one else was.

---

[77] Ibid., p. 35.
[78] Ibid., p. 54.
[79] Ibid.

The CCC based its position on contentions that, firstly, "police should have primary responsibility for dealing with allegations of misconduct concerning police officers" and that would result in the "development of police ownership of responsibility for misconduct" and that that results in "positive cultural and organisational change".[80]

Secondly, that the CCC did not have the resources to do more following up of complaints.[81]

However, the CCC bizarrely suggested that if it had more resources it would apply it to excessive force within the Education Department.

No-one bought these CCC arguments. PI Steytler said:

> The CCC Act contemplates that the CCC ... will play a more active role in investigating police misconduct than other forms of public service misconduct. That was why s 21A was enacted, *requiring* (my emphasis) the Commissioner of Police to notify the CCC of "matters concerning, or that may concern, reviewable police action" ... Moreover, an almost complete failure to conduct independent investigations into allegations of the use of excessive force by police will do nothing to promote a culture of accountability. Rather, it is more likely to have the opposite effect. It will also result in a loss of faith in the justice system by those affected, coupled with disillusionment at the role played by the CCC.[82]

My personal view is that the CCC position was preposterous.

Police culture abused judicial system

History attests to the fact that decades of police investigating themselves had led to the worst abuses in WA judicial experience. The loose and partisan procedures had led to a police culture where the police considered that they were immune from prosecution for murder, through to corruption and even to traffic offences.

---

[80] Ibid., pp. 41-2.
[81] Ibid., p. 55.
[82] Ibid., pp. 33-4.

I would mention by way of explanation that the former head of the WA CIB, Don Hancock, mentioned above in relation to the Ora Banda murder, was never arrested for the crime, although most observers, including police who were closely involved, believe he did the shooting.

How is it possible for the CCC to seriously maintain that there was no need to investigate the wrongful arrest, repeated Tasering and assault of the law professor and his female companion in Fremantle? This case ultimately involved the most severe condemnation of the police witness and the total dismissal of the initial police charges by the courts.

However, much more sinister, it also contained high suspicion of intimidation of witnesses, destruction of video evidence and tampering with documentary evidence. How could the CCC possibly maintain that it was doing its duty by simply allowing the police arresting officers' colleagues to conduct their own inquiry and come to their own unfettered and unsupervised conclusions?

The media was not impressed. Paul Murray, writing in *The West*, stated:

> Blind Freddy can see the CCC has failed one of the key obligations under its enabling legislation, but it offered in response a spurious legalistic interpretation of the Act, arguing that the police should take 'primary responsibility' for investigating complaints against officers.
>
> At the risk of sounding sarcastic, 380 out of 381 does seem to push the term "primary responsibility" to its limits. . . The CCC even tried to run the hoary chestnut of under resourcing as an excuse.
>
> To put the matter into context, Messrs Burke and Grill estimated that the Commission spent $45 million pursuing them. So, the CCC priorities are questionable. And Attorney-General Christian Porter pointed out that the Commission did not spend all its budget over the past several years.

> Even with a political oversight committee and a parliamentary inspector, the CCC has the appearance of an agency out of control. It routinely thumbs its nose at its overseers.[83]

There is a postscript to the Fremantle Tasering case. After an eight-year battle, District Court Judge Felicity Davis ordered the police to pay $1.024 million damages and about $1 million in costs to law Professor Robert Cunningham and his wife, Catherine Atoms. Her Honour actually awarded exemplary damage, which is most unusual and gives an indication of her repugnance of the police actions.

PI Steytler's report mentioned two other matters, but did not give full details. They are fully explored in an addition to this chapter.

It was always appreciated that, next to the police, the one other area of endemic corruption was the prison system, which was awash with illegal drugs. However, the CCC's dereliction of duty and responsibility in relation to WA prisons was every bit as pervasive as it was with the police force.

The issue burst into the public domain in a sensational front-page story in *The West* by Gary Adshead on 29 June 2013. It was an extraordinary narrative based on a leaked jail dossier giving evidence of guards linked to organised crime figures, confidential prison information being disclosed, a list of guards being investigated for misconduct, compromised security, extreme misogyny and special favours for prisoners associated with motorcycle gangs and drug dealers.

Three days later, another article by Adshead implicated the CCC in a clique of investigators employed in at least five State Government agencies who were sharing information and strategies aimed at undermining the management of the Department of Corrective Services. It was publicly stated that CCC officers were involved.

On advice from the Public Service Commissioner, an alarmed Corrective Services Minister Joe Francis, without reference to the CCC, went to the police and requested that they investigate the entirely unsatisfactory situation in WA prisons. On 10 July 2013, he

---

[83] *The West Australian*, 14 September 2011.

dramatically made an unannounced spot check on Hakea Prison over an incident that had happened the previous month, but had been kept from him.

Police Commissioner Karl O'Callaghan set up Operation Ulysses, which, over a 12-month period, resulted in the arrest of 73 people, including three prison staff, over illegal activity associated with WA prisons. As a result of this success, there was a decision taken to set up a special policing unit for prisons.

It is acutely important to note that the CCC was pointedly excluded from this process and from any close ongoing role, although legislatively and notionally it still continued to have responsibilities. The obvious message was that the CCC was not only incompetent in this role, but was not trusted.

I venture the opinion (albeit on limited information) that the genesis of the CCC's problems was that its legislative functions were defined too widely and its resources spread too thin on less important matters – and on "misconceived quests" such as the Smiths Beach and Lobbyists terms of reference, where no corruption was found.

Think about it this way. Contemplate, in respect to the Smiths Beach, Lobbyists and CCC-inspired Parliamentary Committee hearings, the extent of the voluminous material investigated, the complexity of the issues, the number of court cases and appeals the CCC spawned, the avenues it entered (i.e. Parliament, Cabinet, local government and industry), the extensive electronic surveillance, the massive seizure effort, the legal questions raised, the analysis required, preparation of legal briefs, answering Parliamentary Inspector questions and a whole host of ancillary considerations, such as the vast amounts of time, human assets and finance it consumed. In duration, these inquiries and their aftermath extended from at least as early as 2005 to late 2014.

This set of inquiries, which PI Steytler asserted was into Burke and Grill, was a voracious monster that gobbled up resources. As time went on and it attained no tangible results, the CCC in desperation just threw more wasted energy into it. I suggest that there was little left over in the investigation section for any meaningful attention to be applied to police and prisons, which, as we now know, largely went unattended during that relevant time.

What is more, as I shall show in Chapter 12, "Corruption, dysfunction, conflict exposed in CCC", it also meant that the CCC hierarchy lost the ability to detect and control rogue activity within its own organisation.

The Government only gropingly appreciated the problem. Initial plans by the Barnett Government to enlarge the CCC's jurisdiction to give it a real role in respect to organised crime were shelved after the JSCCCC, under the chairmanship of Nick Goiran, strongly recommended against a move that potentially compromised the CCC's role of overseeing the police force.

The Barnett Government had already legislated, with the support of the McGowan Opposition, to remove jurisdiction from the CCC for all but the most serious of public service impropriety. The Government was well aware of the devastating blow the unfair and heavy-handed Smiths Beach and Lobbyists inquiries were to public service morale and did not want it repeated.

I have used the quote attributed to Public Service Commissioner Mal Wauchope elsewhere, but it is salient and worth repeating:

> The WA public service lost its confidence after high-profile Corruption and Crime Commission and other public inquiries, causing it to lapse into risk averse decision making that harmed the public interest.[84]

In New South Wales, in 1996, the Government set up the Police Integrity Commission, which focuses almost entirely on police.

The real quandary, both for those devising an effective anti-corruption system and for those investigating organised crime, is that they both need highly effective eavesdropping powers and the ability to enforce witnesses to testify in certain circumstances. The rub is that very few decision-makers believe that it is responsible to hand extensive eavesdropping powers and similar abilities to the police.

---

[84] *The West Australian* 20 February 2014, p. 17.

Just imagine for a moment how such powers, and the multi-million-dollar computerised equipment necessary, can be misused. We already know that the police central computer and records system is periodically misused and abused.

I maintain that the most intense focus should be put on ensuring that the police force is as free of corruption as possible. Once that is done, you have a chance of addressing wider corruption. If you can't solve police corruption, forget about the whole thing. It is the age-old question of who watches the watchers, or who guards the guardians. I tend to believe that a dedicated anti-corruption commission focused on the police is worth consideration in WA.

Suffice for the moment, in this chapter, firstly to indicate that the initially much-lauded CCC failed miserably in its core and most important duty, and that that failure was in large part due to legislative deficiencies that have only partly been overcome by *ad hoc* means.

Secondly, to look at the mechanism of public hearings used by the CCC. One of the themes of this book relates to the use and misuse of public hearings. It has been recognised by numerous eminent legal bodies that public hearings are potentially ruinous for many innocent witnesses.

If abused, or even if used carelessly, they can and have destroyed reputations and lain waste to careers without due cause. That is especially the case where the hearings were not conducted employing the principles of natural justice and procedural fairness.

Parliamentary committee rejects CCC methods

It can fairly be assumed that the JSCCCC inquiry into the CCC public hearings was largely motivated by the egregiously unfair way that witnesses were treated in the Smiths Beach and Lobbyists hearings. PI Chris Steytler made the point that:

> Experience shows that reputations are far more easily damaged than rehabilitated. It would be a triumph of optimism over experience to think that the Section 86 process provides an adequate mechanism for rehabilitation

of reputation.[85] (I shall deal with Section 86 of the CCC Act shortly.)

The JSCCCC took evidence concerning CCC Public hearings, commencing in 2010 and bringing down a final report on 27 March 2012. This ground-breaking report is available online. Serious problems with CCC public hearings were flagged early on by Malcolm McCusker during the Smiths Beach hearings and later taken up by Nick Goiran MLC as chairman of the JSCCCC. The JSCCCC, at that time, also included MPs John Hyde (deputy), Frank Alban and Matt Benson-Lidholm.

The CCC had essentially adopted public hearings as its default setting until that time. I made oral and written submissions (twice) to the JSCCCC, as did others including Mr Steytler, Mr McCusker, Chief Justice Wayne Martin and Brian Burke.

For me, it was and is a crucial issue, as the stain and trauma created by misdirected public hearings is destructive and indelible. Lesley and I ran into Justice Martin on the way in to the JSCCCC hearing room to give my evidence as he came out. The Chief Justice was friendly and affable, but the transcript would soon disclose that we were on different sides of the debate.

CJ Martin was there generally to give support to the CCC's position. The CCC argued that there should be no restriction on its discretion to use public hearings.

However, there was a heavy caveat on CJ Martin's support; that was that procedural fairness should be extended to witnesses. Messrs Steytler, McCusker, Burke, Grill and others, although not opposing CCC public hearings *per se* where appropriate, did strongly suggest that they should only be used with the greatest of discretion.

It was against this background that the JSCCCC inquiry was held. During the inquiry, the JSCCCC gave recognition to a point that I have long maintained and which I believe had been overlooked by the CCC in affirming public hearings as its default posi-

---

[85] *The Use of Public Examinations by the Corruption and Crime Commission, Joint Standing Committee on the Corruption and Crime Commission*, Report No 5, March 2012. p. 33.

tion. The point was best put by Mr Steytler in page 29 of the JSC-CCC report:

> Hearings in an investigatory phase may be more akin to police interviews (which are strictly confidential) than they are to court proceedings or even royal commissions. In such cases, it might be as inappropriate to air what is said in the course of a hearing as it is to air what was said in the course of a police interview.

In my oral evidence to the JSCCCC, I listed detailed instances to support Mr Steytler's view. For the first time, one after another, I referred to outrageous untrue suspicions raised by the CCC in the Smiths Beach public hearings, the sensational treatment given to these allegations by the media, the subsequent quiet abandonment of them by the CCC in its eventual reports, and the fact that the CCC took no positive steps to correct the record when serious accusations were found to be unsupported by evidence.

This was new material for the JSCCCC. No-one had previously gone back and reviewed the electrifying disclosures by the CCC at the outset of the Smiths Beach hearing in October 2006 and compared them with the ultimate truth. These accusations and innuendo had held the State and the nation spellbound. It caused WA parliamentarians to swoon at the mention of the CCC's name.

I have to concede that I was disappointed at the media response to my message. Although the press were present in force, and I was interviewed outside the hearing room by radio and TV, I received little coverage. In retrospect, I now appreciate that my testimony was a bitter pill for the media to swallow, as it implied that jointly they had been duped, or simply had not properly discharged their duty to inform the public accurately.

The JSCCCC hearings were different to anything that I had experienced since the CCC Smiths Beach and other hearings commenced. I have lost count of the public and confidential hearings with the CCC, Parliament and parliamentary committees I had attended. Although I was always treated with (cold) civility on these occasions, there was invariably an underlying sense of menace and hostility, which sometimes erupted into positive threat and intimidation.

Conversely and contrastingly, at the JSCCCC hearings Lesley and I were made to feel reassured that our presence and my evidence was welcome. For instance, we were given a cup of tea while we waited for my turn to give evidence. Although my testimony was thoroughly questioned and tested, I was, for the first time, not treated like a transgressor or an accused.

For four years to that point, I had been regarded with scepticism and disbelief, and the media, especially in the early months, had been highly aggressive and unkind.

As I gave my evidence to the JSCCCC, with Lesley sitting behind me, I had the impression that the committee was actually taking the trouble to look at the concrete evidence and view it impartially. Of course, we had no indication of how they would find, but I gained the impression that they were looking at these issues afresh with unprejudiced minds.

That impression was confirmed when committee members John Hyde and Matt Benson-Lidholm both came from the front of the committee room to the body of the room to personally greet Lesley and me, and to congratulate me on my contribution.

At later times, I also had some friendly contact with the parliamentary research staff. Brian Burke later told me that he had been similarly treated. The testimony of Mike Allen, Noel Crichton-Browne and myself was referred to in the report with approval. In fact, Chapter 1 of the report lead off with a quote from Brian. Evidence given by Mr Crichton-Browne about the illusory nature of Section 86 of the Act (that is the right for a witness to see and comment on any adverse CCC finding) and its ineffectiveness got a good run.

In fact, the JSCCCC in its report recommended substantial amendment to the section, to try to give it some force and relevance. The JSCCCC additionally referred approvingly of Mr Crichton-Browne's observation that the checks and balances generally in the CCC Act were flagrantly inadequate.

Once the CCC had embarked on a course of action, no matter

how wrong on occasions, it was never deflected in its pursuit or took stock of the situation in the light of contradictory evidence. Counsel assisting seemed to treat the hearings as adversarial.

The CCC's performances appeared to me not to be a search for the truth, but a hunt for scalps.

The first occasion was usually when overzealous counsel assisting outlined the case to be presented, often appearing to forget that they were not presenting a case for the prosecution in a criminal trial. In other places in this book, I have given instances where some witnesses were damned by media leaks before one word of testimony was presented and long before the accusations could be tested, if at all.

Another occasion for character assassination was when a witness was examined by counsel assisting. It needs to be remembered that these hostile examinations were tightly scripted by the CCC and were set up to take witnesses by surprise. In my case, I sat there helpless in the witness box responding to such inquisition, knowing that the line of interrogation was giving an erroneous impression, but unable to say one word to correct the record.

In utter frustration, I would mutely appeal to my counsel by facial gesture. Back would come the return raising of the shoulders and lifting of the open hands. That is, the universal sign for "I know that it is unfair, but there is nothing I can do".

The media loved these one-sided inquisitions. They were like red meat to a tiger and they were that night's TV news and the following day's headlines. Usually, the media story was accompanied by a picture of me, or some other hapless and beleaguered witness, trying desperately to find some way through the media scrum.

The JSCCCC voiced its disapproval of some of the actions by counsel assisting (see page 23 of its report).

Other occasions when witnesses were in jeopardy were when counsel assisting summed up and when the CCC report was tabled in Parliament. On both occasions, the CCC had a free kick. One's only hope was to have it contradicted in disciplinary tribunals or the courts, if one was lucky enough to have such access.

Many people, such as some of the public servants and Busselton Shire councillors, were subjected to derogatory statements, but faced no disciplinary proceedings and therefore no review.

People like the then minister Tony McRae, MPs Anthony Fels and Shelley Archer, and councillors such as Anne Ryan actively wanted court proceedings so they could dispel the cloud over their heads. But there was no avenue for clearing their name.

In Chapter 6, I specifically deal with the case of MP Tony McRae. He lost his career as a result of untested and dubious CCC findings, but never had any avenue of redress. There is no formal process to reply or correct mistakes. The PI, the JSCCCC, Parliament and the courts cannot amend or correct a CCC report concerning alleged misconduct by a witness.

The JSCCCC recognised this fundamental iniquity. It suggested in its report that the least that should be done by the CCC in its reports on misconduct was for the CCC to print in its reports the responses it received from aggrieved witnesses pursuant to the aforementioned Section 86 process. This is a practice followed by the JSCCCC in its dealings with the CCC when the JSCCCC makes a finding or gives a recommendation potentially affecting the CCC.

At least in that way the Parliament, media and public can see and (if they wish) evaluate the counter argument. What happened to Section 86 witness responses in the Smiths Beach and Lobbyists terms of reference, and the parliamentary committees that I have referred to, is manifestly unjust, and it can happen again.

Firstly, almost invariably, the CCC ignores the complaints from aggrieved witnesses. They are not even responded to, except in very rare cases. Secondly, they remain hidden under the secrecy provisions of the CCC Act. You re-publish your own Section 86 defence document under threat of a criminal charge.

I appreciate that my allegations of such inequality and blatant injustice, set out here and in other parts of this book, might sound a bit exaggerated. That is the reason for my use of extensive quotations in this book. I try to cite impartial commentators or contemporary accounts by well-known people. If you feel that I may be gilding the lily, please take a look at the JSCCCC report.

The main findings of the JSCCCC report were a resounding vindication of the submissions by Messrs McCusker and Steytler. The JSCCCC endorsed that:

1. Henceforth, "by default, the CCC misconduct examinations are private".
2. There should be a set of specified criteria "in making a determination as to whether a particular CCC examination will be open to the public".
3. "It should be a very rare case in which the public interest is found to outweigh potential prejudice and privacy interests."
4. Suppression orders to protect witnesses are advocated.

The JSCCCC followed up with a list of statutory amendments to implement these findings, but I am unable to determine the extent to which the Government has gone towards legislating these changes. As far as I am aware, the CCC could presently in its inquiries quite legally regress to its old default position and place witnesses in unfair and unnecessary jeopardy, as it has previously.

I appreciate that some readers will find it troubling that governments have not followed up with the well-considered JSCCCC recommended amendments. It certainly is bewildering.

There is a broad consensus that there needs to be a strong body to fight organised crime and most in the Barnett Government believed that it should be the task of the police. But I am told confidentially by insiders that few trusted the police enough to invest them with the necessary eavesdropping and surveillance powers.

The situation is far from ideal.

Experience so far with the McGowan Labor Government indicates it has not embarked on any legislative change in this area.

Case studies illustrate police-CCC tensions

The two matters mentioned by Parliamentary Inspector Christopher Steytler in his report to the JSCCCC, but not detailed above, involve Indigenous men Ian Quartermaine and Kevin Spratt.

Ian Quartermaine

The case of Ian Quartermaine was deeply concerning. It went back to 1990, had been revived by the Kennedy Royal Commission (KRC) and then referred to the CCC for further investigation.

The circumstances were the subject of a separate report by Parliamentary Inspector Steytler in 2011.[86] As a case study into just how hard, if not impossible, it is for an ordinary person to obtain some redress against the police through the CCC, this report is a must-read.

The main body of evidence is set out in a memorandum prepared by KRC investigator Brian Smith.

The facts are that on 4 December 1990 the police at a roadblock on the Cuballing Road, in WA's South West, shot and injured a driver, Aboriginal man, Ian Quartermaine, who had his nine-year-old son, Phillip, in his car.

The police justified the shooting by alleging Quartermaine was driving towards them and aiming to run them over. Additionally, the police averred Quartermaine had fired shots at them from a rifle during a police car chase. Quartermaine swore he had never fired on the police and that he had been shot by police after his car had been turned around and was stationary in front of the roadblock.

The police charged Mr Quartermaine with wilfully attempting to kill a police officer, two counts of assaulting police with intent to avoid apprehension and one count of attempting to unlawfully shoot a police officer.

At the preliminary hearing, the police produced a witness by the name of Tyson, who, remarkably, said that he was present at exactly the right time and the right place to see Quartermaine fire a shotgun at the police. However, Mr Tyson's evidence was later found to be false and he was convicted on counts of perjury and associated charges.

Further obvious problems at the trial were that no gun belonging to Mr Quartermaine was ever found and the bullet holes from the

---

[86] www.piccc.wa.gov.au

police firearm were on the side of Quartermaine's vehicle, rather than in the front, as would have been expected from the police description of events.

As a consequence, the charges of wilfully attempting to kill a police officer and unlawfully shoot a police officer were dismissed. However, he was convicted on two charges of assaulting police officers with intent to avoid apprehension and sentenced to six years jail.

Despite the huge holes in the police evidence, a police Internal Investigation Branch (IIB) inquiry conducted shortly afterwards into the police shooting of Mr Quartermaine exonerated the police.

Quartermaine complained to the Parliamentary Commissioner for Administrative Investigations (the Ombudsman), Robert Eadie.

His complaints were:

(a) He had been unlawfully shot by police.

(b) He was assaulted after arrest.

(c) Following his arrest, his son Phillip was kept in police custody, assaulted and threatened.

(d) He (Quartermaine) could not obtain proper legal representation.

(e) Four other ancillary accusations (which I shall not detail for the sake of brevity).

The report from Mr Eadie was equivocal, but the bottom line was that he was not prepared to take the complaints any further. The Ombudsman's response was not surprising. He was never invested with sufficient power to effectively examine and prosecute complaints against the police.

Mr Quartermaine again complained to the Ombudsman on 9 August 1994 with more evidence and with the names of witnesses. Mr Eadie declined to investigate, as the matters complained of were more than 12 months old.

But Quartermaine was a surprisingly resolute person, and he again appealed to the Ombudsman with fresh evidence in June 1997. By then, there was a new Ombudsman, Murray Allan. Mr Allan reviewed the files and refused to intervene. He did investigate an allegation by an Aboriginal police aide that the police intended to shoot Quartermaine prior to the police chase, but nothing came of it.

Not to be deterred, Mr Quartermaine took his tribulations to the KRC. Counsel Assisting Stephen Hall QC who, in my opinion, played an unsettling role as a CCC enabler in the Smiths Beach and Lobbyists terms of reference, "did not see the matter as warranting priority".[87] According to the PI Christopher Steytler's report (mentioned above), Mr Hall also wrongly asserted that many of those involved would have already left the police force.

Mr Justice Kennedy apparently thought differently, as investigator Brian Smith was authorised to proceed with a "small and discreet" inquiry on 9 April 2003. Mr Smith's memorandum concluded:

> I believe that there is evidence to suggest that police colluded to construct a version of what took place to justify the use of police firearms. Having done this, they were locked into giving that evidence and perjuring themselves during the preliminary hearing and trial.

Mr Smith also concluded that the appearance of witness Tyson was an "elaborate ruse" and that someone had "coached Tyson . . . in the detail of his statement".

Additionally, he came to the conclusion that police record of interview with Mr Quartermaine was a "sham" and had the hallmarks of a "police verbal". Mr Smith arrived at the conclusion that there appeared to be a disturbing "number of police officers who were prepared to perjure themselves for the common cause".

Despite previous rejections and disappointment, Mr Quartermaine (who was unaware that Mr Smith had prepared a report) made a written complaint to the CCC on 26 June 2006.

It needs to be borne in mind that the CCC was set up with a new set of potent capabilities to take on this very situation; that is, suspected flagrant malpractice involving a number of possible crimes by

---

[87] *Assessment of Procedures of the CCC Used to Assess Complaints of Serious Misconduct Made by Mr Ian Quartermaine*, Parliamentary Inspector of the Corruption and Crime Commission of Western Australia, 21 July 2011, p. 6.

the police, directed at a persistent, but essentially defenceless, Indigenous man and his son.

Clearly, the Quartermaine case represented a significant test for the recently established CCC.

Almost a year later, on 11 May 2007, the CCC curtly wrote to Ian Quartermaine informing him that it was not in the public interest to undertake any further investigation and gave three supporting reasons. For brevity, I will not detail those supporting reasons. But, for succinctness I would advise that PI Steytler later determined that "none of these reasons is supportable". He then went on in his report (available online [88]) to forensically demolish each of the three reasons.

One aspect of the PI's critique of the CCC's reason, which was particularly disturbing, was that the CCC's investigating officers conveyed the impression that both the initial police investigation and the preliminary investigation by the KRC had rejected Mr Quartermaine's complaint. The PI responded:

> ... nothing could have been further from the truth. The KRC investigation had concluded that there appeared to have been serious misconduct by police officers involved and that the internal police investigation appeared to have been a "cover up".[89]

You have to admire Mr Quartermaine for his endurance, at least. Not to be deterred, he telephoned the CCC again on 17 May 2007. He related that a police officer involved had recently boasted to Mr Quartermaine's grandson about getting away with the shooting. Also, that another witness was prepared to admit to perjury at the original trial. The CCC officer he spoke to fobbed him off and suggested that he perhaps go to the Aboriginal Legal Service.

True to his cause, Ian Quartermaine rang the CCC again on the 21 November 2008 inquiring whether anything could be done for him. He was told that his file was closed.

Tenaciously, on 7 August 2009 Mr Quartermaine made a second written complaint to the CCC. On 7 September 2009 he was sent a

---

[88] https://www.piccc.wa.gov.au/_files/Quartermaine_Report.pdf
[89] Ibid., p. 9.

letter by the CCC advising that his letter did not contain sufficient information to act upon.

Mr Quartermaine contacted the CCC by telephone on 10 September 2009 and wrote again on 27 September 2009 indicating that he had fresh evidence. The response from the CCC was once again "File Closed".

There is a saying about the police and the CCC: "The CCC inspectors and the police come out of the same gene pool." That may explain some matters.

Ultimately, Ian Quartermaine appealed to Mr Steytler, the PI, on 9 November 2009, and Phillip Quartermaine took the same step on 18 January 2010. That included an allegation that the police had assaulted him and threatened to kill him on that fateful day of the 4 December 1990.

The PI referred the Quartermaines' complaints to the CCC Commissioner Len Roberts-Smith and, finally, the CCC, conducted an investigation of the Quartermaine accusations. It concluded on 17 May 2011.

The PI's report (referred to above and which is online) makes it clear that the CCC investigation was deficient in a number of pertinent respects. Nonetheless, although the CCC offered the Quartermaines no material redress, it was highly critical of police procedure at the scene of the shooting and concluded for a multiplicity of reasons that, "the investigation of the actions of police by the IIB (Internal Investigation Bureau) officers was not conducted diligently".[90]

I will not enumerate the reason put forward by the CCC in its letter to the Commissioner of Police, but I can assure you it does not make pretty reading, or fill one with confidence about the impartiality, competence or integrity of the police force.

The concern remains, however, that if there is no effective oversight of the police, or if the CCC does not competently and thoroughly probe complaints against the police in these matters, there can be no reform and the old culture will continue.

---

[90] Ibid., p. 16.

In the Quartermaine matter, the ever-discrete and always-understating PI Steytler had this to say on page 19 of his report:

> My investigation of Mr Quartermaine's complaint to me reveals fundamental shortcomings in the procedures adopted by the CCC.

From my perspective, one of the most concerning aspects of the CCC's posture was the way it dealt with the KRC report on Quartermaine. The CCC had a statutory duty to follow up the reference from the KRC.

It appears in advice given to the PI by the CCC that no substantial action was taken by the CCC on the Smith memorandum until after Mr Quartermaine's written complaint of 26 June 2006.

Initially, Commissioner Roberts-Smith said that he could not explain the lack of action because the CCC records were deficient. However, further records were ultimately found and it is apparent that the Smith memorandum had in truth been properly referred to the CCC for action. Mr Roberts-Smith then had to concede that "it was difficult to see why Mr Smith's report and recommendations would not have been acted upon to the extent of requiring some further investigation at least".

Once the KRC documentation was found, it transpired that the copy of the Smith memorandum used when the CCC made the decision to take no action was materially different from the original prepared by Mr Smith. According to Mr Steytler, "a number of sentences (and in some cases whole paragraphs, including those earlier quoted in this report) have been deleted from it. In other cases sentences have been amended".

Mr Steytler doesn't further comment beyond simply laying out the facts, but in my view these alterations are an indication of high-level tampering with a report in an endeavour to forestall and frustrate an incisive and fair inquiry.

Next, by way of excuse, the CCC contended that the file was sent to the CCC for "Intelligence" purposes only and did not require any action. However, the CCC did not follow the procedures required (like notifying Mr Quartermaine) when deciding to discontinue the

KRC inquiry. Nor could it produce any documentary evidence to corroborate its case.

PI Steytler was not a poor marginalised Aboriginal person. He was one of the most astute and experienced legal persons in the State and he was not easily brushed off. His verdict was:

> These justifications offered by the CCC for its conduct are unconvincing.

His reason can be read at pages 19 to 25 of his report. It is not happy reading and even with his art of understatement, it is readily apparent that he was appalled. He concluded his report by saying:

> My assessment is that Mr Quartermaine has been very badly treated by the CCC.[91]

Confronted by the truth, the CCC finally offered Mr Quartermaine a qualified apology. PI Steytler was far from satisfied. He requested that the CCC make an unqualified apology.

There are two unfortunate design aspects of the CCC legislation: One is that all of the CCC's activities are immersed in secrecy; the second is that the CCC does exactly what it pleases. It is not obliged to take directions from the PI or the JSCCCC.

Kevin Spratt

The second case referred to in Parliamentary Inspector Styetler's report of 11 August 2011[92] was the matter of Kevin John Spratt, another Indigenous man.

As you will see, it was a "shocker", in large part because of the use of stun guns, or Tasers.

The 14 deployments of a Taser gun on Kevin Spratt by police officers in the Perth Watch House on 31 August 2008 were captured by camera and then video recordings went viral in the media after ultimately being released by the CCC on 4 October 2010.

---

[91] Ibid., p. 25.
[92] *Parliamentary Inspector's Report Concerning the Procedures Adopted by the CCC When Dealing with Complaints of the Use of Excessive force by Police*, Joint Standing Committee on the Corruption and Crime Commission, 11 August 2011.

It was worldwide news. Pictures of a seemingly helpless Indigenous man writhing in agony and screaming in pain as he was racked by multiple shocks in less than two minutes horrified and sickened viewers in every corner of the globe.

It was later reported that in a second such session by Department of Corrective Services (DCS) on 6 September 2008, the Taser was deployed against Kevin Spratt on 11 occasions. It was only much later, in a CCC report on the Spratt incidents, dated 16 April 2012, that the full horror emerged.

In all, Mr Spratt was subjected to the laser in either "Probe" (immobilisation) or "Drive stun mode" (causes pain rather than incapacity) settings 41 times (see the Daily Magnet, 21 April 2012). I cannot explain the discrepancy in the number of occasions the Taser was reported to have been used and can only conclude that the latter figure of 41 was more accurate because of the accumulation of evidence.

As a result of the events on 6 September 2008, Spratt was hospitalised the next day with what were termed "life threatening injuries that included at least one fractured rib, collapsed lung, pneumothorax, dislocated right shoulder and multiple fractures of the upper arm".

CCTV of the incidents (three such videos were found), although not covering the DCS Taserings in the police cells, disclosed no aggressive action by Spratt. DCS staff initially alleged that on 6 September Spratt's injuries may have been caused by Spratt throwing himself around in the back of the transporting paddy wagon. Later, faced with the Taser evidence, they withdrew this assertion.

Two police officers, Aaron Grant Strathan and Troy Gregory Tomlin, were eventually prosecuted for assault on Spratt and found guilty on 21 January 2014.

Bizarrely, the police officers' defence lawyer suggested in court that Mr Spratt's crying out when Tasered were "screams of joy". Presiding magistrate Richard Bromfield dismissed this assertion as fanciful. An expert witness made it clear that police were under strict instruction that Tasers were to be used to "prevent injury" (mainly to the police), but never for "purposes of compliance" (see transcript).

James MacTaggart, the state prosecutor from the DPP's office, maintained that, "Mr Spratt wasn't posing a threat to anyone", and that was the unqualified opinion of Magistrate Bromfield.

As a consequence of these convictions and its report, the CCC was able to maintain that it had done its oversight job well. This was a highly superficial piece of self-congratulation by the CCC and a more thorough examination of the true facts, which dribbled out over almost six years from 3 August 2008 to 21 January 2014, constituted a narrative of systemic failure and negligence of significant proportion.

Evidence unearthed later revealed that the CCC had ignored an opportunity to deal with the Spratt matter as early as 16 September 2008 – that is, 11 days after the event. On that date, pursuant to the CCC Act, the police formally advised the CCC of the incident. It would appear that the CCC took no action to look into the matter and was quite happy for the police Internal Affairs Unit (IAU) to handle it.

An IAU investigation commenced on 23 September 2008 and a report was sent to the CCC by the police on 10 November 2009. It is clearly surprising and disappointing that the CCC took no independent action on the police statutory advice to it of 16 September 2008. The CCC was well aware that Taser use could cause death and there was enough information to indicate that there had been multiple deployment of a Taser on Mr Spratt over a very short period of time. It clearly was an extreme event.

There is no indication that the CCC took any immediate action on the report. Nor does it appear that the CCC was aware of the further 11 deployments of the Taser by DCS on Mr Spratt on 6 September 2008.

It was only 24 hours after this incident that Mr Spratt was taken to hospital with life-threatening injuries. A problem for a clear understanding of matters was that much of what happened with DCS officers on 6 September 2008 was not caught on video and Mr Spratt, because of his disoriented and stunned state, had no recollection of the events of either 31 August or 6 September 2008.

The reality was that the DCS protected its own by keeping the events secret until they were exposed by external forces in April 2011.

It was a classic bureaucratic cover-up that was never satisfactorily explained even after the CCC was persuaded to examine the matter.

An article in *The West* by Daniel Emerson contained at last an admission of some culpability by DCS.[93] The story stated:

> The head of the Department of Corrective Services unit (James Shiro) which forcibly "extracted" Kevin Spratt from a police cell admits he did not do enough to find out how the Aboriginal man was seriously injured in custody. Mr Shiro also conceded that he had not abided by DCS policy when he failed to consult the department's health services division over the injuries and that he and DCS "abandoned" an "incident hand over form" because it was possible that "we would be responsible for injuries."

However, in the interim, after Mr Spratt's Tasering, but not motivated by that Tasering, the CCC commenced "a research project" on the use of Tasers by police. It was this report that was tabled two years later in the WA Parliament on 4 October 2010. It was accompanied by a video that showed a large part of the Taser deployment on Mr Spratt on the 31 August 2008.

Pertinently, it did not mention Mr Spratt by name and certainly did not disclose the names of his assailants. His was but one of 14 case histories briefly reviewed in the CCC research report.

WA Police Commissioner Karl O'Callaghan must have had it for some time because he responded to it in fairly unremarkable and polite terms, accepting most of the CCC recommendations.

Neither the police nor the CCC seemed to be fully aware of the sensational nature of the 31 August 2008 video, or the storm that would break around their heads. It would not be long before the police and the CCC were at each other's throats.

---

[93] "*Officer admits error over Spratt injuries*", *The West Australian*, 16 April 2011, p. 17.

In a report exclusively on the Spratt issue that the CCC was ultimately forced to make on 16 April 2012, it gave itself considerable credit. This is how the CCC put it:

> Widespread public interest and media reporting followed (tabling of the CCC report), most particularly about the repeated use of Taser weapons on Mr Spratt in the Perth Watch House by WAPOL officers on 31 August 2008.
>
> … The Commission determined that it would not finalise its review of the WAPOL investigation until the aforementioned Commission research project on the use of Taser weapons by WAPOL had been finalised, so that the investigation review could be informed by any findings arising out of the research project. Following tabling of its report on 4 October 2010, the Commission moved to finalise its review of the WAPOL IAU investigation. That, however, was overtaken by events.[94]

This rationale by the CCC was highly suspect. The "research project" was a separate matter from the inhumane treatment of Mr Spratt, and this barbaric conduct should always have been investigated and expeditiously dealt with in its own right. Also, there is evidence that the CCC may never have intended to investigate the Spratt matter, and worse, was well on the way to sweeping the matter under the carpet.

Nonetheless, the CCC was correct in commenting that the CCC's handling of the matter "was overtaken by events". Those "events" were that John Quigley, the then Opposition Shadow Attorney-General, and barrister Steven Penglis took an interest in Mr Spratt's case. This was a turning point for Mr Spratt.

As I have explained elsewhere, Quigley was a high-profile Perth barrister who among other things had been the Police Union's lawyer for more than 20 years before he entered Parliament in 2001. Life membership of the union was conferred on him.

---

[94] *Report on the Investigation of Alleged Public Sector Misconduct in Relation to the Use of Taser* Weapons by Officers of Western Australia Police and the Department of Corrective Services*, Corruption and Crime Commission 16 April 2012.

Quigley is the current WA Attorney-General. He is a long-term cancer sufferer, has considerable flair, is controversial, and sometimes says of himself that he is a little mad (*Australian Story*, ABC Television, 4 April 2011), but he is certainly brave. He took on the egregiously unjust Andrew Mallard case, gathered evidence and later joined Malcolm McCusker in securing Mallard's acquittal against the most ferocious odds after Mallard had spent 12 years in jail for the crime of murder of which he was innocent.

On the way, Quigley had his Police Union life membership withdrawn, he was pursued by the CCC for contact with Brian Burke, and was fined $3,000 for bringing the legal profession into disrepute over a CCC matter.

None of this deterred him. His response was to indicate that he would melt down his life membership badge and have it made into a tiepin with the words "Veritas Vincit" (Truth Conquers) and present it to Mr Mallard.

Quigley and I had become friends when he, the late legendary Brian Singleton QC and Murray Campbell represented me at the time of the WA Inc. Royal Commission. I was well aware of his legal ability and his courage. Hilton Quail, President of the WA Law Society, said:

> He is one of our best criminal lawyers ... and a loose cannon, but a cannon that has the unerring ability to hit targets, anyway ... big targets.

Steven Penglis was my lawyer for most of the CCC and Parliamentary Committee inquiries relating to the Smiths Beach and Lobbyists terms of reference. He was then a partner at Herbert Smith Freehills and he and his associate Ante Golem were a tower of strength to Lesley and me through these legal and emotional ordeals.

Mr Penglis was called to the bar in October 2012. He has a highly tuned sense of justice and was a pioneer of formal *pro bono* programs in WA. In 2009, he was named as one of two winners of the Law Society Lawyer of the Year and has been named by *The Australian Financial Review* as one of the best lawyers in Australia.

Quigley asked him to take up the Kevin Spratt case on a *pro bono* basis in October 2010 when it became apparent that the Tasering was not being adequately investigated. The pairing of these two must have seemed like the CCC's worst nightmare.

Quigley was under no misapprehension that a serious injustice had been done. In a feature article by Alana Buckley-Carr in *The West*, he stated:

> My beef is that police are not judge, jury and executioner and *should not be able to torture prisoners*. (My emphasis)[95]

Just to recap: The problem for the CCC was that the Tasering of Mr Spratt took place on 31 August 2008 and a statutory report was made to the CCC shortly thereafter, but no action was taken by the CCC, even after it received the Police IAU final report on the 10 November 2009.

When PI Steytler publicly reported to Parliament on 13 October 2010, he was highly critical of the CCC in respect of its oversight of the police generally and specifically in respect to the three cases dealt with here.

PI Steytler observed: "The watchdog (the CCC) had failed to respond adequately after internal investigations cleared police of wrongdoing."

And in the three cases that he believed had warranted further CCC involvement, the watchdog had declined to act on one incident (Ian Quartermaine) and had only audited the police inquiries into the other two cases (the law professor and his companion at Fremantle, referred to separately above, and Kevin Spratt).[96]

CCC Commissioner Len Roberts-Smith responded to the Steytler report in the same story concerning Kevin Spratt by saying: "Police were investigating the matter." He said it had become part of the broader CCC inquiry into the use of Tasers, and the CCC was "obviously treating the matter seriously".

I suppose that his explanation appeared credible, except that there had been a delay of more than two years since the event and the CCC

---

[95] *The West Australian*, 23 October 2010, p. 25.
[96] *The West Australian*, 14 October 2010, p. 3.

had not lifted a finger to independently examine the Spratt issue in its own right.

Worse, as became apparent, in a further story in *The West* the next day Police Commissioner O'Callaghan, in a sharp attack on the CCC, claimed the, "CCC had lauded the quality of the internal police investigation into . . . the Kevin Spratt matter . . . in a draft report supplied to police, but those statements were omitted from last week's report".

This attack indicated a major public rift between the police and the CCC, with both sides directing savage media denunciations at each other.

Pointedly, O'Callaghan's statement, which was not contradicted by the CCC, made it clear that the CCC was prepared to endorse and praise the police report until it was informed that PI Steytler was highly critical of the CCC inactivity and Messrs Quigley and Penglis were on the job.

Thus, although the CCC could plausibly assert that the Tasering of Spratt by police on the 31 August 2008 may not have become public unless they tabled their report on the police use of Tasering generally on the 4 October 2010, it was also apparent that at that time the CCC hadn't done any work on the Spratt Tasering specifically; had not discovered the even more extensive use of the Taser on Spratt on 6 September 2008; and was not aware that he had been taken to hospital "naked and wailing" in a wheelchair on 7 September 2008.

The CCC had also accepted a grossly inadequate Police IAU report on the issue that later proved to be misleading. Put succinctly, an outrageously derelict CCC had been used in a squalid cover-up.

One of the first actions Mr Penglis took was to request that the CCC take over the Spratt investigation from the police. Given the public tumult, the CCC duly acceded and it was announced on 16 November 2010 that the police had been ordered by the CCC to "halt their internal investigation into the Kevin Spratt Tasering scandal in a dramatic takeover of the affair".[97]

For the first time, the full extent of the numerous Taserings and

---

[97] *The West Australian*, 17 November 2010, p. 5.

the circumstances thereof was to be examined in public hearings, with the victim represented by Mr Penglis. And then the true facts, which painted a very different picture to the initial Police IAU report, came spewing out.

Mr Penglis also took the matter of Mr Spratt's conviction for obstructing the police on the 31 August 2008 back to court on appeal. Supreme Court Justice Stephen Hall, in overturning Spratt's conviction, stated:

> It is clear that Mr Spratt's plea of guilty was induced by false allegations made by the prosecution.

Mr Penglis said outside the court:

> It (the overturning of the conviction) has the effect of getting rid of suggestions that Kevin was Tasered in the Perth Watch House as a consequence of some unlawful conduct on his behalf. That's now been blown out of the water.[98]

The most disturbing element of this scandal was that the CCC took four years to do its duty and was clearly forced to respond properly by a combination of PI Steytler, the Joint Standing Committee on the CCC, the media and Messrs Quigley and Penglis.

The Spratt scandal was a "systemic failure" of epic proportions that the CCC had been set up and empowered to guard against.

---

[98] *The Australian*, 24 February 2011.

12

CORRUPTION, DYSFUNCTION, CONFLICT EXPOSED IN THE CCC

It is entirely unfortunate that, for a period of at least two years from October 2006, the CCC came to be perceived as the definitive moral arbiter of West Australian public life. Its arrogant and unfair determinations were treated as holy writ.

The fact that its covert methods had grave similarities to those of the infamous Stasi, the former East Germany's secret police, seemed to escape people's attention. Similarly with the CCC public hearings, which were almost indistinguishable in form from Stalinist show trials.

Slowly, during 2007 and 2008 through the brave efforts of lawyers such as Malcolm McCusker QC, Tom Percy QC, senior barrister Steven Penglis, John Price SC, Ante Golem (Herbert Smith Freehills Partner), Grant Donaldson SC (who became State Solicitor General), Chris Zelestis QC, Mark Ritter SC and Stephen Lemonis, and the re-evaluation of CCC "findings" by the Public Service Commission, it became apparent that the CCC processes could lead to serious injustice.

Later, two Parliamentary Inspectors, former Supreme Court judges Chris Steytler and Michael Murray, took up similar issues. In the interim, the Joint Standing Committee on the CCC (JSCC-CC), mainly under Nick Goiran as chairman, actually started doing its designated job. The established lawyers' professional associations remained critical of CCC methods throughout this period, but they were never given much airtime.

Progressively, through a series of forensic examinations of actual CCC findings and a succession of failed CCC initiated court cases, it became apparent that the defective CCC procedures had spawned mistaken outcomes.

However, notwithstanding these repeated legal failures and despite the CCC's inability to retain a Commissioner, the media did not seriously question the integrity (as distinct to the competency) of the CCC. That remained the case until late 2013. How did that come about?

In this chapter I shall endeavour to respond to that question by explaining what brought about changes to perceptions in 2013.

It hurts me to concede it, but the CCC had been able to deliver for itself the mantle of being the most formidable and feared semi-judicial organisation in Australia.

But it was all perception and no substance. The media were for far too long besotted by it and craved this new source of electrically charged copy. After the CCC forced the resignation of several ministers and MPs, the stunned public was in awe and applauded the deployment of the CCC's massive and unprecedented powers against the politicians.

The parliamentarians were intimidated and (in the most part) cravenly surrendered their historically hard fought for independence from the executive wing of government.

At the outset, the parliamentary oversight committee, the JSC-CCC, almost immediately forgot its statutory role, jumped the fence, changed sides and became an enthusiastic cheer squad for the worst excesses of the CCC.

It was reported on the ABC that two prominent Upper House ALP members were seen "high fiving" in the corridors of Parliament House when the news came through that I had been charged by the CCC for allegedly giving false evidence to the Smiths Beach inquiry. I was deeply hurt.

Some elements of the ALP were consistently hostile to Burke. As an example, on 14 and 15 August 2013, Ben Harvey, the business editor of *The West Australian*, wrote stories in *The West* and *The West Business Magazine* respectively, about Brian Burke and me after Harvey and colleague Daniel Emerson interviewed us over lunch.

They were interesting pieces of journalism, but pretty neutral. After both stories were published, Harvey sent us an email in which he made the following remarks:

> BB not 100% happy. The ALP left faction bombarding me with hate mail for "revisionist history" on the Burke/Grill years. Perhaps if everyone is equally unhappy then I may have got close to the middle ground.

Andrew Burrell from *The Australian* described a similar hostile attack-after he wrote a more extensive analysis of Burke in *The Weekend Australian's* magazine of 5/6 June 2013.

My friend, Graeme Campbell, the former long-term Federal Member for the huge seat of Kalgoorlie, puts it this way:

> Burke and Grill were to be treated like Labor rats. The objective truth was irrelevant. Labor rats would be accused forever, seen as literally damned souls.

As if to prove this true, ex-Premier Geoff Gallop, according to many first hand accounts, also attested to by Emerson in an article in *The West* of 26 April 2014, embarked upon a surprisingly vitriolic attack on Burke in a speech at the launch of respected political analyst Peter Kennedy's book, *Tales from Boomtown*.

Emerson relates that Brian was present at the book launch when Gallop "described Brian Burke as wielding power recklessly and leaving a damaging legacy for Labor to clean up".

According to others present, the attack on Brian went on for several minutes. If correctly reported, it represented one of the unkindest assaults ever made by a WA Labor leader on another.

In any event, Gallop's bitter assessment was not endorsed by Kennedy in *Tales from Boomtown* – the very book he was helping to launch. On page 6 Kennedy poses the question: "So who are the standout Premiers?" And answers himself by saying: "Without doubt they are Charles Court and Brian Burke..." He makes his position even more evident when he quotes Keating as saying:

> Intellectually, Burke was very good and he was a bloke who was across all the issues. He had a good public sense of everything and a good executive brain – prob-

ably among the cleverest people to have held the job over there. But I think he was harshly treated.[99]

I wrongly assumed that some in academia would recognise the unprincipled methods employed by the CCC and register an objection. With just a couple of brave exceptions, they were nearly as silent and cowered as the East German collegiate during the Stasi's period of terror.

My research reveals that the only senior academics who seriously questioned the CCC processes were Professor Greg Craven, until January 2021 Vice-Chancellor of the Australian Catholic University and Professor Peter van Onselen, formerly of Edith Cowan and UWA and now a political commentator in *The Australian* and on Network Ten.

And so it was with that other supposed moral bastion, the churches. There was never a word of concern from this quarter or from the Human Rights Commission. How could Parliament's actions in judging and penalising Burke and others, as I have described, not amount to a gross violation of the most basic elements of the United Nations Universal Declaration of Human Rights?

How could the Legislative Assembly, in court session, judge me without allowing me to utter one word in my own defence? How could a Legislative Council committee conduct a secret trial – where no one knew that they were being accused, all the evidence was secret and there was no means of review or redress?

One who questioned aspects of the CCC's oppressive methods was Peter Weygers of the Western Australian Council of Civil Liberties, as did civil liberties campaigner, the late Brian Tennant.

Another was the former Labor premier and barrister Peter Dowding, who sometimes speaks for the Australian Council for Civil Liberties. Commentator and former editor of *The West Australian* Paul Murray was a constant sceptic of the CCC's method, even if he did not always support us personally.

But their voices of concern were lonely and easily drowned out

---

[99] *Tales from Boomtown: Western Australian Premiers from Brand to Barnett*, by Peter Kennedy, p. 146.

by the over-enthusiastic support of almost everyone in politics and a bedazzled media. And I remind readers that the institutions I refer to cannot say that they were not aware of what was going on. These issues and our travails were aflame in the media right across Australia.

The frenzy developed into a kind of madness.

For some years, the CCC had the field to itself. It was a potent cultural dimension not seen since the days of the Lindy Chamberlain trials. The CCC was the uncontested arbiter of right and wrong, morality and immorality, propriety and impropriety.

A similar questionable phenomenon was observed with ICAC in New South Wales. Premiers Nick Greiner and Barry O'Farrell were high-profile, but essentially innocent, victims of this syndrome.

Also, the CCC made its adjudications ruthlessly, without citing objective criteria and often in defiance of the facts. And it was operating on fertile ground. While most social scientists concede that the Australian political scene is relatively free of corruption, a majority of people are sceptical, if not cynical, and primed to believe the worst.

So, who were these people exercising such devastating powers? By statute there is a veil of secrecy cast over the operations of the CCC and its officers. True, the public are made aware of the identity of the commissioner and the director, but the names of the operational personnel are kept confidential unless they are disclosed in official proceedings.

In short, it is inherently-as covert an organisation as its authoritarian forerunners in the secret service. Its day-to-day operations are shrouded in confidentiality. Consequently, there is no easy way of making assessments of the competency or ethics of the CCC's internal operations.

Even Parliament, which created the CCC, can't directly scrutinise the CCC's inner processes and actions and can only endeavour to do so through the limited keyholes of the Parliamentary Inspector (PI) and the JSCCCC. I argue that the powers of these two agencies are insufficiently robust to fulfil their CCC-oversight responsibilities.

The CCC's veil began to slip however when, in a small article on page three of *The West Australian* of 2 November 2013, Gary Adshead wrote a story under the headline: "CCC officers stood down".

In part, the story quoted a brief statement from the CCC Executive Director, Brigadier Mike Silverstone:

> Three officers from the CCC have been stood down over the alleged misappropriation of $1000.

It turned out to be a masterpiece of understatement.

Silverstone reassuringly added that a "thorough investigation" was underway. The alleged incidents had occurred in May 2011. That is, more than two years earlier.

Adshead went on to state: "But the agency refused to reveal other details ..."

That appeared to be the beginning and the end to the matter in a public sense. However, that was clearly unsatisfactory from a community point of view. Why had it taken so long for the CCC to come clean on the incidents and take action? Who were the officers concerned? A plethora of questions arose.

The terse Silverstone press statement, to those with experience in these matters, had all the hallmarks of the age-old police internal custom of getting rid of crooked cops by allowing them to quietly resign, with full entitlements and no mark against their public name. That is, the public were to be told as little as possible and the smallest amount of damage was to be inflicted on the CCC's standing.

As we now know, there was very much more to this incident. Its initial inadequate explanation created a significant conflict between the CCC hierarchy and the Parliamentary Inspector (PI), and between the CCC and the police, who the PI called in to investigate the matter.

Intriguingly, even before the disclosure in *The West* of this improper conduct the dogs were barking about CCC procedural integrity. On 2 August 2013, a Daniel Emerson article in *The West* referenced a speech made by the WA Chief Justice Wayne Martin at the Council of Australasian Tribunals in Sydney.

In delivering the annual Whitmore Lecture, Chief Justice Martin was quoted as saying he was alarmed by the strength and powers conferred on newer "integrity agencies". He argued that, "moves to collectively regard integrity agencies as a fourth arm of government after courts, Parliament and the executive should be resisted". He was concerned at the extraordinary delegation of legislative power to unaccountable agencies.

The Chief Justice pointedly targeted the questionable activity of the CCC when he said:

> It is, however, of some concern to me that these statutory agencies have banded together to promulgate definitions of conduct and standards of behaviour which are separate and distinct from the language used in the statutes creating their agencies...

This activity by the CCC was identical to that I have commented on in relation to the Smiths Beach and Lobbyists terms of reference. I was so relieved when I read this speech by the Chief Justice.

The CCC, in my assessment, had just formulated its own perceived class of offences for purposes of bringing down impropriety "findings". That is, the CCC in the Smiths Beach and Lobbyists inquiries was inventing new subjective forms of impropriety, not found in any statute, regulation or official code of conduct.

Nor were these "improprieties" recognisable in any court of competent jurisdiction. The so-called "findings" against the likes of Anne Ryan, which Malcolm McCusker criticised, and the CCC comments about Wally Cox, Mark Brabazon, Paul Frewer, Mike Allen, Brian Burke, me and others fall squarely within this class identified by the Chief Justice.

Paul Murray took up the same concerns in an article in *The West* on 7 August 2013, under the prophetic headline: "Who is watching the integrity watchdogs?"

Murray quoted Chief Justice Martin in the following terms:

> The cloak which shrouds the activities of many of those agencies stands in stark contrast to long-standing and entrenched traditions of transparency which characterise

the activities of many of the courts and the parliaments which have been responsible for the maintenance of the integrity of governments for centuries longer than the more recently created aspirants to membership of a new branch of government.

Further on:

The opacity which characterises the activities of many of these agencies stands in marked contrast to the very values of transparency and accountability which they espouse as characterising integrity itself.

Chief Justice Martin is then quoted in highlighting a problem that Burke's and my lawyers had previously identified, but which had largely been ignored:

> A number of integrity agencies are subject to ministerial direction, but in almost all instances can decline to comply. Thus they are only accountable politically through committees of the Parliament. However, those committees have no power of direction, and their practical capacity to oversee the actions of these agencies in individual cases is very limited.

Interestingly, the Chief Justice had sat on the bench of the Supreme Court when it decided that it had no power to intervene or review findings of the CCC on Dr Wally Cox in the Smiths Beach matter. The CCC, through Commissioner Len Roberts-Smith, tried to spin this into a Supreme Court endorsement of CCC's outrageous finding against Dr Cox. It was nothing of the sort. It was simply a conclusion by the Supreme Court that the CCC Act excluded its jurisdiction to review the merits of CCC "findings".

It took eight years of intimate observation for the Chief Justice to publicly express these opinions. Nonetheless, they were profound assessments and represent a watershed in authoritative legal opinion on the subject of accountability of government-sponsored "integrity agencies".

The essential point made by the Chief Justice has implication for the administration of justice Australia-wide. These unaccountable tribunals, such as the CCC, are in danger of supplanting important parts of our impartial court system. They are popular in certain austere and oppressive circles as they are seen as dispensing penalty without all of the "niceties" of a detached and fair processed court of law. But for the fair-minded, it is just a step down the road to a police state.

Coincidentally, this speech by Chief Justice Martin was made at the exact time that these very accountability issues were being fought out, in real and explicit terms in WA, between the CCC and Parliamentary Inspector Michael Murray. In a legal sense, it was a titanic battle, with long-term consequences for the justice system.

Paul Murray immediately raised the rhetoric question. He commented after reviewing the Whitmore Lecture:

> So, in our reaction to the excesses of WA Inc, have we created public sector monsters which pose their own threats?

Murray answered his own question when at the conclusion of his 7 August 2013 article, he wrote:

> Something has clearly gone badly wrong with our approach to public service accountability. While there is always tension between the political and judicial arms of government, Chief Justice Martin has gone way beyond that in exposing a dangerous divergence from established democratic principles.
>
> These are serious matters which demand a serious response from Government.

Has there been such a response? We are still waiting.

Murray returned to the same theme in his column on 14 August 2013, exhorting the Barnett Government to give some sort of reaction to the CJ's speech. There was none.

My reading of the situation is that Premier Barnett understood that the CCC Act and other integrity-related agency legislation required serious amendment, however the ALP and a large section of

Barnett's own Liberal Party, headed by the chairman of the oversight committee, would not countenance any extension of the CCC's powers in relation to organised crime, for conflict-of-interest reasons.

That was because of the obvious need, in that circumstance, to have day-to-day operational collaboration between the CCC and the police. That is, between the CCC and the very group it is supposed to be overseeing.

The CCC' chief role is the rooting out of impropriety in the police force. There is already a problem of a crossover of culture between the police and the CCC. That is because they both draw from the same investigatory talent pool. This has been overcome to some extent in NSW with the creation of a completely independent and dedicated Commission of Police Integrity as well as ICAC.

Just three days after *The West's* story of 2 November 2013 about the standing-down of the three CCC officers for allegedly stealing $1000, the CCC Commissioner, former District Court Judge Roger Macknay, announced his retirement.[100] It was a big surprise and at the behest of Attorney General Mischin it did not become effective until 24 March 2014.

This was the third consecutive commissioner who had resigned before his term was up, without any apparent preparation for a successor.

Clearly, there was something deeper here and any half-interested observer could identify that there were endemic problems within the organisation. However, the public was not being informed of what was actually transpiring because of the secrecy provisions of the CCC Act.

Nonetheless, the public was aware that Mr Macknay's period as Commissioner had been marked by friction between the CCC and the police. It was a disagreement played out in the media on a weekly basis. Any hope that these two bodies could work together cooperatively was being damaged.

In a story by Gary Adshead in *The West* on 10 December 2013, it was made apparent that even WA's Attorney-General, Michael Mis-

---

[100] *The West Australian,* 5 November 2013, p. 15.

chin, was only partially informed on what was happening with the suspension of the three CCC officers. He was quoted as saying:

> I was informed several weeks ago that there had been an inquiry that had been going on for quite some time regarding an allegation involving a small amount of money.

A relevant question thus arose: was the Attorney-General being kept in the dark, or was he deliberately playing the issue down? We now know that the situation was more serious than he was indicating. John Quigley, the Shadow Attorney-General, took a much more cynical line when he said:

> It doesn't matter if it's $1,000 or $10,000, having kept it secret in the manner that they have, there should be a public hearing where all of WA can see what is happening inside the CCC.

In spite of Quigley's urgings for some transparency, the matter then went back behind the CCC's veil of secrecy for six months until the week commencing 11 August 2014. A tiny story by Gabrielle Knowles appeared at the bottom of page 27 in *The West* on 16 August 2014, under the headline: "Ex-CCC man on charges".

It comprised only three short paragraphs and it stated:

> A second former CCC officer has been charged by police after misappropriation of funds.
>
> The 43-year-old man has been charged with two counts of corruptly falsifying records and is one of six CCC staff members who have either been sacked, quit or did not have a contract renewed after allegations surfaced last year.
>
> Another 43-year-old man was charged last week with falsifying records and giving false evidence to an internal inquiry investigating his actions.

Ever so slowly the truth was being revealed.

There were no names, but it was apparent the number of CCC officers involved had escalated.

PI Murray's dramatic annual report

Nonetheless, it was not until a front-page story by Emerson in *The West* on 16 October 2014 that the public got a glimpse of a massive struggle going on between the CCC and the PI to uncover what appeared to be truly profound impropriety within the CCC. Emerson's article was a blockbuster concerning an absolutely stunning report (Annual Report 2013/14) that PI Michael Murray had filed in Parliament on this long-running issue.[101]

His article commenced:

> The CCC tried to thwart a police investigation into allegedly corrupt CCC officers by denying access to key documents, witnesses and suspects, State Parliament was told.
>
> An explosive report by Michael Murray, the retired Supreme Court judge who oversees the CCC, includes a claim that delays to the investigation allowed some of the officers to leave WA.
>
> In his annual report tabled in Parliament, the Parliamentary Inspector of the CCC revealed details of the WA Police investigation into six officers who were sacked or quit over alleged misappropriation of funds.

Emerson went on to state:

> In his report, Mr Murray revealed allegations of 'serious misconduct' against officers in the CCC's operational support unit, which provides investigators with surveillance and covert capability.

The number of officers had increased from three to six and they were in the special OSU unit. The allegations were starting to look as though they had real implications for the justice system.

To make it clear, the OSU was the elite unit that gave the CCC its real clout. It was separately housed at a secret location. This was the section that broke into Lesley's and my home to plant listening bugs and eavesdrop on my wife's most intimate conversations. This was

---

[101] *Parliamentary Inspector of the Corruption and Crime Commission Annual Report 2013-14.*

the group who photographed everyone who came into our block of home units by means of a camera secreted in a lamppost outside of our front gate.

This was the cabal which, when the surveillance exercise was completed, refused Lesley's pleas to remove the bugs from our home. She even offered to vacate our home while the OSU did the removal job. They still refused. Also, I suspect, that this was part of a CCC investigative group that swore out secret affidavits to monitor the telephone conversations and emails of Brian Burke, David McKenzie, Lesley and myself.

PI Murray, in his annual report, was revealing not only concerns of serious and systemic misconduct of a criminal nature within the CCC but he was also disclosing a critical difference of opinion between himself and Commissioner Roger Macknay. That dispute was over how these offences should be further investigated, and dealt with.

The PI's report hinted at the CCC impeding the police in their investigation of OSU officers, but gave no names or details of the investigations.

However, shortly thereafter other serious allegations concerning the fetid activities of the CCC came bubbling to the surface. On 18 October 2014, Grant Taylor wrote a front-page story in *The West* alleging that two more CCC staff members were under investigation for "several serious allegations, including claims that they conspired to deliberately mislead a parliamentary committee".

This brought the total to eight officers under a cloud. Premier Colin Barnett, who had already moved to strip the CCC of jurisdiction to investigate other than serious allegations against public servants, was quoted as saying:

> It is a bit rich isn't it, when your most powerful crime-fighting organisation, the Corruption and Crime Commission . . . is in itself under investigation.

The West added that, "…it understands that the watchdog is also struggling to manage morale problems and internal dissent among some staff opposed to what are described as 'root and branch' review of how it does business".

Its hard-line Executive Director Brigadier Silverstone had recently quietly "retired" (more about this later) when, on the 17 October 2014, *The West* editorialised on this subject. *The West's* conclusion was that there was a "leadership vacuum", the CCC was wallowing aimlessly and was a "tarnished organisation". It also stated:

> The perception of ineffectiveness and misconduct within the agency shall be hard to shake.

PI Murray made a special report to the JSCCCC in June 2015. It was a bombshell. Attached to the JSCCCC's Report No. 19 tabled in Parliament on 17 June 2015, it provided more details of probable criminality within the CCC, and of how the CCC had used legal procedures to limit outside access to some-investigations it considered irrelevant to alleged misbehaviour by OSU officers.[102]

The headline of the front page of *The West* of 18 June 2015 (relating to PI Murray's special Report No 19) must have been the ultimate denunciation that the CCC hierarchy could only have conjured up in their worst nightmares. The title of the article simply stated: "CCC Rogues". The sub-title followed: "Allegations of cash theft, fishing trips and falsified records."

The first few paragraphs then went on to state:

> A rogue unit of Corruption and Crime Commission officers allegedly stole cash and property of the watchdog, went fishing in work time, bought or hired 4WD vehicles for private use and falsified records. It is also alleged the officers lied to investigators and the Australian Taxation Office, unlawfully obtained drivers licences under assumed names and used them to rack up more than the maximum 12 demerit points and hid property for a police officer who was subject to an internal affairs search warrant. The extraordinary allegations were among 23 accounts of serious, 'systemic' corruption allegations in an explosive report by the CCC's Parliamentary Inspector Michael Murray that was tabled in State Parliament

---

[102] *Parliamentary Inspector's Report On Misconduct and Related Issues in the Corruption and Crime Commission*, Report No. 19, June 2015.

yesterday after a two-year investigation. They relate to officers in the covert Operations Support Unit, which was set up in 2004 to provide "surveillance and technical services"...

By this stage three OSU officers had been dismissed by the CCC, four had resigned and one officer did not have his contract renewed, on top of the two officers charged in relation to the falsifying records regarding missing money.

The West article then went on to quote PI Murray:

> The systemic nature of the conduct investigated revealed a disturbing culture of entitlement and unaccountability...

The PI's report set out a long list of allegations made against OSU officers including:

1. The theft of $1000 of Commission funds.
2. The theft of glasses from hotels.
3. The improper interference in a Commission tender procurement process for the purchase of telecommunication interception systems.
4. The making of false entries in records representing that officers were working when they were fishing and unlawful claims for meal allowances.
5. The improper interference with a personnel employment selection process.
6. The improper interference with WAPOL investigation.
7. The falsification of meal claims allowances.
8. The misuse of an assumed identity.
9. The repair of a privately owned motor vehicle at the OSU premises during working hours.
10. The unauthorised use of OSU equipment.
11. The false representation to the Commissioner of Police that the Commission had conducted a thorough integrity check of an applicant officer.

12. The failure of an OSU Officer to disclose that he had been arrested and convicted of possession of a prohibited drug during his employment in the Commission.

13. A false representation made to the Australian Taxation Office about the percentage of time that OSU motor vehicles were used for official and private purposes for assessing Fringe Benefit Tax. This included a reassessment of at least $269,533.00 tax liability which personally effected individual OSU Officers.

14. The falsification of motor vehicle log book entries.

15. The improper purchase of two motor vehicles and the receipt of gifts for the purchases.

16. The improper use of a Driver's Licence under an assumed identity.

17. The unlawful obtaining and using of a Driver's Licence under an assumed identity and the subsequent accumulation of demerit points on that licence.

18. Uneconomic and irregular practices in purchasing and hiring motor vehicles.

19. The unlawful installation of Commission property in the construction of a new private residence of an OSU Officer.

20. Multiple allegations of favouritism in recruitment processes for employment with, and promotion in, the OSU.

21. Multiple allegations of bullying, sexism, harassment and racial discrimination by OSU Officers against colleagues.

22. Officers dissuading other officers from cooperation with the Commission's investigation of the allegations.

It was apparent that this alleged systemic criminality was happening within the CCC at a time when most of the media, all of the political class and much of the public were according it a godlike status.

In an associated article on page six, Labor's shadow Attorney-General John Quigley said:

> Mr McKechnie (the new CCC Commissioner) had a

"herculean task" to rebuild the credibility of the corruption watchdog.

Later in the article, Quigley is quoted as saying:

> After gearing up to tackle organised crime, it appears these investigators themselves became involved in organised crime.

Quigley can always be relied on for a colourful phrase, but he was not too far off the mark.

Unfortunately, this exposé came on top of revelations that the CCC had been forced to pay out hundreds of thousands of dollars to three investigators who were victims of harassment and intimidation (see story by Gary Adshead in *The West* of 2 February 2015). It also had to pay out over $200,000 to the Australian Taxation Office as a result of tax fraud committed by the rogue CCC officers.

Perhaps the most insightful observation on Report No. 19 came from Mr Goiran, easily the most astute Chairman of the JSCCCC to that time. He said in the Chairman's Foreword to Report No. 19:

> The fact that these allegations are in relation to a number of individuals within the State's highest integrity body is a timely reminder that whenever greater power and discretion is granted to one or more individuals, it is essential that it is offset by a proportionate increase in the oversight of them.

Similar statements urging better oversight powers had been made by a host of eminent legal practitioners, including all of the Parliamentary Inspectors, Messrs McCusker, Steytler and Murray, and such senior counsel as Tom Percy, Grant Donaldson, Steven Penglis and Mark Ritter. Even previously by the JSCCCC.

However, no publicly discernible action on these recommendations was taken by Government. Others, such as Commissioner Len Roberts-Smith, actively opposed any extension of the PI's oversight powers and tried to limit existing powers for PIs.

It is true that some progress has been made in reforming CCC procedures. After the JSCCCC took extensive evidence on the question of CCC public hearings, following the unjust show trials related to the Smiths Beach and Lobbyists inquiries, and after the severe censure that emanated from the subsequent JSCCCC report, the CCC did not venture to hold any further public hearings until October 2015. For a time, at least, after the JSCCCC hearing, the CCC showed much more discretion in when and how it conducts public hearings.

But as I shall show in Chapter 19, the CCC has since relapsed into some of its old much-criticised ways.

The posture and procedures of the CCC are an entirely voluntary process by the CCC. They could change abruptly and at times they have. Lamentably, none of Malcolm McCusker's recommended policy changes relating to enhanced oversight powers of the CCC by the PI and parliament has been legislated.

Without a change in the Act, it is always possible for a headstrong or headline-grabbing Commissioner of the CCC to quite legally resume the previous travesties of justice. There is always the possibility of pressure of the investigative wing of the CCC, or conceivably, persons of political influence, to reinstitute such questionable processes.

I would also comment that Report No. 19 only dealt with a limited time period mid-2013, (from what can be made of the opaque public record) and examined one unit only, the OSU. There has never been a forensic audit of the larger part of the CCC.

A partial audit of one of the CCC's NSW counterpart units, the Police Internal Affairs Unit, threw up hair-raising evidence of illegality. In an article by Dan Box in *The Australian* of 1 March 2015, under the heading, "NSW Police got warrants with 'false evidence'", it was found that "false evidence" was repeatedly used to obtain warrants for telephone intercept, listening devices and searches. There was also "inappropriate targeting and lack of quality control".

Box added:

> The unit 'did not provide the necessary facts and grounds to justify' naming 46 of 114 people on a court warrant authorising surveillance, the inquiry found.

This is precisely the problem of opacity that I have frequently raised in the context of the (secret) affidavits justifying the surveillance warrants on Brian Burke and me. I am hopeful that the full truth may yet come out.

But additionally, PI Murray makes it clear he believed the CCC attempted to exclude a police investigation of the OSU. He said actions taken by the CCC were aimed at placing its officers above the normal operations of the law, a situation he rejected firmly. He stated on page 19 of the report:

> I know of no provision of the (CCC) Act which gives the Commissioner and its officers' immunity from the use of such (police) powers.

This was clear evidence of a dispute (mainly hidden from public view) between Commissioner Macknay and PI Murray over the level of scrutiny applied to the covert OSU by the police.

Disagreement over the involvement of the police persisted for months. This dispute severely delayed any police investigation of the OSU.

The initial complaint against the OSU rogue officers appears to have come from other OSU officers. This is not surprising given the level of allegations of bullying and sexual harassment for which the CCC had had to pay compensation. Nor was it remarkable in view of the leaks to the media from anonymous sources within the CCC.

An example was a story in *The West* on 18 October 2014 and a special report to Parliament dated 10 December 2014. Throughout 2013 and 2014 it was starting to be apparent that honest officers were becoming disaffected by the level of impropriety within the agency and frustrated by the CCC's implicit toleration of internal lawless activity. It also demonstrated that these honest officers had little trust in some of their superiors.

Returning to the dispute between the Commission and the PI; as required by statute, the CCC reported the initial allegations of stealing to the PI in July 2013. There appears to have been four allegations made against CCC officers relating solely to misappropriation of $1000. From what can be gleaned publicly, the CCC did not raise with the PI any other concerns of suspected criminality within the organisation.

In delivering its report, the CCC advised the PI that its own officers would carry out the investigation and if they thought it appropriate they would recommend he refer the matter to the DPP for assessment and advice on a possible prosecution. In other words, the CCC proposed that, initially, they would keep the matter "in house" and make the crucial decisions, such as whether there was sufficient evidence to refer the matter to the DDP for possible prosecution.

The CCC was in for a rude shock. The PI totally rejected this approach.

In his report to the JSCCCC in June 2015, PI Murray sets out what transpired after he received the information of alleged impropriety within the CCC (see Report No.19, page 18, etc.) and the CCC's actions in dismissing three officers and refusing to renew the contract of another.

In brief, the PI decided on 3 December 2013 that the CCC's preliminary investigations were sufficient to allow him to remove the investigation from the CCC to the police jurisdiction.

The CCC objected, strongly.

Tension between the PI and the CCC appears to have been brought on, firstly, by the PI indicating that he would refer the handing the matter to the police and, secondly, by the PI suggesting in his 2013/14 Annual Report to Parliament that the CCC was impeding the police in an attempt to prevent a more extensive investigation of the OSU's covert activities.

This tension had later repercussions. As did a media release and report to Parliament issued by the CCC's Acting Commissioner, Neil Douglas, on 6 November 2014 disputing critical statements in PI Murray's 2013/14 Annual Report.

According to the Douglas report, the CCC suggested to the PI that, rather than referring the allegations to the police for investigation, police officers could be sworn under the CCC Act so they were bound by the secrecy and other provisions of the Act. Their investigations would be overseen the PI.

Mr Douglas said the CCC also suggested that, alternatively, the PI could request from the CCC the documents wanted by the police, but which the CCC was reluctant to release for legal and operational reasons. It would then be for the PI to make a decision about releasing them to the police, as he was entitled to do.

The PI did not take up either option.

The essential point, from the CCC's perspective, was that the police should have no role in investigating misconduct within the CCC as there could be a conflict of interest and it could compromise CCC investigations of police. Additionally, the CCC argued that the only agency that could make such investigations was the CCC itself and the Parliamentary Inspector.

On the other hand, the PI's position was that there was no dispensation or immunity of CCC officers from police investigation. The PI believed that a process of the CCC investigating itself was highly unsatisfactory.

In the event, the PI ultimately (after a lengthy delay to resolve the issue) made the decision to commit to a police investigation, and the task was given to the then Deputy Commissioner (and now Police Commissioner) Chris Dawson.

Thereafter followed an extended period during which the CCC insisted on complying with its own understanding of the provisions of the CCC Act when responding to police requests for certain documents and to interview certain witnesses. The police believed that this unduly restricted their investigations.

Remember, the PI's Annual Report intimated that the CCC "tried to thwart a police investigation into allegedly corrupt CCC officers by denying access to key documents, witnesses and suspects".[103]

The CCC's unprecedented response, by way of special report to Parliament and a media conference presided over by Acting Commissioner Douglas, was epitomised by Mr Douglas' statement reported in *The West*:

> ... any assertion that the CCC sought to delay or thwart the investigation was "utterly false".[104]

---

[103] *The West Australian*, 16 October 2014, p. 1.
[104] *The West Australian*, 6 November 2014, p. 13.

In other words, the PI was lying. This is pretty strong stuff.

PI Murray and the police saw this statement as a CCC offensive directed at them.

The CCC view of the law was supported by two senior counsels, including Chris Zelestis, regarded with Malcolm McCusker as the authority on the CCC Act.

It was clear that PI Murray was distressed and injured by the CCC offensive. He went on the defence and told the media:

> ... (he) did not mean to suggest that the CCC had deliberately attempted to harm the WA Police investigations and was horrified by the coverage his annual report had attracted.[105]

You sometimes see this type of semi-apologetic response from inexperience media performers such as judges and the like, who are really out of their depth without a media adviser. PI Murray's words appeared to be an unfortunate public back down on a matter of very considerable importance to the State's justice system.

It seemed at the time that the CCC, now without a permanent head again (Mr Macknay's retirement was effective from April 2014), and no doubt, in reality, under the direction of Brigadier Silverstone, (up until October 2014) had had a big media win with its press conference of 6 November 2014 attacking the PI's Annual Report. It appeared that the CCC, in a highly organised and planned manoeuvre, had intimidated and temporarily silenced its main overseeing body, the PI, on a pivotal subject.

It also appeared that the media had been browbeaten, too. For instance, *The West* had given very prominent coverage (front page and editorial) to PI Murray's initial comments in his 2013/14 Annual Report relating to thwarting and delaying the police investigation of the OSU. It had editorialised hard in favour of broad reform of the CCC on 17 October 2014, under the heading: "Leadership just part of overhaul needed at CCC".

Seemingly chastened by the CCC attack on PI Murray, *The West*

---

[105] Ibid., p. 22.

actually ran two stories on 6 November 2014, both by Emerson, on the same affair. I quote the second on page 22, the editorial and opinion page.

It illustrates how completely *The West* had changed position:

> **CCC a victim of misinterpretation**
>
> On the face of its painstakingly outlined defence yesterday, the Corruption and Crime Commission is within its rights to be aggrieved at criticism from its Parliamentary Inspector Michael Murray in his annual report tabled three weeks ago.
>
> Mr Murray has said it was not his intention to imply that the CCC had deliberately "delayed" or "thwarted" a WA Police Investigation into CCC officers accused of misappropriating funds. But that was the way his report was interpreted by the media, as well as by CCC Acting Commissioner Neil Douglas, and the damage to its reputation has been done.

When I read the story I nearly cried. My immediate thought was: "Good God – the CCC is going to escape proper scrutiny again!" Brian Burke told me that he had a similar reaction.

This was not some petty technical disagreement between officials. This was a very serious dispute, the outcome of which would decide the future status of one of the most important elements of the State's law enforcement agencies.

The question was: Is the CCC henceforth to be subject to independent scrutiny, or remain an agency that essentially polices itself?

I have to concede that the CCC attack on PI Murray's Annual Report was well argued and cleverly presented. Additionally, the CCC offensive was supported by two senior counsel. The first was Patricia Cahill SC, who gave opinion on three points. Essentially, her advice was that:

(a) The secrecy provisions of the CCC act were such that information could not be supplied by CCC officers to the police when the requested information went beyond the original allegation referred to the PI by the CCC.

(b) To supply CCC information beyond that "may well be contrary to the public interest" and was therefore unlawful.

(c) Even if the police issued a search warrant (which the police had threatened when they could not obtain co-operation from the CCC) the secrecy clause in the CCC Act could be used to successfully frustrate it.

This advice supported any desires the CCC may have had to prevent a police investigation.

The second senior counsel retained by the CCC was Chris Zelestis QC, a highly respected former acting Parliamentary Inspector. Fundamentally, Mr Zelestis's opinion was that Ms Cahill's advice was correct.

If accepted, that advice would place the CCC in a very strong position to fend off or prevent any outside investigation of any of its activity that it did not itself authorise.

PI Murray pointed out later the effect would be that, if a police officer were investigating an offence referred by the PI, and in doing so came across another offence or offences (as actually happened in the situation under consideration), or another offence was confessed by a Commission officer, then that police officer "is precluded from unilaterally investigating (the second offence) or indeed from arresting and charging the Commission officer who confessed".[106] That is, without going back through the CCC and then the PI.

Consequently, equipped with its legal advice, the CCC asserted that:

1. ... production of some of the documents would be destructive of or extremely damaging to the Commission's ability to oversee WA police; and

---

[106] *Parliamentary Inspector's Report On Misconduct and Related Issues in the Corruption and Crime Commission, Report No. 19,* June 2015, p. 29.

2. ... the Commission could not lawfully disclose to WA Police all the information that it had sought.[107]

As events turned out, the police did obtain most of the documents and information requested.

This is how it happened.

PI Michael Murray did not respond to the CCC special report of 5 November 2014 until he presented his report to the JSCCCC on 10 June 2015.

PI Murray's report, supported by the detail of a comprehensive written police narrative, sidelined the CCC's technical legal defence. The publicised extent of CCC impropriety, was devastating. The CCC did not publicly raise the issues again.

It was starkly apparent that if the CCC had prevailed in its legal argument, based on the secrecy provisions of its Act, only a small proportion of the CCC criminality would have been exposed or prosecuted.

As an example, it was reported by the PI that at a hearing of the JSCCCC on 17 September 2014, Assistant Commissioner Gary Budge, gave the following evidence:

> So there has been significant obstruction, I must say. There has been a reluctance to cooperate with us. Even last week we had a nonsensical situation in regard to another referral, where they (the CCC) provided us some material that we requested and it is quite generic. We were asking for all information that they have in regard to a certain incident. They gave us material, but from reading the material we discovered there was obviously some material that was not provided. We asked them why they had not provided that, and they said because they did not think it was relevant; so they are making a decision on whether it is relevant. We are the investigating officers

---

[107] *Report on an Administrative Matter Relating to the Functions of the Commission Pursuant to Section 88 of the Corruption and Crime Commission Act of 2003,* Corruption and Crime Commission, 5 November 2014, p. 19.

who should be making a decision, I believe, on whether it is relevant or not.

So, when we said, "Well, we want the material", they said, "Tell us what you want then; itemise it and we will then provide you the material." But, of course we do not know what they have got. So, this situation has arisen where we have been restricted in the way we can go about our investigation because of their reluctance to cooperate with us in regard to what is described as serious misconduct, corruption or criminal behaviour."[108]

Also in PI Murray's report was the following paragraph concerning Deputy Police Commissioner (now Police Commissioner) Chris Dawson:

On 6 March 2014, Deputy Commissioner Dawson wrote to me and said:

He had met with Commissioner Macknay QC on 25 February 2014 and voiced his concerns about the lack of information and records being provided by the Commission, and again explained why the materials sought – particularly financial records of the OSU – were necessary for the Police investigation;

Despite Commissioner Macknay QC telling him on 19 December 2013 that the Commission had conducted a thorough investigation of the OSU and had tackled the unit with rigour, an internal financial audit of the unit had only recently been commenced by the Commission, and would take several weeks to conclude...[109]

This statement by Mr Dawson suggests something more worrying. If correct, the CCC misled the police as to the CCC's internal investigations. Also, it appears to indicate that if the CCC did undertake an internal investigation of the OSU, it was almost entirely ineffective.

---

[108] *Parliamentary Inspector's Report On Misconduct and Related Issues in the Corruption and Crime Commission, Report No. 19,* June 2015, p. 7.
[109] Ibid., p. 23.

To do justice to Commissioner Macknay, it would appear from other parts of PI Murray's report of 10 June 2015 that the CCC did ultimately cooperate with the police investigation before he retired on 14 March 2014.

We may never know the full story, but I think that the CCC's eventual cooperation could have come about this way.

In the first instance, Mr Macknay took a very hard line on preventing a police investigation. In fact, the CCC and Commissioner Macknay were prepared to resist a police search warrant and actually threatened to take the issue to the Supreme Court if a search warrant was obtained by the police. This was made public by PI Murray's June 2015 report. But at some point Mr Macknay relented and co-operated with the PI.

It is not clear from the public record whether Executive Director Silverstone and the inspectorate wing of the CCC agreed with the new co-operative posture of Commissioner Macknay as the CCC continued to oppose aspects of the police investigation after the Commissioner resigned. Remember, Commissioner Macknay departed on 14 April 2014 and the CCC launched its legal counter offensive by way of a Special Report to Parliament and media conference on 5 and 6 November 2014 respectively, seven months after his departure.

In respect to the law, it is my view that there was merit in both of the opposing PI Murray and CCC legal arguments. Put simply, there is good reason to believe that PI Murray was correct in persisting to maintain that CCC officers were not immune from police investigation. On the other hand, Ms Cahill and Mr Zelestis are probably are technically correct in asserting that a CCC officer could lawfully refuse to respond to questions relating to "official information".

Putting it briefly, on the narrow legal point Cahill and Zelestis may well have prevailed; but in the broader perspective of the administration of justice it is hard to fault PI Murray. However, this problem can be overcome if the CCC Commissioner issues certificates allowing disclosure of "official information" to the police if it is considered to be in the public interest. And that is exactly what happened.

Commissioner Macknay issued the certificates before he resigned. If the CCC had continued to fight the police investigation, there is doubt as to whether the systemic internal criminality could have been exposed. And where would the State have been then, with possible rogue elements continuing at the very core of the CCC.

PI Murray has to be acclaimed for his persistence and bravery on such a sensitive and acute issue. There was a clear mismatch of resources. The PI has one administrative assistant only; the CCC on the other hand has dozens of officers and tens of millions of dollars annually in funding. It was, in truth, a mismatch and a close-run thing.

If the PI had lost his nerve and blinked while under attack, it may have turned out differently. Or if Commissioner Macknay had not issued the public interest certificates, it could have been a changed outcome. To avert this risk in future, PI Murray recommended that the PI be given the same power to certify public interest as the Commissioner. Thus, if the Commissioner refuses to issue public interest certificates, the PI could.

There is still one unanswered question of considerable importance: What provoked Commissioner Macknay's resignation? He announced it on 4 November 2013 (delayed to 14 April 2014).

As was the case with Kevin Hammond and Len Roberts-Smith before him, Mr Macknay had not completed his term. The explanation provided for his departure was to spend time with his family.

There was no replacement in the wings and he was right at the centre of a critical dispute with the PI over the procedures to be adopted in relation to allegations of serious impropriety within the CCC.

It should not be overlooked that the previous two commissioners had also resigned at similar critical moments. That is, while the CCC was in acrimonious dispute with PIs Malcolm McCusker and Chris Steytler.

It is my contention (and much of this is educated speculation on my part) that Kevin Hammond may have been overwhelmed by a dominant investigative wing of the CCC, aligned with the CCC administrative apparatus, headed up by Brigadier Silverstone. That gives some hint as to why the processes of the Smiths Beach and Lobbyists investigations were the most procedurally restrictive in all of Australia.

Even the notorious ICAC (the NSW equivalent of the CCC) allowed effective legal representation for witnesses. As I have previously contended, it's possible that Mr Hammond ultimately took a more judicious position on alleged wrongdoing in the Smith's Beach and Lobbyist inquiries. My speculation is that this led to a falling out between the Commissioner and overly aggressive elements of the CCC concerning the framing of the Smiths Beach report.

The upshot was that Mr Hammond resigned after he had heard all the evidence and written the report, but before the report was released.

Roberts-Smith – McCusker conflict

Commissioner Len Roberts-Smith, in my view, did not need any capturing. All of his public statements indicate he felt quite at home among the rigid elements of the CCC. However, he soon ran into conflict with PI Malcolm McCusker, who was systematically and forensically dismantling and discrediting the CCC reports.

The CCC in the name of Commissioner Roberts-Smith then tried to disrupt Mr McCusker by taking an injunction application to the Supreme Court.

The Government stepped in and the court case went nowhere. Afterwards, PI McCusker moved on, among other things, to become State Governor.

Commissioner Roberts-Smith then encountered the intellectually formidable former Supreme Court judge, Chris Steytler, who succeeded Mr McCusker. There was almost immediately conflict between the new PI and the Commissioner over a number of CCC perceived excesses. However, the paramount issues were the almost complete failure of the CCC to adequately investigate complaints against the police use of force and the suicide of a proposed witness to an unnecessary public hearing.

The suicide was a truly tragic case. On either 7 or 8 September

2010, a man who had been summoned to give evidence in a public hearing in aid of the CCC's on-going investigation into alleged theft and a contractual manipulation of up to $5 million by former employees of the City of Stirling, committed suicide.

The man had been under physical and telecommunication surveillance by the CCC since February 2010. The CCC had ascertained that after the man had become aware of his proposed public interrogation he took steps to end his life. Some of those steps included inquiries about the level of coverage afforded by his life insurance, access to websites concerning committing suicide, and he bought or tried to buy a scalpel.

Consequently, two CCC officers visited the unsuspecting young wife of the witness in Perth on 30 August 2010 and informed her of their beliefs. The CCC officers refused to tell the wife how they came by the information, or of the CCC hearings. The wife was bewildered and telephoned her husband at his then place of work on Barrow Island. He denied any intention to take his life, but offered no explanation of the situation.

The CCC also informed the witness's employer of its apprehensions, but pertinently did nothing else. The witness took his own life about a week later.

PI Steytler took the strong view that, from an evidentiary position, there was no need for the CCC public hearing because more than enough confirmation of wrongdoing had already been collected. PI Steytler maintained that the matter should have simply been handed over to the police.

In his final report to JSCCCC on 22 November,[110] the PI extensively canvassed the probability that the witness had taken his life, rather than expose his family to the trauma and scandal of a sensationalised public show trial.

The truth seems to be that the CCC behaved quite cynically. Brian Burke points out in his book, *A Tumultuous Life* (page 546):

> Towie and Baker [the two visiting CCC officers] wore lis-

---

[110] Joint Standing Committee on the Corruption and Crime Commission Report No. 14 *Death of a Witness*, 24 February 2011.

tening devices that secretly recorded their conversations with the woman [wife] and her distress, which they later transcribed, leaving the inescapable implication that they thought that the woman might say something that would advance the investigation of her husband."

The widow was heartbroken and desolate, but was in no doubt of the CCC's disastrous handling of the matter. Her public remarks after the death made it clear that she held the CCC responsible for the death of her husband, her sons' loss of their father and the loving parents' loss of their son.

PI Steytler made no secret of the fact that he was appalled by the insensitive and incompetent way the CCC investigating officers and supervising staff had handled the case. While the PI "was in no way implying or suggesting that the CCC was to blame for the suicide" as "he regarded it as being one that fell outside of the scope of his report",[111] he maintained that the suicide may have been preventable and implied that the situation had been provoked by unnecessary CCC heavy-handedness.

The PI determined that the proposed public examination was uncalled for.

The matter was handled by way of a PI report to the JSCCCC, which was tabled in Parliament on the 24 February 2011. The next day, Gareth Parker wrote in *The West*:

> The report states that CCC Parliamentary Inspector Christopher Steytler believed CCC Commissioner Len Roberts-Smith should have used his discretion to postpone the hearing or make it private.[112]

Commissioner Roberts-Smith publicly disputed PI Steytler's opinion, but resigned shortly thereafter, well ahead of time.

In the case of Roger Macknay, a very decent individual, it could be too easy to conclude that he was just worn down with the continual conflict with the Police Commissioner and the PI. While I have no

---

[111] Ibid., p. 13.
[112] *The West Australian*, 25 February 2011, p. 9.

doubt that this was a contributing factor to his resignation, I theorise that there were more profound reasons.

It can be argued that he was, in truth, originally and unfortunately caught up in the ethos and culture of this covert and feared investigative body, the CCC.

Nonetheless, and despite the fact that Mr Macknay appears to have been initially won over to a forceful pro-CCC position, there is evidence that he was ultimately converted to a position of some scepticism concerning the integrity of certain of his officers and some of their more senior supervisors.

Roger Macknay and Kevin Hammond were, as legal practitioners within the CCC, somewhat isolated. There were other lawyers employed within the CCC apparatus, but it is well known that a senior solicitor within the CCC was particularly hawkish and had a decidedly close relationship with Brigadier Silverstone.

There is confirmation of this general problem in an intimation by PI Murray in his annexation to JSCCCC Report No. 19. He was commenting on "The Repositioning Report" (which I shall explain shortly) as follows:

> ... I have been pleased to see that an aspect of the proposals is to strengthen the capacity and independence of the legal section of the Commission. Ready access to reliable legal advice must be of considerable assistance to those officers concerned with operational activities.[113]

The clear implication from these words is the concern that independent reliable legal advice was at risk. It can also be reasonably surmised that, as a result of the weakness of the legal section, and possibly the emphasis on the hegemony of the investigative wing, the potential for excess and abuse was heightened.

Interestingly, it did not feature in the media coverage, except for a line or two. However, the raw facts are that many of the CCC's senior administrative staff resigned once Report No. 19 was presented

---

[113] *Parliamentary Inspector's Report On Misconduct and Related Issues in the Corruption and Crime Commission, Report No. 19* June 2015, p. 36.

in draft for internal Government discussion. That is, before it was tabled in Parliament.

There is no doubt that PI Murray took a very critical view of the CCC administrative hierarchy. He actually named the officers he considered were responsible as managers and had given the following specific comments on this score in Report No. 19:

> The (now renamed) OSU is a discrete unit of the Operations Directorate of the Commission (CCC) which operates secretively from premises separate from the Commission's premises in St Georges Terrace. Its function is to provide surveillance and technical services to Commission investigators who are conducting operations.[114]

Elsewhere in the report he details how Craig McGowan was recruited by the CCC from Victoria in 2004 to form the OSU. The Commission, in 2013, declined to renew Mr McGowan's contract of employment.

Nick Anticich, Director Operations, who held his position from June 2004 to August 2009, was responsible for Mr McGowan and the performance of his professional duties from May 2005 until August 2009. Mr Anticich acted as Executive Director on three separate occasions during this period.

Robert Sutton was Deputy Director Operations from 2004 to his resignation in February 2013. He acted as Executive Director between 29 March 2012 and 5 April 2012 and 30 April 2012. In his role as Acting Executive Director, Mr McGowan and the OSU reported to him and Mr Sutton oversaw the actions for Mr McGowan and the OSU.

Brigadier Michael Silverstone, Executive Director from 2004 to October 2014, was responsible for overseeing and managing Messrs McGowan, Anticich and Sutton "and, ultimately, for the organisational environment in which the OSU culture was created and maintained by Mr McGowan". [115]

---

[114] Ibid., p. 13.
[115] *Parliamentary Inspector's Report On Misconduct and Related Issues in the Corruption and Crime Commission, Report No. 19* June 2015, p. 14.

The clear line of logic was that Mr McGowan had superintended OSU whose officers has serially misbehaved and that the three other superiors had failed to adequately oversee either McGowan or the unit.

If you set aside Commissioner Macknay's resignation, the highest-profile casualty of PI Murray's persistence with the police investigation appears to be Brigadier Michael Silverstone, the long-serving Executive Director of the CCC. He had been appointed in 2004, at the CCC's very inception, and had held his position for a period that easily exceeded the combined periods of service of three commissioners.

The brigadier publicly represented the stringent inflexible face of the CCC. In his media presentations, he invariably took the hard line and was never prepared to acknowledge any fault by the CCC. The Executive Director was a major part of the resistance to the questioning by PI Malcolm McCusker of CCC procedures and findings.

Two members of the JSCCCC have separately expressed the view that Brigadier Silverstone had more to do with the moulding of the culture of the CCC than any other party.

After Commissioner Macknay's resignation had taken effect in April 2014, Brigadier Silverstone had the opportunity, as the senior permanent officer of the CCC, to open up the CCC for a full audit. As the record shows, that did not happen. The police continued to complain that their investigation was being frustrated by the CCC.

Some people question how Silverstone ever got the Executive Director position.

The brigadier played a significant role in the Children Overboard scandal a few years before his appointment to the CCC (see details below).

There are similarities between the Children Overboard affair and the Smiths Beach and Lobbyists inquiries, where I contend that some CCC officers must have known that parts of the pivotal evidence presented to the public were flawed, but made no effort to correct the record. In any event, it was into the hands of Brigadier Silverstone as Executive Director, that the Gallop Government effectively entrusted the administration side of the State's paramount corruption-fighting agency.

In Western Australia, we know that Brigadier Silverstone was not always accurate with his own evidence. When he gave testimony to the JSCCCC on 5 July 2004, he was asked questions about the sensitive matter of the ownership and maintenance of the state-of-the-art CCC telecommunication interception (TI) equipment. Even though he had been extended some notice of the nature of the questions to be asked, he delivered evidence that was incorrect in three important particulars. As a consequence, 10 days later he had to correct the record.

I mention this episode for two reasons. The matter was not all that important, and we are all human and make mistakes. However, first, it is of interest that the brigadier could have handled his evidence so negligently. Was this how he handled the Children Overboard matter?

In the press release announcing his resignation, Brigadier Silverstone tried to give the impression that it was just business as usual at the CCC and that all was going well. There was not the slightest hint in his final public goodbyes that major corruption had been detected within the CCC, that a significant internal scandal was about to be exposed or the seriously impaired morale.

Brigadier Silverstone said he had been in the job for 10 years and his "departure would provide his successor with time in the chair before a new Commissioner was appointed so that he or she was well settled".

It was true that he had been in the chair for 10 years. But, as I shall shortly explain, the rest of his statement gave the impression that all was rosy. There was no indication of the gathering storm within the CCC or the rock-bottom morale that accompanied it. It would appear that, as soon as it became clear that PI Murray could not be deterred from having a police investigation into the OSU, the future of senior members of the administration of the CCC was clouded.

In due course, PI Murray made it clear in two separate sections of his June 2015 report that he considered that Brigadier Silverstone was "ultimately responsible for the organisational environment in which the OSU culture existed".

Brigadier Silverstone has never publicly conceded any element of culpability for the succession of CCC blunders culminating in the OSU scandal.

In conspicuous contrast, John McKechnie QC, who took up the Commissioner's job on 28 April 2015, had a different view. He wasted no time. Through a press release dated 17 June 2015, Commissioner McKechnie emphatically endorsed Report No. 19. By necessity and without any reservations, that media release embraced PI Murray's findings.

Commissioner McKechnie also frankly commented that it would "take the CCC a long time to recover".

Commissioner McKechnie welcomed the appointment of two new senior executives to the CCC in a press release dated 13 July 2015. That is, two-and-half months after he took up his own appointment.

Ray Warnes was appointed Chief Executive from 10 August 2015. He has a long history in the WA Government Justice system. Wendy Enderbrock-Brown was made Director Legal Services after almost 20 years with the Australian Government Solicitor.

These appointments had the potential to start to fill two daunting weaknesses in the previous CCC structure. The first was the almost total ignorance, within the CCC, of how Parliament and government actually worked on a day-to-day basis.

The second weakness was the way in which the investigative and administrative wings of the CCC, in Silverstone's period, appeared to dominate and monster the legal section. This could be an explanation of the CCC's disastrous win/loss ratio in court on the Smith's Beach, Lobbyists and associated matters.

It has been an enduring and unfortunate practice within the police force in WA to allow corrupt and/or criminal police officers, especially if they were in senior ranks, to quietly retire on full benefits and with their public reputations intact.

It was hoped that with the advent of the CCC and with new Police

Commissioners O'Callaghan and Dawson taking firmer control of the police force, this custom would be discontinued. I think that the practice has substantially abated, but, alas, it appears to have moved across to the CCC. The names of the seven or eight rogue CCC officers who were forced out as a result of investigation have not been disclosed.

As an example, I refer to a story by Gary Adshead, in *The West* on 2 November 2013:

> Three officers from the CCC have been stood down over the misappropriation of $1,000, the corruption agency's Executive Director Mike Silverstone said.
>
> But the agency refused to reveal other details, including which section the officers worked in or what area of the CCC the money related to.

There are several other such examples that could be documented.

As far as my research indicates, no rogue CCC officer has ever been publicly identified, but, as PI Murray had indicated, some CCC officers have been allowed to quietly resign and move interstate before they could be interviewed.

Courts do not normally suppress the names of accused unless the welfare of a juvenile is in issue. The immunity from identification is not extended to ordinary members of the public.

In fact, in the CCC interrogations I have referred to the least suspicion was sufficient for the CCC to unleash the most intense and harsh public scrutiny, together with baseless criminally adverse inferences.

The difference was that the hard-pressed witnesses in the CCC inspired Smiths Beach, Lobbyists and Parliamentary inquiries were so outrageously denigrated that their careers never recovered. The dismissed and/or resigned CCC officers on the other hand walked away with their public reputations intact. It is difficult intellectually to reconcile these two positions.

The Chairman of the JSCCCC has since severely questioned the privileged position of the CCC officers, as outlined above. His forthright comments are reported in *The West Australian* of 15 October 2015 as follows:

> **Name, shame rogue officers**
>
> The head of the Corruption and Crime Commission's parliamentary oversight committee wants members of an allegedly corrupt unit of covert investigators to be named and shamed to restore public confidence in the corruption watchdog.
>
> Chairman and Upper House Liberal Nick Goiran told a parliamentary hearing yesterday he found it 'somewhat dissatisfying' that the reputations of the officers whose exploits featured in a damning report by CCC Parliamentary Inspector Michael Murray remained untarnished.

In fairness, I should indicate that the CCC took some internal steps to clean up its act before former Supreme Court Judge John McKechnie assumed the position of Commissioner on 28 April 2015. This essentially took the form of a special "Repositioning Report" under the names of Acting Commissioners Neil Douglas and Christopher Shanahan, which was tabled in Parliament on 21 April 2015. To my mind this report was a shallow attempt to publicly display that the CCC was adopting new and more effective procedures in its "dual jurisdiction in respect of misconduct generally and police oversight".[116]

The Repositioning Report had some hopeful organisational proposals, but it failed to mention the rampant corruption of the rogue investigators or the prevailing maladministration that allowed it to nurture. That is, apart from a fleeting mention of charges "involving two officers and the loss of $1000", while congratulating itself on "responding swiftly to those matters."[117]

---

[116] *Report on an Administrative Matter Relating to the Functions of the Commission Pursuant to Section 88 of the Corruption and Crime Commission Act 2003 ("The Repositioning Report")*, 21 April 2015, p. 1.

[117] Ibid., p. 13.

Afterword

It would be remiss if I left the impression that the events mentioned above and the remedial actions taken have remedied the oversight problems within the CCC.

And it would be wrong to leave readers with the impression that after the trauma of the CCC/PI wars and their stopgap settlements, the underlying issues were expunged. Unhappily, that is not the case.

In summary, I contend that the lionisation of the CCC by the media and critical sections of the political establishment, when the CCC set itself up as the new moral authority in WA during the Smiths Beach and Lobbyists inquiries, was counter-productive. It allowed the organisation to brush off concern at its methods by successive PIs; it sanctioned the invention of new highly subjective categories of impropriety not mentioned in the statutes (as explained by Chief Justice Wayne Martin); and it allowed corruption to fester unchecked in its own ranks.

In short, too much power and insufficient checks and balances.

Nick Butterly ran an article in *The West* of 11 October 20 under the headline: "Parliamentary Inspector savages Crime and Corruption Commission".

It related to the PI's inability to investigate allegations of misconduct by CCC officers in the period before they took up their CCC positions. That meant that CCC officers were left with the job of investigating their fellow officers. In the view of the PI this caused a possible conflict of interest situation.

The PI also went back to the running sore of the CCC's handling of accusations against police. He referred to continuing "flawed" assessments of serious misconduct complaints against police and said that the CCC had refused to hand over relevant documents.

That recurring theme was echoed by a story in *The West* of 2 September 2020 that quoted a JSCCCC report bought down by Chair and Labor MP Margaret Quirk. The report alleged that:

> WA's Corruption and Crime Commission has failed to use its full powers to stamp out systemic police misconduct ...

The report called for legislative change. But, as we know, such calls have been made since 2006 without parliamentary action. Inevitably, such dereliction has consequences. And if I may speculate, this is the area of concern that prevented a majority and bipartisan re-endorsement of Commissioner McKechnie under the CCC Act.

Hon. Michael Murray AM QC

The Honourable Justice Michael Murray passed away on 27 July 2020 after a long and distinguished legal career.

Justice Murray retired from the Supreme Court in 2012 after 22 years of service. He was appointed Parliamentary Inspector of the CCC in 2013, where he presided during a period of considerable turmoil and reform.

Brigadier Silverstone – A man with a past

Michael Silverstone was a 32-year career army officer before he was appointed Executive Director of the CCC in June 2004.

Previously, he had served as Commanding Officer of the Special Air Services Regiment and held a senior position in the Defence Intelligence Organisation. He is academically well credentialled, but does not have a law degree, or, as far as can be seen from the public record, any experience or background of any sort in the justice system.

In the profile released by the CCC at the time of his appointment, there was no mention of the pivotal role he played in what some see as one of the most notorious maritime scandal Australia has experienced.

The disgraceful incident is commonly known as the "Children Overboard Affair". It has featured in two acclaimed books, *Don't Tell the Prime Minister* by Professor Patrick Weller and *Dark Victory* by David Marr and Marian Wilkinson. The latter book deals with both the Children Overboard incident and in detail with the related Tampa maritime affair. It won numerous literary awards.

In commenting on *Dark Victory*, Morag Fraser in *The Australian Book Review* wrote:

...it throws into relief the shabby manoeuvres of a ruthless election campaign and one of the most shameful episodes in Australian political history.

Please be assured: Silverstone was no bit player. Without his critical role there would not have been a Children Overboard affair.

Many political commentators contend that the related controversies of "Tampa" and "Children Overboard" were the turning points for the fortunes of the Liberal Party in the November 2001 election campaign featuring Prime Minister John Howard and Opposition Leader Kim Beazley.

In respect to the Children Overboard affair, the allegation was that seafaring asylum seekers had thrown children overboard in a presumed ploy to secure rescue and passage to Australia.

It was a claim first publicised by Immigration Minister Phillip Ruddock and later repeated by Prime Minister Howard.

Wikipedia stated:

> In the early afternoon of 6 October 2001, a southbound wooden hulled "Suspected Illegal Entry Vessel" designated SIEV 4, carrying 223 asylum seekers and believed to be operated by people smugglers, was intercepted by HMAS *Adelaide* 100 nautical miles (190km) north of Christmas Island and then sunk. The next day, which was the day before the issue of writs for the 2001 federal election, Immigration Minister Philip Ruddock announced that passengers of SIEV 4 had threatened to throw children overboard. This claim was later repeated by other senior government ministers including Defence Minister Peter Reith and Prime Minister John Howard.

Wikipedia also stated in its entry:

> The government's handling of this and other events involving unauthorised arrivals worked to its advantage. The Tampa affair had led the government to adopt stricter border protection measures to prevent unauthorised arrivals from reaching Australia by boat. Polls indicate the

measures had public support. The government was able to portray itself as 'strong' on border protection measures and its opponents as 'weak'. In November 2001, the Liberal-National coalition was re-elected with an increased majority.

The Australian Senate Select Committee inquiry into a certain maritime incident later found that no children had been at risk of being thrown overboard and that the government had known this prior to the election. The government was criticised for misleading the public and cynically "(exploiting) voters' fears of a wave of illegal immigrants by demonising asylum-seekers."

Australian Navy patrols of the waters around Christmas Island were under instructions to detect, intercept and turn back boats bringing unauthorised refugees. Once refugees had landed on Australia they could claim a number of legal rights, consequently the Government opposed their landing.

As far as I can make out, this posture was quite legal. However, there were serious questions about the morality of the Government's public reporting of certain events in the Children Overboard affair.

Brigadier Silverstone, as a senior officer in Operation Reflex (to exclude unauthorised boat-borne immigrants from Australia), was merely an official carrying out instructions in the Tampa affair; but in the Children Overboard scandal, he played a much more central and questionable role.

The allegation that asylum seekers threw their children overboard has been totally discredited. It was false. But how was such an invalid report manufactured and who concocted it? Given the undisputed chain of communication, there are only two candidates for this doubtful honour – the Captain of HMAS *Adelaide*, Commander Norman Banks, or his immediate (reporting) senior, Task Force Commander Brigadier Mike Silverstone.

A second and even more sinister question was how such false statement could be perpetuated for more than a month until after the 10 November election.

Weller's book contains a description of what happened after the *Adelaide* intercepted SIEV 4:

> In the early hours of 7 October, having managed to slow down the vessel by firing across its bows, the *Adelaide* dispatched boarding parties in inflatable vessels. The boat stopped, its engines sabotaged. When the *Adelaide* approached, a number of refugees jumped overboard. The *Adelaide*'s rescue boats pulled them out of the water and put them back on board. During that episode one refugee placed a life jacket on a small child in a yellow suit and walked to the edge of the boat, holding the child over the side. The crew of one of the inflatable boats told him to pull back, and he did so. The whole incident took about 65 seconds. It was not recorded in any of the situation reports that the *Adelaide* sent to base because it was not seen as significant.
>
> The *Adelaide*'s technicians got the engine operating again, pointed the ship away from Australian shores, and sent the refugees on their way.
>
> While these events were taking place, the captain of the *Adelaide*, Commander Norman Banks, received a phone call from his superior, Brigadier Silverstone, who was based in Darwin. Because these were sensitive operations, with instructions on actions against SIEVs sent through the chain of command, it was always necessary to keep up to date with what was happening. But this call was different. The minister for defence (Peter Reith) was to appear on a Sunday current affairs program, and needed to be briefed on recent developments. Silverstone had been instructed to ring the captain of the *Adelaide* and then tell the head of strategic command what was happening – a procedure that was not part of the normal chain of command.
>
> The timing of the call was, perhaps, unfortunate. In his discussion with Silverstone, which took place while he

was overseeing a dangerous and often fraught operation, Banks described what he saw. As best he can recall, he noted that one person was holding a child in a life jacket and was threatening to throw her overboard. He states that he did not say at any time that a child had been thrown overboard. Nor does the officer on the bridge with him during the phone conversation recall him saying a child had gone overboard.

Silverstone took notes during the conversation. His notes record "men overboard", and after the phone was put down he added the word "child" between the two. He wrote "five, six or seven", an indication of the age that Banks thought the child might be. Silverstone has consistently been adamant that Banks said a child had been thrown overboard, and relied on his notes as evidence. Banks was initially unsure, particularly when faced by a senior officer who had taken notes at the time while he, Banks, was mid-operation and overseeing the crew. But as he reflected, and with the support of the officer on the bridge with him at the time, he became more certain that he did not say a child had been thrown overboard. The officer on the Adelaide said he heard Banks tell Silverstone 'that the SUNCs are throwing themselves overboard and threatening to throw a child in the water in an attempt to create a SOLAS [safety of life at sea] "situation".' In retrospect, Banks suspected that 'somewhere in the chain of command' statements about asylum seekers threatening to throw children overboard 'were changed in translation' or alternatively there was a political imperative and it was a deliberate change of the words signalled by the ship.

Precisely what was said in that call will never be known? Each participant sticks to his own version. But that conversation is the only source for the story that a child was thrown overboard. None of the situation reports sent by the *Adelaide* describing the events of 7 October made any mention of children being thrown or dropped into the water.

After speaking to Banks, Silverstone rang the head of strategic high command in Canberra, Air Vice Marshall Titheridge, and recounted what was happening on the *Adelaide*. It is not certain whether he said that a child or children had been thrown overboard. But the threat reported to Silverstone had now become a fact. Silverstone also rang his superior, Vice Admiral Smith, and gave the same report. Smith did not usually advise ministers directly, but that day he was in the company of parliamentary secretary for defence, Brendan Nelson, and when asked, told him that events had been made "much more difficult . . . by people jumping/pushing people into the water". Smith thought Silverstone used the word children, rather than child.

In turn, Titheridge rang the defence minister's chief of staff. That, after all, had been the purpose of the initial call, to brief the minister. He also rang the chief of the defence force, Admiral Barrie, and the head of the people smuggling task force, Jane Halton, a deputy secretary in the prime minister's department. He told her that SUNCs had jumped overboard and that children were being thrown overboard, and insists that he would not have used the term "children" if Silverstone had not used the plural too. Halton asked him if they were all men, and recalls being told "we didn't think any women had gone in". . . Halton made her own note: "throwing kids o/b & trying to disable steering." She says she was told "children", not "child".

And so, it went up the chain of command to the Prime Minister and the other relevant ministers. It only took four hours. If Captain Banks and the naval officer on the bridge of the Adelaide at the time of Brigadier Silverstone's telephone conversation are to be believed, then the "children overboard" allegation was a misunderstanding by, or an invention of, Brigadier Silverstone.

It was clear, almost from the beginning, that there was no documentary evidence to support Brigadier Silverstone's assertion about children being thrown overboard that he passed on to his superiors and to the world. There was only the Brigadier's notes to support his position. However, there were difficulties with those notes. They had been amended, on the crucial point of "children overboard".

Mark Forbes, the Defence Correspondent of *The Age*, put it this way on 28 March 2002 when reporting on the subsequent second Senate Inquiry:

> Notes of the first and only conversation that allegedly reported that asylum seekers threw children overboard were subsequently altered to include the reference to children, material presented to the Senate hearing into the controversy has revealed.
>
> The notes were made by northern commander Brigadier Mike Silverstone, who had claimed the commander of HMAS *Adelaide*, Norman Banks, told him by phone during the October 7 incident that a child had been thrown overboard.
>
> Commander Banks says he only talked of a threat to throw a child and is supported by an officer who witnessed his call.
>
> The Federal Government has claimed, based on Brigadier Silverstone's notes, that Commander Banks made the report.

An obvious comment on this scenario is that the throwing of a child or children overboard is an astonishing event. How could the Brigadier only include it in his notes as an afterthought? Why did he write the word "child" when both of his superiors, Air Vice Marshall Alan Titheridge and Vice Admiral Smith, thought that Brigadier Silverstone had used the word "children" rather than "child" in his separate verbal reports to them. Titheridge was quite adamant on this point.

Another question for the Brigadier is why, when dealing with something as startling as children supposedly being thrown overboard, did he not thoroughly check and double check the purported facts. Clearly, he did not do so, and subsequently came into conflict with both Commander Banks and his superiors on the basic facts.

The reality was that no child was thrown overboard and that there was no hard evidence, documentary or otherwise, to support the claim. Furthermore, this became obvious to those closely involved within 24 hours. These facts were never admitted to the media or the public prior to the election.

However, SIEV4 actually sank the next day, on 8 October 2001, and all of the occupants, including the children, were rescued from the water by the crew of the *Adelaide*. This rescue was captured on film and part of this film was dishonestly used by the Government to muddy the waters and allow the fantasy of the "children overboard" scandal to persist.

This was done, despite the fact that a small group who was intimately involved, including Brigadier Silverstone, knew better. Silverstone did not lift a finger to publicly reveal the truth.

Whatever position one adopts on border protection and refugee entry, you have to concede that, in the Children Overboard issue, honesty and truth were jettisoned.

The integrity of the military was gravely compromised. People in places of trust failed to rectify the public record. Subterfuge was used on a wholesale basis to convey a wholly fallacious impression. Military officers were drawn into the heart of an election campaign.

It is apparent that no one in possession of the true facts was prepared to set the record straight. Brigadier Silverstone did eventually confide to one or two of his superiors that hard evidence to sustain the allegation was not available. Statutory declarations collected almost immediately by Commander Banks from all relevant crewmen on board the *Adelaide* explicitly excluded any possibility of children being thrown into the water.

The declarations were not made public by Brigadier Silverstone or his military and political superiors. Nor did they blow the whistle on the fact that pictures of refugees (including children) in the water after SIEV4 sank on 8 October were misused in the media to bolster the impression that children were supposedly thrown into the ocean on 7 October.

Much of the subsequent commentary has focused on the roles played by the Minister for Defence, Peter Reith, and John Howard, who contrived not to be fully informed on the subject. Their roles have been comprehensively examined and severely condemned by some. But this does not absolve the senior military officers and high-ranking bureaucrats who simply opted to remain silent.

We seem to have forgotten the lessons garnered from the criminal trials of Nazi officials set up at Nuremberg by the Allies after World War II. At those celebrated trials, the morally bankrupt defence that the accused were "merely following orders" was specifically rejected. Also, that the concept of officials simple turning a blind eye was declared ethically reprehensible, and in some cases carried criminal responsibility.

In the case of Brigadier Silverstone, it is clear that he never had the strength to write a memo setting the record straight; even though, by any account, he was a central link in the misinformation.

Norm Marlborough was humiliated during the Smiths Beach inquiry when the CCC played secretly recorded phone conversations with Brian Burke. The chats were irreverent and earthy, but there was nothing incriminating in them. Marlborough was deeply distressed when he left the hearing and required intensive medical assistance in following weeks. He was dumped from Cabinet and resigned from Parliament.

Replaying intercepted phone conversations between Brian Burke and Norm Marlborough during the Smiths Beach inquiry revealed no illegality or corruption, but the CCC's hurtful strategy provided fun for the media. Alston's cartoon was published in *The West Australian* on 9 November 2006.

Julian Grill refused to apologise to the Parliament after an Upper House committee decided he had been in contempt by releasing unspecified documents to Brian Burke. By refusing, Grill risked being sent to prison. Fisheries Ministerial Chief of Staff Nathan Hondros (right) was charged with corruption after assisting Burke and Grill in discussions with the Fisheries Minister about a pearling industry draft policy document. He was acquitted of the charge. Mr Hondros was one of several senior public servants to lose their jobs because they had everyday dealings with Burke and Grill. Although shown to be innocent of any misconduct, they were never reinstated.

As a measure of Brian Burke's perceived notoriety, this Bill Leak cartoon in *The Australian* in March 2007 suggests Australian Al Qaeda terrorist David Hicks would find it less threatening to admit meeting Osama Bin Laden than to having lunch with Burke.

Kevin Spratt (left) is an Indigenous man who made headlines in 2010 when it was revealed that in 2008 police had used a Taser on him about 40 times when he was in custody. He was admitted to hospital with serious injuries. A report by Parliamentary Inspector Christopher Steytler in August 2011 criticised the police performance and the CCC for not taking action in the matter. Jim McGinty (right), as Attorney General, was responsible for the drafting and parliamentary passage of the WA Corruption and Crime Commission Act. He remained a staunch defender of the legislation, despite considerable legal profession and political criticism.

Legislative Assembly Speaker Fred Riebeling found himself in a difficult position when the Carpenter Government decided to use the archaic powers of the Assembly, in court session, to discipline Julian Grill over perceptions of his relationship with Minister for Resources John Bowler. The unprecedented situation was lampooned by Alston in *The West* in August 2007.

Adele Farina, despite owing her parliamentary career to support from Brian Burke, gave inflammatory, but ultimately irrelevant, testimony against him at the Smiths Beach inquiry. She later participated in a Legislative Council committee investigating a CCC-inspired allegation against Burke. Sue Burke (right) shows her relief after husband Brian and Julian Grill were acquitted of the corruption charge recommended by the CCC. The charge related to a pearl industry draft policy.

The pressure on Lesley and Julian Grill created by the CCC's relentless pursuit of Julian starts to show when the failed Smiths Beach inquiry is extended to the business dealings of Grill and Brian Burke. Files and computers seized in raids on their homes were the springboard for new, but fruitless, CCC investigations and inquiries.

Julian Grill's refusal to apologise to the Legislative Council – simply because he had nothing for which to apologise – sparked a lively debate about whether modern parliaments should retain the ancient, but seldom used, power to jail people for perceived contempt of parliament. *The West* supported Grill's call for the power to be abolished, including in this Alston cartoon in February 2008.

Bob Hawke and Brian Burke in Labor's glory days of the early 1980s. Hawke was Prime Minister and Burke was the very popular Premier of WA.

Former MP Shelley Archer was accused by a Legislative Council committee of passing confidential information to Brian Burke, but the DPP declined to prosecute. She resigned from the ALP in November 2007 and retired from Parliament in May 2009. Colin Barnett (right) had a surprise victory in the 2008 WA election after Premier Alan Carpenter called a snap election. The Carpenter Government's demise resulted from the loss of four seats previously held by ministers who had been subjected to high-profile, but misguided, CCC inquiries.

Robert Taylor was *The West Australian*'s chief political reporter for most of the period covered by this book. His stories are quoted extensively. The Legislative Council was so annoyed with one of his stories, which contained "confidential" information, that it established a committee of privilege to investigate the matter. No action was taken against Taylor.

Julian Grill and Brian Burke at lunch in 2013 near the completion of the long series of unsuccessful CCC-inspired prosecutions related to their lobbying and issues management business.

A Legislative Council privileges committee asserted that a number of people had been in contempt of Parliament by discussing with MPs a possible investigation of WA's unwritten "iron ore policy". The group included Brian Burke, Noel Crichton-Browne and Julian Grill, who also was found to have breached parliamentary privilege. On principle, Grill refused to apologise, risking being sent to prison. The matter was highlighted in *The West* on 20 February 2008.

Journalist Paul Murray took a close interest in the CCC from its inception, writing a number of news stories and feature articles about its tumultuous progress.

The first signs of the CCC losing its dominant position in the community came when Parliamentary Inspector Malcolm McCusker QC supported the overturning of CCC impropriety findings against senior public servants and cast doubt on the facts, procedures and ethics adopted by the CCC in the Smiths Beach and Lobbyists inquiries. This enraged CCC Commissioner Len Roberts-Smith who tried unsuccessfully to silence McCusker with a Supreme Court injunction – providing plenty of scope for an Alston cartoon in *The West* in March 2008.

13

CCC LEADERSHIP MARKED BY TURMOIL, CONTROVERSY

This chapter focuses on the extraordinary resignation of the inaugural Commissioner of the CCC, Kevin Hammond.

Mr Hammond resigned after he had heard all of the evidence in the Smiths Beach and Lobbyists terms of reference, and written the draft final report in the Smiths Beach matter, but before he had finished the task.

The significant repercussions caused by Mr Hammond's resignation are examined; the rewording of at least parts of his report after his departure is analysed; and a theory is put forward for this curious departure from normal practice.

This event points to a mystery at the core of the CCC for which there is no clear explanation. Stated briefly, it is that the CCC, for much of its time, has been without a permanent head. For about three years and three months between January 2004 and June 2021 the CCC was without a commissioner. This absence is quite extraordinary as Section 9 of the CCC Act expressly states that CCC performs its functions through its commissioner.

One of those periods was after Commissioner John McKechnie's term expired at end of April 2020 until he was finally reappointed, directly by the McGowan Government, pursuant to special legislation on 25 June 2021.

The JSCCCC had been unable to provide majority and bipartisan support for Mr McKechnie's reappointment, as required by the prevailing CCC Act. In June 2021, the Government announced it would bypass the existing law and introduce legislation to reappoint Mr McKechnie for a second term. It was an extremely controversial second term appointment and had a very rocky road, as I relate at the end of this chapter.

Prior to Mr McKechnie's appointment, the CCC had three commissioners: Kevin Hammond, from 1 January 2004 to 31 March 2007; Len Roberts-Smith, from 5 June 2007 to 31 January 2011; and Roger Macknay, from 21 November 2011 to 4 April 2014. None of the commissioners completed their full term and questions remain concerning the circumstances of their departures.

A CCC Commissioner's appointment is rather special and serious business.

The State Government cannot remove a commissioner. That can only be done by the Governor upon a motion from both Houses of Parliament.

Commissioners are well paid. They received the same salary and allowances as a Supreme Court judge, up until the appointment of Mr McKechnie. With his appointment, the emoluments were very seriously increased, mainly because of problems filling the position.

Mr Hammond held the office of Chief Judge of the District Court before he became the first commissioner. He had served on that court since February 1982 and, as a consequence, was highly experienced in that jurisdiction. However, he had never participated in an investigative body before and he was to find out that it was a very different animal.

Judge Hammond enjoyed respect in the legal profession and was well liked.

I never appeared before Judge Hammond as a barrister as I had given up legal practice for Parliament before he went onto the bench. However, I did have some professional contact with him when he practised law in Northam and I practised in Kalgoorlie. He was courteous and proper.

Intriguingly, and in my view pertinently, our paths crossed again when he launched a book (to which I had contributed) edited by Professor Allan Peachment, entitled *The Years of Scandal*, at the WA University Club in 2006. The book dealt with commissions of inquiry in WA 1991– 2004. It covered a broad canvas, but my contributing chapter dealt with my experience with the "daddy of them all" – the WA Inc. Royal Commission.

This royal commission was called in 1991 by new Premier Carmen Lawrence, partly under pressure from her lawyer brother, Bevan Lawrence, and the People for Fair and Open Government organisation of which he was a leader.

At the function and slightly before the launch of *The Years of Scandal*, Lesley and I spoke briefly to Mr Hammond, who, at the time, was the Commissioner of the CCC. I can't remember details of the conversation, but I expect it contained unremarkable pleasantries. But what Mr Hammond said about my chapter, The Quality of Mercy, when he rose to launch the book has stayed etched in my memory.

Unbeknown to me, the CCC had already commenced a far-reaching inquiry into the lobbying activities of Brian Burke and myself. Mr Hammond must have been acutely aware of that fact.

My offering to *The Years of Scandal* dealt with my wife Lesley's and my experience with the WA Inc. Royal Commission. I was told later by Professor Peachment that it was an entertaining chapter, although the experience I described was among the nastiest episodes in our lives. It was a period of trauma, frustration and anguish when, among other demeaning incidents and for a short period, I was wrongly thrown into jail; and Lesley, the nearest thing to an angel I have encountered, suffered undeserved distressing indignities and torment. For example, we lost our family home, which we were forced to sell to pay my legal bills.

In the chapter I contributed, I tried to explain, gently, the profound injustices that can befall innocent parties who become casualties of an instrument as blunt as a royal commission. That is especially relevant to a royal commission such as the WA Inc. commission, where raw politics was always an unstated, but ever-present, factor.

There is no doubt that the substance of my chapter had a deeply felt effect on Commissioner Hammond. He said, among other relevant things when he launched the book, that he had read my chapter with deepening concern. If it was correct, he said, and he had no reason to believe that it was not, we needed to take stock of where such inquiries could take us. It was an episode that should never be repeated in this State.

I believe that Kevin Hammond was sincere when he made these comments and that they were not invented just for the occasion. Later events confirm my judgement.

Mr Hammond resigned as Commissioner effective from 31 March 2007. He made the announcement on the occasion of a speech to the Institute of Public Administration Australia (IPAA) on 20 March 2007. He was terminating his term almost two years early.

In his IPAA speech, Mr Hammond presumed that some people would be aware of his intended retirement, but there had been no public warning of his departure, as far as I can ascertain, and no arrangements for a replacement commissioner. In fact, he was still publicly hearing evidence in the Lobbyist Inquiry at the beginning of that month.

Mr Hammond's retirement announcement was not accompanied by any press release. Remarkably, there was no public departing eulogy from the Premier or senior ministers. On the surface, Commissioner Hammond's quitting seemed to evoke no particular concern or interest by government.

Mr Hammond stated that the Smiths Beach Inquiry Report would be "tabled sometime in the next couple of months". There was no hint that the report would be anything other than his own authorship. As to the Lobbyists inquiry, he indicated, "it is hoped to have that report tabled by the end of the year".

Mr Hammond came under no intense questioning from the media about the sudden nature of his departure. It is of some implicit significance that the statement from the CCC, on 30 March 2007, formally notifying of Mr Hammond's resignation and indicating that part-time existing Acting Commissioners Christopher Shanahan SC and Neil McKerracher QC would take over his duty's *pro tem*, was about the tersest that I have ever seen in similar circumstances.

The West Australian clearly treated this media release as the first confirmation that Mr Hammond would not be finalising and tabling of the Smiths Beach report.

The media statement was merely five short sentences long, giving just the barest of essentials. It referred to Mr Hammond in the third person and appeared to have been cursorily put out by the CCC media contact, Owen Cole. There was no attempt at a eulogy or even a short summary of Mr Hammond's work as inaugural commissioner. It was just another aspect of this puzzling departure.

The reality was that the Commissioner's quitting was quite extraordinary. He had just presided over the Smiths Beach and Lobbyists terms of reference. He had written the report on Smiths Beach, but had not yet tabled it. He was still sitting on aspects of the Lobbyists term of reference. There had been months of testimony that he alone had heard.

No urgent reason for resignation was ever advanced. There was no indication of ill health. The best that Mr Hammond offered was that he "was looking forward to spending more time with his grandchildren".

Prominent Perth lawyer Tom Percy described the situation as unprecedented.

> If you were looking at it in terms of a criminal trial you'd probably have to start again. Wouldn't that put a cat amongst the pigeons? Everyone would know what to say this time.[118]

Mr Percy pointed out that:

> ... retiring judges usually extended their tenure so that they could write any outstanding judgements and clear up loose ends. The resignation was very strange. The Commissioner observes all the demeanour and reactions of the witnesses. As all good jurists know, there's a lot more to assessing evidence than what the witnesses actually say. It is not just the evidence, it's the way they give it and that will all be lost.

Two days later I had email correspondence and a telephone conversation with Robert Taylor who had written the *The West Australian*'s article containing Mr Percy's comments. He advised me that it had provoked a very hostile response from the CCC hierarchy. It was

---

[118] *The West Australian*, 31 March 2007, p. 2.

obvious that Mr Hammond's resignation and the uncompleted business was an extremely sensitive issue for the CCC.

But it didn't end there. There existed doubt in legal circles whether an acting commissioner could ethically finish off a commissioner's report.

The Australian gave Kevin Hammond the eulogy that the CCC and the Government did not. It comprised a full-page feature with photos of Mr Hammond and four of the "big scalps" during his time as Commissioner – former ministers Tony McRae, John D'Orazio, Norm Marlborough and ministerial chief of staff Graham Burkett.

The story, written by Amanda O'Brien, was replete with a lurid headline,

> "Some like it rotten", and a sub-headline, "Kickbacks and backhanders all the way to Canberra".[119]

The term "All the way to Canberra" was a reference to the ruthless sacking by John Howard of Ian Campbell, the Federal Environment Minister, for an innocuous and almost accidental meeting with Brian Burke.

The highly graphic words "kickbacks and backhanders" referred to nothing that ever emerged, even as opinions or findings, in the subsequent CCC reports. But the terms painted a fallacious and ghastly picture of corruption. The body of the article was florid, exaggerated and quite improper. Here is a taste:

> The bodies of crooked politicians and public servants are piled high in Kevin Hammond's discrete city office in Perth. His filing cabinets are filled with remnants of reputations, his desk stained by evidence against countless crooks and liars... He'll leave an impressive legacy that stretches all the way to the Lodge and a body count that includes state and federal ministers.

Make no mistake, O'Brien was almost exclusively referring to the Smiths Beach and Lobbyists matters. It didn't seem to bother her editor that the reports of these matters had not yet seen the

---

[119] *The Australian*, 29 March 2007, p. 12.

light of day. Or that not one finding had yet been made against any individual.

It didn't seem to be important that there was no proof of the electrifying allegations about "crooks". Or for the damning of the innocent witnesses who she was referring to as "scalps" and "bodies". It did not seem to occur to her that these dooming accusations might be dropped by the CCC before the reports were tabled, which they were. What *The Australian* was doing was the worst form of trial by media.

However, much more pertinent to me at that point in time was the fact that O'Brien did not mention anywhere that Commissioner Hammond was vacating these sensational inquiries before they were complete. Nor did she question the ethics, advisability or efficacy of abandonment of such an important task.

O'Brien, before she was employed by *The Australian*, was Jim McGinty's press secretary. In turn, McGinty instituted the CCC and has been zealously protective of it. O'Brien subsequently worked with the CCC in its public relations section.

The West Australian, on the other hand, in its edition on the very same day, was much more sceptical about Commissioner Hammond's resignation. *The West*, allowed this story to dominate its early pages. It ran the Tom Percy comment quoted above under the headline: "Hammond to leave before CCC reports".

The story began:

> Retiring Corruption and Crime Commissioner Kevin Hammond will not present any of the reports from CCC investigations into activities of lobbyists Brian Burke and Julian Grill despite sitting through every day of recent public hearings.

Taylor's article also contained the CCC's casual view on the problem of the reports being brought down by people other than those who had heard the evidence.

In his telephone conversation with me, Taylor said the CCC anger he had referred did not come from Mr Hammond; it came from CCC Executive Director Mike Silverstone, who said:

> Mr McKerracher (barrister and part-time Acting Commissioner) could get all the transcripts and video tapes of hearings and electronic and documentary evidence.

This statement, of course, was questionable. It was unlikely that a part-time commissioner could adequately wade through and accurately assess months of detailed evidence and make the finely tuned assessments from two major inquiries on his own. In numerous discussions with other lawyers, I encountered the same doubt.

In some instances, nearly two years elapsed before reports were brought down. This limbo circumstance alone destroyed careers.

The report into Smiths Beach had, in fact, already been written by Mr Hammond, and relevant parts had been sent out to public officer witnesses who might have a finding of improper conduct made against them. They received the relevant sections of the draft report on 19 January 2007. Those witnesses had a right of reply and their written responses had to be received by the 9 February.

The timetable for the final Smiths Beach report had been set by Mr Hammond on 6 December 2006. At no time was there any hint that the final report would be delayed or that Mr Hammond would not be delivering it. It also was indicated in the letter of the 19 January that Mr Hammond himself would consider those replies received by the 9 February in preparation of his final report.

By press release dated 2 April 2007 the CCC briefly referred to the Smiths Beach report. The release opened:

> … Mike Silverstone, said Commissioner Hammond (who officially retired from the position on 31st March 2007) has completed his work on the Smiths Beach report.

There are two serious problems for the CCC in this statement. The first is, if the Smiths Beach report was completed or almost complete, as Mr Silverstone implied, why wasn't it released under Commissioner Hammond's name before he retired? If it was going to take a few more days to complete, why didn't Mr Hammond take a few more days, or weeks, and complete it?

The second problem was that Mr Silverstone's media statement didn't fit the facts. If the Smiths Beach report was complete, as he implied, why was it not tabled until 5 October 2007 – that is, more than five months later – under the name of the Acting Commissioner Neil McKerracher QC?

These significant questions have never been satisfactorily answered.

There were two more troubling points of concern. Firstly, why didn't Mr Hammond front up to the media in a press conference and explain his sudden departure? As Tom Percy said, the retirement of the Commissioner with so much important work nearly completed was entirely "unprecedented".

Why did Mr Hammond embark upon a series of (seemingly) important hearings on Lobbyists matters in February 2007 if he was contemplating retirement the next month? Why wasn't an acting commissioner designated to do the job?

These were not "any old" inquiries. They were the biggest and most important tasks that the CCC had touched. Why didn't Commissioner Hammond himself explain the situation to the public? It was clearly his duty.

Why did Mr Silverstone make the announcement? It was not his job. He was an administrative officer who did not have the qualification demanded by the Act for a commissioner's role. These were inquiries that were costing the taxpayers tens of millions of dollars and were raising attention across Australia. Witnesses' reputations, livelihoods, careers and freedoms were in the balance.

For all their sakes and for the sake of the State, the inquiries had to be carried through with coherence and conformity. Removing the hearer of evidence and the trier of the facts and substituting someone who had not been a party to any of the testimony, near the end of the process – although probably legal under the CCC Act – was highly unsatisfactory. It would not and could not happen in a court of law or most other public fact-finding tribunals.

However, there was no opportunity to put these questions to Mr Hammond. There was no media conference. No opportunity to question. No explanation. Then Mr Silverstone neatly closed the door on the subject altogether by saying:

> Mr Hammond, who retires today, could have nothing more to do with the reports under the provisions of the CCC Act.

The secrecy provisions of the CCC Act prevented any questioning of Mr Hammond after his retirement as Commissioner and there was no other avenue to determine the truth. Surely Mr Hammond and the CCC owed some explanation to the people of WA?

Intriguingly, Attorney-General Jim McGinty made no comment on this strange development. As far as I can see from the public record, no one from the Government made any comment. It is hard to believe that the Government did not know more about this situation.

If that was all that there was to the resignation of Commissioner Hammond, I reluctantly would have to conclude that his actions in failing to complete and table the reports were irresponsible. In fact, highly irresponsible.

But I don't believe that. There is nothing in Kevin Hammond's long legal history to indicate any irresponsibility. In fact, quite the contrary. I am suggesting that something more dramatic happened within the CCC. Although there is no clear, unambiguous proof of it, I believe that a case can be made that there was a sharp difference of opinion between the Commissioner and the investigative wing of the CCC about how to handle the evidence from the Smiths Beach and Lobbyists terms of reference public hearings.

The bureaucrats take over

CCC Executive Director Mike Silverstone appears to have become the public presence within the CCC at this point. Perplexingly, he and not the acting commissioners issued critical media releases.

I can assert with more certainty, however, that when Mr Hammond departed his near-completed Smiths Beach report was not the report the public would see. I can produce documentary evidence proving that at least some crucial parts of Mr Hammond's report were re-written by parties within the CCC.

In looking for clues for what motivated Mr Hammond to precipitously resign well ahead of the end of his term, I go back to the speech he made to the IPAA of 20 March 2007. In general terms, the speech was predictable. Centrally, it was a defence of the three years of CCC operations to that date. He was particularly sensitive on the questions of intrusive surveillance in peoples' homes and the procedures employed at public hearings. These were the areas where the CCC had received the most public criticism.

As an aside, I think that Mr Hammond may be a little embarrassed if he reread his defence of public hearings now in the light of the sharp censure that has come from the CCC parliamentary oversight committee, the JSCCCC, and senior barristers such as Chris Zelestis and Malcolm McCusker.

By this time (March 2007), although the politicians, most of the media and the general public were still wildly supportive of the CCC and its practices, there was considerable and mounting disquiet in the legal community at the civil rights-stripping methods being employed by the CCC.

WA's most respected barrister, Malcolm McCusker, was in the vanguard, and the legal profession soon fell in behind him. Professional associations such as the Law Society and the Criminal Barristers Association quickly passed motions condemning the unfair CCC procedures, and sent letters expressing that disapproval to the Premier, Attorney-General McGinty, Mr Hammond and others.

Mr Hammond was indirectly being taken to task by his peers, who were outraged at what was happening. He was part of the profession so it was natural for him to be sensitive to his legal colleagues' views.

The investigative wing of the CCC, however, would have been elated and confident in their positions because of their perceived public success and media acclaim. Notwithstanding that media support, by March 2007 there were also some rumblings among journalists. Senior press commentators such as *The West's* Paul Murray and

Robert Taylor were starting to have doubts about the CCC processes and asking some hard questions.

Joanna Menagh, the ABC's senior court reporter in Perth, had been assigned to the CCC public hearings. Rather than hide from the media, and with Lesley at my side, I would answer questions from the assembled journalists in our apartment block forecourt. They were not always happy affairs. Menagh wept at one of these impromptu door-stops. Later, when we privately asked whether I had upset her, she replied:

> No, it is not you. I have been following this issue for some months now and I find it hard to come to terms with how unjust it is.

I am tentatively persuaded that Mr Hammond was not indifferent to this change in the wind. Although I have no strict proof of this (and may never have) I feel sure that these two possibly conflicting attitudes – on the one hand the Commissioner's sensitivity to his peers and on the other the more gung-ho inspectorate staff – were likely to create tension.

Going back to Mr Hammond's speech of 20 March 2007, there was another small indication of possible conflict. In the last paragraph of his address, he quite properly thanked the CCC staff with whom he had worked since the CCC's inception. The curious aspect was that no individual person was mentioned and, in particular, no mention was made of Mike Silverstone, the CCC Executive Director.

Brigadier Silverstone had worked with Mr Hammond from the outset. This most senior administrative figure had enjoyed a high profile, although for some reason had rarely been photographed. He carried an equivocal reputation because of his uncertain role in the Federal Government's "children overboard" incident (See chapter 12, "Corruption, dysfunction, conflict exposed in CCC".)

The 20 March dialogue turned out to be the one and only occasion where Mr Hammond could single out Mr Silverstone for public comment and praise. He chose not to do so. Mr Hammond is not an ungenerous man, but he failed to make any reference to Mr Silverstone. Quite extraordinary.

It is possible that Mr Hammond could see over the horizon. I am told by people close to him that he was acutely sensitive to a potential danger. One of his close associates told me that Mr Hammond could "smell smoke a mile away". Additionally, for an experienced lawyer there were already enough markers out there then to indicate that the CCC was heading into rough water.

Section 86 of the CCC Act creates an obligation on the Commission, when preparing a report on any matters adverse to a person or body, to extend a reasonable opportunity to that person to make representations concerning those adverse matters. That is normally done when the final draft report is settled by the Commissioner.

Section 86 is one of the much over-hyped safeguards under the Act. It was in that process that the CCC made a revealing mistake, as I shall shortly explain.

Just to recap, by his press release of 2 April 2007, Mr Silverstone had stated that Mr Hammond had completed his work on the Smiths Beach inquiry. He also advised that the responses of the public officers likely to be subject to an opinion of *misconduct* (my emphasis) sent out by Mr Hammond on 19 January 2007 were already considered as part of the report.

He then went on to state:

> The next step is to advise others who have been adversely mentioned in the report, but not subject to opinions of misconduct. They will also have the opportunity to reply. Acting Commissioner McKerracher will consider the replies and decide as to whether adjustments to the report is necessary... The final report will then be tabled in Parliament.

Thus, although Mr Silverstone's timetable was already several weeks behind that of the retired Commissioner, it confirmed the same process. However, Mr Silverstone failed to explain why the report-writing program had slipped by nine weeks. The Commissioner's letter to me of 19 January advises that any final submission from public officers affected would need to be in by 9 February 2007.

The letter also referred to the possibility of receipt by me of a further letter making adverse comment concerning me. If that was to happen, my lawyer expected to receive that shortly after 9 February 2007. That is the final date by which affected public officers had to reply to Commissioner Hammond.

It later transpired that the letters to those adversely commented upon (private citizens like Brian Burke, David McKenzie and me, as distinct from public officers who had findings made against them) did not go out from the commission until 13 April 2007, under the hand of Acting Commissioner Neil McKerracher. That is an unexplained nine-week delay on Commissioner Hammond's indicated time frame.

Why didn't the Executive Director explain the delay? I suggest that this hiatus coincided with the possible time when the dispute within the CCC may have come to a head. What other explanation is there?

Interestingly, because of the format initially adopted by Commissioner Hammond, the media was able to deduce that certain public officers were in the clear, as they had not received advice by letter sent out on 19 January 2007 alleging impropriety. The *Busselton-Dunsborough Mail* as early as 31 January 2007 was able to run a prominent article by Rob Bennett under the headline: "Buswell, Morgan safe from CCC".

It went on to state, in part:

> Vasse MLA Troy Buswell and former shire president Beryl Morgan have not received an adverse submission from the CCC. Neither was asked to provide a please explain to the CCC as had been the case with those who have been told they were adversely affected by the hearings.

The paper was absolutely correct. No adverse findings were ever made against these two. But why did others have to wait for seven months before they were advised of their actual situation?

My barrister, Jeremy Allanson SC (now a judge of the Western Australia Supreme Court) was expecting further advice from the

CCC soon after 9 February 2007, but there was nothing but silence through to the date when Commissioner Hammond announced his impending resignation on the 20 March 2007, and until Mr Silverstone's media release of the 2 April, referred to above.

Even then there was no action on this front for nearly a further three weeks, as explained. The critical question to be answered centres on what intervening event took place sometime after the 19 January letter that coincided with the slippage of Mr Hammond's agenda and prevented the report from being finalised before he departed?

As explained above, there was no opportunity to pose these questions to Mr Hammond prior to his resignation. Thus, there was a duty on the part of the CCC to give some explanation. That duty has never been discharged.

Surprisingly, the Attorney-General, who had a clear responsibility in respect to the administration of the State's legal system, appears not to have made any inquiry or offered any explanation. Some may say it was not the AG's duty to comment on internal CCC processes and that there was a parliamentary oversight committee, the JSC-CCC, for that purpose.

My reply is that the baffling departure of Commissioner Hammond, the abandonment of the published timetable for the report, and the mysterious hiatus in preparation work on the report were quite exceptional and momentous. As a consequence, these matters required inquiry and elucidation by government.

In that respect, it is interesting to note the observations of Alan Carpenter when he made his first major speech on 26 of November 2008 after stepping down as Premier.[120] It was clearly his swan song and was a review of his period as a minister. He expressed distress at the potential damage and injustice at the delay within the CCC.

It seems that he was also alluding to something more tangible: He was hinting that it brought his government down. He did not say so directly, but it is hard to escape the conclusion that he regretted

---

[120] *Hansard* of the Legislative Assembly of Western Australia Parliament, 26 November 2008, p. 555.

putting so much faith in the CCC and the advice he was receiving at the time.

This issue is discussed in more depth in Chapter 14, "2008 Election: A CCC casualty".

It is also relevant that Mr Hammond's departure did not signal his retirement from active employment. A report on the ABC shortly after his resignation indicated that he had taken up the task of reorganising the case list for the Supreme Court. Also, a Thomas More College (UWA) online profile report, downloaded on the 16 September 2014, indicated that he had also accepted a position as a criminal mediator in the Supreme Court.

It was manifestly apparent that there was no urgent haste for Mr Hammond's retirement from the CCC.

I argue that, unmistakably, as at 19 January 2007, the most significant outstanding issue in finalising the Smiths Beach report was how to treat the CCC hearing evidence in respect to Brian Burke, Mr McKenzie and me. Consequently, I am raising the hypotheses that this perplexing set of circumstances had fostered a material difference of opinion between the investigative wing of the CCC and the Commissioner on how the evidence in relation to Burke and Grill should be interpreted and handled.

My hypotheses include the conclusion that the investigative wing won the battle.

I have other evidence for this theory, which I shall reveal later in this chapter.

Just briefly, however, I refer back to Mr Hammond's address of 20 March 2007. Even on that date he expressed the view that he thought the Smiths Beach report would be "tabled in the next couple of months". It was not contemplated by him, even when he knew that he would not be finalising the report, that it would consume nearly another seven months.

Chasing the prize 'scalps'

The explicit premise of this book is that the Smiths Beach and Lobbyists terms of reference were not essentially about alleged corruption of or by public officers. It was about collecting the scalps of Brian Burke and Julian Grill. Remember, the CCC's forerunner had been excoriated for failing to collect any trophy conviction.

There were people both within the CCC and outside who had much riding on its success, and who did not want a repeat of the low-profile Anti-Corruption Commission.

If I am correct in that belief, then on 20 January 2007 the inquiries had reached a critical point. The nature of Commissioner Hammond's comments in the Smiths Beach report were crucial for the aspirations of the investigators. After two years of the most intensive covert surveillance, tens of millions of taxpayer dollars and a host of reputations rested on the words used by him in his final draft document.

I should stress that at the time of Commissioner Hammond's resignation there was zero public evidence of even the most rudimentary steps to find his replacement.

Because of the rigid secrecy provisions of the CCC Act, the contents of Commissioner Hammond's final draft report may never be made public. Therefore, it is not possible for us to know what that report comprised in detail. But I do know, because of the requirements of Section 86 of the CCC Act, that what Commissioner Hammond wrote about me was significantly different to what was incorporated in the Smiths Beach report tabled on 5 October 2007.

So, what did the Hammond report disclose in the way of comment about me? Before I divulge that, I must indicate that there is some personal risk to me in exposing this material. CCC draft reports are confidential and, in this case, a relevant part of the draft report was revealed to my counsel, Jeremy Allanson, and me for the purpose of responding to it.

As broached above, my counsel and I were advised of the possible adverse comment in the draft report (note, adverse comment not adverse finding) by letter from the new acting commissioner, Neil McKerracher QC, dated 13 April 2007. The relevant part of the letter reads as follows:

> ... there is no doubt a possibility that Mr Burke and Mr Grill may seek to give a false impression of the power and

influence they have over senior public officers (like Dr Cox), particularly when talking to clients.

That was it! That was all. Although incorrect, it was utterly benign.

Jeremy Allanson responded on my behalf on 18 April 2007, primarily enquiring if the passage quoted above was "the only adverse comment being made". The answer came back the next day, by letter under the hand of Michael Cashman, the CCC's Director of Legal Services. He wrote:

> The sentence quoted in the matters adverse letter is the only matter adverse to your client in the Commission's proposed report.

It would seem obvious that Mr McKerracher's adverse comment letter to me of the 13 April 2007 quoted Mr Hammond's draft report. For one thing, in the period of less than two weeks since Commissioner Hammond resigned, Mr McKerracher would not have had the time to fully review the voluminous evidence and exhibits of the Smiths Beach term of reference.

Secondly, it was not expected that he would review such evidence, as he was only putting the finishing touches to a draft report already prepared by Commissioner Hammond. Consequently, we would be on safe ground in concluding that the "only adverse comment" came directly from Commissioner Hammond's draft document.

On 24 April 2007, Mr Allanson sent a further letter to the CCC, explaining that a detailed examination of the relevant CCC transcripts did not reveal any actual evidence to support even the proposed benign "adverse comment". It is highly likely that Allanson was correct because the CCC subsequently dropped the accusation.

In the Smith's Beach matter, I appeared to be in no jeopardy. Lamentably, my lawyers and I were in for a considerable shock. About two months later, and contrary to the formal CCC advice above, new adverse comments affecting me were framed by the CCC.

In the absence of any other explanation, I can only conclude that there were dark forces at work within the CCC that were not happy with Mr Hammond's report and were determined to change it, at least in so far as it applied to me.

The first indication that the CCC had rewritten Commissioner Hammond's Smiths Beach report (at least as far as it applied to me) came in a letter to Mr Allanson from Mr Cashman dated 13 June 2007. It contained two pages of completely new adverse comment under the heading: "Messrs' Burke and Grill's influence on Public Sector Agencies."

The CCC was now endeavouring to imply that Burke and Grill had improperly influenced public officers, but it gave no instances or evidence of that supposed influence, or over whom and when it had taken place.

The allegations by the CCC were so ill defined and nebulous that to respond would have been impractical. Consequently, Mr Allanson's essential rejoinder (20 June 2007) was that it was impossible to sensibly respond unless more particulars were supplied.

Mr Allanson's response of 20 June 2007 also sternly reminded the CCC that it was acting beyond its jurisdiction and quite improperly when it implied misconduct by me (as a private citizen), as Section 4 limits its authority to public officers.

The CCC, in its arrogance, simply ignored Mr Allanson's caution. It was manifest that the CCC could not be trusted to administer the basic provisions of its own Act. Much later, the CCC parliamentary oversight committee, the JSCCCC, and Acting Parliamentary Inspector Chris Zelestis were to severely criticise the CCC for similar transgressions. (See Chapter 11)

Mr Cashman's letter of 13 June 2007 containing the new adverse comment did not refer to the previous adverse comment letter two months earlier (13 April 2007) or offer any explanation of how these new adverse comments arose or if the previous ones had been abandoned, and why. That is despite the fact that he had specifically told us in April that there were no other adverse comments relating to me.

Mr Allanson's response of 20 June 2007 raised this issue and invited an explanation. No explanation was forthcoming. There is no doubt that in the interest of natural justice and basic fairness some justification was necessary. We were seeing the CCC at its arrogant best in this correspondence. It could afford to be as high-handed as it liked, because all of this was transacted in secret. It was the CCC's privilege that its actions and the correspondence in this issue were unlikely ever to be made public.

Mr Cashman responded to Mr Allanson's letter of 20 June 2007 on of 26 June 2007. It was little more than an acknowledgement, but was followed by a more substantial letter two days later. But still no details of the alleged improper conduct.

On 11 July 2007, Mr Allanson drafted a long and detailed letter of protest to the CCC. He correctly argued that the CCC had both a statutory obligation and a common law duty to provide me with adequate notice and detail of the adverse comment so that I had an opportunity to answer the charge. Mr Allanson indicated that if the particulars were not forthcoming from the CCC and if natural justice was not extended to his client, then the issue would be taken to the Supreme Court for decision.

It was at this time that Mr Allanson ceased acting in this matter and Herbert Smith Freehills partner Steven Penglis and (then) senior associate Ante Golem took over. They are both highly competent, compassionate individuals, who immediately appreciated the blatant injustice of the CCC posture. Mr Allanson's draft letter was sent off to the CCC on Freehill's letterhead on the same day.

At that stage, I was fighting on several fronts and could not easily afford additional highly expensive Supreme Court proceedings.

As Mr Penglis was concerned the CCC would simply ignore the letter of 11 July and table the report as it was, he additionally wrote to the CCC on 12 July 2007 expressing his indignation at the egregious denial of natural justice.

He also made it crystal clear that if the CCC was not more reasonable, Herbert Smith Freehills would commence proceedings in the Supreme Court where all of the preceding correspondence would be on public display. He gave the CCC 24 hours in which to respond.

This was no idle threat. Mr Penglis, after reading the letter exchange on the Smiths Beach term of reference between Mr Allanson and the CCC, was appalled and dismayed at the outrageous posture being adopted by the CCC.

Consequently, contemporaneous with preparing the above-mentioned letter to the CCC, he drafted an originating summons to be issued out of the Supreme Court requesting that the court make a declaration that the CCC had failed to discharge its obligations properly under Section 86. In other words, the CCC had refused to give me sufficient information to allow me to answer the proposed fresh adverse comment in the new draft report.

Put another way, Mr Penglis and Herbert Smith Freehills associate Richard Lilly, who prepared the court documents, were calling the CCC's bluff and forcing it to abide by its own legislation. And my new lawyers did not mess around; they sent a copy of the originating summons and supporting affidavit to Mr Cashman at the CCC on 12 July 2007.

I don't believe that Brian Burke was treated any better.

Certain clear conclusions can be drawn. Concisely put, they are as follows:

- There was a manifest and dramatic difference between Commissioner Hammond's comment in the draft report and the post-Hammond draft report.
- Our lawyers considered the post-Hammond comments to be "couched in scandalous and pejorative language that were not supported in any factual way".
- The CCC refused to supply the factual basis of their comments and thereby effectively prevented my lawyers from framing relevant answers.

Brian Burke's frustrated solicitor, Stephen Lemonis, and barrister, Grant Donaldson SC (subsequently filling the role of WA Solicitor General), referred the Burke/CCC Section 86 process by way of formal complaint to the Parliamentary Inspector, Malcolm McCusker.

These two actions had almost immediate results. Like classic bullies in the school playground, the CCC started to back off. The very next day (13 July 2007) Mr Cashman wrote to my lawyer asserting that "to agitate these matters would appear to be clearly premature" and that "the Commission is and will be closely considering the representations made on behalf of our client prior to finalising its proposed report in due course".

The CCC letter also assured Mr Penglis that "the Commission had no intention … to finalise its report imminently". This translated into a CCC retreat. However, the CCC climb-down became clearer on 26 July 2007 when Mr Cashman wrote to Mr Penglis indicating "that a more detailed and particularised letter canvassing the possible matters adverse to your client will be sent to you shortly".

Earlier in his letter of 28 June 2007, Mr Cashman stated arrogantly, *inter alia*, "the Commission does not consider there is any further obligation to give you now the precise factual basis on which its conclusions will be drawn". Well, by 13 July 2007, the CCC was commencing to retreat from its former unprincipled position. That was only under duress of a threatened lawsuit and Parliamentary Inspector inquiry.

From there Mr Cashman provided a further letter on 2 August 2007 with a nine-page set of excerpts and passages from the Smiths Beach draft report. It was clearly a work in progress, as Mr Cashman indicated in his letter.

The proposed adverse comment now bore no resemblance to Commissioner Hammond's considered conclusions. The fiction that these draft reports, as they applied to me at least, were one and the same could not reasonably be maintained. It was light years from Commissioner Hammond's assessment.

The unanswered question was how this process could be thought to have any integrity. Obviously, critical determinations about witnesses' credibility were being made by persons who had not been present when the evidence was given. Although Acting Commissioner McKerracher would ultimately affix his signature to the final report, it was far from clear who was now making those critical judgments, and on what basis they were being made.

Mr Hammond's conclusions had obviously been repudiated internally by the CCC after he resigned. To say the least, it was a baffling and unnerving process. It was perplexingly opaque and disturbingly overbearing.

Also, consider this: One group of witnesses – Troy Buswell and Beryl Morgan, for instance – were responding to the initial draft report and I was responding to a different later draft report. What a mess!

The additional new material supplied by the CCC did not give much more elucidation. The relevant parts of the draft report are a rambling diatribe. My lawyers found it hard to make much sense of it because it did not clearly disclose the supposed impropriety or refer to relevant evidence.

They certainly were not opinions that Kevin Hammond shared. This was confirmed when the CCC wrote to my lawyers on 7 August 2007 indicating that the newly provided material was "in substitution for, rather than additional to, the proposed draft material previously furnished".

It was never entirely clear, but there now appeared to be CCC allegations in the latest draft report that I had directly influenced public officer Dr Wally Cox, and indirectly influenced public officers Michael Allen, Paul Frewer and Norm Marlborough so as to cause them to behave improperly simply by virtue of my commercial partnership with Brian Burke. This was very a very dubious legal proposition.

A prime allegation seemed to be that Department of Planning senior officer Michael Allen had "committed misconduct by complying with the wishes of Mr Brian Burke in August 2006, by agreeing to appoint a DPI officer (Barbara Pedersen) to write a DPI report on Smiths Beach, in preference to other DPI officers (Stephanie Clegg)".

The corollary was that Brian had behaved improperly by "influencing" Mr Allen to do just that. This opinion by the CCC was later found by Parliamentary Inspector Malcolm McCusker to be based on an incompetent and erroneous piece of CCC investigation.

Mr McCusker's report on the CCC findings against Mr Allen, tabled in Parliament on 7 March 2008, is the most devastating demolition of a (quasi) legal finding that I have ever read.

The Parliamentary Inspector established that the CCC did not interview the relevant witnesses, relied on hearsay evidence, suppressed exculpatory evidence without explanation, ignored important contradictory evidence, did not have hard data to support its findings, did not identify the crucial elements of the misconduct findings and failed to comply with its statutory obligations under Section 86 of the Act.

Significantly, he found that Ms Pedersen had not been appointed to "write a DPI report on Smiths Beach", as alleged by the CCC; there was no such report; and there was no proposal to write such a report. Although Mr McCusker interviewed the CCC staff, including the CCC's senior investigator Mark Ingham, he was unable to ascertain how the "misconduct" finding found its way into the draft report.

According to Mr McCusker, the misconduct finding was not recommended by Mr Ingham and he was unable to shed any light on how it came about. That was the chaos that followed the departure of Kevin Hammond.

The CCC's "misconduct" finding on Mr Allen met a similar assessment to that made by the Parliamentary Inspector when it was referred by the CCC to the Director General of the DPI for disciplinary proceedings against Mr Allen. Ms Petrice Judge, a senior and experienced public officer from the Department of Premier and Cabinet, conducted the disciplinary inquiry.

Sufficient here to say that Ms Judge unconditionally rejected the CCC opinions of impropriety by Mr Allen.

Without any credible finding against Mr Allen, there should not have been, by law, any adverse comment against Brian Burke. The finding against Mr Allen was shown by two totally independent and respected authorities to be outrageously defective. Mr McCusker actually requested that there be an internal inquiry in the CCC to examine the process whereby the botched CCC conclusions came about and urged the CCC to publicly acknowledge its errors.

It never happened, which is a negative observation on the CCC leadership and on the Government, where there was no support for such an inquiry.

If the process instituted by the CCC against Mr Allen was outrageously defective, then the adverse comments then applied to me by the CCC verged on the preposterous. Remember that these proceedings by the CCC were analogous to criminal proceedings and as a consequence were potentially highly damaging.

As Mr McCusker explicitly pointed out in his report, in these circumstances findings against witnesses should be made only where due process has been accorded the witness and where proper legal standards are applied.

As you can imagine, my lawyers were at their wits end in dealing with a draft report that, even after some particulars were supplied, spoke in vagaries and gave no specifics. Although in due course the CCC was forced to provide further information, it was never adequate to identify the alleged impropriety, much less answer it.

Take as an instance the remarks by the CCC on page 109 of the report:

> In terms of their involvement in the matters considered in this report, Messrs.' Burke and Grill were equal partners as discussed above. The misconduct of Messrs.' Allen, Frewer and Marlborough resulted from the request or influence of Mr Burke.[121]

So, was I also liable for any possible criminal misconduct by Marlborough and Mr Frewer, even though I took no part in it and was not aware of it? Hardly logical, legal or reasonable.

A second damaging allegation in the CCC's Smiths Beach second draft report concerned Dr Wally Cox, the chairman of the Environmental Protection Authority. The CCC found that Dr Cox had committed misconduct by (simply) having lunch with Brian and me in West Perth (page 106 of the report).

As with Mr Allen, Dr Cox was immediately suspended from his position. A subsequent inquiry and disciplinary proceedings under the *Public Service Act* failed to uphold the CCC finding and threw out the allegations unceremoniously.

---

[121] *Report on the Investigation of Alleged Public Sector Misconduct Linked to the Smiths Beach Development at Yallingup*, Corruption and Crime Commission, 5 October 2007.

To complete the quartet of the public officers I was supposed to have influenced, for the purpose of this section of the book I only briefly mention Marlborough and Mr Frewer. I review their cases in more detail elsewhere.

Mr Frewer was found by the CCC to have committed misconduct for failing to record that he had been approached by Brian Burke at a planning committee meeting, but was quickly exonerated by a Public Service Commission disciplinary process.

Additionally, his case was the subject of a separate investigation by PI Malcolm McCusker who found that the finding against Mr Frewer was unjustified and that the CCC officers had suppressed crucial facts that exonerated him.

The process of exculpation with Marlborough took much longer, but was no less decisive.

As far as the CCC findings were concerned, it is common ground that I never spoke to Mr Frewer on the matter in question or was aware of any conversation between Brian and Mr Frewer (innocent as it was) until after the event.

The case against Marlborough was that he supposedly agreed to the urgings of Brian Burke to appoint a certain person (former Busselton Shire President Beryl Morgan) to the board of the South West Development Authority. Ultimately, the Supreme Court decided that that accusation by the CCC could not be sustained. By what bizarre process the CCC involved me is a mystery of legal gymnastics, as I was advocating a completely different appointment.

It is abundantly clear that Commissioner Hammond did not make the comments about me that were ultimately included in the tabled final Smiths Beach report. I conclude that may have been the case with Brian as well.

In respect to the three above-named senior public servants – Paul Frewer, Wally Cox and Michael Allen – whom I was supposed to have improperly influenced, I ask: Who in the Gallop Government gave the instruction to hunt these dedicated career officers out of the Public Service after they were exonerated? And why?

Consequently, one wonders how Mr Hammond reacted when the

tabled report varied decisively (at least in the case of me) from his own findings.

Mr Silverstone's press release of 2 April 2007 (two days after Mr Hammond's resignation) had stated that, "Commissioner Hammond has completed his work on the Smiths Beach Report". The clear implication was that it would be Mr Hammond's report, as he "completed" it, which would be tabled.

There is also some uncertainty concerning the function of Acting Commissioner Neil McKerracher. It is clear enough that it was Mr McKerracher and not Mr Hammond under whose signature the report was finally tabled.

However, did Mr McKerracher painstakingly read all of the evidence, consult all of the electronically gathered transcripts, watch the videos, and listen to the telephone calls recorded and then make judgements that supplanted some of Mr Hammond's verdicts? If so, aren't we entitled to be told that – and given the reasons for it? If not, how did the new finding come about?

Mr McKerracher's actual role in the Smiths Beach report continues to be an enigma to me, despite the fact that his formal role was apparent. He is a competent lawyer (now a Federal Court judge) and decent man.

The advice that I have received from every independent lawyer I have consulted, and a number of others who have volunteered their opinion concerning the standing, status and credibility of the Smiths Beach report, was that, at best, its conclusions were based on very fragile or flawed logic.

A succession of devastating reversals of the CCC's Smiths Beach findings by a procession of inquiries, tribunals and courts has vindicated those opinions. As to Mr McKerracher's role I am unsure.

Quite separately, on 23 January 2015, ex-Senator Graham Richardson wrote an article for *The Australian* on the subject of unauthorised leaks of information from the NSW Independent Commission Against Corruption (ICAC). He also commented on ICAC's failure to gain convictions. The last few sentences of Richardson's article could also be applied to the WA CCC:

> Don't forget the old saying – power corrupts and absolute power corrupts absolutely. The reason there have been few convictions out of ICAC corruption findings is that in a court of law hard evidence from reliable sources is required. Innuendo, hearsay, rumours and speculation are good enough at ICAC but don't stand up in court.

The CCC Smiths Beach report was tabled in State Parliament on 5 October 2007. It was delivered to Parliament by Mike Silverstone, who gave a media conference on the steps of Parliament House. Acting Commissioner Neil McKerracher was not to be seen and, as far as I can ascertain, was not specifically referred to in any way.

Mr Silverstone also put out the accompanying press release and fielded all of the questions from the Fourth Estate. Mr McKerracher was not mentioned in the press release by name or by his title. The release refers to the "Commission" but pointedly excludes any mention of the "Commissioner".

The CCC Act is quite definite as to how the CCC should operate. Section 9 (1) of the CCC Act states:

> There is to be a Commissioner who, in the name of the Commission, is to perform the functions of the Commission under this Act and any other written law.

I am not suggesting that every act done by the CCC has to be done by the Commissioner or Acting Commissioner. However, there is an unambiguous expectation that matters relating to findings, adverse comment, judgments as to credibility and the content of reports, should involve the attention and deliberation of the Commissioner or the Acting Commissioner.

There is no explanation of why Mr Silverstone took over the tabling of the report and the handling of the media. This was easily the most important report that the CCC had tabled and the Acting Commissioner was hardly visible. Why was that?

I have gradually come to the conjecture that Mr McKerracher may have only been peripherally involved in the Smiths Beach report. Further evidence of that comes from the high level of incompetence apparent in the presentation of the report and the media statement that accompanied its tabling.

Put simply, it strains credibility to believe that a highly skilled senior legal practitioner would be centrally involved in such a shoddy and sub-standard piece of work that was almost immediately ripped to shreds by his colleagues in the profession, the judiciary and the public service. Additionally, it was instantly subject to revision, in part from within.

Smiths Beach 'findings' fall flat

Despite the clear legal position stated in the CCC Act that debars the CCC from making findings against private citizens, Mr Silverstone's press release brought Brian Burke, David McKenzie and me into the frame front and centre. It stated:

> Also, in the Commission's view lobbyists (former Premier Brian Burke and his partner, former Minister Mr Julian Grill) acting as agents for Canal Rocks Pty Ltd and its representative, David McKenzie, influenced or attempted to influence public officers to engage in misconduct.

This was the dynamite comment that led the Silverstone press release! Having gone through intellectual and logical contortion to get some vague words into the Smiths Beach report to justify such a statement, the CCC was determined to give it maximum exposure – even if the factual underpinning was more than a bit dodgy.

Although the report made no recommendations for criminal proceedings against anyone, the accompanying Silverstone media release makes reference to damaging allegations against ten people.

Let us look at how misconceived these allegations were:

- Paul Frewer, former Deputy Director of Department of Planning. His alleged misconduct was for failing to declare at a meeting of the South West Regional Planning Committee that he had been approached by Brian Burke concerning a matter on the agenda. A later examination of the record of the meeting by the Parliamentary Inspector revealed, contrary to the hearsay evidence from the CCC, that such a declaration had in fact been made. The CCC finding was contradicted by the PI's report, and the Public Service Commission's disciplinary proceedings did likewise. But it instantly ended Mr Frewer's career. It is difficult to see how either Hammond or McKerracher could have made such a finding.

- Mark Brabazon, senior public servant in the Department of Conservation and Environment. It was stated in the CCC report and by Mr Silverstone that Mr Brabazon was biased in respect to advice that he gave to Brian Burke. Mr Brabazon objected to the finding and the CCC was ultimately forced to withdraw it, while issuing an abject apology.

- Wally Cox, Chairman of the EPA. Mr Silverstone asserted in his media release accompanying the CCC report that Dr Cox had committed misconduct "for having lunch with Mr Grill in a discrete location and denying the Smiths Beach development was discussed". As I detail later, the CCC report conceded in clear terms that there was no acceptable evidence that Smiths Beach had been discussed. Mr Silverstone was in effect claiming in his media release that Dr Cox was a liar. The CCC was forced to withdraw this assertion by Mr Silverstone. In due course the Public Service Commission inquiry quickly and properly dismissed an amended allegation because it did not disclose any impropriety. However, the exculpatory finding came too late. Dr Cox's exemplary public service career was already snuffed out, never to be restored.

- Mike Allen, senior officer with the Department of Planning, committed misconduct "for appointing a particular officer preferred by Mr Burke to write a departmental report on Smiths Beach". As I have previously related, there was not such an appointment and there was no such report. A Public Service Commission and a PI inquiry cleared Mr Allen of any impropriety.

- MS Philippa Reid, MS Anne Ryan and Mr John Triplett were Busselton Shire Councillors who received CCC 'findings' of misconduct for allegedly failing to make proper declarations of interest to the shire. The major problem with these findings was (and this was later conceded by the CCC) that none of the councillors transgressed any law, regulation or enforceable code of conduct. In other words, they acted entirely lawfully. They suffered no suspension from the council or penalty. However, at the time of the CCC 'finding' Ms. Reid was the endorsed Liberal candidate for the Federal seat of Forrest. This seat was a sure Liberal win at the next election. Because of the opprobrium attached to such CCC opinions at the time she was obliged to surrender her endorsement. This was the end of a very promising parliamentary career.

- Norm Marlborough was cited for misconduct, and although the Silverstone press release did not mention the reason, it was clearly the CCC finding that he agreed with "Mr Burke that he would appoint Ms (Beryl) Morgan to the South West Development Commission in circumstances where the relative merit of Ms Morgan holding such a position was unknown".[122] Later, documentary and oral evidence emerged, mostly in court, that Marlborough was never seriously considering the appointment of Ms Morgan. In fact, at the time of the CCC hearings he was completing the formalities to appoint two other candidates.

- Brian Burke and Julian Grill. I know that manipulation of the public hearing process by the CCC was egregiously poisonous for us. There were no facts to support the adverse comment but that did not stop the CCC. As I have mentioned above, my lawyers (and Brian's lawyers) have consistently maintained the opinion that the adverse comments were not only fallacious but outside the jurisdiction of the CCC and hence unlawful. Later, Parliamentary Inspectors Malcolm McCusker, Chris Steytler and temporary acting Parliamentary Inspector Chris Zelestis came to similar views about naming third parties such as Brian and me. Their views on the misuse of public

---

[122] *Report on the Investigation of Alleged Public Sector Misconduct Linked to the Smiths Beach Development at Yallingup*, CCC, October 2007, p. 6.

hearings were adopted and strongly endorsed by the parliamentary Joint Standing Committee on the CCC (JSCCCC).

Lastly, in respect to Mr Silverstone's media release, it was disappointing to note that nowhere did it make the point that the CCC found no evidence of corrupt, illegal or criminal conduct. This is important as the public hearings blatantly implied corruption on many occasions.

Buried on the second page, it almost casually mentioned that there were no prosecutions for substantive issues arising out of the investigations. This posture was a vital opportunity lost. Forget Burke and Grill, it overlooked critical state and national ramifications and interests. The public hearing had unmistakably raised the spectre of wide-scale corruption within the public service in WA.

Those fallacious imputations had gone viral around the world. Not long after, a London-based analyst was marking Perth down on a "liability" basis because of perceptions of corruption.

The persecution of Dr Wally Cox

Until the time of the erroneous CCC finding, Dr Wally Cox had been one of the most respected public servants in the State.

But almost any contact with Burke and Grill was fatal.

The charge against Dr Cox by the CCC (see p. 106 of report) was:

> On 17th May 2006, Dr Cox accepted an invitation from Mr Grill to attend a lunch hosted by Messrs. Burke and Grill, specifically knowing from Mr Grill that Smiths Beach was to be discussed at the lunch. This lunch and the discussion occurred at a time when Dr Cox had before him and his agency a Strategic Environmental Assessment (SEA) lodged by Canal Rocks (our client) and affecting Smiths Beach. In accepting the invitation and attending the lunch Dr Cox deliberately sought to avoid a perception of a conflict of interest by asking Mr Grill to shift the proposed location for the lunch to a more discrete place. The acceptance of the invitation and attend-

ance by Dr Cox to this private lunch, when he knew the agenda for discussion and knew (or should have known) that the Canal Rocks SEA was before him and his agency constituted the performance of functions as a public officer in a manner that was not impartial.

Prior to my telephone conversation with Dr Cox on 17 May 2006, Brian Burke and I had been approached by a senior public servant in an environmental agency who was concerned that possible changes to the environment and planning portfolios would detrimentally affect environmental assessments. He suggested that we might informally campaign against such proposals, in the interest of the State.

Consequently, Brian and I decided that to consult Dr Cox in an unofficial and relaxed atmosphere to discuss the matter.

When I rang Dr Cox's secretary, I sought an appointment (as the CCC agrees) for "lunch or coffee to discuss the environmental portfolio generally and also, possibly to bring Dr Cox up to date on Smiths Beach". During that conversation, Dr Cox personally came in on the call and indicated it was not his practice to socialise with anyone who had a matter pending a decision before him.

However, after consulting his memory, he concluded that there was no impediment in that regard.

I suggested lunch at a restaurant in the Parmelia Hilton Hotel, just over the road in Mill Street, Perth – and opposite Premier Geoff Gallop's office in the Captain Stirling Building. Dr Cox said he would prefer to be further away from his office, so I arranged the lunch in a private area of the well-known Perugino restaurant in West Perth.

During the telephone conversation with Dr Cox, I picked up a sensitivity to any discussion of EPA business matters when it was us paying for the refreshments. I had encountered this hypersensitivity by Dr Cox to any perception of partiality on two previous occasions.

Dr Cox was one of the most ethical officers that I have had the pleasure to meet. Consequently, it was a significant tragedy when the CCC twisted and distorted the factual situation concerning this lunch and Smiths Beach in an effort to make it appear that he was hiding some unidentified "conflict of interest".

In its Smiths Beach report, the CCC made an issue of the fact that Brian and I had paid for lunch. It stated:

> Given the express intention of Mr Grill in the invitation was to perhaps raise the topic of Smiths Beach, it is difficult to understand how Dr Cox could possibly accept such an invitation in these circumstances. This could only be compounded by the fact that Messrs. Burke and Grill paid for the lunch.[123]

Thus, we have a situation in the CCC's Smiths Beach report where there was a career-ending finding (p. 6 of report) that Dr Cox had committed an unspecified "impropriety in acceptance of the invitation and attendance at this private lunch when he knew the agenda for discussion and knew, (or should have known) that the Canal Rocks was before him and his agency".

Under examination in the CCC public hearings, both Dr Cox and I swore that Smiths Beach was not discussed. The third person at the luncheon, Brian Burke, said that he could not remember it being discussed. Even the CCC had to concede in its final report that it had no evidence on this score.

Ultimately, the Public Service Board, after a detailed inquiry, found that there was no transgression and that Dr Cox had acted perfectly properly.

Also, the Strategic Environmental Assessment (SEA) issue was distorted and exploited by the CCC to wrongly imply misconduct. The SEA issue was no longer before the EPA for decision in July 2006; that is, at the time of the lunch.

That decision (even on the CCC's own evidence) by the EPA to assess the Smiths Beach development by means of an SEA was made in August 2005 (see page 57 of the CCC Smiths Beach report). It was a continuous form of assessment and actually contemplated an ongoing dialogue between the developers (and the developer's agents, which included Burke and Grill) and the Department of the Environment. Pertinently, this was a separate agency to the Environment Protection Authority (EPA), which Dr Cox chaired.

---

[123] Ibid., p. 58.

The CCC failed to make this distinction. There was nothing before Dr Cox or the EPA for decision at the time of the lunch. Furthermore, the CCC failed to point to any such decision.

Counsel Jeremy Allanson puts the ridiculous nature of the CCC allegations against Dr Cox (and myself) in focus in a confidential critique of the CCC final draft report (dated 10 August 2007) to Steven Penglis. In summary, Mr Allanson concluded:

> There is no suggestion of improper conduct relating to the exercise of any power or discretion, or any decision or other action by Dr Cox or by the EPA.

As for Dr Cox wanting a more discrete venue for the luncheon than the one I originally nominated, there is a simple, quite innocent explanation. Dr Gallop, for reasons that he never properly disclosed, had banned meetings of his ministers and their staff with Burke and myself. That embargo never applied to public servants as far as I know, but some heads of departments refused to see us.

On page 60 of the report, the CCC refers to a perception of a conflict of interest on Dr Cox's part. However, having raised that perception, the CCC does not give any information as to how that conflict could occur, or where it would lie. The CCC certainly did not point to any evidence to sustain the inference.

Mr Allanson made an assessment of the CCC's assertion that Dr Cox had a conflict of interest in a candid letter to Steven Penglis, of 11 July 2007. He said:

> We are unaware of any evidence, any suggestion in any of the material provided that Dr Cox exercised his powers in relation to Smiths Beach in a biased or prejudiced way.

These were considered assessments made by an acute legal mind. They subsequently proved to be correct. The CCC requested disciplinary proceedings against Dr Cox, but the Public Service Commission refused to come to any unfavourable finding against him.

Furthermore, not one similar such set of proceedings against any public officer in the Smiths Beach term of reference, or the later broader Lobbyist's term of reference, was successful. In terms of criminal proceedings, the score was 40 to 1 against. On the single matter where a conviction was recorded, the issue was a relatively minor matter and resulted in a fine only.

Perhaps this did not unduly concern the CCC. The CCC officers would have been aware of just how devastating the public hearing, reporting and prosecution process could be, even without any successful trial outcomes. In some circles this is referred to as "punishment by process". It is sometimes also referred to as "noble corruption".

In the case of Wally Cox, this "process" destroyed a scrupulously honest and highly competent senior officer.

The aftermath – and media mangling

I readily concede the CCC had a clear duty to investigate vigorously and prosecute corruption of public officers. However, if that corruption was not proved the CCC had a concomitant responsibility to say so. It egregiously failed to do so in its main reports, or in the Silverstone media release in particular.

Almost as importantly, there was not the political milieu or the political will to do so. In truth, the Premier and the Attorney-General took the opposite road. There was not much generosity of spirit there.

The West Australian in a front-page article by Robert Taylor after the release of the Smiths Beach report was honest enough to comment the next day:

> The long-awaited CCC report into the Canal Rocks development at Smiths Beach near Yallingup has found that the much-vilified lobbyists Brian Burke and Julian Grill did nothing illegal in trying to influence the outcome of the Busselton Shire Council approvals for the project.

The Government was not prepared to embrace such a frank assessment. I quote from an ABC news report of 11 October 2007:

> The Western Australian Premier, Alan Carpenter, says the

former Premier, Brian Burke, and his business partner, Julian Grill, should not be allowed back into the Labor Party.

As I explain in Chapter 14, "2008 Election: A CCC casualty", this disposition, largely fostered by Attorney-General McGinty, rebounded surprisingly and dramatically on the Carpenter Government's electoral standing.

Troy Buswell had been a bit player in the Smiths Beach matter as former president of the Busselton Shire, but he had been viciously targeted by the Government in Parliament as he was seen as a future leader of the Liberal Party.

Taylor saw through the superficiality of the adverse comment against Burke and Grill in the Smiths Beach report, and the inaccuracy and desperation in the accompanying Silverstone media release. He also divined the essential truth about Buswell when he went on to state in the article mentioned above:

> In fact, the Smiths Beach report turned into a damp squib, failing comprehensively to nail Mr Buswell and almost vindicating Mr Carpenter's bogymen of choice, Brian Burke and Julian Grill. It came close to reinforcing their claim all along that they were just very good at their jobs.

The radio and television coverage of the ABC on 10 October 2007 into the Smiths Beach report essentially mirrored that of *The West*. The *7.30 Report*, with Leigh Sales and Hamish Fitzsimmons ran the headline: "Burke, Grill in clear over resort lobbying".

However, Andrew Burrell, who wrote a front-page article in *The Australian Financial Review* on 10 October 2007 adopted a line on the report that was sympathetic to the CCC cause. He began his story by immediately tilting the playing field by labelling Brian "disgraced". Burrell began:

> Disgraced former Western Australian premier Brian Burke has again embarrassed the Labor Party after a corruption investigation yesterday found the factional power

broker influenced a Carpenter government minister and two senior public servants to engage in misconduct.

Then Burrell played the guilt by association card in the second paragraph by stating:

> The long-awaited findings of the CCC inquiry into a 2005 local election funding scandal came after federal Labor leader Kevin Rudd admitted he had met Mr Burke – a convicted criminal – three times in the same period that the events that were investigated took place.

The rest of Burrell's article proceeded in the same depreciatory, but superficial, way. He reproduced the Silverstone press release almost verbatim, including the fallacious allegation that Dr Cox had committed misconduct by "denying that the Canal Rocks project was discussed".

I have since got to know and like Andrew Burrell. However, it was clear from his article that he had never properly read the Smiths Beach report and had relied more on the discredited Silverstone media release. Even a cursory reading of the report would have indicated that the Silverstone's Cox "denying of meeting" allegation in the press release was contrary to the report.

Notwithstanding the partiality of the *Financial Review* article, it was with *The Australian* that the flawed Silverstone media release really hit pay dirt. If the CCC had actually found corruption or criminal conduct against Burke and me, it would be hard to imagine a more condemnatory or vicious article. The Amanda O'Brien and Alana Buckley-Carr story ran under the headline: "Stain of Burke, WA Inc. returns". [124]

The front-page coverage commenced with an outright libel:

> The disgraced former West Australian Premier Brian Burke could face the third set of criminal charges since leaving office in 1988 after the state's corruption watchdog yesterday exposed a web of misconduct stretching through government bureaucracy.

---

[124] *The Australian*, 10 October 2007.

As we know, the report made no findings of corruption or criminality against Burke or anyone else. And no charges relating to any opinions of misconduct were ever brought as a result of the report.

The Australian carried on in the same way for two pages and at one point suggested that Burke and Grill could go to jail for five years. O'Brien then followed with an opinion piece on page 4 that lined Brian up and delivered one of the most vitriolic denunciations that I have seen in print.

The first few paragraphs were laced with Jim McGinty complaints against Brian that bore no direct relevance to the Smiths Beach report. In Chapter 10, I reveal that O'Brien apologised to me on 7 November 2013 for some of her coverage of Brian and me. I accepted the apology as sincere. I did not discuss specifics with her and I therefore cannot be sure whether the apology encompassed this particular article or set of articles, but I have presumed it does.

I won't go through all of the extensive media coverage on the Smiths Beach report that followed in the days after its release. However, there is one new line of material that is worth following as it exposed a venomous, internecine encounter between media giants.

On 11 October 2007, *The Australian* (p. 35) launched a campaign with the headline: "West's Burke coverage astounds".

The Buckley-Carr story, in its first two paragraphs, stated:

> Perth's monopoly daily newspaper has been accused of misrepresenting a damning report into the influence of the disgraced former West Australian premier Brian Burke by claiming he had been cleared of wrongdoing when in fact he had been widely criticised by a corruption watchdog. Peter van Onselen, an associate professor of Perth's Edith Cowan University, said he was flabbergasted by *The West Australian* coverage ....

Later in the piece van Onselen is quoted:

> ... the newspaper's claim that the pair had been cleared was premature, if not a bit silly.

Also, in the article he said:

> The door has been deliberately left ajar for follow up to perjury charges, for example. This shows the real problem of a one paper state.

The rest of the story was a regurgitation of previously printed derogatory material.

van Onselen wrote for *The Australian*. He also wrote for the *Sunday Times*, then a sister paper of *The Australian*. At that time, the *Sunday Times* was a committed supporter of the CCC. However, it did not take too long for times to change, as I explain in Chapter 14 dealing with the 2008 Election.

On 12 October 2007, *The Australian*, under the byline of Amanda O'Brien, continued the extraordinary assault against *The West* and to a lesser extent the ABC's coverage of the Smiths Beach report. It was presented under the trite headline "Only in Burke's backyard". The story used former chief of the Institute of Public Affairs think tank, Mike Nahan (later to become WA Liberal Opposition Leader), and Premier Carpenter to prosecute an onslaught on *The West*.

The position of Carpenter was unsurprising and followed the unspecific broad-brush smear that I have detailed elsewhere in this book. He was not at all interested in mentioning the specifics or the actual facts. His quotations were all similar to those made two days before in the *AFR* article: "The forces of darkness had returned to WA".

It was clear that the unfortunate Carpenter had tied his future to his Attorney-General, Jim McGinty, in picking a fight with *The West*. As I elaborate in Chapter 14, it was a fatal decision.

However, it was Dr Nahan who surprised me. He rightly claims some respect for his economics expertise. Early on in the article he is quoted saying:

> In any other town, he (Burke) would have been dead and buried.

Later he makes the statement:

> Not many people in Burke's position would be given a free run on radio to talk up their innocence as occurred this

week. In Perth, even tainted people are given the right to put their spin on events.

It is easy to discern the undemocratic nature of this comment. Surely everyone should be allowed to assert their probity publicly?

However, one of the problems the CCC had now encountered with some of the media was that, from the first day of public hearings, it had projected the spectre of rampant public sector corruption. Counsel Assisting went too far and exaggerated the prospect of proving corruption. Journalists were background-briefed by the CCC with hair-raising stories. Evidence that appeared to show corruption was led at public hearings and then dropped without explanation.

The West and the ABC, who most closely followed the CCC hearings, dutifully ran all of this incriminating and reputation-destroying material. They assigned teams of journalists to the task. Is it therefore not unnatural for these journalists and their editors to feel let down and sceptical when next to nothing materialised?

I mentioned that Dr Nahan was being ungenerous. Brian Burke had endured weeks in public hearings where he and his lawyers were not permitted to utter a word in his defence. That was followed by months of legally condoned defamation and outright calumny, in the form of media articles, cartoons and other media comment.

There was no means of redress as all of this derogatory evidence, although false, was privileged and statutorily protected from defamation action pursuant to the CCC Act.

Is it no wonder than that Brian took the opportunity to assert his lack of guilt when the CCC comprehensively failed to make out any criminal case against him at all for his lobbying role in Smiths Beach?

Also, it was apparent that the CCC had not amended its *modus operandi*. Even with the release of the report, together with an implied admission that they had no substantive case against Burke and Grill, the CCC was still telling susceptible journalists that it would "get us" on perjury charges. That fact was reflected in the contemporary articles in *The Australian*.

The CCC did in fact bring 12 charges, akin to perjury, against Burke, Marlborough, Mr McKenzie, Mr Allen and me. All charges except one minor matter with Burke, basically a misunderstanding for which he was fined, were dismissed by the courts.

When referring to Kevin Hammond, I should briefly mention two other conclusions that I discuss more fully in Chapter 4, "Smith Beach approval frustrated, undermined".

The first was the dropping of the critical allegations of cabinet leaks to Brian and the second was the imputation of bribery of Busselton Shire councillors. After that the CCC had nothing left.

I don't have any hard evidence to support it, but I reasonably postulate that the dumping of these two potential sources of criminal prosecutions into which the CCC had put so much time, effort and resources, would not have endeared Commissioner Hammond to a large section of the CCC apparatus, which was desperate by this stage to find a substantial issue to justify all of the much-hyped publicity coming from the Smiths Beach and Lobbyists terms of reference public hearings.

In summary, it is my strong view that Commissioner Hammond made a significant error in allowing such draconian procedural rules at the hearings and for declaring that the hearings be public. If he had not done so, much injury would have been avoided and more truth would have come out.

Interestingly, I ran into Kevin Hammond at a café in Subiaco on 10 September 2019. I was standing near a table of patrons looking around the cafe for a friend when one of those patrons stood up and introduced himself as Kevin Hammond. I did not need an introduction, but I was slightly surprised when the former Commissioner then went on to introduce some of his family and friends.

We passed some pleasantries, but there was no time and it was too public for any serious conversation. In all, it was a friendly encounter and in no way reflected any of the troublesome issues of the inquiries. Kevin Hammond was always courteous.

The McKechnie reappointment

Lastly, I return to the only recently resolved and highly divisive John McKechnie reappointment as CCC Commissioner.

According to Paul Murray in his column in *The West* of 18 April 2020, the Commissioner's position, "… is one of the most important in WA with the agency's powers of inquiry, compulsion and coercion so awesome, with ability to destroy reputations, careers and livelihoods – that the CCC needs its own parliamentary committee and an independent inspector to oversee its actions."

But there are also very special provisions for the appointments of a Commissioner so that suggestions of political interference are avoided. They are:

1. Selection of candidates is reserved to a three-person nominating committee headed up by the Supreme Court Chief Justice.
2. Three names are put forward by the committee to the Premier.
3. These nominations must be supported by a majority of the JSCCCC.

In April 2020, a majority of the JSCCCC did not support the inclusion of Mr McKechnie on the three person list. This created a stand-off with the Premier, who insisted on the reappointment of Mr McKechnie. Negotiations did not resolve the impasse and the McGowan Government introduced legislation to appoint its candidate directly.

To quote Murray again: "The Government this week embarked upon a bastardised process to reappoint McKechnie that is completely against the long-established apolitical process."

Further on, Murray says in his column that: "… political sources say the committee has had concerns about the CCC's approach to investigating police matters." That is something discussed extensively in this book.

However, initial attempts to get this legislation through the Legislative Council were unsuccessful. And there the matter lay, unresolved, until the 13 March 2021 (Covid 19) state election, when the McGowan Government swept back in with an unprecedented majority, including historic first-time control in the Legislative Council.

With that parliamentary command, the Government's process of reappointing Commissioner McKechnie began anew. When for a second time the Government was unable to achieve the nomination of John McKecknie under the prevailing CCC Act, it introduced – and passed – fresh legislation using its newfound parliamentary control. The legislation provided for direct appointment of Mr McKechnie by the Government.

It was strongly, but unsuccessfully, opposed by what was left of the opposition.

The obvious problem with such direct appointment was that all the political intervention safeguards in the original Act were removed. In the eyes of some observers, this primed the CCC as a potential political weapon.

Opposition Leader Mia Davies said by press release on 24 June 2021 that the Premier "…had tainted the independence of the State's top watchdog …".

Paul Murray, in a two-page spread in *The West* on 3 July 2021, had this to say:

> The McGowan Government, led by Attorney General John Quigley, who was once a leading critic of the CCC's flaws, has trampled on these safeguards against the agencies awesome powers, shamelessly politicising the commissioner's position.

In the Western world, we often talk about the importance of our institutions and the need to safeguard them from gross politics. In WA, in respect to the CCC, we appear to have failed.

14

2008 Election: A CCC casualty

Labor blamed Brian Burke and Julian Grill for the loss of the 6 September 2008 (unloseable) WA election.

ALP State Secretary Simon Mead, referencing a special report prepared by party stalwart former Senator Robert Ray, stated:

> The exposure of the lobbying activities of Brian Burke and Julian Grill and their suborning of Cabinet Ministers, public servants and other key players, contributed more than anything else to the destruction of the Labor Government.[125]

I was stunned and very hurt when I read this statement. Its premise, that we suborned key players, transpired to be demonstrably false and the view that our actions were the main contributor to the election loss was not a conclusion endorsed by any serious impartial commentator.

My belief is that the ALP's surprise loss was a product of the CCC's meddling in Parliament, and the Carpenter Government's refusal to question the CCC's intrusion, prejudicial public hearings and *modus operandi*. I appreciate that this is probably a lonely proposition, but hear me out.

Premier Carpenter called the election six months early and a day after Colin Barnett was dramatically summoned back to Liberal leadership. That was supposed to capitalise on Liberal Party disarray. The Liberal Party was quoted by betting agency Sporting Bet at odds of more than four-to-one against or $4.40.

The ALP was well ahead in the polls.

Pundits will argue for years whether the early opportunistic call-

---

[125] *A Review of the 2008 Western Australia State Election*, by Robert Ray (repeated in a press release issued by Simon Mead on 15 December, 2008, p. 5).

ing of the election was a decisive factor in the shock loss. Former senator Ray was of the view that "the calling of an early election was perceived by voters as a cynical exercise, that it abrogated fair play".[126]

I don't want to give a full analysis of the defeat. I do, however, wish to examine the question of whether the election was significantly impacted by the long and public CCC inquiries, the CCC's intrusion into Parliament and the accompanying explosive publicity.

Months of highly adverse accusations and imputations had taken a heavy toll on Premier Carpenter and consumed large reserves of political capital. Additionally, it had diverted attention from the positive achievements of the Government. Remember, the CCC had been instrumental in the removal of four innocent cabinet ministers.

Where I might offer a different perspective is in how the events given rise by the disastrous CCC inquiries might have been handled to minimise the injurious repercussions.

In that sense, I shall unfortunately have to put myself somewhat at odds with the respected Robert Ray, who stated in his report:

> Alan Carpenter's management of the (CCC) crisis was nothing short of superb.[127]

While I concede that it was important for Carpenter to distance his government from the early fallout from the CCC public inquiries, he blundered when did not take account of profound concerns by the legal profession over prejudicial procedure, public service alarm at the unfair treatment of innocent officers, and the media realisation that the CCC was ignoring acceptable standards of proof and process.

Furthermore, as you might expect, I strongly resist the view that Brian Burke and I were responsible for the loss. Over and above that, I want to raise the question of whether it was proper for the CCC to inject itself so comprehensively and unproductively into the affairs of government and Parliament.

---

[126] Ibid., p. 8.
[127] Ibid., p. 5.

Before I argue my case, I want to set the scene a little.

Firstly, the Liberals were in chaos. They had lost four leaders since the previous election in 2005: Colin Barnett, Matt Birney, Paul Omodei and Troy Buswell. Barnett had announced that he was retiring, would not recontest his seat of Cottesloe and Deidre Wilmott had been preselected for the seat. Dan Sullivan, the former Deputy Leader, had been forced out of the party.

Second, in the middle of 2008 it was unthinkable that the Government could lose. Despite the global financial crisis (GFC), WA was undergoing its greatest-ever mining and energy boom, unemployment rates were very low, Treasury coffers were full and the State was growing at breakneck speed.

Into the bargain, and third, Jim McGinty was telling anyone who would listen that his new, so-called "one vote, one value" reforms would be a watershed in WA's electoral history. He proclaimed that the removal of the malapportioning gerrymander in favour of non-metropolitan seats would dramatically swing the political pendulum in favour of Labor.

Well, despite the general correctness of the reform, it wasn't as ethical as it was portrayed. In fact, the Upper House malapportionment got worse. McGinty and the ALP's faction-dominated State Executive got the electoral psychology wrong, as I will explain.

Fourth, something very substantial changed between the calling of the election and polling day. The two-party preferred vote lead (Westpoll) of 54% to 46% in favour of the Government evaporated. People became convinced that Carpenter was arrogant; his approval rating went down 11 per cent and his disapproval rating went up a devastating 14 per cent.

In losing Government, Labor dropped four seats in the Legislative Assembly.

I have doubts whether Ray really thought that Burke and Grill were responsible for the shock Labor electoral defeat. There are grounds for my belief.

Firstly, it was not referred to as a reason for loss in the overview at the beginning of the report where Ray firmly stated:

A succession of errors and misjudgments by WA Labor led to a narrow loss.[128]

Second, the reference to Brian and me came later in the report under the strange headline: "Round up the usual suspects".

Ray is a political historian and movie buff. He would assume that his readers would be aware that these words had a special meaning derived from the last scene of the Humphrey Bogart/Ingrid Bergman classic, Casablanca. It roughly translates into, "Arrest those who have a bad reputation, but whom we really know are not guilty".

Third, Ray readily concedes that Burke and Grill "didn't rate in the top five issues for voters".[129]

Fourth, the reference to Burke and Grill was only four very short paragraphs in what must have been a 50-page report in its unredacted original form.

The West, maintained in an article by Robert Taylor on 23 August 2008 that Burke and Grill did not show up in polling *at all*.

Last of all, Ray reserves his ire for the ALP factional system, where on page 10 he states:

> Factionalism in the Western Australia Branch of the ALP has been a major negative for the Party's status. *Its modus operandi incorporates hatred, patronage and revenge* (my emphasis). It's not that dissimilar to the Party in other States; just more intense. *Factional instability owes much to the Balkanisation of the Party.* (my emphasis).

You won't find any citation of these latter-mentioned comments by Ray in WA ALP State Secretary Simon Mead's press release of 15 December 2008. That is not surprising as Mead is a product of, and minion of, the faction apparatus.

In fact, the WA Branch censured most of Ray's report. The heavy redactions are clearly apparent.

Any fair reading of the Ray Report indicates that he appeared to believe the following factors were most responsible for the loss:

---

[128] Ibid., p. 1.
[129] Ibid., p. 5.

(a) The calling of the early election, for which he laid responsibility with Alan Carpenter (page 8): "The early election was a decision of the Premier alone, (excluding the urgings of *sycophantic staff members.*)" (my emphasis)

(b) "The overconfident view of certain re-election could only be based on the continued presence of Troy Buswell as Liberal Leader." An identified corollary of that was the re-emergence of Colin Barnett. Ray observes (page 1): "He (Colin Barnett) looked like he had made a personal sacrifice to resume the leadership and had been unfairly ambushed by the calling of the election." This requires no amplification.

(c) Lack of professionalism (page 1): "(The WA Branch) desperately needs to become a professional outfit."

(d) The chronic dearth of primary votes (page 4): "The election was fought against the background of a relatively low primary vote dating back to 1992."

(e) "The loss of Geoff Gallop to WA politics was a major blow." (Page 5) The Labor Premier quit politics less than a year after his 2005 State Election win, citing the need to tackle depression.

(f) The failure of the WA Branch to accept expert political advice (page 6): "Following WA Labor's less than satisfactory performance in the 2007 Federal election, the WA Administrative Committee, in consultation with the National Secretariat, commissioned a Review to be headed by Senator elect Mark Abib … Very few in the WA Branch appear to have read the report."

(g) The Government was wrongly positioned (page 6): "The biggest downside was the failure to properly characterise the Budget surplus."

(h) Ray (page 17) states: "The decision to change the campaign and highlight the issues of uranium and GM crops has been highly criticised by nearly all of those who made submissions or appeared before the review… Another closely linked consideration by Robert Ray was the detrimental and compounding effect of "… the ALP running a very Perth-centric campaign".

My belief is that the Greens have targeted the energy and mining industries in WA and defamed this wealth-producing sector as the "enemy". Unfortunately, sympathetic fellow travellers in WA's "hard Left" have adopted the same posture. The ALP's chronic reliance on Green preferences has exacerbated the situation. That might be an acceptable electoral posture for a central Melbourne or Sydney constituency, but in WA it is poison because most jobs, property prices and standards of living depend on the health of the extractive sector.

There is an unawareness of just how pervasive and close the extractive industries are. Even in the seemingly rural South West of the State, the biggest industries are part of the much-maligned extractive sectors.

Ray identified a number of valid, but less important, issues as contributing to the loss. They included (and I quote Ray here): "Leaking the polling", "Not responding to Liberal Party negative ads", "Not using WA's most experienced campaign operatives in Stephen Smith and Gary Gray", "The 2008 campaign lacked a narrative", "The hubris of the Premier's staff", "Electoral tactics (of) Labor were nearly always reactive, bordering on amateurish", and finally, "Alan Carpenter's naïvety about the culture of the ALP and his lack of central campaign experience would always be a problem, but the rest of the team needed to fill some of those vacuums, and didn't."

There is a last set of factors – referred to in quotes by Ray on pages 11, 15 and 18 of the redacted report – that were decisive to the shock electoral defeat. I deal with them in page order.

On page 11, Ray refers to the "shenanigans" that led to the exclusion of popular sitting member Bob Kucera and the subsequent loss of the Mount Lawley seat:

> Not one witness to this Review suggests that Kucera would not have won the seat.

On the same page, Ray refers to the loss of Morley, where the ALP went to extraordinary lengths to exclude another ALP sitting member who certainly would have given Labor another seat. That was John D'Orazio, who was wrongly pursued by the CCC. Ray declares that there was "a good dose of revenge" associated with this decision.

Ray also refers to former ALP member John Bowler who won Kalgoorlie in 2008 as an Independent. Bowler would have won for any party he stood for, but was ejected from the ALP by the Premier mainly because of his association with me and the (ultimately unsuccessful) CCC campaign against him.

The 2008 election produced an ALP and Coalition locked on 28 seats each. The wanton loss of these three seats requires a lot of explaining. That is especially true considering Alan Carpenter insisted on the boycotting of Bowler as an ALP candidate, but after the election begged him to join him in government.

If one includes Tony McRae (Southern Rivers) who was, with Bowler and D'Orazio, a victim of the CCC, the extent of these miscalculations were conspicuous. These errors are a plank of my case.

On page 15 of his report, Ray refers to the crucial question of the relations between the media and the Government prior to the election. He states:

> Labor's election prospects were constantly undermined by (my emphasis) the intensively negative attitude of the media.

This is where I believe my argument gains more traction.

Further down Ray states:

> In particular, The West Australian *was toxic.* (my emphasis)

And further down:

> It is easy to blame the Premier or Jim McGinty for these poor relations, but any attempts by them to repair the relations were constantly rebuffed.

Attempts by McGinty to repair the relationship were too equivocal and too late, as established below.

Ray referred to the dramatic fall in Carpenter's approval rating during the campaign because of the growing perception of his "arrogance". He states (page 18):

> The biggest factor in the door-knocking feedback was

the perception of the Premier as "arrogant". Much of this can be attributed to the *unrelenting campaign of* The West Australian *and the rest of the media pack.*" (my emphasis).

And that leads me to the linchpin of my case.

In Chapter 7, I comment on the Select Committee of Privilege (SCP) in the WA Legislative Council inquiring into whether there had been any unauthorised disclosure of deliberations of the Standing Committee on Estimates and Financial Operations, which in turn was contemplating an inquiry into WA's iron ore industry.

In an entirely unprecedented turn of events, the CCC had effectively taken over the SCP process in Parliament and, among other things, the Committee had in secret proceedings recommended criminal charges against Nathan McMahon, Shelley Archer, Anthony Fels, Brian Burke and Noel Crichton-Browne.

The Director for Public Prosecutions (DPP) ultimately refused to proceed with charges. But well before that, Malcolm McCusker QC, backed by some of Australia and WA's foremost jurists, had condemned the SCP process and outcomes. The Government's reaction to this was to cause critical damage to itself.

Carpenter-McGinty media rift

The genesis of the toxic relationship between McGinty and *The West* (in fact, most of the media) lay in *The West's* support for McCusker. Though Carpenter and McGinty did not specifically criticise the eminent lawyer, they remained wedded to the CCC – especially in respect to this SCP inquiry.

This was followed by their rancorously unprecedented step of trying to expel Archer from Parliament.

As Robert Taylor put it in *The West* as early as 20 December 2007:

> Mr Carpenter's critics within the Party say the Premier could have hosed the affair down when the report was first tabled, insisting that the Upper House should have its debate (on the SCP report) and Mr Cock (the independ-

ent DPP) make his decision before action (that is, expelling Archer) was taken.

At the urging of McGinty, the Premier took a far more aggressive course (in moving down the path to expulsion). Remember the SCP report had been unreservedly condemned by Mr McCusker.

It was a very dangerous path for the Carpenter Government. Firstly, it was taking on one of the most admired persons in the State in Malcolm McCusker. Mr McCusker was, in turn, supported by some of Australia's best legal minds. *The West* and most of the rest of the media shared Mr. McCusker's concerns.

As it turned out, these events were happening in the lead-up to the September 2008 election. There were other potentially dangerous CCC reports still in the pipeline. Additionally, the Carpenter/McGinty strategy of expelling Archer and pursuing others (McMahon, Burke, Crichton-Browne and Fels) for criminal offences was risky and likely to fail, which it did, as related in Chapter 7).

On cue, the next CCC inquiry, directly involving McGinty, was the subject of a full front-page story in *The West* of 26 January 2008. The headline read: "Fong quits but McGinty digs in".

The body of the story by Amanda Banks then continued:

> Health Minister Jim McGinty yesterday refused to resign after Health Department boss Neale Fong quit his $600,000-a-year job in the wake of an explosive Corruption and Crime Commission report which found serious misconduct over his dealings with disgraced lobbyist Brian Burke.
>
> A defiant Mr McGinty, who appointed Dr Fong and has stood behind him through a string of controversies, dismissed any suggestion he should stand down over the scandal as "silly" but said he accepted responsibility for recruiting the health chief.
>
> The damning CCC report, tabled in Parliament yesterday has accused Dr Fong, the nation's highest paid public servant, of knowingly misrepresenting the true nature of

his contact with Mr Burke and leaves him facing the prospect of a criminal charge …

The editorial in the same paper was highly critical of McGinty and was tantamount to a call for his resignation. *The West* justified this by pointing to McGinty on the one hand defending Dr Fong from a string of criticism about the handing of the Emergency Departments of the State's hospitals, but turning on him for the same complaint once the CCC report was released.

The gist of the editorial was that McGinty opportunistically had "turned Dr Fong into a sacrificial lamb for the short comings in WA's Health system …"

On 28 January 2008, *The West* ran a further front-page story under the headline: "Carpenter refuses to back McGinty".

The story by Amanda Banks went on to state (in part):

Alan Carpenter has refused to take even one minute out of his summer holidays to defend his beleaguered Health Minister …

There were various medical interest groups publicly calling for blood. Carpenter did finally stand by his Health Minister, but it took three days for that to happen.

The Australian also treated the report seriously, featuring it as its main front-page story (by John Lyons) on 26 January 2008, in addition to four other stories on page 2 and a huge spread in the Inquirer section. It included two stories by Amanda O'Brien.[130] Further, it ran a lead editorial in its edition on 29 January 2008.

The Australian's editorial was bizarre. The first half accused Brian Burke of a whole string of improprieties and criminality conduct, without referring to any credible evidence in support thereof. It alleged "potentially ruinous consequences for the State's taxpayers"; it mentioned the possible "illegality of taking people's money to arrange for the political process to be manipulated to their advantage",

---

[130] Amanda O'Brien is a former press adviser to Mr McGinty. She currently works as a liaison officer at the CCC. She has privately apologised to me for some of her writings in The Australian during this period.

"confusing client profit with public benefit", "treating cabinet secrecy as a joke", and "wrecking the careers and reputations of four government ministers and several public servants including Australia's highest paid bureaucrat, former Director-General of Health, Neale Fong, who potentially faces criminal charges as a result of conversations with Burke".

Ultimately, when the dust had cleared, and when the actual evidence could be forensically examined, it became clear that not one of *The Australian*'s denunciations could be supported. The lattermost allegation by *The Australian* was a straight-out lie. Dr Fong was not in any trouble because of contact with Burke. Nor was he ultimately accused of any impropriety by the CCC for anything discussed in his association with Burke.

As even McGinty said at the time: "All the contacts were innocuous." The facts were that Dr Fong had wrongly testified he had no recollections of any email communication between himself and Burke, and he had "no personal relationship with Mr Burke". But emails were found.[131]

The CCC specifically found "that there was no evidence of any impropriety on his part in his (Fong's) contacts or relationship with Mr Burke, nor any benefit received by him nor any personal business dealings between them".

There developed a strong view within the senior echelon of the State bureaucracy that the CCC processes were manifestly unfair and wrong. As a result, the public service went back into its shell and was collectively hesitant about cooperating with the public lest that cooperation be misconstrued by the CCC.

As late as 19 February 2014, in an article the day after by Gareth Parker, reporting in *The West* on a lecture at the University of Western Australia, the former Director-General of Premier and Cabinet and former Public Sector Commissioner, Mal Wauchope stated:

> The WA public service lost its confidence after high pro-

---

[131] *Report on the Investigation of Alleged Misconduct Concerning Dr Neale Fong, Director General of the Department of Health*, 25 January 2008, Crime and Corruption Commission.

file CCC and other public inquiries caused it to lapse into risk-averse decisions that harmed the public interest.

It is very difficult to quantify the effect of loss of public sector morale on the 2008 election, but it once used to be said that no party could win government in WA if the government workers were offside.

Although it was found by the CCC that there was nothing improper in the Fong/Burke association, Commissioner Len Roberts-Smith insisted that Dr Fong be prosecuted for misleading evidence concerning the relationship. However, on 5 June 2008, the DPP announced that it was "not in the public interest to pursue the charges".

It was not to be the only occasion that the DPP refused to do the CCC's bidding.

It was becoming alarmingly apparent by this stage that in pursuit of Burke and Grill the CCC was cutting a demoralising swathe through the innocent ranks of the State's best and brightest public servants. Neale Fong, Wally Cox, Kieran McNamara, Mike Allen, Gary Stokes, Paul Frewer and Mark Brabazon were among the cream of civil service personnel, and those close to them felt very strongly about what these once highly respected public officers had to bear.

The West said the wife of Mike Allen, Beth, complained:

> The CCC process has put her family through hell, ruined her husband's reputation and cost them $50,000 to defend charges which she said had never had any chance of succeeding.[132]

It was easy for the CCC to indict Dr Fong for his untruths, but the CCC (primarily), *The Australian*, *The West* and the rest of the media had induced an environment of dangerous hysteria in the political domain in relation to any contact with Brian Burke. PM John Howard had summarily sacked his Minister for the Environment, Ian Campbell, for a most inoffensive contact with Brian. [133]

Returning to *The Australian*'s editorial of 29 January 2008, the

---

[132] *The West Australian*, 6 June 2008, p. 4.
[133] See Chapter 8.

remainder of that opinion piece was mostly devoted to an absurd onslaught on *The West* for being too soft on Burke and Grill. This accusation came as a surprise for my wife and family who blamed *The West* for unfair and partisan reportage. It also shocked our friends, some of whom had cancelled their subscriptions to *The West* over its coverage.

Nonetheless, *The Australian* (for the moment) had clearly adopted the Carpenter Government line and ignored the concerns of Mr McCusker.

As for *The West* editorial of 26 January 2008 (referred to above) concerning Jim McGinty, it also went too far. It is true there had been an element of hypocrisy by McGinty and it certainly appeared that there was some incompetence in the management and funding of hospital emergency departments. But that is not sufficient to call for a Minister to be sacked, especially as the CCC adjudged him to be an injured party.

There was, however, one other dubious matter concerning the CCC inquiry. When McGinty gave evidence, he did so *in camera*. Most other witnesses had to face the glare of an open public tribunal. Why was the Minister given special treatment and why did he need it? This unexplained anomaly was the subject of a number of stories in *The West*, including a front page on 4 February 2008. The exposure did nothing to make McGinty any happier with *The West*.

The Fong affair is not so important to this particular narrative in its own right and you may think I have laboured the point. However, it is important in appreciating how the CCC inquiries provoked a toxic relationship between the Carpenter Government and *The West Australian*.

For McGinty, *The West's* reaction to the Fong matter was deadly confirmation that he was "at war" with the newspaper. From that point on he seemed to want revenge.

At least part of McGinty's wrath should have been directed at the CCC because its unjustified hearings saw the loss of Dr Fong, the person directing the Government's massive new health building program. The agenda was badly set back and never recovered. Nor has morale within the department been fully restored.

However, McGinty could never publicly question the CCC. It was his own creation and it was systematically destroying his adversary, Brian Burke.

But *The West* did not let up on the Fong inquiry report. On 7 February 2008, it ran a page 5 article by Cathy O'Leary under the headline: "Fong's Elitist Office Closed". The sub-headline said: "Another embarrassment for McGinty as health chief opts to move back to East Perth headquarters".

This was quickly followed up the next day with a front-page story in *The West* with the headline: "McGinty's man blew $1million on Subi empire".

This episode reached a crisis the next day when McGinty refused to answer questions by a reporter from *The West* and walked out of a press conference. *The West* ran the headline: "Questions toe to toe, Minister abruptly takes to his heels."

In the story, *The West* laid it on the line, when it stated:

> It's no secret Mr McGinty has a major problem with *The West Australian*.

On the same day, *The West* devoted its editorial to the subject under the heading: "New chapters in deplorable history of arrogance". The editorial was a scathing critique of the Government's and McGinty's haughtiness, but the really interesting part was the comment on the relationship between Carpenter and McGinty:

> One conclusion that can be confidently drawn from Mr McGinty's behaviour is that he has no fear of being called to account by a Premier who evidently has no authority over him.

As Robert Ray would later report, the perception of the Carpenter Government's arrogance would, a few months later, explain Carpenter's dramatic fall in personal popularity in the polls.

This public perception was not confined to the Premier. McGinty also went close to losing his previously safe Labor seat of Fremantle to Adele Carles (Greens) at the 2008 election. She correctly predicted that the seat would be a loss to Labor and a win to the Greens next time around. She also called on "arrogant" McGinty to resign forthwith.

McGinty takes on *The West*

It was all part of a descent into destructive rancour that continued through to the September 2008 election. To throw fuel on the fire, on 14 February 2008 McGinty massively exacerbated the problem with *The West* by instructing the Government Media Office to delete *The West* from the list of parties receiving alerts for his press conferences.

This is when McGinty "crossed the Rubicon". There was no way back.

The West responded with a front-page story by Amanda Banks on 15 February, which stated in part:

> Health Minister Jim McGinty has taken unprecedented steps to censor *The West Australian* by effectively black listing the newspaper's reporters from his press conferences.
>
> Political commentator Harry Phillips said: "I don't think it's good politics."

The West story stated that McGinty took the decision against Government Media Office advice. The relationship was further inflamed on 22 February 2008 when it was disclosed that the Carpenter Government had a "dirt file" on the editor of *The West Australian*, Paul Armstrong. This information came from John Lyons, a journalist from Rupert Murdoch's Australian operations.

Armstrong seemed to take the matter quite personally. He responded in an article by Robert Taylor by saying, *inter alia*:

> I am honoured that the Government goes to such lengths to attack me, the paper and our reporters . . ..

Taylor's article also drew attention to the fact that Paul Giles, the Government's acting manager of strategic communications, had organised a meeting of senior public servants to "discuss news format, editorial stand and media mix along with advertising opportunities" with the Eastern States-based Fairfax media organisation. You don't have to be particularly astute to appreciate that such a move, if successful, would be a direct attack on *The West's* revenue base.

When Premier Carpenter opened the Fairfax website on the 10 June 2008, it was further confirmation. Put together, the Government's strategy was a dagger at the heart of *The West*.

In the countdown to the 2008 election, much of February and March media coverage was taken up by the effective overturning of all findings of impropriety by the CCC against public servants in the Smiths Beach inquiry. Then the feud between the CCC's Len Roberts-Smith and Parliamentary Inspector Malcolm McCusker burst into spectacular media controversy.

Mr McCusker not only supported the independent tribunals that cleared the public servants, but conducted his own inquiries that cast considerable doubt on the facts, procedures and ethics adopted by the CCC in the Smiths Beach and Lobbyists inquiries. An enraged CCC Commissioner Roberts-Smith took the unprecedented step of challenging Mr McCusker in the Supreme Court.

This was a huge embarrassment to the Carpenter Government and ultimately went nowhere.

In the media, a large part of April was taken up by CCC matters, among which was the brutal struggle by John D'Orazio with Carpenter for D'Orazio to regain entry to the ALP after his forced resignation, and to gain pre-selection for the seat of Morley. The allegations made against D'Orazio by the CCC, and which had seen him excluded from Cabinet and the ALP, had been found to be almost totally baseless.

As such, D'Orazio thought that he could resume his political career. However, Carpenter had earmarked the seat for his "Dream Team" candidate and fellow journalist Reece Whitby. With the help of McGinty and the factions, the Premier had the numbers.

There was a short-lived rebellion by Government Ministers (and members of the Right faction) John Kobelke, Michelle Roberts and Margaret Quirk, but they were outgunned.

Carpenter justified his opposition to D'Orazio's re-entry into Caucus on his assertion that "he (Carpenter) could not trust D'Orazio not to leak information from Caucus".[134] This was an allegation that had not been raised previously and, on the basis of available evidence, was very unfair. D'Orazio countered by responding that he had been in Caucus for six years and had never leaked information.[135]

Apart from the D'Orazio combat, April 2008 was a pivotal month in the hostilities of *The West* versus the Carpenter Government. In the first week of April, McGinty accused a reporter "of failing to appreciate that the winds of change are blowing for his newspaper".

This was a highly inflammatory accusation and not one that you would expect from someone trying to mend fences.

At this time, the board of *The West* was in the midst of a do-or-die struggle with businessman Kerry Stokes, in what was a *de facto* takeover battle. For the board, led by respected Herbert Smith Freehills senior partner and company director Peter Mansell, it seemed clear that the Carpenter Government had backed Mr Stokes, who had already indicated that he would make big changes if he succeeded.

It was an extraordinarily partisan statement by government, which usually steers clear of taking sides in a strictly commercial matter. The issue came to a preliminary head at a highly publicised shareholders meeting on 24 April, where Mr Stokes lost a first attempt to put his people on the board.

Despite *The West's* win with the shareholders, McGinty's "winds of change" remarks were taken very badly by *The West* and its editor. *The West* editorialised on the subject on 26 April. In part, the editorial stated:

> Mr McGinty, who as Attorney-General and Health Minister is a key powerbroker in the WA Government, could not have been more wrong when he also asserted that most other journalists on this newspaper appreciate that his winds of change were blowing, implying that possible change on the newspaper's board could influence their reporting. The proof of his error is in the unchanged re-

---

[134] *The West Australian*, 17 April 2014, p. 5.
[135] Ibid.

porting by this newspaper of government matters during the boardroom battle . . .

With the Government openly barracking for boardroom change it was clear that the McGinty/*West* relationship was now septic.

Intriguingly, however, the McGinty/Carpenter Government strategy may well have come off, except for the fortunes of timing. Mr Stokes was ultimately elected Chairman of West Australian Newspapers' board on 11 December 2008. McGinty's nemesis, Paul Armstrong, was discharged as editor on 16 January 2009.

Nonetheless, the changes at *The West* came too late (after the September 2008 election) to help the Labor Government. If the election had gone full term – to, say, March 2009 – it may have been different. The banning of *The West* was a colossal gamble by McGinty that just did not come off.

On the other hand, McGinty, who resigned his seat on 2 April 2009, was not personally disadvantaged by his aggressive posture towards *The West*. The Stokes-controlled newspaper in 2012 appointed McGinty to a prestigious job on *The West's* Independent Media Council.

D'Orazio's fate was similar to nearly all those wrongly besmirched by the CCC. Despite being cleared by other independent authorities, they never recovered their status or careers. In respect to D'Orazio, he eventually stood for Morley in the 2008 election as an Independent candidate and his preferences helped elect Liberal, Ian Britza, who retained the seat in 2013.

D'Orazio died on 5 April 2011, still bitter at the ALP, as were many of his former constituents.

May 2008 began as a better month for the ALP in the media. *The West* editorialised against the Liberal leader – the talented, likeable, but flawed Troy Buswell. He was the gift that just kept on giving to the ALP. *The West* editorial of 3 May 2008 summed up the Opposition's position neatly:

> Even if Troy Buswell survives as leader of the Liberal Party, the damage has been done. His integrity is damaged

beyond repair and the party's ability to mount an effective challenge to the Carpenter government at the next election has been compromised.

The respite from the media was not to last long. On the very same day, 3 May, the Carpenter Government's Department of Premier triggered a massive raid by police (some of them armed) on *The Sunday Times*. This weekend newspaper, then part of the Murdoch stable and a sister publication to *The Australian*, dominated the media on Saturday evening and Sunday.

Outside of *The West*, it was the only other mass circulation paper based in WA. The Carpenter Government, having angered and insulted *The West*, set about thoroughly alienating the only alternative in town and putting an end to *The Australian* v *The West Australian* conflict.

The incident involved the CCC and revolved around a story written by *Sunday Times* journalist Paul Lampathakis, on 10 February 2008, concerning a request by Treasurer Eric Ripper for $16 million for political funding through a Cabinet subcommittee. It was alleged by the Government that the story was a result of an illegal leak and the CCC had been requested to take up the matter.

Colleen Egan, writing for *The Sunday Times* on 4 May 2008, was highly critical of the police raid.

The Sunday Times took three full pages, including a searing editorial, to express its aversion to the methods adopted. The editorial commenced ominously:

> West Australians today should be fearful of their Government.

And from my personal perspective, that about sums it up and enunciates my reason for writing this book.

The resulting embarrassment to the Government was compounded by the fact that the police were very unhappy about being forced by the CCC to conduct the raid on the paper. It provoked open public hostility between the two law enforcement agencies.

No incriminating evidence was discovered. The Fraud Squad and the police generally were resentful at being ordered to undertake this highly unpopular task. They took the view that the CCC should have used its own powers if it insisted that the probe had to go ahead.

To make matters worse, a later parliamentary inquiry into this questionable event heard the critical evidence in secret. As you would expect, this earned a front-page headline and a scornful editorial in *The West* on 10 June. It was a most unedifying spectacle and it did the Carpenter Government no favors.

However, on 4 June 2008 the ALP lost probably its best election campaigner when Carpenter sanctimoniously banned all lobbyists from managing election campaigns. The loss of the former MP-turned-lobbyist John Halden was a blow to the ALP. Halden was particularly targeted because he admitted to the CCC that he had received Cabinet leaks from unnamed public servants.

The matter was a storm in a teacup, but it was to deprive the Government of much-needed independent advice and expertise when it was needed in the September election.

Interestingly, Halden was at the time running the campaign of Karen Brown, part of Carpenter's "Dream Team". Ms Brown, a lobbyist and former senior journalist at *The West Australian*, had defeated popular MP Bob Kucera in Labor pre-selection when Carpenter threw his weight behind her.

Kucera was deeply hurt and subsequently quit the ALP and sat in Parliament as an Independent, though he did not contest the 2008 poll. The seat was lost by Labor to the Liberals. A totally unnecessary waste of a vital seat.

The situation was mentioned by Robert Ray on page 5 of his report, where he stated:

> His (Alan Carpenter's) naïvety about the culture of the ALP and his lack of central campaign experience would always be a problem, but the rest of the team needed to fill some of the vacuum, *and didn't* (my emphasis). In the case of John Halden, this most likely source of strong in-

dependent advice was sadly removed by Alan Carpenter, before the event.

During May 2008, it became apparent that CCC hearings were going to impact on the next election.

CCC investigations followed a number of State MPs who had had quite innocent contact with Burke. There was more than a hint of McCarthyism about the process.

Some saw this as an attempt by the CCC to intimidate Parliament after the highly-publicised confrontation between Commissioner Hammond and President Griffiths (see Chapter 7, "CCC resorts to Parliament – and fails again").

John Quigley (ALP), Ben Wyatt (ALP) and John McGrath (Lib) were stigmatised by totally unnecessary CCC public inquiries simply because they were lobbied by Burke. It all turned out to be above board and they were all cleared.

However, that was not the point. Without some initial evidence of impropriety, there should never have been the public odium of an inquiry. And the Government should not have been tainted. The frenzy at the time was such that much of the public, and many who should have known better, assumed guilt.

McGrath lost his shadow ministry. Although personally resilient, he did not really recover.

It was a bit different with Quigley, who had several run-ins with the CCC. Controversy and sensation always followed him, so it was nothing new. A legal colleague said of him: "If you want a dogfight in court, John was the 'go to' man".

He just shrugged it off, but Wyatt was hurt. His later attempt to lead the party was badly dented by the CCC inquiry into his quite innocent contact with Burke.

I deal with the case of Anthony Fels (Liberal, Upper House) elsewhere, but most commentators and observers say that this CCC target was entirely innocent. The DPP would not have a bar of prosecuting him despite the urgings of the CCC. Nonetheless, he lost his seat and his career.

Bunbury Liberal MP John Castrilli was badly smeared when a CCC investigation allowed unsupported allegations of corruption to be publicised (see page 6 of *The West*, 26 June 2008).

The tragedy of Tony McRae (ALP) was that he was never allowed an opportunity or a venue to defend himself against a dubious imputation by the CCC that he misled me, for his own benefit, over a lobbying matter. I don't believe that there was any truth in the allegation, but there is no doubt as to why he ever so narrowly lost his seat of Riverton in the 2008 election as a result.

He was unfairly forced to resign his cabinet ministry over the issue in 2007. His political career was confiscated from him. I deal with this in more detail elsewhere.

I also deal elsewhere with the case of Shelley Archer. Suffice it to say here that the CCC tried to prosecute her criminally twice on different matters. On each occasion, the DPP refused to proceed. Her penalty for being a friend of Burke was to lose her cherished vocation.

Norm Marlborough was unfairly made to appear corrupt at his first CCC appearance. I cover this tragic affair elsewhere. He never recovered.

Although the ill-considered CCC intervention in political and parliamentary matters affected both sides of politics, it had a disproportionate detrimental effect on the Government. Premier Carpenter woke up to the danger too late. The Government's reaction was to uncritically and enthusiastically accept every step of the CCC's intrusion into the political domain.

A prime example was the Government's failure to support Legislative Council President Nick Griffiths in his dispute with CCC Commissioner Kevin Hammond over age-old parliamentary privilege. The Government dogmatically embraced every ill-founded CCC finding and acted far too self-righteously and ruthlessly against its own MPs.

Worse, the Carpenter Government stubbornly refused to acknowledge the inherent and fundamental flaws and unfairness in the CCC processes.

However, Carpenter personally appeared to have a genuine change of position after losing the 2008 election. On 26 November 2008 in the Legislative Assembly he gave what was effectively his valedictory speech. He soberly reflected upon his time in Parliament.

He also deliberated on the CCC. His words may be open to some interpretation, but Peter Kerr of *The West* had little doubt about what Carpenter meant. In an article of 27 November 2008 under the heading, "Humbled Carpenter comes out swinging", Kerr stated:

> Mr Carpenter pointedly used his address in reply to launch a thinly veiled attack on the time it took the Corruption and Crime Commission to complete its investigations.

Carpenter told Parliament:

> ... the CCC threw up some horrendously difficult circumstances to deal with and decisions that had to be made. I knew, in my role as Premier that these would have profound ramification for some of the individuals involved, but these decisions really have to be made. I will not go into details about each decision, because if I mention one and neglect another I will create a problem.

Later in his speech he said:

> In the long term, it will undoubtedly produce a better and more accountable and open system of government, but there have been some real issues in its early years of operation. Some individual lives have been extremely affected.
>
> One of the issues concerning the CCC that needs to be addressed is the length of time it takes for it to resolve issues, from the time that matters are raised in a public forum to the time matters are finally dealt with and recommendations are made. The process can take a very long time – up to 21 months in some cases. In the meantime, people's lives and careers are at least put on hold and in some cases destroyed ...

> The CCC will evolve from this point forward and I hope that the people who have been subject to the activities of the CCC and who have been shown to be completely and utterly innocent of any wrongdoing, but who have had their careers put on hold, or others who feel that they are still being unfairly tarnished or stigmatised by the CCC, can eventually move on and rectify that situation.

Given past history, it was a remarkable set of concessions by the former Premier. It was the first time he had publicly questioned CCC procedures. He implied that he may have been wrong in some of his CCC-related decisions. He cast some doubt on the early years of the CCC's operations. This could only be a reference to the Smiths Beach and Lobbyists inquiries.

He conceded that some witnesses' careers had been destroyed. I accept that he was expressing sincere regret when he acknowledged that some, at least, were "completely and utterly innocent of any wrong doing".

Also, I believe that he was genuine when he hoped that those who had been unfairly "tarnished or stigmatised by the CCC" would eventually rectify that situation. Carpenter's dialogue was one of compassion.

There is one thing that Carpenter did not do. He did not mention Burke or Grill. He did not blame us for his loss, or even hint at it.

Although the McGinty "ban" on journalists at *The West Australian* only lasted two months (until 4 May 2008), it caused serious damage with the media generally and *The West* in particular. *The West* printed that:

> The State's media union 'accused Mr McGinty of adopting dangerous' and 'repressive' tactics to avoid answering journalists' questions and to stop the newspaper from reporting on issues relating to his portfolio.[136]

It is hard to judge whether Jim McGinty was just insensitive or intentionally insulting in his public comments when he lifted the ban.

---

[136] *The West Australian*, 5 May 2008, p. 5.

In any event, he did not do his colleague, the Premier, or his party any favours in the churlish language he used. There was no hint of reconciliation when he said:

"I wanted to send a message to The West that I had had enough of what I regard as inaccurate and unethical reporting. I've made that point, hopefully people will be big enough to take it on board in the way in which they approach these things in the future."[137]

What could and should have been a turning point in the ALP/media/*The West* relationship was instead another inflammation point.

There was further bad news for the CCC on 2 July 2008 when Magistrate Michele Pontifex decisively acquitted senior public servant Mike Allen on two CCC charges of false testimony. Costs were awarded against the CCC.

More such reversals for the CCC were to follow. The outcome of the Allen case cracked the monolithic support of the ALP parliamentary wing in upholding even the worst and most blatant excesses of the CCC. The day after Mr Allen's acquittal, Labor backbench parliamentarian and lawyer Ben Wyatt (who went on to be deputy leader and Treasurer in the WA Government) was referred to by Amanda Banks in *The West* in commenting on the Allen exoneration that it:

> ... had highlighted problems identified previously by Parliamentary Inspector Malcolm McCusker, yet the watchdog (CCC) appeared unwilling to acknowledge internal failures.[138]

The acquittal of Mr Allen was predictable in the light of the fatal flaws in the investigation procedure, the omission of key evidence at the CCC hearings, and a departmental inquiry that absolved the public servant for any breach of discipline.[139]

Notwithstanding this growing list of exonerations, the CCC remained obstinate. The CCC's Executive Director Mike Silverstone said immediately after the case that, "the acquittal would not affect

---

[137] Ibid.
[138] *The West Australian*, 4 July 2008, p. 6.
[139] *The West Australian*, 3 July 2008, p. 5.

the Commission's view of other false testimony charges arising out of hearings".

It was a disgrace that the CCC carried on just as Mr Silverstone said it would. With the aid of the CCC's immense powers and ample taxpayers-provided funds, it unmercifully pursued prey in criminal proceedings relating to Smiths Beach and Lobbyists inquiries for another five years – and may have gone on longer if the DPP had not called a halt to it.

The CCC's results were spectacularly unsuccessful. In its wake it left a trail of broken lives.

However, Mike Allen and his loyal wife, Beth, were to be dreadfully disappointed at the final outcome. This quiet, modest and highly respected town planner told the assembled media after the acquittal that he hoped and expected that he would now be reinstated in his old job. To his shock and deep dismay, he was not allowed to resume his old position. In fact, he was excluded from the public service altogether.

It was all done quietly, in a back room, away from public gaze, but it was a ruthless execution nonetheless. He was instructed not to come back.

What Mr Allen and his heartbroken wife may not have fully appreciated at the time was that inoffensive, innocent Mr Allen was not the target in his own right. What only lawyers and a few others fully appreciated was that Burke and Grill could not be attacked by the CCC directly. There had to be findings against "public officers" (i.e. public servants or the like) that implicated Burke and Grill.

Put simply, no findings against public servants, then no findings against Burke and Grill. Mr Allen was an essential scapegoat. What was befalling these blameless office holders may not have been a major issue at the 2008 election, but it did receive abundant publicity and had considerable potential to colour the public's perception of the Government and public servants' attitudes.

The legal profession could clearly see what was happening and expressed its alarm through its professional associations. But despite the highly dubious legal and moral basis of the CCC activity, as explicitly described by Malcolm McCusker, the Government was undeterred. It continued to follow the McGinty strategy of unquestioning commitment to the CCC.

The Governments partisan and ruthless attempt to expel Archer from Parliament was no different (see Chapter 7).

The month of August was the election campaign month proper and that was where it all fell to pieces for the Carpenter Government. The self-righteous stunt of closing the Parliament bar blew up in the Premier's face on 22 August. An article by Amanda Banks the next day refers to comments by Labor MP Nick Griffiths:

> Upper House President Nick Griffiths said it's not the first time the Premier had exceeded his jurisdiction and had 'typically' failed to consult his colleagues about his plans.[140]

Carpenter needed a dressing-down from one of his own members like he needed a hole in the head. It was a devastating front-page story in the penultimate week to the election. It just added to the Carpenter 'arrogance' effect.

As for the CCC, it lost another high-profile criminal prosecution on 29 August. The former chief of King Edward and Princess Margaret Children's Hospital, Michael Moodie, was acquitted of travel claims charges, and signalled in a story in *The West* by Sean Cowan and David Darragh that his lawyers were pursuing a $1 million compensation claim.

The CCC, which had to pay $56,000 in court costs, conceded that it had not sought DPP advice before commencing the actions. It later transpired that such prosecutions by the CCC were illegal (see Chapter 19, "CCC prosecutions 'unlawful' – Senior Counsel").

Someone once said that "history is a cavalcade of bloodshed" and that was the way it was for the hapless Carpenter, with a six per cent swing against the ALP at the 6 September 2008 general election. The ALP lost four seats (total of 28), the Coalition picked up five (total of

---

[140] *The West Australian*, 23 August 2008.

28) and went on to govern (initially with the help of three Independent MPs) for eight years.

The election result came as a big shock to most political analysts. It was a substantial swing that indicated some very persuasive motivating forces were at play.

CCC 'casualties' cost Labor government

Any one of the seats held by CCC casualties and spurned Labor MPs – Bowler, McRae, Kucera and D'Orazio – may have secured an ALP win.

More often than not, governments fall when the economy falters. Remember Bill Clinton's famous line: "It is the economy, stupid". However, despite the GFC, WA's economy was growing at nearly three per cent and was entering its biggest-ever mining and energy construction boom.

On top of that, the Opposition was in disarray. But talk about a Phoenix rising from the ashes. Barnett went on to be Premier for a near record-breaking term.

In the immediate aftermath of the election, there was an avalanche of condemnation from ALP members and candidates critical of Carpenter and the shambolic campaign. ALP members and candidates Jay Radisich (now deceased), Sheila Mills, Paul Andrews (now deceased), Reece Whitby, Bob Kucera, Tony O'Gorman, Judy Hughes and others who did not want to be named sheeted home the loss to an extremely inept campaign. Most, but not all, referred to the Premier's "arrogant" and dictatorial campaign.

The West brought in two analysts to comment on the campaign. One was John Halden, former State Secretary of the ALP, lobbyist and former Member of State Parliament. He was also a long-standing member of the Left faction. He was excoriating of those who ran the ALP campaign, listing all the substantial reasons for the loss, later enumerated in the Robert Ray report. He did not refer to Burke and Grill as causes of the loss.

However, Halden also made some very interesting remarks for a one-time powerbroker in the ALP's Left faction. He declared:

The campaign issues that were made front and centre by the Premier were straight out of an outdated left wing handbook – uranium mining, GM crops, AWAs (Australian Workplace Agreements) and privatisation are clearly not vote-winning issues in 2008. Ultimately Labor positioned itself as a second-rate Green party and not the major progressive political force in WA.[141]

The other "independent" analyst was veteran former Liberal leader Barry MacKinnon, whose remarks reflected the general unfavourable lament. Of Carpenter he said:

> His continual attacks on any media that dared question his Government showed him insensitive and arrogant.[142]

This assessment supports Robert Ray and his comments about *The West*, and my conclusions about the war provoked by McGinty with *The West*, which had its genesis with the battle between Malcolm McCusker and the CCC.

MacKinnon added:

> Finally, his inability to be able to claim leadership in the traditionally key policy areas of health, law and order and education was fatal.[143]

It is pertinent that two of these areas, health and law and order, were areas where the CCC played a heavily destructive role. The controversy surrounding the unnecessary removal of Dr Fong, and the massive dislocation it caused, lay at the door of the CCC.

The intensively publicised feuds involving the CCC – firstly with the very highly regarded Malcolm McCusker and secondly with popular Police Commissioner Karl O'Callaghan – were acute events, played out over months, that sapped public confidence in the law systems.

While generally endorsing the Ray, Halden and McKinnon evaluation of the 2008 election result, I do offer another complementary

---

[141] *The West Australian*, 8 September 2008, p. .
[142] Ibid.
[143] Ibid.

perspective. Firstly, however, I want to dispel any indication that I was (or still am) under any illusions as to the popularity of Burke and myself at the time of the election. We were deeply unpopular with the public, and politicians prudently kept their distance from us.

My alternative view is that McGinty, as Attorney-General and as the most important personality within the controlling Left faction, influenced Carpenter and his Government to adopt a flawed course in respect to the CCC. The flaw was to unquestionably embrace all of the actions of the CCC.

This was exacerbated by the Government adopting an absurdly self-righteous posture in respect to the CCC findings, which simply threw away seats, as I have explained above.

Unwavering support for the CCC, as an election strategy, was initially highly successful for the Carpenter Government in 2006 and for much of 2007 when the media uncritically championed what appeared to be a corruption-busting process. However, as the series of sensational CCC allegations did not stand up to forensic scrutiny, some elements of the media became suspicious and said so.

This was particularly the case in respect to the Standing Committee of Privilege (SCP) matter in the Legislative Council, when *The West* took the side of Mr McCusker and favourably published and commented upon his scathing report of this CCC-inspired fiasco. I cover this crucial battle in more detail in Chapter 7.

Paul Murray, then a broadcaster with radio station 6PR and columnist with *The West*, was foremost among those in the media having doubts.

When Parliamentary Inspector McCusker began questioning the unfair methods used by the CCC and exposing the clearly defective findings against innocent public servants, the wider public started to take some notice, too. Then followed the disciplinary tribunals to which the CCC had referred the public servants and which exonerated them all.

The CCC then made two mistakes that opened them to censure. The first was to impugn the independent public service disciplinary tribunal's findings in exonerating the public servants. It was perceived by the public as akin to a footballer disputing the umpire's decision.

The second error was to apply to the Supreme Court for an injunction against Mr McCusker. It was clearly interpreted as an attempt to silence and gag him. This perception was magnified when it was learnt that the CCC action was *ex parte* – that is, behind Mr McCusker's back.

Quite properly, the Supreme Court refused to hear the CCC application to restrain Mr McCusker in his absence.

Ultimately, the CCC's injunction application went nowhere. Primarily, the episode demonstrated how intolerant the CCC was of any oversight or appraisal.

Then, in 2008, the State's courts started dismissing the criminal actions brought by the CCC. All the while, the legal profession was deeply concerned at the procedure adopted by the CCC and registered protests. When it was learned that the CCC had intruded its way into parliamentary disciplinary committee proceedings and conducted secret trials, a large part of the media split from the CCC.

The West led this revolt and after the CCC raids on the *Sunday Times*, that newspaper followed. Ultimately, as I have already explained, the DPP refused to prosecute. The public embarked on the road to scepticism.

In spite of all of the high-profile legal questioning of the CCC's methods, the Attorney-General and the Carpenter Government did not query the CCC's *modus operandi*.

In fact, the Government's disposition became more sanctimonious and judgmental against the innocent witnesses. In contrast the NSW ICAC hearings, for instance, although denying aspects of natural justice, did not descend anywhere near as far down that slippery slope as did the CCC.

As far as I am aware, McGinty never practised law after he qualified and was admitted as a solicitor and barrister, but he was well enough equipped to understand how egregiously inequitable the CCC proceedings had been.

Mr McCusker had detailed his concerns in his written reports as Parliamentary Inspector. In fact, in some cases he exposed what could be categorised as gross negligence, by the CCC investigating team. The Frewer case, where McCusker proved the CCC was factually incorrect, the Mark Brabazon matter, where the CCC was obliged to apologise, and the example of Mike Allen were glaring instances.

Nor should the Government have failed to apprehend the shell-shocked condition of the senior ranks of the Public Service.

So, this growing perception that the Carpenter Government was too pious and overly judgemental also fed a consciousness that the Government was arrogant and contemptuous of others' sensibilities, and basic rights. It was an ugly look that sustained *The West's* "campaign", if I may call it that.

However, it had an indirect and a more amorphous effect on the election result than the more direct and brutal actions of the Government against some of its own members. I refer to the callous way Bob Kucera, Norm Marlborough, Tony McRae, John Bowler, Shelley Archer and John D'Orazio were excluded and discarded, largely as a result of the defective CCC processes, and in an effort by the Government to appear unsullied by perceived scandals that never in fact materialised when all of the evidence came in.

Kucera was appointed as Health Minister in 2001 and he held that position until 2003 before losing it to McGinty in a Cabinet reshuffle. He was forced to resign as Minister for Sport and Recreation in 2005 after claims of a conflict of interest. He and his wife both held shares in Alinta Gas, an energy supply company, when Cabinet made a $90 million decision that would benefit the company. Kucera maintained that it was an innocent oversight, but he paid the severe penalty of losing his ministry.

However, the Carpenter Government took the issue to a new, higher level. When Kucera sought ALP pre-selection for the seat of Mt Lawley (where he was highly popular) in the 2008 election, Carpenter, with the aid of factional elements denied him the endorsement. Karen Brown, part of Carpenter's "Dream Team", stood for the seat and lost to Liberal Michael Sutherland, who went on to become Speaker of the Legislative Assembly.

There is little doubt in anyone's mind that in 2008 Kucera would have won the seat.

The Independents, elected in 2008 were Janet Woollard (Alfred Cove), Elizabeth Constable (Churchlands) and John Bowler (Kalgoorlie – previously ALP Murchison-Eyre). Given the closeness of the general vote and some predilection by the Nationals' leader Brendon Grylls (dubbed the "Kingmaker") to favour forming Government with the ALP, the decision on who would govern was delayed for nearly a week after the election while Grylls negotiated with Barnett and Carpenter.

It is a matter of recorded history that the Nationals finally went with Barnett, but it was a close-run thing. Clearly, one more seat falling to the ALP could have made all the difference.

A similar story unfolded in respect to John D'Orazio in the seat of Morley.

In Kalgoorlie, by forcing John Bowler to resign from the ALP, Premier Carpenter just threw away a safe Labor seat. Bowler won overwhelmingly as an Independent and later became an unofficial part of the National Party.

Tony McRae's seat of Riverton was slightly different, but it should have been an ALP seat if not for the highly questionable tactics of the CCC and his abandonment by the ALP hierarchy. Counting in the seat was on a razor's edge for days after the election before it was declared in favour of the Liberal candidate Mike Nahan (later Opposition Leader).

I deal with the McRae issue in more detail elsewhere, but a few facts are salient.

Firstly, Carpenter forced McRae to resign from the Ministry over contact with me.

Secondly, at the time of the election there was an overdue and uncompleted CCC report hanging over McRae's head. I believe that Carpenter was, in part, alluding to this when giving his regrets in his departing parliamentary speech, referred to above.

In Norm Marlborough's old seat of Peel (replaced by Kwinana), the ALP candidate, Roger Cook, lost nearly all of the 19.1 per cent margin. The vicious nature of the swing against the ALP was an indicator of the regard for Marlborough in the electorate, and the electors' disapproval of the shabby way in which he was treated by the CCC and his party.

In summary, therefore, I submit that there is no credible evidence that Brian Burke and I were responsible for the Labor Party's 2008 election loss. Such a narrative may only have served the interests of those wishing to avert attention from the real problems within the WA Branch.

As evidence that such systemic problems in the ALP persisted, the Federal Labor Party in January 2014 appointed David Feeney (former State Secretary of the ALP in Victoria) and Cameron Milner (former State Secretary in Queensland) to make further recommendations following the WA electoral performance. After the 2008 WA election, Senator Mark Abib's report into the WA Labor Party, at the behest of the National Executive, and the Robert Ray report, made three federally initiated inquiries in WA in just a few years.

At the July 2016 Federal election, Labor could only manage to win three out of 15 House of Representative seats in WA and one out of six Senate seats. The overarching problem was apparent to all but the willfully blind. That was, a state apparatus out of touch with a largely aspirational constituency. It was not remedied until the State 2017 election. That makes nearly a decade in the wilderness.

The fact that the problem persisted well after Burke and Grill left the scene, speaks for itself.

I am not suggesting that the calling of an early election by Alan Carpenter, the misdirected and very average campaign, and the lack of campaigning skills in his office did not play a part in the loss. But I do assert that the Government's lethally destructive relationship with *The West* and much of the rest of the media, together with the pious dumping of its own members in four of its safe seats, was much more significant in the loss.

On a personal level, I confess that I was distressed and crushed to be condemned, along with Brian Burke, for the ALP's 2008 election loss. Lesley and I have been in the Labor movement for most of our lives. Brian, his brother Terry, their children and their father, Tom, are part of ALP history.

During the CCC experience, we were reviled by members of our own party and I was improperly expelled – without due process or any opportunity to defend myself. ALP members were told by ALP leadership that they should not speak to us because we were "toxic" and "corrupting". These were scathing and very hurtful words used publicly and aggressively applied to us.

It came to the ridiculous point where not only I, but Lesley, was excluded from a long-standing ALP football tipping competition of all things!

15

HELPING ANDREW FORREST CRACK THE IRON ORE DUOPOLY

So that our general lobbying *modus operandi* is better understood, I give commentary in this chapter, on the Fortescue Metals Group (FMG) matter, which was examined by the CCC.

Prior to saying anything else, I want to make it clear that I believe FMG's founder, Andrew Forrest, is an extraordinary human being. Not perfect perhaps, but extraordinary. When we were associated with him, he pulled off some remarkable feats. He succeeded with FMG against overwhelming odds.

But he has his detractors. Paul Garvey of *The Australian* wrote on 23 October 2013:

> Before he became the nation's greatest philanthropist, Andrew Forrest was a fast-talking salesman who borrowed millions of dollars from a convicted drug dealer and employed disgraced former West Australian premier Brian Burke to help him smash the BHP Billiton-Rio Tinto duopoly in the Pilbara iron ore industry.

How's that for an introduction? Nasty, certainly, but quite correct in one respect. FMG actually employed Brian Burke and me to do exactly what Garvey brutally stated.

My personal FMG files were among the many files the CCC seized from my home office in Mount Street, West Perth, on 8 November 2006. No specific reason was given for the confiscation of the material or the seizure from Brian Burke's house in a simultaneous incursion.

Attempts by our lawyers to ascertain the specific grounds for the seizure have been refused by the CCC and denied by the courts.

While the CCC must legally obtain a warrant to enter premises and seize material, or break into your home and plant bugs, the affidavit setting out the evidence and grounds that a judge must seriously consider before granting a warrant remain secret. It is a process that can be egregiously abused.

Whereas the CCC did not feel obliged to give any specific justification for the raid on our homes, it appeared to have alerted the media, who witnessed, filmed and photographed the whole unedifying procedure at the Burke residence.

It was part of a theatrical and highly prejudicial trial by media. The floridly graphic images did immense immediate damage. The pictures of CCC officials removing cartons of material from the home implied and insinuated criminality. They sent indelible messages of illicit transgression that can never be erased. There is no possibility of defending oneself in this situation. That is, where the CCC refuses to disclose the accusation or the basis for the raid.

We had no motive to hide any files or dealings. As it ultimately transpired, there was nothing untoward about our activities for, or with, FMG or anyone else.

The West devoted most of page six to a story by Gary Adshead with accompanying photographs of the Burke raid, showing CCC officers removing material and a very concerned looking Sarah Burke, daughter of Brian, and Burke's lawyer, Grant Donaldson, outside the house. I have no doubt that it would have been front page, except that the page was taken up by another even more hair-raising CCC/Burke/Marlborough/Carpenter story.

Adshead's story began:

> When the Corruption and Crime Commission was dropping its ace on a gobsmacked Norm Marlborough in the St Georges Terrace hearing room yesterday his old mate Brian Burke was at his Trigg home with company.
>
> But his guests were uninvited CCC agents turning his world upside down.[144]

It was all very droll. A put-down, or dangerous speculation of criminal intent, in every sentence.

---

[144] *The West Australian* 9 November 2006, p. 6.

None of it turned out to be correct, but it imperilled any prospect of a fair trial there and then. In due course, the raid led to a full public inquiry by the CCC on our association with FMG and numerous other matters, with all of the usual histrionics and false leads.

Our FMG story is one of both soaring achievement and of despairing disappointment. Brian Burke and I were part of a critical change to the strategic direction of the infant FMG, which in turn laid the foundation of its ultimate dazzling success. With Andrew Forrest and his team, we played an intimate role in overcoming many of the challenges that confronted the fledgling company, and saw off a substantial lobbying effort by BHP and Rio Tinto that was designed to scuttle the company before it could take off.

Our profound disappointment stemmed from the manner in which our contract with FMG was summarily suspended once the CCC public hearings commenced. But looking back, I do not really blame Forrest for cutting us adrift as he could not afford a breath of scandal. Forrest at the time had appointed directors such as Herb Elliott and Cathy Freeman who were Australian icons and sporting royalty.

However, we had been near the core of FMG, had bonded with the senior executives and had an emotional link to their titanic struggle for Australian corporate success as it unfolded. We accepted our dismissal, but we were deeply hurt.

Our engagement by Forrest was a consequence of a meeting on the 2 July 2004. Brian and I were introduced by public relations consultant Paul Downie who was a friend of Forrest. Downie had worked with me on Ric Stowe's Griffin Coal account. He was a high-profile partner in a PR firm Porter Novelli, which he ran initially with the well-known ex-journalist Caroline de Mori and later with even better known print and radio journalist John McGlue.

Downie, Burke and I met with Forrest at his home in John Street, Cottesloe. The house was a large historic residence that was once the dwelling of premier and federal minister, Lord John Forrest, and his explorer brother, Alexander Forrest.

Andrew Forrest is exceedingly proud of that ancestry. It is an interesting comment on him that he has a monumental sense of his family's history and has moved to resurrect that history and all of its adornments and past glory. An example of this is his repurchase the family's pastoral property Mindaroo, the John Street house and other Forrest family heirlooms.

I had met Forrest previously when he pioneered the Anaconda Nickel project, located in what was part of my parliamentary seat of Eyre.

On 2 July 2004, we were ushered into what I presumed was the dining room of the house. It was clear that the dwelling was richly furnished and had an air of grandeur.

At the meeting, Forrest was warmly welcoming, ebullient and highly persuasive in his explanation of the various aspects of his extremely bold Pilbara iron ore project. It was clearly centred on China, both in terms of off-take contracts for the iron ore and in respect to financing. The primary matter that he wanted us to focus on was the question of access to BHP's rail line to Port Hedland and later Rio Tinto's rail line to Dampier.

He explained the frustrations and problems that had accompanied his company's efforts to obtain some agreement with BHP for utilisation of their line. While the agreements between BHP and Rio Tinto and the State Government all contemplated and specified that these rail lines should be used by third parties such as FMG, no company had been successful in achieving that goal. Both major companies had stubbornly resisted all attempts through the National Competition Council (NCC).

It was public knowledge that Forrest had selected the NCC route in his attack on the problem of getting his ore to port and hoped to ultimately convince the NCC to recommend to Peter Costello, the Federal Treasurer, to grant FMG access to the rail lines. He essentially wanted to engage Burke and Grill to map out and execute the political lobbying effort that would complement his company's submissions to the NCC and the Federal Government.

The rail track agreements in the Pilbara have a long history. They were intended by the State Government to facilitate use by mining companies other than the builders. BHP and Rio Tinto saw off attempts by Lang Hancock, and later rebuffed Gina Hancock, for access to their lines. We left the meeting with Forrest with the understanding that it was agreed in principle that we would accept a consultancy contract with FMG.

Brian Burke and I had had some experience of the entrenched and obdurate reluctance of Rio Tinto and BHP to make their railway lines available to third parties. Forrest had sold us on his project and his concept, but we left his house with the firm view that his strategy was flawed, fatally flawed.

Brian saw the problem and the solution in a flash. Near Forrest's front gate on the way out Brian turned at me and said: "This guy is the best salesman I have ever seen, but BHP and Rio Tinto will smash him on rail access. We have to convince him to change tack." He argued, and I agreed, that Forrest and FMG would be better served if we could convince him that the company should negotiate a State Agreement with the WA Government and build its own rail and port infrastructure.

Readers should understand that there are two possible paths to mining in WA. The first and usual way is under the standard provisions of the Mining Act. The second, reserved for projects of State consequence, is by way of a special State Agreement. Rio Tinto and BHP had adopted that latter route. Such an agreement would not only include provisions for the mining of iron ore at FMG's various deposits, but would also approve a pathway for FMG to build its own railway line to Port Hedland and port facilities.

FMG's executive team at that time were Corporate Affairs Manager Julian Tapp, Chief Finance Manager Chris Catlow, Engineer in Charge of Construction Alan Watling and Operations Manager Graeme Rowley. At a meeting on 5 July 2004 with that group and Forrest, Brian and I discussed our proposed engagement and an alternate strategy for FMG. The outcome was that FMG would pursue a State Agreement to cover both mining and rail and port operations for FMG.

There were compelling reasons to pursue this alternate strategy.

Firstly, Forrest and FMG badly needed credibility in the eyes of the Australian media, especially the Western Australian media. Forrest had been the instigator of the Anaconda Nickel Project mentioned above. It was a very ambitious operation designed to produce both nickel and cobalt in largely refined form in the North East Goldfields. The project was primarily financed by bondholders in the United States.

This very challenging project had technical problems during construction and fell on hard times. The unfortunate American bondholders essentially lost their money. Some contractors remained unpaid and acrimony was created. Although Anaconda did limp on after a financial reconstruction and continued under the name Murrin Joint Venture, the exercise very badly damaged Forrest's financial reputation.

In July 2004, when he was endeavouring to promote FMG, he was a targeted pariah of the press. Clearly, a State Agreement would give the FMG Pilbara project the stamp of respectability and a new-found status.

Secondly, Forrest found himself once again in a position where he had to raise more equity funding. This time, not from the Americans, but from the Chinese. It is well known that the Chinese are very impressed with projects that are supported by sovereign governments. The imprimatur of a State Agreement would make fund-raising substantially easier.

Thirdly, the State Agreement would also raise FMG's financial stocks with investors within Australia and suppliers of material and labour.

Focus was placed on passing a comprehensive State Agreement through Parliament before the end of the year.

This time line was very ambitious, as no major State Agreement had ever been settled in such a short period. Nonetheless, Brian and I had both historic and recent experience in this arena and we had some confidence that it could be pulled off.

There was broad scepticism that this very limited time line could be met, but there was no doubt that Forrest was a hard-driving taskmaster. Julian Tapp was delegated to work directly with us on the project and weekly meetings with FMG senior executives were pencilled in.

FMG at that stage did not abandon the option of forcing BHP to accede to third-party rights on the BHP rail line. In fact, that task remained part of our brief.

However, I must say that once the State Agreement decision was taken, FMG moved decisively. On 7 July 2004, Forrest wrote to the Minister for State Development, Clive Brown, formally advising that FMG wished to enter into a State Agreement to support development of its iron ore and infrastructure project.

From the outset, Forrest committed to, and made it public, that his railways and port would be "open access". This commitment is important in the light of later events.

Brian Burke and I had previously worked with consultant Malcolm Carson, who had extensive experience in relation to State Agreements. He was brought on board. Harry Adams, a senior FMG employee, collaborated with Carson.

Julian Tapp, together with Messrs Carson and Adams, immediately contacted senior executives of the Department of Industry and Resources, Greg Dellar and Julie O'Donoghue, concerning the proposed agreement.

The welcome advice from Mr Dellar and Ms O'Donoghue was that the department was in a position to quickly formulate and assent to a State Agreement. Mr Dellar was initially a Kalgoorlie boy and both he and his family were well known to me.

Both officers were of the view that a State Agreement Act would add much-needed credibility to FMG, give it additional status before the NCC and start to overcome the BHP legal argument (which had been supported in part by the WA Supreme Court) that BHP does not even have to negotiate with third parties unless they have demonstrable prospects of establishing a mine.

That task was very difficult for a new smaller miner because without a rail line they were not viable. The old chicken or egg argument. At the meeting between Carson and Adams and the departmental officers, the question of whether there was sufficient time to implement new legislation that year was discussed.

The departmental officers indicated that unless there was an early election, and provided Brian and I could help bring the Opposition on side, the passing of the *State Agreement Act* was just possible within that time frame. In that respect, I advised that we had already contacted John D'Orazio as head of the Parliamentary Public Accounts Committee and mining electorate MPs John Bowler and Matt Birney. We also suggested that Norman Moore, as the Opposition spokesman on resource matters, be approached.

Additionally, Forrest volunteered that he would contact Richard and Sir Charles Court to negotiate their public and private approval for the agreement act. The concept was to bring together a powerful body of support for the project as quickly as possible.

There was no doubt that it was an audacious proposal by any standard. Normally, such developments were only pursued by multibillion-dollar transnational companies, not financially challenged local entrepreneurs with a disappointing recent history.

This process saw a relationship develop between Forrest and Brian Burke. Forrest later somewhat surprisingly commented semi-publically that, "Brian Burke was a "national treasure" and that "he needed to be looked after". It was an affectionate remark and appeared to have been made sincerely.

Ironically, however, Brian did not commence the Forrest relationship as a "believer". He had real doubts about the FMG project. Nor was he initially enthusiastic to take on the consultancy with FMG. He gave some credibility to the sceptical views expressed by his friends and associates in sections of the financial media. They intimated the conviction that the FMG tenements contained unacceptably low-grade iron ore and that it was possible that the whole project was largely exaggerated.

However, not long after we commenced our consultancy with FMG, Brian was completely won over. He commented that Andrew Forrest was the best entrepreneur that he had ever encountered.

I later came to appreciate that when Forrest was around there was a sense of electric urgency about matters. He motivated people and he got things done.

The subject of rail and port access was always in play. Early on, Forrest had made the case that, given the geographic disposition of each company's tenements and the placement of rail lines and ports, there was an argument to be made for sharing infrastructure. It made sense, but it was never going to happen.

In that context, it is interesting to note a letter from Robin Chapple, the Greens WA party Member for Mining and Pastoral Region, supporting FMG's application to the National Competition Council. Chapple was then and remains today a prominent member of the Greens in WA. In view of the hardening Greens' attitude towards mining in this State, and towards Andrew Forrest in particular, it would be interesting to speculate whether Chapple, if requested, would write such a letter today.

Both Alannah MacTiernan, Minister for Planning, and Eric Ripper, Treasurer, were sounded out over a royalty concession in the event that FMG went ahead and built its own railway and port infrastructure. The advice back from the departmental officers was that both MacTiernan and Ripper were supportive of the royalty concession, as long as the concession phased out once the capital costs of the railway infrastructure had been recouped.

In July 2004, Clive Brown, the Minister for State Development, advised FMG he was prepared to take the matter to Cabinet.

In fact, Cabinet approval came quite quickly. ALP Members of Parliament such as Larry Graham (Pilbara) and Tom Stephens (Kimberley) were briefed and came on board supporting the State Agreement process. Julian Tapp handled the day-to-day negotiations with the department and Burke and Grill were brought in on various matters where problems arose.

However, on 15 August FMG received some bad news. We were told that Minister Brown and the Director General of the Department of Industry and Resources, Jim Limerick, had ruled that the State Agreement would need to be split in two: one for the mining operation and the second for the railway, port and other infrastructure needs.

That was not of great concern for FMG, but the worrying news was the view expressed by Brown that the agreement was being rushed and he did not wish it to proceed at this stage. This came as a considerable shock. According to the advice, Brown had said that the prospects of the agreement getting up prior to the end of the year were "300 to one".

Brian and I were told independently by officers within the department that BHP had been lobbying the Chamber of Minerals and Energy, the media and anybody else who would listen, including Brown, to argue that FMG should not be taken seriously and that the FMG proposal was strictly "not viable".

But our soundings within government indicated that the State Agreement could be in place by the end of the year. We further contacted people within the political process who were close to Brown to encourage him to persist with the expedited State Agreement process.

In that context, we communicated with Bill Johnston, the ex-secretary of the WA Branch of the ALP and the then MLA for Cannington (and later Resources Minister), and he agreed to speak to Brown.

We also advised Forrest we were aware that Mr Limerick was a conservative and cautious bureaucrat who was by nature risk averse. We could expect nothing but prudence from him; but there were other officers within the department who could be quite pro-active.

As it turned out, we were proved right. Vince Catania, the then ALP Legislative Council Member for Mining and Pastoral, was also briefed and lent his support to an expedited process.

Early on, in mid-August 2004, we realised that it was important to have the Opposition on side, and in that context we brought in former senator Noel Crichton-Browne as an additional lobbyist. Despite Crichton-Browne's estrangement from the Liberal Party, he retained some close friendships and associations.

There was always going to be war between FMG and BHP and in the early days it was perceived as an asymmetrical David and Goliath battle. But, as in the biblical tale, the agile David won the day. However, relations between FMG and BHP were never good. Forrest just had too much chutzpah for his own good.

Meanwhile, and throughout the process, there was continued media speculation on how Forrest intended to finance what now appeared to be a 40 million tonnes a year iron ore mining process with independent port and rail network.

There was significant scepticism concerning the grade of iron ore in the FMG deposits, the ability of Forrest to raise sufficient funds to exploit the resource and the question of take-off agreements for the iron ore. In *The West* of 21 of August 2004, it was incredulously reported as follows:

> Last week, Mr Forrest said FMG expected to fund its mine development plans by 'virtual equity' in the form of pre-payment for iron ore.

I concede that such airy-fairy statements did not do much to add to FMG's credibility. The funding arrangements at that time were just too vague to be taken seriously and there was no doubt that BHP would employ this vagueness as a weapon in what became a lobbying war between FMG and itself. If one took into account that, at that particular time, the market capitalisation of FMG was a very modest $78 million and it required $1.85 billion in either equity or loan funds to get the project going, it was clear that FMG had taken on a Herculean task.

Many believed that BHP and Rio Tinto had come to consider that the vastly rich Pilbara iron province was their own exclusive fiefdom.

Forrest had decided to challenge that hegemony. It was a very brave decision and was destined to antagonise some very powerful enemies.

FMG was advised by solicitor Gary Lauden, Damian Edwards, in-house Tenement Manager for FMG, and Malcolm McCusker QC.

For unrelated reasons, there was also opposition within Government to BHP and Rio Tinto on a broader political front. For instance, Tom Stephens, the former MLA for Pilbara complained in late September 2004 that the big two iron ore companies were not even paying rates on their tenements in the Pilbara municipalities where they operated and made a minimal contribution towards the community facilities. It was the beginnings of a movement that would culminate in the "royalties for regions" program under Nationals' leader Brendan Grylls some years later and would be echoed in Kevin Rudd's super profits tax.

Both Rio Tinto and BHP publicly mounted counter attacks directed at FMG.

On 22 September 2004, *The West* carried an article [145] featuring Leigh Clifford (one of the big hitters of the mining industry) from Rio Tinto under the headline "Rio chief lashes ore hopefuls" in what was essentially an attack on Andrew Forrest.

Mr Clifford said that these hopefuls had both a "glib" and "superficial" understanding of the question of infrastructure sharing. He went on to say:

> Though Rio's Pilbara business was highly efficient, its success hinged on the company having total control over all aspects of the business (meaning its rail and ports)... Those who see such infrastructure as a public good simply have not grasped the nature of our industry.

He also stated in the article:

> It is far from obvious that the industry cannot now meet the challenges that lie before it.

What Mr Clifford was asserting was that there was no need for, or room for, any other companies in the Pilbara iron ore trade.

This statement, from a touted expert, needs to be contrasted with the truth of what followed. That-reality was that Chinese demand almost immediately went through the roof, both Rio Tinto and BHP massively increased their export tonnages.

The Clifford comments make it clear that not only did the big two want to thwart third-party access to their rail and other infrastructure, but they intended to keep new Australian companies out of the market altogether. This attitude was made explicit in an article in *The*

---

[145] *The West Australian* 22 September 2004, p. 57.

West Australian of 23 September, where BHP's Iron Ore Manager Graeme Hunt (at that time, another exalted name in the industry) is quoted as mocking FMG's plans to set up a $1.8 billion mining and infrastructure project in the Pilbara. Mr Hunt said:

> To the best of our knowledge, it (FMG) has yet to prove sufficient resources at its Christmas Creek location to establish a mine, it has no mining leases, no State Agreements and no government approvals.[146]

Behind the scenes, BHP senior officials were hinting to anyone who would listen, that FMG was all smoke and mirrors and destined to fail.

Despite this BHP attack, the negotiations for the State Agreement proceeded with some small qualifications. Brian and I had painstakingly built up a body of support within the department and we had recently achieved a State Agreement for another client, so we knew the ropes.

Additionally, Julian Tapp turned out to be a gifted lobbyist in his own right. To almost everyone's surprise, a draft of the FMG's Pilbara Infrastructure Proprietary Limited Railway and Port Agreement was ready by 13 September 2004. This was all at a time when FMG corporately was still very frail.

A story in the *WA Business News* asked the question whether the FMG project was "another ambitious dream".[147] The same article reminded readers that Andrew Forrest had essentially failed with the Murrin Murrin (Anaconda) mining operation and as a result he had been ousted from the company in 2002. While the article conceded that Forrest had his supporters, it still gave the general impression that the Pilbara iron project was unlikely to get up.

During the month of October, various versions of the draft State Agreements were produced. It was not all plain sailing. The department was having difficulty in keeping a consistent line on timing. By the end of October, the State was maintaining that, as there was a linkage between the infrastructure agreement and the mining agree-

---

[146] *The West Australian*, 23 September 2004, p. 47.
[147] *WA Business News* 16-22 September 2004, by Jim Hawtin, pp. 1, 6.

ment, they would both have to be executed and ratified at the same time.

FMG correctly argued that the linkage would negate the benefit of the previously agreed two-stage process and that it would effectively delay the actual implementation of the critical infrastructure agreement. Minister Brown, in support of maintaining the linkage, gave an undertaking to Forrest that the mining agreement would be executed prior to Christmas.

Startlingly, almost immediately thereafter, Jim Limerick effectively countermanded his Minister's instruction and said that it was impossible for the department to have the agreement ready within that time line. Ultimately, in the spirit of compromise, FMG agreed that if Cabinet would approve the infrastructure agreement by 1 November 2004, the date for execution of the mining agreement could slip to 15 January 2005.

But there was an underlying concern about BHP's lobbying capacity and its reach within Government. Later events graphically demonstrated that BHP had very considerable lobbying clout, both within the department and with the Minister's office.

This was epitomised when Brown retired from Parliament on 26 February 2005. He immediately took up an unpublicised lobbying consultancy with BHP. It lasted for six months after his retirement.

Although legal at the time, such a lobbying contract is no longer accepted under the State's lobbying statute, which prescribes a one-year prohibition period after retirement of a minister.

I believe that, while legal, questions of appearances and ethics should have been considered even then. Brown later justified his actions by asserting that his BHP consultancy was approved by Premier Geoff Gallop. But his actions were kept confidential from the rest of the world.

It is important for me to indicate that I have no evidence that Brown did anything improper at this time. He has never been other than honest, in my experience. However, it is my strong sentiment that the appointment with BHP should never have been allowed.

As the date for the last parliamentary sittings in 2004 approached, the question of whether there was sufficient time to pass the infrastructure agreement through both houses before Christmas became critical. Brian and I realised that the legislation could not be negotiated through Parliament without active cooperation of the Liberal-National Party Opposition.

This was where Noel Crichton-Browne's old Liberal Party associates came to the fore, especially in the upper house where his former colleague Norman Moore was the Leader of the Opposition. The Opposition commanded a majority in that house and could set the order of business. It was agreed by Moore that the Coalition would give support to expediting the legislation.

Cabinet had approved the Infrastructure State Agreement on 6 November and Minister Brown had issued the press release announcing that fact. The statement gave special mention to the detail that the new 520km railway to be built from FMG mines to Port Hedland would be multi-user third-party access infrastructure.

While this was highly encouraging, we were receiving advice through the officers of the department that the Minister had not given any go-ahead for the linked Mining Agreement. That was puzzling, as the operation of the Infrastructure Agreement depended on the execution and ratification by Parliament of the Mining Agreement.

What invariably happens at the end of a parliamentary year is that legislation begins to bank up and comes on to the notice paper with a rush. It means late and sometimes all-night sittings of Parliament. It often results in legislation being left over until the next session.

As time went on in late November, it became apparent that the Infrastructure State Agreement could well meet that fate and be delayed into 2005 under the Government timetable. In this end-of-year situation, what often happens is that there is a hiatus where the Upper House sits around doing very little waiting for legislation to be passed in the Lower House.

What we decided to do, with the cooperation of the Opposition and the state bureaucrats, was reverse the normal legislative process and put the Infrastructure State Agreement through the upper house first. Consequently, the agreement was listed for debate in the Upper House on 22 November and ultimately passed through both houses of Parliament that session. This procedure came as a surprise to the Government, but was quite legitimate.

The accelerated process set a record for a State Agreement of this nature and Minister Brown was himself stunned at the speed of progress. Remember that Brown had told Forrest (on 15 August) that the odds of legislating an agreement before the end of the year were 300 to 1 against.

In November 2004, at the time the Infrastructure State Agreement went to the Lower House, Brown told Norm Marlborough:

> I can't understand how this legislation got before Parliament so quickly. It has surprised me. There appears to be some other forces at work here.

Marlborough told me this in a private conversation at the time and has repeated it on several occasions since.

The speed of passage did not impress either Rio Tinto or BHP. They were outraged. In a story by John Phaceas on the front page of the business section of *The West Australian* on 11 November 2004, under the headline "State miners at odds with FMG" it was stated:

> BHP and Rio Tinto, which together paid more than $550 million to the State last year, were seething yesterday that the State Government had fast tracked approval of the State Agreement for the port and rail development plans of Mr Forrest's Fortescue Minerals Group.

The story quoted Premier Gallop as supporting the agreement. The story continued:

> Both BHP and Rio believe that government has become too close to FMG, which has been advised by former Labor powerbrokers and professional lobbyists Brian Burke and Julian Grill.

Nor did it please BHP and Rio Tinto that the Government had also thrown its support behind FMG in its application to the NCC for access to Rio Tinto and BHP's railway and port infrastructure. This trenchant public accusation of partisanship by Rio Tinto against the Government, and the singling out of Burke and Grill for special comment, was clear evidence of a new and more aggressive lobbying posture by the two major iron ore producers. They were effectively throwing down the gauntlet to FMG. It would be a fight to the finish, with the continued existence of FMG at stake.

I should point out that the realignment of government support behind FMG was not primarily due to the efforts of Brian and me. We detected in our various discussions with senior officers within the department – including Noel Ashcroft, who later became WA's Agent General in London – that there was a deep-seated frustration within a significant number of the department's officers. They thought that the two big companies were arrogantly thumbing their nose at government ambitions for shared infrastructure, treated the Pilbara as their own exclusive domain and were indifferent to value-adding to their raw material.

They were also disturbed that Rio Tinto and BHP royalty concessions continued for long after the capital costs of the mines and infrastructure were recouped.

While the negotiations over the State Agreement were going on and proceedings were afoot before the NCC, Forrest had also ramped up progress on the construction and financing fronts. The progress that he had made since buying into FMG in July 2003 had been breakneck and breathtaking. He was a fearless risk-taker and a compelling motivator.

As an aside, I would mention that I saw his profound faith in God at work on two occasions.

The first was when he was negotiating by telephone with the Tasmanian Independent senator Brian Harradine over an aspect of legislation affecting the Anaconda development. Forrest was able to make a connection with Senator Harradine through faith that I had not witnessed before and which astonished me. The second was when he built a chapel at Anaconda and thereby brought the deeply religious local Indigenous community firmly onside.

I suspect that this faith allowed him to take chances that other businessmen would avoid.

Within a period of a few months, he had negotiated the first iron ore off-take agreements. He had entered into an agreement with China's largest construction company, China Engineering Railway Corporation, to build the Pilbara rail infrastructure, then secured financial support from JP Morgan Fleming. The share price had gone up from about 25 cents to about 90 cents by October 2004, but escalated to $2.40 by the middle of November.

The support the WA Government put behind FMG with the State Agreements had worked magic. Chinese companies such as Jiangsu Fengli and others now clamoured to invest in, and enter into iron ore agreements with, FMG. It had all happened just as Brian and I had predicted before we first met the FMG executive on the subject on 5 July 2004.

But you cannot take any credit away from Forrest as he later turned that State Government support into hard financial agreements.

In effect, the Chinese Government-connected agencies would ultimately put up 90 per cent of the $1.85 billion cost of developing the new iron ore mines and building the 400km rail line and port. Overnight in November of 2004, Forrest became one of the richest people in Australia.

Contemporaneously, Gina Hancock's rival Hope Downs Project, which had been more advanced (in 2004/5) in terms of resource definition and partners (Anglo American, Kumba Resources) was out-paced. Our advice from other informed sources was that the Chinese, always more comfortable dealing on a government-to-government basis, became quite enthusiastic about the project once they knew that FMG was being supported against Rio and BHP. A graph of FMG's share price shows that it took off like a rocket.

However, the process did not end there. Gradually, over the weeks and months, Brian Burke and I became more and more enmeshed in the operations of FMG.

'Binding contracts' causes problems

On a fateful 5 November 2004, Forrest and FMG issued a press statement stating:

> Binding contracts announced and signed this afternoon in Beijing commit Chinese financing and construction support for the Australian $1.85 billion iron ore and infrastructure project proposed by FMG.

It was a use of words that would later come home to haunt Forrest and change the structure of FMG. Brian and I were not aware of the press release at the time, but the use of the words "binding contracts" caused immense problems for FMG and for Forrest personally in the months and years to come.

At this time, BHP and Rio Tinto were enhancing an already very strong adverse campaign against Forrest. Additionally, there was conspicuous evidence that large sections of the financial media continued to have considerable doubt about the ability of the project to succeed. It meant the continuation of a very threatening atmosphere for the would-be miner. The backdrop to this new dangerous situation for FMG was vicious corporate politics.

On 26 February 2005, the State Government went to the polls. The Gallop Labor Government was returned, but Clive Brown did not seek re-election. His position of Minister for State Development was taken by Alan Carpenter.

This development was to have important implications for FMG.

On 3 February 2005, Julie O'Donoghue, the lead departmental negotiator on the Mining State Agreement with FMG, while discussing a range of problems relating to the mining agreement, including physical access to Port Hedland port, said that there was "no political will" (my emphasis) to overcome the problems or to get the second State Agreement (mining) up.

It was a very enigmatic statement and she refused to enlarge upon it. My belief is that she was alerting FMG to the possibility that the parliamentary road ahead may be rocky. Perhaps that state of affairs could be attributed to the amplified lobbying effort by BHP.

I was later disturbed by the fact that Brown had taken a contract with BHP immediately after retiring from the Ministry. He had told me personally that he had been engaged on a short six-month contract with a resource company. He did not name the company, but I understood that it was BHP. I make it clear that I have no evidence and I don't suggest that he worked on FMG related matters.

FMG's financial model had a critical path which required the first shipments of iron ore to commence early in 2007. As problems of access and delay mounted up, it started to threaten that timetable, the financial model and, as a consequence, the whole viability of the project.

The question of the "binding contract" statement started to come to the fore when the Chinese parties commenced a vigorous process to persuade Forrest to grant them an enhanced equity stake in the FMG project.

After the first Infrastructuree State Agreement went through, Forrest resisted this coercion as he was then in a relatively stronger position. But as part of this intense negotiation process the Chinese were prepared to play hardball.

It was at about this time that allegations were raised in the financial media that the agreements with the Chinese were not binding at all. This was a stunning allegation, as much of the progress of the FMG project was premised on the binding nature of those contracts. The allegation electrified the media, which could now smell Forrest's blood. If proved, this was a significant corporate crime.

On 28 March 2005, *The West* ran a major story on page 32 (the front page of its business section) under the headline: "Chinese run ruler over rival ore plans".

The suggestion was that the Chinese were walking away from the project. FMG's share price began to fall dramatically. To the financially uninitiated that may sound relatively inconsequential, but in reality it could be cataclysmic as the FMG project was at that stage mostly unfunded and share price is one of the basic determinants of future funding.

A few days later, on 31 March, *The West* once again on the front page of its business section ran the sceptical headline: "I did not mislead: Forrest".

The question of the "binding nature" of the Chinese contract was now starting to become very serious. In a smaller story on the same page under the headline "Questions over exchanges role", John Phaceas, who had written the main story, queried whether the investors had sufficient information to make a judgement about the nature of the contracts between FMG and the Chinese.

Of course, Phaceas was raising a very critical question. One which would be pursued by ASIC, the corporate watchdog, and result in court proceedings commencing against FMG and Andrew Forrest personally that could have seen him banned as a director of an ASIC listed company.

It was readily apparent to financial insiders that FMG's future was very much in the balance. Phaceas' stories of Thursday, 31 March 2005, echoed in other financial papers, caused a major crisis for FMG. *The West's* stories of 31 March reported "industry news service Steel Business Bulletin claimed that two Chinese steel mills were also denying that the supply deals struck with FMG last year were legally binding".

Those allegations saw FMG's share price fall from $5.55 to $3.19 in two weeks.

Worse was to come. *The West's* editorial of 1 April was devoted to the question of the "binding nature" of the contracts. The headline "Questions over Fortescue deal are no help to WA's reputation", started:

> Escalating disquiet about the details of the deals struck between FMG Chief Andrew Forrest and the Chinese consortium is damaging the State's reputation as a place to do business. FMG investors are faced with heavy paper losses …

The editorial claimed that the use of the words "binding contracts" was misleading. It suggested that Forrest had been dishonest. This assertion considerably raised the stakes by turning the issue into one of national prestige and standing. Forrest now had his back to the wall and was forced either to fight or go under (for the second time).

To give you some flavour of the precarious situation FMG was now in, and the miserable atmosphere that pervaded, I quote briefly from a two-page story by Phaceas in *The West* under the headline: "Twiggy's buoyant fortune at breaking point". It was almost as though Phaceas was writing Forrest's epitaph:

> The spectacular fall from grace over the last week of his latest business foray – Fortescue Metals Groups grandiose plans for a $1.85 billion iron ore mine, railway and port empire in the Pilbara – has created a sense of *deja vu* on St Georges Terrace.[148]

Mark Drummond, *The West's* Chief Reporter, wrote a similar story under the headline: "Share hustler or pioneer with vision?".[149]

In the *Australian Financial Review* of the same day (page 15), veteran journalist Trevor Sykes had a full-page story under the heading: "How Forrest got burned by the dragon".

Sykes appreciated instinctively that the real issue was a power play by the Chinese Government agency to lever more equity in the project. The first paragraph of the article went as follows:

> On the face of it, the Chinese have Andrew Forrest over a barrel. He faces the choice of either surrendering majority control of his cherished Fortescue Metals or have the grandiose project stalled indefinitely.

Later in the story Sykes commented:

> Fortescue – talking big and sitting on a tiny equity base – was a soft target.

Forrest properly treated the matter as a major crisis and it later became public knowledge, because of the CCC hearings, that he reacted by calling an emergency meeting of his senior people on Saturday 2 April 2005. This was crunch time. At the suggestion of Brian

---

[148] *The West Australian* 2 April 2005, pp. 14-15.
[149] Ibid.

Burke, the meeting was arranged at a little cafe opposite my residence in Mount Street, West Perth. The venue was chosen to allow easy attendance by Marlborough, Burke and myself, but was immediately adjourned for privacy reasons to the less public nearby apartment of in-house lawyer Peter Huston.

At the meeting there was tension in the air. We were all digesting the grave media attack of that very morning. There were no recriminations, but it was a long and difficult meeting where far-reaching decisions were taken. I shall not disclose the discussion that took place, but, as a lawyer, I took particular notice that Mr Huston bravely continued to maintain (as he did at previous senior executive meetings where Brian and I were present) that the sales contracts were legally binding.

Shortly after this meeting the following public actions took place:

1. Forrest stood down as Chairman and was replaced with Gordon Toll.
2. Forrest met with the new Minister for State Development and the Premier, with a view to confirming and strengthening the satisfactory position taken by Alan Carpenter in respect to FMG on the State Agreement (Mining) and the NCC proceedings.
3. The Opposition was briefed on the situation by Noel Crichton-Browne.
4. Grill contacted *The West's* John Phaceas to discuss the affair and present FMG's perspective.
5. A conciliatory, explanatory letter was sent by Forrest to *The West Australian*.
6. The relevant Chinese companies were requested to confirm that the sale contracts were binding.

These open actions amounted to a public relations and lobbying exercise to garner support within the media and within government, and show the Chinese that Forrest would fight.

The obvious goals were to emphasise the *bona fides* of the FMG project, the importance of breaking the Rio-BHP duopoly in the

Pilbara, expose the real motives of the Chinese and stress the importance to the WA economy of establishing a third major iron ore company in the State.

Importantly, the Chinese companies immediately cooperated as they appreciated the dire situation Forrest was now in and that it was not in their interest to see FMG fail. The truth was that the Chinese needed FMG as a market counterfoil to BHP and Rio. Accordingly, they made public statements indicating their continued support for the contracts.

These statements were picked up by Phaceas in *The West* and the other business media almost immediately on 4 April.

I had spoken at some length to Phaceas and I was hopeful that I had made some impact.

Andrew Forrest met with the new Minister for State Development, Alan Carpenter, on 8 April 2005. To our great relief Carpenter played the issue with a straight bat. The reportage of that meeting in the media and a strong letter by Carpenter on 14 April 2005 helped to stabilise FMG.

The decisions taken at the crisis meeting were beginning to pay off, as the share price started to rise again.

An article by Drummond on 9 April 2005 and a further story by Phaceas on 15 April indicated that the paper was taking a more sympathetic line on FMG.

The immediate crisis was thus averted, but the legal question of "binding contracts" was to dog FMG and Forrest for some years. ASIC pressed on with the proceedings, firstly in the Federal Court in 2009 before Justice John Gilmour, who found in Forrest's favour. Next in the Federal Appeals Court in 2011 where Gilmour's decision was overturned and, finally, in the High Court of Australia in October 2012, where FMG and Forrest were ultimately exonerated.

It was a long grinding business, but in the final analysis Peter Huston's dogged determination to stand by his opinion that the "contracts were binding" was vindicated.

But Forrest's opponents were far from finished. A fair assessment in mid-2005 was that the future of FMG continued to be dubious and it appeared for some time that Forrest's combined antagonists could pull him down.

In the interim, BHP and Rio, jacked up the price of iron ore on the international market by 70 per cent and signalled further possible increases in price. Chip Goodyear, BHP's CEO, was pressing for a 100 per cent increase.[150]

How did this fit in with the official BHP position that there was no room in the industry for new players? The price increase certainly raised the stakes and caused media speculation that it made FMG an attractive buy-out target. But it was also serendipitous, as it motivated the Chinese to ensure that FMG did not fail.

But FMG remained under close scrutiny by the financial media and the regulatory authorities. In *The West* on 2 May 2005, Phaceas referred to the fact that FMG had been quizzed by the ASX in respect to its categorisation of shipping grade ore.

On 9 May, also in *The West*, Neale Prior ran a big story under the headline: "Exchange pressures Forrest on cost, ore". The story referred to a blowout in some costs in the FMG project and mentioned the "troubled Pilbara iron ore and infrastructure project".

In the meantime, the war between BHP and Rio Tinto on the one side and Forrest and Gina Rinehart on the other, in respect to third-party access to infrastructure was unremitting.

In July 2005, Forrest's perceived rival, Rinehart's Hancock Prospecting, changed course and compromised with the giant Rio, entering into an agreement with the titan to develop the huge Hope Downs deposit, a legacy from Lang Hancock's estate. They were to be 50/50 partners.

It was seen by the media as doing little if anything to weaken the Rio-BHP stranglehold on the Pilbara. It was perceived as a coup for Sam Walsh, the CEO of Rio.

Also in July of 2005, FMG was hit with considerable problems relating to environment and EPA approvals. The initial focus of attention was the mangroves that might have to be removed in Port

---

[150] *The Australian Financial Review* 13 April 2005, p. 63.

Hedland harbour. Additionally, it was reported in *The West Australian* of 13 August that: "Fortescue faces a tussle over native title deal".

The story, once again by Phaceas, stated:

> Andrew Forrest's Fortescue Metals Group is facing a fresh battle to develop its $2 billion plus Pilbara iron ore project, with the Pilbara Native Title Service accusing the company of unconscionable conduct over a land access deal signed this week.

In the body of the story, Phaceas wrote:

> There has clearly been no informed consent given by the Nyiyatarli people under these alleged agreements.

Phaceas appeared to be setting himself up as an immediate authority and arbiter on Native Title matters. It was just one more debilitating attack on FMG's credibility. FMG maintained that the agreement had been negotiated fairly, with the full knowledge and consent of the Aboriginal people.

While the issue lingered for quite some time, nothing ever came of the allegations of unconscionable conduct. Much of the background briefing to the journalists on the Native Title issue appeared to come from sources close to BHP.

In respect to the NCC hearings over third-party access to the BHP infrastructure, by 4 November 2005 FMG was tipped by the media to win.[151]

Importantly, both the Gallop and Carpenter Governments supported FMG's application to have the Mt Newman-Hedland line "declared" for open access. In brief, the government submission to the NCC stated:

> The government is of the view that the services to which FMG is seeking access satisfy all of the criteria for declaration.

---

[151] *The West Australian* 'Forrest Tipped to Score Rail Win Over BHP' by Mark Drummond 4 November 2005, p. 4.

Although successive governments had always been inclined to support third-party access to BHP and Rio Tinto infrastructure, they had never previously made such a strong submission to a tribunal.

Our lobbying efforts extended to the Federal Opposition in the persons of Martin Ferguson, Joel Fitzgibbon and Stephen Smith. It is public knowledge that Julian Tapp and I made more than one trip to Canberra for that purpose.

As a consequence, on 23 January 2006 the *Australian Financial Review* (AFR) reported under the headline "Labor backs BHP on rail line", that:

> Labor has strongly supported BHP Billiton retaining control of its Mt Newman iron ore railway. But Labor is also seeking a mechanism to force the world's biggest miner and small player Fortescue Metals Group to negotiate iron haulage on the Mt Newman railway.

The story quoted resources spokesman Martin Ferguson who said, "haulage negotiations would force BHP Billiton to act".

While this was encouraging in one sense, Ferguson also exhibited lingering scepticism concerning FMG's motivation and viability, as he went on to say it was "also testing whether Fortescue was a genuine miner or just playing games in a bid to be bought out".[152]

There was still plenty of healthy doubt about FMG, but the Labor Party owed BHP and Rio Tinto no favours and appeared to be prepared to give Forrest a chance.

At the same time, Crichton-Browne lobbied Peter Costello through his old colleagues for support of FMG. However, political incredulity was shared with, and fanned by, the media, which continued to doubt the essential viability of Forrest's project. An article by Jennifer Hewett in the AFR stated:

> It's crunch time for the man they call Twiggy as the funding deadline for his iron ore venture looms.

---

[152] *The Australian Financial Review*, "Labor backs BHP on rail line", 23 January 2006, p. 2.

The story was run under the headline: "Forrest out of the woods, but not home yet".[153]

Although it was presented as a pun, it was correct, as the FMG project remained largely unfunded. Hewett was not unfair, but like the rest of the media she was fashionably sceptical.

The problems for FMG continued to come unabated during 2006. It was as though the project was never destined to get a clear run.

In the meantime, ASIC had commenced proceedings, claiming FMG had engaged in deceiving and misleading conduct with the "binding contracts" statement referred to above. At the same time, Phaceas continued to write articles in *The West* suggesting that FMG was under financial pressure and might fold.[154]

On 20 May 2006, there came a bolt out of the blue. A story in *The West Australian* by Phaceas, under the headline: "Ripper asks Costello to reject Fortescue". It announced that the State Government had dramatically changed its position on third-party access. The sub-headline stated: "First it backed Rio Tinto, now the State Government is dancing to BHP Billiton's tune".

This eleventh-hour about face by the Government was a nasty surprise to FMG. Deputy Premier Eric Ripper said that the State Government did not want to see the National Competition Council declare BHP railway line under Commonwealth legislation, but wanted to start direct negotiations with BHP for "a state-based access regime for haulage services".

The State Government had been fruitlessly endeavouring to negotiate such an outcome with BHP for at least 20 years and should have been well aware that BHP was not likely to agree to such a scenario. Of course, no such "state-based regime" ever materialised.

The fact that this dramatic change of direction took place just prior to Treasurer Costello giving a ruling on the NCC recommendation pointed to a very heavy lobbying process on the part of BHP within government as a whole.

---

[153] *The Australian Financial Review*, 8 February 2006 by Jennifer Hewett, p. 45.
[154] *The West Australian*, 29 March 2006, p. 45.

On 22 May, another bombshell was dropped by Treasurer Costello when, despite two years of research and toil by the NCC, he overturned the NCC's recommendation in favour of FMG by refusing to "declare" the BHP railway for use by third parties.

That decision by Costello appeared to entrench the lucrative duopoly of the mining kings BHP and Rio Tinto and proved that the high-powered lobbying effort by BHP was extremely potent.

At the same time, it underlined the crucial nature of the "new strategy" adopted by FMG when Burke and Grill came on board. Without that "new strategy", whereby FMG owned its own rail and port infrastructure pursuant to a State Agreement, Costello's decision would have closed the curtain on Forrest's Pilbara dreams.

Additionally, every little approval required pursuant to the Mining State Agreement between the State and FMG was delayed for a host of technical reasons. Until all of these small matters were decided, it was legally impossible for FMG to commence work on their mining tenements.

It had always been my belief that there was a dichotomy within DOIR: on one side, those officers who supported the *status quo* and the big two; on the other, those who supported new entrants. The Government's reaction confirmed my belief when the Government and the department were reluctant to see the agreement terminated.

The State simply vacillated.

These matters were critical because Forrest was in the process of raising funds (reportedly $2.5 billion) to continue to finance the project.[155] The department was aware that these delays were critical to FMG, but it refused to expedite matters.

However, notwithstanding this host of bureaucratic delays, on 15 August 2006 Forrest was able to report that he had been successful with a major $2.7 billion debt package to finance the project. It was a tribute to his drive, staying power and salesmanship.

This was a fairy tale outcome. Australia had never seen anything

---

[155] *The West Australian*, 5 July 2006, p. 51.

like it. Sir Charles Court had determined that the Pilbara iron ore province was for the massive transnationals and that had led to deadly enmity between Lang Hancock and Court.

Impoverished individuals such as Andrew Forrest were not supposed to beat the system and develop giant new projects. Reporter Michael Weir in *The West Australian* correctly stated:

> Fortescue's bond issue represents *the last and most important step in the funding of its $3.7 billion Pilbara iron ore project* (emphasis added).[156]

Forrest was extremely grateful for the work and effort that Brian and I had put in on his behalf. An email that he sent to us on 14 August 2006 stated:

> I had an email written to you, but was a little emotional to send it on Friday, soon after the deal closed. In the end I started it again.
>
> I just wanted to express my gratitude deeply for the work and innovation of you both. Thank you very much.

Julian Tapp had previously written to Brian and me:

> Gentlemen, your advice and support has been invaluable. Thank you.

Since then, the 45mtpa (million tonnes per annum) operation has been expanded several times and the management has steadily brought down the operational costs so that it is one of the lowest cost operators in the world.

In short, we were very happy to be part of a winning team. However, with the CCC commencing public hearings into Smiths Beach in 2007, events were soon to take a very unpleasant turn for us. Those dramatic events, and being abruptly cut adrift by Andrew Forrest, were very depressing.

However, in hindsight, and putting the experience of working with Forrest in perspective, it was hard not to feel some satisfaction. The great winners were the citizens of Australia. Rivers of gold, by

---

[156] *The West Australian*, 15 August 2006, p. 42.

way of an array of taxes and royalties, have flowed to governments from well before operations commenced.

One might criticise the brashness of entrepreneurs like Andrew Forrest, but they are the people who build nations.

16

BRIAN BURKE – THE 'GODFATHER'

No Australian public figure has been so trenchantly and incessantly condemned and publicly excoriated as Brian Burke. In that sense alone, he is unequalled.

A number of books and countless articles have been written about him.

The books include: *Burkie*, by John Hamilton; *Burke's Shambles: Parliamentary Contempt in the Wild West*, by Anthony McAdam and Patrick O'Brien; *The Years of Scandal: Commissions of Inquiry in Western Australia 1990-2004*, edited by Allan Peachment; *The Burkes of Western Australia*, by Brian Peachey; *The Burke Ambush: Corporatism and Society in Western Australia*, by Patrick O'Brien; *The Business of Government: Western Australia 1983-1990*, edited by Allan Peachment; and *The Godfather: The Life of Brian Burke*, which I discuss in some detail below.

In 2018, Brian Burke released his autobiography, *A Tumultuous Life*, which, in part, sets about debunking the false allegations made in some of these books. It also provides an entertaining account of his most interesting life and career as a successful politician, strong family man and notable Australian.

It is no over-estimation to conclude that Brian makes good copy. Most of the material in the biographies and articles is highly unflattering of him. Much is vicious and malicious. Rarely is it accurate or fair. He has been good for cartoonists, too. They have cruelly exploited his bald dome, and his sad (previous) obesity.

If he has transgressed, the scribes and the caricaturists have made him pay and pay, and extracted a terrible toll. Prison, social exclusion, years of being the pariah, family shame and political expulsion have been his lot.

The years since 1988 have not been easy for Brian Burke. He has lost his lobbying and company advisory business, was unemployable, has consumed most of his finances on the CCC's public and secret hearings, and in defending 14 CCC-inspired criminal charges.

I am not sure how he supports himself and his wife. He has no parliamentary pension.

It is well publicised that the Brian Burke and Julian Grill lobbying business was decidedly profitable, but most of the high-profile companies that beat a path to our doors abruptly departed in late 2006 when the CCC commenced its extraordinarily well-promoted Smiths Beach public and secret hearings, moved on to the much more extensive "Lobbyists" terms of reference, and the WA Parliament (at the behest of the CCC) established its own politically-charged Committees of Inquiry.

History shows that all of this highly frenetic activity, which was followed greedily in a scandal-maddened media, was succeeded by more than 50 highly dubious criminal charges. This quasi-judicial and blatantly political activity was all dressed up in pseudo legal garb, but it had the propensity to result in long prison terms and so required full-time legal representation.

Good legal representation does not come cheap. Over nearly eight years from 2006 to February 2014, it ran into millions of dollars for Brian and me.

As a consequence, he and I were slowly bled dry. In 2006, Brian was starting the process of planning and constructing a new house in the Perth northern suburb of Trigg. Such was the financial drain on him and his angelic wife, Sue, that the bank was threatening foreclosure on the uncompleted house.

Brian doesn't live on charity, but I have noticed that he has to be careful.

The last book written about him, *The Godfather: The Life of Brian Burke*, was authored by Quentin Beresford, an academic in political science at Edith Cowan University. It was published in 2008 by Allen and Unwin and capitalised on the CCC inquiries.

Friends and associates of Brian, like me, refused invitations to contribute as they feared that it would be a sensationalised hatchet job.

Brian rejected an opportunity to bestow his imprimatur on the exercise. It was also a time, with the impending CCC charges, when it was fully expected by many in the media that both he and I would go to jail.

The process to that time, in both the CCC and parliamentary inquiries, had deprived Brian and me of any notice of the so-called evidence, denying us the opportunity to give explanation of it or deliver any testimony in rebuttal. It was also a process that was deeply unjust for another reason: we had little if any idea of what we were being accused.

According to sworn evidence of the chief CCC investigating officer, Mark Ingham, we were deliberately kept in the dark about what the underlying CCC accusations were because the CCC wanted to take us by surprise in the witness box!

The compilation of the Beresford book also came before Parliamentary Inspector Malcolm McCusker QC had completed his rebuttal of the sensational findings about public servants made by the CCC, and before Mr McCusker's strong criticism of the methods, false assumptions and unfair procedures employed by CCC officers during the Smiths Beach term of reference.

Additionally, it was largely prior to the criminal allegations against Brian Burke, me and our associates being subjected to the cold hard requirement of factual evidence.

Defamatory observations about us were coming so thick and fast at the time that they were too hard to document, let alone respond to.

Beresford did not let his publishers down. But, as I illustrate below, his research and analytical skills were poor for an academic, and even his memory let him down.

His book wasted no time in slating Brian. The title, *The Godfather*, set the scene. It epitomised and brought to mind the highly toxic mental images of the Mafioso, with all of the associated metaphors of graft, illegality, corruption and murder. Tucked away in the last paragraph of the Acknowledgements section of the book, Beresford denies that he means these inferences apply to Brian Burke.

However, the disclaimer is no better than the fine print in a shonky contract. Few are expected to read it. Beresford clearly was aware of the detrimental implication of his title, but used it nonetheless.

Did Beresford impartially lay out any of the facts in his book and invite the reader to draw conclusions? No, that was not his way. In the seven-page Introduction to the book, Beresford shows his true colours and goes about as good a character assassination of Brian Burke as one could possibly imagine. The flow of derogatory words and traducement is torrential.

Beresford is nuclear in his demolition of Brian's character. Without producing any evidence to support the description, Beresford refers to him as the "hatchet man", writes of his "nefarious lobbying activities", his "influence peddling", his "string pulling", and his "acting as a mole for business in the very bowels of government" (that despite the fact that Brian had been out of Government for 15 years before he became a lobbyist).

Beresford refers to Brian Burke as a "dodgy character", a "malevolent influence", "a person whose public persona concealed his private actions", a person who had an unhealthy "fascination for both wealth and power" and whose "secretive dealings" resulted in "staggering billion dollar losses to the taxpayer".

The accusation of "losing billions of dollars" is a serious defamation in its own right. Unfortunately, it is an urban myth that Beresford and Allan and Unwin were either too lazy to check, or they simply didn't care.

The little-known truth about Premier Burke's so-called "deal making" is that the transactions left the State overwhelmingly better off financially.

It is correct that the State lost $175 million on the Rothwells Merchant Bank bailout, which was triggered by the 1987 Stock Market Crash when Brian was Premier. However, it cannot correctly be called a deal. Its genesis was a government guarantee of additional private sector funding while Rothwells tried to work out its problems.

It was approved by a properly constituted Cabinet meeting with only one dissent. It was supported by most of the media, the Chamber of Commerce and the National Party, and not formally opposed by the Parliamentary Liberals.

The guarantee saved important institutions such as the Catholic education system and several municipal councils, as well as "mom and dad" investors. And it was a much smaller bailout than occurred in Victoria at about the same time when its state bank was faced with bankruptcy. That bank was taken over and rescued by the Commonwealth Bank (1990) after intervention of then Prime Minister Paul Keating. It was also much smaller than the later (1991) calamitous failure of the state bank of South Australia.

It was tiny when compared with the guarantee by Prime Minister Kevin Rudd of Australia's banks during the Global Financial Crisis (GFC) of 2007/8, and miniscule compared with US President Barack Obama's similar efforts in America.

Typically, Beresford gives no factual details of how Premier Burke's supposed $1 billion losses occurred. One can only guess that he may have been referring to the $1 billion loss by the State on the PICL (Petrochemical Industries Company Limited) project.

Large sections of the media have ascribed this loss to Brian because it was embarked upon by the Dowding Government to negate the probable loss on Rothwells. The dubious logic was that if the Dowding Government hadn't been faced with a loss on Rothwells it would not have embarked upon PICL.

That probably is correct, but it is an erroneous leap of logic to suggest that Brian Burke would have launched the PICL project in partnership with the Bond Corporation. That was strictly the action of the Dowding Government, which executed it with the help of consultants Malcolm Turnbull and former NSW Premier Neville Wran. Brian had no knowledge of, or part in, the PICL project.

The problem with most of the malignant stories run at that time was that they were not supported by credible evidence. The journalists must have thought that the taxpayer-funded (to the tune of tens of millions of dollars) CCC would do all the heavy lifting and supply all the justifying hard facts.

Well, that is not how it ultimately worked out. True, the CCC did do some misconceived investigation. With multi-millions of taxpayer-funded dollars, the CCC unleashed the most intrusive and extensive set of covert surveillance, confidential and public hearings, criminal prosecutions and investigations over nine years. This represented one of the biggest forensic inquiries ever seen in the State.

But the initial high-profile public allegations of impropriety that electrified the Australian media fell to the ground and were dropped. No prosecutions of matters of substance were successful. The incriminating evidence did not materialise.

Lack of hard evidence did not stop Beresford. He resorted to the broad-brush smear. That is obloquy of the worst kind, without the facts to support it.

Beresford was not on his own. Premier Geoff Gallop banned Burke and Grill from lobbying without a shred of public justification and without any process of inquiry to legitimise the action. Gallop considered it sufficient to refer to us as "poisonous". Premier Alan Carpenter later used the term "toxic" for the same process.

In the introduction to *The Godfather*, Beresford accuses Brian Burke of the full spectrum of political crimes. He insinuates that Brian "gained personal benefit from donations" even though a court of law had expressly found that that was not the case. Beresford claims that in our lobbying business, Brian "ruthlessly exploited contacts in the State Labor Government and bent the processes of government decision-making to achieve outcomes for his clients".

Relevantly, Beresford does not indicate who was "ruthlessly exploited" or where or how the government decision-making was "bent".

Beresford claims that Brian was "a masterful but deceitful lobbyist", but gives no indication of "deceit". Beresford asserts that, "Burke's character goes beyond a Machiavellian framework". It is a very dramatic contention, but once again he produces no facts to support it.

'Old money' turns hostile

Leading up to his five-year premiership and during that period from February 1983 to February 1988, Brian Burke made two sets of trenchant enemies. The first was Perth's old money establishment that had previously controlled WA business and politics. They had not been impressed when Ray O'Connor succeeded Sir Charles Court. They were privately hostile when Burke became Premier.

Two events epitomise this disaffection. The first was the setting up of the John Curtin Foundation, touched on in page 60 of *The Godfather*. Beresford refers to it as a "new elite" and correctly brands it "essentially a fund raising body for the Labor Party". He mentions Vice-Patrons such as Alan Bond, Laurie Connell, John Roberts from Multiplex, Sir James McCusker (head of Town and Country Building Society), mining magnate Ric Stowe and former Perth Lord Mayor Sir Ernest Lee-Steere.

It also loosely embraced Lang Hancock, who believed that Charles Court had tried to lock him out of the Pilbara iron ore province in favour of big money from overseas.

This was the first time that the ALP, anywhere in Australia, had put together such an illustrious and wealthy support group. The old Perth money saw it as traitorous and the ruling class wing of the Liberal Party was affronted. The hard Left wing of the Labor Party was appalled, but accepted the money.

The second matter that exemplified the hatred that existed between Brian Burke and elements of the old Perth establishment and which inflamed that animosity was the provocative "four on the floor entrepreneurs" remark made on several occasions by Premier Burke. These remarks amounted to a homage to entrepreneurs who were now spearheading WA development and risk capital generally. It was also an uncomplimentary critique of the contribution being made by Perth's traditional, insipid and risk-averse old money.

The Perth establishment had never been taken on in such a forthright way and Burke's remarks created quite a stir and no small amount of rancour. It needs to be borne in mind that from Federation until about that time, in terms of state revenue as against state expenditure, WA could not pay its own way and was forever being fiscally bailed out by the Commonwealth Grants Commission.

However, the new entrepreneurs were building a new dynamic

WA that could more than pay its own way. The "four on the floor" comment was both brave and naïve. Many of the "old money" people had lots of influence and long memories. They lay in wait.

Another powerful group that Burke irrevocably distressed was the hard Left wing of the WA Labor Party. The Broad Left, as it was known, had dominated Labor politics since shortly after the Second World War until Brian Burke took over leadership of the State Parliamentary Labor Party on 18 December 1981.

The long period of dominance of the Left was crafted by Joe Chamberlain, who was State Secretary of the WA Branch of the ALP from 1949 to 1974. Chamberlain was also Federal President from 1955 to 1961 and Federal Secretary from 1961 to 1963. He had a vicious public dispute with Labor Premier Bert Hawke, a very uneasy relationship with Labor Premier John Tonkin, and a well-publicised dispute with Gough Whitlam.

Significantly, he moved the motion at the Hobart National ALP Conference in 1955 that resulted in Brian Burke's father, Tom, being expelled from the party and thereby triggering the great ALP split.

The ALP did not regain office nationally until Whitlam reformed the party and won the election in 1972. After Whitlam's demise in 1975, Bill Hayden set up the moderate Centre Left faction in most States, including Western Australia.

There had long been a Right faction in WA, but it was much smaller than the Broad Left. When Brian Burke became the leader, he was part of the arrangement for a group of highly motivated young organisers from the Labor Right to come to WA from the Eastern States. The Right faction rejuvenated and restructured itself, so that with the numbers from the Centre Left they had the aggregate to outvote the Left for the first time in my experience.

This was a seismic shift in factional power. This challenge to the Left's hegemony upset and infuriated some prominent elements of the faction, and they, like Perth's old money establishment, had a serious axe to grind with the ALP leader.

Jim McGinty, as one of those Left members, is extensively quoted in *The Godfather*.

It is relevant to appreciate that the Left faction had become accustomed to having a deciding say on party policy, choice of candidates, allocation of campaign funding and selection of party office bearers. The resentment at Brian Burke in some hard Left faction circles was deep and enduring.

Twenty-five years after Brian became Premier, in 2008, Beresford quotes McGinty (p. 58 of *The Godfather*) as "expressing concern over the way Burke stacked the Government with loyalists", interpreting this "as the creation of a private power base to ensure arguments over tactics and party platform could easily be controlled by Burke".

Previously, Chamberlain pulled the strings in much more decisive way than Brian Burke.

However, Brian had been conspicuously impartial on important appointments during his five-year period as Premier. At this time, the largest faction was the Left, followed by the Right and then the Centre. It is a matter of open public record that, when it came to Cabinet appointments, the Centre was the recipient of the largest contingent, with the Left second and Burke's own Right faction coming a long last.

The truth was that this was a time when appointments were mostly made on merit. It was a similar story on the succession to the premiership on Burke's retirement. There is no argument that Brian essentially selected his own replacement. Nor was there any contention about whom he considered the four most preferred replacements. They were Peter Dowding, David Parker, Bob Pearce and me.

Brian supported Dowding as the best person to lead the ALP as Premier. Parker was induced to take the Deputy's position with the suggestion that as the youngest of the four he would have other opportunities for the top job. After a specially conducted opinion poll, which indicated that Pearce may not have sufficient support, he agreed not to stand.

Surprisingly, the large Left faction group within Caucus approached me with support. Despite Dowding's attractiveness as a candidate, the Left numbers had some concerns about certain of Dowding's personality traits – specifically, his ability to get along with his colleagues and his capability to cohesively hold the various disparate (sometimes warring) elements of the party together.

Brian Burke had never been close to Dowding (a Centre faction member) and the reality was there had never been much love lost between the two. He was much closer to me and shared my pro-development, pro-mining disposition. Despite that, on a strictly impartial basis, Brian's then assessment was that Peter Dowding was preferable.

Consequently, Brian successfully went to the likes of Jack Marks, a doyen of the Left industrial wing, to prevail on the Caucus Left to withdraw its support of me. Brian was later to apologise formally to me over this action, but it reflected his determination to do his best to give his party what was, in his opinion, its best chance of success.

Brian has publicly disclosed that he initially approached Kim Beazley to take his place as Premier. The approach was rejected by Beazley. I never thought that it had a serious chance of success for a range of practical reasons, and as Beazley always had his sights on Federal leadership.

Chapter 8 of *The Godfather*, entitled "Back From The Brink", deals largely with the Burke and Grill lobbying business and reflects the wholly prejudicial and jaundiced tone of Beresford's book. On its first page, Beresford viciously maligns Brian, and without factual justification, he denounces our partnership in the cruelest terms. To wit:

> Just as he (Burke) had disfigured the world of politics, Burke would turn *consulting into the latest dirty word in the business* (my emphasis).[157]

On page 204 of *The Godfather*, Beresford laments that ALP members were fearful of going on record because of Burke's "reputation for litigation". This is a sheer invention by Beresford. Brian once commenced defamation proceedings against Channel 9 (discontinued), but has never sued any member of the ALP and has no reputation as a litigant.

---

[157] Quentin Beresford, *The Godfather*, p. 198.

Beresford goes to some lengths to demean our lobbying methods and ascribe dubious activity. These assertions are always made without specific evidence and inevitably are unsourced. On page 205 he asserts:

> Grill often arrived early at meetings with clients so he could introduce Burke with the respect befitting a former Premier. On at least one occasion he suggested that they stand when Burke swept into the room.

Brian and I are not fools and we would appreciate that such incredibly stupid acts would be highly counterproductive for client relations. Beresford had no source of knowledge of the dynamic within the partnership. He was not witness to the very robust discussions between Brian and me on how certain accounts were handled. Without evidence, he had no grounds to make false and adverse assertions about the relationship between us.

On the last page of Chapter 8 (page 214) Beresford commences to lay the grounds for an astonishing claim. By way of opening, he explains:

> In April 2003 he (Gallop) announced a ban on his ministers dealing with Burke and Grill ... There are few, if any, precedents for such action.

Beresford is correct, Gallop's actions were quite without equal. The hallmarks of Gallop's premiership was his continual proclamation that his "was a process-driven government". This self-righteous mantra was repeated again and again to all and sundry. However, in the case of the "ban" there was no discernible procedure. It was simply announced. As far as can be ascertained, it was never put in writing. It was never justified publicly.

My wife, Lesley, perplexed, wrote to Gallop seeking an explanation of this unparalleled blackballing. She received no reply or acknowledgement from him. It was readily apparent that the ban had the propensity to put Burke and me out of business. At that time, the lobbying business was Brian's only source of income. It was my main means of a livelihood. Our clients were left in the dark as to the reasons for the ban.

We were deprived of any means of questioning the decision or defending ourselves against the implied impropriety. So much for procedure!

But it was not until later on page 214 that Beresford draws an astounding temporal connection between the "ban" and the setting up of the Corruption and Crime Commission. He states:

> Only months after Gallop's ban was imposed, Attorney-General Jim McGinty introduced legislation to create the Corruption and Crime Commission.

So far, so good, but a few sentences later comes an outrageous bolt out of the blue:

> Lurking in the minds of both McGinty and Gallop was the uncomfortable thought that the new commission could 'come back to bite' the ALP, but they also knew that the Corruption and Crime Commission might lay a trap that could catch Burke. While they had some understanding of his business activity, importantly they also knew his style and were all too aware that he maintained an active network in the party. The irony was that for all Burke's political nous he failed to see that he now had to tread very carefully.

If true, this passage from *The Godfather* has very concerning implications. The first is that, in setting up the CCC, Gallop and McGinty had the ancillary and ulterior motive of investigating Brian Burke. Never before has any potentially penal Australian legislative mechanisms been focused on one individual in this way.

Secondly, if true, and extraordinarily, the suggested use of the CCC is illegal. The CCC's purpose by virtue of Section 7 is strictly limited to combatting organised crime and reducing misconduct in the public sector. Pursuant to Section 4, misconduct is defined as misconduct by "public officers" only.

It is not alleged that Brian Burke is, or was, part of organised crime or was a public officer at any relevant time. It is totally outside of the jurisdiction of the CCC to investigate or pursue private individuals.

That is a job for the police. If Gallop and/or McGinty had any evidence of illegal conduct by Brian, the clear and proper pathway was to report it to the police.

According to Beresford, Gallop and McGinty apparently contemplated the improper use of the CCC to "lay a trap that could catch Burke".

One immediately wonders how Beresford was moved to make such a startling and stupid assertion. The acknowledgement and attribution sections of *The Godfather* do not reveal any interviews of Gallop, but the extensive collaboration of McGinty is declared and readily apparent.

There is no evidence that the claims by Beresford have been denied or corrected by either Gallop or McGinty. But there are some highly germane questions that remain outstanding and require some exploring. These include:

1. Upon what basis did Gallop ban Brian Burke and me?
2. Why have these reasons never been disclosed?

Let me be clear, at the very least Beresford's assertions add impetus to my continued apprehension that the nature (and the specific focus) of the CCC's public and *in camera* hearings leads to the clear conclusion that the Smiths Beach and the following Lobbyists terms of reference were improperly directed at private individuals (Burke and Grill) and not at public officers.

In Chapter 9 of *The Godfather* (page 215), Beresford attributes Burke and Grill's ability to do deals within government to the fact that, "Many of the people he (Burke) had personally leap-frogged into senior positions in the bureaucracy were still there".

This is a very superficial and distorted analysis. First, it ignores the relatively short time that Burke was Premier. It was a self-imposed five years, exactly to the day. Secondly, it overlooks the fact that Burke was out of politics for 15 years before entering into an effective lobbying partnership with me.

That can be contrasted with former Premier Alan Carpenter who took up a corporate affairs position with Wesfarmers almost immediately after he lost the WA state election in 2009. Another example was Clive Brown, who retired from the Gallop Government to immediately take up a lobbying contract with BHP.

There is a strong view in academic public policy circles that there should be a cooling-off period of (say) two years and that immediate appointments like that of Carpenter and Brown should be outlawed. The Barnett Government's 2016 legislation enacted a one-year moratorium after leaving Parliament.

Also, of Brian Burke's 15-year absence from politics, the great majority was spent in relative isolation, where influence could only be wielded with difficulty by telephone. This was not as successful as generally thought. To give but one example, Brian supported Ian Taylor to replace Peter Dowding as Premier, but Carmen Lawrence got the nod.

Beresford makes reference to Burke's time in Ireland and Rome as ambassador, his period in jail and his years working in a steel factory in Siberia when no one would give him a job in Australia. This was a very hard time for Brian because he had spent all of his savings in defending himself in the WA Inc Royal Commission and the subsequent trials and appeals. He still had a dependent wife and children. I had an 11-year absence from the Ministry before embarking on lobbying.

Beresford's superficial assessment overlooks the knowledge, intuition, intensity and sheer hard work that Brian brought to the job. Most of our clientele were taken up on a project-by-project basis. At one time, we had 40 clients on the books, which meant that over the course of a year we probably had 60 clients and 80 or more projects. We dedicated ourselves to these clients and, in terms of time and effort, we always put their interest before our own.

The intensity and strain of the practice was such that when, on two occasions, while Burke was in Ireland visiting two of his boys and their families, I had to seek medical treatment as a result of overwork and work-related stress.

At the same time, Brian greatly feared flying and, although he would dose himself up with sedatives for the outbound leg, it appears the phobia would build up in Ireland and out of dread he would delay the homeward trip. In the interim, the partnership work would accumulate to such an extent that I could barely cope, even with 16-hour days. Lack of proper sleep ultimately took its toll on me.

The problem was that both Burke and I had obsessive personalities and we could not bring ourselves to let a client down. The consequence was that we became emotionally and intellectually involved in our clients' problems.

On page 217 of *The Godfather*, Beresford makes the accusation that, "Burke and Grill were also particularly aggressive in poaching clients from other lobbying firms". This is simply untrue.

The problem with broad-brush smears of this sort, which litter *The Godfather*, is that they are never accompanied by facts or evidence.

However, it is true, as Beresford asserts on page 216 of Chapter 9, that Brian and I (especially Brian) established links with elements of the media. But by dressing this up in derogative language, Beresford seeks to make such activity sound sinister.

As anyone in politics knows, there is always give and take between journalists and MPs. The same applies to lobbyists, who are often called upon to put their clients' public case fairly and in the best light. A lobbyist who does not cultivate media contacts is of little use to his clients and should think about another vocation.

On page 219, again without attribution, Beresford repeats the defamatory remark that, "selected senior bureaucrats, some of whom it was alleged were prepared to do deals with him (Burke)".

Such assertions have no factual base and cast serious aspersions over innocent and honest public servants. Most damagingly, it wrongly gives the highly damaging impression that the higher echelon of the WA public service is corrupt.

The only minor example of where Beresford is correct was in the passing of a letter about the proposed fate of a Mundijong mineral sands deposit to Burke by Gary Stokes, the Deputy Head of the Department of Resources. The letter simply confirmed a situation that was well known to all the interested parties.

Stokes was found guilty of passing on "confidential information", but no conviction was recorded because (among other exculpatory factors) the action was so minor. The episode may have been a technical misjudgment by Mr Stokes, but there was not one iota of evidence that any "deal" was done.

Cabinet confidentiality emerges as an issue

Beresford also implies (page 220) that Brian Burke and I had access to confidential deliberations of the WA Cabinet. For authority he quotes Stephen Hall as follows:

> As Stephen Hall, lawyer for the Corruption and Crime Commission, later argued, improperly disclosed Cabinet discussions conferred "an unfair advantage over others in the community or over government itself".

Brian and I would readily and emphatically agree that, if true, it would confer such an advantage. However, despite some of the most expensive and sophisticated surveillance equipment in the world, the CCC was not able to come up with any tenable evidence that there were unlawful leaks of confidential material from anyone in Cabinet.

This spectre was canvassed by the likes of Stephen Hall and the CCC in its headline-grabbing accusations during the public hearings, but were dropped after doing devastating harm.

Disclosing confidential Cabinet information is a serious criminal offence punishable by imprisonment. On page 220, Beresford flagrantly insinuates that I received or may have received such information from Minister John Bowler. It was a line that originated from the CCC.

Beresford draws from the CCC inquiry to quote me as saying to Bowler: "So, how'd Cabinet go?"

This is particularly dishonest as it gives the fallacious impression that all discussion of Cabinet matters are unauthorised and consequently subject to the provisions of the Criminal Code. The truth is that most of Cabinet business is not confidential or secret. The content and nature of Cabinet submissions is often explicitly public prior to Cabinet deliberations. Most Cabinet decisions are disclosed and explained to the waiting media immediately after Cabinet.

At the commencement of the CCC inquiry into the Lobbyists term of reference, it appeared that the CCC, through statements like the one above by Stephen Hall, was shaping to take action in respect to unauthorised Cabinet disclosures. However, when it became apparent what a legal and jurisdictional quagmire it was about to enter, wiser heads prevailed and the CCC engaged in a strategic retreat. That did not prevent Beresford from maliciously using some of the discarded material.

Also on page 220, Beresford unfairly suggests that Bowler, as Resources Minister, displayed bias in favour of me. Beresford states:

> Bowler gave approval for a number of multimillion-dollar projects to companies employing Burke and Grill.

The truth was very different. Bowler's staff actually did an audit after the issue was raised by the CCC. Brian Burke and I fared far worse with Bowler than we did with any other minister. Of the seven matters that Bowler was approached on by Brian and myself, he rejected our clients' applications on six.

Even worse for our clients was the entirely unprecedented use by John Bowler of Section 111A of the *Mining Act*. This section allows a Resources Minister to summarily refuse or terminate an application for a mining tenement and allow a late renewal by a previous owner, even if the application being summarily refused or terminated is completely legal and in total conformity with the Act and regulations.

Sounds strange? It is, and as a consequence, is only ever used in the rarest of occasions. It is an extreme fallback provision that most Resources Ministers never use. In international law terms, it is akin to resorting to the nuclear option. Bowler used this option three times against the clients of his "friends" – a point apparently overlooked by Beresford.

True to form, Beresford gives no scrap of information on his claim about the "number of multimillion-dollar projects Bowler approved for companies employing Burke and Grill".

On page 221 Beresford deals with the mobile phone that Burke had asked Minister Norm Marlborough to use for private conversations between the two of them. Beresford writes:

> Burke arranged for Marlborough to have a mobile phone for exclusive, *and clandestine*, (my emphasis) communication with him...

Beresford, for a change, actually produces some evidence, in the way of a transcription of a CCC-intercepted call between Burke and Marlborough. Of all of the issues that were highlighted by the CCC, this one probably did the most damage to Brian in a PR sense.

However, it is also the most misunderstood. Beresford was on strong grounds when he said that the mobile was for the exclusive use of Burke and Marlborough. However, the transcript elicited no evidence of *clandestine* communication.

The CCC, in its public hearings, cultivated the impression that the phone was used for improper purposes. It was another of those instances where the CCC misleadingly fomented the impression of criminality, but ultimately dropped it without explanation or apology.

In fact, there would have been actual evidence in the hands of the CCC demonstrating that the mobile was *not* used for clandestine purposes. As it turned out, there were very few calls made to or from the Marlborough mobile. And the CCC, because it was bugging Brian's phone, should have known the content of every one of those calls. It never produced a single transcript that had proof of criminality.

There are two simple reasons for Burke arranging for Marlborough to use an old telephone belonging to Marlborough's wife, Ros, for their exclusive use. First, Burke and Marlborough were best friends and often spoke together. Marlborough's parliamentary phone became so busy as his workload increased that Burke could never get through.

Federal ministers and most state ministers have had similar problems. As a result, their mobile numbers are restricted to a select few and even then the numbers are changed frequently. Some, like Marlborough, have a second phone for use by family and close friends.

The second was that the phone record of parliamentary-financed phones are available for scrutiny and publicity. Gallop had already banned ministerial contact with Burke (and me) and, although that ban had no legal status, contact between Burke and Marlborough would invariably be used by the Opposition for political purposes, no matter how benign the subject of the conversation.

As for Brian wanting to keep the phone confidential from all others, including me, that was a matter that did not bother me in the least.

Beresford makes the point on page 223 that Brian Burke is manipulative. It is not a new allegation and has some truth to it. In fact, Burke has admitted publicly to the fault.[158] It is always hard to define the difference between persuasiveness and manipulation. Brian's stock in trade was to be persuasive and no one doubts that he did that well.

One page 224 Beresford accuses:

> On one occasion, at least, he (Burke) held out the incentive of joining his Dream Team to a young Labor hopeful working as a ministerial staffer while at the same time requesting this person forward sensitive government documents to Burke about a multimillion-dollar pearling industry.

This of course was directly out of the CCC playbook. The unnamed ministerial staffer was Nathan Hondros, Chief of Staff for Fisheries Minister Jon Ford. The CCC followed through on the accusation and on two occasions commenced criminal proceedings against Burke, me and Hondros in the Supreme Court. That happened after *The Godfather* was published.

This was just another case when the CCC's claims, subject to proper procedures and analysis, couldn't stand up. In fact, they couldn't get past first base. On the first occasion Judge Michael Murray found

---

[158] *The West Australian*, 15 August 2015.

that there was no case for the accused to answer. On the second, the DPP withdrew the charges before proceedings commenced. See 18, "'Corruption' – No case to answer".

After seven years of frantically motivated and misguided effort by the CCC, it was another abysmal and embarrassing rout. The ultimate predicament for Beresford's credibility was that he accepted the CCC accusation as fact, even though the CCC hearings in 2007 had denied Burke, Grill and Hondros even the most rudimentary legal procedural fairness. "Print and be dammed" is an old print media maxim. In using this untested evidence and presenting it as truth, Beresford abandoned any pretence of fairness.

The maxim can also be applied to Beresford's printing of some of Adele Farina's CCC evidence. On page 224 of *The Godfather*, Beresford had this to say:

> Burke had an obsessive need to control all aspects of the careers of those he believed were in his personal orbit. Labor MLC Adele Farina, for example, earned an angry outburst from Burke when she applied for a vacant parliamentary secretary's position without seeking his prior approval. As she explained to the commission: "I received a phone call from Brian who was very indignant and annoyed with me that I would nominate for the position without seeking his consent . . . I expressed the view that it wasn't normal for lay faction powerbrokers to get involved in caucus elections."

To give Beresford some small credit, he could have used the more derogatory epithets like "blackmailer, bully" and "intimidation", which Farina actually used in her evidence. But the fact that he relied on any of her evidence in his book is open to significant question. The CCC omitted it entirely from its report.

Farina's evidence to the CCC was given on 6 December 2006. Sean Cowan and Daniel Emerson, in their story in *The West Australian* the next morning, called it "a sensational final day of evidence" on the Smiths Beach terms of reference. The story was accompanied by a big picture of Farina leaving the tribunal after giving evidence.

The CCC had commenced its public hearing on 23 October 2006 with a number of dramatic accusations that electrified the media.

On 6 December 2006 the CCC was intent on bookending the Smiths Beach hearings with claims that were just as astounding. The Farina testimony fitted the bill and was accompanied by Hollywood-style drama and histrionics.

The CCC let the media know that they were calling an explosive mystery witness whose name could not be disclosed. In spite of the fact that the CCC's lawyers had given a clear undertaking to Brian's lawyer, Grant Donaldson, a Senior Counsel (SC) who would later become Solicitor General for WA, that they would inform him if they were going to call a witness who may give evidence adverse to Burke, the CCC gave no name or detail.

When Farina arrived in the CCC to give evidence, she was flanked by two CCC officers in a way that gave the (false) impression that she was under protection. She was not allowed to be cross-examined nor her evidence tested in any way. It was not surprising, therefore, that her narrative went viral and any hope of a fair or balanced assessment of Burke's personality went with it.

The story served its dubious purpose, but the CCC eventually realised that it had gone far too far. Even the CCC finally appreciated that one cannot egregiously traduce a person's character so violently without giving the defamed person some ability to defend themselves.

Additionally, the evidence had no relevance. In its eagerness to smash Brian and me, the CCC had completely stepped out of its jurisdiction. I reiterate: it is not legal for the CCC to pursue private citizens. Its statutory concern is public officers, who in the main part are public servants. Farina's testimony was a vituperative personal attack directed at one target alone and did not reflect on the activity of any public officer.

When these facts were politely conveyed to the CCC by Brian's lawyer, Stephen Lemonis, the CCC dropped all reference to its star secret witness.

The question arises of why Farina would give such damaging

character evidence about a former friend and crucial political ally, even if we assume that she was compelled to do so under a summons from the CCC. Farina was no stranger to the formality of giving evidence. She had been through a harrowing prior incident that had left its mark on her. She had been accused of misusing the stamps allowance when she was working in the office of a previous minister, the Minister for Planning, Bob Pearce. At her trial, the jury was split and there was no verdict. She was well represented by the then high-profile QC Brian Singleton (now deceased) and he convinced the DPP that it was not worthwhile going through with a retrial. But I think that the process unnerved her.

Also on page 223, Beresford refers to Minister Tony McRae. He states that McRae's fall was due to us:

> Environment Minister Tony McRae also became entangled in Burke's web of power and influence.

It was well known that McRae was forced to resign from Cabinet after the CCC hearing. The unstated insinuation was that McRae's demise was due to his vulnerability to possible influence by Burke and me. This was quite misleading, as was the actual finding of the CCC that McRae behaved improperly by misleading me on the status of an application that I had made to the Minister on behalf of a client. There was no suggestion of impropriety by me. How Beresford could turn the situation on its head is not explained.

Lastly on this subject, Burke and I are both emphatically of the view that the evidence of impropriety by McRae was particularly flimsy. Also, as former Premier Peter Dowding vehemently commented publicly, the way the McRae matter was handled by the CCC deprived McRae of any fair trial or any means of redress.

He was just another poor victim of the CCC's loss of proper process and dubious motivation. See Chapter 2, "CCC 'court' revives Star Chamber procedures".

At page 230 of *The Godfather*, Beresford tries to give the false impression that we tried to improperly lobby Wally Cox, the Chairman of the EPA, during the planning and approval process for the Smiths

Beach development. The true facts and circumstances are set out in Chapter 13.

On page 233, Beresford endeavours to follow the pernicious example of the CCC by trying to poison public opinion against Burke and Grill by making us out to be motivated by greed. It related specifically, on this occasion, to our mining company client Echelon and its related company Cazaly, in the dispute with Rio Tinto over Shovelanna, referred to in detail in Chapter 6, "'Lobbyists inquiry' – CCC v Burke & Grill, Round 2".

In respect to our motivation in supporting our client's call to set up a Legislative Council committee of inquiry (Standing Committee on Estimates and Financial Operations) into the Government's semi-secret policy that allowed multinational companies to hold vast areas of mineral prospective land to the exclusion of others in apparent contradiction of the provisions of the State's Mining Act, Beresford has this to say:

> Burke and Grill stood to gain significant riches for themselves if they succeeded in intimidating Rio Tinto. The pair had been purchasing shares in both Cazaly and Echelon and monitoring their share prices. Anticipating a significant leap in Cazaly's share price, they negotiated a payment with McMahon (Cazaly director), of 100,000 fully paid Cazaly shares if they succeeded before Christmas 2006.

As demonstrated below, Beresford was exaggerating.

Beresford on page 234 states:

> Burke's plan to use parliament to force a settlement for Cazaly came to an abrupt end in December 2006 when it became publicly known that he and Grill were caught up in the Corruption and Crime Commission's investigation into Smiths Beach. The ruse that they were operating in a legitimate manner for Cazaly could no longer be maintained.

It is a downright libel to state that our representation of our client was a ruse or illegitimate and, as usual, no substantiation was offered for it. When Minister Bowler exercised his special ministerial discretion in favour of Rio Tinto on Shovelanna, he expressed the first (and primary) ground of so doing as follows:

"(a) termination of the Cazaly application would further the objectives of the State's iron ore policy which was to facilitate the development of iron mines by ensuring secure long-term tenure."

Extraordinarily, little was known about the policy because it was not embodied in a publicly available policy document. There was even doubt, at that time, that "the policy", so relied upon for Australia's biggest industry, was committed to writing.[159]

On page 234 Beresford writes:

> The entire operation, as conceived by Burke, and authorised by McMahon was underpinned by questionable practice.

While it is appreciated that this was exactly the impression that the CCC was promoting, it was nonetheless a harsh and unfair conclusion by Beresford for a number of reasons.

First, the subject matter was highly appropriate for committee consideration. For instance, is it equitable that smaller Australian companies be excluded from the biggest iron ore province in the world?

Another obvious question was whether the titans of the mining industry effectively should be exempt from some of the most important principles of the governing legislation. If they are to be favoured, shouldn't that special "policy" be transparent and open for scrutiny?

Secondly, although it may not have been known to Beresford, in moving to set up the committee of inquiry our clients were acting strictly in accordance with the law. Cazaly had retained well-regarded law firm DLA Philipps Fox (Robert Edel and Alexander Jones) to advise and they in turn had retained WA's best known QC, Malcolm McCusker. Wayne Martin QC, later to become Chief Justice, had provided a legal opinion.

---

[159] Robert Edel and Alex Jones, "Western Australia Developments Shovelanna Dispute", *Australian Resources and Energy Law Journal,* 26 2007, p. 26.

Thirdly, Beresford insinuates that Burke, Noel Crichton-Browne and I behaved incorrectly in giving no advice about Shovelanna or Cazaly to the committee members when we pushed our client's call for the inquiry.

Contrary to that insinuation of impropriety by Beresford, the clear legal advice to Cazaly was that no reference by us to committee members on the Shovelanna case was appropriate and that the committee's deliberations should be free of any bias caused by Shovelanna, which in any event was *sub judice*. That is, it was before the court and should not be the subject of separate specific consideration.

Beresford's allegations of greed on the part of Burke and Grill are highly prejudicial and simply ill-considered. First, there was no evidence that Burke and Grill's fees were any different to those asked by most lobbyists.

Also, Beresford says that, "…they negotiated a payment with McMahon of 100,000 fully paid Cazaly shares, if they succeed before Christmas 2006". I deal with this elsewhere, but the short answer was that Mr McMahon did make an informal offer of shares to us in a conversation with Brian Burke, but it was never accepted by me as the principal of our lobbying company.

Additionally, because of the grossly unfair nature of the CCC hearings, Brian and I were helpless to counter the untrue picture of rapaciousness being so assiduously painted by the CCC and so faithfully replicated by Beresford.

And, finally, I bought no shares in either Cazaly or Echelon.

The extent of Beresford's partisanship is demonstrated again on page 237. Buried in page after page of severe calumny and obloquy is the one isolated sentence:

> In its consideration of the Smiths Beach matter, the commission made no adverse findings against either Burke or Grill.

This was also to prove the case in the many-headed Lobbyists term of reference.

Beresford also (page 239) briefly referred to the plight of Norm Marlborough after the CCC public hearings:

> Having resigned from parliament in disgrace once his slavish relationship with Burke had been exposed in the Corruption and Crime Commission, Marlborough fell into a deep depression and flirted with the idea of killing himself. Three times he went to a bridge with the intention of jumping off. Each time he stood there 'looking at the water and imagining what his crumpled body would look like after it smashed against the concrete below'. Each time he was dragged back from the brink by the emotional pull of his family. He told the Sunday Times that psychiatric help and anti-depressants had helped lift the emotional fog that had enveloped his life. He realised that he had to take responsibility for his own actions and not blame Burke for his demise. 'I still love Brian like a brother.' Marlborough is not the only Burke loyalist to have been damaged by their association with him, although few appear to be as forgiving as Marlborough.

This patently lays the suicidal state of Marlborough at Brian Burke's door – that is, at his best friend's door. It is an exceptionally damning allegation, but also one that does not bear scrutiny. It is only true in the wider sense that Marlborough would not have been in that perilous state of suicidal mind if he did not know Burke and was not his close friend.

However, that is a sophist's argument and one needs to look at the actual causes of Marlborough's sacking as minister and his resignation from Parliament, which I deal with in Chapter 5, "Where it all began: Smiths Beach and Busselton Shire election shire".

Beresford, apart from mentioning that no adverse findings were made against either Burke or Grill (page 237), does report that disciplinary charges were recommended against three senior public servants (Mike Allen, Wally Cox and Paul Frewer) and adverse findings were made against Marlborough and three Busselton Shire councillors. Beresford appears to be leading one to believe that the massively expensive and highly damaging CCC exercise was justified on the basis of these recommendations.

Public servants, councillors cleared

However, as advised above, the subsequent Public Service hearings cleared all three public servants and Parliamentary Inspector Malcolm McCusker was scathing in his condemnation of the methods used by the CCC in coming to the disapproving conclusion that it made in the Smiths Beach Report.

Further, Beresford does not mention that no disciplinary action was taken against the Busselton Shire councillors. Despite the CCC's prejudicial comment about the councillors and the enthusiastic supportive comments of the serried ranks of the ignorantly unquestioning media, it soon became apparent to any impartial observer that the councillors had all acted quite legally.

The Godfather was not published until 2008 and by that time it was clear that the councillors had broken no law, regulation or enforceable policy.

Additionally, Beresford fails to mention that the CCC Smiths Beach Report made six recommendations. Three were in respect to disciplinary action against Mark Brabazon, Paul Frewer and Michael Allen, and they all failed. The other three were in respect to local government procedures on conflict of interest and election donations. They have been implemented only in very small part. The report was an embarrassing fizzer.

Despite that failure, on page 236 Beresford breathlessly asserts:

> The (Smiths Beach) hearings would expose, like no other official inquiry ever has, the inner workings of a ruthlessly effective lobbying business.

There are real problems with lobbying. But they are not those that were the focus of the CCC in either the Smiths Beach or Lobbyists inquiries, which were ill conceived and ultimately spectacularly unsuccessful witch-hunts bereft of intellectual merit.

The potential problem with lobbying is mainly in the area of political donations, a problem now belatedly being tackled in NSW as a result of the ICAC inquiries into the Obeid family activity, subsequent stunning donations made by "foreign citizens", to the ALP and Senator Sam Dastyari, and cash from Chinese billionaire Huang Xiangmo.

In partial response, the Turnbull Government passed the *Electoral Funding and Reform Act 2018*, but much more needs to be done.

Brian Burke and I were more than happy to cooperate with the CCC on any serious inquiry on this subject. Unfortunately, the CCC was simply not interested in any contribution from Brian or me.

As a consequence, many years passed before WA enacted rudimentary lobbying legislation in 2017. Unfortunately, this legislation is not adequate in the modern world. It only covers a fraction of lobbying activity and, in particular, has no oversight of the big end of town.

Beresford reports on page 243 of *The Godfather*:

> No one has been more determined to undermine Burke than the current Premier, Alan Carpenter. As if to atone for his original decision to lift the ban on Burke and Grill's lobbying business Carpenter has taken Burke head-on, labelling him, in barely concealed anger, 'an unstoppable manipulator' and warning everyone, including the media, to steer clear of him.

Further, on page 240, Beresford gives the view:

> . . . Burke thought he would face an adverse finding as, indeed, he did. The committee recommended that the attorney-general assess the false evidence Burke gave to the committee and determine whether he should be prosecuted under the Criminal Code. Similar recommendations were made against Shelley Archer, Noel Crichton-Brown and Liberal backbencher Anthony Fels.

Chapter 7 describes the utter failure of these recommended charges.

Given this background, Beresford at page 241 reports:

> Upon its release (the committee report) Labor parliamentarian Bon Kucera (he means Bob Kucera), a former assistant commissioner in the Western Australian police force, addressed the Select Committee's report in a speech to parliament. Emphasising that he had "investigated many of these kinds of complaints", he explained that the Cazaly affair constituted, in his view, "an attempt to pervert the course of justice".

Remember, here Beresford and Kucera were referring with approval to a secret trial, with secret witnesses and secret evidence! At the time, Kucera was unaware that Cazaly and its consultants, including Burke and I, had acted on some of the best legal advice available in the State.

Despite his position as a former policeman, Kucera was not a lawyer. It was an extraordinary attack by a Labor parliamentarian on a highly successful Labor Premier. One has to wonder whether Carpenter and Attorney-General McGinty were aware Kucera would make such a speech.

Ordinarily such a speech, with a bald accusation of criminal behaviour, would not have been permitted by the Speaker of the House, especially as the matter of a charge was under consideration by the Director of Public Prosecutions.

But these were not normal times and the speech appears to have been encouraged. Certainly Beresford quotes the speech with approval. Brian, quite properly considering the facts, attacked the parliamentary committee as a kangaroo court. However, given the adverse media frenzy, no one of relevance would listen.

Despite that, and although it took some time, sanity finally prevailed. Very quietly, and with little public announcement, all consideration of criminal charges was discontinued and dropped. Despite the fanfare that accompanied the release of the original committee report, there was no media coverage when the recommended charges silently dropped off the agenda.

This had become a feature of CCC-inspired charges and must have been a disillusionment to Beresford, who had implied that criminal charges would result.

What is by far the most disappointing aspect to *The Godfather* is Beresford's unquestioning endorsement of the inexcusable removal of the normal legal safeguards extended to accused persons. Put simply, the CCC in the Smiths Beach and Lobbyists terms of reference and Parliamentary Committees applied tens of millions of dollars of taxpayer resources for no tangible results in circumstances where many totally innocent parties were badly and irrevocably damaged.

Witnesses might have been aware that they were being deprived of the normal right against self-incrimination when they entered the tribunal, because that is what the CCC legislation allowed. What most did not know was that at the whim of the Commission and its lawyers, those testifying would be subject to indignities worse than Soviet show trials. The English-speaking world had not seen any denial of procedural fairness on this scale for more than 200 years when the infamous English Star Chamber was abolished.

The public is still largely ignorant of this state of affairs. In the Smiths Beach, Lobbyists and parliamentary hearings, testifiers were *deceived* into believing they were mere witnesses, when, in fact, they were the accused. They had no idea of what they were accused, were actually deprived of all normal means of defending themselves, and were effectively prevented from using legal representation.

They had to listen in disbelief as the CCC's counsel assisting made the most outrageous and untrue accusations against them, without any ability to question, give evidence in their own right, or call independent evidence in rebuttal.

Beresford, as a political science lecturer, on the other hand, was all too aware of potential for abuse, if not the actual abuse, at the hearings. The CCC procedures were not only a clear traducement of a citizen's fundamental rights, but also a brutal form of oppression.

Some like the Joint Standing Committee on the CCC (JSCCCC), whose only job was to act as a watchdog over the CCC, initially sat on the sidelines and applauded. As Noel Crichton-Browne commented in a letter to the editor in *The West Australian* in early 2007, this committee, as it was constituted at the time, became "a cheer squad for the CCC's worst excesses".

Beresford's position can be contrasted with that of his former colleague from Edith Cowan University, Peter van Onselen. Van Onselen has moved on to take up a professorship at the prestigious University of Western Australia, has a regular column in *The Australian* and hosted a program on Fox Television. He has become increasingly disillusioned and sceptical of bodies like the New South Wales Independent Commission against Corruption (ICAC) and the Western Australian CCC.

His growing cynicism is of considerable persuasive value because he was employed in an ICAC-type body in NSW in his younger years. I believe that he is the only serious commentator who has had this inside experience and it gives him a unique perspective that he partly passed on to me when we met for coffee in 2007.

ICAC in NSW has collected the scalps of two Premiers. First, Nick Greiner who was judged guilty of corruption, but who was later completely exculpated of wrong doing. Too late, however, to save his career. The second, Barry O'Farrell, who had a memory lapse and failed to recollect the gift of a $3000 bottle of Penfolds wine. There was no question of corruption on his part and ICAC later conceded that it was a genuine lapse of memory. Writing in *The Weekend Australian* of 17-18 April 2014, van Onselen had this to say:

> This (O'Farrell's demise) is yet another reason why the Star Chamber that is ICAC should conduct hearings behind closed doors, if they must go on, so that they retain some legal integrity rather than resemble a modern version of the Salem Witch trials.

Among a number of trenchant criticisms, van Onselen went on to say:

> ... there is little or no oversight of the way that ICAC uses the media to tar and feather politicians publicly, even those who have not been found to have engaged in wrongdoing. Anyone reading transcripts from ICAC

hearings would be able to see that counsel assisting the enquiry has used the proceedings now to mock witnesses, in my view playing to the media as a key objective.

Apologists for Beresford could say that his errors in *The Godfather* were simply solecisms, due to timing, and that if he had had access to the trials and events that followed the CCC reports on Smiths Beach and Lobbyists, he would have produced a more accurate document. But the reality is that Beresford went off half-cocked and, armed with the untested and manifestly procedurally unfair CCC reports, he fashioned a narrative about Burke's character that left nothing more than a smoking ruin.

In mid-2017, I attended a forum at the QE2 Health Campus in Perth. It featured former Prime Minister Tony Abbott. There I ran into Bill Hassell, the leader of the WA Liberal Opposition at the time Burke was Premier.

Hassell, who I have known since my university days, was very keen to tell me that he had recently read *The Godfather* and that he assessed it as complete demolition of Burke. I was a little taken aback as I was under the impression, until then, that the Beresford book was not taken that seriously. Clearly, in some circles, at least, it has had impact. That made me very sad, as it is a vicious and partisan chronicle, as far as it deals with the central CCC matters.

I would like to finish this chapter on a positive note. The CCC hearings and their aftermath may have left Brian wounded, lacerated and politically radioactive, but he could still generate emotional connection like an electric current. That is partly because he has genuine character strengths. One of them is bravery. In that context, I reflect on the following events.

In the lead up to the game-changing 1983 election, Arthur Tonkin, who was a shadow minister in Burke's Opposition, was charged with indecently assaulting a 16-year-old boy, whom he had been mentoring. That created headlines.

Brian was urged by party insiders to desert Tonkin and leave him to his fate. But Brian, on the contrary, believed in Tonkin's innocence, publicly supported him and actually attended at court in an open show of loyalty. The case was dismissed. It was the bravest political act that I have witnessed.

Years 1981 and 1982 had been recession years in WA. The Burke Government inherited a dire budgetary situation. It had similarities to the plight in which Premier Mark McGowan found himself in 2017. Severe belt-tightening measures had to be taken.

McGowan, as one of those measures, limited Government pay increases to $1000. That paled into insignificance against Premier Burke's 10 per cent and 15 per cent (for senior figures) cuts in salary for public servants. Make no mistake, that could have been a career-ending move, but Brian got out, took full responsibility and sold the measures.

Whatever else you say, Brian Burke's bailout of Robert Holmes à Court and his Bell Group with $495 million through the State Government Insurance Commission, in return for Perth CBD land and buildings and BHP shares, was breathtakingly audacious. What's more, it was highly profitable.

Few politicians, anywhere in the world, voluntarily give up power. Brian said when he became Premier that he would be there for five years only. No one believed him. Five years later, to the day, he retired, near the peak of his popularity. In my experience, it was a unique act that sets him apart.

Something else that sets Brian Burke apart is that current Premier Mark McGowan has publicly proscribed contact between his Ministers and Burke. Given the significant debt that the ALP owes Burke, this does appear to be ungenerous.

After the Second World War up to the arrival of Burke as Premier in 1983, Labor had been out of power for nearly two-thirds of the time. The party had an ill-fated bond to the Chamberlain Left faction vision of the "socialist objective", which, in a word, meant nationalisation.

For instance, just after the war the Federal ALP unsuccessfully tried to nationalise the banks. It did not go down well with a newly minted, aspirational class of citizens who had had their horizons widened by that war. This was the time when Robert Menzies was evangelising individual liberty, personal responsibility and free enterprise.

Not long after, Liberal grandees such as Sir David Brand in association with Sir Charles Court began opening up WA to massive iron ore, alumina, nickel and petroleum extraction and treatment. This created vast new sources of national wealth and made WA the export dynamo of the country.

On top of that, Charles Court was an irresistible salesman for the State and his Liberal Party. It was no wonder that good men leading the ALP, like Bert Hawke, John Tonkin, Colin Jamieson and Ron Davies were successively swept aside by Court, who was articulate, persuasive, disciplined and had an aura of power.

It was not until Brian Burke emerged that Labor had a champion who could compete with Court, in debate, organisationally, in the minds of business people, in the media, with fundraising and on the hustings. The modern Labor Party, in substantial part, is a tribute to Brian Burke.

17

BURKE AND BRYCE – WA'S BEST LABOR GOVERNMENT

Almost as soon as Brian Burke stood down as Premier, he invariably drew unfair and unflattering media. As a consequence, I fear it might be difficult for people to appreciate the contribution of the government he led without some mitigation of impressions at large. This chapter aims to do just that.

Part of the challenge is that Brian Burke has been both the most popular and most unpopular figure in WA political history.

A majority of pundits would nominate the tenure of the Brand/Court (Charles) State Government as the most successful period of political management in Western Australia's history. David Brand was Premier from 1959 to 1971, with Charles Court as his powerful Minister for Industrial Development.

This period was interrupted from 1971 until 1974 when the Tonkin Labor Government held office. But it only just held office, relying on the casting vote of the Speaker in the Lower House and having its legislation torn to strips in a hostile Upper House.

In May 1972, there was a smooth change of the leadership of the WA Liberal Party from the country-based and conservative Sir David Brand to Sir Charles Court, who became Premier in 1974 and continued until 1982. The finances of the State were prudently managed throughout.

It was the era when WA made the Cinderella-type transition from an impoverished mendicant state to a resources-rich powerhouse. Until then, the State's economy was held hostage to the vagaries of the fickle winter rains for the annual grain crop and a declining gold mining sector.

The Brand/Court administration has credit for breaking the

Federal embargo on iron ore exports, beginning exploitation of the huge petroleum reservoirs on the North West Shelf, encouraging the extensive alumina mines and refineries in the South West, witnessing the birth of the nickel industry and opening up huge new tracts of agricultural land with the help of trace elements. These are world-class assets that engendered sustained wealth for Australia for decades.

Notwithstanding these magnificent nation-building achievements, it can be contended that, for its relatively short five-year life from 1983 to 1988 (compared to the 13 years and nine years of the Brand and Court Governments respectively) the Burke Government was just as (or more) successful.

Certainly the economy flourished during the Burke period. To use a boxing term, pound for pound it arguably had no peers. Certainly it was the best Labor Government the State had ever seen.

It is hard not to feel some sympathy for Brian Burke and his deputy, the late Mal Bryce. They have never been judged publicly on the normal criteria; that is, their record. The pair – and Brian in particular – have always had their very significant successes overshadowed by media-generated perceptions originating in the WA Inc. Royal Commission and CCC hearings – particularly the CCC hearings, which generated an extraordinary amount of unfriendly media coverage over a long period.

As an example of how the media had fallen under the CCC's spell, journalist Tim Treadgold wrote in an article in *Business News* on 10 October 2016 that the "government led by former WA premier Brian Burke was the most corrupt that he had encountered". Treadgold at the time was no novice; he had been a journalist for more than 45 years and specialised in business and resources reporting.

Brian wrote to *Business News* editor Mark Beyer in November 2016 objecting to Treadgold's characterisation of the Burke Government. He requested a retraction on one of the forward pages of the publication. Beyer agreed to a "clarification" which was published in *Business News* on page 3 in late November 2016. It stated:

Clarification

In the edition of this *Business News* of the 10th of October, an article by Tim Treadgold said the "government led by former WA premier Brian Burke was the most corrupt that he had encountered".

Brian Burke has complained that this allegation and its associated implications are untrue and defamatory.

After consideration of Mr Burke's complaint, this paper totally retracts the offending allegation and apologises for the hurt and damage caused to the reputation of Mr Burke and his associates. This paper withdraws any imputation that Mr Burke personally was corrupt or that his Government was similarly inclined.

In making this **clarification** this paper is informed by the conclusions of the Royal Commission into WA Business Dealings (WA Inc) wherein it was specifically stated that "it is appropriate that we should report that there has been comparatively little evidence of illegal or corrupt conduct".

(See WA Inc Royal Commission into WA Inc, Conclusions, Chapter 27, Term of Reference 2.1, 27.1.3. Report 1, Volume VI).

Does a correction such as this have an impact on negative community perceptions built up over years by relentless adverse media? One can only guess.

On the positive side, some of the Burke Government's major milestones are listed below.

After John Tonkin, the ALP tried a number of leaders, but with little success. Burke and Bryce had enough support between them in the Caucus to change leader, but with fierce rivalry between the two and with about equal numbers, they cancelled each other out and were never in a position to mount the crucial challenge. It was ultimately Bryce who sublimated his ambitions and convinced his Caucus group to support a Burke/Bryce ticket on 18 September 1981.

It was a talented Ministry they finally presided over after Labor won the state election in February of 1983. However, they jointly put their stamp on Cabinet and Government in their first term and again after re-election in 1986.

Exactly five years to the day of the 1983 election win, they both resigned from Parliament and made way for a new team led by Peter Dowding. This was largely driven by Burke's promise prior to becoming Premier that he would only remain in the job for five years. There is a famous newspaper picture of them both, at about twilight, wandering off with their fishing gear and rods through the sand on a west coast beach to take up a new life in retirement.

Of course, it did not work out that way, as both took up very active second and later third and fourth careers, in and out of the State.

The Burke/Bryce Government was very supportive of the resources sector as evidenced by the establishment of the world's biggest diamond mine, Argyle Diamond Mine, in the remote East Kimberley region of the State. The WA Diamond Trust, a public trust floated by the Burke Government in 1984, bought five per cent of Argyle from the Bond Corporation for WA citizens.

Another example of the Government's pro-resources nature included its critical renegotiation of the North West Shelf "take or pay" gas agreement.

But Premier Burke believed there was more to WA's future prosperity. The first imperative was to broaden the base of the economy beyond resource extraction and the annual grain crop.

The most natural place to start was to build a substantial state tourism industry. That began with plans for WA's first (legal) casino and the Burswood Peninsula entertainment and sporting precinct. Only by looking back to the media of that time can one appreciate how controversial such a proposal was for a staid state like WA.

The peninsula was a vast low-lying swamp in a loop of the Swan River at the eastern entrance to Perth City. It was then mainly a major landfill rubbish dump with James Hardie manufacturing asbestos fibre cement products in the same area. But from such humble beginnings, the peninsular soon became WA's foremost tourist destination.

A second early goal was the establishment of a major marina and tourism area at Hillarys Nodes on the north metropolitan coast. The case was easy to make, but there was fierce opposition from the Greens, who maintained that immense beach erosion would be the consequence.

That contention was backed by four internationally known marine environmentalists who opined that the engineers from the Department of Marine and Harbours had badly under-estimated the potential for coastal erosion. To add to the government's problems, the Greens were able to mount anti-marina demonstrations on the beach of between 2000 and 3000 people.

Worryingly, the two major daily newspapers, *The West Australian* and the *Daily News*, strongly supported the opponents.

The three-minister cabinet subcommittee overseeing the development, comprising Burke, Bob Pearce (the Minister for Education and Planning) and me (as Minister for Transport) was put on the back foot, with some other Ministers expressing doubt as to whether the fight was worth the effort.

A two-part strategy was agreed upon. Bob Pearce suggested and arranged for a representative poll of metropolitan voters to be taken; and I organised for University of Western Australia's Professor Jorg Imberger to make an independent assessment of the erosion risk.

Professor Imberger's subsequent report indicated that the risk was minimal. The poll showed that, contrary to widespread impression, only 2 per cent of the population opposed the development. On that basis, the Hillarys project went ahead and became Perth's second most popular entertainment destination. Erosion has never been a problem.

Another massive boost to tourism was the Alan Bond-led campaign that won the America's Cup yacht racing trophy in 1983 after it had spent more than 100 years in US hands. The Australian defence of the trophy in 1986 required the creation of a new challenger yacht harbour and the expenditure of huge sums of money to revamp Fremantle.

The defence of the Cup in WA in 1987 was the first time the series of races had been held outside of the US, and it made Perth and Fremantle a centre of attention for the world's media.

The removal of the army from Rottnest, our only substantial tourist island, and the handing back of the land for recreation and leisure also was a significant step.

Another enormous project was the tourism-related, but essentially environmentally driven, Peel-Harvey Estuary Cut to the open ocean at Dawesville, which saved this big and important waterway from putrescence.

Also, in respect to the environment, the Burke/Bryce Government put in place the largest forest and flora preservation system ever seen in the State. It included the whole of the mostly virgin Shannon River Basin and the gazetting of big new national parks, such as the D'Entrecasteaux National Park on the South Coast and Rudall River National Park in the Pilbara.

At the same time, WA's very extensive range of marine parks and fisheries reservation protection zones were legislated.

In town planning, the Government took two big new initiatives. The first was to set up a new regional authority in the South West to promote the area, economically and socially. This South West Development Authority had many achievements, but its biggest was to completely redevelop Bunbury's central city area, remove the railway-related industries, the old sewerage ponds and the oil storage tanks, reintroducing Bunbury to beautiful Koombana Bay.

In Perth, the Government tried an equally new concept for WA: developing the down-at-heel and environmentally blighted East Perth industrial area across the river from the Burswood Peninsular development. The East Perth Development Authority (EPDA) was given statutory jurisdiction to take on the redevelopment program.

To do that, a new road crossing of the Swan River was constructed north of the old rail bridge so the area could be consolidated for an attractive European-style residential area, focused on a new water haven based on a very much enlarged Claisebrook inlet, with hotels and cafes on its banks. Beautiful parks and gardens were a feature.

The EPDA went on to replan and redevelop Subiaco's industrial area and, given the success of the model, the entity has since been renamed the Metropolitan Redevelopment Authority.

Very importantly for the environment of the State's South West, the Burke Government put an end to opening up new land for farming, previously running at the rate of more than 400,000 hectares per annum. The result of the Brand/Court Government's massive land release program was a marginal increase in grain production on the plus side, and WA's greatest environmental catastrophe on the negative side.

Most of the streams in the Wheatbelt, which formed a part of the greater South West, turned from fresh water to salt. Even under the best conditions, this catastrophe will take hundreds of years to reverse.

The decision to discontinue new land release was effective immediately. Not one more hectare was opened up. Even new land farms around the Fitzgerald River National Park, which had been sub-divided, did not proceed to release and the land instead was incorporated in the park.

Initially, there were many critics of the Government's decision, but few would poke their heads above the parapets these days.

Economically, the Government set up the twin corporations of the WA Development Corporation and the Exim Corporation. These agencies attempted to establish wealth-creating industries that the private sector was reluctant to enter.

The WADC reestablished the Perth Mint and introduced the highly successful gold coin and bullion programs. They continue today.

Exim, among other international initiatives, was the first Australian government agency to market tertiary academic courses to overseas students. That industry is now the country's fourth biggest export earner. This was a spectacular, but largely unheralded, Burke Government success.

Mal Bryce was particularly interested in the newly evolving information technology (IT) and technology arena. He presided over the establishment of Bentley Technology Park next to Curtin University.

At this extensive precinct, the big resources players, international technology companies and WA universities have built billion-dollar facilities that have placed the State at the forefront of important aspects of mining and petroleum extractive industry research.

In terms of transport infrastructure, the Labor Government changed the face of the State's capital. The previous Court Government was not supportive of passenger rail transport. It closed the Perth to Fremantle passenger service and indicated that the two other suburban services (to Midland and Armadale) would go the same way.

Almost immediately after the 1983 election, the Labor Government reinstated the Perth to Fremantle service and thereafter there was a rail revolution. A new line north to Joondalup was planned and all services were electrified.

In due course, the Richard Court-led Government adopted the new philosophy and planned a Perth-to-Mandurah line. The Gallop Government ensured that the program was implemented, on a new more direct route over the Narrows Bridge and down the Kwinana Freeway spine.

On the social front, the Burke-led Government was also active. There had been no hangings in WA since that of mass murderer Eric Edgar Cook in 1964. But capital punishment remained on the statute books. The Burke/Bryce Government quickly removed it.

It also passed moderate Native Title legislation through the Legislative Assembly, but opposition from Opposition Leader Bill Hassell and the Liberals in the Upper House saw its defeat. The irony was that most of the other States enacted similar legislation. The failure to do so in WA caused activists to initiate a significant push for more comprehensive national legislation, which was enacted by the Hawke/Keating Government.

Some political scientists and commentators would rank the Charles Court Government ahead of the Burke/Bryce Government in respect to financial prudence, but in one dramatic sense the Burke/Bryce Government saved the Court Government's bacon.

When the North West Shelf was developed, it was clear that its liquefied natural gas (LNG) operation could not stand on its own feet as an export industry and required a substantial domestic gas market. In turn, that demanded a 1000-plus kilometre pipeline from Dampier to Perth to deliver the gas.

The Court Government committed to guaranteeing the domestic market by agreeing to take a substantial amount of the gas, whether it was used or not. It became known as the "take or pay" contract.

It also agreed the State would finance and build the pipeline.

This was a huge financial gamble and the State was in uncharted territory. Less than two years into the Burke/Bryce Government, Treasury officials came to Cabinet to disclose that as events had unfolded the "take or pay" contract was about to put the State into bankruptcy.[160]

Prime Minister Bob Hawke became involved and the governments responded to the crisis by setting up a four-way conference to renegotiate the contract. It comprised the North West Shelf partners as one party, the Federal Government as a second party, and the WA Government as a third party. Fourth was Alcoa, which, as the second largest gas customer, had an important interest.

Gareth Evans, the then Federal Minister for Resources and Energy, represented the Commonwealth; David Parker, the then State Minister for Minerals and Energy, represented the people of WA. Kevin Gosper and Charles Allen spoke for the Shelf Partners.

The resulting new contract was dubbed the "sharing the pain agreement" because all parties had to make significant concessions. However, its purpose was achieved: the State was saved from bankruptcy, the contract was put on a sound financial basis, and the North West Shelf went on to become a major export and financial success.

The Burke/Bryce Government, despite its significant list of achievements, was extremely conservative in its handling of the State's finances. It brought down balanced budgets and did not significantly increase state debt. It reformed the public service superannuation fund in a way that made it a national and international model.

---

[160] Brian Burke, *A Tumultuous Life*, pp. 202-5.

In this chapter I have dealt with the salient financial matters that set WA on a more comprehensive and certain economic footing.

But I have not dealt here with the array of accomplishments that stemmed from the big expenditure in health and education, including the massively successful world leading Quit (smoking) campaign under Minister Barry Hodge and Director Mike Daube.

Rather, I have tried to give a flavour of the excitement and entrepreneurship of this exhilarating period. The State Government had a scope and flair that set it apart from its contemporaries, while at the same time exhibiting a general financial responsibility that Labor Governments are not always famous for.

I may be biased, but my view is that the Burke Government was outstanding.

However, it suffered grievously from what is called in financial and technical circles a Black Swan Event – that is, a circumstance or event no one could have predicted. I refer to the Black Monday stock market crash on 9 October 1987, which saw the biggest one-day losses in history.

The resulting loss of liquidity in Australia's financial system was disastrous. It enfeebled (and ultimately terminated) the Rothwells merchant bank. Later, the state banks in Victoria, SA and our own R&I Bank went under and had to be subsumed in bailouts and takeovers.

The detrimental knock on from Rothwells, although far from catastrophic in itself, led to the PICL (Petrochemical Industries Company Limited) disaster and then to the WA (Inc) Royal Commission into Government Business Dealings. These later events, from the final failure of Rothwells onwards, all happened after Brian Burke departed, but it has unfairly been hung around his neck.

The reality is that Brian left at the wrong time. I urged him – and Mal Bryce – in the strongest of terms not to depart when they did. I did not argue it specifically, but they should have brought about a complete solution to Rothwells before departing. However, Brian had made a public commitment not to let his premiership extend beyond five years, and he stuck to it.

He has since conceded that he made errors on crucial aspects of his departure.[2] Thus, what was a character strength, in keeping his commitment to retire in difficult and unforeseeable circumstances, led to a calamity.

Finally, an assessment of Brian Burke cannot be made without mentioning his fund-raising ability, which was prodigious. As a result, WA was able to contribute substantially to federal and eastern states Labor campaigns.

This gave Brian even higher status in ALP forums, but he came to believe it was his Achilles heel. It attracted too much attention from the WA Inc. Royal Commission and allowed him to be portrayed in a bad light, which in turn tarnished his brilliant governmental and political records.

18

'Corruption' – No case to answer

The touchstone for CCC-type bodies is successful prosecutions. Some CCC apologists may say otherwise, but they are not to be believed.

It was not until 6 November 2008 that any corruption charges emerged from Operation Tiberius, which appears to be the CCC's internal code name for its long and extensive investigation of Brian Burke and Julian Grill.

On that day, in the Perth Magistrates Court, Nathan Hondros (the young chief of staff to Jon Ford, Minister for Fisheries), Brian Burke and I were each formally accused by the CCC of corruption and, in the alternative, that we were guilty of being involved in the unlawful disclosure of official information.

Of the many prosecutions the CCC initiated against us, this was the only one for an alleged offence carrying anything like a minimum jail sentence of seven years and for which the CCC could claim it had the evidence needed for permission to tap our phones. But it met the same fate as the others.

Due to the secrecy surrounding CCC operations, there is not much that is public about Operation Tiberius. I don't think there was any media reference to that name and I only became aware of it from copies of warrants obtained by the CCC to carry out its extensive surveillance of Burke and Grill.

The choice of the code name is curious. Tiberius Caesar was the second Roman emperor. Historians say he was a great general, but in his later years became a tyrannical, ruthless and cruel ruler. So perhaps the name was a cynical and childish reference to Brian Burke.

The fact that the CCC had an operation which, from all appearances, specifically focused on Burke and Grill again raises the important question: What was the CCC doing chasing after two people who were not public officers?

The long delay in bringing the corruption charges after the CCC hearings were completed in February 2007 has never been explained. It is almost as though the charges were an afterthought when the CCC finally realised that nothing of consequence had come out of the long, destructive and expensive inquiry circus.

And the delays did not stop there. The trial commenced in the Supreme Court on 20 April 2010 and was not finalised until 2 February 2012. Yes, that is seven years from the date the investigation commenced.

The CCC appeared to plan these prosecutions as their *magnum opus*. That is, their justification and payoff for years of spying, eavesdropping, snooping, probing and public mud-throwing.

Up to that point, the CCC had not prosecuted any issue of serious criminality or corruption in relation to us. It was a bit like the notorious Al Capone gangster case in Chicago during prohibition. The police pursued Capone for very serious crimes, without success, but finally jailed him for tax evasion.

Stripped of their legal verbosity, the charges against us were essentially that: Burke and Grill corruptly induced Nathan Hondros to unlawfully give them a confidential copy of a draft Fisheries Department Pearl Oyster Hatchery Policy document so that they could amend it in a way that would unfairly give their client, Norwest Seafoods, an additional quota allocation (Section 83 of the Criminal Code).

The inducement to Mr Hondros was alleged to be an undertaking from us to assist him to enter the WA Parliament as part of a "dream team" concept that Brian was contemplating.

In all, there was one charge of corruption against each of us and alternative charges relating to disclosure of official information (the Draft Hatchery Policy) by Mr Hondros to Burke and Grill (Section 81 of the Criminal Code).

There was one further charge, unconnected with hatchery policy, which alleged that Mr Hondros unlawfully released a copy of a letter between Minister Jon Ford and the Federal Minister for Fisheries that dealt with a compensation claim by two of Brian's fishing industry clients. I won't tire the reader with details of this averment as it was never a significant matter.

It was apparent that the CCC meant business, as the charges were followed by the delivery to our lawyers of six bulging lever-arch files of the CCC's pre-trial documents. However, it also testified to the complexity and ultimate fragility of their case.

It was true that Mr Hondros gave us a copy of the draft hatchery policy and that we suggested amendments to it. However, our proposed amendments were designed (with the consent of the Minister) to restore the Minister's control of the pearl hatchery industry and give him the discretion to make it fairer to small producers like our client, and to allow Indigenous people to enter the industry.

We vigorously rejected any suggestion that our actions were other than legal and proper, or that any inducement was offered to Mr Hondros.

Like the other accusations made against us, these charges were accompanied by the CCC's usual failings demonstrated during this extended period. The charges would ultimately misfire and founder. Nonetheless, the manner in which they were flamboyantly presented and publicised would do lethal damage to reputations, destroy Mr Hondros's public service career and leave his family deeply in debt.

On the day we were formally charged, we were obliged to negotiate a full media gauntlet both going in and out of the courtrooms. The CCC provided the magistrate and the media with a "statement of material facts" which sought to inform and justify the accusations. This was not necessary and was blatantly unfair, as it was likely to cause bias in the media right from the beginning. It later had to be mostly withdrawn when the DPP took over.

It was not a document that was kind to the accused and, even before any hearings commenced, the so-called facts were found to be inaccurate in important aspects. The CCC "statement" included sensational, but unprovable, allegations that had become emblematic of the CCC's unfair processes.

Prominent in the "statement of material facts" was the assertion that we effectively bribed Mr Hondros by making him part of the "dream team" concept. It took no genius to appreciate that this sensational statement would become the basis of headline-grabbing media coverage across the country.

The TV news made it the lead story the same night and radio was alight with the accusations.

On 7 November 2008, *The West Australian* ran the story on its front page. The banner headlines screamed: "Burke, Grill charged by corruption watchdog".

Below the headlines were three unflattering picture portraits of Burke, Marlborough and Grill. Underneath each picture was the word: CHARGED.

It was set up to look like a wanted poster. Norm Marlborough was actually charged on a completely separate matter, which I have dealt with in Chapter 5.

Much of the lurid front-page story dealt with the "dream team" concept and the implication that a parliamentary seat was used by us as a bribe to Mr Hondros. Among *The West's* reference to the "dream team" was the following:

> *The West* understands the corruption charges relate to Mr Burke's and Mr Grill's promotion of a Labor Party 'dream team' of future candidates, among them, Mr Hondros ....

The Australian's lead article on the front page the same day had banner headlines screaming, "Burke charged with corruption", and pictures of Brian and myself.

The Australian was also quick to point out that we were all possibly going to jail for seven years on the corruption charge or five years on the others. Their front-page story traversed the whole Smiths Beach and Lobbyists inquiries from the perspective of Nick Anticich, the CCC's Director of Operations, and painted a picture of profound corruption and a plethora of criminality.

As I disclose in Chapter 12, this was one of the officers mentioned by Parliamentary Inspector, the late Michael Murray, in his report on rogue CCC activities.[161] It was not alleged that Anticich was a rogue officer, but it was made apparent that the rogue activity happened on his watch.

The condemnatory media euphoria was epitomised by Simon Beaumont, the 6PR radio station "shock jock", when he said on 7 November 2008:

> I have said many times on this program their (Burke and Grill) actions in influencing elected members and public officials were immoral. They were... Their actions were an abuse of power. The courts will decide if these acts were criminal.

Later the same morning he said:

> The stain of Burke and Grill will forever remain etched on our – on the public office of State Parliament and on lobbyists and advocates.

A reader might correctly question why we did not sue for the clearly defamatory comment. But we were well and truly on the back foot and desperately defending ourselves from multiple untrue allegations. We did not have the time or the money to open another battlefront.

With these sorts of poisonous comments pouring forth from the media generally, a fair trial by jury was problematic. We had to reluctantly accept that as a result of months and years of toxic media we were reviled and considered odious. Outside of our lawyers, there was not one public voice in our defence.

We were just too hot to handle. It was a lonely landscape.

Specifically, we should note here, as it later had considerable legal repercussions, that although the DPP took over the case before trial, the CCC highhandedly assumed dubious prosecution powers to frame, commence and prosecute the initial charges.

It took longer than we expected, but by letter from the DPP's de-

---

[161] Parliamentary Inspector's report on misconduct and related issues in the Corruption and Crime Commission, Joint Standing Committee on the Corruption and Crime Commission, Report No. 19 June 2015, p. 37.

puty, Bruno Fiannaca SC, dated the 15 June 2009, my solicitors received advice that the DPP had taken over the case. Also received was notification that the charges had been very substantially amended and the "statement of material facts" built around the "dream team" assertion had been largely abandoned. That is, the allegation in the initial charge, that Burke and I had effectively suborned Mr Hondros was "not part of the purpose which the prosecution alleges was to be achieved by the corrupt conduct".[162]

By any standards it represented a major restructuring of the charges. Also, it was an implied admission that this sensational aspect of the prosecution case would be difficult to prove.

As I have explained in previous chapters, this subsequent quiet down-playing of startling allegations by the CCC was almost standard practice. But the damage had already been done in the media. I should record for clarity that Mr Fiannaca indicated in his letter that the "dream team" assertion would be used as a claim of motivation. However, such evidence did not seriously emerge in the DPP's case.

But the substantially amended charges immediately created problems for us. The redrawn charges were so vague in their details as to be largely incomprehensible to our lawyers. Until that time, they had battled with the CCC to obtain some particulars of the allegations. Over the following months, letters went backwards and forwards between our respective solicitors and the DPP seeking particulars and clarification.

Unfortunately, this situation was not resolved by the time we were due to go to trial in April 2010. Before any evidence was heard, argument raged in court as to what actually constituted the essential elements of the charges. It was difficult to discern what "improper purpose" was alleged against us. Without an "improper purpose" the charges could not stick.

It is my opinion that once the "dream team" allegation was largely discarded as part of the charge, the rest of the CCC's argument was very brittle and had the appearance of being held together by gossamer. As events eventually transpired, I was not far off the mark.

---

[162] Letter the DPP's Bruno Fiannaca, 15 June 2009.

For more details on the chaotic nature of the CCC's prosecution process, the reader can check a speech made by Margaret Quirk MLA in State Parliament in 2010.[163] She was appalled by the unfairness of the situation and said so in very explicit terms. For the reader's information, Quirk was appointed chair of the Joint Standing Committee of the CCC in June 2017.

The media, although showing great interest in every aspect of the proceedings and turning up *en masse* at the original charge process, the committal and bail applications and the other preliminary proceedings prior to trial, never appeared to understand the true nature of the process.

The radical amending and redrawing of the charges did not receive any comment by the media. Apparently it did not strike any of the journalists that anything was slightly amiss when so dramatic an amendment of the charge was made. They did not, throughout the long process, ask the obvious questions: "What was actually being alleged in the new replacement charge? Why was such a wholesale change to the original charge necessary? Why did it take seven months to notify the accused of the amendments?"

It was not as though these issues were not raised. At the doorstop media interview, just after we left court following the hearing when the new charge was accepted by the court, I said clearly to the assembled media: "The precise nature of the new charge is not apparent. We do not know what we are supposed to have done wrong."

Even though I could discern that some individual journalists were now decidedly more sympathetic to out general plight, I could also see in a flash from their faces and their reaction that they were sceptical of my lament. That was confirmed on the following Saturday when I ran into Paul Murray (columnist and former editor of *The West*) at our gym.

He told me frankly: "Jules, up until the time that you were charged, it was legitimate for you to say that it had never been made apparent to you by the CCC exactly what you had done wrong. Some of us who have examined the various material from the CCC over

---

[163] *Hansard*, Parliament of Western Australia, 25 May 2010, pp. 3282-5.

the months have come to ask the same questions. But now that you have been charged, and the elements of the offences specified, your complaint no longer has any traction. You are doing yourself damage among the media by repeating it."

I was shocked by this advice, as it was far from clear what the crucial elements of the corruption charges were. In fact, our lawyers would have to do a lot more work on this subject to ferret out the truth; never with complete success.

Nonetheless, I took Murray's advice because it was obviously well meant and it represented a perspective on the part of the media that I was unlikely to be able to change.

Hearing of evidence ultimately commenced on 20 April 2010 in the Supreme Court of WA. This court sits at the top of the hierarchy of courts in WA. In its criminal jurisdiction it only deals with the more serious criminal matters, such as murder. Technically, the charges against us could have been heard in the lower courts. It was suggested by our lawyers that our cases were dealt with in the Supreme Court because of our notoriety. Also, I suspect, that the CCC preferred the higher court as it added gravitas and hype.

In the Supreme Court, criminal charges are mainly dealt with by judges and juries sitting together. The 12-person jury decides the factual issues, including ultimate guilt or innocence. The judge presides over issues of law and guides the jury members on questions of procedure. In certain circumstances, the accused may make application for hearing by a judge sitting alone without a jury.

It was the strong, unanimous advice from the three sets of legal counsel for the accused that we should apply for hearing by judge alone. The view was powerfully put that, given the duration of the acid rain of the trenchantly adverse comment in the media, especially in relation to Brian Burke, that a fair trial by a jury was highly unlikely, if not impossible.

Interestingly, the DPP agreed and did not oppose our joint application. Not that trial by judge alone was without substantial risk. The common law takes the position that while the public is susceptible to media-manipulated public opinion, judges and magistrates are not.

As a veteran lawyer of many jury trials, I have doubts about this legal principal. While judges do tend to be more impartial and are versed in judicial principal, it needs to be appreciated that judges are human beings who have some of the array of sentiments and prejudices held by members of the public.

Consequently, the allocation of judges to particular cases is critically important and takes on the trappings of a lottery.

In the case of The State v Burke, Grill and Hondros, we waited in some considerable trepidation as the hearing date of the trial came nearer and the time for allocation of a judge came closer. When Judge Michael Murray was appointed, we were relieved as he was considered by our lawyers to be well experienced and fair-minded.

Judge Murray, who died in mid-2020, had superintended a rewriting of the Western Australian Criminal Code in the 1980s and was an acknowledged expert in the arena. Michael Murray and I were at Law School at the University of Western Australia (although not in the same year) at about the same time, but we had never been close friends. I knew him to be a person of considerable legal and personal principle. Thus, the crucial, but intangible, matter of the demeanour of the judge appeared to be, at worst, neutral.

The sun was not always to shine on us, however. DPP Deputy Bruno Fiannaca SC assumed the role of prosecutor of the CCC's case. Even at that time it was apparent that this competent, but ambitious, senior prosecutor had clear aspirations for appointment to the WA Supreme Court. He was a career prosecutor.

In the classical British common law tradition, as distinct from the much more partisan American model, prosecutors are expected to be impartial and fair. It is often said that the DPP is bound to be a "model litigant" with all that that entails. That includes disclosing evidence to the defence that is not helpful to their own prosecution.

In the case of Andrew Mallard, for instance, where the accused was wrongly imprisoned for 12 years, the DPP failed to disclose exculpatory evidence. I am not for a moment implying that Bruno Fiannaca would commit that sin, but it was well known that the accused would never have any quarter from Mr Fiannaca.

To shed a little more light on Mr Fiannaca's personality, I relate the following vignette. Some time ago, my counsel, Tom Percy QC, was discussing with Mr Fiannaca the latter's possible elevation to the WA Supreme Court. Mr Percy said: "Bruno, before you take on any position on the bench, it would be of some benefit to you to see the law from the perspective of defence counsel."

Mr Fiannaca responded: "Not likely. You don't have to put your head in a sewer to know that it stinks."

There was a sharp-edged singularity of attitude and focus that appeared to tinge all of Mr Fiannaca's actions as our trial proceeded.

It might appear obvious, but it is worth saying here that the mere bringing of a serious charge like corruption against an accused is enough, in itself, to ruin an accused's reputation, status and finances. In the end, it was entirely up to Mr Fiannaca as to whether the charges against us proceeded. The DPP himself, Joe McGrath, declined to become involved as he may have done for high profile cases because he had once acted in a matter which involved Brian Burke's youngest son, Joseph.

In the absence of any involvement by the DPP himself, this left Mr Fiannaca making all the vital decisions. It can be safely said that he never did us any favours. In Bruno Fiannaca, the CCC had their man.

The defence legal teams were made up as follows:

For Brian Burke – Grant Donaldson SC and Ms L. Christian.

For Nathan Hondros – Mark Ritter SC and Ms P. M. Tantiprasut.

For Julian Grill – Tom Percy QC, Ante Golem and Ben Gauntlett.

Although not appearing at trial, Steven Penglis, then Senior Herbert Smith Freehills Partner, exercised a supervisory role over the preparation and conduct of my defence. Steven Penglis is a very special man. He has a profound sense of justice, has decisive judgment and the courage of a lion. He gave his services *pro bono*.

The Crown's case took 11 days to present. It was accompanied by all of the media attention we had learned to expect. Some among our family and friends attended court on every day. Lesley, in her concern, would not miss a session. My children, Siobhan and Shannon, attended whenever their work permitted. Brian's wife, Sue, and lawyer daughter, Sarah, were also constantly in attendance.

For Mr Hondros, the trial and other ancillary proceedings were poignant family affairs. His wife, Katie, attended each day, along with his mother and father, his grandparents and their extended Greek-derived family. This kinfolk group was always friendly and convivial and believed implicitly in Nathan's innocence. They adored him.

It was during one of the many adjournments at this trial that I learnt Mr Hondros' parents had mortgaged their home to help pay for his defence.

Lesley and Sue gracefully weathered the media attention and were polite to everyone, but one could see that they were profoundly distressed. The CCC was always in attendance, with sometimes up to six officers. It was clearly a contest of some importance to them.

Those readers who have been involved in criminal proceedings will know the feelings of fear, uncertainty and trepidation that accompany such procedures, especially if it produced saturation media coverage, as this did. It may not sound much, but it is a strange alienating feeling that, as an accused, you are segregated from the rest of the court, like lesser beings.

I know, some people who may read this book are conditioned by American movies and TV to believe that the accused sit next to their counsel at the bar table in the centre of the court, close to the judge. In British criminal courts, the accused sit conspicuously like "untouchables" in the "dock", well away from the judge and their lawyers.

Our trial was not in the Supreme Court proper, which is in Supreme Court Gardens, but two blocks away on the 14th floor of the AXA Building on the corner of St. Georges Terrace and William Street. In the set-up of the courtrooms, the accused's lawyers essentially have their backs to their clients and there is no way to have contact with counsel while the trial is in progress.

It is a strange process and even stranger feeling. As an accused, you are the subject of the whole procedure, but you are barely involved. You are rarely addressed directly by the judge. You are not in a position to speak to your lawyers and you certainly can't speak to the public. In essence, you are an interested observer of a process that takes place between the counsel and the judge.

The judge and counsel refer to documents, which we accused mostly don't see. Some documents are exhibited on an overhead screen that is in public view. I have defended clients in similar circumstances in my earlier incarnation as a trial lawyer, but I have never appreciated just how segregated and divorced an accused can feel.

It is also extremely frustrating and rather depressing because you feel left out of the process. There are occasions during a trial when you can see a wrong impression being given, facts misused, or distorted, or a relevant point being omitted. By necessity, an accused often has a better command of the facts of a case than his or her counsel, who doesn't live with the issues day in, day out. However, when you see some aspect of the case clearly being misconceived there is nothing you can do about it until you have access to your lawyers at lunch and other breaks, or at the end of the day.

Preliminary, but highly important, legal argument took a considerable time before evidence was commenced on 20 April. We lost every legal point. I won't take you through this as it is not essential for this narrative, though it was desperately disappointing at the time.

However, it is salient to appreciate that if the case had not been cut short, as I explain below, it would have revolved around who was to be believed, and as to what transpired in a conversation between Fisheries Minister Jon Ford, Nathan Hondros, Brian Burke and me at the Minister's office on 16 August 2006.

If we, the accused, had been obliged to give evidence, those at the meeting other than Mr Ford would have given sworn testimony to the effect that the Minister had expressed deep regret concerning his mistaken endorsement of a copy of the policy that relinquished his control over the hatchery part of the pearl industry; that he was intensely unhappy with the quality of advice coming from the Fisheries Department; that there had been a breakdown of trust between himself and the department; that he was concerned about the plight of small producers; that he wanted to see some opportunity for Aboriginal people to enter the industry; and lastly, that some elements of the bigger operators had threatened him and his family.

We did not know what to make of this last allegation, but the Minister went on to say that he was putting Mr Hondros in charge of a review of the policy and asked Brian Burke and me to work with Mr Hondros to restore the ministerial discretion over hatchery production.

Unfortunately, Mr Ford, some months later, denied making such a request of us. However, outside of that disputed request and the Minister's allegations about the threats from the industry, there was clear documentary evidence to support the truth of our recollection of this pivotal meeting.[164]

At the commencement of evidence, and to justify an offence of unauthorised disclosure (Section 81), the prosecution had the task of proving that the draft Hatchery Policy endorsed by the Minister and given to us by Mr Hondros was an official secret and that Mr Hondros had no authority to disclose it to us.

Crown's case faced problems

To prove the graver charge of corruption, the Crown had to go much further and establish that we intended to amend the document in a way that favoured our client and that we planned to have it approved by the Minister, the Fisheries Department, the Department of Premier and Cabinet and Cabinet without anyone noticing the nature of the suggested changes.

To put it mildly, this presented significant challenges to the State. In my opinion, those challenges were insurmountable, for numerous reasons, but I shall mention only a few:

1. Within two days of the meeting of the 16 August 2006, the Minister authorised Mr Hondros to make an endorsed copy

---

[164] A letter written to the CCC by the Minister, dated 24 January 2007; an undated letter that the Minister wrote to Premier Carpenter after Mr Hondros gave evidence to the CCC on the 28 February 2007. The letters confirmed a lack of trust between the Minister and his departmental head, whom he forced to resign not long after the meeting with us.

of the draft hatchery policy document available to Burke and Grill. This was never disputed.

2. The policy was never secret. Mr Donaldson pointed out in his opening that, "…a copy of that document, your Honour, had been provided to every member of the Pearl Producers Association on 7 June 2006. It was everywhere, your Honour, and there was nothing confidential about that document."

3. It was stretching credulity beyond endurance to assert that the amended policy could be slipped past the Minister, the Fisheries Department (which normally had to prepare the Cabinet submission), the Department of Premier and Cabinet (which always thoroughly examines and vets every cabinet minute and produces a report for the Premier prior to Cabinet consideration) and the Cabinet ministers, without detection of the suggested amendment.

It is unnecessary to give a blow-by-blow rendition of the evidence given and cross-examination of the CCC witnesses. But as I have mentioned, in the early days of the case, the State won all the initial legal argument.

This was very concerning for us. It appeared that Mr Fiannaca's case was gaining traction with the judge. We accused sat on the edge of our seats, straining at times to hear the evidence, but always hoping for some sign from the bench that the judge had some empathy with our position.

Brian, who is a more sensitive judge of human emotion than I, made the extremely pessimistic assessment nearing the end of day four that the judge was adverse to our position and that we were in deep trouble. I was not prepared to argue with him as I saw nothing in the judge's demeanour that indicated otherwise.

However, from about day five onwards what I could see in a strictly logical sense was that the CCC's case was gradually falling to pieces.

Jon Ford (the Fisheries Minister) was the prosecution's most crucial witness. I am sure that his evidence did not live up to CCC expectation. His testimony did not fully tally with his earlier written statements, he could not recollect on numerous occasions and forgot important matters. I shall not go through it all, but as an example, Minister Ford did not name me as being present at the all-important 16 August 2006 meeting. The other evidence showed that I was there and the State case actually relied on it.

Such a lapse in memory by the Minister reflected adversely on his ability to recollect the more contentious aspects of the meeting. Why did the Minister's evidence potentially differ from that of the three others at the meeting?

But in the end it did not come down to one person's evidence against another. We accused were never required to testify. Our lawyers made a submission of "no case to answer" on 5 May 2010, at the conclusion of the prosecution evidence. These submissions continued on 6 and 7 of May when Mr Fiannaca responded. The case was then adjourned over the weekend to resume on Monday, 10 May, when Judge Murray delivered his ruling.

It made for an agonising wait, when all of us were distracted and apprehensive. We were praying that the judge would find in our favour, but his stern exterior made it difficult to predict his decision.

Brian rang me on the weekend. He was still convinced that we would lose, and wanted my view. I told him that I was very impressed with the strength and coherence of our lawyers' arguments and, although not giving anything away, it appeared that the judge had followed the logic with interest. Consequently, I had hope that Judge Murray would find for us. I did not appreciate then just how disconcerted and apprehensive Brian really was.

When the court reconvened on the morning of 10 May, Judge Murray did not prolong the agony. He read his judgment immediately and declared that he had found that there was no case to answer. We were each acquitted of all charges.

Before I could register any reaction, or even catch Lesley's eye, I was startled by a heart-rending sob from next to me in the dock. I looked and it had come from Brian who was clearly in a state of emotional distress. Mr Hondros, who was sitting on the other side of Brian, displayed his innate humanity by immediately putting his arm around Brian and giving him his genuine support.

If I had thought about it a bit more, I would not have been so surprised at this cry of anguish and relief. I do not know of another soul who has been so interminably and hurtfully maligned. It had been a long and sustained fall.

When he retired as Premier, he was one of the (if not *the*) most popular politicians in Australia. Thereafter, he was unfairly made an ogre in the WA Inc. Royal Commission (see chapters 16 and 17), had spent a good stretch in jail, forced to travel to Siberia to find work to support his family, and was shunned in many circles. As a consequence of the subsequent CCC pursuit, he was abusively and publicly scorned and again lost his source of income.

A finding of "no case to answer" is unusual. It entails an assessment by the judge that the evidence presented by the prosecution, taken at its highest, was not capable of establishing the charge beyond reasonable doubt. In other words, it amounted to a finding that the charge did not even meet the threshold for prosecution.

From our perspective, Judge Murray was finally exposing the CCC's grossly inadequate competence and unprincipled methods. He would later, in another role, lay bare the entrenched illegal conduct within parts of the organisation and the inadequate supervision that allowed it to prosper. It shook the whole rotten edifice to its foundations.

The judgment was a devastating assessment of the CCC's evidence and, although it was not specifically raised in the decision, by implication, opened up the question of whether the charges should have been brought in the first instance.

I have been critical of the media in the manner in which the CCC matters were covered and I do not apologise for that, but I have to concede that the media gave prominent coverage to the acquittal. For instance, it took up the entire front page of *The West* and was unusually fair to us.

The story, by Christina Jones and Peter Kerr, prominently referred to the CCC's failure in a string of cases against us. That would not have pleased the CCC, which now began to say that convictions were not all that important.

Naturally, we were all jubilant and Herbert Smith Freehills threw a small party in its office immediately after. Lesley and I profusely thanked Steven Penglis, Ante Golem and Ben Gauntlett, who had been magnificent and had always believed in us. That night, friends flocked to our house and we celebrated until late. All of our lawyers, including my initial lawyer, Sharad Nigam, and his son, Sash, attended and Tom Percy made a great speech.

But the celebrations were premature, because at the death knock for appeals (in fact two weeks late, with an application to extend time), the Crown took the matter to the Supreme Court Appeals Court to overthrow the judgment.

I always believed that the CCC would press the DPP's office for an appeal. It had invested too much resources and prestige in the case to simply give it away. However, as a seasoned criminal lawyer in my first vocation, I had doubts as to whether the DPP would be similarly enthusiastic. Drawing from the lateness of the appeal and informal reports that I had received back from well-placed friends, I have formed the view that the decision to appeal was attended by some ambivalence on the part of the DPP.

The appeal was heard on the 3, 4 and 5 May 2011 before Chief Justice Wayne Martin, and Appeal Court Judges Michael Buss (President) and Robert Mazza. On 14 September 2011 they delivered their judgment, unanimously finding against us and sending us back to trial. The 99-page decision was long and complicated; but, boiled down, it concluded that there was sufficient evidence to make us face another hearing.

The appeal had been a long and expensive business and it was very disappointing to be facing another trial and all of the cost and dislocation that that entailed. Until that time, we had had nothing but a continuum of hearings and trials for six years. However, I was not personally devastated, because we had seen the prosecution case now and I knew that it would not stand up when fully tested.

I should explain that the Appeal Court decision did not find us guilty. We were sent back for a retrial of the facts. That is, the same old prosecution case that had seemed to impress Judge Murray at the commencement of our trial, until the wheels started to fall off at about day five.

I desperately desired that the matter be finished – either by appeal to the High Court, or to go back to the Supreme Court and have the case quickly retried, with our evidence being given this time. For the sake of my family, I had to see an end to the matter. Lesley was greatly concerned that I was going to jail. It had badly affected her wellbeing and was starting to impair her health and (very disturbingly) the health of our daughter Siobhan.

Intriguingly, our lawyers had other ideas. They wanted to submit to the DPP that the cases should be dropped altogether. At that time, I could not see the point. The DPP and CCC had won the appeal and a new trial had been ordered. Why would the DPP stop now? It didn't immediately make much sense and I was not inclined to take that path. Consequently, I told my lawyers to seek leave of the High Court to appeal. They followed my instructions and filed and served the necessary papers specifying the grounds.

However, my lawyers and the other counsel for my co-accused persisted with advocating the course of seeking the DPP's cooperation in discontinuing the case.

At a later session with my lawyers, I asked them point blank why they were advising an approach that, on the face of it, had no prospect of success. I said: "You have previously told me that Bruno Fiannaca is unremitting. Why would he give up, having come this far? Do you have any reason to believe that he would abandon the case now?"

The response I received from Steven Penglis was strangely elliptical. He did not answer directly, but said: "Bruno Fiannaca has won his appeal. This is probably his high point. If he goes further, he risks the embarrassment of losing the case altogether."

I still wasn't convinced. It was only then Penglis finally said: "We have received a hint from the DPP's office indicating that 'a submission would be seriously considered.'" That was enough for me.

So, I agreed, as did Brian and Mr Hondros. Our lawyers made written submissions to the DPP for a discontinuance of the prosecutions. I shall spare you the details. Mr Fiannaca concurred with the thrust of our lawyers' submissions and on 2 February 2012, before Judge Lindy Jenkins in the Supreme Court, the charges were discontinued.

Thus, this flamboyantly presented and conducted case ended with a whimper. It was not an ideal outcome for us as, once again, we had no opportunity for our side of the case to be presented. The public had been regaled for days at trial, and before trial, with the more sensational aspects of the charges against us without hearing any response.

Also, it disturbed me that at the discontinuance hearing the DPP still maintained that there was a prospect of convicting us and that their withdrawal of the case was motivated by public interest considerations. Nonetheless, we were *acquitted,* and that was a tremendous relief for our respective families.

But, oh, the wreckage. The human toll was immense. Humiliation upon humiliation had been heaped on Brian Burke and his family. He had lost his last source of income and his family had stoically and silently suffered alongside him.

Nathan Hondros and his family had mortgaged everything they had and taken out loans to pay the legal costs. Successful accused in the Supreme Court are not awarded costs. That financial burden was with the Hondros family for many years. To add to the misery, Mr Hondros, although innocent, could not get back a job in government, or anywhere else.

After years, and changing his occupation, he obtained employment out of Perth. He limped on with hope that he would finally overcome the setback. And his perseverance has triumphed. From small out of town beginnings he has become a respected and brave journalist with a special compassion for the underdog.

Lesley, my wife, is an angel, but highly sensitive. She feels other people's pain much more acutely than most. There were days when she would have preferred to run away, but she was graceful and ever supporting throughout.

I won't itemise the trauma, but my daughter, Siobhan, was never to recover fully. Because of her position in Parliament House, she was too close to the action; too exposed to the animosity and the engendered hatred for Brian Burke and her father to survive unscarred.

Those in the CCC who conducted the investigations, formulated the case, strung together the barely credible accusations, spoke to the media in the most prejudicial terms and commenced the prosecutions, remain largely anonymous. They take no public responsibility for the failed cases. They are protected by their Act, in a way that the police can only dream of. They just walk away without any consequence or concern for the destroyed lives they leave behind.

19

CCC prosecutions 'unlawful' – Senior Counsel

Throughout the never-ending CCC-inspired quasi-judicial processes, we witnessed an abundance of moral preening by the CCC. But how did their actions measure up against their words? I have given instances in this book where the CCC's exploits have fallen short of acceptable standards.

This chapter briefly outlines one of the more egregious instances.

On 15 July 2016, the WA Court of Appeal, in the case of A v Maughan [2016] WASCA, held, *inter alia*, that the CCC does not have, nor has it ever had, the function or power to commence and prosecute criminal proceedings against any person.

The (then) Chief Justice, Wayne Martin, stated:

> If it had been the intention of the legislature that the commission itself undertake such prosecutions specific reference to that function would be expected in the (CCC) Act.

The decision created quite a storm in the media and in judicial circles. For instance, the ABC's Joanna Menagh filed a long story (online) on the day of the judgement, which stated, *inter alia*:

> In a unanimous decision today, the Court of Appeal ruled the proceedings against the former police officer 'must be quashed' because according to the legislation, the CCC's functions did not include the prosecution of offences.

The ABC followed this up with a story by Andrew O'Connor on 20 July 2016 (online) where the validity of "more than 50 convictions" was said to be in doubt.

The West ran several stories, commencing with a front-page article by Grant Taylor and Gabrielle Knowles on 20 July 2016 under the headline: "Ruling puts CCC convictions in doubt".

From my perspective, the most interesting section of the article related:

> The State Government was made aware last year of the issues surrounding the CCC's prosecution powers when a parliamentary committee (JSCCCC) recommended the watchdog's Act be retrospectively amended to enshrine the power to bring prosecutions. But the recommendation was not acted on.

Many readers would appreciate what a potent weapon the power to prosecute can be in the wrong hands. It can be used vindictively. The punishment can be in the process, not in the verdict. In Australia, that power, in respect to serious criminal matters, is limited to an independent Director of Public Prosecutions.

Daniel Emerson and Gareth Parker in *The West* of 21 July 2016 (page 12) followed up on this issue by reporting that Attorney-General Michael Mischin had rejected suggestions the Government should have acted to amend the CCC's prosecution powers in the face of "several official recommendations to do so". The article went on to report:

> Amid the fallout from the Court of Appeal ruling that CCC lacked the power to bring prosecutions, questions turned to why the Government failed to legislate to put the issue beyond doubt.

They quoted Mr Mischin as responding:

> It's never been drawn to my attention such a significant doubt attended upon (the CCC's) power to prosecute.

I can only comment that it makes you wonder whether Mischin was sheltering under a rock somewhere. He appeared to be unaware of Gail Archer SC's recommendation in 2008 to amend the Act to clarify the situation, or the qualified support the JSCCCC gave to this course in 2011.

The article went on to state:

> Mr Mischin said previous District Court convictions should be safe because though they might have been initiated by the CCC, they were prosecuted by the DPP. But he admitted Magistrates Court convictions were "in doubt."

These comments gave rise to media speculation that the Government might legislate retrospectively to cure the problem by deeming the unlawful prosecutions to be legal.

Paul Murray, in a full-page (page 29) article in *The West* of 20 July 2016 under the headline, "Reckless act to reward CCC", began:

> The CCC has put the State Government in an unenviable position through its prosecution of people it investigated.
>
> For more than eight years, the commission and the WA Parliament have been aware that the power of the CCC to launch prosecutions was at best under a cloud.

Murray strongly opposed retrospective legislation to cure the defects, and finished his article by stating:

> And rewarding a beleaguered agency that must have the worst track record in the WA public service just to solve a problem it has so recklessly caused would be reprehensible.

"Reckless" is a heavy duty word to apply to a vital cog in the State's justice system, but later analysis proved that the expression was not misapplied.

In July 2016, Brian Burke made complaint to the Parliamentary Inspector Michael Murray (ex-Supreme Court judge) that on 6 November 2008 the CCC committed misconduct by commencing and prosecuting criminal proceedings against him.

Mr Murray investigated the complaint and delivered a report to State Parliament on 28 June 2017. It confirmed the CCC illicitness, but did not ultimately take the next step and find actual "misconduct" against the CCC officers. However it lifted the lid on some very disturbing conduct.

This report revealed that the relevant CCC Commissioners, Kevin Hammond and later Len Roberts-Smith, were aware, as a result of an internal legal review made on 21 July 2006, that the CCC's powers to prosecute criminal matters had some significant question marks.

Such powers had to be derived from the CCC Act. That statute explicitly enumerated the CCC's powers, including the ability to refer criminal matters to the DPP for prosecution. There was no mention of any capacity for the CCC to prosecute in its own right.

In confirmation of that situation, the Second Reading speeches did not breathe a word about conferring prosecution powers.

There was a circuitous contention, favoured by the CCC's Hammond and Roberts-Smith, that, as Section 184 of the CCC Act allowed for the appointment of "authorised officers" who had the functions of special constables and therefore could prosecute criminal matters, the CCC could thereby launch and pursue prosecutions.

If this argument had prevailed, it would have amounted to a back door contrivance to confer criminal prosecution powers on the CCC.

The PI's report of 28 June 2017 commented on page 3 that:

> The Commission's documents established that at various times throughout the Commission's history its executive was faced with conflicting views as to whether the Commission was empowered to commence and prosecute criminal proceedings.

Also on page 3 that:

> The sources of the legal advice were within and outside the Commission, and included the State Solicitors Office, two Acting Commissioners in the Commission, the then Parliamentary Inspector and a senior Queen's Counsel.

The PI reviewed some 14 opinions on the subject, drawn from the CCC's internal files. Both Commissioners Hammond and Roberts-Smith were in the "Yes" camp, as was the Solicitor General's office, the former PI, some internal CCC lawyers, and two unnamed senior counsel.

Registering opinions that the CCC could not launch prosecutions were two unnamed senior counsel on the 7 July 2006 and another QC specially briefed by the CCC on 10 April 2007. But the real surprise was that both Acting Commissioners, although not identified in the report, strongly opined against CCC prosecutions on 6 March 2007.

On 16 March 2007, one of those Acting Commissioners presented a further written opinion confirming his judgment that the CCC lacked power to prosecute. In fact, he went so far as to warn that, "If asked to authorise a prosecution by the Commission under the Act he could not do so".

That Acting Commissioner recommended, for the second time, that independent legal advice be obtained. That suggestion was accepted and a further senior counsel was briefed.

The subsequent opinion from the senior counsel, armed with all of the previous legal advice, was obtained on 10 April 2007. It essentially stated that *the CCC did not have criminal prosecution powers by virtue of the authority in its Act,* and that, if the Section 184 "authorised officers" route was adopted by the CCC to commence prosecutions, it was a very constrained route and would be open to legal challenge.

Despite that independent opinion, and further advice from Gail Archer SC (who shortly afterwards became an Acting Commissioner) that the CCC's power to prosecute was at least questionable, Commissioner Robert-Smith authorised criminal prosecutions against Brian Burke, me and an array of other CCC witnesses on 6 November 2008.

This action was surprising to say the least, given the uncertainty of the state of the law and that other reasonable and available courses of action were not adopted, or seemingly not seriously considered.

Other options included having the police commence the prosecutions; refer the matters to the DPP as the Act clearly contemplated; seek a declaratory decision from the Supreme Court as to the CCC's powers; seek a declaratory amendment to the Act to confer the powers; or request the Government to appoint a Special Prosecutor for Corruption and Crime.

In fact, Ms Archer, in communication with Commissioner Robert-Smith, actually recommended consideration of these last two options in her review of the CCC Act in February 2008 (page 9 of report).

PI Michael Murray in his report (page 10) referred to these potential procedures in these terms:

> The Commission, when providing the relevant documents to me, confirmed that after making its submission to Ms Archer SC it did not make a formal application for a declaratory amendment to the Act. Nor did the Commission provide me with any evidence that, before it commenced criminal proceedings against Mr Burke on 6 November 2008, it took an action in the Supreme Court for a declaration to determine whether the Act empowered it to commence and prosecute criminal proceedings.

Judges and ex-judges are not discourteous to each other and normally go out of their way to convey their opinions in the most civil of language. Such was the case in this instance. But please make no mistake, the PI was saying in his conclusions to the report that Commissioner Roberts-Smith had acted unlawfully in prosecuting Burke.

For instance, on page 15 of his report the PI declares:

> ...his (Brian Burke's) complaint requires my assessment to focus on how and why the Commission decided to act in the way it did, and why its procedures were ineffective in preventing it from acting unlawfully, despite the judicial and parliamentary processes available to it to authoritatively determine any uncertainty as to the existence or scope of its powers.

It is apparent from PI Murray's report that the criminal prosecution of Burke was unlawful, but, to prove misconduct, the bar is set much higher in that corruption must be proved. I quote from page 17 of the report:

> The relevant actions of the Commission were unlawful, but that is insufficient of itself and in my view it cannot be said that the conduct in prosecuting Mr Burke, supported

> as it was by the opinions of eminent lawyers, despite the opinions of other eminent lawyers to the contrary, was a corrupt perversion of the proper performance of the misconduct function of the Commission …

Apologists for the CCC may argue that in the final analysis PI Murray made no finding of misconduct and that consequently the breech was technical only. I do not believe that this argument would in any way be tenable.

In fact, PI Murray specifically rejected that view. On page 15 of the report he trenchantly maintains:

> …the unlawful commencement of criminal proceedings by a State instrumentality is an extremely serious matter, the consequences of which, for the individuals involved and for the State's criminal justice system, are difficult to measure.
>
> The Commission's documents, as described above, clearly establish that its executive officers, prior to initiation of the proceedings the subject of the complaint, knew of the differences of opinion as to whether the Commission had the power to do so.

This to me amounts to a censure of Commissioner Roberts Smith, who launched the prosecutions against the advice of the senior counsel who had been specifically briefed to give a recommendation on the commencement of proceedings.

Paul Murray was correct; at the very least these prosecutions were reckless.

Because of the opacity of the CCC, there is still no explanation from Mr Roberts-Smith as to how this happened.

And, as a postscript, I pose the question: Why would any conscientious legislator grant the CCC, with its disastrous track record of abuse of its existing powers, the additional powers to prosecute criminal matters? For self-evident reasons, most other similar jurisdictions do not grant its CCC-type investigative bodies such powers.

Additionally, I make the obvious point that A v Maughan placed a cloud over the one clear recorded conviction that the CCC achieved during the long, unhappy mess. That is, a minor finding against Brian Burke for giving misleading evidence (on a matter of no import) in the Smiths Beach inquiry.

Since Maughan, that miserable dividend from months of snooping, tens of millions of dollars of public funds, truncated careers, broken lives and years of litigation remains in question.

Index

A v Maughan, 130, 268n1, 558, 564–565
Abbott, Tony, 30, 32, 232, 238, 242–243, 275, 524
Abib, Mark, 431, 460
Adams, Harry, 468
Adshead, Gary, 42, 60, 72, 267, 302, 336–337, 363, 463
Alban, Frank, 306
Alcoa, 535
Alinta Energy, 458
Allan, Murray, 313
Allanson, Jeremy, 19, 21, 26, 396–397, 400, 401–403, 417
Allen, Beth, 172p1, 438, 452
Allen, Charles, 535
Allen, Mike
    CCC (Corruption and Crime Commission)
        allegations against, 405–406, 412, 519
        findings against, 333, 423
        inquiry consequences, 407, 452
    damage to reputation, 438, 452, 518
    photo with Beth Allen, 172p1
    role in Smiths Beach project, 124–125
    testimony at JSCCCC (Joint Standing Committee on the Corruption and Crime Commission) inquiry, 308
Allen & Unwin Publishing Company, 496
Alston, Dean
    cartoons
        on Bowler-Grill relationship, 177c1
        of Burke and Grill, 174c1, 176c1, 178c1
        of Fred Riebling, 377c1
        on Grill's refusal to apologise, 379c1, 381c1
        on intercepted phone calls, 375c1
        of McCusker on CCC (Corruption and Crime Commission) findings, 382c1
        on McRae dismissal, 168
    media as ally, 221
    of media-perceived infamy, 233
AMC Consultants Pty Ltd, 146
AMEC (Association of Mineral Exploration Companies), 202
Anaconda Nickel Project, 465, 467, 478
Anderson, Rosemary, 286
Andrews, Paul, 454
Andrusiak, Kevin, 230
Annandale, Lynette, 297
Anticich, Nick, 359, 541–542
Anti-Corruption Commission, 280, 291
Anwyl, Megan, 252
Archer, Gail, 12, 268, 559, 561, 562, 563
Archer, Shelley
    in CCC (Corruption and Crime Commission) inquiries, 2, 11, 179, 181, 190, 205, 206
    effect on career, 185, 204, 214, 216, 310, 434
    photo, 380p1
Argyle Diamond Mine, 530
Armstrong, Paul, 441, 444
Ashcroft, Noel, 478
ASIC (Australian Securities and Investments Commission), 482, 485, 489
Atoms, Catherine, 295–297, 302
Austic, Scott, 292, 293
Australian legal justice system, 15, 16–17, 24, 62
Australian Serial Killers, Paul B. Kidd, 281n2
AWU (Australian Workers Union), 72
Azad, Usman, 79

Baddock, Wayne, 83–84
Baker, 356–357

Banks, Amanda, 40, 42, 58, 67–68, 141, 150, 233, 435, 436, 441, 451, 453
Banks, Norman, 368, 369, 370, 372–373
Barass, Tony, 65
Barnes, Greg, 297–298
Barnett, Colin, 6, 72, 335–336, 339, 380p2, 427, 429, 431, 454, 459, 506
Barrie, Christopher, 371
Bartlett, Liam, 31–33
Barzotto, Emiliano, 72
Bates, Ken, 288
Beahan, Michael, 32
Beamish, Darryl, 280–288
Beaumont, Simon, 542
Beazley, Peter FitzSimons, 54
Beazley, Kim
 Beazley, 54
 cartoon, 55
 friendship with Burke, 52, 53–55, 60, 251
 role in Labor party, 41, 227, 229, 232, 367, 502
Belmont Park project, 240–241
 . see also Ian Campbell
Bemax Resources Ltd, 145, 146, 148–149
Bennett, Rob, 396
Benson-Lidholm, Matt, 306, 308
Bentley Technology Park, 533
Beresford, Quentin
 The Godfather: The Life of Brian Burke, 494–495
 interpretation of events, 496–498, 499, 502–524, 518
 shortcomings of *The Godfather: The Life of Brian Burke*, 519, 522, 524
Beyer, Mark, 252, 528
BGC, 235–236
BHP
 as adversary, 239, 471–472, 473–474, 478, 479, 480, 485, 486
 bid for state-based access regime, 489
 binding contracts, 480, 481–482, 485, 489
 duopoly with Rio Tinto, 187, 188, 462, 466, 472, 473, 478, 486, 489–490
 on fast-tracked Cabinet approval, 477–478
 lobbying, 464, 471, 475, 480, 489–490
 media about Native Title matters, 487
 opposed by government, 472–473, 474–475
 royalties for regions, 473
 sharing of infrastructure, 465, 466, 468, 477–478, 488
 Yeelirrie Tenement matter, 156–157
Birney, Matt, 252, 429, 469
Bishop, Mark, 59, 230
Black, David, 216
Blackburn, Estelle, 280, 281
 Broken Lives, 286
Bond, Alan, 499, 531
Bond Corporation, 274, 497, 530
Bowler, John
 allegations
 by Beresford, 508–509, 516–518
 breach of information, 50–51, 153, 154
 role in Whitby development, 140
 ban, 155, 433
 Bowler Bookkeeping Inquiry, 153–154
 cartoons, 177c1
 damage to reputation, 154–155, 162, 181, 185, 247, 433, 458
 effect on career, 1, 433, 454, 458, 459, 469
 investigated by CCC (Corruption and Crime Commission), 1, 11, 139–141, 153, 181, 509
 photos, 173p1
 role in project approvals, 65, 139, 140, 145
 Shovelanna matter, 6, 187–189, 516
 Yeelirrie Tenement matter, 155–158
Box, Dan, 344
Boys, Alan, 81

Brabazon, Mark, 126, 129, 333, 412, 438, 458, 519
Brand, David, 526, 527–528, 533
Brewer, Jillian, 281–282, 283, 285, 286
Britza, Ian, 444
Broken Lives, Estelle Blackburn, 286
Bromfield, Richard, 319, 320
Broome pearling industry matter
  alleged role of Hondros in, 539–541, 549
  Beresford allegations about Burke in, 511
  trial, 547, 548–549, 550–555
Brown, Clive, 468, 470, 471, 475, 477, 480, 481, 506
Brown, Karen, 446, 458
Bryce, Malcolm, 32, 528, 529–530, 532–535
Buckeridge, Len, 235–236
Buckley-Carr, Alana, 324, 420–421
Budge, Gary, 351
Bunbury 2000 project, 120
The Burke Ambush: Corporatism and Society in Western Australia, Patrick O'Brien, 493
Burke, Brian
  after CCC (Corruption and Crime Commission) inquiries to present day, 57–59, 60, 493–495, 505–507, 553
  antipathy towards, 33, 153, 232–233, 498–500, 501
  apology, 217
  associations
    Adele Farina. see Adele Farina
    Andrew Forrest, 462. *see also* FMG (Fortescue Metals Group)
    BGC, 235–236
    Bob Hawke, 379p1
    Cazaly Resources Limited, 202–203
    City of Wanneroo, 158
    Gary Stokes, 149
    John Bowler, 154–155

John Quigley, 323, 447
Kevin Rudd, 227–233
Mark Brabazon, 126
Smiths Beach project, 75, 93–94, 95, 124, 398–399, 414–416, 513, 515. *see also* Burke CCC allegations in Canal Rocks scandal; Burke coastal development projects
Tony McRae, 159–160, 162, 163–164
Wally Cox, 127
ban, 41, 43, 52–54, 155, 229, 245–246, 273–274, 417, 511
Beresford allegations, 496–498, 516–518, 520
Beresford interpretation of events, 502–503, 504, 505, 506–507, 508–509, 510–512, 515–517
blamed for election loss, 427, 428–430
books about, 356, 493, 494, 524, 535n1
cartoons, 48, 55, 174c1, 176c1, 178c1, 375c1, 376c1
CCC (Corruption and Crime Commission)
  adverse comments by, 401
  charges, 1, 275, 423–424, 511–512
  consequences of inquiries, 59–60, 63, 65–66, 68–70, 71–72, 89, 185, 418–420. *see also* Burke damage to reputation
  electronic surveillance operations. see Burke home raid
  inquiries affected family, 11, 12, 31, 234, 378p2, 494, 548
  lack of clarity in allegations, 495
  methods used by, 22–23, 306
  Smiths Beach Inquiry findings against, 35–36, 129–130, 411, 418–420
  treatment at hearings, 308, 548–549
  unlawful prosecution by, 560, 562–563
CCC (Corruption and Crime Commission) allegations
  breach of confidence with Bowler, 153–154

breach of confidence with Grill, 207
breach of confidence with Marlborough, 43, 44, 45, 47, 50–52
breach of confidence with Stokes, 147–150
in Broome pearling industry matter, 64, 135, 538–540, 543–544, 551–553
in Canal Rocks matter, 37–39, 112
influence on Busselton Shire Councillors, 19, 411
in iron ore policy inquiry, 189
in Lobbyists Inquiry, 63, 131–132
in McRae matter, 160, 162
in mortgage brokers' scandal, 66–69
in Smiths Beach Inquiry, 22, 89, 129–130, 401, 405, 411–414
in Whitby matter, 140, 148–150, 151
characteristics of, 7, 8–9, 42, 55, 174p1, 240, 329–330, 536–537
coastal development projects, 69, 96–97, 101–102
damage to reputation. *see also* Burke cartoons
by books, 493–495, 510. *see also* Burke ban; *The Godfather: The Life of Brian Burke*
by media, 238–239, 245–248, 328–329, 420–423
in public life, 29–30, 268, 461, 556
'dream team,' 511, 541, 543
FMG consultancy, 466, 490. *see also* FMG (Fortescue Metals Group)
friendships, 11, 43, 47, 53–54, 55–56, 71, 205, 230, 381p1, 469, 491, 511
home raid, 8, 137, 138, 144, 462–463
legal costs for, 493–494, 503, 506
lobbying by, 65, 239, 248–250, 252, 269, 273, 494, 498, 502, 503
media allegations about, 31–32, 49–50, 58–59, 60, 64, 206–207, 236–237, 528–529, 541
media as ally, 220–221, 260, 439
photos, 171p1, 173p2, 378p2

as premier, 31, 57–59, 60, 102, 166, 276, 496–497, 498–499, 525, 526, 527, 528, 529–530, 530–536, 553
SCP (Select Committee of Privilege) findings against, 197, 209–210
A Tumultuous Life, 356–357, 493, 535n1
Burke, Grill, and Hondros, State v, 546
Burke, Joseph, 547
Burke, Sarah, 112, 463, 548
Burke, Sue, 11, 171p1, 234, 378p2, 494, 548
Burke, Terry, 31, 32, 461
Burke, Tom, 53, 461, 500
The Burkes of Western Australia, Brian Peachey, 493
Burke's Shambles: Parliamentary Contempt in the Wild West, Anthony McAdam and Patrick O'Brien, 493
Burkett, Graham, 388
Burkie, John Hamilton, 493
Burrell, Andrew
allegations by, 231, 329, 419–420
on Marlborough-Burke phonecalls, 51, 52
media vilification by, 29, 49–52
on Smiths Beach report findings, 419–420
Twiggy, 268–269
Burt, Frances, 284–285
Burton, Hamish, 111, 113
The Business of Government: Western Australia 1983-1990, Allan Peachment, 493
Buss, Michael, 554
Busselton Shire Council
alleged improper payments to, 9, 19, 27, 39, 89, 107–108
in CCC (Corruption and Crime Commission) inquiry findings, 1, 35–36, 128–129
election funding to candidates, 107–111, 110–112, 113, 114, 115

on Smiths Beach project, 82, 85, 105–106, 108
. see also Beryl Morgan; Canal Rocks; Smiths Beach project
Busselton-Margaret River Times, 81
Buswell, Troy, 108, 396, 405, 419, 429, 431, 444–445
Butterly, Nick, 261, 365
Button, John, 286, 287, 288

Cahill, Patricia, 349, 350, 353
CALM (Conservation and Land Management), 83–84, 126, 249
Campbell, Graeme, 329
Campbell, Ian, 154, 237–239, 241–243, 250, 388, 438
Campbell, Kate, 220–221, 222
Campbell, Murray, 323
Canal Rocks Pty Ltd
  CCC (Corruption and Crime Commission) inquiry into, 35, 125, 411, 414–415
  environmental assessment by Cox, 127
  lack of critique by newspapers, 40
  loss of resources for, 40, 76, 104
  development opposed, 80, 84, 90–92, 94, 98. see also SBAG (Smiths Beach Action Group)
  proposals by, 77–78, 80–81, 85–86, 87, 98–99, 105
  role of Busselton Shire Council, 107, 108, 111–112
  Smiths Beach project, 73–75, 80, 91, 93–94, 99–101, 105–106
Cape to Cape Alliance, 83
Caporn, David, 288
Caporn, Dylan, 72
Carles, Adele, 440
Carpenter, Alan
  bans by, 41, 52–53, 155, 177pl, 446, 520
  on Burke and Grill, 36, 58, 178cl, 243–244, 418–419, 422, 498
  Carpenter-McGinty media rift, 31, 434–440, 441, 443–444, 445–446, 458
  on CCC (Corruption and Crime Commission) inquiries, 45–47, 182, 397–398, 448–449
  dismissals by, 42–43, 168–169, 170, 459. see also Ian Campbell
  as premier, 33, 58–59, 223, 224. see also Carpenter government
  restrictions on ministers by, 53, 70, 163, 251–252, 433
  at WA 2008 election, 429, 431, 432, 506
  . see also Burke ban; Grill ban; Jim McGinty
Carpenter, WR, 110, 111
Carpenter government
  affected by CCC (Corruption and Crime Commission) inquiries, 48, 275, 435, 442, 448–449, 460
  conflict within, 442–443
  errors by, 211–214, 216
  on SCP (Select Committee of Privilege) report, 208–210, 220, 224
  support for CCC (Corruption and Crime Commission), 457–458
  WA 2008 election loss, 3, 427–428, 429, 432, 434, 445–446, 453–455, 459, 460, 506
Carson, Malcolm, 468
Cash, George, 219, 223
Cashman, Michael, 400, 401–402, 403–404
Castrilli, John, 448
Catania, Vince, 471
Catlow, Chris, 466
Cazaly Resources Limited, 187–190, 195–198, 202–203, 515–517, 521
CCC (Corruption and Crime Commission)
  accountability, 334–335, 349, 360, 365, 418, 455
  Act, 128, 161, 162, 253–255, 257, 260, 268, 279, 300, 334, 344, 347, 383, 395, 411, 557, 561, 563

Act secrecy provisions, 89, 121, 310, 318, 336, 337, 346, 349–350, 351, 391–392, 399, 538. see also CCC officers implicated
Act secret hearings, 12, 18–19, 27, 73, 494, 521
adverse comments by, 396, 400, 401–402, 403, 404, 406–407, 413–414
allegations
  in Broome pearling industry matter, 64, 135, 538–540, 543–544, 551–553
  in Canal Rocks matter, 37–39, 112
  in iron ore policy inquiry, 189
  in Lobbyists Inquiry, 63, 131–132
  in McRae Inquiry, 160, 162
  in mortgage brokers' scandal, 66–69
  in Smiths Beach Inquiry, 22, 89, 129–130, 401, 405, 411–414
  in Whitby matter, 140, 148–150, 151
allegations against
  Bowler, 153–154
  Burke and Grill, 2–3, 6–7, 20–21, 129–130, 202, 207, 401–402, 407, 411, 538–540
  Busselton Shire Councillors, 19, 107–108, 110–111, 112, 113–114
  CCC (Corruption and Crime Commission) officers, 336, 337, 338–339, 340
  Frewer, 125, 405, 408, 411
  Marlborough, 43, 44, 45, 47, 50–52
  Stokes, 147–150
allegations cleared, 38, 92, 126, 128, 172, 296–297, 324, 412, 442, 444, 447, 519, 552, 554–556
appeals against, 16, 162, 164, 194
appeals by, 16, 152, 554–555, 558
charges by, 16, 18, 36–37, 121, 123, 128, 130, 135, 151, 158, 185, 209, 219, 328, 414, 420, 423, 494
code name for Burke and Grill investigation, 538
comments by Carpenter on, 449–450

conflicts
  with Parliamentary Inspector, 338, 345–349, 355, 360. see also PI (Parliamentary Inspector) annual report
  with police, 311, 312, 314, 332, 336, 347, 350–351, 353–355
consequences of inquiries
  on business, 2, 7, 10, 36, 60, 65, 70, 234, 464
  on CCC (Corruption and Crime Commission) officers, 331–332, 337, 363–364
  on families, 1, 3–4, 5, 10–12, 34, 36, 55–57, 61, 91–93, 137, 270, 438, 555, 556, 565
  on lawyers, 5, 11, 13. see also CCC critique
  on media, 307, 528, 540–542, 543–544. see also media CCC
  on politicians, 1, 29, 139, 154, 158–159, 186, 228, 447–448, 514, 565
  on the public, 4, 7, 60, 181–182, 310, 456, 515
  on public servants, 12–13, 29, 35, 63, 126–127, 150, 152, 169–170, 435–436, 437–438, 452
  on WA 2008 elections, 45, 427–428, 437, 447, 454, 456–457, 458
costs
  of Burke and Grill investigations, 143–144, 293, 303–305, 498, 522, 548
  of inquiries, 343, 345, 453, 565
critique. see also CCC critique by Murray; CCC shortcomings; Murray report to JSCCCC
  by Fitzgerald, 260–261
  by Grill, 123–124, 332, 333–334
  by JSCCCC, 255, 307
  by McCusker, 393, 405
  of methods, 62–63, 142, 167–168, 198–199, 261, 333, 339, 342–343, 393–394, 401–402, 437. see also McCusker CCC misgivings
  by Murray, 348–349, 560

of police procedures, 294–298, 299, 301, 316, 320–321. *see also* CCC police use excessive force; WA Royal Commision into police corruption

damage to reputations by, 35, 36, 73, 253–254, 261, 263, 268, 349, 411–414, 437–438

delays by, 139, 152, 157–158, 213–214, 220, 326, 338–339, 386, 391, 395–397, 398, 400–401, 404–405, 539

differential treatment by, 363, 439

effect on Carpenter government, 448

electronic surveillance operations by, 12, 28, 33, 34, 37, 47, 73, 92–93, 138, 162, 194, 270, 338–339, 390, 409, 462, 510

Grill comments on inquiries, 143–144, 147, 263–265

home raids, 8, 13, 136–138, 144, 159, 462–464

information
  demands for information, 179–184, 195
  incomplete material from, 112, 113–114, 135–136, 145, 146, 190, 350–352, 403, 404, 405, 406–407, 408

inquiries
  Bowler Bookkeeping Inquiry, 153–154
  Broome pearling industry matter, 64, 135, 155, 512, 536, 547–548, 550
  Exmouth Shire Inquiry, 261, 262
  FMG (Fortescue Metals Group) Inquiry, 152–153, 462, 483–484
  iron ore policy inquiry, 186–189, 190, 200, 202, 206
  Lobbyists Inquiry, 61–62, 131–133, 142
  McRae Inquiry, 158, 161, 162, 165, 169, 459
  parallels with other inquiries, 17–18, 120–121, 344–345
  Smiths Beach Inquiry, 9, 74, 76, 89, 107, 120, 121, 123n1, 135, 179–181, 410, 411–423, 509
  Wanneroo Council Inquiry, 141, 158
  Whitby Inquiry, 139–140, 141, 144–146, 147, 147n1, 148n1, 149, 150, 150n1
  Yeelirrie Tenement matter, 155–158

internal conflicts, 361, 395–396, 397–398. *see also* OSU

internal investigations and reviews, 302–303, 345–346, 352–353, 451–452, 453, 457, 561

jurisdiction, 2, 9–10, 24, 132, 195, 289–290, 304, 339

justifications of findings by, 125, 142, 202, 255–256, 318, 463, 539

lack of action by, 42, 316, 317–318, 320–322, 324–325, 344, 345–346, 355–356

lack of clarity in allegations, 18, 21, 24, 270, 495, 513, 522, 543–544

lack of evidence, 6, 19, 21, 28, 33, 34, 39, 73, 121, 131, 138, 154, 158, 165, 262

lack of explanation allowed for defendants, 4, 162, 164, 309–310, 503, 513, 522

lawyers, 358

leadership
  commissioners, 24, 256, 360, 362, 384, 386, 390, 410, 424–426, 561. *see also* Kevin Hammond
  officer appointments, 291–292, 425–426
  resignations, 340, 348, 354–355, 383, 386, 389–390, 392

media role in. see media CCC

methods used by, 21–23, 44, 46, 138, 340

officers implicated, 331–332, 337, 364

OSU (Operational Support Unit), 129–130

police use excessive force, 295–297, 302, 312, 314–316, 314n1, 318–326, 319–320, 321–322, 322n1

power abuse safeguards, 25, 395, 425–426
power restrictions in, 331, 343–344
powers, 3, 6–8, 25–26, 182–183, 201, 254–255, 279, 293, 332–333, 334, 335–336, 345, 347, 359–360, 538, 558–559, 561–563. *see also* CCC Act; CCC home raids
powers need amendment, 559–560, 562–563
procedures, 183, 208–210, 212, 256–257, 262, 267–268, 271, 299–300, 308, 310, 330–331, 344, 347, 353–354, 364. *see also* McGinty CCC defence of track record; Repositioning Report
process, 4, 12, 26–27, 29, 36, 62, 89, 121, 124–125
public perception of inquiries, 12, 20–21, 24, 36, 47, 73, 299
purpose of, 278, 279–280, 295, 303, 314–315, 336, 428–429, 504. *see also* WA Police miscarriages of justice; WA Police mishandled cases; WA Royal Commision into police corruption
resources, 297, 298, 300, 301, 303–304, 354
response to Murray report, 349–350
role of SCEFO (Select Committee on Estimates and Financial Operations). see SCEFO (Select Committee on Estimates and Financial Operations)
role of SCP (Select Committee of Privilege). see SCP (Select Committee of Privilege)
shortcomings, 13, 267, 279, 292, 302–303, 305, 320, 325–328, 336, 358, 362, 365–366, 416–417, 457
CFMEU (Construction, Forestry, Mining and Energy Union), 214, 235
Chamberlain, Joe, 53, 500, 501, 525
Chamberlain, Lindy, 284, 331
Chance, Kim, 213, 216, 223
Chandler, Bob, 83
Chappell and Lambert, 76, 76n1, 94
Chapple, Robin, 470
Charitable Collections Act, 118
Children Overboard Scandal, 360–361, 366–374, 368
China Engineering Railway Corporation, 479
Christian, Bret, 282n1, 284, 285, 286
  Presumed Guilty, 281
Christian, L, 547
Christie, Rory, 286, 289
Clarke, Tim, 293
Clegg, Stephanie, 124, 405
Clifford, Leigh, 473
Clough, Peter, 189–190, 204
Cock, Robert, 434–435
Cohen, Sasha Baron, 55
Colbung, Ken, 240
Cole, Owen, 387
Cole Royal Commission, 25–26
Collison, Bayfield Ian, 114–116
Commonwealth Grants Commission, 499
Commonwealth Royal Commission into 'The Stolen Generation,' 283
Concerned Citizens Group, 119–120
Connell, Laurie, 499
Constable, Elizabeth, 459
Cook, Roger, 70, 459–460
Cooke, Eric Edgar, 280–282, 283, 284, 285, 287
Corrigan, Simon, 153
Costello, Peter, 178c1, 231, 232, 238, 241–243, 465, 488, 489–490
Court, Charles, 276, 329, 469, 491, 526, 527–528, 534
Court, Richard, 84, 85, 218–219, 235, 469, 534, 535
Cousins, Ben, 104
Cowan, Sean, 5, 38–39, 43, 139–140, 162–163, 233, 453, 512

Cox, Wally
   association with Smiths Beach project, 155, 414–416, 417
   Beresford interpretation of events, 514
   CCC (Corruption and Crime Commission)
   allegations against, 126–128, 405, 407
   findings against, 334, 412, 416–417, 518
   persecution of, 414–418, 438
   photos, 172p2
Craven, Greg, 59, 168–169, 330
Creating Communities, 103
Crichton-Browne, Noel
   Beresford interpretation of events, 516
   CCC (Corruption and Crime Commission) allegations against, 434
   at iron ore policy inquiry, 185, 189, 206, 207
   at JSCCCC (Joint Standing Committee on the Corruption and Crime Commission), 308, 522–523
   at Legislative Council Privileges Committee, 220, 222
   as liaison for Canal Rocks Pty Ltd, 108, 109, 111
   as lobbyist for FMG (Fortescue Metals Group), 471, 476, 488
   SCP (Select Committee of Privilege) report on, 197, 209, 217, 222
Criddle, Murray, 185, 192, 208, 209, 212
Criminal Lawyers Association, 30
Crimp, Glyn, 110, 111
Crowe, David, 231
Cuneen v NSW ICAC (Independent Commission against Corruption) (NSW), 132
Cunningham, Robert, 295, 302

Daly, Tim, 72
Dance, Chris, 95–96
Dark Victory, David Marr and Marian Wilkinson, 366–367

Darragh, David, 453
Dastyari, Sam, 520
Daube, Mike, 536
Davies, Mia, 426
Davies, Ron, 526
Davis, Felicity, 302
Dawson, Chris, 347, 352, 363
de Mori, Caroline, 464
Dean Greg, 110
Dellar, Greg, 468
DLA Phillips Fox, 197, 199, 516
DOIR (Department of Industry and Resources), 146, 148, 149, 490
Donaldson, Grant, 17, 22, 23, 218, 327, 343, 403, 463, 513, 547, 551
Don't Tell the Prime Minister, Patrick Weller, 366
D'Orazio, John, 1, 1n1, 134, 162, 388, 432, 433, 442–443, 444, 454, 459, 469
Douglas, Neil, 346, 349, 364
Doust, Kate, 223
Dowding, Peter, 32, 161, 274, 330, 501–502, 506, 514, 530
Downie, Paul, 109, 464
DPP (Director of Public Prosecutions)
   action on SCP (Select Committee of Privilege) findings, 224–225
   application for discontinuance, 555
   disclosure of evidence by, 546
   not consulted by CCC (Corruption and Crime Commission), 453
   refusal to proceed with charges by CCC (Corruption and Crime Commission), 130, 134, 179, 203–204, 207, 225, 434, 438, 447, 448, 452, 457
Drummond, Mark, 235, 246, 483, 485, 487n1

Eadie, Robert, 313
Easterday, Clark, 286, 289
Easton, Brian, 218–219, 224

Easton, Penny, 218
Echelon Resources Ltd, 187, 189, 196, 202, 203, 515, 517
Edel, Robert, 185, 189, 197, 199, 516, 516n1
Edwards, Damian, 472
Edwards, Graham, 228
Egan, Colleen, 288, 445
   Murder No More, 286
Egan National Valuers, 98
Electoral Funding and Reform Act, 520
Elliot, Herb, 464
Emerson, Daniel, 38–39, 40, 72, 147, 168–169, 295, 321, 328–329, 332, 338, 348–349, 512, 559
Enderbrock-Brown, Wendy, 362
EPDA (East Perth Development Authority), 532
Evans, Gareth, 535
Everett, Ian, 94
Exim Corporation, 218, 533

Fairfax Media, 442
Farina, Adele
   association with Burke, 88–89, 94–95, 192–193
   divided loyalties, 86–87, 89, 98, 513–514
   evidence in Smiths Beach Inquiry, 89, 512–513
   photo, 378p1
   role in Smiths Beach project, 84, 89, 94, 96
   as SCP member, 185, 192–194, 209
Feeney, David, 460
Fels, Anthony
   CCC (Corruption and Crime Commission) allegations against, 181, 185, 204, 209, 434, 447, 520
   consequences of CCC (Corruption and Crime Commission) inquiry, 179, 214, 216, 224, 435
   efforts to clear name, 310
   as SCEFO (Select Committee on Estimates and Financial Operations) member, 190, 206
Ferguson, Martin, 488
Fiannaca, Bruno, 151, 543, 543n1, 546, 547, 551, 552, 555
Fiocco, John, 112
Fiocco Lawyers, 112
Fisheries Department Pearl Oyster Hatchery Policy, 539
Fitzgerald, Greg, 260
Fitzgerald Commission, Queensland, 291
Fitzgibbon, Joel, 488
Fitzsimmons, Hamish, 419
FitzSimons, Peter, *Beazley*, 54
FMG (Fortescue Metals Group)
   adversaries, 471–472, 473–474, 482, 485, 486–487
   approvals, 474–476, 477, 486, 490
   ASIC (Australian Securities and Investments Commission) allegations against, 489
   association with Chinese companies, 467, 473, 479, 480, 481–482, 483, 485
   binding contracts, 480, 481–484, 485–486, 489
   credibility, 467, 468, 474, 479, 482–483, 484–485, 487
   financials, 480, 481, 483, 486
   government support for, 470, 478, 479, 487–488, 489–490
   grade of deposits, 469, 472
   infrastructure access for, 465–466, 468, 470, 476, 490
   linkage agreements, 465–466, 474–475, 476–477. *see also* FMG (Fortescue Metals Group) State Agreement
   lobbying, 469, 470, 471, 474, 476–477, 478, 488
   Pilbara Infrastructure Proprietary Limited Railway and Port Agreement, 474

Pilbara Native Title Service, 487
royalty concessions, 470, 478
State Agreement for, 467, 468–469, 470
. see also Andrew Forrest; FMG (Fortescue Metals Group) Inquiry
FMG (Fortescue Metals Group) Inquiry, 152–153, 268–269, 462, 464
Fong, Neale, 435–436, 437, 437n1, 438–440, 455
Forbes, Mark, 372
Ford, Jon, 155, 511, 538, 549–550, 551
Ford Jon, 540
Forrest, Alexander, 464
Forrest, Andrew (Twiggy)
  adversaries, 473–474
  advised on State Agreement, 468, 469, 470, 471
  ancestry, 464–465
  association with Burke and Grill, 152, 239, 268–269, 464, 466, 469, 491
  challenged duopoly, 462, 464, 472
  equity funding by, 462, 466, 467, 472, 474, 479, 483, 489, 490–491
  personality traits of, 462, 464–465, 466, 467–468, 469–470, 472, 478–479
  . see also FMG (Fortescue Metals Group)
Forrest, John, 464
Forte, Andrew, 261
Francis, Joe, 302
Fraser, Morag, 366–367
Freeman, Cathy, 464
Fremantle Tasering Case, 295–298, 301, 302
Frewer, Paul, 98, 125–126, 125n1, 333, 405, 407, 408, 411–412, 438, 518, 519

Gadens Lawyers, 188
Gageler, Stephen, 218
Gallop, Geoff
  about Burke, 31, 32, 33, 329
  actions by, 39–40, 41, 431, 503
  antipathy towards Burke and Grill, 53, 70, 244
  bans by, 30, 155, 245–248, 251, 273, 417, 498, 503–504, 511
  photo, 178p1
  on Smiths Beach development, 77, 85, 86, 87–88
Gareth, Parker, 236, 357, 559
Gartrell, Adam, 183
Garvey, Paul, 462
Gauntlett, Ben, 21, 547, 554
GFC (Global Financial Crisis), 429, 454, 497
Giffard, Graham, 94, 219
Giles, Paul, 441
Gilmour, John, 485
Gleeson, Murray, 164
The Godfather: The Life of Brian Burke, Quentin Beresford, 493–498
Goiran, Nick, 20, 142, 295, 299, 304, 306, 327, 343, 364
Golem, Ante, 21, 26, 197, 222, 323, 327, 402, 547, 554
Goodyear, Chip, 486
Gosper, Kevin, 535
Gracetown Progress Association, 83
Graham, Larry, 470
Gray, Deb, 251
Gray, Gary, 251, 432
Greer, Arthur, 287
Greiner, Nick, 331, 523
Grierson, Billy, 288
Griffin Coal, 65, 70, 110, 139, 464
Griffiths, Nick
  CCC (Corruption and Crime Commission)
    conflict with, 448
    critique of, 209
    resistance to, 11, 180, 182, 184
  comment about Carpenter, 453
  not lobbied by Burke and Grill, 248–249

at SCP (Select Committee of Privilege) inquiry, 199–201, 215–216, 223

Grill, Julian
  anonymous letter about CCC (Corruption and Crime Commission) to, 134–135, 136
  as accused, 544–545, 548–549
  allegations by media, 50, 150, 270–271
  apology refusal by, 207, 217, 218–219, 222, 379c1
  associations
    Adele Farina. see Adele Farina
    Ben Wyatt, 244–245
    BGC, 235–236
    Broome pearling matter, 64
    Cazaly Resources Limited, 202–203
    City of Wanneroo, 158
    David Johnson, 250–251
    FMG (Fortescue Metals Group), 239, 470, 474, 490, 491. see also Andrew Forrest
    John Bowler, 153–154
    John Quigley, 323, 447
    Kevin Merrifield, 120–121. see also Smiths Beach project
    Kevin Rudd, 227–233
    Mark Brabazon, 126
    mortgage brokers' scandal, 66–69
    Shirley McLeod, 282
    Smiths Beach project, 75, 88, 91–94, 95, 124, 398–399, 409, 414–416, 513, 515. see also Canal Rocks Pty Ltd; Smiths Beach project
    Tony McRae, 159–160, 162, 163–164. see also Tony McRae
    Wally Cox, 127. see also Wally Cox
  ban by Carpenter on, 41, 43, 52–53, 155, 417, 511
  Beresford interpretations of Grill events and allegations, 502–503, 505, 506–507, 508–509, 511–512, 515–518
  cartoons, 3, 48, 55, 174c1, 176c1, 177c1, 178c1, 377c1, 379c1, 381c1

CCC (Corruption and Crime Commission)
  adverse comments on, 396, 400, 401–402, 403, 404
  appeals, 554–556
  charges, 34, 423, 511–512
  cost of Burke and Grill investigation, 143–144, 293, 303–305, 498, 522, 548
  critique, 123–124, 322, 333–334
  electronic surveillance operations by, 138, 270, 339. see also Grill CCC home raid
  home raid by, 8, 136–138, 144, 159, 462–464
  lack of clarity in allegations, 495
  lack of evidence, 28, 40
  lack of information, 403, 405
  treatment of defendants, 4, 162, 164, 307–308, 309–310, 503, 513, 522, 548–549
  unlawful prosecution by, 562

CCC (Corruption and Crime Commission) allegations
  breach of confidence with Bowler, 153–154
  breach of confidence with Grill, 207
  breach of confidence with Marlborough, 43, 44, 45, 47, 50–52
  breach of confidence with Stokes, 147–150
  in Broome pearl industry matter, 64, 135, 538–540, 541, 543–544, 551–553
  in business charging structure and success fees, 6–7
  in Canal Rocks matter, 37–39, 112
  corruption, 11–12, 538–540
  false evidence, 21, 130
  influence on Busselton Shire Councillors, 19, 381p1, 411
  in iron ore policy Inquiry, 189
  lobbying, 502
  in Lobbyists Inquiry, 63, 131–132

in McRae matter, 160, 162
in mortgage brokers' scandal, 66–69
in Smiths Beach Inquiry, 22, 89, 121, 129–130, 401, 405, 407, 411–414
in Whitby matter, 140, 148–150, 151
in Yeelirrie Tenement matter, 156–158
CCC (Corruption and Crime Commission) inquiry consequences
on business, 2, 7, 10, 36, 60, 65, 70, 234
damage to reputation, 5, 10, 196, 231, 234–237, 248, 544–545
on family, 10, 12, 34, 61, 63, 68–70, 71–72, 89, 185, 233–234, 378p3. see also Lesley Grill affected by events
as media headlines, 234–235, 270–272, 418–419
on social relations, 10, 92–93, 244–245, 251, 461
characterisitics of, 6, 7, 8, 10, 59–60, 506–507
coastal projects experience, 69, 96–98, 102, 531
as contributing author, 385
damage to reputation, 244, 246–248, 268–269, 305–306, 328–329, 461. see also Grill media damage to reputation
'dream team,' 541, 543. see also Nathan Hondros
friendships, 29, 110, 139, 153, 238–240, 241, 243, 244, 248, 249, 251, 282, 323, 329, 554
Julian Grill Consulting, 152, 252
lobbying by, 65, 239, 248–250, 252, 269, 271, 273, 474, 494, 498, 503, 519–520
media
as ally, 220–223, 439, 507
damage to reputation by, 50, 150, 171p2, 270–271, 421, 541–542.

see also Grill cartoons; Grill damage to reputation
family affected by, 10–11, 233–234
as minister, 101, 106, 120–121
photos, 171p1, 173p2, 175p3, 376p1
questions and comments by
on Beresford interpretations of events, 496, 504–524, 522, 523
on Broome pearling industry matter, 550–552
on CCC (Corruption and Crime Commission) inquiries, 563–565
on CCC (Corruption and Crime Commission) processes, 259–260, 301, 542, 559–560
on CCC (Corruption and Crime Commission) Smiths Beach report, 123, 124–125, 129–130, 390–391, 396–397, 408–409, 411
on Hammmond's final report and resignation, 390–392, 394–395, 395–396, 403
on hypothesis about CCC (Corruption and Crime Commission) and commissioner conflict, 398–399
on SCP (Select Committee of Privilege) procedures, 192–195, 205–206
theory about McGinty, 273–274
on SCP (Select Committee of Privilege)
allegations and findings, 197–199, 207–208, 217–220
iron ore policy inquiry, 189, 202
on WA 2008 election loss, 427, 428, 455–460
Grill, Lesley
effect of electronic surveillance on, 12, 270, 339
effect of inquiries on social relations, 10, 92–93, 95, 244–245, 251
financial uncertainty for, 233–234
home raid, 136–138
letters, 134, 155, 273, 503

photos, 171p1, 175p3, 378p3
SCP (Select Committee of Privilege) demands on, 195–196
as supportive wife, 34, 308, 385, 394, 548, 555, 556
working for the Labor party, 72, 160, 166, 244, 460–461
Grill, Shannon, 11, 137, 166, 548
Grill, Siobhan, 10, 11, 34, 166, 270, 548, 555, 556–557
Grylls, Brendon, 182, 459, 473
Gutteridge, Adrian, 111, 113

Halden, John, 50, 446, 454–455
Hall, Malcolm, 18
Hall, Stephen, 27, 46, 50–51, 59, 61, 62, 107, 113, 131–132, 137, 314, 326, 508, 509
Hallett, Nigel, 185, 190
Halligan, Ray, 219
Halton, Jane, 371
Hamersley Iron Pty Ltd (Rio), 187
Hamilton, John, Burkie, 493
Hammond, Kevin
  as CCC (Corruption and Crime Commission) commissioner, 132, 291, 384, 394–395, 405, 424. *see also* Hammond's resignation
  CCC (Corruption and Crime Commission) internal conflicts, 393, 561
  demands for information at inquiry, 180, 183–184, 186, 195
  final reports for Smiths Beach Inquiry, 383, 390–391, 392–393, 395, 396, 399, 401, 403, 404–405, 408
  on Grill contribution to The Years of Scandal: Commissions of Inquiry in Western Australia 1990-2004, 385–386
  Grill hypothesis about CCC (Corruption and Crime Commission) and commissioner conflict, 398–399

IPAA (Institute of Public Administration Australia) speech, 386, 393
justifications for Lobbyists Inquiry processes, 142–143
photo, 175p2
questions by Grill about, 123
resignation, 354–355, 383, 386–389, 392, 394, 398, 406
on Smiths Beach Inquiry, 17, 28, 63
Hampson, Clint, 292
Hancock, Don, 288, 301
Hancock, Lang, 60, 466, 486, 491, 499
Hancock Prospecting, 486
Haratsis, Brian, 95, 98
Hardie, James, 530
Harradine, Brian, 478
Harvey, Ben, 328–329
Hassell, Bill, 524
Hawke, Bert, 500, 526
Hawke, Bob, 32, 379p1, 535
Hayden, Bill, 500
Hearne, Shannon, 293
Hemsley, Ann, 68
Herbert Smith Freehills, 26, 197, 198, 224, 264, 323, 327, 402, 443, 547, 554
Herron, Mark, 255n2, 297
Hewett, Jennifer, 488, 489n1
Hicks, David, 376c1
HMAS Adelaide, 367–373
Hodge, Barry, 536
Holmes à Court, Robert, 525
Hondros, Katie, 548
Hondros, Nathan
  Beresford interpretation of events, 511–512
  Broome pearling industry matter, 550–551
  CCC (Corruption and Crime Commission)
  allegations against, 538, 539–540, 541, 543–544, 549

consequences of report on family, 548, 556
corruption charges, 135, 155
defence team, 547
photos, 376p2
Hope Downs Project, 479, 486
Horizon Power, 258, 259, 262
House, Barry, 65, 185, 192, 209, 220
Howard, John, 227, 228, 237, 238, 241–243, 367, 374, 388
Howes, Paul, 72
Hughes, Billy, 32
Hughes, Judy, 454
Hunt, Graeme, 474
Huston, Peter, 484, 485
Hyde, John, 86, 278–279, 306, 308

IAG (Independent Action Group), 110, 111, 112, 113, 114, 115
IIB (Internal Investigation Branch), 313, 316
Iluka Resources Ltd, 145–146
Imberger, Jorg, 531
IMF (litigation funding company), 66–68, 69
Ingham, Mark, 21–23, 24, 25, 125, 406, 495
IPAA (Institute of Public Administration Australia), 63, 386, 393
iron ore policy (WA), 185, 186, 187–189, 190, 197–198, 202, 462–479, 475, 516
. *see also* BHP; Rio Tinto
Irwin, Jim, 284

Jackson, Liz, 88
Jakovich, John, 83
James, Clive, 189
Jamieson, Colin, 526
Jenkins, Lindy, 556
Jiangsu Fengli, 479

Jinks, Beth, 119
John Curtin Foundation, 499
Johnson, Chris, 232, 250
Johnson, David, 240, 250–251
Johnston, Bill, 471
Jones, Alexander, 185, 189, 197, 199, 516, 516n1
Jones, Christina, 553
Jones, Clive, 197
JP Morgan Fleming, 479
JSCCCC (Joint Standing Committee on the Corruption and Crime Commission)
  critique of CCC (Corruption and Crime Commission)
    methods, 183, 254–255, 256–259, 262, 266, 299, 309, 327, 340, 350–352, 401–402
    officers, 346, 363–364, 393
    process, 183, 254–259
  CCC (Corruption and Crime Commission) justifications to, 255
  conflict about commissioner nominations, 383, 425
  different from CCC (Corruption and Crime Commission) investigations, 306, 307–308, 310
  findings, 62, 254–257, 266, 311, 356, 358, 365–366
  incomplete material received by, 351–352
  lack of questioning by, 20, 254, 328
  limitations, 331
  public hearings, 142, 305–308, 344
  purpose of, 180, 278–279, 397, 522
  recommendations, 308, 310, 343–344, 365–366, 414, 559
  Repositioning Report, 358
  role of Silverstone in, 359–360
Judge, Petrice, 124, 406

Kafka, Franz, *The Trial*, 17–18
Kailis Brothers, Leederville, 228

Karpa Gold Swindle, 289
Karvelas, Patricia, 231
Keane, Bernard, 143
Keating, Paul, 32, 178c1, 329–330, 497, 534
Kennedy, Elicia, 81
Kennedy, Geoffrey, 290, 291, 314
. *see also* Kennedy Royal Commission; WA Inc Royal Commission
Kennedy, Peter, *Tales from Boomtown*, 276, 329
Kennedy Royal Commission, 264, 280, 290–291, 294, 312–318
. *see also* CCC purpose; Geoffrey Kennedy; WA Police miscarriages of justice; WA Royal Commission into police corruption
Kerr, Peter, 449, 553
Keys, Bruce and Grania, 241
Kidd, Paul B., *Australian Serial Killers*, 281n2
Kierath, Graham, 84, 85, 85n1
King, Rhianna, 60
Kipling, Rudyard, 15
Knowles, Gabrielle, 337, 559
Kobelke, John, 442
Korda Mentha, 79
Kucera, Bob, 432, 446, 454, 458–459, 521
Kumba Resources, 479

Lampathakis, Paul, 445
Langer, Justin, 104
Lauden, Gary, 472
Lawrence, Bevan, 385
Lawrence, Carmen, 30, 218–219, 275, 385, 506
Lawrence, Pamela, 209, 287
Leak, Bill, 376c1
Lee-Steere, Ernest, 499
Leeuwin Conservation Group, 83
Leeuwin–Naturaliste Ridge Planning Policy Review Steering Committee, 77, 84–85, 90
. *see also* LNRP (Leeuwin Naturaliste Regional Plan)
Legislative Council Privileges Committee
president, 12, 65
resistance to CCC (Corruption and Crime Commission), 181, 191, 199, 425. *see also* Nick Griffiths; Taylor Privileges Committee Inquiry
standards, 195
Leitch, Owen, 282–283, 285
Lemonis, Stephen, 327, 403, 513
Levine, David, 151
Lewandowski, Tony, 288
Lewis, Steve, 231
Lilly, Richard, 403
Limerick, Jim, 146–147, 146n1, 148, 470, 475
LNRP (Leeuwin Naturaliste Regional Plan), 75–77, 82–83
. *see also* Leeuwin–Naturaliste Ridge Planning Policy Review Steering Committee
lobbying
ban, 273, 498
Beresford interpretation of lobbying activities, 496, 498, 502–503, 507, 517, 519, 520
by BHP, 464, 475, 480, 489–490, 506
by Burke and Grill, 49, 55, 65, 67, 195, 239, 245–246, 248–250, 381, 419, 427, 462, 465, 488, 494, 505–506
problems, 519–520
for various projects, 82, 90, 103, 249, 271, 448
Lobbyists Inquiry
CCC (Corruption and Crime Commission) findings in, 1, 417–418
as extension of Smiths Beach Inquiry, 9, 10, 28, 42, 61–62, 131, 133, 142, 179–182

Logan, Fran, 59
Lombardo, David, 159, 160
Lorre, Peter, 235
Los Angeles Board of Inquiry of 2000, 291
Lovell, Avon, *The Mickelberg Stitch and Litany of Lies*, 288
Lupton, Wayne, 111, 113, 115–116
Lyall, Rewi, 159–160, 164n1, 169–170
Lyons, John, 436, 441

MacDonald, Kim, 71
MacKinnon, Barry, 455
Macknay, Elizabeth, 264, 272, 273
Macknay, Roger, 264, 266, 336, 339, 352, 353–354, 357–358, 360, 384
Macquarie Bank, 140
MacTaggart, James, 320
MacTiernan, Alannah
  FMG (Fortescue Metals Group) support by, 470
  personality traits, 96
  on Port Coogee development, 69–70
  on rezoning for mining, 146
  role in Smiths Beach project
    amended proposal, 84, 90, 99–100, 102, 123
    proposal, 89, 94, 96, 98, 99, 100–101
Madrill, Constance Lucy, 281
Malcolm, David, 287
Mallard, Andrew, 209, 286, 287, 323, 546
Mansell, Peter, 443
Marks, Jack, 502
Marlborough, Norm
  Beresford interpretation of events, 510, 518
  in Canal Rocks scandal, 37–39
  cartoon, 375c1
  CCC (Corruption and Crime Commission) inquiry
    allegations against, 41, 42–43, 45, 46–47, 58–59, 64, 128, 405, 407, 408
    consequences of, 1, 56–57, 63, 388, 459–460
    findings, 128, 413, 423, 463
    lack of questioning in, 46, 47–48
    friendship with Burkes, 43, 57, 510, 518
    in media, 3, 48, 56, 162, 246, 541
    phone calls with Burke, 43, 44, 47, 50–51
    photo, 375p1
Marlborough, Ros, 44, 56, 510
Marr, David (and Marian Wilkinson), *Dark Victory*, 366–367
Martin, CJ, 306
Martin, Gregory, 148
Martin, Wayne, 188, 306, 332–333, 334–335, 365, 516, 554, 558
Mason, Graham, 58, 139
Maughan, A v., 130n2, 268n1, 558, 564–565
McAdam, Anthony (and Patrick O'Brien), *Burke's Shambles: Parliamentary Contempt in the Wild West*, 493
McCusker, James, 499
McCusker, Malcolm
  CCC (Corruption and Crime Commission)
    letter to commissioner of, 163–164, 164n2
    misgivings, 13–14, 30, 135, 210, 211, 266, 306, 348, 360, 382c1, 393, 405–406, 456, 457–458
  conflict with Len Roberts-Smith, 355
  as eminent lawyer, 112, 218, 280, 288, 292, 327, 343
  on findings from inquiries, 34, 406–407, 408
  on iron ore policy, 188–189
  JSCCCC (Joint Standing Committee on the Corruption and Crime Commission) endorsed views of, 413–414
  media support for, 434, 435

as Parliamentary Inspector, 291
photo, 176p2
SCP (Select Committee of Privilege)
report misgivings, 198–200, 201,
209, 214–215, 435
on Smiths Beach planning report, 124
on Spratt case, 323
support for overturned findings, 442
McGinty, Jim
antipathy towards Burke and Grill, 36,
53, 59, 263, 274
as Attorney-General, 5, 210, 377p2,
444, 455–456
Beresford interpretation of events,
504–505. see also Quentin
Beresford
CCC (Corruption and Crime
Commission)
track record defended by, 167–168,
264–266, 267–268, 269, 272
purpose of, 292, 389
on confiscation of
public servants' property, 230,
233–234, 237
superannuation, 61, 62, 234, 535
damage to reputation, 46, 169, 268,
269, 274
errors by Carpenter government, 211
feud with *The West Australian*,
275–276, 441, 450–451
Grill's theory about, 273–274
media criticism of, 435–436
media rift, 434–440, 435–436, 439,
440, 443–444, 450–451, 455. see
also McGinty feud with *The West
Australian*
in mortgage brokers' scandal, 66–69
quoted by Beresford in *The Godfather*,
500–501, 502, 505
on reforms, 223–224, 429
on WA leadership, 33, 275–276
. see also Carpenter government errors
McGlue, John, 464
McGowan, Craig, 359–360

McGowan, Mark, 70, 72, 525
. see also McGowan government
McGowan, Michael, 289
McGowan government, 70, 311, 383,
425–426
McGrath, Joe, 547
McGrath, John, 447
McGregor, Alan, 111
McKay, Bob, 81, 84–85, 104, 116, 118
McKechnie, John, 168, 261, 342–343,
362, 364, 366, 383, 384, 424–426
McKenzie, David
in Canal Rocks scandal, 37–38, 75,
111–112. see also Smiths Beach
Inquiry
CCC (Corruption and Crime
Commission) inquiry
consequences on business and
family, 91–93, 122
lack of evidence against, 37, 39
Lobbyists Inquiry, 63. see also
Lobbyists Inquiry
role in Smiths Beach project, 9, 21,
76–77, 109
photo, 176p1
McKenzie, Fiona, 92–93
McKerracher, Neil, 123, 386, 390–391,
395, 399–400, 404, 409, 410, 412
McLeod, Denis, 282
McLeod, Shirley, 282
McLernon, Hugh, 67–68, 69
McLure, Carmen, 281
McMahon, Nathan, 2, 185, 189, 197, 202,
203–204, 209, 434, 515
McMullen, Vince, 98
McNamara, Kieran, 438
McQueen, Paul, 98
McRae, Tony
allegations in Gingin land decision,
159, 160, 161–162
Beresford interpretation of events, 514
CCC (Corruption and Crime
Commission) inquiry,

consequences for, 1, 158–160, 163, 310, 388, 433, 454, 459
damage to reputation, 159, 160, 168, 169, 310, 448, 514
helped by Grill, 163–164
photo, 178p2
Tony McCrae Inquiry, 158–164
Mead, Simon, 3, 427, 427n1, 430
media
as ally, 220–223, 247–248, 260, 434–435, 544–545, 553
cartoons in, 48, 55, 56, 174c1, 176c1, 177c1, 178c1, 375c1, 376c1, 377c1, 379c1, 381c1, 382c1
CCC (Corruption and Crime Commission)
media role at inquiries, 20–21, 309–310
media unit, 142–143
methods critiqued, 258–259, 261–262, 393–394
statements to media, 140, 141, 212, 253–255. *see also* Hammond resignation
as CCC (Corruption and Crime Commission) conduit
before Burke and Grill home raids, 8, 138, 463
at inquiries, 4–5, 142–143, 227, 328, 348, 423
before public hearings, 138
conflicts in, 180–181, 349, 418–423, 441–444. *see also* Carpenter-McGinty media rift
damaged reputations, 209, 229, 420–423, 436–437. *see also* media cartoons
effect on families, 10–11, 56, 233–234
lack of questioning by, 20–21, 276–277, 386–387, 392
public opinion influenced by, 4, 7, 9, 10, 50, 61, 138–139, 140–142, 167, 168, 423
scrutiny
The Sunday Times raid, 445–446, 457

Taylor Inquiry, 212–213. *see also* Carpenter-McGinty media rift
vilification by, 3, 8, 29, 48, 49–50, 55, 56, 234, 418, 423
media comments
on Austic acquittal, 292–293
on Beazley distancing Burke, 52–55
on Busselton Shire Council (BSC) election funding, 112–113
on Carpenter comments on Burke, 58–59
on Carpenter-McGinty media rift, 434–441
on CCC (Corruption and Crime Commission)
adverse comments letters, 396, 419
investigations, 66, 183, 449
on conflict between members of Parliament, 180–181
on FMG (Fortescue Metals Group), 472. *see also* Andrew Forrest; FMG (Fortescue Metals Group); FMG (Fortescue Metals Group) Inquiry
on Gary Stokes, 150
on Hammond, 183, 386–389, 392
interview with Burke and Grill, 246–247, 328–329
on Lobbyists Inquiry, 131, 136–137, 227
on Marlborough phone calls with Burke, 41, 43–46, 50, 51–52
on McGinty feud with *The West Australian*, 441–444. *see also* Neale Fong
on McRae Inquiry, 162, 163, 165
on misconduct by officers, 258–259
on Murray report, 348–349
raid on *The Sunday Times*, 445–446, 457
reaction after SCP (Select Committee of Privilege) report, 208–210, 209, 212. *see also* Taylor on SCP report
on Smiths Beach Inquiry, 9–10, 35, 37–42, 418–423
on Spratt case, 325

media sources
  ABC (Australian Broadcasting Corporation)
    4 Corners, 88, 121
    7.30 Report, 419
    Australian Story, 323
  The Age, 372
  The Australian
    on Burke and Grill, 65, 196, 221, 230, 231, 421–422, 541
    on Carpenter ban, 243, 250–251
    cartoon, 376c1
    on Crichton-Browne, 222
    on Forrest, 462
    on Hammond retirement, 388
    ignored McCusker CCC (Corruption and Crime Commission) critique, 438–439
    on McGinty and Fong, 436–438
    on Smiths Beach and Canal Rocks, 40
    Star Chamber references, 166
    on *The Sunday Times* raid, 445
  The Australian Book Review, on *Dark Victory*, 366–367
  Australian Financial Review
    on Andrew Forrest, 483
    on Burke and Grill, 49, 231, 246
    CCC (Corruption and Crime Commission) sympathies, 419
    on Labor support for BHP, 486n1, 488
    on Marlborough phone calls to Burke, 52
    on Penglis, 323
    on Smiths Beach and Canal Rocks, 5, 40
  Busselton-Dunsborough Mail, 396
  Crikey, 143, 297
  Daily News, 531
  Kalgoorlie Miner, 176c1, 177
  News Weekly, 274
  Perth Now, 152n1, 183
  Steel Business Bulletin, 482
  The Sunday Times
    on Burke cleared by CCC (Corruption and Crime Commission), 422
    on Carpenter government, 31
    CCC (Corruption and Crime Commission) critique, 167
    distorted images of Marlborough, 48
    on election donation scandal, 41–42
    raided, 445–446, 457–458
    on Smiths Beach project, 66, 82
    on West Australian government, 445
  WA Business News
    on Burke as premier, 528–529
    on FMG (Fortescue Metals Group), 474
    on Kalgoorlie election, 252
    on Smiths Beach project, 7, 7n1, 40
  The West Australian
    as an ally, 220–222, 247–248, 553
    on Beazley distancing Burke, 53–54
    on Burke, 57–58, 463
    on Burke and Grill charges and acquittal, 541
    on Burke and Grill finances, 236–237
    on Burke's associations, 58–59, 71, 243–244
    on Campbell dismissal, 237–238
    Carpenter ban on lobbying, 52
    Carpenter dismissal of Marlborough, 43
    Carpenter-McGinty media rift, 434–440, 446, 449, 460
    cartoons, 174c1, 178c1, 375c1, 377c1, 379c1, 381c1, 382c1
    on causes of WA 2008 election loss, 430, 433–434
    on CCC (Corruption and Crime Commission) commissioner appointments, 425–426
    on CCC (Corruption and Crime Commission) critique, 261, 301, 330–332, 333, 337–341, 357, 365, 558–560
    changed outlook on CCC (Corruption and Crime Commission), 347–349

on FMG (Fortescue Metals Group), 472–473, 477, 481–483, 486, 488
on Gallop antipathy towards Burke, 245–246, 329
on Hammond demands from SCEFO (Select Committee on Estimates and Financial Operations), 18, 180, 183, 186
on Hammond resignation, 387, 389
on John Bowler Griffin Coal approval, 65, 139–140
on the JSCCCC (Joint Standing Committee on the Corruption and Crime Commission) report, 258–259, 365
on Marlborough and Burke in Smiths Beach Inquiry, 37–40, 42, 56
on Marlborough phone calls, 43–44, 45, 50
on McCusker CCC (Corruption and Crime Commission) critique letter, 209
on McGinty confiscation of public servant assets, 233
McGinty feud with *The West Australian*, 211–214, 223, 267, 275, 422, 441–445, 450–451, 454–455, 460
on McRae inquiry, 163, 165, 168
media in conflict, 421–422
on Parliamentary privilege, 181
on Rudd-Burke association, 229–232, 243
on SCP (Select Committee of Privilege) report, 208–210
on Smiths Beach Inquiry, 5, 35–36, 37–40, 42, 56, 136–137, 418–419
Steytler critique of CCC (Corruption and Crime Commission), 299
on Stokes breach of confidentiality, 147–148, 150
on *The Sunday Times* raid, 445–446, 457–458
Taylor Privileges Committee, 212–214, 216

Meeuwig, Jessica, 116–117
Megaw, Mike, 246
Meiklejohn, Bill, 83–84
Menagh, Joanna, 293, 394, 558
Menzies, Robert, 525–526
Mercer, Bob, 94
Merrifield, Kevin
  Busselton Shire Council candidates challenged by, 114–115
  as CCC (Corruption and Crime Commission) witness, 103, 104
  consultant for Busselton Shire Council, 104
  friendship with Adele Farina, 94
  Millbrook property owner, 104, 119, 120
  opposition to Smiths Beach project, 86, 87, 88, 90, 118, 119–120
  property development record, 81, 81–82, 95, 120–121
Mickleberg brothers (Brian, Peter, Ray), 86, 209, 287, 288–289. *see also The Mickelberg Stitch and Litany of Lies*
The Mickelberg Stitch and Litany of Lies, Avon Lovell, 288
Middlemas, Ian, 189
Mills, Sheila, 219, 454
Milner, Cameron, 460
Mining Act, 156, 157, 187–188, 189–190, 204, 466, 509, 515
Mischin, Michael, 336–337, 559–560
Mitchell, Bill
  as Busselton Shire Council consultant, 104
  friendship with Adele Farina, 94
  opposition to Smiths Beach project, 86, 87, 88–89, 90, 118
  property development record, 81, 82–83, 84, 90, 95
Mollen Commission, New York, 291
Moodie, Michael, 453
Moore, Norman, 219, 223, 469, 476
Morfesse, Luke, 69, 235

Morgan, Beryl
  appointment to South West Development Commission, 413
  as Busselton Shire Councillor, 38, 43, 44, 85, 108, 109, 408
  in CCC (Corruption and Crime Commission) inquiry, 38, 396, 405
mortgage brokers' scandal, 66–69
Murder No More, Colleen Egan, 286
Murdoch, Rupert, 441
Murphy, Kieran, 247
Murray, Michael
  annual report as Parliamentary Inspector, 338–339, 340–342, 348–349
  CCC (Corruption and Crime Commission)
    incomplete material from, 352, 353
    lack of evidence at inquiry, 511–512, 564
  critique of CCC (Corruption and Crime Commission)
    hierarchy, 358–359, 361–362
    investigations, 350, 546, 547
    officers, 560
    procedures, 129, 260–261, 266, 327, 343, 345, 553, 563
  report to JSCCCC (Joint Standing Committee on the Corruption and Crime Commission), 351
Murray, Paul
  advice to Grill, 544–545
  on Beazley distancing Burke, 54
  critique of CCC (Corruption and Crime Commission), 301, 333–334, 335, 394, 425, 426, 560
  photo, 382p1
  on Taylor Privileges Committee, 213–214
Murrin Joint Venture, 467
Murrin Murrin (Anaconda), 474

NAB (National Australia Bank), 76, 79, 98
Nahan, Mike, 169, 422–423, 459
NCC (National Competition Council), 465, 468, 477, 478, 484, 487, 489–490
Nelson, Brendan, 371
Newman, Peter, 240
Nigam, Sash, 554
Nigam, Sharad, 21, 554
Noongar Elders (South West WA Indigenous Clan), 240–241, 242
North Metropolitan Health Service, 258
North West Shelf 'take or pay' Agreement, 530
NSW ICAC (Independent Commission against Corruption)
  critique, 166–167, 254, 331, 336, 523–524
  Cuneen v, 132
  similarities with CCC (Corruption and Crime Commission), 138, 151, 331, 355, 409–410, 520
NSW Police Integrity Commission, 304
NSW Police Internal Affairs Unit, 344–345
Nyiyatarli people, 487

O'Brien, Amanda, 183, 221, 222, 243–244, 251, 272–273, 388–389, 420–421, 422, 436, 436n1
O'Brien, Patrick (Anthony McAdam and), *Burke's Shambles: Parliamentary Contempt in the Wild West*, 493
O'Brien, Simon, 219
O'Callaghan, Karl, 303, 321, 325, 363, 455
O'Connor, Andrew, 558
O'Connor, Ray, 499
O'Donoghue, Julie, 468, 480
O'Farrell, Barry, 331, 523
O'Gorman, Tony, 454
O'Leary, Cathy, 440
Omodei, Paul, 63, 64, 214, 429

Operation Reflex, 368
Operation Tiberius, 135, 538
Operation Ulysses, 303
OSU (Operational Support Unit), 129–130, 338–339, 339–342, 345, 359

Pagliaricci, Giuseppe, 228
Parker, David, 31, 32, 49, 501, 535
Parker, Gareth, 236, 357, 559
Parliamentary privileges, 182, 184–185, 191, 221–222
Parmelia Hilton Hotel, 415
Peachey, Brian, *The Burkes of Western Australia*, 493
Peachment, Allan (editor)
  The Business of Government: Western Australia 1983-1990, 493
  The Years of Scandal: Commissions of Inquiry in Western Australia 1990-2004, 384, 493
Pearce, Bob, 75, 87, 501, 514, 531
Pedersen, Barbara, 124, 405, 406
Penglis, Steven
  comments on findings by
    CCC (Corruption and Crime Commission), 21, 327, 402
    JSCCCC (Joint Standing Committee on the Corruption and Crime Commission), 343
    SCP (Select Committee of Privilege), 197, 198, 200, 202, 217–218
  on defence team for Grill, 26, 323–324, 417, 547, 554
  role in Spratt case, 322, 325–326
  at Transparency International Australia, 264
Pennells, Steve, 245, 247–249
People for Fair and Open Government, 385
Percy, Tom
  CCC (Corruption and Crime Commission) critique by, 21–22, 135, 167
  comments on
    Hammond resignation, 387, 389, 391
    SCP (Select Committee of Privilege) findings, 218
    JSCCCC (Joint Standing Committee on the Corruption and Crime Commission) findings, 343
  on defence team for Grill, 26, 327, 547
  exposed police mishandling of cases, 280, 281, 286
  on *Presumed Guilty*, 281, 286
Perth Mint Swindle, 288, 533
Perugino, 71, 228, 229, 239, 415
Petchell, Lee-Anne, 78
Phaceas, John, 477, 482–483, 484, 485, 486, 487, 489
Phillips, Harry, 441
PI (Parliamentary Inspector)
  critique of CCC (Corruption and Crime Commission)
    investigations, 261, 305–306, 354, 365
    procedures, 294–298, 335, 405–406
    prosecution powers, 561–563, 564
    self-investigations, 345–346
  conflict with CCC (Corruption and Crime Commission), 343, 345–347, 348, 350–351, 353–354, 355–357, 358–359, 360
  critique of police procedures in Spratt case, 324–325
  on lack of resources, 354
  reports by
    annual report, 338–339
    other reports, 315–316, 341–342, 348–349
PICL (Petrochemical Industries Company Ltd), 30, 274, 497, 536
Pilbara iron ore project, 465
PMA (Precious Metals of Australia), 156–157, 196, 230
Pontifex, Michele, 451
Poprzeczny, Joseph, 274
Porter, Christian, 297, 301

Porter Novelli, 109, 464
Portman Mining, 246, 249
Presumed Guilty, Bret Christian, 281, 282n1
Price, Bill, 261
Price, John, 327
Price, Matt, 238
Price, Richard, 199, 218
Priest, Gail, 85n1
Prior, Neale, 79, 486
Probyn, Andrew, 53–54, 229, 232, 238
Public Sector Management Act 1994, 150

Quail, Hilton, 221, 323
Quartermaine, Ian, 299, 311–318, 324
. see also WA Police mishandled cases
Quartermaine, Phillip, 313, 316
Quigley, John
    as Attorney-General, 426
    critique of CCC (Corruption and Crime Commission) by, 269, 325, 337, 342–343
    damage to reputation of, 447
    photo, 175p1
    role in exposing police mishandling of cases, 288, 292, 322–324
    at Transparency International Australia seminar, 264
Quirk, Margaret, 365, 442, 544

R&I Bank, 536
Radisich, Jay, 454
Ravlich, Ljiljanna, 1, 48, 162
Ray, Robert
    on causes of WA 2008 election loss
    campaign strategy, 429–432, 446–447, 454–455
    Carpenter government attitude, 432–433, 440
    CCC (Corruption and Crime Commission) inquiries, 3, 428
    instigations into Burke and Grill, 427–428
    report, 460

Rayney, Lloyd, 286, 289
Read, Pippa, 185
Regency Beach Club, Dunsborough, 81, 82
Reid, Philippa, 128–129, 412–413
Reid, Sid (bikie Gypsy Joker), 288
Reith, Peter, 367, 369, 374
Repositioning Report, 358, 364, 364n1
Reynolds, Kevin, 2, 169, 205, 214, 235
Richards, Phillip, 110
Richardson, Graham, 242, 409–410
Riebeling, Fred, 180, 181, 182, 184, 377c1
Rimes, Matthew, 189
Rinehart née Hancock, Gina, 466, 480, 486
Rio Tinto
    duopoly with BHP, 187, 188, 466, 472, 473, 478, 486, 489–490
    fast-tracked Cabinet approval for, 477–478
    as FMG (Fortescue Metals Group) adversary, 473–474, 478, 479, 480, 485, 486
    Hope Downs Project compromise, 486
    lobbying, 464, 478
    opposed by government, 472–473
    royalties for regions, 473
    SCP (Select Committee of Privilege) findings against, 198
    on shared infrastructure, 465, 477–478
    Shovelanna matter, 187
Ripper, Eric, 59, 246, 248, 445, 470, 489
Ritter, Mark, 327, 343, 547
Roberts, John, 499
Roberts, Michelle, 31, 33, 67, 69, 72, 442
Roberts Day, 100, 103
Roberts-Smith, Len
    critiqued on CCC (Corruption and Crime Commission) standard of proof, 161
    on McRae Inquiry, 161–162, 164, 164n1

CCC (Corruption and Crime
  Commission) prosecution powers
  for, 561, 562–563
report on Whitby matter, 150
conflict with McCusker, 266, 269, 355,
  442
on investigation of mishandled police
  cases, 298, 317, 324
resignation, 354
on Steytler opinion, 343, 357
Rockford, Simon, 287
Rothwells Merchant Bank, 496–497, 536
Royal Commissions
  Cole Royal Commission, 25–26
  Commonwealth Royal Commission
    into 'The Stolen Generation,' 283
  different from CCC (Corruption and
    Crime Commission), 26
  investigation into Brian Burke, 31
  Kennedy Royal Commission, 264, 280,
    294, 312, 314–315, 317–318
  process, 25–26
  Royal Commission into Commercial
    Activities of Government and
    Other Activities, 275
  WA Inc. Royal Commission, 29–30,
    49, 528, 529
  WA Royal Commission into
    Government Business Dealings,
    536
  WA Royal Commission into police
    corruption, 288, 290
Rudd, Kevin
  Howard antipathy towards, 245
  cartoon, 178c1
  consequences of associations,
    227–233, 236–239, 242–243,
    251–252, 420
  leadership, 53, 274, 276, 497
  on super profits tax, 472–473
Ruddock, Phillip, 367
Ryan, Anne
  as Busselton Shire Councillor, 34, 35,
    111, 113, 116

CCC (Corruption and Crime
  Commission) allegations against,
  128–129, 333, 412–413
challenged Merrifield on Millbrook
  property, 104
efforts to clear name, 310
. see also Smiths Beach project

Sales, Leigh, 419
SBAG (Smiths Beach Action Group)
  as consultants for Busselton Shire
    Council, 90, 103–104
  differential treatment of projects by,
    81–82
  operational methods, 115–116
  opposition to Smiths Beach project
    by, 77, 78, 81, 84–86, 88–89,
    91–92, 97, 105–106, 114, 115–116,
    121–122
  as an organisation, 73–74, 80, 90, 115,
    116, 118, 119
  supporters' letter to Busselton Shire
    Councillors, 114
  website, 116–118, 121–122
SBDGP (Smiths Beach Development
  Guide Plan), 73–75
SCEFO (Select Committee on Estimates
  and Financial Operations)
  on breach of deliberations, 179,
    185–186, 192, 205
  CCC (Corruption and Crime
    Commission) demand agenda
    from, 180
  on iron ore policy, 189–190, 202
  on SCP (Select Committee of
    Privilege) findings, 197–199
  . see also Giz Watson
Scott, Garry, 247
SCP (Select Committee of Privilege)
  Carpenter government action on
    report by, 434–435, 456
  concerns about, 199–200, 205, 212
  DPP (Director of Public Prosecutions)
    action on findings of, 224–225

findings, 196–202, 204, 206–207, 208, 218
on iron ore policy, 187–188
procedures, 194, 197
recommendations, 185–186, 190–192, 202, 204, 224–225
report consequences on politicians, 208–209, 216–217
report critiqued by McCusker, 435
shortcomings, 192, 194–195, 202
Shanahan, Christopher, 164n1, 364, 386
Sharp, Tim, 67–68, 69
Shea, Syd, 57, 249
Shelf Partners, 535
Sherville, Mal, 288
Shiro, James, 321
Shorten, Bill, 71–72
Shovelanna matter, 187–189, 203, 516–518, 516n1
SIEV 4 (Suspected Illegal Entry Vessel), 367, 369, 373
Silverstone, Michael
  background, 366–374
  CCC (Corruption and Crime Commission)
    internal conflicts in, 332, 353, 354–355, 358, 451–452
    practices shaped by, 360–362
  on Hammond resignation
    final report, 389–390, 392, 394, 395, 409
    press conference, 9–10, 123, 129–130, 348, 391–392
  at media release of Smiths Beach report, 410, 411–414, 418, 420
  responsible for OSU culture, 359–360
  retirement, 340, 361–362
  role in Children Overboard Affair, 368–372
Singleton, Brian, 323, 514
Smith, Brian, 312, 314
Smith, Fraser, 37, 109, 111
Smith, Geoff, 371, 372

Smith, Stephen, 3, 432, 488
Smiths Beach Inquiry
  Beresford interpretation of events, 515
  CCC (Corruption and Crime Commission)
    allegations in, 18, 107, 141, 405, 411–414
    hearings, 27–28, 33, 35
    lack of evidence in, 39, 73
    processes, 42
    purpose of, 179–182, 398–399
    report and findings by, 110–111, 386, 392–393, 411–418
  JSCCCC (Joint Standing Committee on the Corruption and Crime Commission) findings in, 266, 307
  Marlborough role in, 51
  questions about Smiths Beach report, 123, 334
  role of media in, 47, 66–67
  . see also Busselton Shire Council election funding to candidates; Lobbyists Inquiry; SBAG (Smiths Beach Action Group); SBDGP (Smiths Beach Development Guide Plan)
Smiths Beach project
  amendments to, 89–90, 98–99, 100–101, 102, 103, 104–106
  development issues in, 78–79, 80
  environmental assessment for, 82, 127, 414–415
  investors, 39, 73, 76, 78–79, 92, 101
  limitations, 75–79, 80–81, 86, 105–106
  local supporters of, 105–106
  Marlborough role in, 46
  opposition to, 75, 76–77, 80–82, 84, 86, 97, 98–99, 103, 104, 105–106. see also SBAG (Smiths Beach Action Group)
  proposal, 2, 74–75, 76, 80, 101
  public perception of, 78–79, 107
  role of Busselton Shire Council elections. see also Busselton Shire

Council election funding to
candidates
viability, 79, 91–94, 95–96
. see also CALM (Conservation and
Land Management); Canal Rocks
Pty Ltd; Smiths Beach Inquiry
South West Development Authority, 75,
106, 120, 532
South West Development Commission
(SWDC), 38, 43, 44, 125, 128, 413
Spagnolo, Joe, 41, 66
Spooner, Rania, 151
Spratt, Kevin, 311, 312, 318–322,
324–326, 377p1
Square Kilometre Array, 65
Standing Committee on Procedures and
Privileges, 212n1, 215, 215n1
Star Chamber references, 25, 26, 166,
195, 522–523
State Agreement Act, 469
approvals, 471, 474–476, 490
government support for, 478, 479
linkage agreements, 474–475, 476–477
split in, 470–471
State Parliamentary Labor Party (SPLP),
263
State v Burke, Grill, and Hondros, 546
Stein, Les, 98
Stephens, Tom, 470, 472
Stevens, Clifton Coney, 100, 103
Steytler, Christopher
on CCC (Corruption and Crime
Commission) public hearings,
306, 306–307, 356
critique of CCC (Corruption and
Crime Commission) procedures
by, 266, 267, 299–300, 314–316,
318, 324–325, 327–328, 357
critique of police procedures,
294–298, 302, 305–306
as eminent lawyer, 281, 343
JSCCCC (Joint Standing Committee
on the Corruption and Crime
Commission)

endorsed views by, 413–414
report, 311–312
role in clearing Brabazon, 126
Stokes, Gary
Beresford interpretation of events,
507–508
CCC (Corruption and Crime
Commission) allegations and
findings against, 132, 147–148,
149–150, 151–152, 438
Stokes, Kerry, 443, 444
Stowe, Ric, 70, 464, 499
Strathan, Aaron Grant, 319
Strutt, Jessica, 48, 56
stun gun. see Taser use
Sullivan, Dan, 429
super profits tax, 473
Sutherland, Michael, 458
Sutton, Robert, 359
Swift, Mike, 85n1, 109, 119
Sykes, Trevor, 483

Tales from Boomtown, Peter Kennedy,
276, 329, 330n1
Tampa controversy, 366–367, 368
Tantiprasut, PM, 547
Tapp, Julian, 239, 464, 468, 470, 474,
488, 491
Taylor, Grant
on CCC (Corruption and Crime
Commission)
convictions, 559
officers under investigation, 339
Taylor, Robert
on 2008 WA election results, 430
on Bowler role in Burke land deal,
139–141
on CCC (Corruption and Crime
Commission)
demands for information, 180–181,
186
Lobbyists Inquiry, 136–137

process, 210–212
reports, 223, 394
Smiths Beach Inquiry, 45, 137, 418–419
on Hammond resignation, 387–388, 389
on Marlborough phone calls, 43
on McRae Inquiry, 162–163
media rift with McGinty, 434, 441–442
photo, 380p3
on SCP (Select Committee of Privilege) report, 208–212, 215–216
on WA Australian Labor Party leadership, 58
. *see also* Taylor Privileges Committee Inquiry
Taylor , Ian, 506
Taylor Privileges Committee Inquiry, 212, 213, 220
Tennant, Brian, 330
Thomas, Steve, 69
Thorn, Stacey, 292
Tingay, Alan, 94
Titheridge, Alan, 371, 372
Tomlin, Troy Gregory, 319
Tonkin, Arthur, 524–525
Tonkin, John, 500, 526, 529
Transparency International Australia, 264
Tranter, Allan, 103, 108
Travers, Ken, 190
Treadgold, Tim, 7, 40, 528–529
Trenorden, Max, 61, 182
The Trial, Franz Kafka, 17–18
Triplett, John, 111, 113, 116, 128–129, 412–413
Trounson, Andrew, 230
A Tumultuous Life, Brian Burke, 356–357, 493, 535n1
Turnbull, Michael, 497, 520
Tutu, Desmond, 15
Twiggy. see Andrew Forrest

Twiggy, Andrew Burrell, 268–269

Urban Pacific (subsidiary of Macquarie Bank), 140, 145–146
Urquhart, Phillip, 159, 186, 194–195, 196, 202, 223

van Onselen, Peter
critique of
CCC (Corruption and Crime Commission) processes, 216, 330
media articles, 421–422
NSW ICAC (Independent Commission against Corruption), 166–167, 523–524
on the McRae Inquiry, 165, 166
Vanadium Resources, 181
Verstegen, Piers, 117

WA 2008 Election
as CCC (Corruption and Crime Commission) casualty, 208, 454, 458
comments on, 454–455
reasons for loss, 427–430, 429–434, 458, 460. *see also* Grill perspective on WA 2008 election loss; Ray causes of WA 2008 election loss
relations with media, 433, Carpenter-McGinty media rift. *see also* McGinty feud with *The West Australian*
status of major parties for, 427–430, 433–434, 454
. *see also* WA Royal Commission into police corruption
WA Diamond Trust, 530
WA Inc. Royal Commission, 30, 31, 49, 290, 323, 384–385, 506, 529, 536, 537, 553
WA Labor Party, 53, 499–501, 500
WA Law Society, 30
WA Legislative Assembly (Lower House), 108, 179

WA Legislative Council (Upper House), 179, 434
WA Mining Act, 156
WA mining pathways, 466, 469
WA Police
  allegations against, 279–280, 282–283, 285–286, 287–288
  CCC (Corruption and Crime Commission)
    creation for, 266–267
    investigations by, 300–301, 347, 362–363
    tensions with, 312, 314, 332, 336, 338, 339, 347. *see also* Ian Quartermaine, Kevin Spratt
  complaints against, 295–301
  miscarriages of justice by, 280–289, 292–293
  mishandled cases by, 324. *see also* specific cases Beamish, Mallard, Mickleberg brothers, Spratt, Quartermaine, Cunningham
  procedures critiqued, 302–303, 304, 318–321
  self-investigations, 300–301, 302, 303, 313, 315, 321–322. *see also* OSU; Steytler critique of police procedures
  WAPS (WA Police Service), 290, 291
WA Trotting Association, 247
WA Turf Club, 240–241
WADC (WA Development Corporation), 533
Wainwright, Janet, 82, 83
Walsh, Peter and Rose, 251
Walster, Timothy, 153
Warnes, Ray, 362
Warnock, Diana, 86
Water Corp, 98, 100
Watling, Alan, 466
Watson, Giz, 179, 190, 205, 209, 219, 223
Wauchope, Mal, 155, 304, 437
Weir, Michael, 491

Weller, Patrick, *Don't Tell the Prime Minister*, 366, 369
Weygers, Peter, 330–331
Wheeler, Christine, 281
Whitby, Reece, 442, 454
Whitby matter, 139–141, 144–151, 150n1
White, Joe, 109, 111
White, Karl, 96, 99, 101
Whitlam, Gough, 32, 500
Wilkinson, Marian (David Marr and), *Dark Victory*, 366–367
Wilmott, Deidre, 429
Wilson, Ronald, 283–284
Wolff, Albert, 283, 284
Wood and Grieve (engineering firm), 94
Wood Commission, NSW, 291
Woollard, Janet, 459
Wran, Neville, 32, 497
Wyatt, Ben, 222, 241, 243–244, 447, 451
Wyatt, Cedric, 244
Wyatt, Vivian, 244

Xiangmo, Huang, 520
Xstrata, 230

The Years of Scandal: Commissions of Inquiry in Western Australia 1990-2004
Allan Peachment (editor), 384, 493
Grill contribution to, 384–385
Yeelirrie Tenement matter, 155–157
Young, Robert, 151–152

Zelestis, Chris
  critique of CCC (Corruption and Crime Commission), 62, 183, 255–256, 327
  as eminent lawyer, 348, 350, 353
  JSCCCC (Joint Standing Committee on the Corruption and Crime Commission) report concurred with, 254, 257–258, 262, 413–414

www.ingramcontent.com/pod-product-compliance
Lightning Source LLC
Chambersburg PA
CBHW070004010526
44117CB00011B/1418